WILD
swimming

wild-swimming *(n.)*

1. Swimming in natural waters such as rivers, lakes and waterfalls. Often associated with picnics and summer holidays.

2. Dipping or plunging in secret or hidden places, sometimes in wilderness areas. Associated with skinny-dipping or naked swimming.

3. Action of swimming wildly such as jumping or diving from a height, using swings and slides, or riding the current of a river.

Third Edition 2025

Daniel Start
et al

Esthwaite Water, p279

WILD
swimming

Wadenhoe, R Nene p160

Contents

Overview

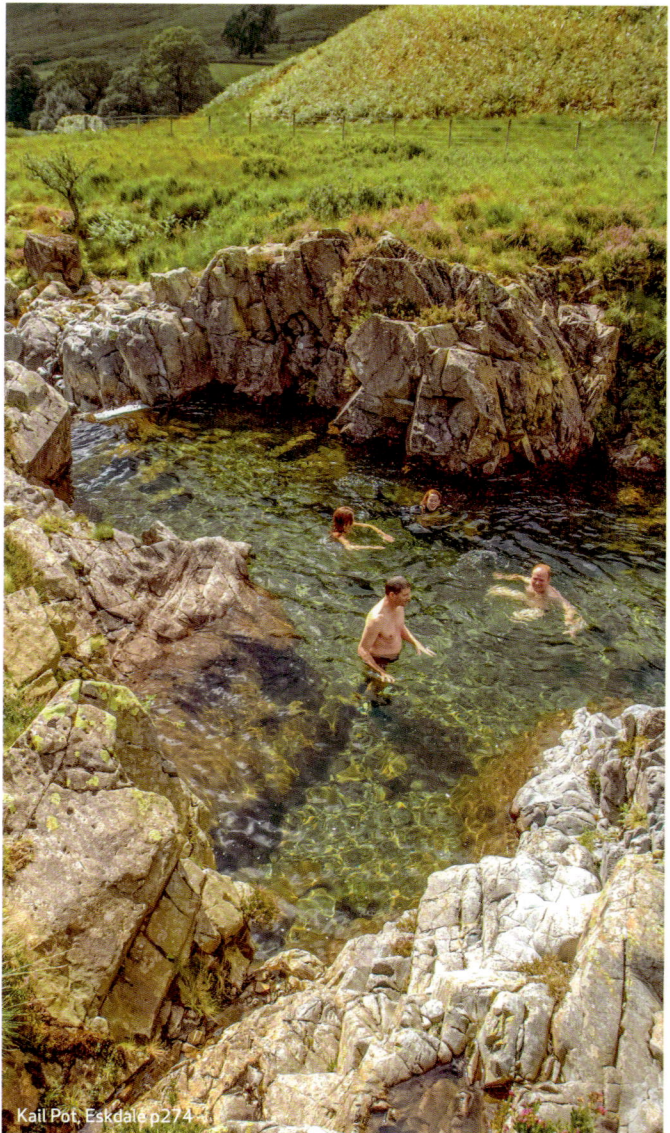

Kail Pot, Eskdale p274

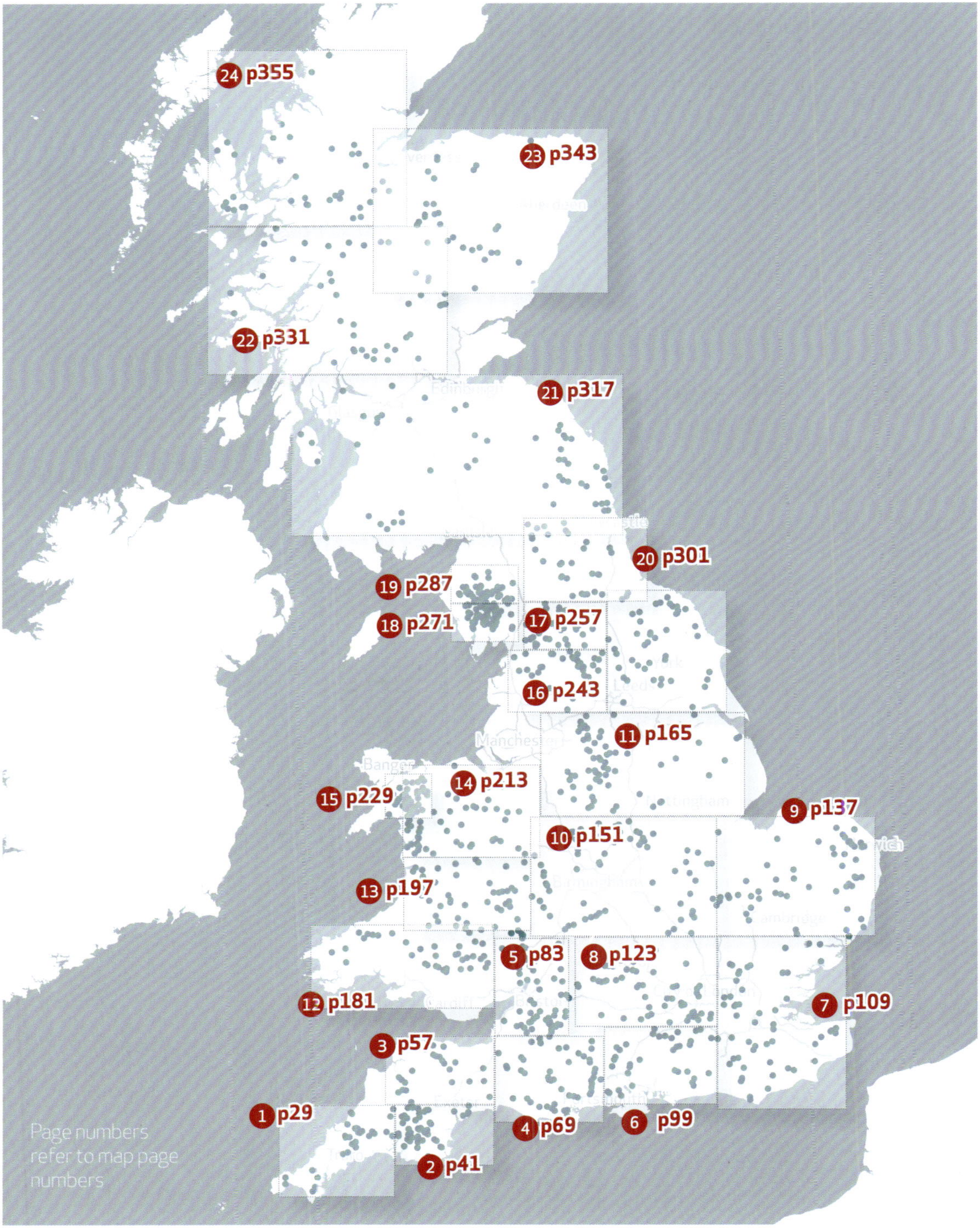

24 p355
23 p343
22 p331
21 p317
20 p301
19 p287
18 p271
17 p257
16 p243
11 p165
15 p229
14 p213
9 p137
10 p151
13 p197
5 p83
8 p123
12 p181
7 p109
3 p57
1 p29
4 p69
6 p99
2 p41

Page numbers
refer to map page
numbers

Dundas Aqueduct, p92

Introduction

One branch of evolutionary theory, expounded by Sir Alister Hardy in the 1950s, suggests that being by and in water is more than just a pleasure; it is at the core of our human condition. During the ten million years of the Pliocene world droughts, while our species was busy evolving into uprightness, we did not, suggests Hardy, choose the arid deserts of Africa as our home, as mainstream evolutionists believe, but the more tempting turquoise shallows of the nearby Indian Ocean. There, we became semi-aquatic coastal waders. Our subsequent life on dry land is a relatively recent and bereft affair.

Could this explain some of our more peculiar habits and features? Apart from the proboscis monkey, we are the only primate that regularly plays in water for sheer joy and whose offspring take to water naturally from birth. We are also unique in having subcutaneous fat, like a whale's blubber, for buoyancy and warmth. We are almost hairless, like the dolphin, and what little hair remains is arranged to make us streamlined for swimming.

Perhaps this is why Greek art and mythology abound with stories of water nymphs, naiads, and sirens as magical, sexual, mischievous creatures inhabiting their wild 'nymphaea': natural pools, rivers, and swimming holes, so beautiful that they lure unwitting mortals to their watery ends.

Pools and springs have long been revered by our Celtic and pagan ancestors. Even the Romans built shrines to water goddesses, and several accompany the bathhouses along Hadrian's Wall. Fresh water was seen as a sort of interface with the spirit world, a place where miracles—or curses—could manifest. 'Mermaid Pools' dot our Pennine mountain tops, and ancient holy wells and springs are found across the Welsh and Cornish hills. No wonder then, that when Christianity came, the Britons were quick to embrace river baptism as a doorway to a new god.

The Romantics and the Picturesque

As the nineteenth century dawned, a new era of contemporary European artists was rediscovering the appeal of the swimming hole. The waterfall, surrounded by trees and mountains, was now regarded as the quintessence of beauty. Wordsworth, Coleridge and De Quincey spent much time bathing in the mountain pools of the Lake District. The study and search for the 'picturesque' and 'sublime'—an almost scientific measure of loveliness and proportion in the landscape—had reached epidemic proportions. The fashionable tours of Provence or Tuscany

9

Galleny Force, p294

Wastwater, p290

Llanwenarth, p190

were replaced by trips to the valleys of Wales and the dales of Cumbria and Yorkshire, as Turner and Constable painted a prodigious flow of falls, tarns, and ponds.

As the Romantic era took hold, water held its place in the artists' gaze. Ruskin and others moved south to paint the river pools of Cornwall and Devon. Meanwhile, Charles Kingsley was dreaming of water babies on the Devon Dart, and Henry Scott Tuke was opening his floating studio in Falmouth, painting scenes of children swimming in the river. Soon, Francis Meadow Sutcliffe gained notoriety for his Water Rats photograph of naked boys, while across the Atlantic, Thomas Eakins was creating a stir with his homoerotic painting of the Swimming Hole. Water and nudity were pushing at the boundaries of rigid Victorian society, creating space for new ideas, freedoms, and creativity.

Health and Hydrotherapy

Alongside this change, a widespread craze for hydrotherapy swept the country, promoting the healing powers of water—particularly cold water—as a cure for everything from nervous disorders to digestive complaints. Inspired by European practitioners like Priessnitz and Kneipp, the movement encouraged treatments such as cold plunges, wet sheet wraps, and sitz baths, all aimed at stimulating circulation and restoring natural balance.

Indeed we now know that cold immersion soothes muscle aches, relieves depression, and boosts the immune system and all wild dippers known the natural endorphin high that raises mood, elates the senses, and creates an addictive urge to dive back in. However the world seems before a swim, it looks fantastic afterwards. The long-term impacts are also well researched: NASA studies have shown that, over a 12-week period, repeated cold swimming leads to substantial bodily changes known as 'cold adaptation'. These bring down blood pressure and cholesterol, reduce fat disposition, inhibit blood clotting, and increase fertility and libido in both men and women. Far from quelling passion, a cold shower will boost vitality and desire.

George Bernard Shaw, Benjamin Britten, Charles Darwin and Florence Nightingale were all advocates of regular cold baths to strengthen the mental constitution and physical state and its popularity gave rise to spa towns like Malvern, Harrogate and Matlock, where visitors flocked to drink or bathe in mineral-rich spring waters. At the same time, seaside resorts like Margate and Brighton boomed, as sea bathing became a fashionable form of cold water immersion. Bathing machines allowed for modest dips, while the bracing air and saltwater were thought to fortify both body and mind. More than a medical fad, hydrotherapy embodied Victorian ideals

Appletreewick, p250

Llyn Eiddew-bach, p216

Aberfeldy, Tayside, p339

of self-control, natural living and moral purity. Though it declined with the rise of modern medicine, its legacy lives on in today's sauna and spa culture, and renewed interest in cold-water therapy.

The Halcyon Era

By the 1870s, river- and lake-based recreation was entering mainstream culture. London was expanding at a rapid pace, and the middle- and working-class population woke up to the potential of the Thames, with its villages, boats, and watering holes lying only a cheap rail fare away. 'We would have the river almost to ourselves,' recalled Jerome K. Jerome, 'and sometimes would fix up a trip of three or four days or a week, doing the thing in style and camping out.' In 1889, he wrote the best-selling Three Men in a Boat, which was a manifesto for a simple way of living: close to nature, with river swimming before breakfast. Ratty declared in The Wind in the Willows that there 'was nothing, simply nothing, more worthwhile than messing about in boats,' and by 1909, Rupert Brooke was writing poems about bathing in Grantchester.

It was an idyllic period. Europe had been relatively peaceful for a hundred years. It was an age of relaxed elegance, of 25-mile-a-day walking tours, sleeping under canvas, and bathing in the river. Brooke spent his days studying literature, swimming, living off fruit and honey, and commuting to Cambridge by canoe. His passion for the outdoor life was shared by writers Virginia Woolf and E. M. Forster, philosophers Russell and Wittgenstein, economist Keynes, and artist Augustus John. As they swam naked at Byron's Pool in moonlight and practised their 'belly-floppers' in picnic diving practice along the Cam, this nucleus formed the emerging Bloomsbury Group, whom Woolf later dubbed the 'Neo-Pagans'.

Grantchester Meadows became the site of one of the first formal bathing clubs in the country, with an elegant pavilion, separate changing areas, and stone steps down into the warm waters of the River Cam. Similar clubs, 'Parson's Pleasure' and later 'Dame's Delight', quickly followed at the Cherwell in Oxford. Soon, every major public school was following suit with its own special riverside swimming facilities. By 1923, over 600 informal river swimming clubs were in existence around the country, with regular inter-county river swimming competitions and galas. Henry Williamson was swimming with Tarka the Otter, and Arthur Ransome immortalised the Lake District in Swallows and Amazons. Wild swimming had reached its heyday.

Rivers on the Brink: From Sewage to Restoration

In the decades following the Second World War, the rivers of England fell into crisis. Once vital arteries of trade, recreation and biodiversity they had become dumping grounds for untreated sewage and industrial waste.

Torrington Common, p62

Warleigh Weir, p92

'I can go right up to a frog in the water and it will show more curiosity than fear. The damselflies and dragonflies that crowd the surface of the moat pointedly ignore me, just taking off for a moment to allow me to go by them, then landing again on my wake. In the water you are hidden and submerged, enveloped in the silkiness of a liquid that is the medium of all life on earth.'

Roger Deakin, author of *Waterlog*, naturalist and forefather of wild-swimming, describing swimming in his moat in Suffolk.

By the 1950s, the Thames – once a proud symbol of Britain's capital – was declared biologically dead. By the 1970s, many rivers across the country were not much better. Fish populations had collapsed, oxygen levels were critically low, and raw sewage routinely fouled urban waterways.

But from the 1980s onward, change began to stir. The environmental movement gathered pace, new European legislation took hold, and water companies – now privatised and heavily regulated – were forced to invest in cleaning up their act. A turning point came with the European Union's Water Framework Directive (WFD), adopted in 2000, which mandated that all rivers should achieve 'good ecological status'. Its roots lay in earlier directives targeting urban wastewater and bathing water, but the WFD was broader, more ambitious, and science-led. For the Thames and many other rivers, it marked the beginning of a long, difficult recovery.

Over the next two decades, sewage treatment works were upgraded, industrial discharges curbed, and oxygen returned to the waters. Fish, including salmon and sea trout, reappeared in the Thames. Otters began to return to rural rivers long thought poisoned beyond repair. By the early 2000s, the Thames was being hailed as one of the cleanest major urban rivers in Europe.

Yet beneath this recovery lurked an older problem, one not easily solved by treatment plants alone: the Victorian sewer system. In many English towns and cities, stormwater and foul sewage still share a single pipe. Known as a combined sewer system, it works adequately in dry weather. But during heavy rain – increasingly common with climate change – the system becomes overwhelmed. To prevent sewage backing up into homes and streets, excess waste is discharged, untreated, into nearby rivers. These events are known as Combined Sewer Overflows, or CSOs.

Raising Awareness for Action

The publication of *Waterlog* by Roger Deakin in 1999 began a new wave of interest in swimming in rivers. It inspired the first edition of this book in 2008, *Wild Swim* by Kate Rew and the foundation of the now hugely popular Outdoor Swimming Society. During the Covid epidemic, lock down inspired a huge new wave of outdoor swimming too. For years, the CSC spills had largely hidden from public view, permitted as an emergency measure. But as public awareness of environmental issues grew, so too did scrutiny. Campaigners such as Surfers Against Sewage and The Rivers Trust began publishing historic and real-time CSO data in their sewage apps and maps. Citizen scientists tested local waters. Public anger mounted as it became clear just how often sewage was being discharged: not once or twice a year, but often hundreds of times per site, per year. Water companies blamed the Victorian infrastructure and worsening

Hembury Woods, p49

Teifi Gorge, Cilgerran, p184

Cornish Tipi Holidays, p37

storms. Critics, meanwhile, pointed to decades of underinvestment, where shareholder dividends and executive pay had taken precedence over the renewal of crumbling systems. The tension between long-standing structural problems and short-term financial choices became a central part of the national conversation about river health.

Cleaner Rivers - Looking to the Future

Today a whole sweep of new legislation is in progress, much brought by private members, to hold companies to account, impose massive fines and hold back bonuses for executives who pollute. Local groups are also applying for 'bathing water status' for their river, which brings additional legal protections. In response, some of the most ambitious infrastructure projects in generations have been launched.

The Thames Tideway Tunnel – dubbed London's "super sewer" – is a £4.5 billion project designed to intercept and store sewage overflows from 34 CSOs that currently spill directly into the river. The tunnel runs 25km beneath the Thames, capturing waste during storms and holding it until it can be properly treated. When finished, it is expected to prevent more than 90% of sewage spills into the central Thames, transforming the river's health and safety. In Leamington Spa, Severn Trent Water has begun installing new storm tanks and overflow diversions to prevent CSOs from polluting the River Leam. Projects like these aim to hold back rainwater and delay its entry into the sewer system, reducing the pressure that causes overflows in the first place.

Increasingly, though, the emphasis is shifting from grey to green infrastructure. Rather than just building bigger pipes and tanks, many towns are exploring reedbeds, artificial wetlands, tree planting, rain gardens, swales, and green roofs – all designed to absorb, slow, and filter rainfall before it reaches the drains. On a city scale, Sustainable Urban Drainage Systems (SuDS) can mimic natural hydrology, allowing rainfall to be absorbed into the ground or filtered through vegetation.

The fight for clean rivers is far from over. In England today, over 90% of rivers still fail to meet "good ecological status", with agricultural runoff, microplastics, pharmaceuticals and persistent CSO discharges continuing to degrade ecosystems. But public awareness is now high, and pressure is growing on both regulators and water companies to act. Climate change will continue to stress the system. Heavier, more intense storms will test the limits of both old infrastructure and new investments. But with sustained investment, stronger regulation, and a turn towards greener solutions, plus new hopes that water companies will open up our reservoir lakes to public swimming, England's waters can once again become clean, vibrant spaces – not just for wildlife, but for swimming, paddling, and all life.

Getting started

Using this book

Most places listed are on a public right of way, permissive path, open-access land or benefit from long-use rights. However, some places, usually marked ❓, may not have such clear rights. You will need to make your own judgement about whether to proceed or seek permission from the landowner.

Decimal coordinates are provided in WGS84 (latitude, longitude), the definitive global reference system. They can be entered into any online map site, including those with OS maps such as Bing or Streetmap. Print out the map before you go or save a screen grab. Bing will not show OS maps on a mobile browser unless the 'desktop view' is requested. Sadly, OS paper maps still do not provide decimal WGS84 (only imperial). If a parking place is mentioned, use your own judgement and be considerate. Where two places are named in the title, the listing coordinate refers to the first. Walk-in times are one way only, allowing 15 mins per km, which is quite brisk. For Left and Right river banks, this is facing downstream. Abbreviations also include north,

Joining a local group This is a great way to learn the basics and make friends in a supportive setting. National networks such as the BlueTits Chill Swimmers and Mental Health Swims offer welcoming, informal swim communities across the country with online maps to find your local group. While the BlueTits began as a women-led movement in West Wales, founded by Sian Richardson, they are now fully inclusive and welcome men, non-binary swimmers, and people of all ages and backgrounds. Their focus is on fun, body positivity, and connection, and you can find your nearest group on their website or through social media. The Outdoor Swimming Society also has a good page on local groups, and the NOWCA Wild app (below).

Managed venues & NOWCA Another approach is to visit a venue with lifeguarded OWS (Open Water Swimming) sessions. You'll usually have to wear a wetsuit and cap, trail a tow float and swim a marked circuit. It might be better for keen swimmers transitioning to the outdoors, and those looking to swim a distance. All venues are lakes, many are beautiful and most would otherwise be No Swimming outside of sessions/membership. Most are insured as part of NOWCA (National Open Water Coaching Association) so you will also need to join for a small annual fee. They provide insurance and basic safety protocols to adhere to. They also have the Wild app to find venues and book online.

Finding your own swim This guide describes some of the best known or most beautiful freshwater wild swims, but there are many more and conditions change, so learn to use a map and find your own. River bends often create shallow beaches on the inside and deeper pools on the outside. Small weirs and waterfalls create pools in rivers that would be otherwise too shallow. A narrowing of a mountain river, or a bridge across, suggests a gorge or canyon. Ordnance Survey maps provide a huge number of clues and are still free on bing.com and streetmap.co.uk. Satellite imagery on Google can also help. Any waterside footpath, ford, footbridge or open-access land is a good place to start, as it suggests historic access and use to the water, to bathe, boat and swim.

What are my rights?

Make your own decisions Except in Scotland, there are few clear formal rights to swim in non-tidal British waters. That doesn't mean there aren't historic use rights, but they may be contested. So always make your own judgement about whether to access land and water. Seek permission if unsure, leave if challenged and be polite. Never swim near anglers, particularly on expensive salmon and trout rivers. They have paid for their use; you have not.

No Swimming You'll see many such signs in popular bathing places, but often these are erected to cover against liability in case of an accident (to stop the landowners from being sued). And there may be overriding historic use to bathe, bring animals, or to navigate. Over 20 years' use counts as 'time immemorial' and supports a common law/prescriptive 'customary' right. And a public right of way to the banks suggests such an historic use.

Riparian property Further, nobody owns the water itself. The riparian owner controls the banks and bed, but the water is free to float in. Any water that was navigated in the past, and an extraordinary number of tiny rivers certainly were, enjoys navigation rights in perpetuity, which includes the right to launch and swim. Many bigger rivers have statutory navigation rights (Thames, Avon, Severn, Medway, Ouse, Trent, Cam, Lea, Lugg & Wye).

Trespass Despite misconceptions, trespassers cannot be prosecuted, and the police can only be called in certain circumstances: when there are more than six vehicles on the land, when damage has been done, or when abusive language has been used.

Reservoirs are almost always No Swimming, sometimes under bylaws, even where locals have historically swum. We question their moral and legal right to deny swimming (see box). So do something, join a local 'Swim Trespass' each April to commemorate the 1932 Kinder Scout trespass and sign up to the Right to Swim Manifesto on the Outdoor Swimming Society website. Reservoirs should be open access for swimming.

Swimming in Reservoirs: 500 beaches campaign

Thatcher privatised our country's reservoirs but new owners were legally obliged to 'facilitate' recreational access and use, and 'promote' amenity by the public where 'reasonably practicable'. (1989 Water Act), more recently emphasising the duty of preserving public freedoms of access (1991 Water Industry Act, s3).

It's extraordinary that while the Water Companies pollute our rivers, they also deny us the right to swim in our lakes, all of which were built with public money. They complain of safety, yet the upper shores of reservoirs are by far the safest waters in the UK (no currents, no pollution, not too cold) They complain of contamination but far more comes from bird poo, run-off and motor boats.

On the continent swimming is allowed in all reservoirs. How amazing it would be if a beach on each of the 500 British reservoirs were opened. No lifeguards, just 'swim at your own risk'. Write to your MP or join a Swim Trespass.

Safety & water quality

5 ways to stay safe

1. Enter cold water slowly if you don't know how you will react
2. Stay close to the shore; cold water limits swimming ability
3. Check for depth and obstructions before every jump or dive
4. Check your exit before you get get in, especially if currents
5. Stay away from the bottom of weirs and waterfalls
6. Avoid urban areas and rivers after heavy rain

Checking water quality

Install the SSRS (Safer Seas & Rivers Service) app. It provides real-time sewage overflow alerts for some rivers. Search 'live sewage map' for more comprehensive data about every sewage treatment unit on your river. Both The Rivers Trust and Surfers Against Sewage publish excellent maps using the same publicly available CSO data.

theriverstrust.org/sewage-map

sewagemap.co.uk/

For more detailed information on water safety visit wildswimming.com or outdoorswimmingsociety.com

Hypothermia Swimming in cold water saps body heat. Shivering and teeth-chattering are the first stages of mild hypothermia, with disorientation and stumbling. Get warm before you go in. Don't stay in too long. Warm up with a combination of dry clothes, hot drinks and activity. Wear a wetsuit if you want to stay in for more than a quick dip.

Cold shock is the involuntary gasp and rise in heart rate that occurs as the body enters very cold water, especially if you are not used to cold water. Test the temperature and wade in slowly unless you are already acclimatised to outdoor swimming.

Weak swimmers Shallow water can deepen suddenly. Cold water can surprise even strong swimmers. Drowning happens silently. If any of your group cannot swim, or is not used to cold water, make sure you scout out the extent of the shallows and currents, set clear boundaries and keep constant supervision. Buy a good quality buoyancy aid for non-swimmers.

Cramps and solo-swimming Cramp is not more likely after eating but dehydration, or a poor diet in general, can make you especially prone. If you are prone, shout for help, lie on your back and paddle back to shore with your arms. Swimming alone in deep water has risks so use a tow float.

Slips, trips & falls It sounds obvious but this is the most common hazard. Never run. Go barefoot to get a better grip or wear watershoes.

Jumping and diving Always check the depth of the water, even if you visit the same spot regularly. Depths can vary and new underwater obstructions (sand, rocks, branches, rubbish) may have been brought downstream the night before. A broken neck from a diving accident could paralyse you for life.

Water weeds Common in semi-shallow areas during summer. It's quite possible to swim/float through them safely but panicking and thrashing about don't help. Avoid them if you don't like them, or practise being in them in a safe area.

Blue–green algae Can develop in lakes after warm weather in late summer, caused by eutrophication, usually from fertiliser runoff from fields. The algae multiply and a powdery, green scum (the blooms) collects on the downwind shores. It's pretty obvious but can give you a skin rash or irritate your eyes if you bathe in the scum itself.

Swimmer's itch Uncommon but 'cercarial dermatitis' can be caught from contact with little snails that live on the reeds around marshy lakes and stagnant ponds. It creates a temporary but sometimes intense itching sensation that can last for up to two days.

E-coli Most lowland rivers contain traces of treated sewage effluent, or raw cattle faeces, especially after heavy rain. Although many people never get ill, a few do and the result is unpleasant diarrhoea and vomiting. Rivers do clean themselves however, through the action of UV from the sun and ozone from the flow. So the further you are from upstream development or cattle grazing, the better. Don't swallow the water when you jump in and keep your head out when swimming.

Weil's disease In urban areas sewers and storm drains may harbour colonies of rats whose urine may carry the bacterial infection Leptospirosis. It's very rare and caught early it can be treated with antibiotics, but if left to develop can be very serious. Avoid urban waters after heavy rain, and if you are concerned cover any open wound with a waterproof plaster and keep your head (eyes, nose and throat) out of the water as much as possible. If you get flu or jaundice-like symptoms three to fourteen days after swimming in high-risk water ask your doctor for a Leptospirosis test.

Life-saving If you go swimming regularly why not learn how to save someone? The basic principle is to turn the person on their back, put your hand under their chin, grasp them to your front and backstroke to shore with a breaststroke leg kick. Practise it on a friend for fun then be ready to save someone's life for real.

Understanding currents

Swimming with the flow can be great fun and is a helping hand on a longer swim, and if you have planned for it. But always consider what's downstream and where you will I get out. Scout around for downstream hazards (obstructions, waterfalls or weirs). As a river shallows or narrows the speed increases but 'still waters run deep'.

Faster rivers pose additional risk. In uplands, if it's moving fast enough even shallow water can knock you off your feet and carry you away. Riding river currents with a float or ring is a sport, so search for river boarding, hydrospeed or whitewater sledging.

Where a river drops, over weirs and waterfalls, strong re-circulating currents ('hydraulics' or 'stoppers') can form in the pool directly under the chute. Semi-circular or 'box' weirs, which have three sides, are worse. So don't go and jump into the bubbling whirlpool below a big waterfall, and if you are ever caught in a stopper, throw out an arm, change your position, or swim down or to the side, so you are hopefully caught by the exit currents, which will eventually sp t you out..

Best for Families

Mainly shallow with paddling and minnows

Best for Literary Swims

Where famous poets, writers or artists once swam

Best for Skinny-dipping

Remote and secluded, perfect for a natural dip

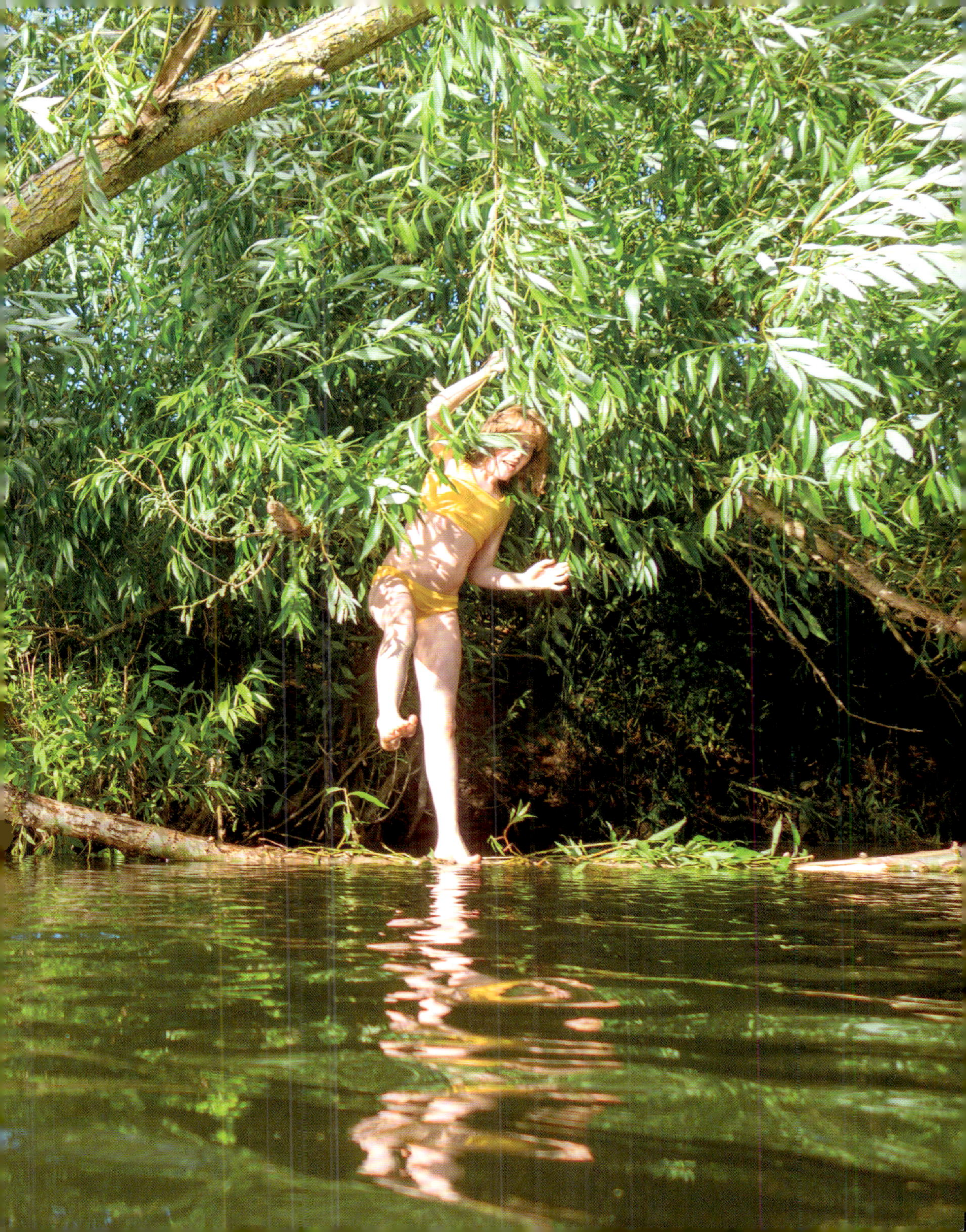

Best for Picnics

Beautiful places, not far from parking with good picnic areas or grassy banks

Best for Train Access

Within walking distance of a train station

Best for Cycling

On dedicated cycle trails or routes

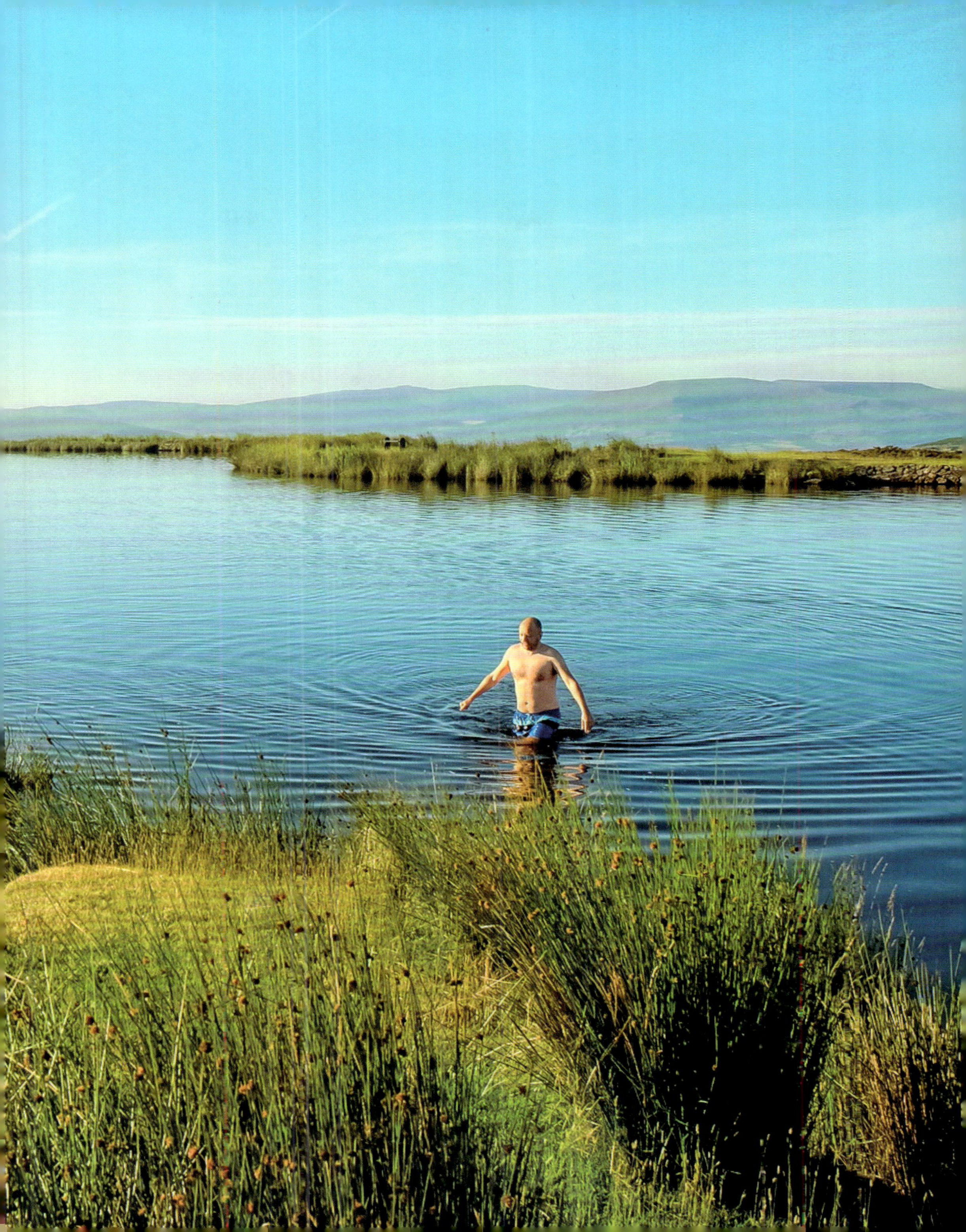

Best for SUPs & Canoes

Good, legal access with your canoe (or possibility to hire a boat *)

Best for Pubs

A cosy, warming pub just a splash away

Best for Camping

Fantastic river or lakeside camping.

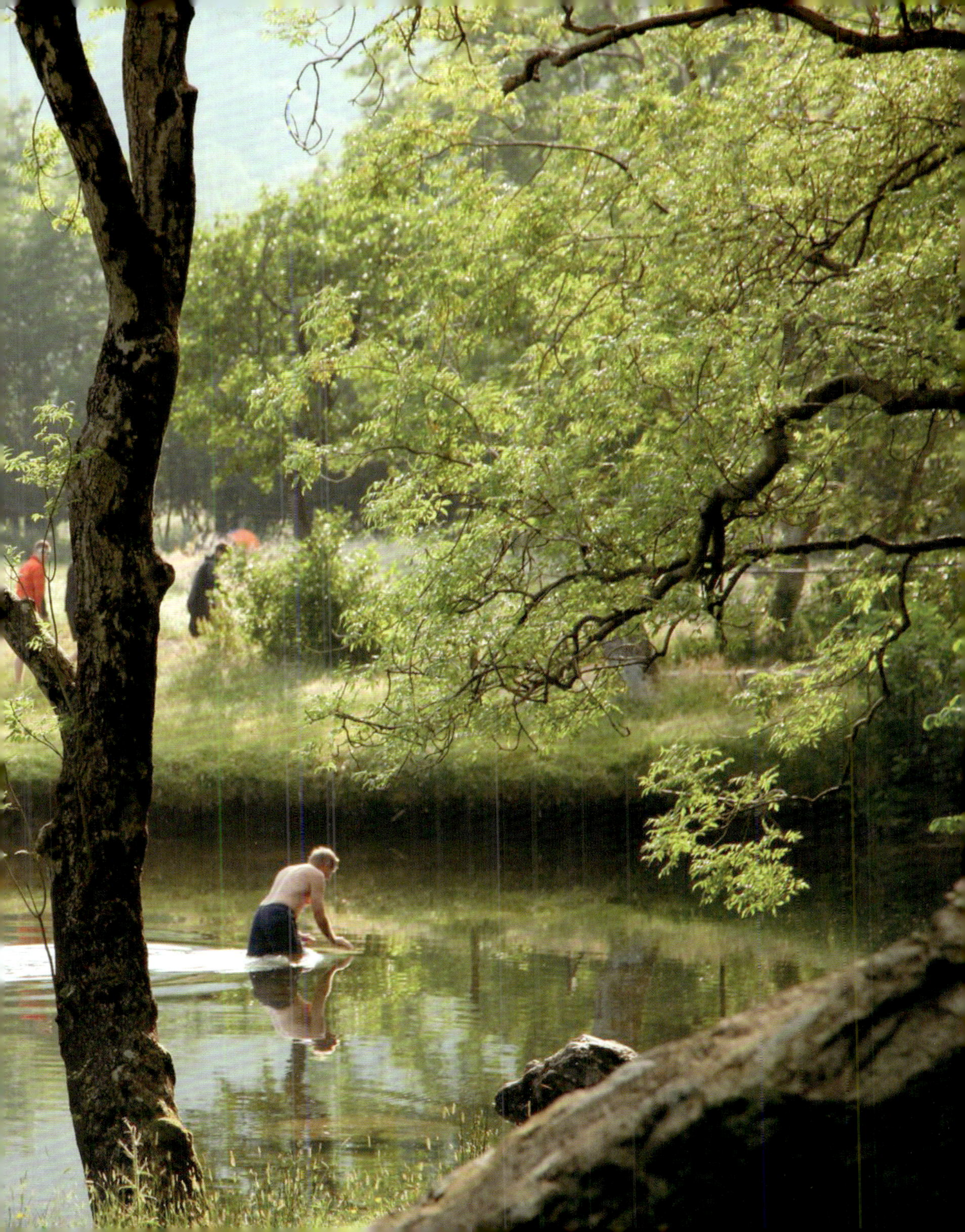

Best for Jumping

Check the depth every time - depths and obstructions change

Best for Tubing & Chutes

Play in the current, or use a rubber ring, if flow level is safe

Best for Waterfalls

Magically situated under waterfalls, big and small

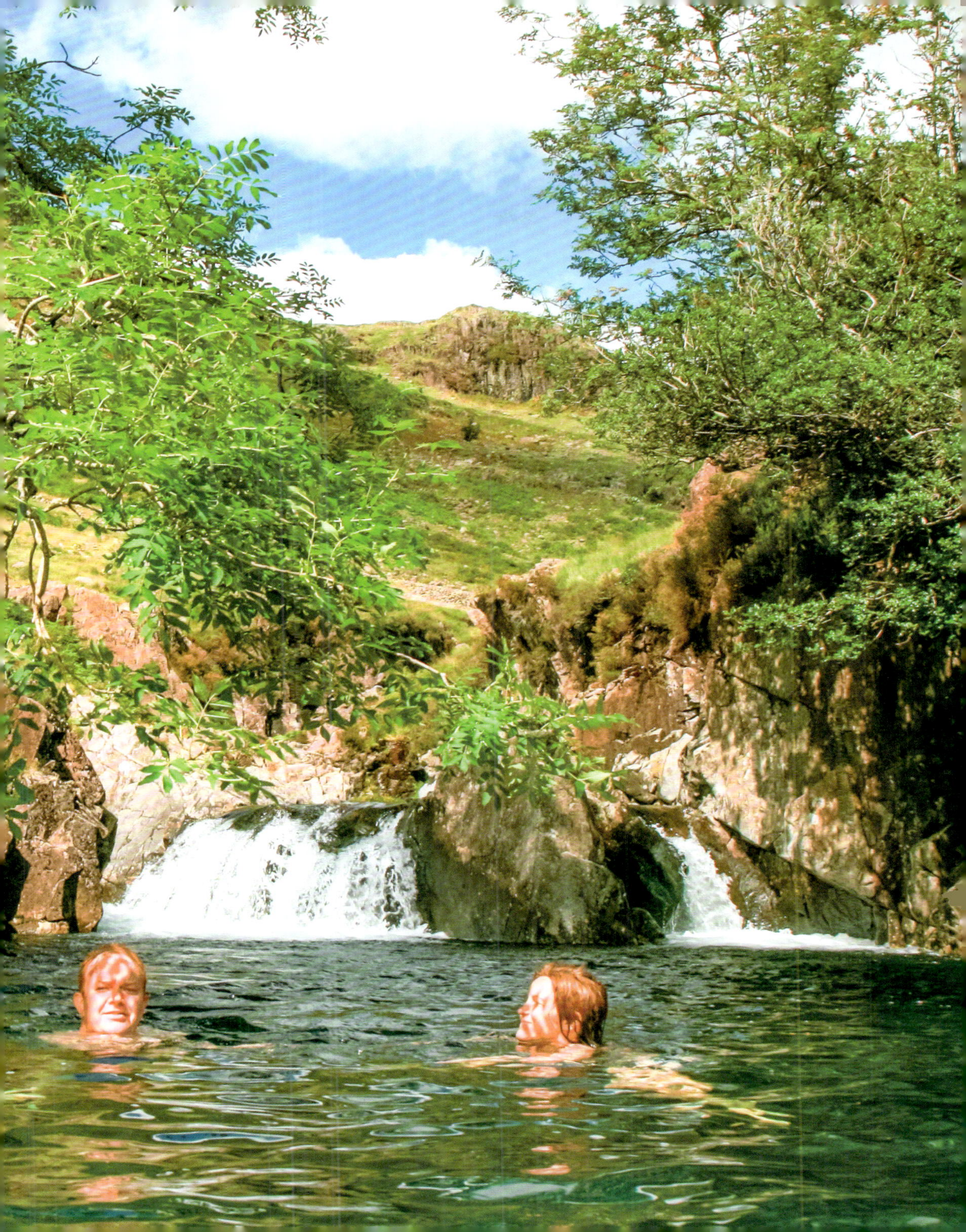

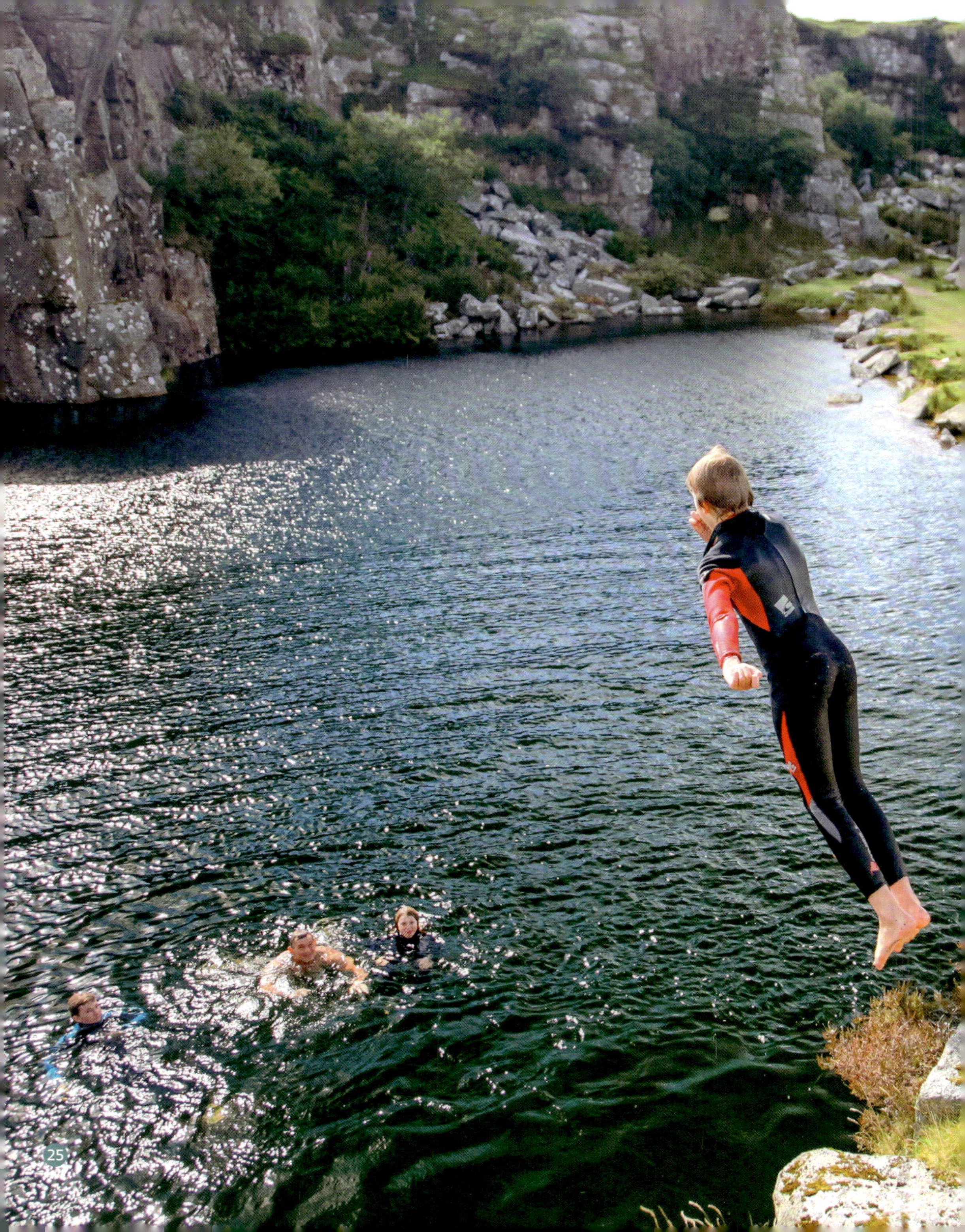

CORNWALL

The River Fowey cascades down through dense, sessile oak woodland on the edge of Bodmin Moor. There are humid, aromatic glens, and the trees are draped with rare ferns, mosses, and ivy. This area, known as Golitha Falls (24), is home to otters, which live among the river roots, and bats, which sleep in the old mine workings and maybe even the 'Beast of Bodmin', thought to be a species of small wild cat similar to a puma. In 1995, a big cat skull was found in the woods and claimed as the final proof, although the skull turned out to be that of a leopard taken from an exotic leopard-skin rug and planted by a hoaxer.

Where the main path ends, at the beginning of a series of shallow falls, pick your way further down one of the narrow trails. Wagtails criss-cross the stream, and a small, gladed pool opens up a few hundred yards below, out of sight of any crowds. When I was there, the yellow sand of the stream threw up a golden light on the rocks around as I eased myself into the pool. It was hot and I was tired, but the babbling moorland water soon cut through the sweat and grime. It wasn't large or particularly deep, but the stream picked me up, and I found a part of the current which, with some careful balancing, held me in position as I swam. Then I flipped onto my back and let the flow carry me down into the shallow rapids and ground me in the sand, the water rushing over my shoulders and shins like a spa.

After a little doze in the dappled light of the rocky ledges, I found a wooded weir pool about another mile or so downstream and camped there discreetly. As dusk gathered around me, I sipped whisky and kept a silent vigil for bats and owls. As the evening drew late, I thought I saw the luminescent blurs of will-o'-the-wisp in the shadows of the wood before I fell asleep under the trees, looking up at the pale midsummer night sky, with total darkness never quite descending.

Padstow
St Columb
Major
Newquay
Truro
Redruth
3
8
St Ives
Camborne
7
Hayle
Penryn
1
6
Falmouth
St. Just
Penzance
Marazion
2
Helston
5
Porthleven
4

Launceston
Camelford
Tavistock
Wadebridge
Callington
Bodmin
Liskeard
Lostwithiel
Plymouth
St Blazey
Looe
St Austell
Fowey
9
10
11
12
13
14
15
16
17
18
19
20
21
22
23
24
25
26
27
28
29
30
31
32
33
34

Waking early, I had a quick splash in the water in bright sunshine before trekking back to the car. I was heading ten miles downstream for the National Trust estate of Lanhydrock House, a Jacobean country house built in the early 17th century by the Robartes family. It is now one of the Trust's most visited properties. The gardens are filled with magnificent magnolia and camellia, and the estate stretches for many miles along the Fowey.

Downstream from Respryn Bridge (13), once the lowest crossing point on the Fowey, there are bankside decking areas which make a good place to change and swim. The water is fast-flowing and refreshing, about five feet deep in places and completely clear. I practised some shallow diving and then swam along the bank, searching for otter holes and examining the oak roots that grow down into the water.

As the morning drew on, the path became busy with dog walkers and families playing Pooh Sticks, so I got dressed and headed upstream. This path is even more beautiful for swimming and arrives, bizarrely, at a white gate leading into the back of Bodmin Parkway Station car park (14). This was the terminus of the first steam railway in Cornwall, built to bring lime-rich sea sand from Wadebridge for use as fertiliser. A wooded stretch of riverbank here is home to a dark but magical stretch of the river, completely overshadowed by trees and foliage. I swam and floated several hundred yards downstream and then had to tiptoe back barefoot through the undergrowth and creepers to find my pile of clothes. Here, only a mile from the main line and the 08:36 to London, you can pretend you're lost in a tropical jungle.

Much of the wealth of the Robartes family came from mining, and the landscape is dotted with their pools and lakes. Often, they are old granite workings, but there are areas with relics from tin and copper too, such as at Caradon. One of the best-known pools is a turquoise quarry lake near Port Isaac, the old Tregildrans Quarry. The land has been in the same family for generations, but when the quarry went out of business forty years ago, the owner, Lizzie, decided to let it go wild, creating a network of forest clearings with tipis all around the lake, now called Cornish Tipi Holidays (30).

When I visited, the lake was alive with families swimming and having fun. Leaving my clothes in a heap, I dived in to join the melee, the late afternoon light shining through the leaves. The underwater zone felt white, opaque, and was flavoured with minerals. Almost before I had surfaced, someone dive-bombed me from a tree, and I raced for control of an abandoned lilo. At the far end of the quarry, a willowy boy stood alert at the prow of his canoe, searching for trout below. Later that evening, we prepared a small fire, and I retired to my tipi at the edge of one of the clearings. Towels were being hung out on the guy ropes to dry, swimming costumes adorned the totem poles, and I could still hear the sound of splashing from the lake. This is a little lost world of canoes, swimming, and Hiawathas.

Those interested in legends should visit Dozmary Pool, where the ghostly hand reputedly appeared to take the sword Excalibur when the knight Sir Bedivere returned it to the lake. Whirlpools are said to rage here to this day. On top of Bodmin Moor on a sunny August day, clouds racing across the sky, Dozmary seems rather benign and the swimming a little shallow. The shores of Colliford, lying across the field, would provide a more satisfying swim, if it were permitted. This is Cornwall's largest and highest lake. It is also situated close to the famous Jamaica Inn, setting for Daphne du Maurier's evocative novel of smugglers and pirates, and now a mystical labyrinth, constructed using traditional Cornish hedges (23).

For more Arthurian legend, visit St Nectan's 'Kieve' — a Cornish word meaning tub, vat, or natural basin — often used to describe circular or hollowed-out pools (29). Found in a hidden valley only a few miles from the Arthurian castle of Tintagel, St Nectan, the hermit who lived here in the hermitage around 480 AD, was one of the holiest of Cornish saints. Treading gingerly down the wet slate steps, I descended into the veil of mist that rises from St Nectan's Kieve; it's easy to see why this place was revered. The flow of the water has sculpted a deep cylindrical well and a perfect man-sized hole through which the water spills. This upper pool is out of reach, but the lower pool is deep enough for an exhilarating splash and plunge. This has long been a place of pilgrimage and immersion, and it was here that King Arthur's knights were baptised before they set out on their quest to recover the Holy Grail. Today, small shrines of cairns and photographs of loved ones have been set up on the surrounding rocky ledges. Little light filters down here, but hundreds of coloured ribbons tied to branches and rocks give the cavern a fluttering glow, like a pagan May Day.

PENWITH TO ROSELAND

1 BAKER'S PIT LAKE & FOLLY ❓

Once a china clay works, now nature reserve with deep freshwater quarry popular for a quite but No Swimming. There's a ruined engine house on the way up. Afterward continue 1km SE to Roger's Tower, a quirky folly inside Castle-an-Dinas hillfort with ruined farmhouse adjacent. Turn L off the B3311 from Penzance at Nancledra. After 1 mile turn L to Georgia and park at the road end then SW on track.

15 mins, 50.1667, -5.5295 🖼🚶

2 JUBILEE POOL LIDO, PENZANCE £

UK's largest seawater lido, an Art Deco classic right on the shore with super café and a geothermally heated pool too. Locals also swim all year round off Battery Rocks below; steps lead into the water. Battery Road, TR18 4FF, 01736 369224.

2 mins, 50.1151, -5.5313 £

3 CARN MARTH POOL & THEATRE

Old granite quarry amid heather, with smooth flat rocks and deep spring water, near summit of Carn Marth. There's also an outdoor theatre in the quarry below. The Great Flat Lode cycle route passes close by. Near top of Lanner Hill, A393, take Carn Marth lane by the bus stop (dead-end). Continue up, bearing R then L at Wheal Amelia mine. After 250m park outside the old quarry/theatre, TR16 5TA and continue up track on foot 250m.

5 mins, 50.2233, -5.203 🖼🚶🌾

4 TREVASSACK LAKE, HELSTON £

Beautiful freshwater lake for swimming, paddleboarding or sailing. Run by the Children's Sailing Trust. Café and come accommodation on site. £6.50 per swim. Trevassack Lake Garras, Helston TR12 6LH. 01326 702326

2 mins, 50.0560, -5.1981 £

5 TREMAYNE QUAY, HELFORD

Tidal stone quay reached downstream path through ancient woodland. High tide only, S side of estuary. Parking on lane TR12 6DB. On N side is an even more remote tidal quay, Scott's Quay. Bear E down on lane from Trengilly Wartha Inn, Nancenoy, (TR11 5RP, 01326 340332) and find path on R after 300m (50.1026, -5.1647)

20 mins, 50.0908, -5.1681 🚣🚶🌾

6 CARNSEW POOL, MABE BURNTHOUSE ❓

Spring-fed quarry with sheer granite sides.

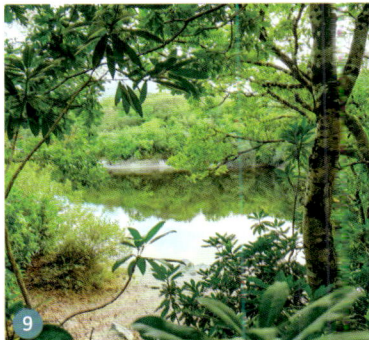

300m W of Mabe Burnthouse on Antron Hill find bridleway on R, after Estuary View cul de sac (where you could park).
5 mins, 50.1661, -5.1387 ▣

7 KENNALL VALE NATURE RESERVE
Deep water-filled quarry, plus streams waterfalls, leats and old waterwheels from the ruined mills where gunpowder was manufactured. Entrance track through wall on R on tiny Cot Hill, Ponsanooth, TR3 7HG. Park on Kennall Vale and walk up 150m. Respect signage, this is a nature reserve
5 mins, 50.1954, -5.1488 ▣▣▣

8 ROUNDWOOD QUAY & HILLFORT
Impressive old stone quay area with ruins, hillfort, woods and swings. High tide only Limited parking at end of rough track, signed as Byway, on lane S of Cowlands.
5 mins, 50.2237, -5.0313 ▣▣

ST AUSTELL ALPS

9 BURNGULLOW COMMON LAKE
Completely wild clay lake with white beaches, surrounded by rhododendron woodland. It may be private so observe any signage. Turn off A3058 between Lanjeth and Trewoon (dead-end) and continue ¾

mile to find layby on L at 50.3498, -4.8315, PL26 7TR. A trail opp leads down into woods. After 300m find lake up on R.
5 mins, 50.3498, -4.8262 ▣▣▣

10 CARN GREY ROCK & LAKE, TRETHURGY
It's fun to climb the granite tor of Carn Grey. Below is a small pretty quarry lake. 400m S of Trethurgy on St Austell road, bear off R on track to car park at PL26 8TE, 50.3629, -4.7647. There are more clay pit pools to admire in the area, though mostly fenced and No Swimming. This one is frequented by swimmers 50.3659, -4.7706.
3 mins, 50.3628, -4.7666

RIVER FOWEY

11 COULSON PARK, LOSTWITHIEL
The Fowey meanders through Shirehall Moor meadows. Easy parking and access make it a handy place to launch a canoe or quick dip. At the bottom of Quay Street, PL22 0BY, drive under the low railway bridge (far R end) to find car park after 250m and river adjacent. More remote meander section 300m downstream, beyond the quay/embankment.
1 mins, 50.402, -4.6689 ▣▣▣

12 RED MOOR LAKE, TREDINNICK PITS ▣
Remote woodland and glades surround a large lake with island, formed from open-cast tin mining until the late 19C. Follow the path around to the S shore where there's a rooty way into the peaty, amber water. People do swim discreetly here but it is also an SSSI and part of the Helman Tor Nature Reserve. Park at the grassy triangle where dead-end lane is signed (50.4287, -4.7091), or elsewhere, and find wooden gate and sign on R 100m down lane. Continue 350m.
5 mins, 50.4277, -4.7149 ▣▣

13 RESPRYN BRIDGE DOWNSTREAM

Wooden, bankside decks (for fishing) and a beach shingle area by the lower footbridge (also good for Pooh sticks). Cross river and continue for a full ¾ mile to reach river islands (50.4337, -4.6816) and old weir. Up to 2m deep in sections and fun to swim against the current. There's a large car park downhill E on lane from Lanhydrock House entrance, PL30 4AH.

20 mins, 50.4391, -4.6795 🏊🚲➕

14 RESPRYN BRIDGE UPSTREAM

Dappled light reflects on the river as it flows briskly through the woods. This is the less-visited section but has rope swings and deeper pools, particularly on the meanders. From car park head upstream on R bank path ½ mile, or you might get lucky with much closer parking at the red gate R on the narrow, unsigned '7.5t' sign lane, turn L just before car park. Another 400m upstream is a secret, secluded river beach in woodland, perfect for a skinny dip. Keep on R bank. There's a pond too. Or it's accessible just through the back gates of Bodmin Station car park (50.4461, -4.6668).

5 mins, 50.4443, -4.6713 🏊🚲➕🅿🔥⬇

RIVER CAMEL

15 POLBROOK BRIDGE CYCLE, R CAMEL 🚲

Picnic and paddling by little bridge, also on cycle path. There's also a large, deep pool in the bend, right next to the bike path 400m N – look out for the wooden gate and bike rack, 50.4954, -4.8024. Non-cyclists can park at Bishops Wood car park, PL30 3AN.

2 mins, 50.4918, -4.8015 🏊🚲➕🅿🏊

16 GROGLEY MOOR, R CAMEL

A wooded deep pool with small beach just below the gauging station and cabin, with pulley cables across the river. On open access land. The Camel Trail runs along R bank, or park on lane and find small opening for L bank, 50.4787, -4.7982. Further S down the lane are mountain bike trails in Grogley Woods.

2 mins, 50.4795, -4.7959 🏊

17 DUNMERE WEIR & OTTERS

Deep in Pencarrow Woods the weir and salmon leap make a shady, secret, dappled place for a swim. This is also the perfect territory for the secretive but clever otters. Watch for them at dawn and dusk and if you get a sighting, do log it with the Cornwall Wildlife Trust to be added to their research.

500m upstream is Crabb's Pool (50.4850, -4.7458). ½ mile NW of Bodmin A389 park behind Borough Arms, PL31 2RD. Head E on trail, dir Bodmin, but take first L dir Wenford Bridge and continue ½ mile.

20 mins, 50.4817, -4.747 🏊🚲➕🏊

BODMIN MOOR

18 DELPHY POOL, BODMIN 🏊

Jade green quarry pool with OWS, diving and spear fishing. Weekend sessions with 'wild spa' hot tub and sauna sessions. Members only. £35 per year plus £10 swim/£22 with sauna. Delphy Pool, St Breward, Hantergantick, PL30 4NH. 07817 326223.

2 mins, 50.5500, -4.6788

19 DELFORD/DELPHI BRIDGE, DE LANK 🚲

Pretty moorland stream and clapper bridge with a shallow, soft, sandy pool and large area of beach for children. Explore upstream for more picnic spots. Leave A30 St Breward/Temple, follow signs for St Breward, turning R after 4km, PL30 4NL.

2 mins, 50.5524, -4.6632 🚲

20 CARBILLY QUARRY POOLS

Three deep, spring-fed quarry pools lie among the tors, together with the ruins of several mine houses, including one with the remains of an impressive hearth and chimney. The little-known Trippet Stones circle is to the SE. Leave A30 St Breward/ Temple, follow signs for St Breward. After 1km the first track on R leads to the circle (50.5450, -4.6390) but continue another 400m to farm gate on R with some parking on verge, PL30 4LE. The land is open access, but be respectful and discreet. Walk up the track and bear off R after 150m, which leads to the ruined hearth and the first two pools where people often swim. Continue N up to the top which leads around the back of the biggest quarry pool, with high cliffs and views. Obey any No Swimming signage.

10 mins, 50.5486, -4.6469 ⬛?

21 CARDINHAM MOOR POOL
On open moorland, just by the A30, the perfect place to blow away the cobwebs on a drive to west Cornwall. St Bellarmin's Tor parking layby is on A30 W bound (dir Temple Fishery) or via Temple/St Breward exit E bound, PL30 4HW. Hop over the fence and it's 400m on open access land W.

5 mins, 50.5191, -4.6413 ⬛

22 THE LAKE CABIN, GLYNN VALLEY ⬛
A remote flooded china clay quarry in open-access moorland with fascinating mine ruins to explore. You can touch the water, but No Swimming unless you rent the simply converted, off-grid shipping container perched right on its shore (PL30 4DW). Book at canopyandstars.co.uk

5 mins, 50.5147, -4.6188 ⬛

23 KERDROYA LABYRINTH, COLLIFORD
Explore the new Kerdroya labyrinth, the largest of its kind in the world, made using traditional Cornish hedging techniques, right by the lake shore (PL14 6PZ). Colliford is a huge moorland reservoir, the highest and largest in Cornwall, just off A30. The whole W shore shore is open access with chalky, shelving beaches. No Swimming signs, but people do sometimes paddle.

2 mins, 50.5283, -4.5926 ⬛?

24 GOLITHA FALLS, REDGATE
A popular spot where the young river Fowey tumbles down through ancient oak woodland. There is paddling before the river cascades down over boulders and small falls. At the bottom there is a small, secret plunge pool with golden sand, beyond the

mine ruins. Car park at PL14 6RJ.

15 mins, 50.4907, -4.5071 ⬛⬛⬛⬛⬛⬛

25 GOLDIGGINS QUARRY, MINIONS
A spring-fed quarry lake, out on the open moors hidden in a small grassy amphitheatre. Flat rock ledges for jumping. Popular with youngsters in summer. No Swimming signs. From the Hurlers car park, PL14 5LW, follow the vehicle track that heads N onto the moor, past the stone circle. After 15 mins bear L at the junction and continue another 750m to find the quarry.

25 mins, 50.5248, -4.4711 ⬛⬛⬛⬛⬛⬛

26 THE PONY POOL, MINIONS
Beachy areas, gently shelving shallows and a waterfall make this small, sheltered lake nice for kids. As for Goldiggins but bear R at the junction. After the stream (about 300m) turn R off the track to find the lake and dam on the stream valley above.

20 mins, 50.5223, -4.4629 ⬛⬛⬛

27 CARADON HILL POOL & RUINS
Deep, clear quarry pool with remains of a submerged crane and big views, good for a sunset dip and maybe even a wild camp. From Minions take the road by the shop

up toward Caradon Hill Transmitter, PL14 5LT. After 700m park in layby on L and walk up track on R 250m to quarry. Fascinating and little-visited ruins of engines houses, chimneys and the old reservoir 600m to the SW, 50.5043, -4.4471). Also accessible from The Crows Nest to the S, PL14 5JQ (good traditional pub, 01579 345930).
5 mins, 50.5085, -4.4421 ☒ⓥ

TINTAGEL STREAMS

28 ROCKY VALLEY, TINTAGEL ☒
Follow the ancient, wooded stream valley down to the sea. There are waterfalls towards the bottom, and the pools are big enough for a dip. Look out for the ruins of Trewethett Mill with old millstones in the undergrowth halfway down. On rock face behind are two beautiful carvings of labyrinths, possibly ancient. Park on B3263, ½ miles E of Bossiney, at layby on R just after tiny lane junction, PL34 0BB. Cross road and find signed path by white house.
10 mins, 50.674, -4.7299 ☒🚶☒🚶

29 ST NECTAN'S KIEVE, TINTAGEL ☒☒
At the head of a wild glen with prayer flags adorning the trees, a tall, slender waterfall falls into a high basin, flows through a

circular hole and drops into a plunge poo
(the kieve). Above in the hermitage is a
shrine room and tea room. Park on B3263,
¾ miles E of Bossiney, in layoys on L in
Trethevy, PL34 0BG. Cross road and take
track by postbox, bearing R with St Pira's
church on L (do look inside – there's a ho y
well too). Continue a mile along the stream
(the same one that flows on down into the
Rocky Valley, see listing). The stream bec
continues straight to the waterfall, and
could possibly be followed, but take the
steps up to the hermitage at the top (£8/£4
entrance fee) and descend via the steps to
waterfall for the full experience.

20 mins, 50.6644, -4.7168

30 CORNISH TIPI HOLIDAYS

The original tipi and wild-swimming
campsite. 16 acres of woodland and
meadows and its own beautiful, spring-fed
quarry lake. Now with a pop-up cafe and
wood-fired pizzas. Pendoggett, PL30 3LW,
01208 880781, cornishtipiholidays.co.uk

5 mins, 50.5815, -4.7708

TAMAR VALLEY

31 KIT HILL QUARRY

Enjoy the view, tower and various ruins
then find the disused quarry lake for a dip.
Blocks of quarried stone surround the lake,
including many pieces once destined for
London bridges. Turn L off A390, 2 miles
NE of Callington, PL17 8HR. Park at the
first parking on R, and 50m beyond descend
on trackway on R. After 300m turn R for
tailings lookout or L into the old quarry.

15 mins, 50.522, -4.295

32 COTEHELE, R TAMAR

Launch your canoe or start a long adventure
swim from the historic quay at Cotehele,
swim with the outgoing tide from Calstock
to Cotehele, or float upstream on the
incoming. Explore further upstream with

the tide as far as the weir at Gunnislake.
Pass below steep woodlands and beneath
the famous Calstock viaduct, to view old
quays and ruined wharfs, relics of a once-
thriving copper industry. The quiet stretch
above Morwhellam, beneath the crags of
Morwell Rocks is beautiful. Watch out for
deer, kingfishers and peregrine falcons.
PL17 8BY, £2 launch. Organised trips are
offered by Canoe Tamar, 01822 833409.

240 mins, 50.4913, -4.2234

NORTH EAST CORNWALL

33 SPRYTOWN WEIR

A remote countryside dip at a weir on the
River Lyd, 4 miles to S of A30 Roadford
junction, PL16 0AY. Walk down through the
farmyard and take path on L, 400m.

10 mins, 50.6426, -4.2471

34 ROADFORD LAKE

Beautiful pastoral reservoir surrounded by
meadows and woods with a path around its
entire shore. No Swimming, but to admire
the most secluded parts from the shore,
away from fishing and bird hides, take the
Headson Trail from lane along E side.

3 mins, 50.7019, -4.2136

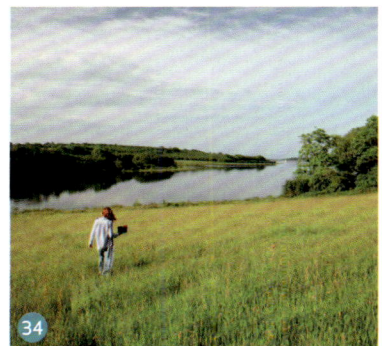

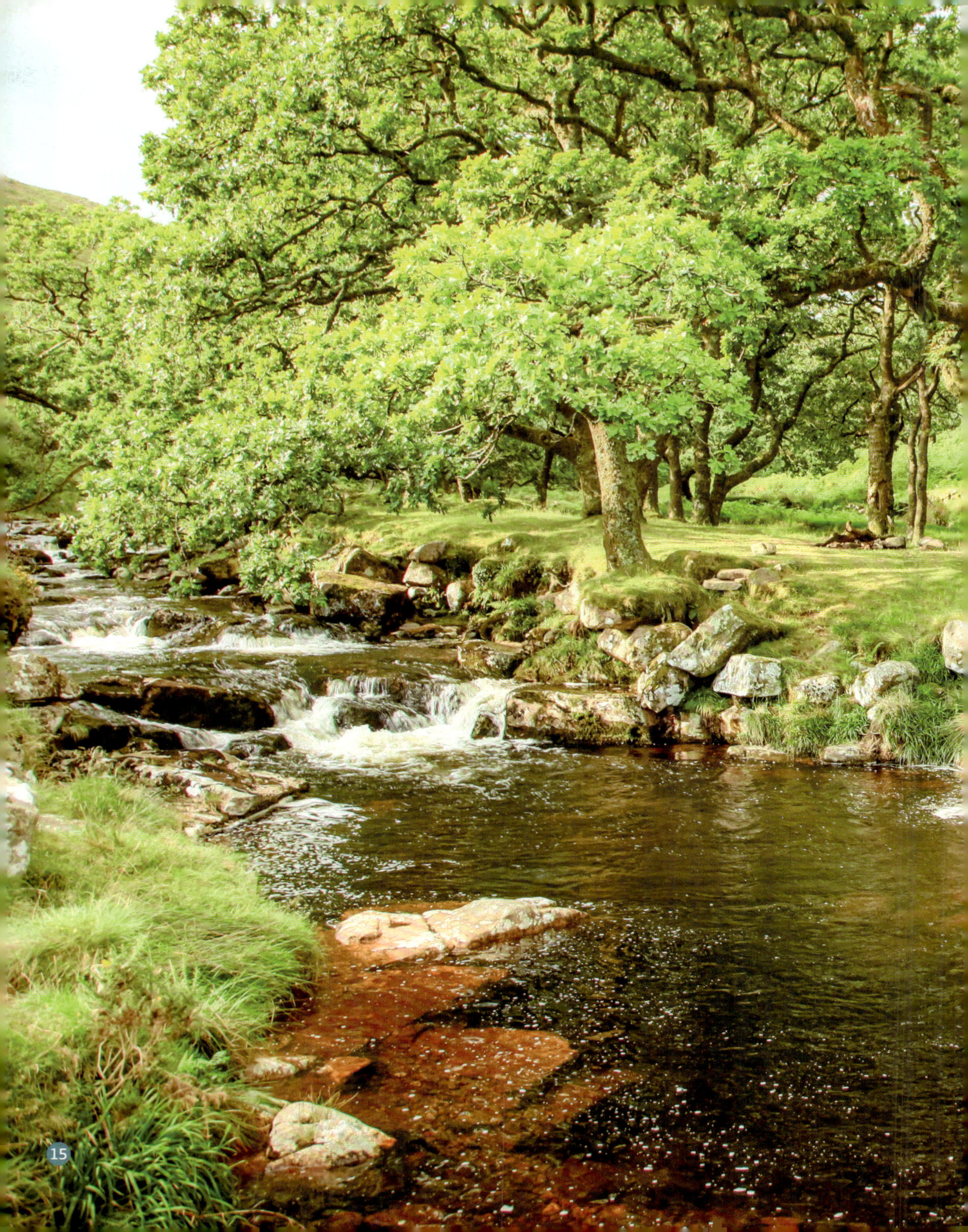

DARTMOOR & SOUTH DEVON

In the early 19th century, Dartmoor emerged as a destination for Romantic travellers drawn to its wild beauty, tumultuous rivers, and sense of sublime isolation. As road and rail access improved, poets, clergymen, and educated walkers ventured onto the moor and found in Dartmoor's rivers and waterfalls a perfect embodiment of the picturesque: fast-flowing streams carving through wooded valleys, moss-covered boulders strewn across rocky gorges, and waterfalls like Lydford's White Lady plunging through shadowed clefts. Lydford became a regular stop on the alternative Grand Tour, particularly when Europe was closed for business during the Napoleonic Wars. Prior to that, it was famous as a hideout for a large family of outlaws – the Gubbins – who terrorised the neighbourhood and stole sheep from the farms of Dartmoor.

The main part of the gorge is hugely impressive but certainly no place to enter the water, even if you were allowed. A narrow chasm cuts deep into the grey Devonshire slate, where the grinding gyrations of river stones churn out huge, smooth cavities. The National Trust has repaired a Victorian viewing gangway that takes you right into the heart of one of the pots, allowing you to stand over and gaze down into the almighty whirlpools of the great Devil's Cauldron. Further downstream, there are paddling places and the impressive White Lady Falls, which tips a thirty-metre plume on sightseers below, its great white globules as hard as hail. To swim in the Lyd gorge, you'll need to seek out the quieter upstream parts, such as Tucker's Pool (2), a small plunge pool that shelves into the deep entrance of a narrow ravine. It's reached through an old Victorian gate and may have once been part of the show gorge. When I swam into it, large droplets of water fell on me from the vegetation and forest above. It was only a few feet wide in places, and the rock walls were smooth and sheer with few handholds, but it gave a visceral sense of the sublime.

I dreamt of waterfalls that night as I camped on the moors. A persistent drizzle had started, pattering gently on the tent and

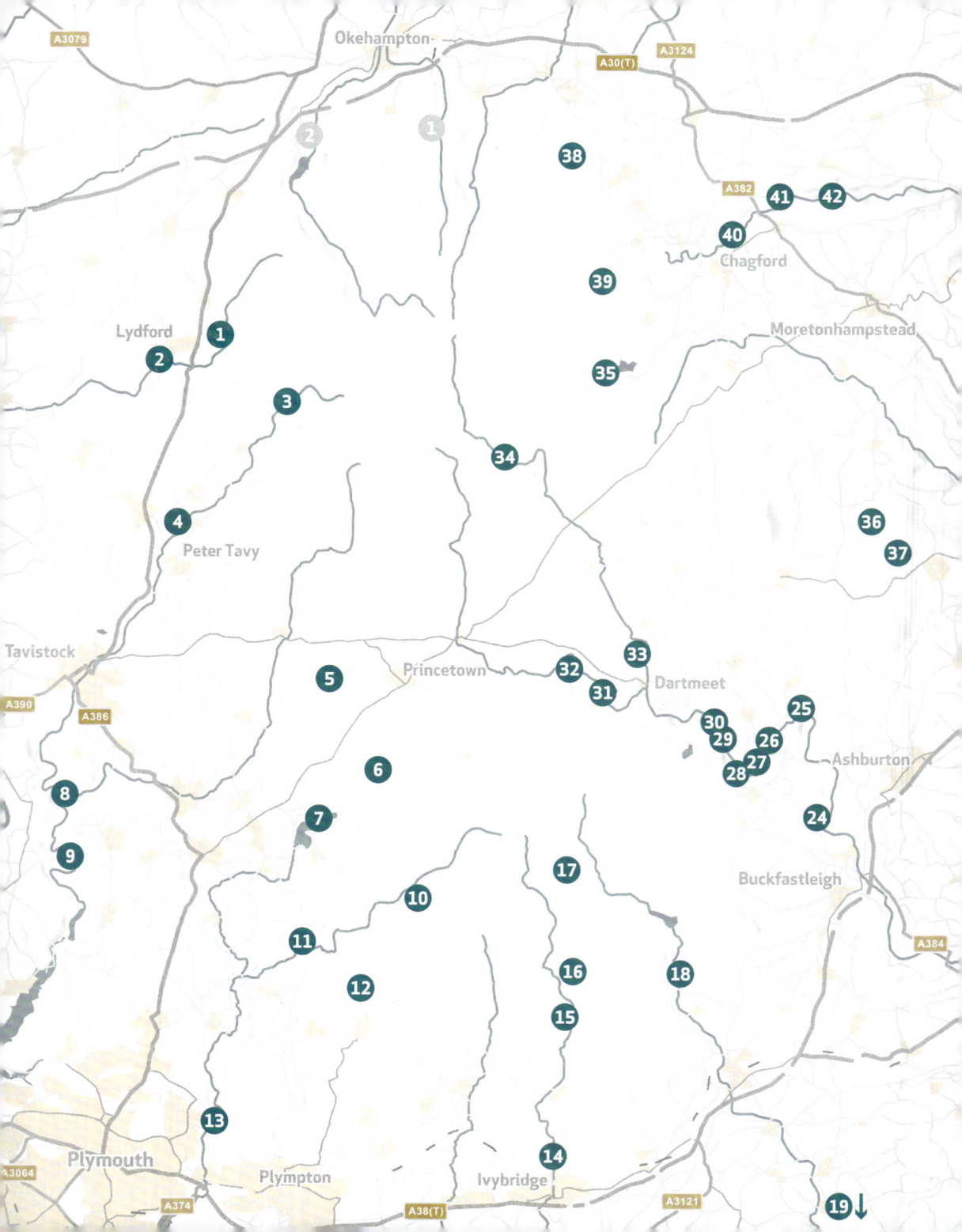

Ottery St Mary
Exeter
A30(T)
47
A3051
A3052
Topsham
M5
43
46
A376
45
44
Budleigh Salterton
Exmouth
A38(T)
Chudleigh
A380
Bovey Tracey
Dawlish
Teignmouth
A383
Newton Abbot
A379
A380
Torquay
3
22
A381
Paignton
Totnes
A3022
21
20
Brixham

raising the river to a roar. By morning, it had abated, but a warm, sloth-like mist had descended. A local friend had arrived, and after a hot pot of tea and a warming, thoroughly waterproof fry-up at the hotel in Lydford—coats and maps hung out to dry on radiators all around—the waitress explained the route to some lovely pools she knew further upstream on the moor beneath the stone-built landmark of Widgery Cross (1). This 1887 commemoration of Queen Victoria's golden jubilee proved elusive to find in the muggy mist, but we were feeling rather determined. We followed the small river for several hundred yards, startled sheep looming out of the bracken. Finally, beneath a craggy outcrop and a memorial to a lost soldier, we came to the most beautiful of mountain pools. As the rain thickened, the surface broke out in a melody of concentric rings, and we leapt about among the rocks, splashing and squealing.

By midday, the skies were clearing, and we made for Crazywell Pool, high on the moor above the prison at Princetown, and the headwaters for the Meavy and Tavy (6). This is a tin-mining area dating back almost a thousand years. Tin was so important to the Dartmoor economy that three independent 'stannary' parliaments were established in the sixteenth century, with a dedicated stannary prison at Lydford. Crazy Well is a quarry that was probably dug around the same time. Now it's one of the few 'natural' lakes on Dartmoor. As such, it has collected more than its fair share of legends. Its level is said to change with the tides at Plymouth, and, of course, it is said to be bottomless (ten sets of weighted bell ropes from Walkhampton Church were tied end-to-end, and still no bottom was found). To us, though, on a blustery August afternoon, with clouds racing across a blue sky, it was simply a wonderful moor-top lake—sheltered, wide, and finally sunny, with views out over the world.

The western flanks of Dartmoor have many more streams and valleys to explore, all blessed with the afternoon and sunset light. The Tavy Valley is particularly rich in hidden waterfalls and pools for those who like to explore, while the Plym is a popular weekend bathing spot for those who drive up from Plymouth and park by their picnic at Cadover Bridge (11). The Erme Valley, due south through Ivybridge, is home to one of the richest concentrations of Bronze Age monuments in Europe, featuring an extraordinary number of stone rows, cairns, hut circles, and stone circles dating from around 2500–1500 BC (14,15,16). However, for many, the River Dart itself will be the main draw. With river pools and sandy bays, oak gorges and towering tors, the Dart was the setting for Charles Kingsley's The Water Babies and is one of the most beautiful wild-swimming rivers in the UK. In a deep gorge far upstream of Newbridge, lying on the flat, hot rocks by a gurgling river, I was miles from anywhere. Dense woodland tumbled down the side of the moor, a light spray lifts off the water, and the forest twitters with birdsong (30). Somewhere along here, the hero of *The Water Babies*, Tom the chimney sweep, was lulled into the water by the fairies. Wrongly accused of theft, he escaped across Lewthwaite Moor before falling into a deep, exhausted sleep by the river. In his new life underwater, he goes in search of the other water-babies and meets many river creatures along the way: the foolish trout, the wise old salmon, the crafty otter, and the trumpeting, happy gnats. He learns many things from them before eventually finding the girl he truly loves.

Holne, the birthplace of Charles Kingsley, is a good starting point for river walks. The river is a ten-minute walk down through the fields. You'll find a large rock by a small waterfall, partly in sunshine, partly in shade—a place made for lazy picnics and sunny afternoons. Exploring further downstream brings you first to Horseshoe Falls (27) and then to Salters Pool, and within twenty minutes, you'll arrive at the car park of Newbridge, where a narrow medieval bridge crosses the river. There's a National Park visitors' hut and an easy walk downstream to the green lawns of Spitchwick Common (26). With its easy access, gentle pools, and good swimming, it's almost too popular and can be busy on a summer day, creating parking and litter problems. So, head back up the other side of the river for a good half an hour, and you'll arrive at Wellsfoot Island. On the far side of this picturesque piece of woodland, there's a red sandy beach in a bend of the river under Holne Cliff. This is a fabulous deep pool by a coppice of spindly birch. Feel the fine-grain sand running with the current between your toes. But the best pools are also the most remote, miles upstream from Newbridge, in the forest halfway to Dartmeet, below Mel Tor. These legendary swimming holes are surrounded by large flat rocks with chutes between them for floating down on rubber rings. Whether you walk up the river from Holne, down from Dartmeet, or scramble over the steep slopes from Mel Tor, it's quite a trek. You should be able to find your own pool – there are plenty to choose from (29).

While I mused, I suddenly saw three wet-suited swimmers on rings riding the river current, who must have come from Dartmeet, at least two miles upstream. 'Is there anywhere good to swim up there?' I called out, ever searching for the perfect pool. 'Everywhere's good to swim!' they replied. Apparently, the Dartmeet-to-Newbridge run is popular with the most daring local swimmers but not generally recommended unless water levels are very low and you know where the waterfalls are. The sport of 'hydrosurfing' is catching on in France, where they gear you up with helmets and padded suits. One local told me that the best swimmers here do it without anything at all, just in their trunks, and have learned to curl their bodies like eels to pass in between the rocks and slip unharmed over the waterfalls. They can feel the micro-currents with their skin

'Tom…was so hot and thirsty, and longed so to be clean for once, that he tumbled himself as quick as he could into the clear cool stream. And he had not been in it two minutes before he fell fast asleep, into the quietest, sunniest, cosiest sleep that ever he had in his life…' from *The Water Babies*, 1863

and move through the water like otters. If you're looking for the Dartmoor water babies, all grown up, I think these might be them.

The Teign flows down the eastern valleys of the moor. Perhaps the most spectacular pools are the Victorian 'Salmon Leaps' in the woods beneath Castle Drogo (41). Three rectangular pools cascade into one another, resembling stacked glasses of champagne. Castle Drogo was the last castle built in England. Constructed in the 1920s by merchant millionaire Julius Drewe—self-styled as Baron Drogo de Teign—it stands high above the wooded gorge of the Teign. As part of his landscaping project, the 'Baron' installed several weirs to create river pools to help stock the river with salmon. The first pool is a long, peaceful stretch of river that runs beneath an elegant suspension bridge. Drewe faced a problem because the dam that creates the pool also impeded the upward migration of spawning salmon, so to solve this, he built an impressive series of salmon 'leaps'. While the peaceful pool above is popular with the local girls, the salmon leaps are favoured by the lads. Each pool is about four feet deep, with a flat concrete bottom. The turbulence literally lifts you off your feet, but you soon get the knack of bobbing about in these mountain jacuzzis. The water bubbles wildly as it tumbles from one pool to the next, massaging and pummelling all the muscles in your body.

Another mile or so downstream, you'll find a second weir and river pool before arriving at Fingle Bridge and its pub (42). This narrow, medieval packhorse bridge was built to service the gorge's once-busy industries: corn milling, charcoal burning, and bark ripping. It has long been a local beauty spot for paddling and picnicking, and even in 1894, the unknown author of *A Gentleman's Walking Tour of Dartmoor* suggested it was a 'great place for picnics. Little has changed, and if you want more peace and quiet, the weir behind Chagford is charming. Or why not visit the town-run swimming pool? It's fed by the river, which comes straight off the moor, though the health and safety officials still insist that chlorine is added (40). It was dug in 1947 as a co-operative effort by the village, and some of the original old boys still come down to make tea. These days, it has solar heaters and an indoor café, in case it rains.

An important source of the Teign is Blackaton Brook, which rises by the windswept stone circle of Little Hound Tor, back up on the moor. From here, it gathers momentum through Raybarrow Hill and Throwleigh Common before arriving at the tiny and rather secret Shilley Pool. In this sheltered and sunny glen, bathers and nymphs have built a low dam to create a perfect bath (38). The water flows in across wide stone slabs, perfect for sunbathing, and the depth reaches about three feet. Lying in the stream, with the current creating eddies along one's length, in the warmth of the afternoon sun, you feel a very small part of some much larger, more wonderful thing. Dartmoor has many secret bathing spots, often difficult to find, and this is one of its most special. Bathe here, and

UPPER TAVY & LYD

1 WIDGERY CROSS, R LYD

Small tumbling plunge pools in moorland glen with gorse and heather, aka Black Rock Falls or Witch's Pool. Turn off A386 by Dartmoor Inn opp Lydford turning (good food, EX20 4AY, 01822 820221) and continue to car park. Follow track up onto the moor and after 800m meet stream and follow its R bank 400m to find bench and plaque under tall rocky outcrop with pool below.

20 mins, 50.65, -4.0772 🧍🏔🏊🚷

2 TUCKER'S POOL, R LYD

Secret, jungly pool in a narrow canyon just upstream of the famous NT Lydford Gorge. Take dead-end lane opposite Lydford war memorial (EX20 4AT) to 50.6456, -4.1031. Follow path to old viaduct and steep path down to old Victorian gates at the bottom (sometimes locked) then hard R, over fence into woods and downstream along wooded gorge for 200m.

5 mins, 50.6423, -4.1064 🚂🔔🏊🏊🅿🏊🚷

3 TAVY CLEAVE, R TAVY

Beautiful walk up among tors and views into this wild valley of waterfalls and plunge pools. Follow lanes from Mary Tavy

4 miles NW via Horndon and Willsworthy for Lanehead car park at end (PL19 9NB. Follow track E to Nattor Farm then bear up L and join the leat for 1 mile until it ends at pump house (the leat runs 3 miles W to Wheel Jewell reservoir and could be fun on a rubber ring). Follow stream 500m further and just after it turns L into the cleave find a big pool, followed by another 200m further along. More swimming downstream on Tavy, at Creason Woods and United Mines (see listings).

40 mins, 50.6296, -4.0453 🧍🏔🏊🚷

4 HORNDON, R TAVY

Explore the streamside remains of the Devon United Mines then head upstream through a little-known wooded valley with many secret waterfall pools. From Mary Tavy park at lane-end, beyond hydro power station (50.5872, -4.1069). Follow path to the bridge and cross. Downstream 250m is a plunge pool below Longtimber Tor. Or upstream, take footpath up through the woods, but follow informal path L along the wooded valley with mine ruins to find pool with rope swing after 500m. The stream path continues to bridge at Horndon, and then on through Creason Woods.

30 mins, 50.5923, -4.0974 🧍🏔🏊🚷

MEAVY & LOWER TAVY

5 FOGGINTOR QUARRY & SWELLTOR

Impressive flooded quarry with cliffs and ruins, and the source of the granite used for London Bridge. Close to Merrivale stone row (see listing) and on the mostly off-road Princetown Railway cycle trail (Princetown to Yelverton). 2½ miles W of Two Bridges on B3357, and ½ mile from the telephone box at the B3357 junction (signed Princetown), find a farm track and parking on L (Yellowmeade Farm). Follow track for a mile. Make time to explore

Swelltor quarry ½ miles SW. Find the line of abandoned granite corbels, cut in 1903 and intended for London Bridge but left on the railway siding just to the W of the quarry at 50.5424, -4.0392.

20 mins, 50.5444, -4.0245

6 CRAZY WELL POOL
A spring-fed, mystical, moor-top lake excavated by medieval tin miners and reputedly bottomless. Look for Crazy Well Cross which marked the Monk's Path from Buckfast Abbey to Tavistock Abbey. From Norsworthy Bridge PL20 6PF follow forest track/bridleway 1½ miles up onto the moor. along the edge of the plantation forest. 300m after the end of the forest find a small stream bed which leads 200m up to the lake. The cross is 150 m E at 50.5161, -3.9989.

35 mins, 50.5167, -4.0011

7 BURRATOR RESERVOIR
Secluded little beach areas where people paddle, despite No Swimming. From Dousland follow the lane over the dam to Sheepstor, turning L 200m before church. Various paths down from the lane.

2 mins, 50.5018, -4.0293

8 DOUBLE WATERS, R TAVY
Enchanting oak woodland walk along the Walkham as it winds down to meet the Tavy. Shallow at the actual confluence but small pool 200m upstream on Walkham, or 300m downstream on Tavy. Grenofen Bridge parking (50.5189, -4.1312).

30 mins, 50.5090, -4.1508

9 DENHAM BRIDGE, R TAVY
On narrow lane between Buckland Monachorum and Bere Alston, a very deep-section pool below stone arch. Or find downstream path into woods on R bank (50m above bridge) for a wide, open, pebble beach and deep, secluded corner pool. Car park is beyond PL20 7EF. Upstream 1km is another beautiful deep stretch of river and a remote old weir: follow lane back up towards Buckland for 300m, then following driveway down to L, past house and along river for 10 mins 50.4944, -4.1539.

2 mins, 50.4899, -4.1481

PLYM VALLEY

10 SHAVERCOMBE WATERFALL, R PLYM
A very wild and remote, rowan-clad glade with a small pool and waterfall. Continue E through Sheepstor to the road end 1 mile to

Gutter Tor car park, PL20 6PG. Follow track S to Ditsworthy Warren House (a bleak, shuttered bunkhouse where Warhorse was filmed). Follow the Plym upstream 750m, bearing R up the Shavercombe brook for 500m to find the fall.

50 mins, 50.4776, -3.9818 🚶🏊📷⛺👣

11 CADOVER BRIDGE, R PLYM

Open moorland stream with shallow pools and grassy banks. There is ample parking and safe paddling upstream for a mile. Attracts crowds on hot August weekends, but about 20 mins downstream there is an excellent, large, deep pool with a high rope swing and cliff for jumps, plus several secluded smaller pools along the way. Well-signed from Plympton (6 miles) via Shaugh Prior. For the deep pools follow the path downstream about a mile from the bridge, keeping on the near side of the river, through North Wood, to reach the waterfall and main pool (50.4557, -4.0589).

20 mins, 50.4644, -4.037 🏊🐟🏊📷🚻

12 BIG POND, CADOVER BRIDGE

A large, shallow lake in open moorland with pebble beach. Warms up on hot days and usually deserted but No Swimming signs - so this is for info only. Take dead-end lane at

Cadover Bridge. Continue 1km to car park and stone cross at end then 300m.

5 mins, 50.4503, -4.009 ➕❓

13 PLYMBRIDGE & BICKLEIGH, R PLYM

There are wooded pools galore along the river Plym, all connected by the old railway cycle path or a riverside path. There are car parks on either side of Plym Bridge at PL7 4SR. Upstream in Bickleigh Valley there's a weir, viaduct and ruined quarry house and it's a bit more adventurous (50.4180, -4.0798). Or simply relax downstream of the parking – there's a big beach and some pools by the stepping stones and footbridge.

5 mins, 50.4096, -4.0788 🚴📷🏊

ERME & AVON

14 IVYBRIDGE WATERFALLS, R ERME

Series of fun jacuzzi pools, waterfalls and small weirs in Longtimber woods. Look out for the remains of the old swimming baths, a series of concrete walls in the woods. Park underneath the railway viaduct on Station Rd, Ivybridge PL21 0AG (on road to Cornwood), then follow track down to the river in woods and continue upstream 500m.

5 mins, 50.399, -3.917 🏊🚻🚲

15 PILES COPSE, R ERME

Precious remnant of ancient oak woodland with exquisite stream, small pools and waterfall. Quickest access is from road end NE of hamlet of Tor (via Ivybridge then Cornwood, 50.4337, -3.9377). Follow track up around waterworks and around hillside 1.5km dropping down to the stream.

60 mins, 50.4417, -3.9113 🥾🏊🏞📷

16 LEFTLAKE MIRES POOL

High on the old tramway below Red Lake, and with far-reaching views over Piles Copse and the Erme Valley (see listings),

this is a deep, dark and silky lake. Climb the moorland path from Harford Moor Gate (20 mins), then bear N to follow the Two Moors Way over Piles Hill until the old mine works are reached (45 mins). Harford is 2 miles N of Ivybridge.

60 mins, 50.4555, -3.9076 🔒🏊🏞🏔

17 RED LAKE, HUNTINGDON WARREN

Possibly the most remote swim on Dartmoor. Two large lakes with dramatic hillocks. Easy 6-mile route, possible on a bicycle, along the old mineral tramway (Two Moors Way) from Harford (see Leftlake Mires). NB no access from Lud Gate road to E but possible from Scorriton also 6 miles. If time, find Huntingdon Cross and clapper bridge. Also Huntingdon Warren wheelpit and mine ruins (50.4832, -3.8819).

60 mins, 50.4863, -3.9107 🔒🚩🏔🏊🏞

18 SHIPLEY BRIDGE, R AVON

As easy path along the stream to the reservoir. There are only shallow pools, the best after 500m, but the woodland is beautiful. Easy parking and toilets make this popular for overnighters. Beyond Didworthy, dir TQ10 9ED.

10 mins, 50.4549, -3.8562 🏊🚗

19 TOPSHAM BRIDGE, AVON

Follow the river down towards Loddiswell through idyllic, ancient woodland. From Topsham Bridge itself continue 1.5km downstream to find a deep swimming spot on a right-hand bend after about a mile, or try above the weir, a bit further down.

20 mins, 50.3305, -3.7857 🏊🚗

LOWER DART

20 STOKE GABRIEL MILL POOL

Idyllic place in summer. Canoe launch from the pontoon or simply swim from the dam into the mill pool/quay. Also one of the UK's top crabbing spots. Watch the action from the River Shack café (TQ9 6RD, 01803 782520).

1 mins, 50.4015, -3.6228 🏊🚗

21 ASHPRINGTON POINT

A wild, remote beach on this secluded and seldom-visited stretch of the tidal Dart, downstream of Sharpham estate. Camping here in summer (Point Field, TQ9 7UT, 01803 732542). Find path opposite church and follow for 1.5km.

20 mins, 50.4048, -3.6343 🚶🏔🏊

22 DARTINGTON HALL, R DART

Take time to enjoy the alternative scene at the college and a snack at the vegan Green Table café (TQ9 6EE), then wander down through fields to a bucolic riverside with swimming up- and downstream. Downstream eventually leads to Totnes weir and the station. Take Dartington Lane on the L from the main road as it enters Totnes from A30. From Park School car parkcontinue to little roundabout at end and take path down to the river.
5 mins, 50.4525, -3.6843 ▣

23 STAVERTON & STILLPOOL, R DART

This fun stretch of river is perfect for train lovers and can be reached from Totnes or Buckfastleigh by steam (South Devon Railway). Otherwise park at the station car park (50p), cross the tracks and head down path to reach the river. It's rather straight, with steep banks, but there are lots of places to swim, right up to the old weir. Beyond the weir is a footbridge (before the path goes under the railway bridge) leading onto Nappers Field private conservation area, open on weekdays only. It gives access to Stillpool, once very popular with secluded little beaches and a big tree jump into a deep pool on a bend (50.4600, -3.70170)

but this riverbank is now fenced off. You can still access Stillpool down a steep track from the opp bank however: park on the roadside bend above Staverton Bridge by Riverwood (50.4594, -3.7132) and follow the permissive paths through Dartington Estate land E for 750m.
10 mins, 50.4622, -3.71 ▣◢▧▨

UPPER DART

24 HEMBURY WOODS, R DART

Ancient oak woodland leads down to a deep, secret stretch of the river Dart. From A38 Buckfastleigh, cross Dart bridge, turn immediately R, signed Buckfast, then R fork, signed Hembury Woods. After bridge, park on L.
10 mins, 50.5026, -3.7912 ◤▧▣

25 LOVER'S LEAP, NEW BRIDGE

One of the most enigmatic and remote of the Dartmoor pools, set beneath a 12-metre cliff deep in ancient woodland. 1 mile downstream from Spitchwick (see listing): swim across the river and walk down on the woodland track opposite, along the R bank.
30 mins, 50.5359, -3.7989 ▣▽

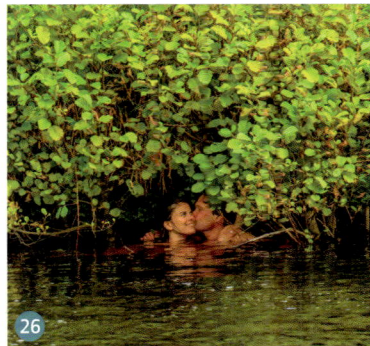

26 SPITCHWICK COMMON, NEWBRIDGE

The most popular and accessible Dart swimming location, especially in summer, when crowds and litter can be a big problem (take some away). Flat, grassy areas lead to river with deeper section on far side and high cliffs, from which some people jump. From Ashburton A38 follow signs to River Dart Country Park. Cross Holne bridge, then park at Newbridge (TQ13 7NT). Cross road and follow path downstream 300m.
5 mins, 50.5261, -3.8141 ▣◢▨

27 HORSESHOE FALLS, R DART

This horseshoe-shaped waterfall has a big pool below, great for jumps. Large rock for sunbathing. Follow path on the river's R bank from Newbridge car park (500m) or on path down through fields from Holne (on R as you enter Holne from Holne bridge direction).

15 mins, 50.5195, -3.82

28 WELLSFOOT ISLAND, NEW BRIDGE

Wooded island reached by footbridge, with red-sand beach shelving into a deep river-bend pool below a cliff. Follow the river upstream from Newbridge car park side (river's L bank) just under 1 mile.

20 mins, 50.517, -3.8274

29 BELL POOL, R DART

This deep hidden pool on an S-bend on the E side of the island has an old iron ladder for scaling an outcrop and jumping back in. 300m downstream of Sharrah Pool (see listing) on L bank.

30 mins, 50.5265, -3.8363

30 SHARRAH POOL, R DART

A legendary pool on this wild and wonderful stretch of the valley. As for Horseshoe Falls (see listing) but head upstream 1½ miles. The path climbs and then down then it's

about 500m beyond the stile, obvious on the R. 500m upstream are the Mel Pools (50.5346, -3.8447) and a range of smaller pools, including a few good chutes if you have an inner tube. There is a L-bank path back which takes in Bellpool and Wellsfoot (both only accessible from L bank) so this could make a good loop back to Newbridge. It's also possible to descend from Aish ⁻or or Venford, on each side of the valley. Check OpenStreetMap for paths.

40 mins, 50.5301, -3.8396

31 HEXWORTHY BRIDGE & WEEK FORD

One of the easiest and most beautiful West Dart swims; a large sandy pool below a stone bridge, with grassy banks and easy parking by the lane. From B3357 W of Dartmeet, turn L at The Forest Inn sign and continue down (past Huccaby Farm camping, PL20 6SB) to parking on R before the bridge. Wild campers sometimes head downstream to the wooded glades around Week Ford (50.5364, -3.8895), a pretty walk down from Combestone Tor.

1 mins, 50.54048, -3.8939

32 SWINCOMBE MEET, WEST DART

A large sandy pool and beach with huge stepping stones where the Swincombe joins

on a bend. From Hexworthy Bridge (see listing) continue ½ mile, past The Forest Inn (PL20 6SD), and turn R at the top (dir Sherberton). Park by cattle grid at end. Continue W down the lane with open-cast gully and other remains of Gobbet tin mine L. Pass Wydemeet House (an upmarket B&B, PL20 6SF) and take bridleway gate R after bridge over Swincombe. Cross the stream by stepping stones, and continue 500m to the West Dart.

20 mins, 50.5476, -3.9098

33 YAR TOR, DARTMEET

Head upstream 750m to escape the crowds at Dartmeet and find this sandy beach and pool by a grassy meadow, below Yar Tor. From the far end of the car park, beyond the toilets, take the path to the R of Badger's Holt holiday accommodation (PL20 6SG) and then drop down again to follow the riverside path 500m.

15 mins, 50.5522, -3.8774

EASTERN TORS

34 EAST DART WATERFALL & SANDY HOLE

A moorland walk to a granite-lined plunge pool below a waterfall. 500m upstream is a deep peat-cut circular pool, just before

Sandy Hole Pass (50.6143, -3.9472); tinners straightened the stream just above so it flows faster. Following the bridleway/track N from the National Park Visitor Centre in Postbridge (PL20 6TH, paid parking) over the saddle of Broad Down and then N down to the rocky section of the river straight ahead.

45 mins, 50.6128, -3.9411

35 FERNWORTHY RESERVOIR

Remote reservoir surrounded by woodland with a stone circle. Silty shores, depending on water level, and often warm, but No Swimming, so for info only.

3 mins, 50.6387, -3.893

36 BECKA BROOK LAKES

Hidden lakes hidden in woodland on Becka Brook open access land. From Hound Tor ancient village (50.5954, -3.7726) continue on path 500m to descend to stream. Find gate door into woods on R and head upstream 300m. It is private land, so be very respectful. Opposite bank is open access land.

30 mins, 50.5931, -3.7655

37 HAYTOR QUARRY

Sheltered, sun-trap quarry pools, just big

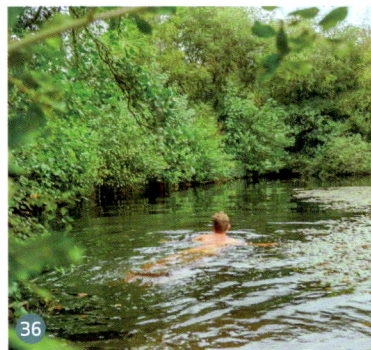

enough for a dip, but quite busy. Scramble about on Haytor afterwards and look for the granite tramway that runs from here, made entirely from stone – rails points and all. B3387, 3 miles from Bovey Tracey, find free car park on L just after the Visitor Centre (TQ13 9XT). It's about 500m, beyond and to R of Haytor Rocks.

10 mins, 50.5835, -3.7529

RIVER TEIGN

38 SHILLEY POOL, THROWLEIGH

Series of small plunge pools in brook at the edge of the moor. Paddling for children

51

and a great place for picnics. 1km NW of Throwleigh, at junction, find rough track on L, 100m before cattle grid and stream bridge. Follow Blackaton Brook up onto moor 750m.

10 mins, 50.705, -3.9093 🏊

39 SCORHILL DOWN, R TEIGN
Set amid heather-covered moorland, some secret pools, stone bridges and a stone circle. Follow tiny lanes 4 miles W of Chagford. 170m past the Round Pound settlement circle on roadside R park on R. There is a little hidden swim spot in the cleave directly below; follow the wall then scramble down to 50.6666, -3.8946. From parking walk on 20 mins to find the Teign-e-ver clapper bridge. There is pool 100m downstream, at the stone bridge (50.6677, -3.9053) and another at the Tolmen hole stone, another 50m down. It's then 300m N to the circle, crossing another stone bridge.

5 mins, 50.6666, -3.8946 🧗

40 CHAGFORD SWIMMING POOL 🅿
Community run, river-fed swimming pool on the banks of the Teign. £5.50 per adult. Rushford, Chagford, Dartmoor National Park TQ13 8DA. 01647 432929

2 mins, 50.6810, -3.8326

41 SALMON LEAPS, R TEIGN
Long river pool above weir in woods beneath Hunter's Tor, Castle Drogo. Three square tubs then cascade down – great for a spa bath. 150m S of Sandy Park Inn, TQ13 8JW, find gates/path on L before Dogmarsh Br. Follow river downstream 750m. Continue another mile to Fingle Bridge. Also explore upstream, path from parking leads to hidden weir and pool in woods (50.6865, -3.8267).

10 mins, 50.6926, -3.8097 🏊🅿🔻

42 FINGLE BRIDGE, TEIGN
A popular, thickly wooded gorge with stone bridge and riverside pub. Walk upstream 500m to find a deep stretch above a small weir. Or 2km to the Salmon Leaps. Follow signs 1 mile E of Castle Drogo/Drewsteignton (Fingle Bridge Inn, EX6 6W, 01647 281287).

5 mins, 50.6929, -3.7848 🅿🏊ℹ

EXE & OTTER

43 TOPSHAM &TURF LOCK
The Exeter ship canal is prettier and cleaner than it sounds, fed from the Exe and surrounded by nature reserve. No Swimming, but locals jump and swim here, and paddle board. Pass the Swan's Nest pub, Station Rd, EX6 8DZ, to the car park at the road end. Follow the towpath 600m upstream/N to find footbridge/quay. The little Topsham ferry is just beyond. The superbly located Turf hotel/pub is 2km S on the towpath, with another popular lock (50.6651, -3.4675).

10 mins, 50.6819, -3.4701 🏊🛶ℹ❓

44 SQUABMOOR RESERVOIR, BUDLEIGH
Lily pond and reservoir high on East Budleigh Common. No Swimming and anglers, so be discreet if you choose to dip. Walkers can also view the fenced-off sand lakes at Black Hill 1km N (50.6620, -3.3694).

5 mins, 50.6486, -3.3592 📷🏊❓

45 OTTERTON, R OTTER
Riverside meadows and deeper pools both above and below the weir with shallower gravel beaches further along. On an evening walk downstream from the bridge you might spot otters or beavers. From Otterton Mill shop (EX9 7HG) cross the river and head upstream on riverside path 300m.

5 mins, 50.662, -3.3022 🏊🏊

46 COLATON RALEIGH, R OTTER
Lovely little beach and deep corner pool beneath red cliffs strung with ivy and ferns. Turn down Church Rd off B3178, opposite Woods Village Shop. Pass church and follow path from bottom of road (near farm) to river and downstream for 5 mins. You could also try the beaches 1 mile N at the bend 50.6862, -3.2957 (path off Church Rd).

10 mins, 50.6745, -3.2925 🏊🏊

47 FLUXTON WEIR, TIPTON, R OTTER,
Good pool and weir by ancient mill in pastures. Calm, deep water and a flume like a jacuzzi. Take path at 50.7213, -3.2944 on Tipton Vale, EX11 1RW (car park behind bus stop 80m S). Follow river upstream ½ mile to weir, bridge and mill. To explore more: Continue 2km mile upstream along the river to find a deep corner pool on the inside of a bend with rope swing 50.7435, -3.2835 (or quicker access to this from S end of Ottery Saint Mary Millennium Green, off Mill Street, EX11 1YA). Or downstream, a mile S of Tipton St John, easy river beach and paddling at Harpford Bridge, EX10 0NQ (50.7052, -3.2913)

10 mins, 50.7267, -3.2891 🏊🧗

43

43

46

47

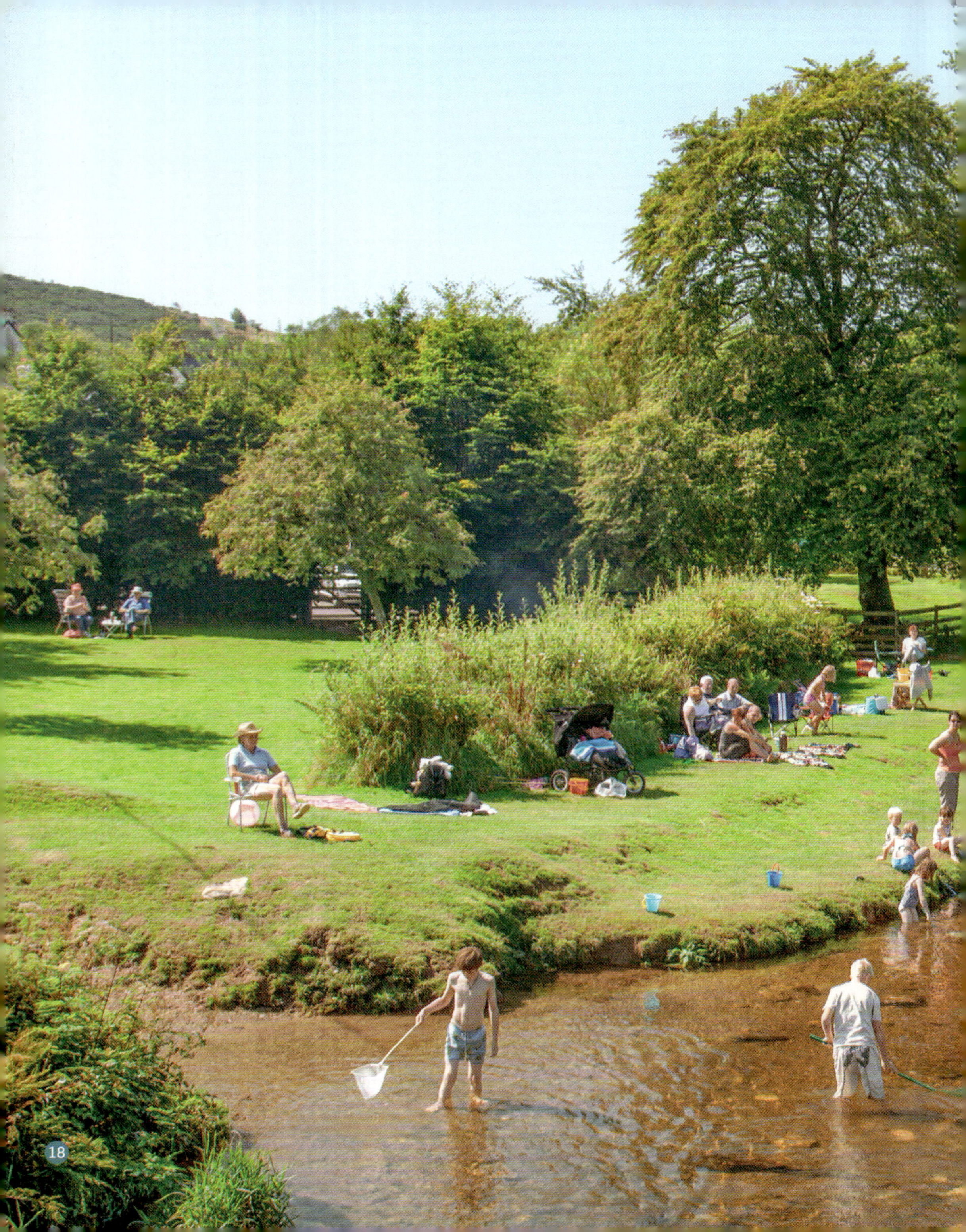

EXMOOR & NORTH DEVON

Tarka the Otter, one of Britain's best-loved nature stories, is set along the north Devon rivers of the Torridge and Taw. I followed the rivers, from highland pools to wooded river valleys, swimming in Tarka's paw-steps.

Henry Williamson was a disillusioned young man when he arrived on his racing motorcycle from London to live in a tiny cob cottage on the north Devon coast. He had just returned from the horrors of the First World War, weary and nerve-wracked, at odds with his family and desperate to be a writer. He lived alone, hermit-fashion, tramping about the countryside, swimming in brooks and often sleeping out. The doors and windows of his new cottage were never closed, and his strange family of dogs, cats, gulls, buzzards, and magpies were free to come and go as they pleased. This was to become the sanctuary for the real-life Tarka: an orphaned otter cub that took refuge with Williamson.

High on north Dartmoor, the headwaters of the Torridge and the Taw provide an excellent vantage point to survey Williamson's famous 'Tarka Country'. Here, on the East Okement, an important tributary of the Torridge, the army blew out a small but beautiful pool at Cullever Steps, just below Scarey Tor, as a place for servicemen to cool off during hot summers (1). It can still be reached via the decaying network of moorland military roads. As you bathe here, among the grazing wild ponies, Devonshire's rolling countryside unfolds like a soft counterpane below, with the steep wooded river valleys of the Torridge and the broader, gentler reaches of the Taw just discernible to the north.

At Halsdon Nature Reserve, ten miles away on the Torridge, the otter population is almost back to its pre-1950 levels. Historically, Devon has been an international stronghold for otters, but in the 1950s and '60s their numbers crashed as industry and farming intensified. Watercourses became

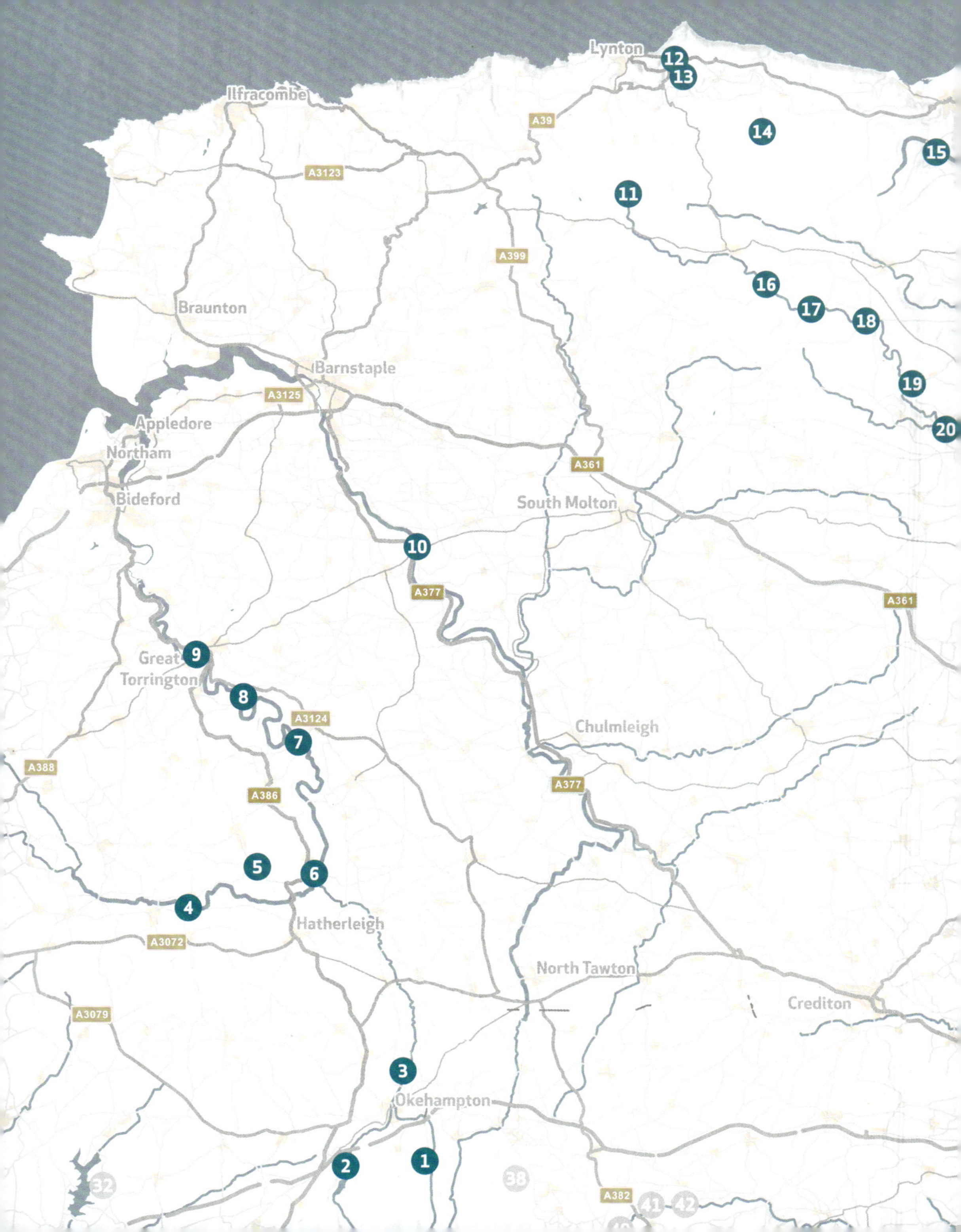

Lynton
Ilfracombe
A39
A3123
A399
Braunton
Barnstaple
A3125
Appledore
Northam
Bideford
A361
South Molton
A377
A361
Great Torrington
A3124
Chulmleigh
A388
A386
A377
Hatherleigh
A3072
North Tawton
Crediton
A3079
Okehampton
A382
1
2
3
4
5
6
7
8
9
10
11
12
13
14
15
16
17
18
19
20
32
38
41
42

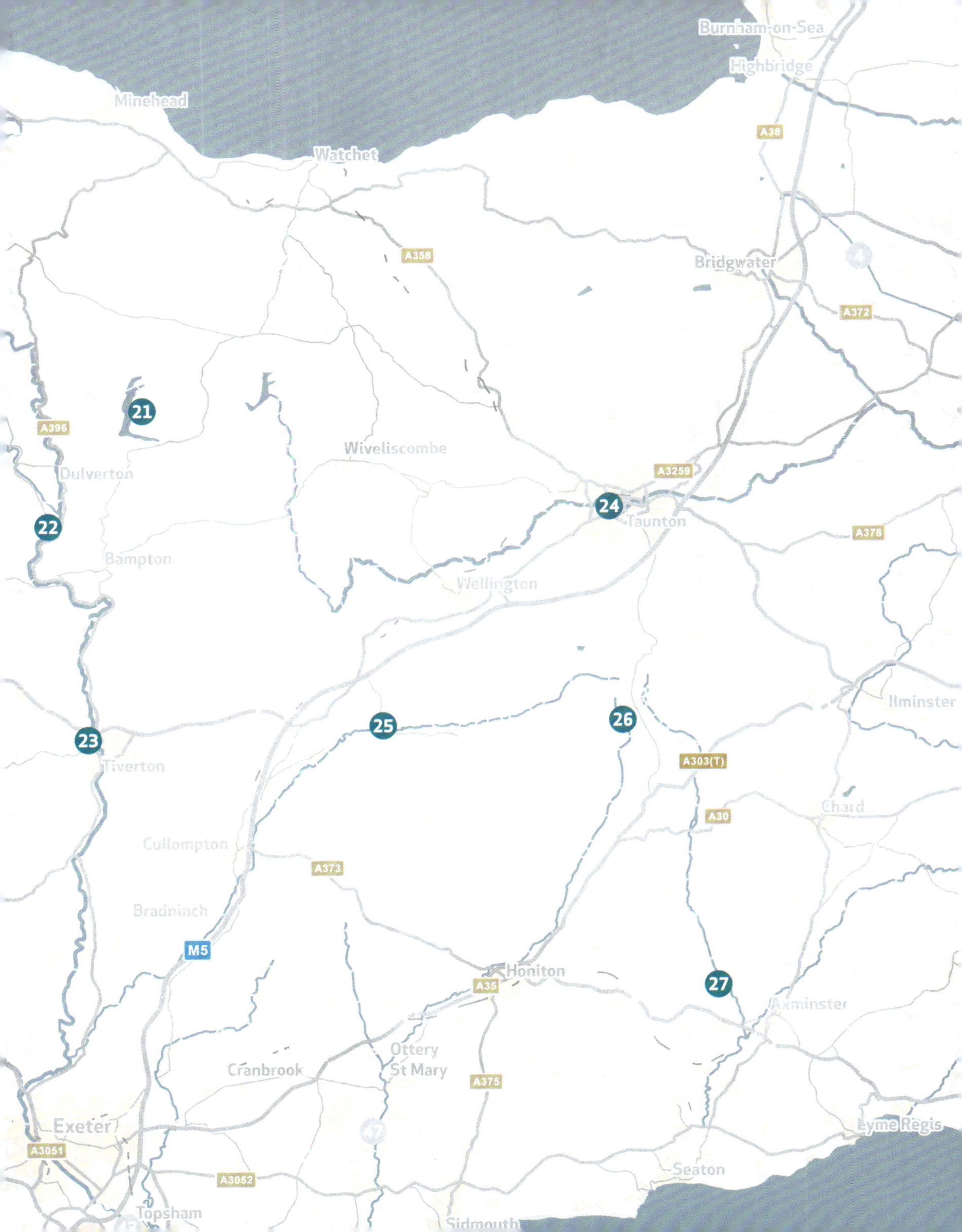

Burnham-on-Sea

Highbridge

Minehead

Watchet

A38

A358

Bridgwater

A372

21

A396

Dulverton

Wiveliscombe

A3259

22

24

Taunton

A378

Bampton

Wellington

Ilminster

25

26

A303(T)

Chard

23

Tiverton

A30

Cullompton

A373

Bradninch

M5

Honiton

27

Axminster

Ottery St Mary

Cranbrook

A375

Lyme Regis

Exeter

A3051

A3052

Seaton

Topsham

Sidmouth

contaminated with chemicals and farm runoff. By the late 1960s, the local otters were almost extinct. A massive clean-up over the last thirty years has had a major impact on the health of all British rivers. Now, at Halsdon, you'll see white-legged damselflies, kingfishers, sand martins, herons, dippers, and grey wagtails. There are even freshwater pearl mussels.

Halsdon won't welcome you to swim, as it disturbs the wildlife, but downstream, near Little Torrington, you can wade across the river at the old ford near Undercleave. This is a remote spot where the river runs wide, fast, and shallow under a tunnel of tall trees. Great Torrington Common, below Great Torrington town, is an accessible stretch of fast-flowing, shady river with some deeper holes. It was here that Tarka learned to swim, to play, and to hunt, and he also first encountered the poachers with their trap lights like 'little moons which he could touch and bite'.

Seven miles to the east, the Taw also rises below Dartmoor, but is a very different kind of river, running through flatter, more open countryside. Behind the remote Chapelton Station on the Barnstaple line, you'll find a meadow and footbridge with good access to the river from open fields. The river is wide, flowing across smooth gravels with a perfect current against which you can swim, but fishing takes precedence here so walk upstream to Umberleigh, or down to Bishop's Tawton (10).

Bathing in the rivers and streams of this area was one of Henry Williamson's greatest pleasures. He brought up his children at Shallowford, six miles to the east, and spent much of his time in the river Bray, a tributary of the Taw, fishing or swimming. He describes in his memoirs lying still in the golden gravels of the ford, watching the clear, cold water foaming over his body. It took him a long time to get over his experiences of the war and feel at peace with his world, but it was at moments like this, he said, that he could finally feel 'a part of the great stream of life'.

Williamson often roamed Exmoor, which rises up to the north of Brayford. The main river is the Lyn, that drains the moor to the north coast. The upper reaches of the River Lyn's east and west branches sweep through the peaceful Doone Valley, the setting for the famous novel Lorna Doone, and also Watersmeet, with its pools and waterfalls.

The rain can be extreme on Exmoor and Lynmouth was the site of one of the most devastating floods in British history. The River Lyn took on ferocious force on the night of 15th August 1952. An intense tropical storm rolled in from the Atlantic and dropped nine inches of rain on the already waterlogged moors. None of the rivers could cope, and banks burst all over Exmoor. At Hawkridge, the massive Tarr Steps were washed a hundred yards downstream (19), and in another village, a row of ten cottages was completely swept away. ut the worst devastation was on the Lyn at Lynmouth, where an avalanche of churning trees and boulders destroyed over 100 buildings and 29 bridges. Thirty-eight cars were washed out to sea,

I was back beside the little river in North Devon, under the alders and hazels, watching the otters play, hearing the hiss of water over the weir, and the humming of bees in the foxgloves. There was peace there, and joy, and the smell of warm fern and mud and sunlit water... I used to swim in the Barle, where the trout darted like quicksilver and the water was so clear it seemed like floating through light itself

Henry Willaimson in
The Wet Flanders Plain (1929)

and in total, 34 people died. New evidence now suggests that the extreme weather events of August 1952 may have been a result of top-secret cloud-seeding experiments taking place at the time off the Devon coast.

As you stand at Watersmeet, a Victorian fishing lodge on the West Lyn, now a quaint National Trust-run tea shop, it's sobering to think of the force of this water and debris piling down the hillside. Yet, ironically, the Lyn has a long history of water power. In 1890, it was one of the first places in the world to install a hydroelectric generator, which provided lighting and powered an ice-maker for the local fishing crews.

The main attractions at Watersmeet now are the simple waterfalls and woodland walks (12). Follow the river path a couple of miles upstream to the little-known Long Pool, a deep narrow gorge found in the woods beneath the path (13). Further on, the path continues to Rockford, and before you get there, you'll find several more pools with small cliffs to jump from. As I was exploring, I met two families kitted out with wetsuits and rubber dinghies. They had spent much of the afternoon playing in these shady pools and said it was more fun than being on the nearby beach.

Follow instead the East Lyn, upstream to Malmsmead, to discover the notorious setting of Lorna Doone: an Exmoor Romance by R. D. Blackmore, one of the bestselling books of all time. The church at nearby Oare is where the novel's famous conclusion was set. his land of murder and outlaws has tumbling streams and dense woods. Wildlife abounds throughout the area. Red deer, ponies, and sheep graze freely, watched over by falcons, buzzards, and even the rare merlin. Cloud Farm is a great place to stay, with pony trekking, a campsite, and river paddling in the Badgworthy, a tributary of the Lyn. But on a hot summer day, Deer Park Pool is the place to be, a mile further up the stream (14). As you come out of the woods and into an open grassland clearing, you'll find a circular plunge pool flowing under a large ash tree. Although small, it's deep enough for a good splash, as my friend Hue and his dog, Felix, demonstrated. The path continues on and up to more Doone country on Brendon Moor, or you may prefer to return to the farm shop for one of their famous après-swim cream teas.

Heather-topped hills, bracken-covered combes, tumbling waterfalls, and wooded river valleys prompted the Victorians to name the magnificent scenery and quiet charm of Exmoor the 'Little Switzerland of England'. The ancient landscape of Iron Age barrows and hut circles on its high flat moors suggest it was popular with ancient man too, after the ice age. But Exmoor is now Britain's least-visited National Park. To the east it become Somerset county and the river Barle steals the show. An old friend, Hue, and his dog, Felix, had offered to take me to one of their swimming holes near Cow Castle, a prehistoric hill fort in the remote upper reaches of the valley (16). We met at Simonsbath, an auspicious-sounding place for the job at hand, and dropped down through Birchcleave Woods to the river. The Barle runs in a narrow vale lined with bright orange asphodels for much of the two miles to Cow Castle.

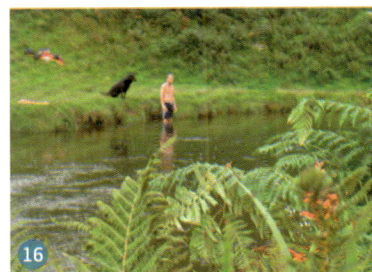

It is a shallow stream that twists and turns between avenues of birch and the ruins of old mine workings. As it reaches the conical hill of the fort, it deepens and slows into a pool.

Swimming against the current of this small, buffeting stream was harder than we had anticipated, and soon we had a competition going to see who could beat the river and make it upstream. We then tried to out-swim the dog. Once we were all thoroughly exhausted, we ran up to the top of the castle knoll and collapsed on the grass, the wet dog panting and the evening sun glowing low.

From here, the course of the Barle winds its way another two miles before it reaches Sherdon Hutch and Landacre Bridge (17). These have long been popular Exmoor bathing and picnicking spots, with shallows by the bridge and a deeper hole at the confluence of the Sherdon brook upstream. According to Hue, locals believe there is a hot spring somewhere along its course near here that makes the water especially warm. Perhaps the hot spring was broken the next day because the water was pretty invigorating at Landacre. Despite this, several families had taken up positions along the bank. At Withypool, a few miles further on, barbecues and picnics were in full swing, and a small flotilla of inflatable boats was in operation.

At Tarr Steps, there were even more people (19). The clapper bridge here is truly impressive. Constructed from megalithic flat stones laid end to end and propped up on boulders, it is one of the best-known monuments on Exmoor, and several theories claim it dates from the Bronze Age, although others date it to around 1400 AD. One myth has it that the Devil built it to win a bet and swore he would kill anyone who tried to cross it. To test his curse, the villagers sent a cat across. That was promptly vaporised, so the terrified locals sent the parson across next. Although the Devil swore and intimidated him, the parson swore back, and finally, the Devil succumbed and allowed people to pass, except when he wanted to sunbathe.

Between, above, and below the flagstones, children were chasing minnows, skimming stones, and getting thoroughly wet. I decided to find some peace and headed upstream a couple of miles through the beautiful National Nature Reserve. The woods here are internationally renowned for their mosses, liverworts, and lichens, including a type of moss found in burrows, which appears to glow in the dark. They are also home to the rare barbastelle bat, which breeds in the cracks of old trees. Feeling wonderfully relaxed away from everyone, I found a perfect pool, not too deep, some way down from a footbridge. Here, I swam, disturbed by no one, not even the Devil.

OKEMENT STREAMS

1 CULLEVER STEPS, EAST OKEMENT

Small, deep, popular pool by large flat rock in a pretty little valley below Scarey Tor with banks for a picnic. From Okehampton centre follow red army signs S to 'Camp', past range warden hut, to park at top of track on L (50.7105, -3.9846, EX20 1QR). Descend 600m to T-junction and continue straight over onto grass and down to pool 50m.

15 mins, 50.7132, -3.9766 🏊🏼

2 MELDON QUARRY

Impressive wrought-iron viaduct built in the 1870s (now on the Granite Way/NCN27, between Okehampton and Lydford) towers above a milky-green quarry pool with steep rock cliffs, popular among local swimmers. The land is private and access is permissive. Park at Meldon Reservoir car park, 3 miles SW of Okehampton on B3260 (EX20 4LU). Descend L on path 500m for quarry. The reservoir and West Okement stream are further up the valley to explore.

10 mins, 50.7109, -4.035 🏊‍♂️🚸❓🏊

3 ABBEYFORD WOOD, R OKEMENT

Bubbly stream pool and rapids in the woods,

waist high. Park at S car park (EX20 1RJ) and follow forestry track with barrier 750m to find just off to R.

12 mins, 50.7552, -3.9925 🏊‍♂️🚶

TORRIDGE & TAW

4 SHEEPWASH WOODLAND, R TORRIDGE

Pretty section of the young Torridge with a large, deep swimming hole below Boyton Bridge, the old sheep dip. Find parking and path on downstream L bank. Upstream on the L bank the land is community-managed with dormice, mature trees and barn owls at dusk (Sheepwash Woodland, donated by the Pedrick family) and there are many more sandy beaches and deep pools. Find path 100m N along lane, over stile in fence. Good pub in village (Half Moon Inn, EX21 5NE, 01409 231376).

5 mins, 50.8314, -4.1507 🏊‍♂️ℹ️🐾🚸

5 MEETH QUARRY

Explore the newly reclaimed clay lakes - deep, clear and beautiful. Just off the Tarka Trail. No Swimming. Park on W side of reserve, the quietest entrance point, EX20 3QN.

5 mins, 50.8505, -4.0999 🚸❓

6 BONDSTONES FORD, R TORRIDGE

An historic byway fords the river here, a rare point of public access, with a confluence pool 100m upstream. You can fish for trout and salmon (permits Stafford Moor Fishery, £10). Remote lane/byway beyond EX19 8SN with tricky parking, so best on foot/by cycle.

5 mins, 50.8474, -4.0578

7 BEAFORD BRIDGE, R TORRIDGE

Remote wooded stretch of river with ladder steps down to deeper water above old weir. Between Merton (A386) and Beaford (A3124). Climb lane 300m from Beaford Bridge (dir Beaford) and follow path on R for 10 mins down through woods. Also a good place for canoe launch.

10 mins, 50.9083, -4.0699

8 BLINSHAM, GREAT TORRINGTON

A small, secluded, sandy bay on the lively Torridge. Once a ford, so it is mainly shallow with boulders and rapids but also deeper sections. A good place to launch a canoe. Turn R off A3124, 2 miles SW of Torrington, signed Blinsham and conifer nursery. After 800m find gates on R with parking area. Follow middle trackway down to river 200m.

2 mins, 50.9295, -4.1105

9 TORRINGTON COMMON, TORRINGTON

A long stretch of quiet riverside meadow below the town, fast flowing and stony but the setting for many of Tarka's adventures. Access from Castle St car park EX38 8HB, through archway and down to the riverbank admiring the sweeping views. Downstream, Ladies Pool has a concrete platform, built in 1928 for the swimming women of Torrington; a second pool 200m along has a rope swing, and you can also swim below the weir beyond the road bridge. For closer access to the weir, park near the road bridge and Torridge Inn (EX38 8AW); for medieval Rothern Bridge, further downstream, park near Puffing Billy café (EX38 8JD), though this is a bit close to the sewage plant. Bring river shoes.

10 mins, 50.9491, -4.1453

10 UMBERLEIGH, R TAW

Pastoral stretch of the lively Taw, accessible by train. Pass train station N on B3227. Park at the primary school on R (EX37 9AD). Cross road and take path opp, on R of the tabernacle, down to the river and upstream. There's an even more beautiful river stretch at the next station, Chapelton (51.0173, -4.0228), but No Swimming so go downstream to tidal Bishop Tawton, towards Barnstaple.

5 mins, 51.0001, -3.9826 🏊❓

NORTH EXMOOR

11 PINKERY POND, CHALLACOMBE

High, lonely, open stretch of moor known as The Chains, with a large lake. Look out for the overflow tunnel hewn through the rocks on the SE side. The lake was created for landowner John Knight in 1830 by damming the headwaters of the river Barle, and intended to feed a large waterwheel via canal, powering an inclined railway carrying iron ore from Exmoor to Porlock Weir. Between Challacombe and Simonsbath (TA24 7LL on B3358) find layby car park on L, just after the gated entrance to Pinkery Centre for Outdoor Learning. This driveway/track takes you past the centre and all the way up to the pond.

30 mins, 51.1658, -3.8275 🏊⛺🏕🚶🔥

12 WATERSMEET HOUSE, R EAST LYN

A fine series of pools, waterfalls and woods upstream of a Victorian fishing lodge, now a NT tea room. Cash-only pay car park on the road just above, EX35 6NT. Descend and cross both footbridges. 300m upstream, on

the R bank (L as you go upstream), there are a series of rocky pools beneath the path. Another ½ mile, about 500m before Ash Bridge, find several beachy areas and deep corner pools with lots of paddling for kids.

5 mins, 51.2262, -3.7908 🍴🏕🔥🚶🌲🍽

13 LONG POOL, R EAST LYN

A deep, dark, long pool in a small, verdant ravine beneath a waterfall. Some good jumps for the brave. Park as for Watersmeet House (see listing); this is closer to the Rockford Inn end of the woods (EX35 6PT, 01598 741214) but parking there is even trickier. From Ash Bridge on R bank, it's another ½ mile upstream, just below a wooden bench on the opp bank. There are further pools below another small waterfall a further ½ mile upstream (Ash Pool).

15 mins, 51.2204, -3.7871 🍴🌲🏕🔥🍴

14 DEER PARK POOL, BADGWORTHY WATER

Charming little plunge pool underneath a shallow waterfall on the popular Doone Valley woodland walk. Start at Malmsmead, a tiny NT village with stone bridge, ford, riverside tea room and car park, EX35 6NU past Cloud Farm campsite/shop. A further 1.5km upstream on L bank, when woods

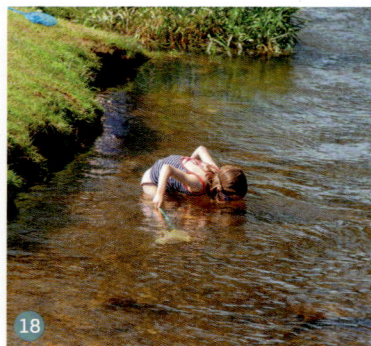

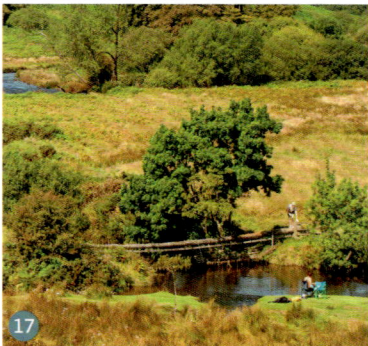

clear and path bears R up onto moor, find pool down on L under big tree.

20 mins, 51.1948, -3.7288

15 HORNER WATER POOL

A beautiful walk into ancient woodland to find a remote plunge pool beneath a small waterfall, just above a path and confluence. If camping at Pool Bridge, TA24 8JS, just follow the stream down 1km. Or start at the remote church and hamlet of Stoke Pero, TA24 8JT, and follow bridleway through farm, then down to L after 750m (open access woodland).

15 mins, 51.1854, -3.6002

RIVER BARLE

16 COW CASTLE, R BARLE

Small pool in the babbling stream at foot of the impressive Cow Castle hillfort. The walk follows the river through beautiful moorland and the riverside ruins at Wheal Eliza. There are several little places to bivvy along the way. From the Exmoor Forest Inn, Simonsbath (TA24 7SH, 01643 831341), walk down road 100m and take path (Two Moors Way) and continue for 2 miles.

40 mins, 51.1237, -3.7254

17 LANDACRE BRIDGE, R BARLE

Grassy river banks below old stone bridge up on the moor - a popular spot for summer picnics and paddling. For deeper pools follow the R bank upstream 400m to where the river bends with shale beaches. Or continue up moor road and take track on R after 500m. Park and follow track 500m down to Sherdon Hutch (51.1119, -3.7078). Signed off B3223, to TA24 7SD.

2 mins, 51.1121, -3.6922

18 WITHYPOOL, R BARLE

Popular kids paddling spot upstream of the bridge in pretty riverside village - the village post office even sells inflatables and nets. Downstream 3km into Bradley Wood (Two Moors Way) find small weir and island, just before path turning signed Winsford Hill (51.0919, -3.6351) and another deeper section after 300m.

30 mins, 51.1066, -3.6517

19 TARR STEPS, BARLE

Ancient stone clapper bridge in woods at the end of a pretty lane with popular inn. There is a deeper pool with open grassy banks about 750m upstream on L bank, through woods to a corner bend below footbridge, 51.0816, -3.6293. Well signed off B3223, Liscombe, and park in car park 500m before Tarr Steps Farm Inn (TA22 9PY, 01643 851507).

15 mins, 51.0772, -3.6176

20 BREWER'S CASTLE, BARLE

Deep in remote ancient forest, the Barle wraps itself between two ancient hillforts creating pools along the way. Park on verge of dead-end lane, before bend R to Hinam Farm, 51.0490, -3.5936, TA22 9QQ (respect any no parking signs, so tractor can enter field). Turn L on track/byway down to river and explore upstream 500m, past the footbridge and ford.

10 mins, 51.0557, -3.5929

21 WIMBLEBALL LAKE, UPTON
Large reservoir lake on the fringes of Exmoor. No Swimming, so for information only. The W shore has a campsite, visitor area and easily accessible shore for paddle boarding. The E shore is secluded, shallower and more gently shelving – the most secluded car park is Lyddons at 51.0617, -3.4473.

10 mins, 51.0639, -3.4568 🏊🚲♿❓

22 ANCHOR INN, EXEBRIDGE
Find car park opp the bridge and pub, B3222, TA22 9AZ. There's a big beach and deep pool here but it is by the road. For a quieter spot head upstream on riverside path 750m to a viaduct arch remains, also with beach, 51.0129, -3.5230. You might also try Brushford/Beasley Weir 51.0315, -3.5414, deep above the weir, but near the road.

10 mins, 51.0096, -3.5264 🏊🚶❓

23 TIVERTON, R EXE
Pretty meadow beach on the outskirts of town. Park by dog centre (EX16 5AA) then follow Loughborough Lane along leat/canal. Cross the leat on the footbridge and bear R for 150m along river to find beach.

5 mins, 50.9103, -3.4976 🏊❓

R CULM & EAST DEVON

24 LONGRUN MEADOW, TAUNTON
Plenty of places to dip along these popular meadows on the River Tone. There's the community barn or cross the river footbridge for The Weir cafe – the entry steps where canoes launch was originally the town bathing club. Free parking at Tesco, TA1 4AB.

5 mins, 51.0181, -3.1129 🏊

25 CULMSTOCK & HUNKIN WOOD
Riverside meadows with places to paddle and dip. For deeper meanders explore upstream from the church, path alongside cottages. Or for paddling, start at Culmstock Bridge EX15 3JJ and follow path downstream for up to a mile to Hunkin Wood, various bridges and little weirs. Or from the woods, park by the wooden gate on lane bend NE of Uffculme (50.9157, -3.3076, EX15 3AZ).

5 mins, 50.9163, -3.28023 🏊🚶

26 OTTERHEAD LAKES, ROYSTON WATER
Two spring-fed lakes at the source of the River Otter, tucked into a valley in the Blackdown Hills. Created as a series of ornamental lakes for a large Victorian

house. It's now a local nature reserve with No Swimming signs, but if there are no anglers people do dip in S lake. There's a car park at the N end, TA3 7EE. Or from the S end, park at 50.9113, -3.1025.

15 mins, 50.9188, -3.1C37 🏊

27 HIGHER WESTWATER, R YARTY
Small weir pool and salmon leap on pretty stream. Further paddling and picnic spots upstream, as far as Beckford Bridge. From centre of Axminster turn L at George Hotel, and L again (Castle Hill, signed Membury). Continue over river/railway line a mile and turn L, signed Westwater. After a mile, heading up hill, find lane to ford on L (public byway, unsuitable for cars further on). From ford follow path upstream 400m.

10 mins, 50.7954, -3.0342 🏊🚶

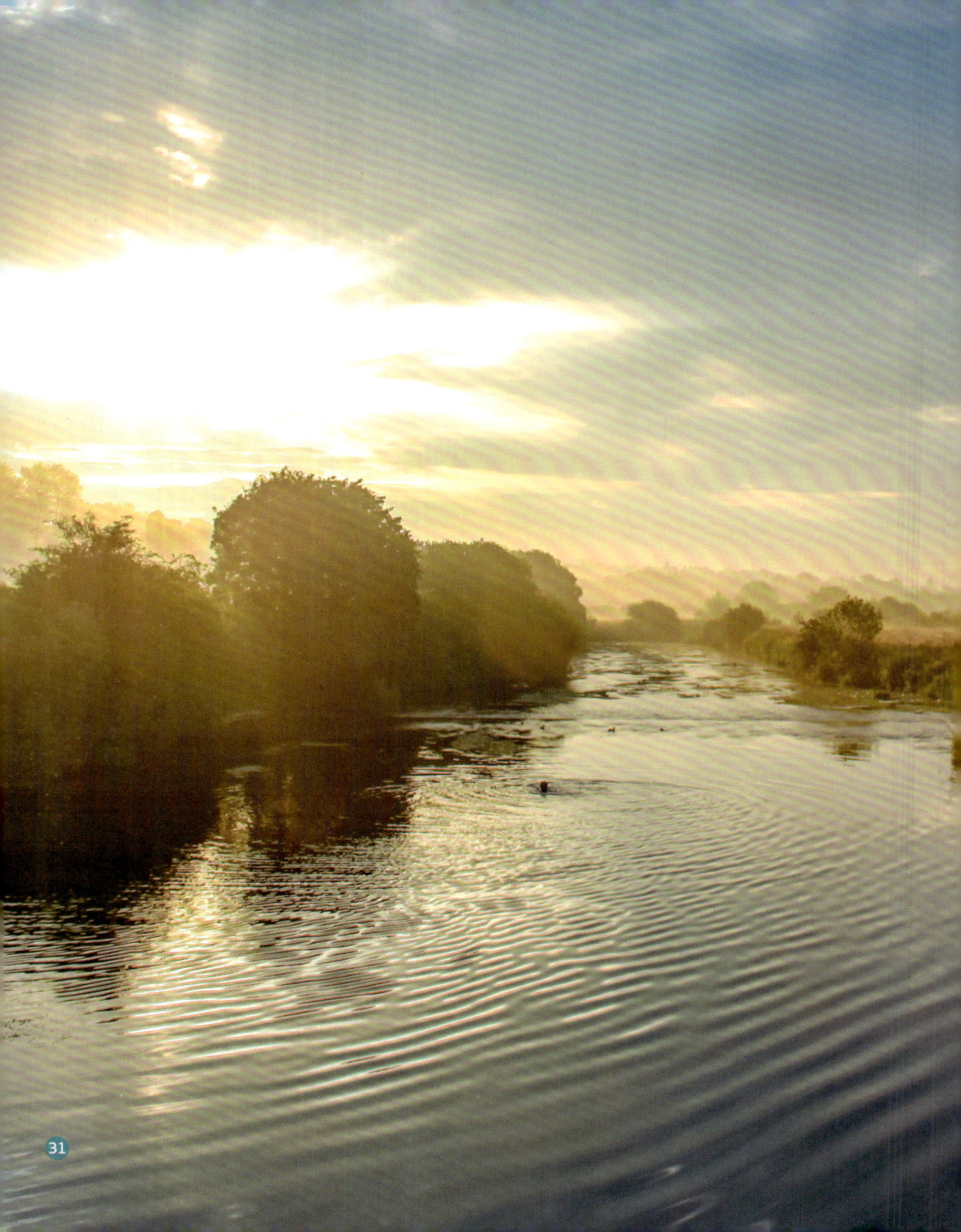

DORSET, WILTS & SOUTH SOMERSET

The meandering rivers of Thomas Hardy's Wessex twist and turn through lush pastures and cider-growing levels. Blossoms line the Somerset Brue in spring, and yellow water lilies fill the Dorset Stour in summer. Camping in fields close to the River Stour, I awoke to a glorious morning mist, with dew-clad spider webs hanging in the dried husks of cow parsley and tall brown bulrushes lining the banks. After sipping a hot mug of tea, I walked up to Colber Bridge on the common beneath Sturminster Newton (26). With little sign of life from the village above, I slid down the muddy bank and into the cool water. The shadow of gudgeon darted through the murk, and the odd weed tickled me as I swam under the bridge and down towards Bather's Island, the site of the old river swimming club.

Sturminster Newton is situated at a historic fording point of the Stour as it flows through the Blackmore Vale, classic Dorset dairy country. It was at Colber Bridge that Thomas Hardy and his wife Emma spent their happiest years walking and swimming by the river. Their friend, English poet William Barnes, also lived nearby for many years and wrote about the 'cloty Stour' – filled with its yellow water lilies and arrowhead much as it is today – in his *Poems of Rural Life in the Dorset Dialect*, written in the rich, wonderful old Dorset tongue.

Another popular Dorset Stour swimming hole is ten miles downstream at Pamphill towards Wimborne Minster Here, an old Roman ford, footbridge, and weir create a large space for swimmers to paddle and play (31). Upstream, the waters are wider and deeper. Like many other southern English rivers, the Stour's wildlife suffered a great decline with the intensification of dairy farming in the 1970s. Lapwing, snipe, and redshank all became rare. The river has largely recovered, but a new project – organised by the rural heritage charity Common Ground – is raising awareness of river ecology with a project to create music inspired by the river.

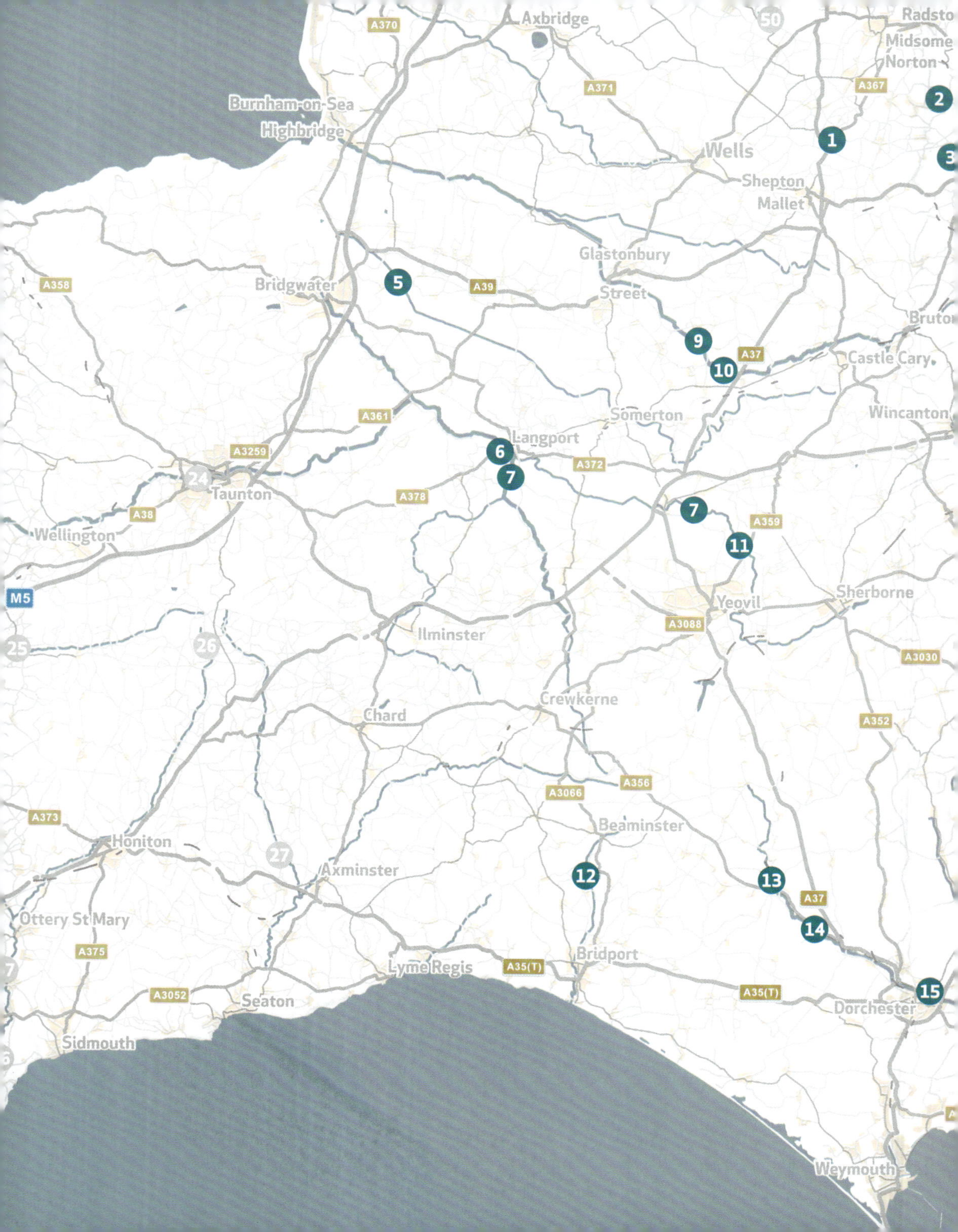

Axbridge
A370
Radsto
Midsome
Norton
A367
A371
2
1
3
Burnham-on-Sea
Highbridge
Wells
Shepton
Mallet
Glastonbury
A358
Bridgwater
5
A39
Street
Bruton
9
A37
10
Castle Cary
Somerton
Wincanton
A361
Langport
6
A3259
7
A372
24
Taunton
A378
7
A359
A38
Wellington
11
M5
Yeovil
Sherborne
A3088
25
26
Ilminster
A3030
Crewkerne
Chard
A352
A356
A3066
A373
Beaminster
Honiton
27
Axminster
12
13
A37
Ottery St Mary
14
A375
Bridport
Lyme Regis
A35(T)
15
A3052
Seaton
A35(T)
Dorchester
Sidmouth
Weymouth

Westbury
Ludgershall
Tidworth
Frome
Warminster
Andover
Amesbury
Stockbri
Mere
Wilton
Salisbury
Gillingham
Shaftesbury
Romse
Sturminster
Newton
Fordingbridge
Verwood
Lyndhurst
Blandford Forum
Ringwood
Wimborne
Minster
Ferndown
New Milton
Christchurch
Highcliffe-on-Sea
Poole
Bournemouth
Wareham
Swanage
A342
A346
A3026
A362
A3098
A360
A3028
A303(T)
A343
A345
A3057
A3094
A30
A36(T)
A27
A338
A3090
A354
A31
M27
A36
A336
A350
A357
A337
A347
A341
A35
A349
A3049
A3060
A3040
A3054
A351
16
17
18
19
20
21
22
23
24
25
26
27
28
29
30
31
32
33
34
35
36
37
38
39
40
41
42
43
44
45
46
47
48
49
50

If river music is your interest, then St Peter's Church, set alongside the River Brue at Lydford, is noted for its choral tradition (10). While the Stour drains Dorset south to the English Channel, the Lyd drains the Somerset Levels west to the Bristol Channel. Dorothy, an energetic silver-haired woman in her 60s, has swum here since she was a child. 'I loved listening to the choir practise as we glided past the blossoms in spring. It was like a natural baptism.' The smell of ozone from the tumbling water and the swooping manoeuvres of the damselflies are sure signs of how clean the river is today. Directly below the old weir is a small pool where children paddle and play. On warm weekends in the past, you might have found the neat lawns of the churchyard laid out with deckchairs and towels, and a mixture of swimmers and spectators of all ages jumping in from the bridge or swimming breaststroke back and forth along the blossomed reach, pulling themselves out between the two cherry trees, then sipping Earl Grey tea on the grass. Sadly, access to the river has been fenced off from the graveyard due to anti-social behaviour during lockdown and parking problems, but you can access the weir from below and there's a huge weir pool upstream through the meadows.

Somerset literally means 'land of the summer people' because the area could not be populated in the winter due to the great sea floods that inundated the levels. Lydford stands on the edge of this floodplain. From here, it's only a couple of miles to Baltonsborough Flights, another swimming hole, where the river drops down a weir into a large pool before beginning its journey to the sea through the heady blossoms of cider groves, willow, and teasel (9).

Salisbury Plain to the east is the headwater for three chalk streams – the Nadder, Wylye, and Hampshire Avon – that all descend on Salisbury and continue along the edge of the New Forest to Christchurch. Percolating from the hills, they are fabulously clean, clear, and cold!

I arrived at the Avon in Figheldean, just south of Stonehenge, to find bikinis hung on a Morris Minor, a picnic hamper spread out under a willow tree, and a mother and her three children paddling and shrieking in delight (38). This is a beautiful pool above a footbridge at the end of a little lane, again by a pretty church. The water is exceptionally clean and clear, rushing in over a simple sluice-type arrangement, first into a deep hole, and then over white pebble shallows and flint sandbanks with views over hay fields.

An' zwallows skim the water, bright
Wi' whirlèn froth, in western light;
zi' whirlèn stwone,
an' streamèn flour,
Did goo the mill by cloty Stour.'

William Barnes, 1862

Two young men in shorts and wellies had also just arrived from across the fields and were racing each other to be the first to dive into the deep pool beneath the small waterfall weir. Elizabeth, an elderly resident of the village, was spectating from a deckchair, calling out comments and clapping at all the action. In the old days, she said, the pool was always packed in the summer, particularly with servicemen from the airbases. During the war, there were Land Army girls here too. Some said their naked bathing distracted the village from the war effort, and the local policeman, who also ran the village swimming lessons, ordered that bathers should be suitably clothed for decorous bathing.

The Nadder, some miles away, is a much quieter, smaller stream splashing down through the uplands of the Cranborne Chase. I was quickly lost among the narrow lanes searching for a public footpath that might give bankside access. There, on a hill brow, with a sign pointing down through a billowing wheat field to a little bridge, I finally found a tiny map-marked public right of way. The Teffon Evias riverside is neatly mown and cordoned off, clearly prepared for some very well-organised fishing. I dare say fishermen would not welcome wild swimmers, so I followed the footpath gingerly, not wishing to disturb the peace, but I saw no one, save a dipper and a wagtail, and I arrived alone, hot but delighted, as the river widened into a clear shelving pool behind shrubs (35). A chute of the purest spring water poured in over an old hatch. Making a neat pile of clothes on a fishing bench, I climbed down the soft grass bank, tiptoed along the deepening riverbed, and swam breaststroke into the pool. Pebbles of whites, greys, and reds formed a wobbling mosaic on the cool river pool floor.

The third chalk stream – the Wylye – runs between the Nadder and Avon. I had initially been attracted to Steeple Langford by a series of lakes I spied from the main road late one evening. What were once gravel pits are now a nature reserve, and just as I was preparing to head home disappointed that a silent dip wasn't allowed, I spied a tiny lawn with a bench opposite the nature reserve entrance and a small sign (36): 'Entry to the pool is prohibited to those unable to swim.' With these magic words, a small but beautiful pool appeared, turning a silver-green hue in the fading evening light! A mother swan was collecting some final weedy titbits before tucking up her cygnets for the evening, and the church warden was cycling by on her bike, making her way home for supper. I tiptoed excitedly over the white shingle and waded into the pool. Here, floating like Ophelia, I lay in perfect stillness, staring up at an indigo sky and the first stars of the evening.

MENDIP LAKES & STREAMS

1 OAKHILL PONDS, SOMERSET ⬛

Two large, spring-fed swimming ponds and saunas, linked by an 18th-century grotto and surrounded by woodland and wildflower meadows. Accommodation and retreats. Winter membership £120 (Sep-May). Oakhill, Somerset, BA3 5AS, 07970541875.

2 mins, 51.2212, -2.5242

2 VOBSTER QUAY, RADSTOCK ⬛

Swimming, paddleboarding and diving quarry in beautiful surroundings. Look for deer on the banks and peregrine falcons overhead as you swim. Annual membership ~£52. Upper Vobster, Radstock BA3 5ZG. 01373 814666

2 mins, 51.2457, -2.4246

3 ASHAM WOOD LAKE

This vast, wildland area of regenerating open-cast stone quarry is full of forest, cliffs and wildlife. Deep in the heart is a peaceful wooded lake, perfect for a dip on the hottest of days, though completely hidden (use satellite maps to find). Park at the blocked-off entrance, 51.2138, -2.4066, opp 'weight limit ½ miles ahead'

sign (people also park along that road). Inside, bear R up steep track, then first L at top; paths down to the L lead to the old separating structures. For more organised swimming, Vobster Quay lakes are 4 miles to the N (BA3 5SD, 01373 814666 – members only).

10 mins, 51.2115, -2.4135 ⬛⬛⬛⬛

4 MELLS' STREAM, GREAT ELM ⬛

Some initial dipping pools along a wooded stream, leading to a footbridge with rope swing and shallow pool. Fussell Iron began smelting in 1804 along the Wadbury Valley and there are impressive ruins 1.5km upstream towards Mells, plus a rare resurgence waterfall that spews from the side of the valley into a shallow pool (51.2378, -2.3808). Cycle on NCN24 or park near the bridge, below the village (BA11 3NY, 51.2411, -2.3613) then upstream 500m.

10 mins, 51.2411, -2.3659 ⬛⬛

SOMERSET LEVELS

5 PARCHEY BRIDGE, CHEDZOY

King's Sedgemoor Drain is actually a very pleasant river, albeit straight and a bit silty. It runs through a vast, empty landscape.

Head downstream and take a dip opposite Pendon Hill (cycle on NCN 3) or explore upstream towards Greylake Bridge (A361, 51.1061, -2.8617) – you will see no one for miles. Car park is on Ward Lane, TA7 8RW.
5 mins, 51.1353, -2.9278

6 LANGPORT, R PARRET
Wild swimming capital of Somerset, this is a town that actually makes swimmers and SUP users welcome with a series of pontoons along the town riverbanks. Park in the main town car park, Parrett Close, TA10 9PG, and follow signs for Cocklemoor. Or park near the bridge café and cross the footbridge. Just upstream, Huish Bridge slipway is also an easy place to launch, 51.0335, -2.8220, TA10 9HE.
3 mins, 51.0356, -2.8315

7 MUCHELNEY ABBEY, R PARRETT
Visit the NT abbot's house and abbey ruins on the E bank, then take a picnic and swim or SUP along the river in deep open countryside. You can explore both sides, up or downstream, from the path. Law Lane bridge is 350m from the abbey with parking adjacent, TA10 0DQ. There's also a floating pontoon for boat launching or jumping!
10 mins, 51.0201, -2.8214

8 YEOVILTON WEIR, R YEO
Easy weir pool by the roadside. Just S of the village, before the bridge, find parking beneath trees on L with bench leading down to pool, BA22 8EU. Just before parking a bridleway by last house leads upstream ¼ mile for meadows and riverside meanders.
2 mins, 51.0012, -2.6504

9 BALTONSBOROUGH FLIGHTS, R BRUE
Large, stepped weir cascade with pool beneath, alone in fields off the lane. Follow riverside path downstream from East Lydford 2 miles or, heading S out of Baltonsborough on the Barton St David lane, find path on R after ¾ mile, BA6 8PQ.
5 mins, 51.1019, -2.6473

10 WEST LYDFORD WEIRS, R BRUE
This pretty stretch of river runs alongside St Peter's churchyard, from the road bridge down to the weir. Access to weir from the churchyard over fence is not encouraged anymore but people do still jump from the road bridge, and it is possible to reach the river below the weir via the footbridge (through churchyard). Or head to a big pool below the upstream weir, about 250m on path through the field (51.0834, -2.6181) but avoid if there are anglers and obey

signs. Avoid the church car park on Sunday, it's private, TA11 7DH.
5 mins, 51.0846, -2.6236

11 MUDFORD BRIDGE, R YEO
Deep meanders and a weir in quiet meadows. Off A359 S of bridge. Park by church, BA21 5TJ. Take path opp across field 500m.
5 mins, 50.9802, -2.6078

DORSET FROME

12 NETHERBURY, R BRIT 2
Just off the Hardy Way, next to Hugh Fearnley-Whittingstall's original River

16 WOODSFORD, R FROME

A pretty pastoral stretch of the Frome. Park by bridge at 50.7179, -2.3279 and follow the path upstream 500m to find two pools on the bends. You can float back down to the bridge or continue another 1km upstream to another pool at 50.7149, -2.3454.

5 mins, 50.7188, -2.3329

17 MORETON FORD, R FROME

A wide, gravel ford and shallow pool, lined with willows and tree swings. Very popular with families. Park in the free car park at the Walled Garden, where there's also a good tea room (DT2 8RG, 01929 462243).

5 mins, 50.7047, -2.2763

18 TURNERS PUDDLE, R PIDDLE

Paddle in the 'Puddle' on the Piddle – too shallow for more than a paddle, but a pretty chalk stream with ford, footbridge and rope swing. Signed R heading S from Bere Regis, then dead-end R. Park at end of lane, just before church, DT2 7JA. Cross first ford to reach main ford, 150m.

3 mins, 50.7389, -2.2428

19 BOVINGTON, R FROME

Remote pool with wooden footbridge surrounded by water meadows. Park on Bovington Ln, 100m W of the tank museum entrance, BH20 6NX. Take the path here, by the house gates, with MOD access sign. It's 750m S, across two tank tracks and a small footbridge. Come out onto a large meadow with the river the opposite side, 300m.

15 mins, 50.6863, -2.2398

20 WEST MILLS, WAREHAM, R PIDDLE

An idyllic little mill pool and beach on common land a short walk from town. Bear R on rough track over cattle grid, after hospital and before school, and park. Continue 500m on foot, under the A351 to the mill at BH20 6AA.

10 mins, 50.6881, -2.1233

21 WAREHAM, R FROME

Deservedly popular for swimming, picnics and boating on a hot summer day. There's a car park on The Quay by the bridge, A351 by the 1,000 year old Saxon church. Cross the road for Abbot's Quay, where there's a slipway plus canoe/SUP/rowing boat hire (BH20 4LW, 01929 550688). Otherwise head downstream on Priory Meadows, the R bank path, and swim from anywhere, for 1km until the boat club and Redcliffe Farm camping (BH20 5BE, 07859 911795).

2 mins, 50.6839, -2.1095

OAA walk up through the river meadows to a pool by the old railway (2km, crossing stream once). Follow line W and turn L at end on lane back to village. Cross footbridge over river opp and paddle on the little beach on R Hooke just upstream 50.7769, -2.5759, or continue downstream for 1km (Frome Ln) to find pools on meanders near footbridge at 50.7701, -2.5653.

5 mins, 50.782, -2.575

14 FRAMPTON & NUNNERY MEAD

Enjoy a pretty riverside paddle and picnic on the Millennium Green by a white timber-railed bridge. Turn off the A356, signed Southover, DT2 9NH, parking alongside.

1 mins, 50.7533, -2.5346

15 TEN HATCHES & STINSFORD, R FROME

The pool below the ten Victorian sluice gates where the river splits (only five remain today) was the town's original river swimming baths, with diving boards. Park in London Close, DT1 1SX. Turn R, over traffic lights and bridge to find path on L and continue 100m. There's another set of sluices and a pretty pool 1.5km away at Stinsford, 50.7165, -2.4083, 200m behind the church (or small church car park, DT2 8PT).

5 mins, 50.7172, -2.4265

Cottage, this little weir has a deep pool below and a good rope swing. From the bottom of Crook Hill, Netherbury, DT6 5LZ follow bridleway opp by the stream ¾ miles (dir Oxbridge) to find weir. From here the path bears R and continues through riverside parkland lakes (Slape Manor) to Waytown and the Hare and Hounds (DT6 5LQ, 01308 488203).

15 mins, 50.7839, -2.7484

13 MAIDEN NEWTON, R FROME

A three-swim walk, accessible by train. From the back of St Mary's church, DT2

22 SWINEHAM LAKE, DORSET 🅴

Large swimming lake close to Wareham with three swimming loops. NOWCA booking/ members, £7 per visit. Swineham Farm, Wareham, BH20 4JD. 07739 960 202

2 mins, 50.6911, -2.0918

23 SWINEHAM POINT, WAREHAM

A longer walk exploring the N bank of the Frome out to a large gravel lake and back along the L bank of the R Frome. Park at end of East St, Wareham (BH20 4JA) at East Walls junction, by dead-end signs. Continue on foot ¾ mile to where river meets path – there are several pontoons in the reeds for a swim (best at HT), and the river leads out into the wilds of Poole Harbour.

20 mins, 50.6906, -2.0854 🚶🏊

DORSET STOUR

24 STOUR PROVOST, R STOUR

Peaceful village with pool below the old mill, with machinery still intact. Park considerately on junction of Church and Mill Lane, SP8 5RX, and walk down to bottom of Mill Lane to find path on L at bend around bottom of garden. Walk upstream to footbridge and deep sections for swimming. Another option upstream is the path from

opp the Ship Inn, West Stour (SP8 5RP, 50.9993, -2.3050). Follow it through fields 400m SE to the footbridge.

2 mins, 50.9928, -2.2991 🏊

25 CUTT MILL, R STOUR

Large weir pool by ruined mill. In the old days youngsters used to leap from the top floor! Walk up from Sturminster along the river 1½ miles, Stour Valley Way, swimming as you go. Or at the N end of Hinton St Mary, B3092 find unsigned dead-end on L. Park on splay and walk ½ mile down the lane to the mill.

5 mins, 50.9479, -2.32 🏊🏊

26 COLBER BRIDGE, STURMINSTER

An open stretch of the Stour with grassy banks by decorative, white iron Colber Bridge. Water is a little weedy and slow, but clean and deep so perfect for long swims. Upstream is a beautiful stretch, beyond the old viaduct, to grassy banks all the way up to Cutt Mill. Park at the recreation ground, Ricketts Lane, DT10 1BY, then follow path down to the river (site of now overgrown 'Eather's Island') and upstream to the bridge.

5 mins, 50.928, -2.3105 🏊🏊🏊

27 FIDDLEFORD & STURMINSTER MILLS

Free car park and entry to the beautiful c14 stone manor house. It has extraordinary ancient roof timbers, some of the best in Dorset. The massive adjacent mill pool and sluices, set among meadows, are a popular place for locals to swim on a hot day. Signed Fiddleford Manor or L, a mile E of Sturminster Newton on A357, DT10 2BX. People also swim at Sturminster Mill pool just upstream but it has a cafe/visitor centre so is a bit busy, DT10 2DQ, 50.9212, -2.3112.

5 mins, 50.9215, -2.2855 🏊🏊

28 HAMMOON, R STOUR

Secluded stretch of the Stour with grassy areas and meanders. A mile E of Fiddleford, A357, take next L and continue 1½ miles through village, DT10 2EB, to park by bridge. Take path downstream on L bank about 200m to the river (or just swim in deep pool under road bridge).

5 mins, 50.93, -2.2532 🚶🏊

29 OLD VIADUCT, BLANDFORD FORUM

The Stour meadows run along the S side of the two with ample places to swim or canoe. The remnant of old viaduct provides a fascinating reminder of the bygone days of rail and provides deep swimming below – climb up to the top to admire the river first. Head upstream to Mortain footbridge with deeper swimming above the weir. Park at M&S Foodhall to find the river directly behind, DT11 7EN. Another pretty and easy spot, downstream of town off A350, is the ford behind the church in Charlton Marshall, DT11 9NQ, 50.8366, -2.1421.

3 mins, 50.8546, -2.1594

30 WHITE MILL, STURMINSTER MARSHALL

Over 1km of river pools downstream of the medieval arched bridge, below NT White Mill (£3.50). For a longer walk follow the Stour Valley Way for two more miles of delightful riverside all the way to Shapwick, with a riverside church and gastropub (The Anchor Inn, DT11 9LB, 01258 857269). Signed Sturminster Marshall from the B3082 E of Badbury Rings, find the NT White Mill car park, BH21 4BX.

2 mins, 50.8048, -2.0613

31 PAMPHILL, WIMBORNE MINSTER

A wide, popular river pool with a riverside beach, footbridge and a small weir. There are good walks and swims upstream too. Heading W out of Wimborne on St Margarets Hill, dir B3082 and Blandford,

turn L down Cowgrove Rd, signed cycle route. Continue 1km to find car park and river on L, BH21 4EL.

2 mins, 50.8, -2.0076

32 HATCH HOLE, CANFORD MAGNA

Cross a beautiful Victorian suspension bridge to reach a large weir pool in meadows opposite the grand buildings of Canford School. Perfect for SUP/canoe too. Park on Canford Magna Lane (No Through Road, dir church/school, BH21 3AD) and walk up to the school entrance. Head upstream, over bridge and downstream 100m to weir. Continue downstream for up to a mile along the river through meadows (Castleman Trailway, path of old railway, open for cycling). Upstream on R bank the cycle trail leads to the extraordinarily ornate Lady Wimborne Bridge (50.7905, -1.9745). Or upstream on L bank for a mile, path only, to Wimborne Canoe Club jetty and boat hire (07761 816796).

10 mins, 50.7903, -1.9568

WILTS CHALK STREAMS

33 LONGBRIDGE DEVERILL, R WYLYE

Large weir pools below sluice gates, just off A350. Park in layby the almshouses with a

clock, BA12 7DL. Take path in front of them.
2 mins, 51.1706, -2.1912

34 HEYTESBURY MILL, R WYLYE

Surprisingly deep and lovely willow-lined pool, just outside the kitchen windows of the mill house. It's incredibly popular with local kids who like to jump in from the footbridge above the sluices. In Heytesbury, follow High St E, bend R on Park Lane, then continue 300m for limited parking on bridge, BA12 0HE. Find riverside path on R, then 50m.
2 mins, 51.1791, -2.1002

35 TISBURY & FONTHILL, R NADDER

Deep stretch above the old mill. Turn R out of Messums, first L into Chicksgrove Rd and find path on R before cottages. Follow for 150m. Or get in from the road, 50m upstream, and float down (Swallowcliffe road, 150m on L before bridge). For another set of hatches, Teffont Evias is hidden and gorgeous, 4km E, and you can jump in, but is contested by anglers (51.0704, -2.0192). For a longer swim some people go to majestic Fonthill Lake 3km N (51.0843, -2.0965) but this is surprisingly shallow and No Swimming.
5 mins, 51.0658, -2.0694

36 STEEPLE LANGFORD, R WYLYE

Pretty village weir pool with shelving chalk beach, grassy banks and bench. Turn off A36 dir The Langfords 8 miles W of Salisbury. In Steeple Langford centre turn L down Duck Street. Langford Lakes Nature Reserve is 500m on L, just over bridge, with some parking. The pool is opp, through little gate.
2 mins, 51.1328, -1.9485

37 GREAT WISHFORD, R WYLYE

It's always fun to dip in the lively Wylye. This shady, deepish, fast-flowing section is just upstream of the footbridge. Follow Station Rd 850m S from Royal Oak, past R turn under railway, to find tarmac path signed on L with layby, SP2 0NX. Follow 100m to bench.
3 mins, 51.1103, -1.8827

SALISBURY AVON

38 FIGHELDEAN & FIFIELD

Popular but pretty pool with chalk shingle beneath a small weir from which people jump; sometimes closed off due to overcrowding and bad parking. Turn off A345 into Figheldean and park on the High St. Continue N to where road bends R and

take small lane L (SP4 8JJ). A footbridge lies at the end with the pool on R. Alternatively walk from the other end of the byway/path on the A345 at the Netheravon sign (layby opp). Upstream there is a good stretch of open access riverbank below the MOD tank bridge at Fifield, but shallow (51.2504, -1.7907).
5 mins, 51.2262, -1.7846

39 HAM HATCHES, AMESBURY

Deep, clear pool with concrete platform below sluices and a pretty beach above. Heading W out of Amesbury, cross river and turn L down Recreation Rd on bend R.

There's a car park and playground; a path leads down to the river bridge.
5 mins, 51.1682, -1.7885 ▣▧▾🍴

40 STRATFORD BRIDGE, SALISBURY

Large area of open access river meadows in the centre of the city. Park near the tennis courts on Coldharbour Lane (SP2 7DG) and head upstream ½ mile to an S bend in the river with a deep pool (about 150m beyond end of the boardwalk). Or access from Stratford/Old Sarum upstream: park at top of Mill Lane (SP1 3LJ, 51.0900, -1.8135) and walk downstream via Stratford

footbridge. A further 3 miles upstream, the Bridge Inn, Upper Woodford (SP4 6NU, 01722 783203) is a nice riverside pub.
10 mins, 51.0842, -1.8118 ▣

41 OLD MILL, R NADDER

On hot summer days kids jump into the deep race below Harnham's c13 mill, now a pub (SP2 8EU, 01722 656999). The water is cool, clear and great for paddling. Parking is tricky on the back streets near the pub, but it's a lovely ½ mile walk or cycle across Queen Elizabeth Gardens and Harnham water meadows, from Crane Street/ Lush House car park on Cranebridge Rd (SP2 7TD).
15 mins, 51.0638, -1.8082 ▣ℹ🍴

42 CHARLTON ALL SAINTS

Superb pool below a weir in a beautiful setting with a long deep, pastoral stretch above (private fishing, do not swim there). The prettiest approach is from E bank, Trafalgar Park. Pull off at the wooded bend 300m W of Standlynch Farm entrance, SP5 3QU (51.0095, -1.7374). Follow track down bearing R to the mill, past Standlynch Chapel (where many of Nelson's relatives are buried), then upstream 200m.
15 mins, 51.0128, -1.7424 ▣🚶❓

43 DOWNTON & THE MOOT, R AVON

The Millennium Green is a community meadow with mown grass pathways leading to picnic tables by a river beach on a wide, open stretch of the Avon. A riverside path leads upstream to more dipping spots and after ½ mile The Moot, an 8-acre Georgian ornamental public garden built on the remains of a Norman motte-and-bailey castle, with an amphitheatre and rope swings and good paddling on the mill stream. Limited parking on the corner of Moot Gardens/Avondyke SP5 3LW (50.9862, -1.7498). Or park upstream at The Moot itself and walk down (car park opp Downton House, SP5 3JP).
5 mins, 50.9845, -1.7526 ▣🐾▾🍴◨⊞

44 CASTLE HILL, R AVON

A beautiful woodland of fine mature oaks, with a steep wooded descent to rope swings and deep river swimming, well away from the crowds. Heading S out of Woodgreen, turn R opp cemetery. Continue ½ mile to car park (SP6 2LU, 50.9494, -1.7587). Walk S on lane and descend to the river on any path. Or dip at the bridge N of Woodgreen off Moot Lane (50.9672, -1.7491, near SP6 2AN).
10 mins, 50.9468, -1.7624 ▣🍴

45 EYEWORTH POOL, FRITHAM

Among Forestry Commission owned open access heathland, a little lane leads down to a shallow warm lake. Leaving Fritham past the pleasant Royal Oak pub (SO43 7HJ, 023 8081 2606, large garden) continue just under 750m down the hill to the pond car park. Occasional No Swimming signs.

1 mins, 50.9308, -1.6761 🚶🚗🏊🅿️❓

46 FORDINGBRIDGE, R AVON

Swim from the riverside car park by the sports ground, or swoosh down to here from the main town river beach in the Memorial Gardens (car park SP6 1AN) 300m upstream. To explore more, 4km downstream by A338 at Ibsley Bridge is a beautiful weir pool by main road (50.8858, -1.793), a traditional wash pool used by the community, with deep meanders in pretty meadows along the footpath downstream. Swimming now prohibited due to fishing interests, so please only picnic and walk.

5 mins, 50.9234, -1.7898 ❓🚶

47 NEW FOREST WATER PARK 🅴

OWS and inflatables in lovely gravel lakes off A338. SP6 2EY, 01425 656868, via NOWCA.

5 mins, 50.8997, -1.7824 ❓🚶

48 ELLINGHAM, BLASHFORD LAKES 🅴

Lifeguarded OWS in a beautiful clean lake set in a nature reserve in the New Forest, BH24 3PJ ellinghamwaterski.co.uk. Book via NOWCA.

2 mins, 50.8718, -1.7876

49 RINGWOOD, R AVON

Lush wide meanders in remote water meadows – very beautiful and rural. Follow B3347/Christchurch Rd a mile S of Ringwood. Take R fork (dead-end) just after L turn signed Burley. Continue a mile down Hampshire Hatches Lane, past BH24 3AT, until parking at end. Follow path N over footbridge 300m.

5 mins, 50.8352, -1.7913 🏊🚶

50 WATTON'S FORD & LEYBROOK

An untamed stretch of heath and common land borders the Avon where a shallow ford crosses from Dorset to Hampshire – a byway since at least Roman times. The bank to the N is Leybrook Common. Downstream is 7 miles of some of the most remote, meandering river in Dorset (first possible get out at 50.7796, -1.7894, Avon Bridge). Approach the ford from the W bank, BH24 2AZ.

2 mins, 50.8156, -1.8064 🏊⛰️

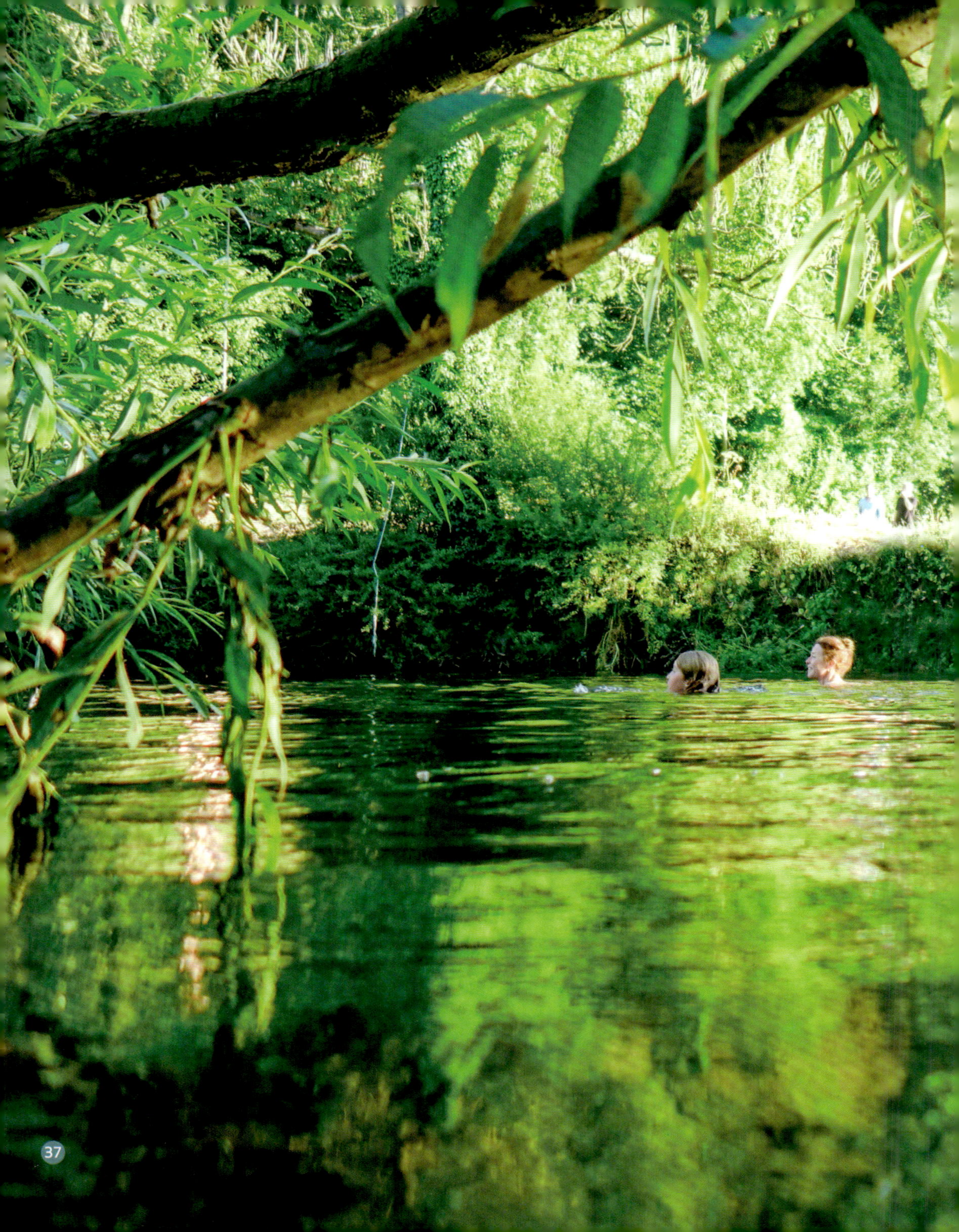

WYE VALLEY & SOMERSET AVON

I spent my early childhood close to the Herefordshire Wye, near Hoarwithy (5). We were two families and a gang of five children. I was the youngest and would trail along behind as rafts were built and lanes explored by bicycle. It's easy to be nostalgic about a river when it flows through the heart of your formative years.

When I tried to remember some of the places I had swum on the Wye, however, I realised many were lost in the fog of early memories, so I decided to return to Hoarwithy for a week and retrace old steps. I based myself at Tressacks campsite, a plain but pleasant stretch of riverside with a little beach, roaring campfires, and an excellent gastro pub. Each morning I tiptoed sleepily down to the river and plunged groggily into the shallow waters, brought to life with a judder of adrenaline. I had played near here as a young boy, I thought, though the river seemed so much wider and deeper then. On really big expeditions, we would cycle the three miles to Sellack Common (5), and it used to take all day. The height of excitement was standing on the white iron suspension footbridge, bouncing up and down to see if it would swing and dropping blackcurrants on canoes as they went by.

The Wye is fortunate to be one of the several rivers in England with an Act of Parliament that enshrines the right to navigate and to swim. Some suggest that all rivers navigable by small craft have automatic rights of navigation, but even here on the Wye, one of the most famous canoeing rivers, there are still occasional conflicts between fishermen and other river users.

From Sellack Common, the river completes a five-mile loop to Backney (6) through mainly private fishing estates, but a mile-long lane, over the brow of a hill, cuts off the corner and brings you to Backney Common. This area of meadow has age-old commoner rights and occupies the inside of a large, deep meander. A wide pebble beach has been deposited over time on the inside bank, and

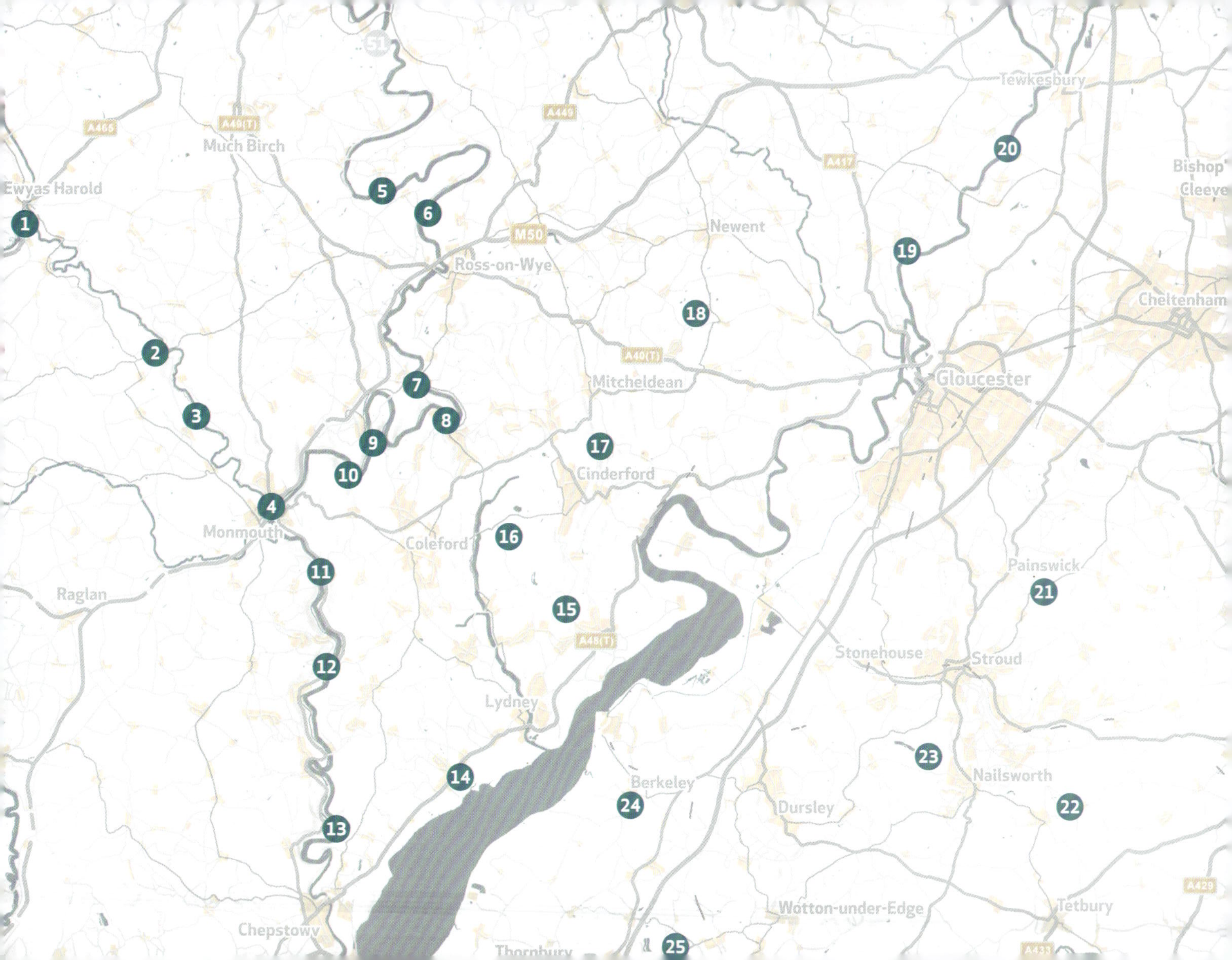
Tewkesbury
Bishop's Cleeve
Cheltenham
Gloucester
Ewyas Harold
Much Birch
Newent
Ross-on-Wye
Mitcheldean
Cinderford
Coleford
Monmouth
Raglan
Lydney
Painswick
Stonehouse
Stroud
Nailsworth
Berkeley
Dursley
Wotton-under-Edge
Tetbury
Chepstow
Thornbury
A465
A49(T)
A449
A417
M50
A40(T)
A48(T)
A429
A433
51
1
2
3
4
5
6
7
8
9
10
11
12
13
14
15
16
17
18
19
20
21
22
23
24
25

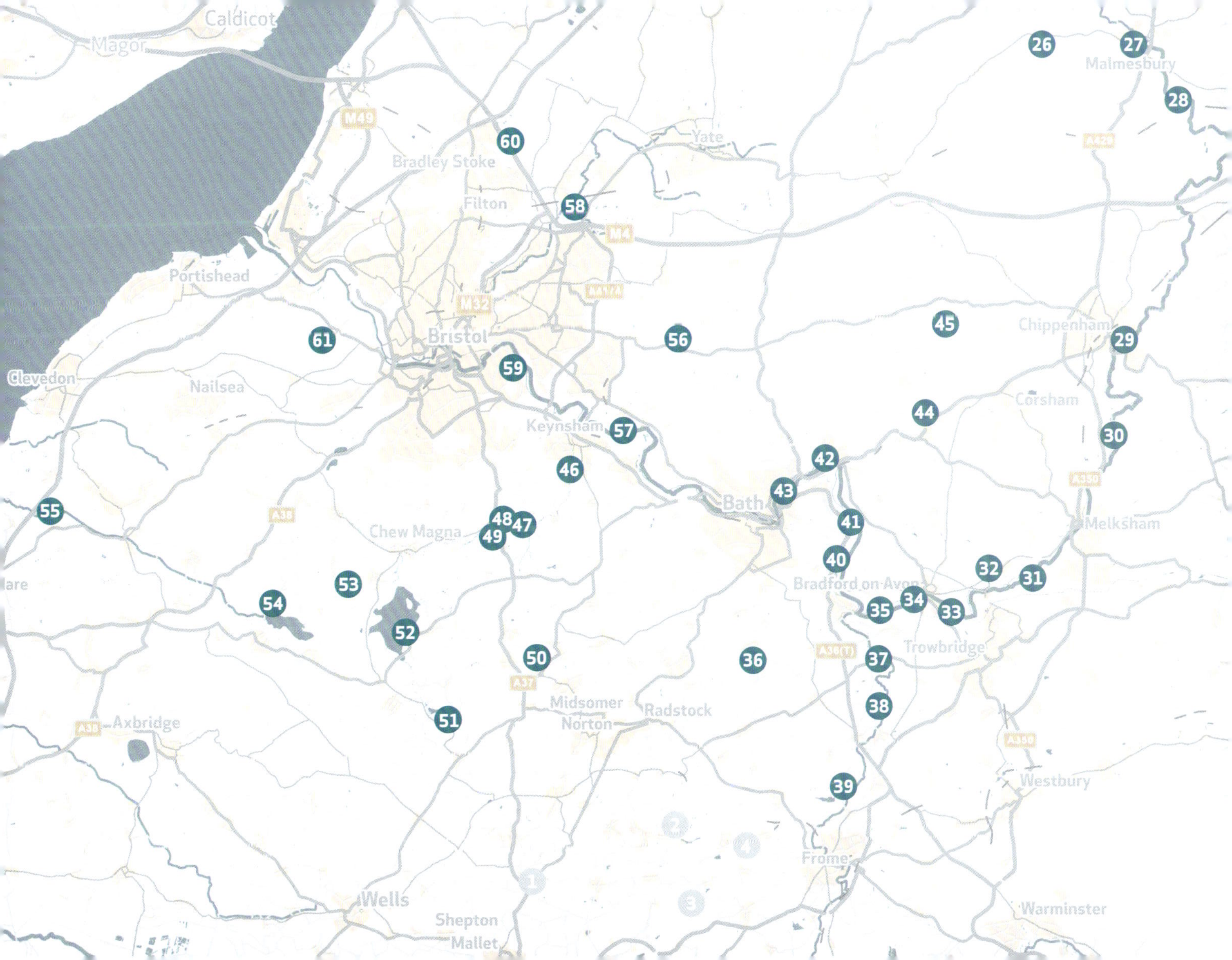
Caldicot
Magor
M49
Bradley Stoke
Filton
Yate
M4
Portishead
M32
A4174
Bristol
Clevedon
Nailsea
Keynsham
Bath
Chew Magna
A38
A37
Midsomer
Norton
Radstock
Axbridge
Wells
Shepton
Mallet
Malmesbury
A429
Chippenham
Corsham
A350
Melksham
Bradford on Avon
Trowbridge
A36(T)
Westbury
Frome
Warminster
26
27
28
29
30
31
32
33
34
35
36
37
38
39
40
41
42
43
44
45
46
47
48
49
50
51
52
53
54
55
56
57
58
59
60
61

large deep swimming holes have been eroded on the outside. The sand and pebbles are beautifully graded, so you can even bring your bucket and spade.

Some seven miles downstream, the river comes to its most splendid reach as it enters the great wooded ravine of Symonds Yat (9). Beech-forested cliffs rise on all sides, and King Arthur's and Merlin's Caves can be spied high on the limestone walls, cut by the river many thousands of years ago. The village is squeezed onto the narrow rising banks of the gorge, and the east and west sides are joined only by two rope ferries. It is possible to swim across, but most inhabitants use canoes. Many homes – and even the church – have river landing stages, which double up for river swimming in the summer. The village is equally famous as a place for learning about rivers and the great outdoors: the Biblins forest camp in Symonds Yat has been providing inner-city children with wild experiences for over 50 years.

The Wye is the most popular canoeing river in Britain, and many companies will arrange everything needed for a few days of canoe camping through the countryside. There is also the beautiful Wye Valley Walk, and it was at Symonds Yat that I met an elderly couple from Lincoln who had walked for over thirty miles, swimming along the way. They had come rather unstuck skinny-dipping one lunchtime just as a flotilla of canoes helmed by a stag party in fancy dress came by! Despite that, they had a strict routine of swimming three times a day: 'Before breakfast, lunch and tea we agreed – it's very good for you, you know, going in the cold water. And we haven't missed an opportunity yet.'

The Wye reaches the sea at the Severn Estuary, nearly opposite the mouth of the Avon, which rises in the Cotswolds before winding down through Wiltshire and Somerset, enriching towns along its way, many of which harnessed the power for mills, such as at Bradford-on-Avon (43). Warleigh/Claverton Weir, five miles downstream and on the outskirts of Bath, forms a long, meandering waterfall across the River Avon (41).

The weir looks a little like a miniature Victoria Falls stretching into the distance. At over one hundred yards long, it was built in 1810 to power a pump that would lift water from the river to the nearby Kennet and Avon Canal. It has created a huge pool in the Avon and a spectacularly wide waterfall. Children play under the dam and in the shallows. Adults can take a long swim above the weir for the best part of a mile.

In Bath, a different water created wealth through the hot springs (which once also emerged in Bristol at Hotwells). The water fell as rain around 10,000 years ago and then sank to a depth of about 2km. Here, it is heated by high-temperature rocks before rising back up through one of the three hot springs in the centre of the city: the Cross Spring, Hetling, or King's Spring, which supplies the Roman Baths. The actual source of the waters remains a mystery. It was believed that the source was in the Mendip Hills, 30 miles to the south of Bath, but more recent findings suggest that the rainwater enters through the carboniferous limestone closer to the city and the Avon Valley.

The Frome joins the Avon from south of Bath and definitely does come from the Mendips. This river is home to one of the country's last surviving river-swimming clubs, with stories of camping galas and wild swimming parties. The Farleigh and District Swimming Club occupies a great sweep of south-facing meadow by an old diving frame and gravel-bedded weir pool on the Frome (37). With over 2,000 members, people come here from far and wide to experience real swimming and to sunbathe on the grassy banks.

The club was founded in 1933 during the great boom in British river swimming. The village was already popular with the people of Trowbridge, a few miles away, who would walk over to Farleigh at the weekend to swim, visit the castle, and have a drink at the Hungerford Arms. The four Greenhill brothers owned the farm on the opposite side of the bank and also loved to swim. One day, they invited some of these regular bathers to form a swimming club, and for the next 20 years, the club flourished. Summers saw a regular group who would camp out on the banks, rise at six for an early-morning dip, and then go off haymaking for the day. There were Wednesday evening swimming galas, great bonfires, and general summer antics, all with the enthusiastic support of the Greenhills. In more recent years, the club has swapped banks. The new landlords are just as enthusiastic, and they run a campsite and tea shop a mile upstream. This river is a beautiful setting for a summer afternoon, with children swimming among the moorhens and alder roots, and the spray from the weir catching the floating dandelion seeds. There are no galas or bonfires here anymore, but the big-hearted welcome still exists.

Two miles upstream at Tellisford (38), the landowners have also been modernising with a sensitive eye for wild swimmers. A beautiful weir pool is located a little way up from a medieval packhorse bridge among wide fields and an old Second World War bunker – this was a position on the 'Salisbury West Stop Line' where the British planned to defend the country against an attack coming from the south coast. This weir was originally constructed in the eleventh century to power the village mill. Although it stopped working in 1912, the weir pool has been saved by a local project to generate 60kW from the renovated mill race – enough to power the whole village. This is an exciting green initiative that has preserved the weir pool, provides a more reliable supply of electricity than wind, and is less unsightly than a turbine.

RIVER MONNOW

1 LLANGUA BRIDGE, MONNOW GAP
A deep pool on the border next to the road bridge, with ledges for jumping. The perfect spot for a hot day cool-down. On A465 just S of Pontrilas, right on the England/Wales border. Park in lay-by 50m down fork dir NP7 8HD and walk to bridge and signed footpath down, L on English side.
2 mins, 51.934, -2.8809

2 SKENFRITH CASTLE
Follow the path through the beautiful ruins of the 13th-century castle to the riverbank to find a number of perfect spots for a dip or a dive. Great community shop and pub across the lane. Signed just off the B4521 at Skenfrith, NP7 8UH, with grass parking outside the castle.
5 mins, 51.8787, -2.7898

3 TREGATE BRIDGE, RIVER MONNOW
A quiet, wooded stretch of the Monnow flowing down to an old weir and bridge. Other deep pools, islands and beaches can be found up and downstream. Take turning next to Bell Inn/bridge at Skenfrith (see listing). Continue 2½ miles S dir NP25 5QG, then turn L to bridge (signed). Parking limited, don't block

gates. Follow footpaths on far side.
5 mins, 51.8516, -2.7607

4 THE WYE AT MONMOUTH
Deep section of the Wye with easy access next to the Rowing Club, stay visible with a tow float and coloured hat and look out for boats. More secluded swimming downstream near the confluence with the Monnow, near ruined ancient stone viaduct and newer iron bridge. Parking with height restriction at Rowing Club (NP25 3DP) or park at Wyebridge Street car park and take subway to river. For viaduct, cross Wye Bridge on foot E and take riverside path along sportsfield 800m to deep section near old viaduct.
10 mins, 51.81289, -2.7083

LOWER WYE

5 SELLACK BOAT & HOARWITHY
A shingle beach shelves to a deeper swim on the far bank under a beautiful suspension footbridge, named for the ferry service it replaced. From Kings Caple (HR1 4TY), head S at crossroads signed Sellack Boat and park on R as road turns sharp L after 800m. Or 2km W you can swim from the riverside path below Hoarwithy Bridge, or

from Tresseck campsite (HR2 6QH, 07901 127097) by the New Harp Inn.
8 mins, 51.9485, -2.6327

6 BACKNEY COMMON, RIVER WYE
This piece of ancient common land juts out onto a tight meander of the river Wye. Good shingle and sand beach, shelving to a large pool at the far end. From A449 Ross take A49 Hereford road then first R, signed Backney. After 2 miles, bear R to Foy and find car park on R after 250m (just before HR9 6QX). Height limit with barrier. Track to meadows is adjacent. Continue

500m upstream to beach.
10 mins, 51.939, -2.6009

7 KERNE BRIDGE, R WYE
The ideal start to a 2¼-mile swim, kayak or float downstream to Lower Lydbrook. Slow, meandering curves in the river, with a few shallow rapids, pass through beautiful countryside in sun and dappled shade. On B4234 in Kerne Bridge, 350m after passing B4229 junction to Monmouth, park in car park R (before HR9 5QX). Follow slipway down to launch. Exit at Stowfield Road in Lower Lydbrook (see listing).
2 mins, 51.8655, -2.6081

8 LOWER LYDBROOK PARK, R WYE
A little grassy park giving easy access to a bend in the river with beaches, picnic tables and benches. The whole stretch here is swimmable, from Kerne Bridge (see listing) down to Symonds Yat. Shortly N from the village, where the B4234 turns R along the river (GL17 9NU). One car park is at the junction, another just 60m along the road L both close at 8pm.
2 mins, 51.8502, -2.5875

9 SYMONDS YAT EAST & BIBLINS
On the site of the vanished railway bridge,

steps lead down into the water for canoe launching or swimming. A short way upstream through the meadow is an old stone landing stage, perfect for a secluded swim. On B4234 from N into Kerne Bridge, 300m after the Inn on the Wye and 100m past turn to HR9 5QT, find pay car park on R.
2 mins, 51.8404, -2.6383

10 THE BIBLINS, RIVER WYE
On a gentle meander of the Wye, this beach under an old, wooden suspension bridge offers shelving access to deep pools. For more spots, follow river downstream on either bank. From A40 interchange for Whitchurch (or just S of it if travelling S) follow signs for Symonds Yat (West) then Crockers Ash, S on E side of A40, past service station, then turn L onto Sandiway Lane past HR9 6D. Go R at fork by cream house, then L signed Biblins at T-junction. After 800m turn R on hairpin at Doward Campsite on signed track to Biblins, park R in lay-by after 150m. Follow Biblins track to river.
20 mins, 51.8266, -2.6553

11 LOWER REDBROOK & BOAT INN
A gentle, deep swim under the imposing old iron railway bridge by a superb, hidden

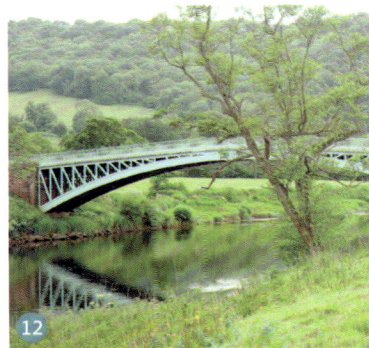

riverside cider pub, the Boat Inn NP25 4AJ, 01600 712615). Follow the riverbank path 150m upstream through meadows to the first of several fishing piers and over 2 miles more riverbank beyond. Downstream are the remains of an old loading quay after 600m (51.7794, -2.6762), and beyond that Prisk Wood with myriad old gritstone quarry workings and mossy millstones to be found. Park in pay car park (opp NP25 4LP) and follow path from corner alongside the pitch, turning R to cross bridge.
4 mins, 51.7849, -2.6739

(photo 11)

(photo 17)

(photo 13)

14 COURT FARM LAKES, LYDNEY £

Beautiful series of small lakes for swimming, paddle boarding, sauna and lakeside yoga. Onsite café. £8 per swim session. Main Rd, Lydney GL15 6PJ. 07718229732

2 mins, 51.6969, -2.5765

15 BLACKPOOL BROOK, WENCHFORD

Perfect for kids and picnics: a pretty stream flowing through the forest with a small weir for paddling, tables for picnicking, and bluebells in May. Turn off A48 at Nibley signed Parkend. After 2 miles turn R over narrow bridge then immediately L to Wenchford forest parking R after 200m (charges April–October, open 8.30am–dusk). Follow paths L into trees. For a deeper swim, Bathurst Pool is nearby, a small community-run lido set in fields on the S approach to Lydney (GL15 5DP, 01594 842625)

2 mins, 51.7694, -2.5032

16 SPEECH HOUSE LAKE & ARBORETUM

One of the larger and more hidden forest lakes for secret dippers (No Swimming). Originally for royal fishing (still popular with anglers), in the 2000s it appeared as the magical Lake of Avalon in the BBC Merlin series. The access is through the Cyril Hart Arboretum, a century-old collection with over 200 exotic fir, redwood and pine species, mainly from China. Turn off B4226 at the Speech House hotel (GL16 7EL), then first L to find Spruce Ride car park on R. Walk 500m on broad track, then turn R. Main Arboretum entrance with car park is 300m further E on B4226 from hotel and also has broad tracks to lake.

7 mins, 51.8004, -2.5433

17 ST ANTHONY'S WELL

You can completely immerse yourself in this famously cold, crystal-clear forest bath It's a substantial, stone-lined holy well said to benefit those suffering from arthritis and skin complaints – but nine visits in the month of May were recommended for a full cure. At the Flaxley/Littledean junction, take the lane past the Asha Centre and park on the bend after 500m (51.8392, -2.4788). There's a good path into woods W, follow the stream 100m.

2 mins, 51.8394, -2.4802

18 BAREFOOT & BOWER, NEWENT £

Two spring fed lakes set amongst ancient woodland. Absolutely stunning scenery and

12 BIGSWEIR BRIDGE, R WYE

The lowest non-tidal section of the Wye, this was once the limit for the larger sea-going 'trows' from Bristol; iron and timber from the Forest of Dean were shipped out from here, while imports were transferred onto smaller boats and pulled upstream by bow hauliers. Pretty riverside meadows with paths upstream on the right bank and downstream on the left are perfect for picnics, swimming and canoe launching. Just off the A466, with easy parking on the Whitebrook turn off (NP25 4TS) on W bank.

2 mins, 51.7441, -2.6697

13 LIVOX QUARRY WALK TO WYE GORGE

Deep down in the gorge of the Wye an azure quarry lake is edged with white quartz beaches and cliffs in a vast, abandoned amphitheatre patrolled by circling buzzards. A public path skirts its S edge for wonderful views into it (quarry access is banned) and then continues on down to a very remote, untouched stretch of the tidal Wye for a high tide dip (beware currents). The footpath starts on A466 (51.6747, -2.6749) at bus stop, but no parking.

20 mins, 51.6744, -2.6625

one-of-a-kind swim. Open daily for NOWCA members. Popular social swim on a Sunday with a free hot drink and a biccy, £8. Judge's Ln, Newent, GL18 1JY. Call Bronwen, 07940 500 345

2 mins, 51.8965, -2.4133

SOUTH COTSWOLDS

19 ASHLEWORTH QUAY, RIVER SEVERN

At the end of a pretty little lane is a delightful swim from a jetty. The NT Ashleworth tithe barn is a short walk away. Park at Ashleworth Quay (GL19 4HZ) and choose your swim spot.

1 mins, 51.9236, -2.2645

20 ODDA'S CHAPEL, RIVER SEVERN

Swim against the current, below the Anglo-Saxon charms of the chapel and adjacent St Mary's church. Lovely walks in both directions. Deerhurst (GL19 4BX) signed off A38, 2.4km S of Tewkesbury. Pay car park opposite chapel. Walk to Severn Way footpath to find beached area and jetties downstream. Alternative swim upstream at 15th century Lower Lode pub (also has small camping and caravan site), signed from A38 about 4km W of Tewkesbury.

8 mins, 51.9676, -2.1944

21 SLAD BROOK

Hidden away in the trees of Longridge Wood lies this tranquil body of water, where the brook pools to form a pond. Part of the Laurie Lee Way. Take B4070 NE from Stroud dir GL6 7QT. After 4.8km park in lay-by R at Bull's Cross, GL6 7QF. Head to N end of lay-by to follow sign for the Laurie Lee Way down to the brook at the bottom of the glade. Can be overgrown in summer.

15 mins, 51.7775, -2.1673

22 CHERINGTON POND, CHERINGTON

Fantastic lily pond in a beautiful wooded valley, constructed in the c18 on the line of the Avening stream to provide fishing for the manor. It has been popular as a quiet place for bathing ever since. Today it is a nature reserve and there are 'No Swimming' signs, but local swimmers still swim discreetly. In Cherinton, 500m E of St Nicholas church, take Avening turning and find some parking at T-junction after 500m. Two short paths to lake: one L walking back 30m, one up hill R after 100m.

5 mins, 51.6851, -2.1484

23 PARKMILL POND, WOODCHESTER PARK

This unfinished gothic mansion masterpiece is being restored, and the NT estate includes a series of five sheltered lakes,

beautiful woodland walks and an intriguing boathouse. There are new No Swimming signs, partly because of the herons, but locals have swum discreetly in the bottom lake for years (Kennel and Parkmill ponds). Closest parking is NT pay car park with a café at Tinkely Gate entrance 51.7048, -2.27147, GL10 3UH, turn off at Nympsfield, B4066).

40 mins, 51.7065, -2.2479

24 BERKELEY BRIDGE, HAM

The tiny 'Little Avon' (Berkeley Pill) passes through the grounds of Berkeley Castle on its way to the Severn Estuary. It's a cooling paddle on a hot day with rope swing and jumps, dependent on water level. Park near the castle gatehouse in Berkeley (GL13 9BQ). Walk S on road and take path through field on L, 50m after crossing white iron-railed bridge.

15 mins, 51.6851, -2.4577

25 THE LAKE AT CROMHALL QUARRY

Clear waters and friendly community at the dive/swim quarry lake. £6 for 2 hour session. Wotton Road, Wotton-under-Edge GL12 8AA, 01454 260130

2 mins, 51.6242, -2.4256

MALMESBURY AVON

26 EASTON GREY, R AVON

Lost in the woods next to the ruins of Foss Mill, an unexpected spot with a weir and large stony pool. Park in the layby on S side of B4040, 200m E of Easton Grey. Follow the path through field gate, and keep to R side of second field to arrive at woodland.

10 mins, 51.5837, -2.1645

27 DANIEL'S WELL, MALMESBURY

A pretty stretch of river below the ancient market town, with numerous springs, long regarded as holy. The area is named for a monk who is said to have bathed in the freezing waters daily to cool his passions. Head for long-stay car park (SN16 9JT) where there is a riverside picnic area above weir on the Tetbury Avon. Then follow Mill Ln over R up to Gloucester Street, turn L past abbey, and find Kings Wall (51.5837, -2.0988) an alley that leads down to the Sherstone Avon and crosses the river. There's no well but a big pool downstream.

5 mins, 51.5835, -2.1003

28 LITTLE SOMERFORD, R AVON

Idyllic deep pools in a woodland orchard upstream of an old mill house, with many

more riverside areas in meadows upstream. The path passes near private gardens, so be respectful. Leave Little Somerford past church (SN15 5JW) and take Mill Ln on R at village hall (before railway bridge). There's a small layby after 900m, before road end (51.5584, -2.0595). Continue on track/path ½ mile, around R side of Kingsmead Mill, over bridge and into woodland glade and field beyond. There's also a good weir pool at the footbridge, a mile's riverside walk from here downstream towards Great Somerford (51.5504, -2.0622).

15 mins, 51.5594, -2.0693

29 CHIPPENHAM, R AVON

It's a suburban setting, but there are large areas of open access meadow and riverbank upstream from the footbridge. The river here is good for swimming and paddle boarding but also popular with the angling club. Park on Long Close (SN15 3JY) and walk across the meadow. The track to the sailing club is by the playground at SE end, if you fancy joining. A bridge downstream at Baydons Wood takes you to the N bank (can also park at end of Sunningdale Close, SN15 3XH, for this), but there are more anglers on this side, especially upstream around Riverside Drive.

5 mins, 51.456, -2.1075

30 LACOCK ABBEY, AVON

A pretty river beach beside the famous NT abbey. From the main NT pay car park at SN15 2RQ turn R and continue 600m along road to find gate and path into field on L, between two bridges. Veer off path to L to riverbank. 300m upstream, opp abbey, is a tree kids jump from into a deep pool.

15 mins, 51.4146, -2.115

BRADFORD-ON-AVON

31 WHADDON, R AVON

A pastoral and remote section of the river with almost no buildings along it for miles. Park opp church and take stile on R and follow down to the banks. Just to the L is simple access to a deep bend, while ½ mile upstream is a medieval packhorse bridge. Or from church go through Whaddon Farm on corner and follow bridleway downstream 1 mile to find a secret (and perhaps private) little riverside area with hut and diving board (51.3486, -2.1932).

5 mins, 51.3529, -2.1721

32 THE GLOVE DIPPERS £

Friendly community of swimmers with sauna, café and shared workspace. £70 annual membership. 1 Brook Lane, Holt Village, Bradford-on-Avon, Wilts, BA14 6RL, 01225 784080, glovedippers.com

2 mins, 51.3571, -2.2029

33 BRADFORD-ON-AVON SAILING CLUB

This little club is no more than a wooden hut and collection of sailing boats, alone on a pastoral stretch of riverbank with good access. Just downstream is the old golf course, a riverside wilderness area with mature trees, tall grasses, and more swimming opportunities. There are hopes to save it from development and turn it into a community nature reserve. Easiest access is from end of Mythern Meadow at the SE edge of town (BA15 1HF). Follow tarmac path next to number 30 and continue along edge of field. On the L is the old golf course (also accessible from Avon Cl, BA15 1JJ). Continue to third field for the sailing hut and meadows.

10 mins, 51.3383, -2.2295

34 BRADFORD-ON-AVON TITHE BARN

One of the largest medieval barns in England, built in the mid-14C for Shaftesbury Abbey in Dorset, the richest nunnery in medieval England. Explore inside for free and enjoy the beach and paddling area for children, a pretty stone bridge and plenty of deeper sections downstream for a long swim or canoe. Signed down Pound Ln from B3109 about 220m S from the railway, with car park at end, BA15 1LF

3 mins, 51.3437, -2.256

35 AVONCLIFF WEIR, BRADFORD ON AVON

Large, fun river pool above weir, with rope swing. There's a long deep stretch upstream leading to a willow maze. Continue further into Barton Farm riverside park to find several more places to swim on route to the Tithe Barn river area in Bradford on Avon (see Wiltshire chapter). Use the canal cycle/

path or alight from train at tiny Avoncliff station, cross aqueduct and 200m along canal, behind pub, find a path on L that drops down through woods to the weir. The maze and a dew pond are a ½ mile further upstream (51.3426, -2.2599). The Cross Guns riverside pub, BA15 2HB, 01225 862335 and No 10 Tea Gardens, 01225 727843 are here and also accessible by road from Westwood, but the car park is small.

5 mins, 51.3391, -2.2797

RIVER FROME & WELLOW

36 WELLOW BROOK

Delightful beach and corner pool, hidden in a wooded glade. Perfect as part of a loop walk to Stoney Littleton Long Barrow tomb from the Fox & Badger village pub (BA2 8QG, 01225 832293). Descend to the ford and take river path upstream 600m.

15 mins, 51.3182, -2.3777

37 FARLEIGH HUNGERFORD, R FROME

Sunbathe on the lawns below the changing hut and step down into the pool above the weir. Above is a tree-lined avenue of still waters. This is England's last river-swimming club. Upstream the path leads

to Stowford Manor camping and tearooms. Downstream a ruined castle sits atop the hill. Signed from traffic lights on B3109 S of Bradford-on-Avon. Pass Stowford Manor Farm and then turn in through gate on L, before corner/bridge, BA2 7RS.

2 mins, 51.3179, -2.281

38 TELLISFORD, R FROME

A lovely, leafy pastoral aspect. The large weir pool has tall trees from which youngsters leap. Downstream is a medieval packhorse bridge. Popular. B3109 S of Bradford-on-Avon, turn R at crossroads,

dir Tellisford Bridge and BA14 9NA, park at end of lane, walk down hill and head upstream through field on L, 300m.

10 mins, 51.2975, -2.2807 🚶🏊

39 LULLINGTON & ORCHARDLEIGH

A pretty footbridge over the River Frome by a meadow. It's a private field and people do pay to fish here, so please be respectful and discreet. A path also leads up Orchardleigh Lake which is now fenced except at one spot on its dam wall (51.2571, -2.3142) – again this is private, but people do dip here. Continue along S shore of lake ¾ miles to the magical lakeshore/island church (51.2576, -2.3258). From Oldford (1 mile N of Frome on B3090), turn L signed Lullington/Stapleton. After ½ mile find narrow layby parking / wooden kissing gate on L up to lake, BA11 2PW. Another ½ mile find path to river footbridge on R.

2 mins, 51.2626, -2.3061 🚶❓

BATH AVON

40 DUNDAS AQUEDUCT, AVON

Descend to this bucolic stretch of the river Avon on the steps of the boatclub and downstream all the way to Warleigh, perfect for secluded riverside picnics and swims. Or hire a Canadian canoe/electric boat and pootle along the canal above (01225 722292). Cycle here or canal/ path. Or turn off A36 onto B3108 signed Canal Visitor Centre at traffic lights/ Brassknocker Hill and find car parks on L, BA2 7JD. Walk up to the aqueduct ¼ mile and descend on the steps to the boathouse below. Buses D1 & D2x half-hourly from Bath stop.

5 mins, 51.3613, -2.3104 🚶🏊

41 WARLEIGH WEIR, CLAVERTON

Long curving weir with cascades and pools and ferryman steps below, and long deep section above. There a beautiful meadow island area and the old Claverton Pumping Station (open inside 2 days a month). This has always been an immensely popular swimming place and is now owned by the Warleigh Weir Project. Best reached on the canal cycle/path from Bath or from Dundas Aqueduct (see listing), or via Bus 264/265. Alternatively people park on the A36 verges and walk down Ferry Lane, 3 miles E of Bath on A36. No access from Warleigh on R bank! Take any litter you find home – it's a big problem.

10 mins, 51.3772, -2.3003 🚶🏊🏊

42 BATHEASTON SECRET GARDEN

This pretty walled riverside garden was once part of Batheaston House but is now a community garden with little car park (BA1 7NB). Follow steps to the river for swimming and canoe launches, or a new NT river path across the bridge down through Bathampton meadows. There's deep swimming from many points along this, or below the weir after ½ mile at Bathampton Mill riverside pub (BA2 5TS, 01225 469758) – cross on the tollbridge to find the path to a little beach opp. The green riverside continues a further mile on this bank down to Kensington Meadows footbridge, where beavers can often be seen (BA1 6BH, accessible on canal cycle/path or from Grosvenor Bridge Rd or Morrisons car park). Another ¼ mile down is the newly restored Cleveland Pools riverside lido, accessible via a jetty, or on foot from Hampton Row (L bank, BA2 6BJ, book at clevelandpools.org.uk).

5 mins, 51.405, -2.3182 🏊🚣🅿🚻🚻

43 CLEVELAND POOLS, BATH 🅢

Built in 1815, this is the UK's oldest outdoor swimming pool. Art Deco at it's best. Unheated and lovely for a swim. £6 per session; £35 monthly swim pass. Cleveland Pools, Hampton Row, Bath BA2 6BJ.

5 mins, 51.3908, -2.3474

BOX BY BROOK

44 BOX, BY BROOK

A delightful valley walk taking in deep meanders of the By Brook, returning in a loop on opp bank for a view of Box Tunnel portal. Follow the Macmillan Way path upstream from Mill Lane, to L of the entrance to old mill, now Peter Gabriel's Real World Studios (SN13 8PL). First pool is after about ½ mile. Continue to cross river at road 400m further up and walk back on path between houses R in to Box. Cross AF at The Wharf (51.4189, -2.2489) into Lacy Wood to view tunnel.

15 mins, 51.4245, -2.2476 🚶🚣❓

45 RAG MILL, BY BROOK

One of the loveliest and most interesting stretches on this bubbly Cotswolds stream. 150m S of Slaughterford church park on bend and find the riverside path (SN14 8RG). The mill ruins are 400m upstream and date from the 17C, when it processed wool, though the iron water wheel and boiler are from the 1890s, when it was converted to pulp textiles for paper – it only closed in the 1960s. You can swim at the footbridge/sluice here, about 100m upstream, or continue onwards for the very best spot, a large pool with a bench beneath the footbridge a further ½ mile or (51.4693, -2.2346); there are No Swimming signs, but locals have swum here for generations. Finally, arrive at the White Hart, Ford (see listing).

20 mins, 51.4629, -2.2331 🏊📷🚻❓

RIVER CHEW VALLEY

46 CHEWTON PLACE, R CHEW

A meadow walk following the river upstream for over a mile. Park on lane by wall and path, just upstream of bridge (BS31 2SU). Look out for the owlery tower in the gardens on opp bank.

5 mins, 51.4003, -2.4972 🚣❓📷

47 WOOLLARD, R CHEW

A secluded secret pool beneath an old weir on edge of meadows. It once powered the tin mill, one of the largest mills of its kind in the Chew valley, the remains of which can still be seen. Park at E end of Woollard bridge by noticeboard and just up hill, follow path on R over stream, opp Brock Cottage, BS39 4HU. The ruins are 150m along fence which links to Stephen's Vale nature reserve. Turn L off Greyfield Rd, ½ mile NW of High Littleton and find car park at BS39 6YE, 51.3236, -2.5196.

5 mins, 51.3188, -2.5205 🌼🚶🚵

51 LITTON RESERVOIR
A path follows the N shores of this long, hidden lake. Primroses, wood anemones, violets and red campions in spring. It's No Swimming, but people do dip if there are no anglers. Entering Litton from Chewton, park in village and take the second R after The Litton pub (pretty stream-side garden, BA3 4PW, 01761 241301). Take R at end, and find path on L after 200m, BA3 4PS.

10 mins, 51.2921, -2.5821 🚶🚵❓

52 CHEW VALLEY LAKE, SUTTON WICK
Beautiful remote beach shore, perfect for sunset, but no access without fishing permit, Better stick to the NE shore with full public access: Picnic Area 2/Grebe Trail are less busy. No Swimming. Walley Lane 51.3435, -2.6038.

3 mins, 51.3301, -2.6115 ❓

53 BABYLON BROOK/STRODE WATERFALL
A hidden waterfall in the woods just off the public footpath. It's on private land so please respect any signage. Park near St Andrew's church in Chew Stoke, BS40 8TU. Take track through gates (dir Long House Farm) then turn L at barn. Continue on track, then path, through three fields ¾ mile to the woods. Waterfall stream is adjacent just to S. See strodewaterfall.earth for future wild spa and sauna events by the waterfall.

20 mins, 51.3509, -2.6513 🚵❓

54 BLAGDON LAKE, BUTCOMBE
A beautiful reservoir, nestled in the folds of a long, lush valley, with the Mendip escarpment rearing up to the S. Early in the season this meadow it is a blissful place to picnic and, despite 'No Swimming' signs, people do swim here. Later in the season the water levels fall and weeds proliferate. Park at N end of the dam, BS40 7UN, and follow the shore path NE. After about 10 mins, having crossed two footbridges and passed through some woodland, find the lakeside meadow on R. It's a lovely cycle ride out here from Bristol via Long Ashton, Barrow Gurney and Felton. Do not disturb the anglers.

15 mins, 51.3427, -2.7039 🚵🚶❓🌼

55 RIVER YEO, YATTON
Small meandering river with steep, grassy embankments, a great place to sunbathe

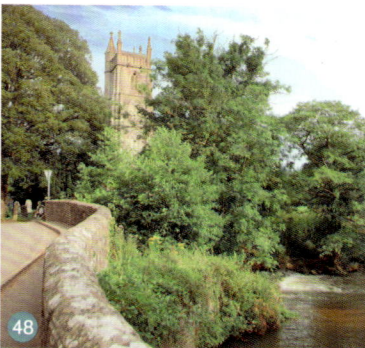

on L, then cross field to find pool.

3 mins, 51.3765, -2.5301 🚶🖼

48 PUBLOW BRIDGE, R CHEW
Large, pretty pool with shelving beach and rope swing, under bridge next to church. Park at church, BS39 4HP. The L bank path by church follows the river all the way to Woollard with a beautiful pond just along the way (private fishing, 51.3732, -2.5352).

1 mins, 51.3754, -2.5433 🚶🚵

49 PENSFORD WEIR, R CHEW
A little path crosses the arches of the village weir to garden of The Rising Sun pub with a little pool beneath, popular for paddling and a dip in summer, and railway viaduct above. The path continues upstream under the towering viaduct arches so you can explore other pools too – look on the bends. The pub has a very small car park to rear (BS39 4AQ, 01761 490006), so best to walk from Publow.

2 mins, 51.3712, -2.5508 🚶🚵🚵

UPPER CHEW & MENDIP

50 GREYFIELD WOOD & WATERFALL
Stream and waterfalls to explore in this mix of ancient woodland and newer planting,

out of sight and on the site of a Roman villa. The water is clear, silky and reedy – perfect for a long swim – though it can weed over later in the season. From Yatton station/ NCN route 26 take Wembersham Lane and continue a mile to the end (tricky parking BS49 4BT). Follow path/track along until the ditch reaches the river then head downstream 300m.

10 mins, 51.3827, -2.8587 🏊🚶🏔

BRISTOL AREA

56 GOLDEN VALLEY, WICK

Follow the wooded valley nature reserve along the R Boyd to find the ruined buildings of the old ochre works, closed in 1968. There's a weir and waterfall as the path heads steeply up on steps to Raven's Rock lookout. The water is a natural and harmless red colour from the iron oxide.

10 mins, 51.4567, -2.4215 🏊➕🏔🚶🔵↕

57 BITTON PICNIC AREA & SALTFORD

This grassy riverside picnic site is easy to reach by bicycle from Bath or Bristol. There's a wooden boat landing stage from which it's fun to jump in. Or watch local kids leap from the railway bridge. On cycle path a mile S of A431 Bitton station, BS30 6HD. The Jolly Sailor in Saltford, BS31 3ER, is also a very popular swimming spot nearby, with a good rope swing on the opp bank above the weir, 51.4094, -2.4435.

20 mins, 51.4171, -2.46 🏊🅿🚶▼

58 FROME VALLEY, BURY HILL

A quick Bristol escape to a pretty river walk with paddling and a dip. Turn sharp R off Worrell's Ln as it enters Winterbourne Down (BS36 1BS) into Bury Hill (lane signed Frome Valley Walkway), and park L after bridge. Follow signed path upstream. After ½ mile (150m after crossing main road at Damson Bridge) there is a deep dip on the bend, and Huckford Quarry Nature Reserve 500m beyond. Also, 200m further along lane from parking is a path up on L past a house to Bury hillfort.

20 mins, 51.5138, -2.4933 🏊🚶

59 CONHAM RIVER PARK

The river runs through a mini gorge for almost a mile here, a green-blue corridor into the suburbs of Bristol. What quality is alright, as it's upstream of the city, but keep to breaststroke. On the S bank head for Beese's riverside tea room and pub, established in 1846 by the wife of a ferryman (BS4 4SX, 01179 777412, parking on Wyndham Crescent). For N side

51

start at the car park on Conham Rd, BS15 3AW. Another good city spot is downstream near Hanham Lock. From the big car park by the Chequers Inn on the river at, BS15 3NU, head downstream to the point (51.4250, -2.5079).

10 mins, 51.4444, -2.5365 🏊🚶

60 WEST COUNTRY WATER PARK 💷

Man-made freshwater lake with swimming course and plunge platform. Beautiful floating sauna with lake views. £8.50 per swim, £15 per swim/sauna. The Lake Trench Lane, Bradley Stoke, BS36 1RY. 01454 538538.

2 mins, 51.5424, -2.5374

61 ABBOT'S POOL, ABBOTS LEIGH

A large, dark lily-pad pool in the woods with a little stone grotto. One of a series of pools used by medieval monks for fish farming. No Swimming signs due to anti-social behaviour and parking issues but still popular among local families in summer. From Abbots Leigh (A369) turn down Manor Road, by the George Inn (BS8 3RP, 01275 376985), and find track on R after about 1 mile (signed to the pool, BS8 3RR).

5 mins, 51.4566, -2.669 ❓

53

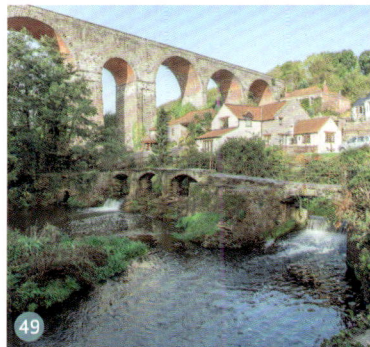
49

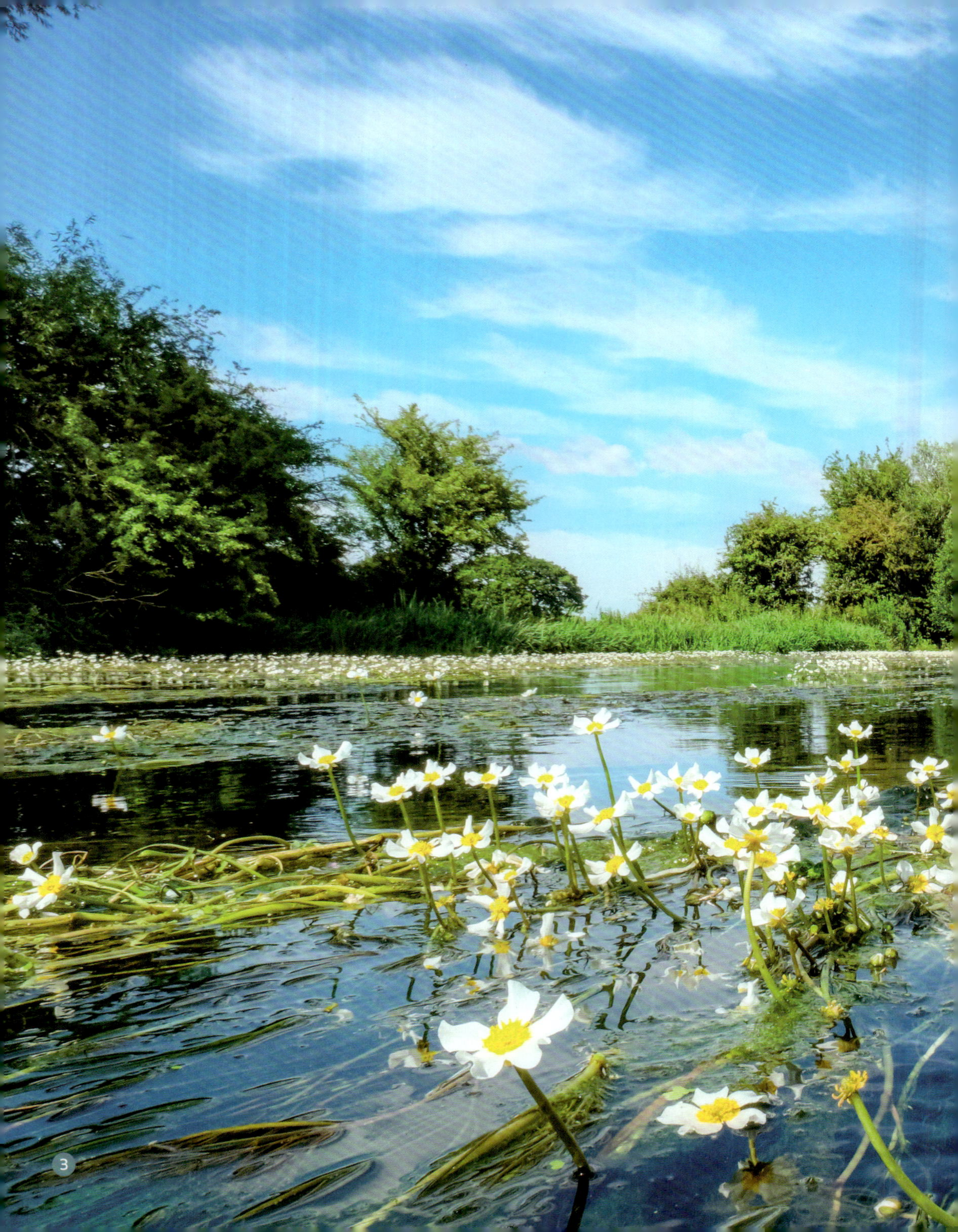

3

HAMPSHIRE, SURREY & SUSSEX

The wide braids of the River Test run through some of the least developed parts of the South East. Wily and fast, the stream winds its way through the most tranquil parts of Hampshire as it heads for the sea. Watership Down, the chalk downland immortalised by Richard Adams, is the headwater of the River Test. These were the hills down which Pipkin and Hazel fled, first from the bulldozers, then from Efrafan rabbit soldiers, before jumping onto a punt moored on the river at Laverstoke. Like the Salisbury chalk streams, public access to the bankside is rare, with fishing rights costing up to £1,000 per day. However, at Chilbolton Cow Common, near Cherwell Priory, there has been public access since ancient times (3). The little footbridges here are a magnet for families paddling and playing Pooh Sticks on a hot summer day, but as I arrived at seven o'clock on an early evening in June, the last picnickers were leaving. The clear waters of the chalk stream are home to many unique plants, and as I dipped my toes in the shallow waters, it felt like bathing in an underwater flower meadow. The long fronds of yellow starwort rippled in the current like buttercups, and the white water's crowfoot waved like daisies. The downland mineral water flowed through my hair and created rivulets around my fingers.

The chalk shingles of these streams were laid down long ago. Coral reefs and sea plankton collected during the landscape's time as part of an equatorial archipelago millions of years ago. Back then, the water would have been a balmy 30°C, but the temperature now is far from tropical – a chilly 12°C. Rising from aquifers deep beneath the hills, the temperature remains remarkably constant throughout the year, so that even on frosty winter mornings, the Test is relatively warm, famous for its steaming river mists. A bath here feels almost balmy. At Houghton, another favourite paddling location five miles away, a white shingle bay opens onto a large shallow pool under a bridge where you can swim against the current (5). The old trackway crosses water meadows to John of Gaunt's deer park and the ancient

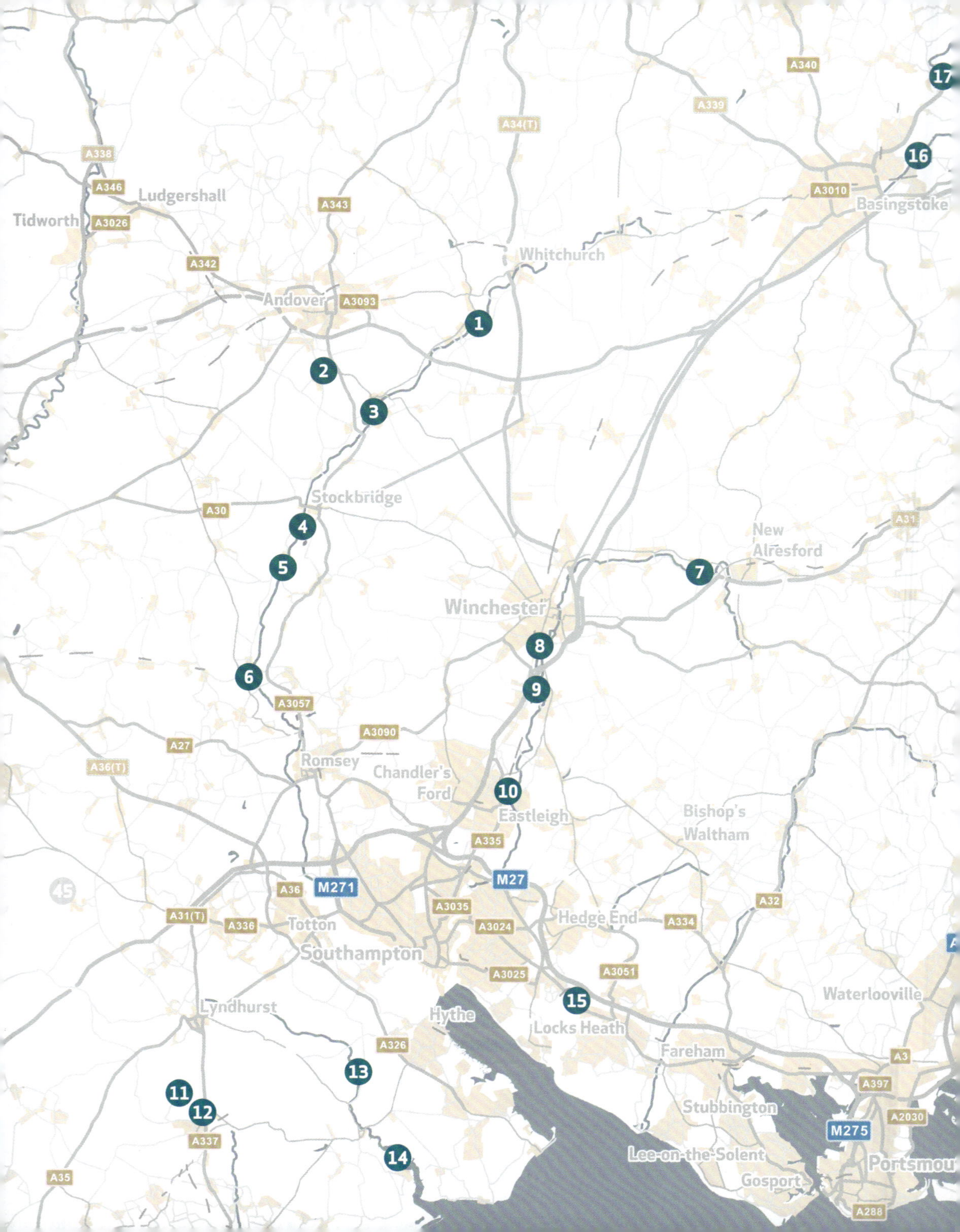
A340
17
A339
A34(T)
16
A338
A346
Ludgershall
A3010
Basingstoke
Tidworth
A3026
A343
Whitchurch
A342
Andover
A3093
1
2
3
Stockbridge
A30
4
5
A31
New
Alresford
7
Winchester
8
9
6
A3057
A3090
A27
A36(T)
Romsey
Chandler's
Ford
10
Eastleigh
Bishop's
Waltham
A335
M27
45
A36
M271
A32
A31(T)
A336
Totton
A3035
A3024
Hedge End
A334
Southampton
A3051
A3025
15
Waterlooville
Lyndhurst
Hythe
Locks Heath
A326
Fareham
A3
13
11
A397
12
Stubbington
A2030
A337
M275
14
Lee-on-the-Solent
A35
Gosport
A288

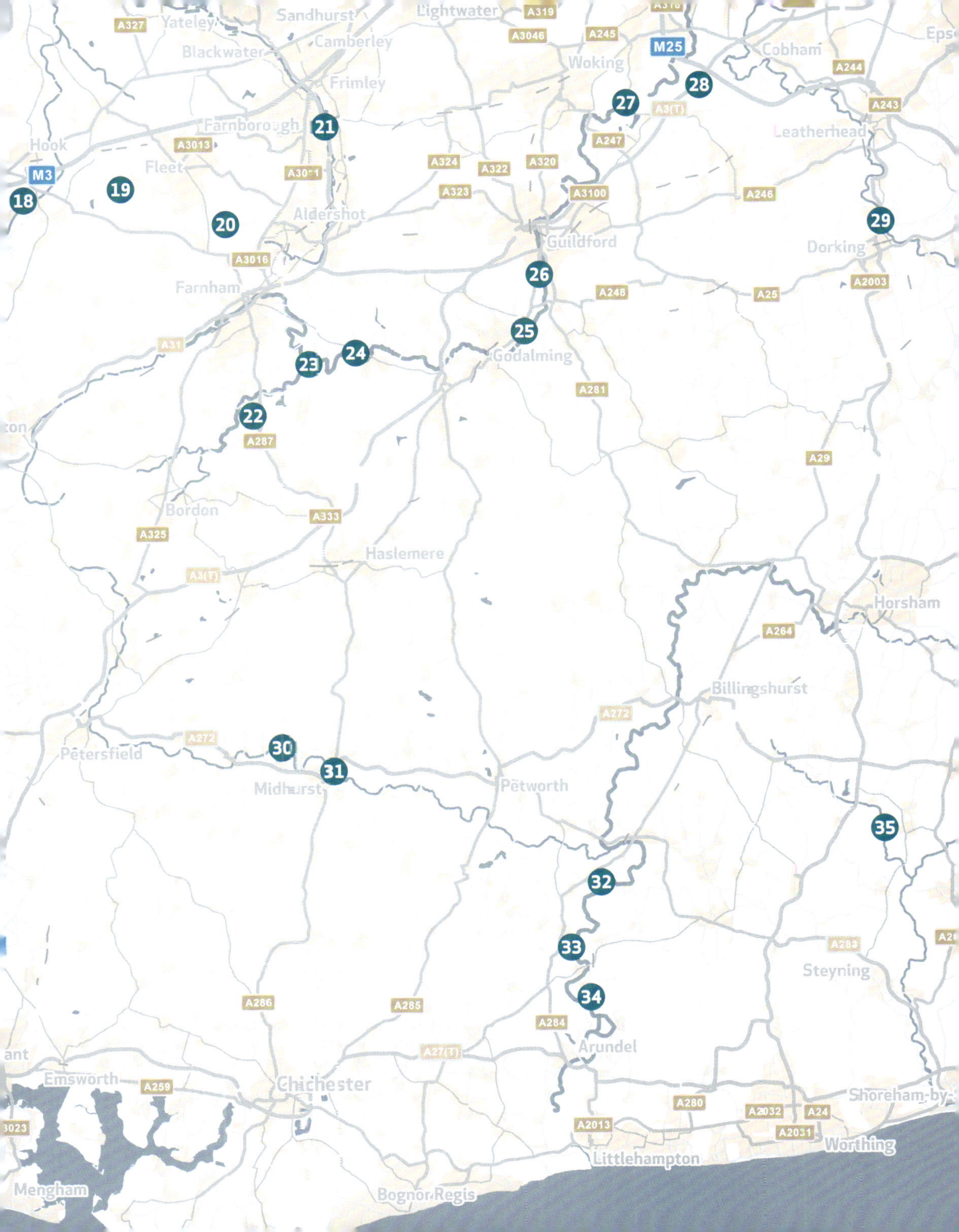

Sandhurst
Lightwater
Yateley
Blackwater
Camberley
Frimley
Woking
Cobham
Farnborough
Hook
Fleet
Leatherhead
Aldershot
Guildford
Dorking
Farnham
Godalming
Bordon
Haslemere
Horsham
Billingshurst
Petersfield
Midhurst
Petworth
Steyning
Arundel
Emsworth
Chichester
Shoreham-by-
Worthing
Littlehampton
Mengham
Bognor Regis
M3
M25
A327
A319
A3046
A245
A244
A243
A3013
A3011
A324
A322
A320
A247
A3(T)
A323
A3100
A246
A3016
A248
A25
A2003
A31
A281
A287
A29
A333
A325
A264
A272
A286
A285
A284
A27(T)
A259
A280
A2032
A24
A2013
A2031
A283
18
19
20
21
22
23
24
25
26
27
28
29
30
31
32
33
34
35

yews at King's Somborne. The river course has changed significantly in the last three hundred years. In John's time, new channels were being cut for the creation of 'floating' water meadows. A system of sluices encouraged the river to flood the fields, nourishing the grass and protecting it from frost to enable earlier lambing and increased sheep stocking. It's now difficult to determine which is the original river course and which is an old irrigation path.

Running through nearby Winchester, the Itchen is another chalk stream that has been much altered by man. It was deepened for barge navigation in the eighteenth century, facilitating barge transport between Winchester and Southam, but most of it has returned to shallows. Twyford Lock still remains – a deep pool beneath a small waterfall. It is one of the few surviving turf-sided locks in the UK (9). With their sloped grassy sides, they were cheaper but less durable than brick or stone designs. A path follows the Itchen all the way to Winchester, making for a pleasant two-mile walk, despite the noisy motorway overhead. The Twyford Downs, site of the road protests of the 1990s, are on your right, and you might like to take a dip in Tumbling Bay. Eventually, you'll reach the water meadows of St Cross, where there are also some deeper pools by the Hospital of St Cross in Winchester (8). Founded around 1136 by Bishop Henry of Blois, it is England's oldest charitable almshouse still in use. Established to care for elderly men and offer hospitality to travellers, it continues this tradition today with its "Wayfarer's Dole"—bread and ale given to any visitor who asks. The site features a magnificent Norman-style church and historic buildings set in peaceful gardens, all located beside the river and its water meadows.

The Winchester connection reaches 30 miles to the north-east to Frensham Great Pond in Surrey (22). This shallow, warm lake has two bays with natural sandy beaches designated for swimming. Built as a fish pond by the Bishop of Winchester during his prolonged stay at his nearby castle in Farnham in 1246, it was drained every five years to cleanse it and grow barley. The last time it was emptied, however, was in 1942, during the Second World War, as it had become a prominent moonlit landmark for German bombers. I first glimpsed the pond on a foggy summer afternoon, with the smell of reeds and heath in the air and the crunch of dry heather underfoot. Placid and large, dark columns of cumulus clouds were rising high above it, and two clinker dinghies were moving languidly near a far bank. The clouds above me were turning, stacking up against the hills, the heathland pines deep green against the grey of a pre-storm sky as I slipped gingerly into the mauve waters of Frensham Great Pond. A cheerful moorhen paddled happily some distance from me before she took off in a frantic dash across the waters, her feet dangling as she struggled to become airborne just as the first rain began to fall. A kaleidoscope of concentric circles rippled across the glassy surface as I glided through the cooling waters, the humidity purged from the day.

You'd be forgiven for not being too excited about the prospect of wild swimming in Surrey, but it does have its wilder pockets. Strangely, it's the most wooded county in England, which means fewer nitrates from farmers and less watershed pollution. Much of its downland is protected within an Area of Outstanding Natural Beauty, and the ancient chalk ridgeway of the North Downs runs across its hills. Frensham Little Pond is on the other side of the A287, and both ponds feed into the Wey, which flows down into Tilford (23). This is a truly English scene, with a cricket green and pub, river paddling above a ford, and a bridge built by medieval monks. It's a perfect place to while away a summer afternoon with lunch and a paddle or swim – there is a rope swing below the weir and some deeper sections above the bridge.

The River Wey, flowing through Hampshire and Surrey into the Thames at Weybridge, also has a rich history of navigation, milling, and recreation. One of England's first navigable rivers, it supported trade from the 1600s and powered numerous mills, while also inspiring writers like Belloc. Swimming has long been part of local life, especially around Tilford, Elstead, Shalford, and Guildford (24,-26). However some are also managed for nature. Thundry is a Site of Special Scientific Interest (SSSI) run by Surrey Wildlife Trust, so if you do decide to dip, it's best to slip into the water silently and carefully, with a view to blending in (24).

Moving east, there are several more wooded lakes. Bolder Mere on Ockham Common near the M25 is a rare remnant of the heathland ponds that used to cover much of Surrey. It's an important site for dragonflies and damselflies, and also for the rare hobby – one of the few birds that can actually catch a dragonfly. Wildlife here is definitely the main priority - when two common tern chicks were found by the side of the lake, people were asked to refrain from swimming too close to them. This is a Site of Special Scientific Interest (SSSI) run by Surrey Wildlife Trust, so it's best to slip into the water silently and carefully, with a view to blending in.

4 COMMON MARSH, STOCKBRIDGE

Common land, good for picnics or paddling (SO20 6JA). Park in Stockbridge (51.1101, -1.4909) and follow river downstream. Most popular spot is 800m.
10 mins, 51.1040, -1.4973

5 HOUGHTON, R TEST

A wide, white chalk stream and wooden footbridge. Crowsfoot and water buttercup in spring. Once very popular now partly fenced off. Entering Houghton (SO20 6LL) from Stockbridge, find footpath at end of village on L, signed Clarendon Way, and follow it to bridge.
2 mins, 51.0843, -1.5119 ▰

6 MOTTISFONT, R DUNN

Delightful, secluded stream tributary of the Test, near lovely Mottisfont House and water gardens. However the fishermen here might not smile upon you if you go swimming but we saw someone having a plunge. Walk down Church Lane from Mottisfont village (SO51 0LP). Continue on Test Way 750m to meet river and footbridge.
10 mins, 51.0325, -1.5372 ▰▰

ITCHEN CHALK STREAM

7 OVINGTON, R ITCHEN

Lush meadows praised by William Cobbett as 'one of the prettiest places in the country'. Riverside pub with footbridge and riverside walk, shallow. Idyllic but No Swimming, just paddling. Bush Inn (SO24 0RE, 01962 732764).
5 mins, 51.0831, -1.2003 ▰▰

8 ST CROSS WINCHESTER, R ITCHEN

Water meadows and deepish pools behnd this wonderful ancient almshouse and church (more like a cathedral). Park on Garnier Rd (51.0519, -1.3172, SO23 9QG) and walk S along the river meadows 600m.
10 mins, 51.0477, -1.3197 ▰▰▰

9 TWYFORD, R ITCHEN

Once an old turf lock, this is now one of the few deep pools on the Itchen. Footbridge and waterfall chute, partly lined with concrete. Clear and cold! Some people like to jump. 800m walk from Shawford station. Or Berry Lane (SO21 1NS) and continue from church over footbridge, 500m along fence boundary to pool. Tumbling Bay sluices 800m upstream. Continue downstream for lively, bubbly but mainly shallow stream with lots of trout fishing. One of the biggest pools is after 3km at the river and navigation confluence,

TEST CHALK STREAM

1 LONGPARISH, R TEST

Exquisite stretch of the young Test alongside a tiny lane leading to a footbridge. Or follow lane down past millhouse, across water meadows and into Longparish (Cricketers Inn, SP11 6PZ, 01264 720335). Mainly shallow but lots of grassy banks and perfect for picnics.
30 mins, 51.2011, -1.3661 ▰▰

2 GOODWORTH CLATFORD, R ANTON

Community riverbanks. Shallow but great for kids. Park alongside Royal Oak (SP11 7QY, 07958592021). 4km downstream is the riverside Mayfly where the Anton meets the Test, with bridge across to its own island (SO20 6AX, 01264 860283).
2 mins, 51.1784, -1.4819 ▰▰

3 CHILBOLTON COW COMMON, R TEST ▰

Ancient rural common ans SSSI with paddling in crystal-clear pools by footbridge. Park at end of Joy's Lane (51.1578, -1.4428) then footbridge is 200m N. Or cross over from S end of Wherwell (SP11 7JS) over a much longer wooden footbridge/walkway.
20 mins, 51.1591, -1.4442 ▰

Otterbourne 51.0068, -1.3307
10 mins, 51.0272, -1.3221 🍴🐟🅿

10 EASTLEIGH, R ITCHEN
Open and pastoral section of this glorious chalk stream, hidden behind railway siding. Car park on B3037 rugby club, then up to 1km upstream.
10 mins, 50.9790, -1.3431 🍴🐟🅿

NEW FOREST EAST

11 BOLDERFORD BRIDGE & QUEEN BOWER
Footbridge and paddling from a shingle beach with rope swings. Upstream are ancient oaks in a grassy clearing. Paddling only. Adjacent to Long Meadow Campsite or 500m walk from Ober Corner forest car park (SO42 7QD 50.8309, -1.5968).
15 mins, 50.8357, -1.5882 🐟➕🔥

12 BALMERLAWN, BROCKENHURST
Very popular for picnics and paddling. Grassy banks with deeper pool near the bridge. Right by the road with car park.
2 mins, 50.8266, -1.5707 🐟🅿

13 KING'S HAT, R BEAULIEU
Footbridge, pools and paddling in the little stream, deep in the enchanted woods. Children love it. A mile N of Beaulieu on B3056, before SO42 7YP, turn R (signed Ipley Cross). Large woodland car park.
2 mins, 50.8462, -1.4543 🐟➕

14 BUCKLERS HARD, R BEAULIEU
A short walk upstream from this famous 18th-century boat-builders' village are quiet wooded bends in the river, perfect for a secluded dip at high tide. A bit muddy. Follow the Solent Way footpath upstream, past all the boats and boatyard. 500m beyond the last find a little path on the R, to a bird hide which leads to the shoreline beyond.
10 mins, 50.8053, -1.4249 🅿ℹ

15 ANDARK LAKE, SOUTHAMPTON 🅴
Small pretty lake with OWS, sauna and cafe. Oslands Ln, SO31 7FL, 01489 581755
2 mins, 50.8803, -1.2913

NORTH HAMPSHIRE

16 OLD BASING, R LODDON
The young Loddon is only a stream here, but there's a fun rope swing from the old tree and a deep corner pool where the tributary enters. Park by Village Hall (RG24 7DA) and take Newnham Lane for 500m to find drive with footpath on L, then 150m.
10 mins, 51.2815, -1.0379 🐟🍴

17 SHERFIELD-ON-LODDON
Mill pool in meadows behind Longbridge Mill pub (RG27 0DL, 01256 883483).
5 mins, 51.3189, -1.0199 ℹ🐟

18 ODIHAM CASTLE & GREYWELL
Spring-fed crystal clear canal with ethereal hues by pretty Odiham Castle. Descend to canal and old tunnel from Greywell (Fox & Goose, Hook RG29 1BY) and N 1km to swim just before the ruins. Or behind the village church (RG29 1DB) explore the banks of the Whitewater chalk stream. S 300m along the stream there are pretty clear pools, before the millhouse, but these are also popular with trout fishermen (51.2510, -0.9734).
10 mins, 51.2606, -0.9629 ❓⛰

19 TUNDRY POND, DOGMERSFIELD
Open parkland with lake and picnic tables. Warm but rather shallow. Head S from Domersfield and 500m past the church find footpath on R, through white garden gates of Double Bridge Fm (RG27 8TB). Or E of Basingstoke Canal.
10 mins, 51.2656, -0.8901 ❓⛰

20 BOURLEY BOTTOM, ALDERSHOT
Series of abandoned reservoir lakes in pine forest on MOD training land. Popular with

locals and kids in summer. Layby parking at 51.2520, -0.8108 then follow the gated forest track up.

15 mins, 51.2488, -0.8117 ▣

21 THE QUAYS, MYTCHETT ▣

Former gravel pit fed by four underground springs, which keep the lake fresh and clean. The depth of the water ranges from 2.5m to 3m at the deepest. OWS throughout the year with lifeguards on duty. Wetsuits are not compulsory. Coleford Bridge Rd, GU16 6DS, quayswim.co.uk.

6 mins, 51.2946, -0.7370

SURREY WEY

22 FRENSHAM GREAT POND, FARNHAM

Sandy lake with beaches and buoyed-off swimming area. Set within forest and open heathland. Parking, café and small museum. Popular with families.

5 mins, 51.1575, -0.7919 ▣▲▣▣

23 TILFORD GREEN & STOCKBRIDGE POND

Popular village green and pub. Paddling and pools just downstream of the bridge. Also try nearby Stockbridge Pond and the River Wey. Parking opposite Barley Mow pub (GU10 2BU, 01252 792205). For the pond,

head S (dir Rushmoor) and after 200m find track byway on L (500m, 51.1793, -0.7419). If fishermen here head on 300m, bearing L into Yagden Heath, to find the R Wey with tree and rope swings on L (51.1797, -0.7353).

10 mins, 51.182, -0.7499 ▣▣▣

24 ELSTEAD & THUNDRY, R WEY

The Mill at Elstead is a famous riverside pub with working wheel (GU8 6LE, 01252 703333). Just 100m E along road is a riverside footpath which leads to a large meander and pool (500m). Or 600m W along the road, just after turning for Seale on R, find layby, gate and footpath on L into beautiful Thundry riverside meadows and nature reserve 951.1873, -0.7149).

5 mins, 51.1899, -0.7056 ▣▲▣

25 GODALMING, R WEY

Meadow, ancient oaks and deep water. From Ragged Robin hotel (A3100/ Guildford Rd, GU7 3BX) follow river path downstream to open fields and meadow (300m). People also swim in town from the Phillips Memorial Park near the bandstand 51.1878, -0.6152.

10 mins, 51.1974, -0.5887 ▣▣▣▣

26 ST CATHERINE'S HILL, R WEY

Bridge for jumping from and a ruined chapel on the old Pilgrims' Way. Steep sandy banks kids love to run down. Access down Ferry Lane near Ye Olde Ship Inn, A3100 (GU2 4EB) but very limited parking. Better to walk there 30 mins from Shalford Station on the towpath, crossing over at St Catherine's Lock. You could swim anywhere along here, but the bank is steep.

20 mins, 51.2243, -0.5772 ▣▣▣▣▣▣▣

27 NEWARK PRIORY, R WEY

The Wey runs broad through the open water meadows and the romantic ruins of the Augustinian priory stand silent on a river island. There's a handy car park near the river bridge (GU23 7ES). The meadows are upstream to the L, 750m to Papercourt Lock with salmon-leap stepped pools. The ruins are downstream, visible across the field from the lock.

5 mins, 51.3052, -0.5119 ▣▣

28 BOLDER MERE, OCKHAM COMMON

Just off the M25 near RHS Wisley, a nature reserve but a popular spot for a discreet dip, though a bit muddy, and road noise. Car park for Ockham Common, KT11 1NR.

5 mins, 51.3135, -0.457 ▣▣

29 STEPPING STONES, RIVER MOLE ▸

Famous stepping stones on the River Mole at Box Hill Country Park. Deeper sections upstream, or in the meadows downstream. Drop down from the main viewpoint and car park for Box Hill, following the North Downs Way. Or walk down the A24 for 5 mins from the Stepping Stones pub (RH5 6BS. 01306 889932) to find footpath on L. Box Hill & Westhumble train station.

10 mins, 51.2488, -0.3216 🚶🚗🚂

SUSSEX ROTHER

30 STEDHAM, R ROTHER

Open fields downstream and some deeper pools, on the way to Stedham Mill. Path and parking at 50.9977, -0.7734 200m N of Stedham Bridge. After the mill it's beautiful below the stepping stones and weir but too shallow. But another 1km brings you back to the river again with more pools upstream of Woolbeding Bridge (50.9916, -0.7625).

5 mins, 51.0003, -0.7715 🏞️🚶

31 MIDHURST, R ROTHER

Sandy Bay is the traditional place for a paddle and dip, in front of the wonderful Cowdray ruins. Or for much deeper swimming explore upstream. From main car park in Midhurst (GU29 9DJ) walk to ruins. Swim spot is 100m upstream from the bridge. To explore the deep and secret wooded river upstream head NE out of Midhurst, L at roundabout signed Fernhurst and Haslemere and take the footpath by the medical centre after 50m (GU29 9AW).

10 mins, 50.9890, -0.7329 🚶🚗

RIVERS ARUN & ADUR

32 GREATHAM BRIDGE, R ARUN

Good access to Arun and views of the medieval stone bridge. Steep banks. Leading to Waltham Brooks Nature Reserve. A mile E of Coldwaltham (A29). Parking by bridge (before RH20 2ES)

5 mins, 50.9363, -0.5336 ⛑️🚶🏞️

33 BURY, R ARUN

A tiny dead-end hamlet with lovely grassy riverbanks downstream. Some people like to swim with the current up or downstream depending on the tide. 4 miles N of Arundel on A29, turn R at Squire & Horse (RH20 1NS) down into Bury and then Houghton dead-end hamlet (limited parking). Take footpath downstream 300m. Or explore upstream from Amberley riverside park (BN18 9GY).

5 mins, 50.9055, -0.5562 🚂🚶🏞️🏊

34 SOUTHSTOKE BRIDGE, R ARUN

Quiet hidden stretch of the Arun, up narrow lanes N of the castle, or a pleasant walk upstream from the castle. White metal footbridge. High tide only. From Arundel, follow Mill Rd past castle and lake, for a mile until T junction. Turn L signed 'S Stoke' and continue a mile to church (BN18 9PF). Limited parking.

5 mins, 50.8817, -0.5417 🚶🏞️🏊

35 HATTERELL BRIDGE & KNEPP

Knepp Estate, home of the famous rewilding project, won't thank you for swimming in their huge mill pond, one of the largest stretches of water in Sussex, but downstream on the young, narrow River Adur is a bucolic stretch of remote meadows. From the Green Man pub (B2135, Partridge Green, RH13 8JT) find the bridleway which leads 1km W to the river, crossing the old Downs Link railway (NCN223). Best swimming downstream 400m. Or follow upstream 2km through West Grinstead into the Knepp Estate (50.9783, -0.3542).

5 mins, 50.9650, -0.3232 🚶🚶

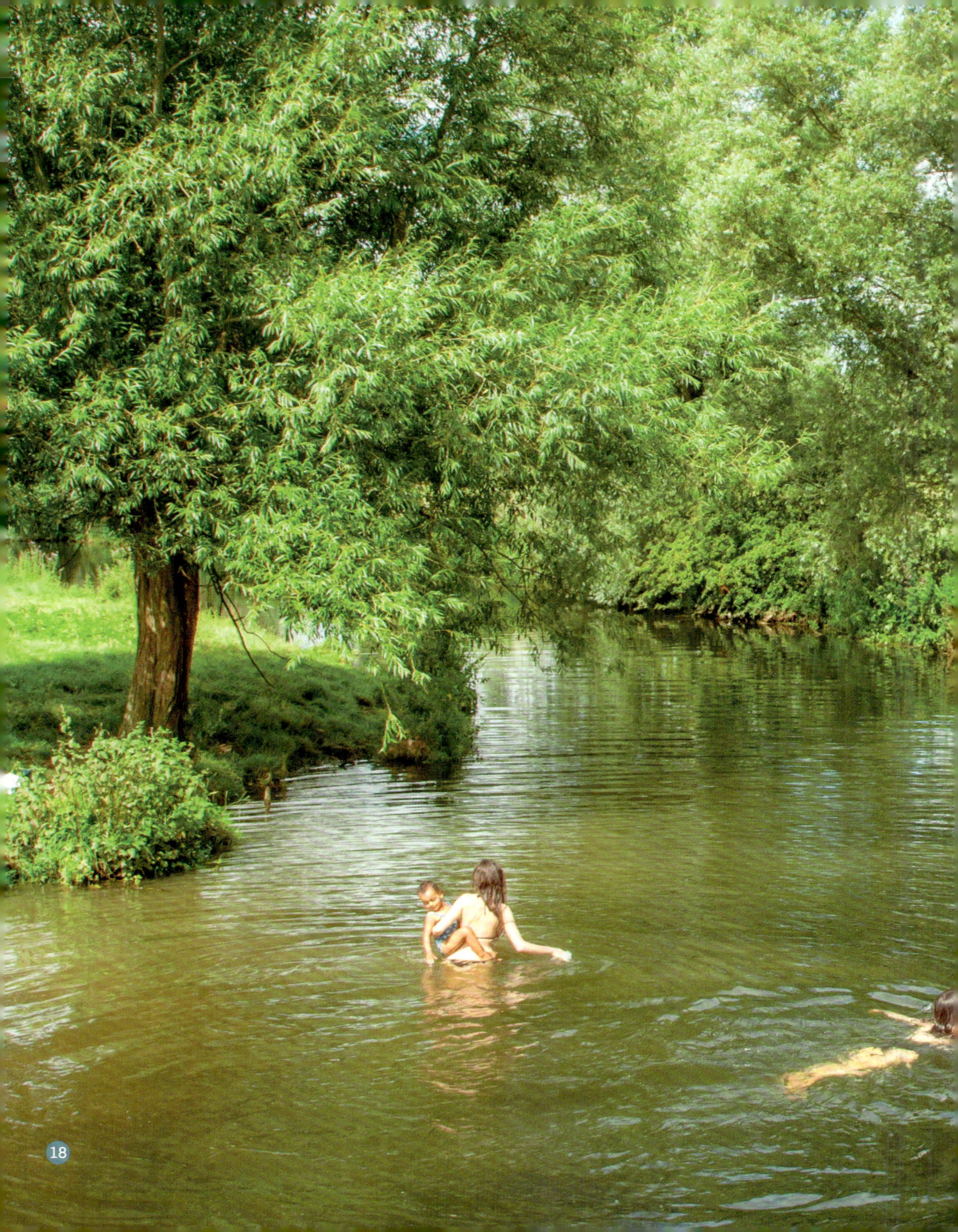

LONDON & SOUTH EAST ENGLAND

Two hundred years after Constable painted it, Willy Lott's cottage still sits prettily by the banks of the pastoral Stour in Essex, the spire of Dedham church rising above the meadows as ever, and the majestic sky filled with purple-tinged clouds (18).

The horse-drawn hay wain may no longer trundle across the river's millstream at Flatford, but there is still a sense of antiquity and calm in this little vale. As a boy, John Constable spent his childhood fishing, swimming, and exploring, the soft light and wide skies inspiring him to become a painter. 'I may yet make some impression,' he wrote, 'with my "light", my "dews", my "breezes" – my bloom and my freshness – none of which qualities has yet been perfected on the canvas of any painter in the world.' From Dedham village, it's a mile's meander down to Flatford Mill via Fen Bridge. I was to meet a friend, Rosy, and her little girl. They have swum in the pool beneath the bridge all their lives.

Further downstream, on our way to find chocolate cake and tea at Flatford Mill, we swam again. The distinctive bank-side willows, planted and pollarded over a hundred years ago, have grown into fat, sinewy bundles. The water is dark with occasional strands of weeds floating up from the bottom, but the river is warm, clear, and clean. There also used to be barges on the river, and though the locks and wharfs have disappeared, the public still retains the right to navigate from Sudbury to the sea. The Stour is now a popular canoeing and swimming river, and you'll find many clinker rowing boats filling its reaches in summer (14-18).

The River Chelmer in Essex flows from Debden through Chelmsford to Maldon, where it joins the Blackwater. Canalised in the late 18th century as the Chelmer and Blackwater Navigation, it was once a key transport route but is now used mainly for leisure. While not officially designated for bathing, the river is popular with wild swimmers in rural spots like Ulting, Hoe Mill, and Paper Mill

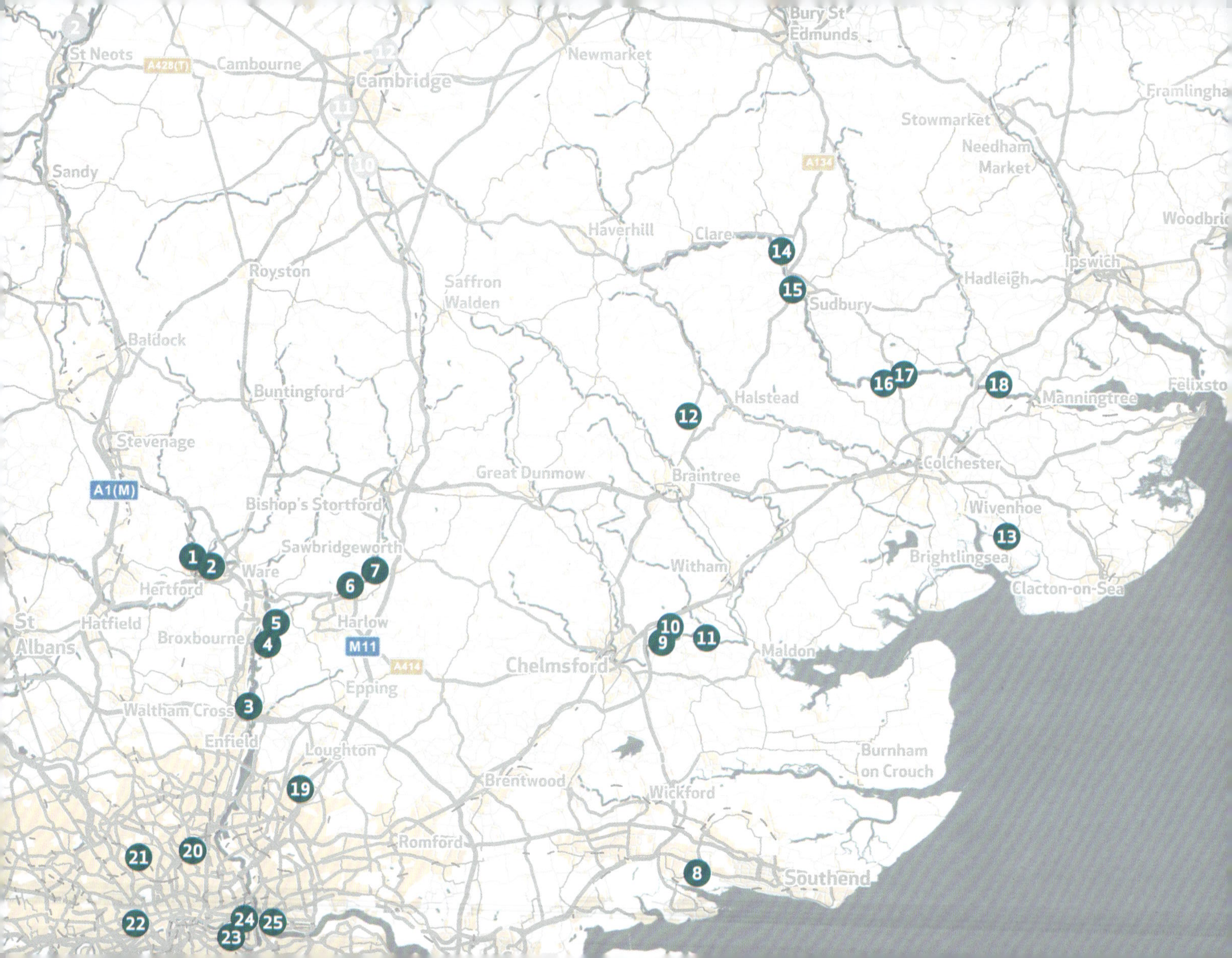
St Neots
Cambourne
A428(T)
Cambridge
Newmarket
Bury St Edmunds
Framlingham
Stowmarket
Needham Market
A134
Sandy
Woodbridge
Haverhill
Clare
Ipswich
Hadleigh
Royston
Saffron Walden
Sudbury
Baldock
Buntingford
Halstead
Manningtree
Felixstowe
Stevenage
Great Dunmow
Braintree
Colchester
A1(M)
Bishop's Stortford
Wivenhoe
Sawbridgeworth
Brightlingsea
Ware
Hertford
Witham
Clacton-on-Sea
Hatfield
St Albans
Broxbourne
Harlow
M11
A414
Maldon
Chelmsford
Epping
Waltham Cross
Enfield
Loughton
Burnham on Crouch
Brentwood
Wickford
Romford
Southend
1
2
3
4
5
6
7
8
9
10
11
12
13
14
15
16
17
18
19
20
21
22
23
24
25

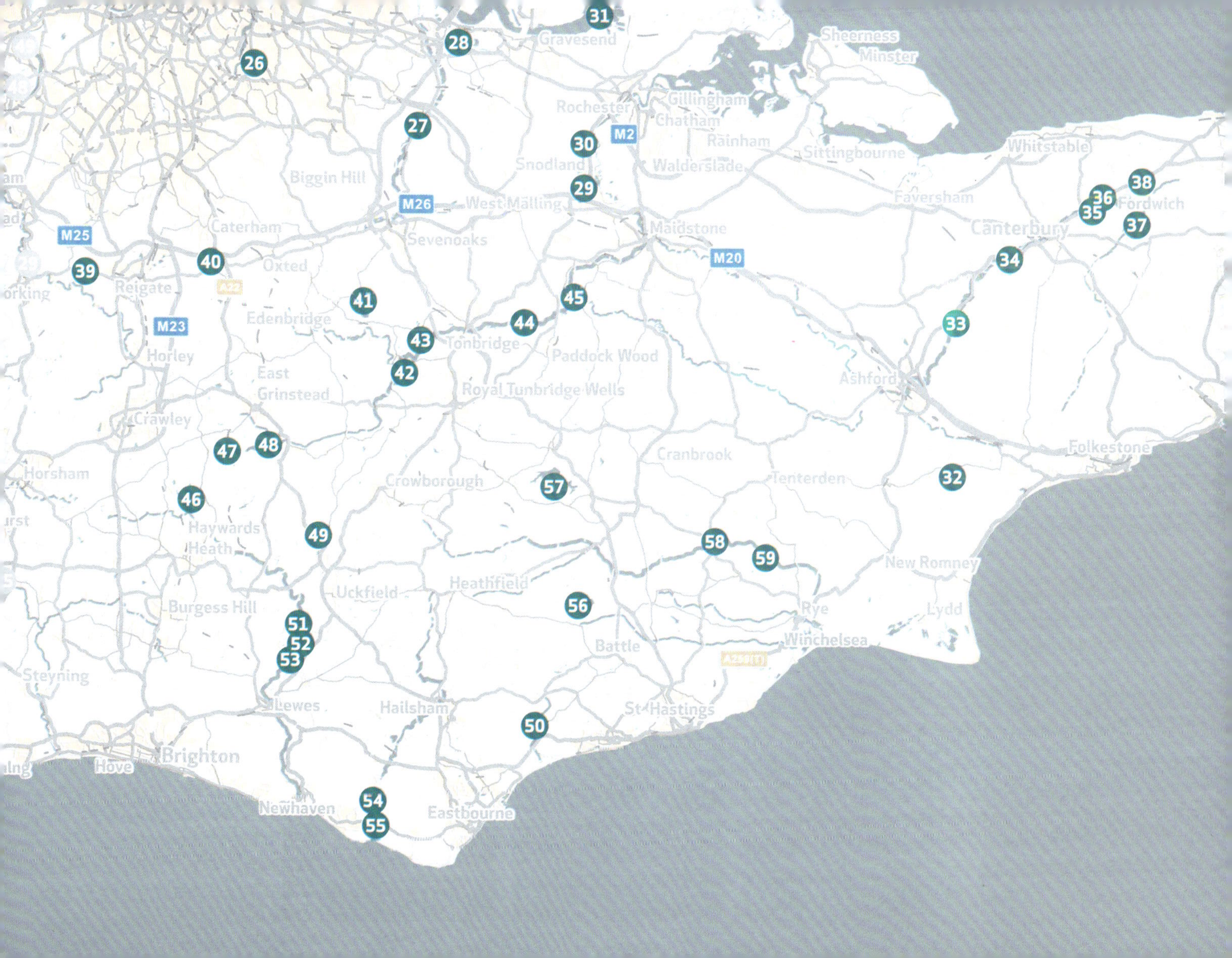
31
Gravesend
28
26
Sheerness
Minster
Rochester
Gillingham
Chatham
M2
27
30
Rainham
Sittingbourne
Whitstable
Snodland
Walderslade
Biggin Hill
29
38
36
Fordwich
35
M26
West Malling
Faversham
Canterbury
37
Caterham
Maidstone
M25
Sevenoaks
40
M20
34
39
Oxted
Reigate
A22
45
41
M23
Edenbridge
44
33
43
Tonbridge
Horley
Paddock Wood
42
East
Grinstead
Ashford
Royal Tunbridge Wells
Crawley
48
47
Cranbrook
Folkestone
Horsham
Tenterden
32
Crowborough
57
46
Haywards
Heath
49
58
59
New Romney
Uckfield
Heathfield
56
Burgess Hill
51
52
53
Rye
Lydd
Battle
Winchelsea
Steyning
Lewes
Hailsham
St Hastings
50
Brighton
Hove
54
Newhaven
55
Eastbourne

'I associate my careless boyhood with all that lies on the banks of the Stour. Those scenes made me a painter, and I am grateful...'

John Constable to a friend, 1814

Lock, where the water is slower and cleaner (9-11). Access is generally good via towpaths and lock-side paths.

Within London's great concrete sprawl, there are a surprising number of hidden green oases, and efforts by local authorities to prohibit swimming have catalysed a number of campaigns to reclaim wild-swimming rights. The three Hampstead Heath swimming ponds are probably the best-known of central London's wild swims (21). The Mixed Pond is the closest to the tube and always has a holiday air. Groups loll about on the lawn, picnics are consumed, and friends breast-stroke between the avenue of trees, catching up on old news and gossip. The Men's Pond is bigger and the Ladies' Pond wilder, but both are a little more difficult to reach if you don't have a bike.

The ponds date back to the end of the seventeenth century when the Hampstead Water Company dammed two brooks that drain the Heath, piping the water down to the city in hollowed-out elm trees. When the 'New River' from Hertfordshire to Islington superseded the ponds, they became important for recreation, and a painting by Constable depicts people bathing at Hampstead as early as 1829. Given this long tradition, it's not surprising that the Hampstead Heath Winter Swimming Club was up in arms when health and safety officials told them they could no longer swim there in the winter months. The club, which includes several prominent public figures, won their case to swim in a landmark ruling in 2005. The judge spoke out in favour of 'individual freedom' and against the imposition of 'a grey and dull safety regime'. This 2005 ruling has inspired other swimmers to reclaim their London ponds too.

South of London, the Medway has a long history of river swimming, especially around Tonbridge and Maidstone (42-45), though access declined due to pollution and safety concerns. In recent years, wild swimming has quietly returned. The Sussex Downs also provide respite for Londoners, with beautiful swimming opportunities, from the reaches of the upper Ouse to the warm lake-land meanders of the Cuckmere Vale (51-55). The great winding paths of the river Cuckmere became separated from their stream in the nineteenth century when a bypass 'cut' was built to stop the vale-land meadows flooding. The abandoned curves are now warm, safe lagoons, ideal for paddling, rafting, and swimming. With panoramic views of the Seven Sisters cliffs and the sea, this is a stunning location to combine saltwater and freshwater swimming. How long the meanders will survive is now in doubt as there are plans to let the sea flood these flatlands again and return them to their original ecology.

This area was the rural heartland of the Bloomsbury Group. Above the Vale and over the Downs is Charleston Farmhouse, where Vanessa Bell lived after her separation from her husband. From here, she could walk to visit her sister, Virginia Woolf, at Rodmell, on the Ouse. The houses and area became the rural retreat of one of the most influential literary and artistic groups of the twentieth century, known for their love of nature and wild swimming. E. M. Forster, schooled and brought up in nearby Tonbridge, visited more than once. Known to wild swim with Rupert Brooke in Grantchester, one of Forster's more famous literary scenes is of Freddy George, and Mr Beebe rebelliously dipping into the Surrey 'Sacred Lake' in A Room with a View. Mocking the world of Edwardian manners and social codes, it symbolised the great liberation of thought and feeling that Forster and his contemporaries believed natural bathing provided. Forster grew up swimming in the Medway, fed by the dark waters of the Ashdown Forest – home of Winnie the Pooh – between Kent and Sussex. You can still swim in the Medway, near Penshurst Place, to this day (43). The banks of the river slope steeply into rich, clean, and weed-free water. The peaty smell and brownish hue are flavoured by the Wealds of Kent. To swim here is to be infused with an elixir of leaf litter and pine cones.

If you do visit Virginia Woolf's Rodmell, the Ouse there is not a great place to swim. The straight, tidal channel has swampy edges and a slick current as it runs under a bleak, open sky, and its lack of charm is not helped by being the site where, just a few hundred yards from her home, the writer chose to take her own life. Woolf had suffered from periods of manic depression throughout her creative and brilliant life. She felt she was going mad again, and after months of suffering, she did not believe she would ever recover.

Just north of Rodmell and Charleston, upstream on the Ouse, the open fields of Barcombe Mills are a perfect place for cricket, leapfrog, and other riverside games. The Ouse here is deep with pretty grassy banks, ideal for cooling down after cartwheels or diving in for a long swim among the rushes (53). The well-known Anchor Inn is nearby, just a mile upstream, at the bottom of a dead-end lane (52). You can hire one of its fleet of blue rowing boats or swim for over two miles through remote countryside, the spire of Isfield church the only building in sight for the entire journey (51).

The three gentlemen rotated in the pool breast-high, after the fashion of the nymphs in Gotterdammerung. For some reason or other, a change came over them. They began to play. Mr Beebe and Freddy splashed each other. A little deferentially, they splashed George…Then all the forces of youth burst out.

E. M. Forster, A Room with a View

LEA VALLEY

1 WATERFORD MARSH, R BEANE
Pretty meadow and young willow-lined river for paddling and a dip. Waterford is 2 miles N of Hertford on A119. Take first R (Vicarage Ln) to find footpath on R after 200m onto common (SG14 2QA).
10 mins, 51.8141, -0.0937 🏊

2 BENGEO, R BEANE
River meadow and footbridge with good swimming spots up or downstream, including a weir and waterfall. Find St Leonard's Church (SG14 3JW). Pass through

gate onto Hartham Common 100m to footbridge for a little beach. Or cross and continue for more deep stretches. Close to Hertford East station (head N via Mill Rd, across the canal, 500m) or Hertford North Station.
5 mins, 51.8063, -0.0687 🏊

3 LEE VALLEY WHITE WATER CENTRE 🅴
I'm not sure how they pump all that water, but you can swim down the huge artificial rapids on a hydrospeed board – good practise for your white water swimming skills! Or just book an OWS session. Waltham Cross, EN9 1AB, 0300 0030616, better.org.uk/destinations/lee-valley
2 mins, 51.6888, -0.0171

4 NAZEING MEAD LAKES, BROXBOURNE
Three pleasant lakes used for fishing and sailing, on cycle route S of Dobb's Weir. Good footpath access to shores. Between Broxbourne and Lower Nazeing, B194, turn off N on National Cycle Route 1 from B194/Nazeing Rd (up Nursery Rd, EN9 2HU). First lake is after 200m on L. Or access from Dobbs Weir. Watch for blue-green algae in late summer.
10 mins, 51.7411, 0.0079 🅴🄿🅱

5 GLEN FABA, DOBBS WEIR
One of the most secluded and cleanest lakes in the Lea Valley area. From Fish and Eels pub, Dobbs Weir Rd (EN11 0AY, 01992 466073) take footpath upstream NE and cross the footbridge on R to reach lake shore after 500m, under pylons. Or from end of Glen Faba Rd (CM19 5JW).
10 mins, 51.7592, 0.0194 🄿🄱🏊

6 REDRICKS LAKES, SAWBRIDGEWORTH 🅴
Beautiful lakes with lifeguards amid the natural beauty of the Hertfordshire countryside. The Dancing Crayfish Café offers breakfast rolls, pizzas and hot beverages, and a good vegetarian selection. Glamping is available nearby at Cre8 Glamping (cre8-glamping.co.uk). CM21 0RL, 07815 294712, redrickslakes.co.uk
2 mins, 51.7908, 0.1200

7 SAWBRIDGEWORTH, R STORT
A pretty rural stretch of river for a mile down to Feakes Lock. Follow the Stort Walkway S from Sheering Mill Lane (CM21 9LR) in Sawbridgeworth, or via Pishiobury Park Car Park (height restrictions), A1184 (CM21 0AL).
15 mins, 51.8035, 0.1538 🅱🏊

CHELMER VALLEY

8 HADLEIGH COUNTRY PARK 🅴
Small but perfectly formed man-made supervised lake with spectacular views across the Thames Estuary. SS7 2PP, hadleighplungersows.co.uk
5 mins, 51.5503, 0.597

9 LITTLE BADDOW LOCK, R CHELMER
Dip with the local swim groups near the lock and weir, a beautiful quiet stretch. Park at bridge (CM3 3DS, 51.7486, 0.5524) then upstream W on towpath 300m. Or continue upstream 1km to Stonham's Lock. Downstream from the bridge is Papermill Lock with tearooms. CM3 4BS, 01245 225520.
5 mins, 51.7463, 0.5476

10 TRIFARM, BOREHAM 🅴
Family and dog-friendly lifeguarded lake, with showers and cafe. Hosts its own annual sprint triathlon. Church Road, CM3 3DS, 07546 560765 trifarm.co.uk. Access to the lake is by a ramp or steps.
5 mins, 51.7503, 0.5511

11 ULTING & HOEMILL BR, R CHELMER
Lovely clean swimming and canoeing, for up to two miles downstream of bridge, or opposite pretty All Saints Church. Watch

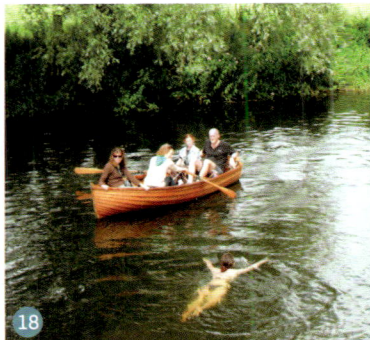

out for boats. Signed Nounsley/Ulting off B1019 at S end of Hatfield Peverel. From Ulting (after CM9 6QU) head S to the causeway and lock. Follow the footpath downstream. Limited parking, cycle route 1. Also explore downstream from Boreham Bridge, upstream (51.7485, 0.5596).

5 mins, 51.7485, 0.6081

12 GOSFIELD LAKE RESORT, HALSTEAD

Enjoy a lake swim in the gentle rolling hills of rural Essex and pitch your tent next to the lake afterwards. Lifeguards, cafe and toilets. Great for those starting out as the lake is mostly 5ft deep. Access to the lake is via a jetty. Take Church Rd E off the A1017 going through Gosfield and continue for 750m. Church Road, CO9 1UD, @ gosfieldlakeopenwaterswimming

5 mins, 51.9345, 0.5806

13 THORRINGTON TIDE MILL AND POND

This restored water mill (open bank holidays and last Sunday of month April–September) stands by a pretty mill pond and creek. Sign on entrance, L on B1029 one mile N of Brightlingsea (CO7 8JL).

5 mins, 51.8350, 1.0204

STOUR VALLEY

14 LONG MELFORD, R STOUR

Follow the St Edmund Way path past the weir pool and through meadows along the river. Follow Liston Ln W out of Long Melford (CO10 9RF) to find footpath on R after 200m to weir and footbridge.

5 mins, 52.0728, 0.708

15 SUDBURY, R STOUR

Many good spots in the meadow on the W edge of Sudbury, including this large weir pool with beach, behind the hospital and church. Signed Sudbury Meadows from the main church (down Croft Rd, CO10 1HR) then explore downstream 50m to weir pool, or upstream for over a mile into meadows. Much quieter and more rural sections of the river are at Borley (52.0530, 0.7129, behind CO10 7AB).

10 mins, 52.0408, 0.7235

16 WISSINGTON, R STOUR

Lovely walk past pretty church. In Nayland, take Wiston Rd off A134 at Nags Corner (CO6 4LS), then after a mile L signed Wiston Church. Walk past church to river and footbridge, exploring downstream all

the way to the weir. More remote spots 2 miles upstream at Wormingford (51.9615, 0.8086).

10 mins, 51.9628, 0.8495

17 NAYLAND, R STOUR

The river winds through open water meadows here, with deep sections and a waterside pub where you can land a canoe. Follow the footpath from behind the lovely Anchor Inn, Court St (CO6 4JL, 01206 262313). Stroll downstream as far as the footbridge and walk back on the other bank.

10 mins, 51.9675, 0.8725

18 DEDHAM VALE, R STOUR

A beautiful, open and historic vale, site of Flatford Mill, where people row boats and occasionally swim. Fen Bridge is a quiet spot with deep pools and shelving access. Some weeds to watch for. Park at Dedham Bridge, opposite the Boatyard (restaurant and rowing boat hire, CO7 6DH, 01206 323153). Follow footpath downstream 1km (L bank) to Fen Bridge. Or 45 mins walk on the St Edmund Way from Manningtree Station via Flatford Mill.

15 mins, 51.9623, 1.0079

Ladies' pond (beautiful and enclosed by trees) are ½ mile away, on opposite side of Heath, or via Millfield Lane off Highgate West Hill (N6 6JB).

15 mins, 51.5608, -0.1655

22 SERPENTINE LAKE, HYDE PARK £

Seasonal 40-acre lake in central London fed by underground springs. Extends between Lancaster Gate and Knightsbridge tube stations. On S side of lake, to E of bridge, with changing rooms. Lido Café Bar (W2 2UH, 020 7706 7098).

10 mins, 51.505, -0.1692

23 SURREY DOCKS WATERSPORTS £

OWS in the vibrant urban oasis and lively community of the docks (Rope St, SE16 7SX, 03330050409, southwarkleisure. co.uk/watersports)

5 mins, 51.4939, -0.0394

24 CANARY WHARF, LONDON £

Perhaps best known for its towering skyscrapers and bustling financial district, Canary Wharf is located on a graceful oxbow curve of the meandering River Thames on the Isle of Dogs in East London. As you kick your way around the basin you can marvel at the juxtaposition of your peaceful swim against the frenzied backdrop of the city. An opportunity to experience Canary Wharf from a unique perspective. Seasonal swims organised by NOWCA (Mackenzie Walk, E14 4PH, loveopenwater.co.uk/canary-wharf)

10 mins, 51.5045, -0.0232

25 ROYAL DOCKS, LONDON £

Dive into what was the largest enclosed docks system in the world. The water quality is good, and it's checked every two weeks. To fully appreciate the grandeur of the place, arrive by the Emirates Air Line from Greenwich. loveopenwater.co.uk

5 mins, 51.5067, 0.0170

GREATER LONDON

19 LUXBOROUGH LAKES £

OWS at the far-eastern end of the Central Line in a wooded gravel lake. Book on NOWCA app. Chigwell, IG7 5DF, beenduranceopenwater.com

2 mins, 51.6193, 0.0535

20 WEST RESERVOIR, HACKNEY £

A Victorian former pump house stands proudly on its embankment overlooking the large sparkling oasis that is West Reservoir. Urban life is kept at bay. Accessible toilets and changing rooms for swimmers with disabilities, and ramp access into the water (Green Lanes, N4 2HA, 0208 442 8116 better.org.uk)

10 mins, 51.5667, -0.0919

21 HAMPSTEAD PONDS, THE HEATH £

Three beautiful woodland swimming lakes set in the rolling hills of Hampstead Heath. Deep, dark and green. Changing areas and lifeguards. Close to train and tube. From Hampstead tube turn L down High St, then L after 500m down Downshire Hill (NW3 1PA). Cross onto Heath, bear L to pass first then second pond (both non-swimming). Mixed pond is next one up. Men's pond and

26 BECKENHAM PLACE PARK ⊟

A small lake once part of a mansion and estate. All year round OWS. BR3 1SY, 07736 930823, ptpcoaching.co.uk

10 mins, 51.4205, -0.0143

NORTH KENT

27 EYNSFORD, DARENT

A short walk from Eynsford Station, popular clear chalk stream, shallow pools and ford run through this pretty village. Great fun for kids. The Plough Inn is adjacent (DA4 0AE, 01322 862281). Upstream on lane is Lullingstone Castle gardens, Roman villa and lovely lake. Downstream along High St is Eynsford Castle (free).

3 mins, 51.3680, 0.2092 🏊🖼️🏠🚆

28 BLUEWATER LAKE ⊟

Year-round supervised OWS in dramatic high-walled quarry on W side of the massive shopping centre, Also inflatables and zip wires. Book online hanglooseadventure.com

2 mins, 51.4387, 0.2641

29 LEYBOURNE LAKES ⊟

Country Park with network of many paths and gravel lakes, some wild. OWS session run by the watersport centre near the main car park (ME20 6JA, 01634 246006). eybournelakewatersports.co.uk

5 mins, 51.3154, 0.435

30 ST ANDREWS LAKE, HALLING ⊟

A former chalk quarry. Turquoise water, chalky-white floor and a sandy beach. Verdant cliffs and deep, clear, cold azure water. Aqua park, paddle boarding and more. OWS all year around via 200m and 500m loops (NOWCA only, Book: standrews watersports.co.uk or 01634 926 204)

15 mins, 51.3531, 0.4350

31 CLIFFE FORT, HIGHAM

Adventurous, industrial walk out past sand lakes to an abandoned fort and torpedo station among marshes. Old sand quarry lakes or high tide only swim at sea wall side (watch currents). Reached from the pretty church at Lower Higham, which helped inspire Great Expectations (ME3 7LS).

45 mins, 51.4616, 0.4563 🚆🅿️❓

EAST KENT & GT STOUR

32 ROYAL MILITARY CANAL, BONNINGTON

Open and quiet stretch of this Napoleonic Wars defensive canal, near pretty Saxon church, one of the oldest on the Marshes.

Signed St Rumwold church/Newchurch (TN25 7JY) S from Bonnington (B2067) 400m.

5 mins, 51.0707, 0.9435 🏕️🚶

33 OLANTIGH, R WYE

Pretty stretch of the young Stour by footbridge, for picnic and paddling. 2km N of Wye, find footpath on L by junction, 100m after gates for Olantigh House (TN25 5EW). River down below in the meadows.

5 mins, 51.2017, 0.9479 🏊🚶

34 CHARTHAM, R GREAT STOUR

Popular stream pool with rope swing and hidden lake beyond. Park at Chartham village hall and follow the path 300m down along the stream to find small weir, deep pool beneath and rope swing. Continue on 300m to find lake on L. Chartham has a train station or is 3 miles SW of Canterbury on A28. NCN 18.

5 mins, 51.2562, 1 0215 🏊🚆🚶🅿️🍴🚻

35 FORDWICH, R GREAT STOUR

Flowing through England's smallest town, the river is first open and sunny, with a bench and little beach after 1km. It then becomes wooded and secretive (a wooded glade on R, 51.3001, 1.1513 after 900m),

leading to a wild gravel lake. From King St, CT2 0DE (51.2963, 1.1247) see signs for CanoeWild hire (07947835688, canoewild. co.uk) and follow the river's N bank. Leads to Westbere Marshes lake (see entry).
40 mins, 51.2988, 1.1365 ▲▤◪⊿⬤

36 WESTBERE MARSHES
Large, wild, unfrequented gravel lakes with S facing bays. From Westbere village, cross the railway and bear R along the N shore, to the first bay. Or continue straight to reach the Stour.
10 mins, 51.3047, 1.1479 ▥❓⊿

37 WICKHAMBREAUX, R LITTLE STOUR
Pretty stream and shallow weir pool, near this picturesque village. Turn at the 16th-century Rose Inn (CT3 1RQ, 01227 721763) then first R after school down Seaton Rd. After 300m find footpath on L. Cross field to find stream and pool after 500m. Or follow riverside path 2km down the Newnham Valley to Blue Bridge.
10 mins, 51.286, 1.1961 ➳▮▮🚶

38 UPSTREET, R GREAT STOUR
Upstream is clean and silky after four miles meandering through the Stodmarsh nature reserve. Opposite Grove Ferry Inn (CT3 4BZ, 01227 860302) signed off A28, find NNR/Stodmarsh gate and river path. Swim upstream from path.
5 mins, 51.3226, 1.2029 ▤▲⊿▮🚶

SURREY HILLS

39 BUCKLAND PARK LAKE, THE SHAC ☰
Superb, spring-fed lagoon, fringed with silver birch. Flanked by steep, white cliffs on two sides. OWS sessions, book online theshac. co.uk. For a sit-down meal, visit The Reverie (RH3 7BQ, 01737 843023), which offers panoramic views of the lake.
30 mins, 51.2426, -0.2445

40 DIVERS COVE, GODSTONE ☰
A turquoise, seven-acre reservoir surrounded by a dense wood of silver birch. The water is exceptionally clean and clear due to the sandy floor. OWS run by knowledgeable and enthusiastic staff all year round. Wood-fired saunas and hot tubs are available seasonally. Hot and cold drinks and homemade sausage rolls are served from a small on-site café. N Park Ln, Bletchingley, RH9 8ND. Book at diverscove. co.uk
2 mins, 51.2515, -0.0735

41 BOUGH BEECH LAKE
Quiet, hidden, wooded reservoir, previously a nature reserve, with some beach areas at this point. Park and walk SW 1km from old oast house (TN14 6LD, 51.2245, 0.1402) or 500m E from 51.2172, 0.1314 (tricky parking).
5 mins, 51.2190, 0.1353 ❓▲🏠

RIVER MEDWAY

42 POUNDSBRIDGE, R EDEN
In remote fields, a bridge with some deep pools under red earth banks, popular for jumps with local kids. Take bridleway track N from All Souls church on narrow

44

lane, limited parking (TN11 8AJ, 51.1541 0.1968). No Swimming signs.
30 mins, 51.1580, 0.1914

43 ENSFIELD BRIDGE, R MEDWAY
Open, sunny stretch of river by lane. Steep banks and muddy but good for a longer swim. Explore downstream for another 1km of river to weir, footbridge and hidden lakes among trees (51.1894, 0.2230). On Cycle Route 12. W of Tonbridge, 2km S of Leigh Station on lanes (TN11 8RZ).
2 mins, 51.1857, 0.2133

44 EAST LOCK, R MEDWAY
This long stretch of bucolic river E of Tonbridge. Perfect for canoeing and swimming in summer, if you are careful to avoid the bigger boats and locks. There are open meadows and mainly easy banks into deep water. Large network of gravel lakes on S shore too, which could be explored. From Golden Green (The Bell Inn, TN11 0BD, 01732 851748) take Kelchers Ln to East Lock. Cross over for footpath to lakes (circular loop) or continue along riverside path 300m E along river for main swim. Further downstream leads to Oak Weir lock with more gravel lakes to S, all on footpaths
15 mins, 51.2009, 0.3537

45 YALDING LEES, R MEDWAY
Kids muck about at the weir, despite the signs and dangers, but local swim groups swim from the ancient common land, downstream the medieval bridge. Council parking by the bridge (ME18 6HG).
5 mins, 51.2227, 0.4214

ASHDOWN FOREST

46 ARDINGLY LAKE, BALCOMBE
A beautiful two-pronged reservoir. Good path along N shores. No Swimming, so avoid fishermen and be discreet if you choose to dip at this little beach - 300m S from parking on the lane (RH17 6QY). Or from Balcombe Station follow Mill Lane (signed Ardingly) from mini-roundabout/postbox. Pick up footpath from parking layby at bottom, beyond bridge to 51.0526, -0.1144. Or 500m N is a footpath to Balcombe Lake, an historic hammer pond (51.0631, -0.1237).
15 mins, 51.0489, -0.0991

47 GRAVETYE LAKE, KINGSCOTE
Lovely little Forestry Commission lake, hidden in deep woods, though sometimes fishing and can get weedy/muddy. 2km walk S from Kingscote Station on wooded

46

42

footpaths via Hastings Wood, or 1km N on footpath from West Hoathly (bring map!)
10 mins, 51.0902, -0.0505 🚉🏔❓

48 WEIR WOOD RESERVOIR
Lifeguarded swim sessions 3 times a week and night swims during the summer. Wetsuit only venue. Swim from sailing club (RH18 5HT) on S side. Book on 01342 621271, weirwood.co.uk
10 mins, 51.0960, 0.0062 🚉🏔

49 BORINGWHEEL, HORNEY COMMON 🚉
Small fishing lake used for OWS in heart of Ashdown Forest. Allows children from

8 years and no wetsuits required. Cackle St, TN22 3DU, 07973 437234, eequ.org/ashdownforestleisure
10 mins, 51.0191, 0.0748 🚉🏔❓

50 WALLERS HAVEN, WARTLING
Very remote, wide river, around 15 feet deep in places with the reed-lined banks. Amazing wild swim experience. From Wartling (3 miles N of Pevensey roundabout) head past church to Horsebridge. Footpath heads upstream. Or explore anywhere on the river.
3 mins, 50.8569, 0.3697 🚉🚶🏞

SUSSEX OUSE & CUCKMERE

51 ISFIELD, R OUSE
Arrive by steam train on the Lavender Line. It's a short walk to the river on the bridleway (TN22 5XJ). Cross the footbridge and head upstream 100m to swim at bend. Or follow the path downstream, swimming all the way to the Anchor Inn.
10 mins, 50.9396, 0.0532 🚉

52 ANCHOR INN, R OUSE
Remote riverside pub. Bucolic swimming and boating for two miles upstream to Isfield. Hire boats from the Anchor and

paddle past grassy meadows for the afternoon. Leave Barcombe Cross dir Spithurst, after ½ mile turn R down single-track dead-end Anchor Lane to find pub at end past BN8 5EA (01273 400414). Or walk upstream 1 mile from Barcombe Mills (above).
5 mins, 50.9264, 0.0513 🚉🍴🚶

53 BARCOMBE MILLS, R OUSE
Popular stretch of grassy riverbank and meadows. Steep banks and deep water 2km N of Lewes, turn L signposted Barcombe off A26. Find car park on R after 1km, after road to BN8 5BY, and head upstream past sluices to meadow.
5 mins, 50.9151, 0.0411 🚉🚶

54 LITLINGTON, R CUCKMERE
Wide grassland vale beneath white horse. Fun at high tide. Approaching from A259 E of Seaford, footpath to river is on L as you enter Litlington village, 200m before the excellent Plough and Harrow (BN26 5RE, 01323 870 632). Head downstream to footbridge.
10 mins, 50.7920, 0.1505 🚉🍴🚶

55 CUCKMERE MEANDERS

Wide, shallow, warm oxbow lakes cut off from the main river. Stunning setting with option of sea swimming too. On A259 W of Seaford. Park in the 'overflow' car park opposite the visitor centre at Exceat. Follow the path down on the L side of the valley 750m.

10 mins, 50.7707, 0.1544 🏊🏖️

HIGH WEALD

56 DARWELL WOODS

A bridleway leads down through ancient woods 2km to the isolated silty shores of Darwell Reservoir. There's a little car park just N of Darwell Hole at 50.9501, 0.4119 TN32 5JB.

30 mins, 50.9599, 0.428 ♻️🌸🏖️❓

57 BEWL WATER

The South East's largest water body. For organised OWS visit bewlwater.co.uk. The lake is surrounded by orchards and no end of secret beaches people dip from discreetly (No Swimming). There is footpath access around the entire perimeter and a 20km mountain bike route. From the main visitor centre head W along the N shore to Bramble Bay. Or try Rosemary Lane off

the A21 (51.0630, 0.4205) at the E end. Our favourite is from Three Leg Cross (51.0613, 0.3948) – from the Bull Inn (TN5 7HH) head down Boarders Ln, then turn R at crossroads, downhill to car park and dead end. Camp at Cedar Gables off A21, Flimwell (TN5 7QA, 01892 890566). The footpath behind leads down to a sunset-facing wooded cove (20 mins, 51.0675, 0.4097). Scotney Castle is also close by.

5 mins, 51.0613, 0.3948 🏊⛺🚶❓

58 NEWENDEN, R ROTHER

Pleasant river swim and café with campsite and canoe hire. Very clean and lined with reeds, purple loosestrife and marsh marigolds. Park at the boating station (Newenden, TN18 5PP, 01797330025) and swim either up or downstream of bridge.

3 mins, 51.0148, 0.6153 🏊⛺🍴🏖️

59 BLACKWALL BRIDGE, R ROTHER

Very wild and remote fenland swim or canoe. Head off in either direction for several miles without sight of a building. 2km N of Peasmarsh (TN31 6TB) in direction of Wittersham.

5 mins, 51.0010, 0.6854 🏊⛺🏖️

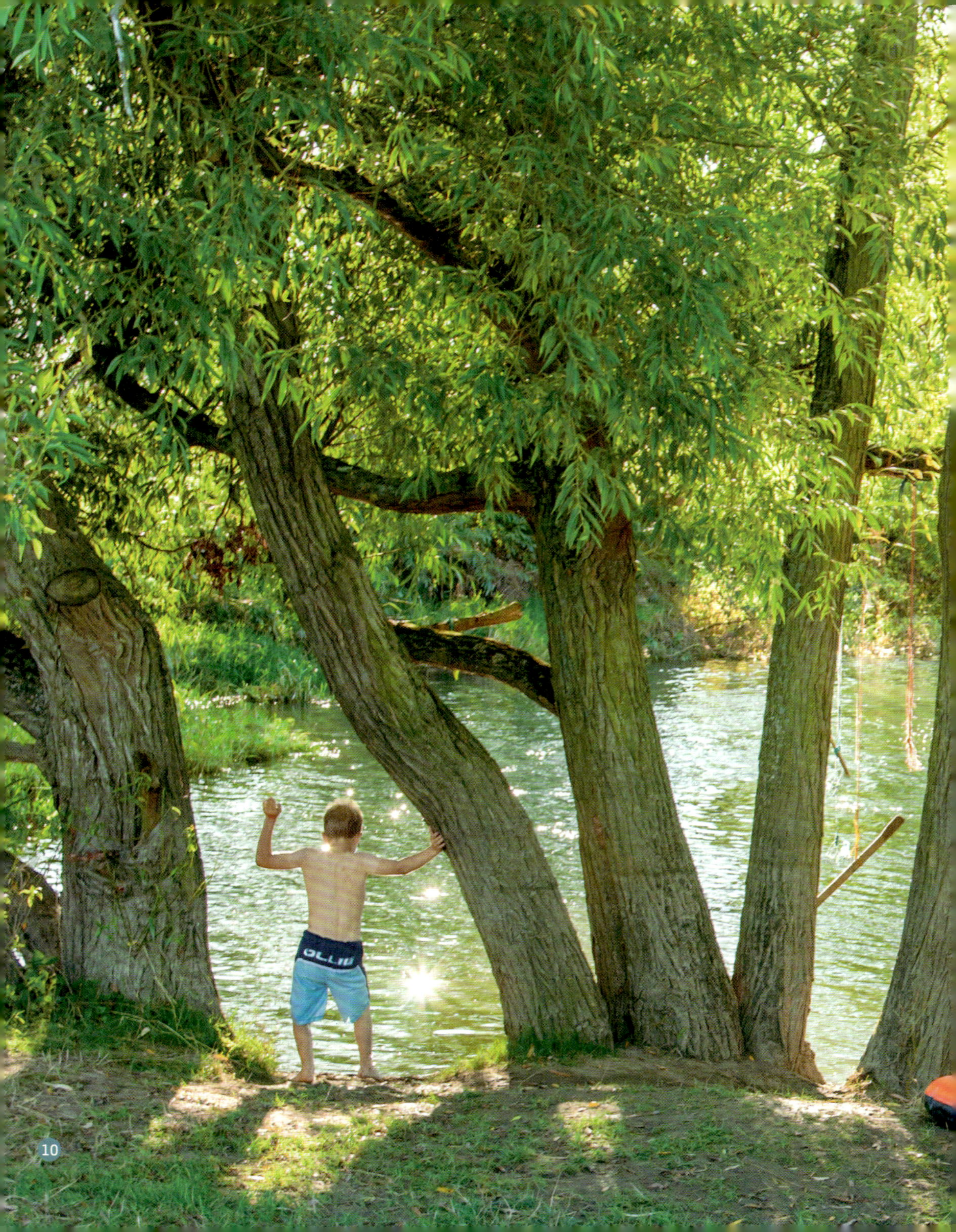

RIVER THAMES & OXFORDSHIRE

The young Thames is a quiet river, rising in the Cotswolds and flowing peacefully through the Oxfordshire plains. Distant church spires peek over billowing wheat fields and wild flowers wave in the hedgerows.

Three hundred years ago things were a little busier on the upper reaches of the Thames. Lechlade was a bustling port, loading Cotswold stone and Gloucester cheese, and the new Thames and Severn Canal had just opened where the Round House now stands. But with the decline of the canals more recreational pursuits took over: Lechlade became renowned for its water carnivals and swimming galas. The Ha'penny Bridge, built famously high to accommodate eighteenth- century sailing barges, was popular for diving competitions. Though the organised activities have now gone, boys still jump from the bridge and the area is still a designated Riverside Park providing swimming and boating for hundreds on hot summer weekends (8).

The open fields of the Riverside Park are a pleasant and convenient place to swim but downstream, around Buscot and Kelmscott, the real beauty and charm of the Upper Thames begins. At the Cheese Wharf in Buscot, once a loading bay for twenty tonnes of cheese a day, there is a rope swing and deep pool for swimming and diving (9).

A mile or so on, past the graceful riverside gardens of the Old Parsonage and church, the old weir at Buscot has scooped out a deep and clear natural pool, lined with weeping willow (10). Swimmers splash about among the tendrils, appearing through the leaves that brush the water. The older children climb the low boughs and use them as platforms to jump in from while the younger ones play among the deep roots and use them as handrails to pull themselves out. This is a justifiably popular place for swimming. The National Trust lawns that border it are dotted

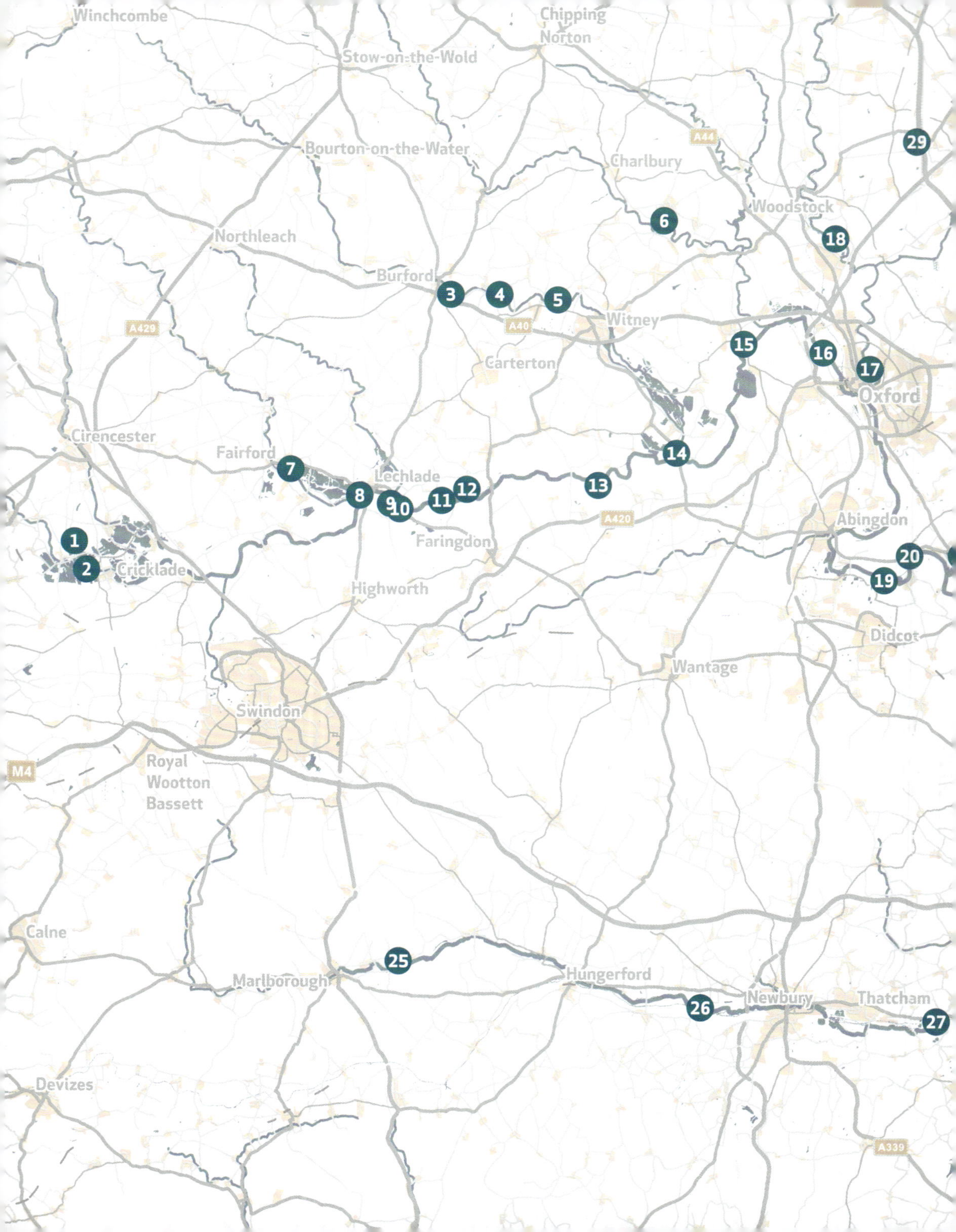
Winchcombe
Chipping Norton
Stow-on-the-Wold
A44
29
Bourton-on-the-Water
Charlbury
Woodstock
6
18
Northleach
Burford
3
4
5
A429
A40
Witney
15
16
17
Carterton
Oxford
Cirencester
Fairford
7
Lechlade
14
13
8
9
10
11
12
A420
Abingdon
1
Faringdon
20
2
Cricklade
19
Highworth
Didcot
Wantage
Swindon
M4
Royal Wootton Bassett
Calne
25
Hungerford
Marlborough
Newbury
Thatcham
26
27
Devizes
A339

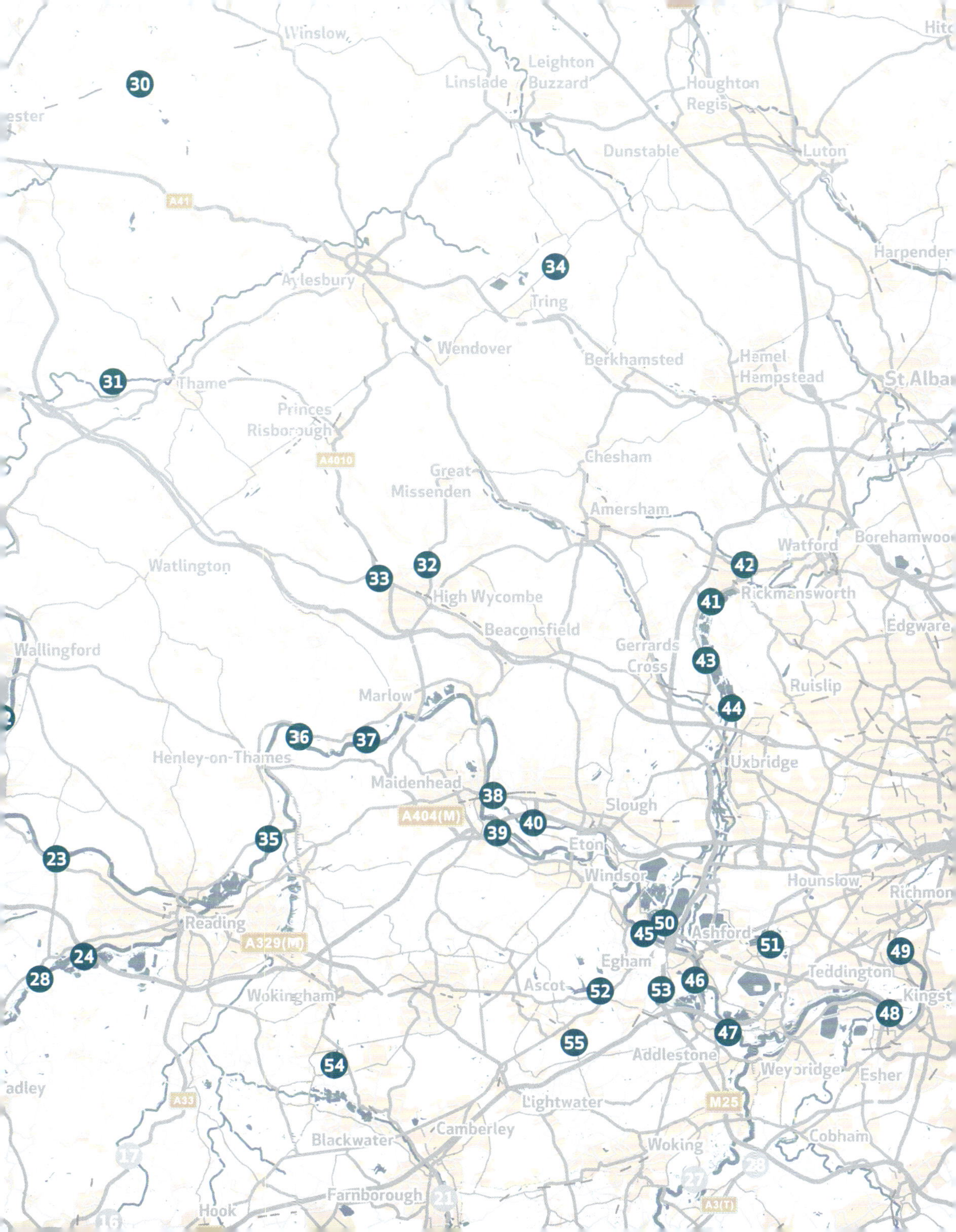
Winslow
30
Leighton Buzzard
Linslade
Houghton Regis
Dunstable
Luton
A41
Aylesbury
34
Tring
Wendover
Berkhamsted
Hemel Hempstead
31
Thame
Princes Risborough
A4010
Great Missenden
Chesham
Amersham
Watford
Watlington
33
32
42
41
High Wycombe
Rickmansworth
Beaconsfield
Edgware
Wallingford
Gerrards Cross
43
Ruislip
Marlow
44
36
37
Henley-on-Thames
Uxbridge
Maidenhead
38
A404(M)
Slough
40
39
35
23
Eton
Windsor
Hounslow
Reading
50
45
Ashford
51
49
A329(M)
24
28
Egham
Teddington
Ascot
52
53
46
Wokingham
48
47
55
Addlestone
Weybridge
Esher
54
A33
Lightwater
M25
Camberley
Blackwater
Woking
Cobham
17
27
28
Farnborough
21
Hook
16
A3(T)

with inflatable boats and deckchairs and the lock keeper is tolerant as long as you stay away from the weir itself. Further downstream is the honey-stone village of Kelmscott, once home of William Morris, the founder of the Arts and Crafts movement (11).

By Chimney Meadows bulrushes tower overhead like wheat in a children's cornfield and the wild flowers of Chimney Meadows, populated by wild grasses since Saxon times, break through; meadow barley, buttercup, crested dog's tail, lady's bedstraw and bird's-foot trefoil (13).

As you approach Oxford the Windrush joins the flow, the idyllic Cotswold stream. In Bourton-on-the-Water there are ducks and high street riverways. In Little Barrington there are perfect riverside pubs and in Minster Lovell it flows past the remains of a fifteenth-century manor (5). Here, alongside the great old arches and ruined walls, you can bathe in the blue- tinged waters and catch crayfish big enough for supper.

The Evenlode is another beautiful river which runs parallel a little way to the north (6). It was at Stonesfield, famous for its honey- coloured stone quarries, that the first ever dinosaur remains were found in 1824. The Jurassic limestone dates back 160 million years to the time of the Megalosaurus, or the 'Great Lizard of Stonesfield', whose discovery changed the face of history. Dinosaur bones had, in fact, been found prior to the 1800s, but were thought to be the fossilised remains of some giant human, now extinct, or the bones of elephants brought to Britain by the Romans. The river here is only shallow but the vale through which it runs is beautiful, with sunny steep banks, a footbridge, pool and the remains of a Roman villa too. If you're lucky and search the riverbed you may even find your own dinosaur bones.

The Thames, from Oxford downstream, has inspired generations of charming tales from *Alice in Wonderland* to The Wind in the Willows. Meandering through rolling countryside and stone villages, these are some of the most civilised swims in England and in many places the river is as unspoilt as it was 100 years ago, and a whole lot cleaner.

The Thames enters Oxford along Port Meadow (16), England's largest and oldest continuous meadow; recorded in the Doomsday Book of 1086. It has never been ploughed, and is older than any building in Oxford. At the northern end near Wolvercote there is swimming under the bridge and beneath the weir with grand views of the dreaming spires. This is the setting and inspiration for the opening lines of Alice in Wonderland who was 'beginning to get very tired of sitting with her sister on the bank…' and the closing lines where Alice sees 'an ancient city and a quiet river winding near it along the plain'. At the southern end of the Meadows, closer to the train station, the river has cut out little shallow beaches along its course, popular with families. In early summer it is awash with daisies and by evening you'll see flocks of lapwing and plover rising into the sky.

Oxford has long been a wild-swimming university and the dons established a naked bathing site on the Cherwell in 1852. Christened 'Parson's Pleasure' one story tells how a number of dons were sunbathing on the banks when a group of students floated by in a punt. The startled dons covered their modesty, all except one who placed a flannel over his head explaining: 'My students know me by my face'. A site just downstream for women – 'Dame's Delight' – followed in 1934 but both were eventually closed in 1991. All that now remains of Parson's Pleasure is a beer named in its honour, but you can still swim nearby (17).

Towards the end of the nineteenth century the river downstream of Oxford had already become a playground for London society. Clifton Hampden, six miles south, was a favourite with Jerome K. Jerome for boating trips (20). 'Sometimes we would fix up a trip of three or four days or a week, doing the thing in style and camping out.' In 1888 he wrote *Three Men in a Boat*, which became a manifesto for a simpler way of living with nature – river swimming before breakfast, kippers after and a snooze before lunch. Today the long grass and river banks are set against billowing hay fields and the area is a wonderful piece of bucolic tranquillity close to London.

Below Reading the river is still clean enough for swimming. The stretch between Hurley and Marlow is the inspiration for much of Kenneth Grahame's *The Wind in the Willows*. This is where Ratty spent so much time swimming with the ducks, and Mole so much time trying not to fall in. Kenneth Grahame's own childhood was spent with his grandparents being rowed out to little islands and other riverside haunts near Cookham Dean – Toad's dungeon is based on the Ice House in Bisham Woods and Badger's Wildwoods is based on the Quarry Woods nearby (35-37).

Grahame moved to live by the Thames after his retirement from the City in 1908. He was probably the most unlikely – and most unhappy – moneyman ever appointed to the post of Secretary of the Bank of England. But within months of his early retirement he had written The *Wind in the Willows*. 'As a contribution to natural history, the work is negligible,' The Times wrote stiffly. But Grahame's fable has become one of the best-loved works in literature.

'...we all talked as if we were going to have a long swim every morning. George said it was so pleasant to wake up in the boat in the fresh morning, and plunge into the limpid river. Harris said there was nothing like a swim before breakfast to give you an appetite...'

Three Men in a Boat, 1906

6

5

8

THAMES SOURCE

1 COTSWOLD COUNTRY PARK BEACH
A popular and safe place with cafe and facilities to introduce children to the delights of open-water swimming and other sports. Best to book ahead. Signed from B4696 just E of Somerford Keynes, GL7 6DF. Open 10am - 7pm, Apr - Oct.
1 mins, 51.6622, -1.9604

2 FREETH MERE, COTSWOLD WATER PARK
Explore this complex of 180 marl lakes, created by gravel extraction in the c20 and interlaced with heath and woodland. Much of the area, especially to the W of Ashton Keynes, is now a nature reserve; lakes to N and E have more watersports, including waterskiing. Take the Thames Path W off the B4696, 250m S of the church SN6 6QR. There's a small layby by the gate or walk on the path from the village itself. After 300m continue straight or take R path for more lakes. Use satellite view for orientation. Keen explorers could also try Cleveland Lake (51.6458, -1.9033), now a nature reserve, from Waterhay pay car park. There are also more formal lake swimming options at Lake 86 or Lake 32 (£10 membership).
10 mins, 51.6462, -1.9494

RIVER WINDRUSH

3 BURFORD, RIVER WINDRUSH
An idyllic, rural section of the Windrush, featured in Roger Deakin's book 'Waterlog'. Take Swan Lane out of Burford centre and turn R onto Witney St at end. Lay-by on L by stile after 800m (past OX18 4DR). Follow footpath to meander by the willow tree.
2 mins, 51.8021, -1.6227

4 ASTHALL, R WINDRUSH
Bucolic village and meadows with shallow swimming and lovely pub. Signed from A40, 4kmE of Burford. Pass the Three Horseshoes pub (OX18 4HW, 01608 692880, threehorseshoesasthall.com) to find river bridge and footpath after on R.
3 mins, 51.8021, -1.5790

5 MINSTER LOVELL HALL, RIVER WINDRUSH
This pretty Cotswold river runs through the romantic grounds of the ruined hall. Just deep enough to swim, with a deeper section downstream at weir and footbridge in meadows. In Little Minster turn past Old Swan pub (OX29 0RN) to parking on R at turning. Follow signs down to church, ruins and river below.
5 mins, 51.7992, -1.5265

6 STONESFIELD, RIVER EVENLODE
Several deep swimming spots are to be found on this beautiful, quiet stretch of the river, though it is shallow at the bridge. From S end of village follow footpath at the end of Brook Lane (beyond OX29 8PS). Cross bridge and head R to find deeper sections on bend in middle of field.
10 mins, 51.8438, -1.4311

YOUNG THAMES TO OXFORD

7 LAKE 104, FAIRFORD
Crystal-clear water in a beautifully rural location, Lake 104 forms part of an extensive range of old gravel pits, now returned to nature. Park in Fairford and follow footpath down Waterloo Lane (GL7 4BW), turn L across bridge and continue with river to R, bearing L to Lake 104, with smaller lakes to R.
30 mins, 51.7033, -1.7663

8 LECHLADE-ON-THAMES
There are many places to dip into the young Thames around Lechlade, but this is the perfect stretch for longer immersion: walk upstream to the pool and drift down, or kayak down to a pub. Head S over Ha'penny Bridge on A361 (past GL7 3AG), car park

R after 450m. Pool 1.2km upstream, above footbridge, near the Round House at junction with River Coln.

15 mins, 51.6885, -1.7042 🚗🏊🎣🅿️

9 CHEESE WHARF, RIVER THAMES

A delightful little roadside picnic area with river swing, this was once an old cheese-loading wharf. Head E and S from Lechlade on A417, dir Buscot, past The Trout Inn (GL7 3HA), continue for 800m to parking on L.

1 mins, 51.6839, -1.6765 🚗🏊🎣🅿️🍴

10 BUSCOT WEIR, R THAMES

A wonderful large, deep weir pool with trees, rope swings and lawns in pretty NT hamlet. Continue S from Cheese Wharf and turn L in Buscot to find car park (SN7 8DA) after 150m.

2 mins, 51.6809, -1.6683 🌊🍴🏊🚗

11 KELMSCOTT, R THAMES

Wild open stretch of Thames downstream from famous gardens and tea room. S from charming Plough Inn (GL7 3HG, 01367 253543) pass the Manor and onto trackway, parking at very end. Follow the river up to 2km downstream through endless open fields and many riverbank pools.

20 mins, 51.6857, -1.6303 🌄

12 GRAFTON LOCK TO RUSHEY LOCK

Grafton Lock is a wonderfully remote and pastoral stretch of Thames. Tiny lane signed to lock (bridleway), with access to park down on riverside field. There follows the most beautiful 4 mile stretch of the Thames, past Radcot Bridge A4095 (Ye Olde Swan, OX18 2SX, 01367 810220), then the Old Man Bridge wooden footbridge, at Radcot Lock (51.6997, -1.5681), Rushey Lock with island camping (51.6982, -1.5341), finally arriving at The Trout at Tadpole Bridge (SN7 8RF, 01367 870382).

2 mins, 51.6920, -1.6079 🌄🚶🏕️🅿️🏊🅿️

13 CHIMNEY MEADOWS, R THAMES

Meadows and nature reserve bordering a remote stretch of the Thames with wooden Tenfoot Bridge (51.6939, -1.4898). Beautiful 2km walk downstream from Trout Inn at Tadpole Bridge (SN7 8RF, 01367 870382). Also Duxford 3km downstream, a shallow glade pool and ford: from opposite bank across meadow (51.6990, -1.4660).

40 mins, 51.6945, -1.4900 🚶🏊🅿️🍴🌿

14 NEWBRIDGE & APPLETON

There's a fun pool in the Windrush here, with shallow paddling and a swing. Park on farm track (51.7136, -1.4207) on bend in A415,

400m N of Rose Revived pub (OX29 7QD) and follow footpath 50m downstream. About 3km downstream along the Thames is our favourite riverside campsite (Barefoot, OX13 5JN, 51.7162, -1.3757) - book at barefootcampsites.co.uk. Car access via Appleton.

2 mins, 51.7129, -1.4196

15 SWINFORD BRIDGE, R THAMES

Beautiful meadows and quiet river, just outside Oxford. Explore downstream along the edge of ancient Wytham Great Wood and on to King's Weir. Or upstream, all the way beyond Pinkhill Lock (OX29 4JH) a lock island with camping.

10 mins, 51.7746, -1.3594

16 PORT MEADOW, R THAMES

Oxford's largest area of grazing common land. Two miles of river with beaches and grassy meadow on both banks, burial mounds and migratory birds. For N end by car, park in Godstow Road car park, OX2 8PU . This is the Wolvercote Bathing Area with a rope swing and pool under the bridge. The riverside Trout Inn, OX2 8PN, is a little further on with parking for customers only. Or from Oxford station, explore the S end, turn R onto main road and after 300m drop

down to Thames footpath on R. Follow for 1km upstream. First footbridge leads to E bank (open meadow), next leads to W with path and access to The Perch (OX2 0NG, the-perch.co.uk).

15 mins, 51.7698, -1.2881

17 PARSON'S PLEASURE, R CHERWELL

Historic university river-bathing pool, though water quality can be variable. Take cycle path at lights on corner of St Cross Rd and South Parks Rd by Linacre College (OX1 3JA) and continue behind college 200m to the punt rollers, or anywhere upstream. For the riverside Victoria Arms, OX3 0PZ, 01865 251174, at the corner of St Cross Rd and South Parks Rd turn into the University Parks, cross the river by the footbridge in the parks, and continue upstream along the river for about 2km.

5 mins, 51.7606, -1.2458

18 KIDLINGTON, R CHERWELL

Remote and meandering, through meadow and common land with many kingfishers. There's a car park behind Kidlington church (OX5 2BA). Walk N 300m towards Hampton Poyle to swim at the footbridge, or explore upstream on the riverside footpath. Or take the cycle route E 800m downstream to

another bridge (51.8290, -1.2673).
10 mins, 51.8339, -1.2772 ⛰️🏊

MID THAMES TO READING

19 APPLEFORD, R THAMES

Open field and quiet beach behind a church, just a short walk from Appleford station. Follow footpath behind church (near OX14 4PA) 200m, or continue on to Little Wittenham. Also Sutton Pools upstream (51.6466, -1.2739).
2 mins, 51.6411, -1.2327 🚂🏊

20 CLIFTON HAMPDEN, R THAMES

A pretty bridge and pub, frequented by Jerome K. Jerome. Downstream for many miles there are sandy bays shelving to deeper water bordered by open meadows. Off A415 between Abingdon and Wallingford. Park opposite Barley Mow pub (OX14 3EH, 01865 407847). Continue downstream on river's S bank for up to 3km through meadows towards Dorchester.
2 mins, 51.6551, -1.2099 🚂⛰️🚶🏊

21 QUEENFORD LAKES, WALLINGFORD 🅿️

Two organisations provide all year round OWS sessions, supervised by a safety team, owsc.co.uk or oxfordwetnwild.com, OX10 7PQ.
2 mins, 51.6551, -1.1634

22 CHOLSEY, R THAMES

A long stretch of rural riverside with no locks and little overhanging vegetation, so great for a longer swim or canoe or a moonlit swim. Head S from Wallingford on A329 and at about 3km find Ferry Lane (dead end, OX10 9GZ) on L, opp the South Moreton turning. Continue to slipway at end. Explore downstream. Beware fast-moving rowing teams. Cholsey train station nearby.
5 mins, 51.5649, -1.1339 ⛰️🚂🏊

23 PANGBOURNE MEADOWS & GORING

Downstream of Whitchurch bridge, with car park or short walk from station, these popular swimming meadows stretch for over 3km (RG8 7DA). Or walk upstream to Goring on the NE bank and return by train - it's a beautiful, peaceful route.
About halfway is a pretty wooded section with rope swings. From bridge climb hill for 750m to find bridleway on L, then 2.5km to Hartslock Wood descending to riverbank (51.5080, -1.1108). Or access opp bank from Lower Basildon church (RG8 9NH, signed 'Church' off A329

3.5km NW of Pangbourne).
40 mins, 51.4860, -1.0849 🚶🏊⛺🅿️✕🚲

24 SHEFFIELD BOTTOM LOCK LAKE
This is one of the huge spring-fed lakes that can be seen from the M4 near Reading. The gravel was used to build the new city. From M4 J12 head towards Sheffield Bottom Lock picnic area and car park (Hangar Road, Theale, RG7 4AP). Follow the canal downstream and after 300m lake is on R. Keep clear of sailing dinghies. Or walk in from Sulhamstead. National Cycle Route 4.
5 mins, 51.4312, -1.0604 🅿️🚲

RIVER KENNET

25 AXFORD, R KENNET
A lively little weir pool below a footbridge on the young R Kennet. Don't swim if there are fishermen. On the Ramsbury road 5km E from Marlborough, entering Axford, turn R opp the MOT garages (SN8 2EY, Stone Ln name sign on brick house R). Pull off to park after bridge, by path sign. It's 300m W to small path R next to Coombe Farm gates to footbridge.
3 mins, 51.4270, -1.6679 🅿️❓

26 MARSH BENHAM, R KENNET
A large junction pool in the River Kennet. Signed Marsh Benham off A4, 3km W of Newbury edge. Continue 1km to Hamstead Lock (RG20 0JE) and follow the towpath upstream 300m. Cycle route 4 to Newbury. Food at the Red House (RG20 8LY, 01635 582017).
5 mins, 51.4010, -1.3963 🍺🅿️🚲🏊

27 WOOLHAMPTON LAKE & R KENNET
Secluded riverbanks and a secret lake; super handy with a pub, train station and cycle path. Head upstream 300m from The Rowbarge (RG7 5SH, 01189 712213) and turn L at footbridge to find track leading

to gravel lakeshore (200m). Or follow river downstream; a quiet wooded stretch passes the footbridge and continues about 1km arriving at an open area above the weirs, perfect for a picnic and dip (51.3920, -1.1549).
10 mins, 51.3934, -1.1844 🅿️🚆🏊🚲🍺🚶

28 SULHAMSTEAD, R KENNET
Beautiful open meadows and good access up and downstream of lock. Turn off A4 at Spring Inn, 3.5km W of M4 J12 at Reading, and find parking at second bridge (RG7 4BS). Old willows upstream. Path downstream past pretty swing bridge leads eventually (20 mins) to Sheffield Bottom Lock Lake (see above). Canoeing. National Cycle Route 4.
10 mins, 51.4186, -1.0999 🅿️🏊🚲

NORTH EAST OXON

29 BICESTER OUTDOOR SWIMMING LAKE £
Bordered by bulrushes, 200m rectangular, purpose built lake provides the perfect place to swim long lengths in the open air. Wooden saunas, cold plunges, hot showers and heated changing rooms. The post sauna cold bucket rinse is not to be missed, Green Lane, Chesterton, Bicester, OX26 1TH,

01869 241 204, bicestergym.co.uk
2 mins, 51.8880, -1.2044

30 CALVERT JUBILEE LAKE, CHARNDON
Quiet, remote wildlife-reserve lake, once a clay pit, now with blue waters. 1km NE of Charndon (on School Hill) turn L at junction (OX27 0BQ). 100m N of entrance to Great Moor Sailing Club find small parking on R. Be discreet and avoid if birdwatchers in hides. NT Claydon House close by.
5 mins, 51.9208, -1.0085

31 SHABBINGTON, R THAME
Pub with paddling and deeper swims downstream. Opp The Old Fisherman, Mill Road (HP18 9HJ, 01844 201247).
5 mins, 51.7538, -1.0330

32 HUGHENDEN STREAM
Lovely paddling in meadow, with deeper sections and a shallow lake just downstream, 200m. The NT estate also contains the largest horse chestnut in the UK, and was once home to Benjamin Disraeli. As you enter the estate (HP14 4LA) the stream is to your left, and you can park and walk down from the church.
10 mins, 51.6497, -0.7512

33 WEST WYCOMBE, R WYE
Downstream of the grand ornamental lakes, in the parkland below, is a secret river pool. Drop down to the meadow, by the waterfall and 'haha'. Follow the stream to the footbridge at the bottom. National Trust property (HP14 3AJ), with entrance fee.
10 mins, 51.6421, -0.7942

34 TRING BLUE LAGOON, FOLLY FARM
Popular but controversial chalk pit blue pool. Often fenced, sometimes accessible No Swimming, for information only. Chinnor pit lakes are also amazingly azure, but fenced off too (51.6919, -0.9055).
5 mins, 51.8179, -0.6354

HENLEY THAMES

35 SHIPLAKE, R THAMES
The rowing club quayside provides easy access to a huge lake-like stretch of the river. Parking end of Church Lane, RG9 4BS.
3 mins, 51.4968, -0.8941

36 ASTON FERRY & HENLEY, R THAMES
Open grassy river meadows and quiet lanes near a pub – great for family picnics. Or a walk downstream from Henley, past famous Temple Island at Remenham. It's a pretty drive to Aston on lanes from Henley via Remenham. Aston is signed off A4130 2km E of Henley. At Flower Pot Hotel (RG9 3DG, 01491 574721) follow Ferry Lane to small car park at end. Meadow is upstream to L.
3 mins, 51.5540, -0.8666

37 HURLEY ISLAND, THAMES
A historic village with wooded river islands and ancient pub. Park near the village hall and Olde Bell (SL6 5LX, 01628 825881). Follow lane to church and cross footbridge/lock to island. Bear R 200m to find beach and shallows on far side. Or don't cross but explore upstream for several places to swim, beyond the weir and Hurley Riverside

Campsite (SL6 5NE, 01628 824493).
15 mins, 51.5522, -0.8061

38 TAPLOW LAKE
Open-water swimming was introduced at Taplow Lakeside in 2020 and has gone from strength to strength. Taplow Lake is the result of one of the many gravel pits excavated to supply the road and construction industry. Loops of 100m and 400m are offered, as well as a variety of open-water swimming courses. Lifeguards are in attendance onshore and on paddleboards. On-site, Lake House Café dishes up tasty post-swim breakfasts, including imaginative vegetarian and vegan options. From Taplow station, head W on Approach Road for 600m; turn R and take Bath Road/A4; after 200m, turn L onto Amerden Lane bridleway. Taplow Lake will be on your L after 300m: taplowlakeside.co.uk
10 mins, 51.5210, -0.6927

39 BRAY LAKE, MAIDENHEAD
A whopping 50-acre stretch of water in the heart of the Berkshire countryside. Five swim loops are on offer: 150m, 250m, 400m, 750m and 1km. The lake is open Saturday and Sunday mornings during even the coldest months of the year. Teas,

coffees and brunch are served in the on-site clubhouse. Monkey Island Lane, SL6 2EB, 01628 638860, braylakeswimming.com
2 mins, 51.5000, -0.6887

40 DORNEY, JUBILEE RIVER
A wonderful wide offshoot of the Thames, lined by open fields, in an otherwise very built-up area by Slough and M4. Head for the bridge just past The Pineapple (SL4 6QS) on B3026/Lake End Rd between Slough (M4 J7) and Eton Wick, and find car park just after it. Explore up or downstream. Retire afterward for lunch at Crocus at Dorney Court, (SL4 6QP, 01628 669999). Cycle path 61 between Maidenhead or Windsor stations.
5 mins, 51.5056, -0.6566 ♿🏊🏄

COLN VALLEY

41 RICKMANSWORTH LAKES & R COLNE
Bury Lake was once a very famous swimming lake, now banned. To the W are three wilder lakes: Stockers, Springwell and Inns, where people dip discreetly if no anglers. Turn L off Uxbridge Rd (A412) on Drayton Ford/Springwell Ln, and find small car park on R after 300m (by WD3 8UR). Small wild fishing lakes are on either side

of road. Or continue another 300m to find track on L (Springwell Metal Recycling) along Colne stream (not the canal) NE to the shores of Stocker's Lake (51.6307, -0.4913). Rickmansworth tube is 2.5km (WD3 1FL).
10 mins, 51.6288, -0.4964 ❓🚉

42 RICKMANSWORTH, R CHESS
Pretty chalk stream deepens by a big willow on a bend with rope swing. Park at Scotsbridge play area or the Steakhouse carpark (WD3 1AT) and continue N 600m. It's also possible to dip in the little R Gade on Croxley Common (beach at 51.6414, -0.4421).
5 mins, 51.6494, -0.4662 💧

43 DENHAM WATERSKI CLUB 🅿
Superb Scandinavian log clubhouse, changing facilities, bar and spacious lakeside decking area give the swimming sessions a warm, friendly feel. Onsite shack supplying burgers and sausages. UB9 5HE, 01895 820007, denhamwaterski.com
2 mins, 51.5960, -0.5011

44 DENHAM LOCK WOODS
Four beautiful lakes alongside the Colne Valley Way. Sometimes used for fishing.

Country Park and nature reserves. All close to Uxbridge and Denham train stations. Park at Uxbridge Golf Club (with public bar and basic carvery, UB10 8AQ, 01895 272457) and follow footpath bearing L to lakes. Or access from Denham station on W side, 30 mins.
5 mins, 51.5695, -0.4782 🍴🅿❓

LONDON THAMES

45 ANKERWYCKE & RUNNYMEDE
Pasture and ancient trees along the banks of the Thames. Find the ruins of St Mary's Benedictine Priory, and a 2,000-year-old yew that was mentioned in the Domesday Book. Park in the NT Ankerwycke car park, Magna Carta Lane, off the Staines Rd/ B376 (TW19 5AD) then 700m walk. For something completely different, on the opp bank, about 10 mins drive (or swim), are the Runnymede 'Pleasure Grounds' park. It's a busy spot but there's a car park and cafe with a sweeping meander for a dip near the paddling pool, 200m (TW20 0AE, 51.4433, -0.5510).
10 mins, 51.4433, -0.5572

46 SILVERY SANDS, R THAMES

Wide, grassy meadows with sandy river beaches on the banks of the Thames. In summer the riverbank is alive with children messing around in boats and inflatables. Wholesome, free family fun. Wheatsheaf and Pigeon on Penton Road (TW18 2LL, 01784 452922) for a swift half on the way home. Turn R out of Staines station and walk 600m to end of Gresham Road; turn R onto Laleham Road; after railway bridge, turn L down path to find river; follow Thames Path downstream (left) for 1.6kmto Silvery Sands.

30 mins, 51.4172, -0.5114

47 CHERTSEY BRIDGE, R THAMES

Dumsey Meadow – a large area of undeveloped meadow and river bank – with several beaches, downstream of bridge. Find small car park 200m E of bridge on S side of Chertsey Bridge Rd (KT16 8LF).

5 mins, 51.3879, -0.4817

48 ALBANY REACH & HAMPTON CT

Quiet riverside beach with a gentle slope into the water. Be careful as the current can be strong here. Also keep an eye out for passing boats. The meadow overlooks Hampton Court Palace across the river and is a fine place to spend a family afternoon. From Thames Ditton station, take Speer Road, on E side of railway bridge; after 800m, at the roundabout, take second exit onto Aragon Avenue; after 300m, at the end of the road, walk through metal gate onto Albany Reach.

10 mins, 51.3985, -0.3365

49 HAM LANDS, TEDDINGTON OBELISK

Local nature reserve on edge of Richmond Park, with some beachy areas, upstream of Teddington Lock. Park on Riverside Drive (TW10 7NB) then 250m. Or 20 mins walk from Teddington station via the lock bridge island (which has a beach) and The Anglers pub (TW11 9NR, 020 8977 7475).

5 mins, 51.4333, -0.3266

LAKES & PONDS

50 WRAYSBURY & HORTON LAKES

Former gravel pits, rich in wildlife. People have swum here discreetly for decades but it's not officially permitted. From Wraysbury station southern platform exit, do not go up to the road but walk through a black-and-white metal gate 20m away on L. After 120m at clearing take path on R. After 30m follow path on left of RK Leisure sign. After 400m, at clearing, cross over the bridge on your L and follow path for about 400m to reach the lake. Or explore Horton lakes to the N of the station. Walk or park at end of Douglas Lane and head N on footpath, across rail tracks (51.4658, -0.5465).

30 mins, 51.4493, -0.53861

51 THE HAVEN, FELTHAM

Heavenly lake in a beautiful location. Hot and cold drinks and light refreshments are available at every session. Challenge Rd, TW15 1AX, loveopenwater.co.uk

20 mins, 51.4370, -0.4434

52 BOTANY BAY, VIRGINIA WATER

The lake beach at evocatively named Botany Bay overlooks the Roman ruins brought from Leptis Magna in Libya. However, for a discreet swim, the S bank of this huge lake is a bit quieter. A footpath follows the lake around the shore. Easiest entry from the car park by the Wheatsheaf Hotel (GU25 4QF) then bear R for Botany Bay or L for the S bank. 1 hour walk from Virginia Water station.

15 mins, 51.4112, -0.5965

53 LONGSIDE LAKE WATERSPORTS

A lovely huge expanse of water to swim in. You can swim around the island. TW20 8FA, 07894 153395, cjmskiandwake.com

5 mins, 51.4118, -0.5416

54 HEATH POND, CROWTHORNE

Birch and pine line this little lake in the woods. An island of pine trees beckons you to swim. Turn L from Crowthorne station and head to A321 roundabout (100m). Cross to R to find footpath. After 700m at diagonal crossroads by gate, take byway L into Simons Wood to find pond after 200m at crossroads (S of Hollybush Ride, RG40 3QL).

15 mins, 51.3697, -0.8352

55 CHOBHAM COMMON, SUNNINGDALE

Wild lake, an old fishing pond, among heather-filled heathland. About 2km S of Broomhall on B383, past SL5 0HY, find car park on L for Victoria Memorial. Cross road and find rough path W to lakes, 500m.

10 mins, 51.3824, -0.6198

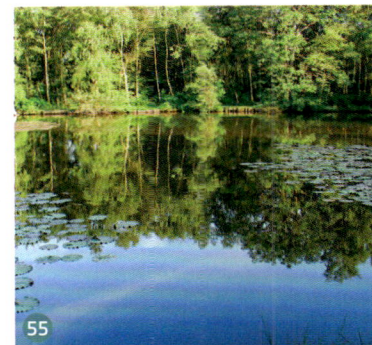

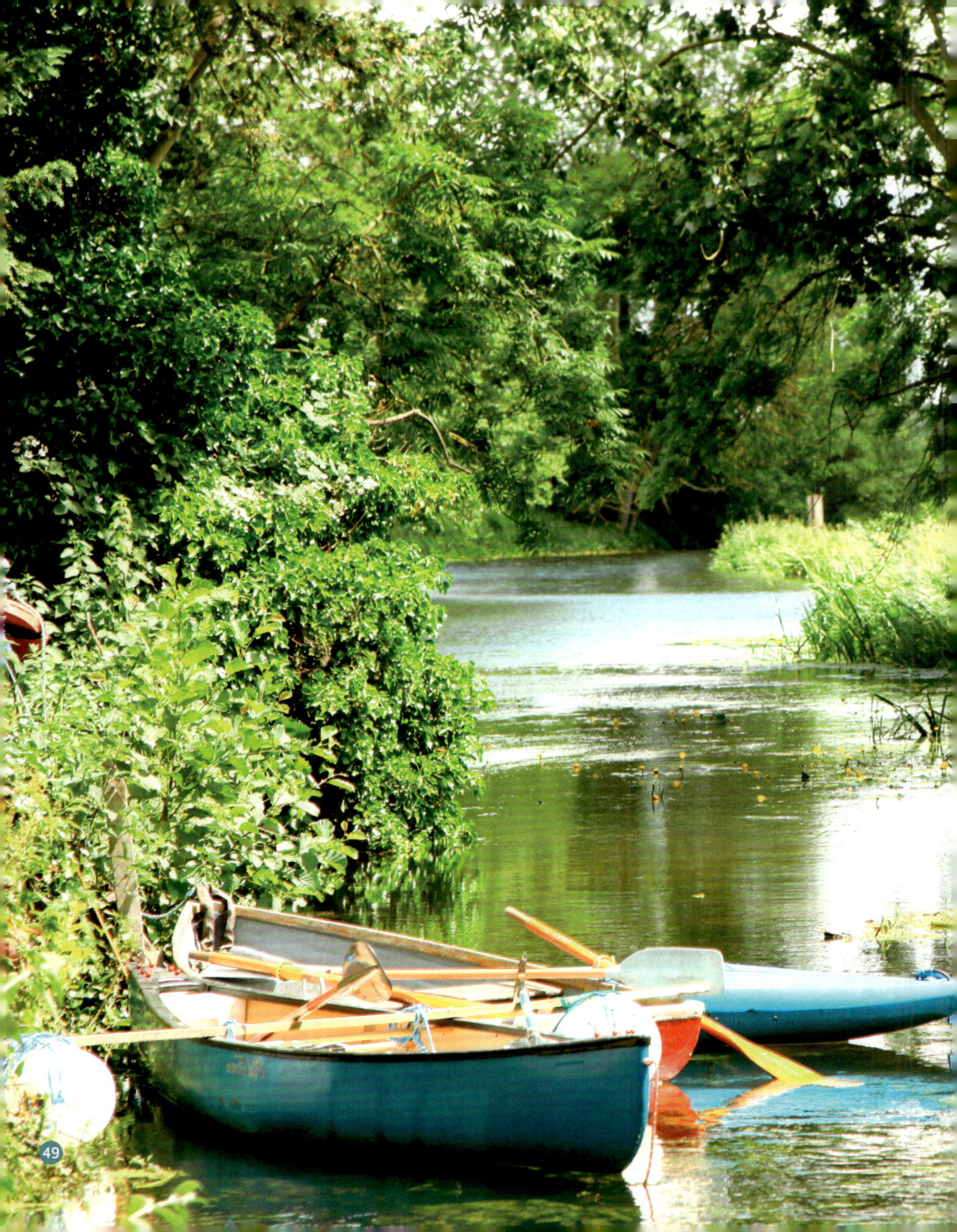

EAST ANGLIA

Take tea in the charming village of Grantchester and enjoy a long stretch of river and meadows that have changed little since Edwardian times (11).

Grantchester was already a fashionable location for Cambridge students when the boyish, charismatic, 22-year-old graduate Rupert Brooke became a resident in 1909, commuting to and from Cambridge in his canoe and often 'sitting in the midst of admiring females with nothing on but an embroidered sweater'. In Cambridge, it was an age of relaxed elegance: long walking tours, sleeping under canvas, picnicking on the grass, and naked bathing. Many brilliant young minds gathered around Brooke and his outdoor lifestyle.

Today, it seems little has changed along Grantchester Meadows. On a hot summer day, the languid mile-long stretch of river is dotted with leisurely picnic parties. Punts and canoes glide by, some heading downstream towards Cambridge's famous Backs, while others head upstream to the tea gardens in Grantchester village. You can hear the occasional splash as punters and picnickers jump into the river to cool off.

Paradise Pool is a narrow wooded area on the edge of town at the top end of the Meadows. There's a curly tree ideal for diving, but anywhere along the Meadows is good for swimming, particularly on the wide bends where the river deepens, often to over six feet. Be warned, though: while the river is clear, clean, and warm, the banks and bed are muddy and squelchy.

Many of East Anglia's rivers suffer from siltation and high quantities of fertiliser run-off, a side effect of the alluvial soils and intensive agriculture in the region. The Cam is actually one of the cleanest rivers in the area, though you should never swim in the actual city or along the Backs, where the sewers can harbour rats and Weil's disease.

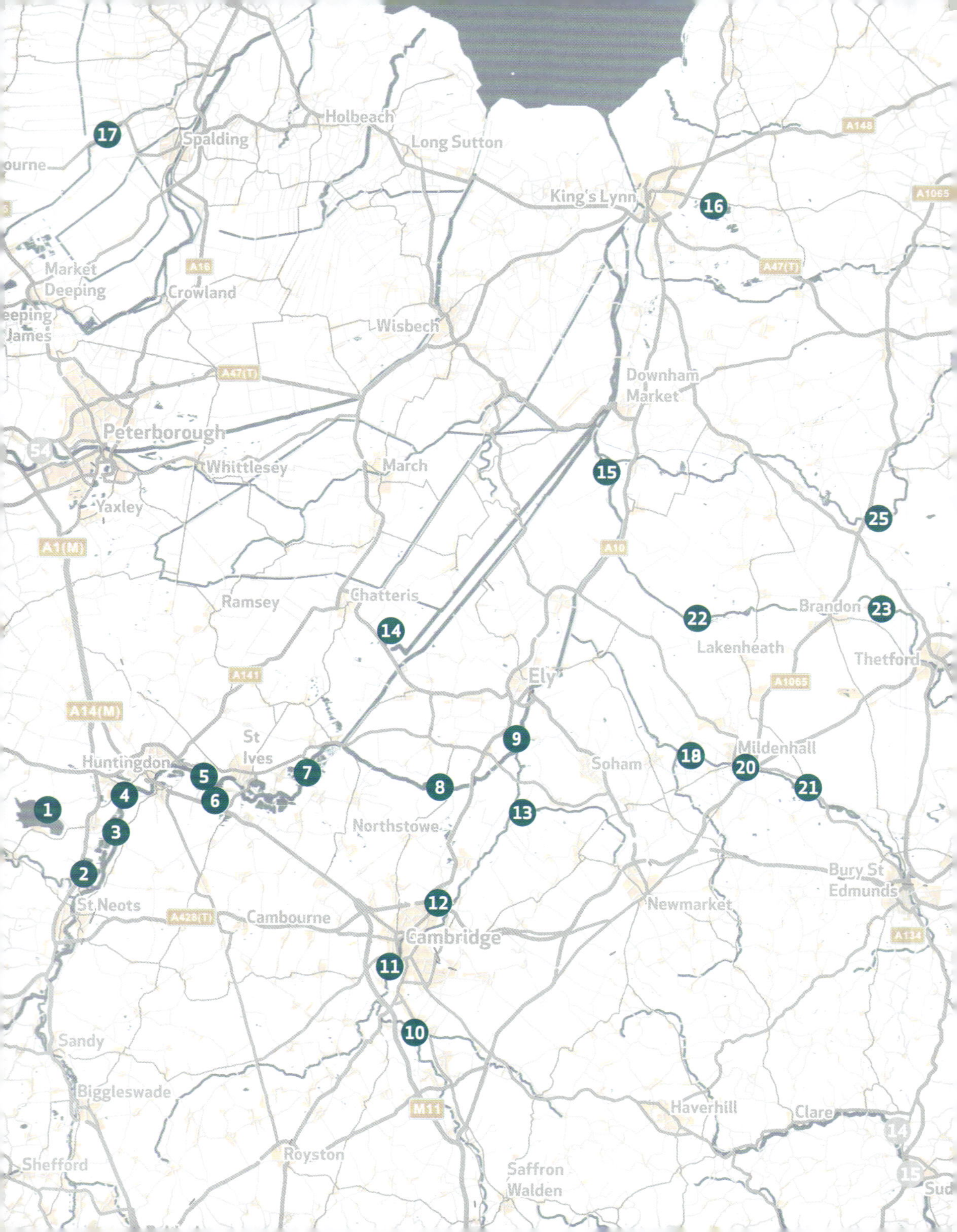

Holbeach
Spalding
Long Sutton
17
King's Lynn
16
A148
A1065
A16
Market Deeping
Crowland
A47(T)
Wisbech
A47(T)
Downham Market
Peterborough
54
Whittlesey
March
15
Yaxley
25
A1(M)
A10
Ramsey
Chatteris
14
22
Brandon
23
Lakenheath
Thetford
A141
Ely
A1065
A14(M)
9
St Ives
Huntingdon
Mildenhall
Soham
18
20
21
5
7
8
4
6
1
13
Northstowe
3
2
Bury St Edmunds
St Neots
A428(T)
Cambourne
12
Newmarket
Cambridge
A134
11
10
Sandy
Biggleswade
Haverhill
Clare
M11
14
Royston
Shefford
Saffron Walden
15

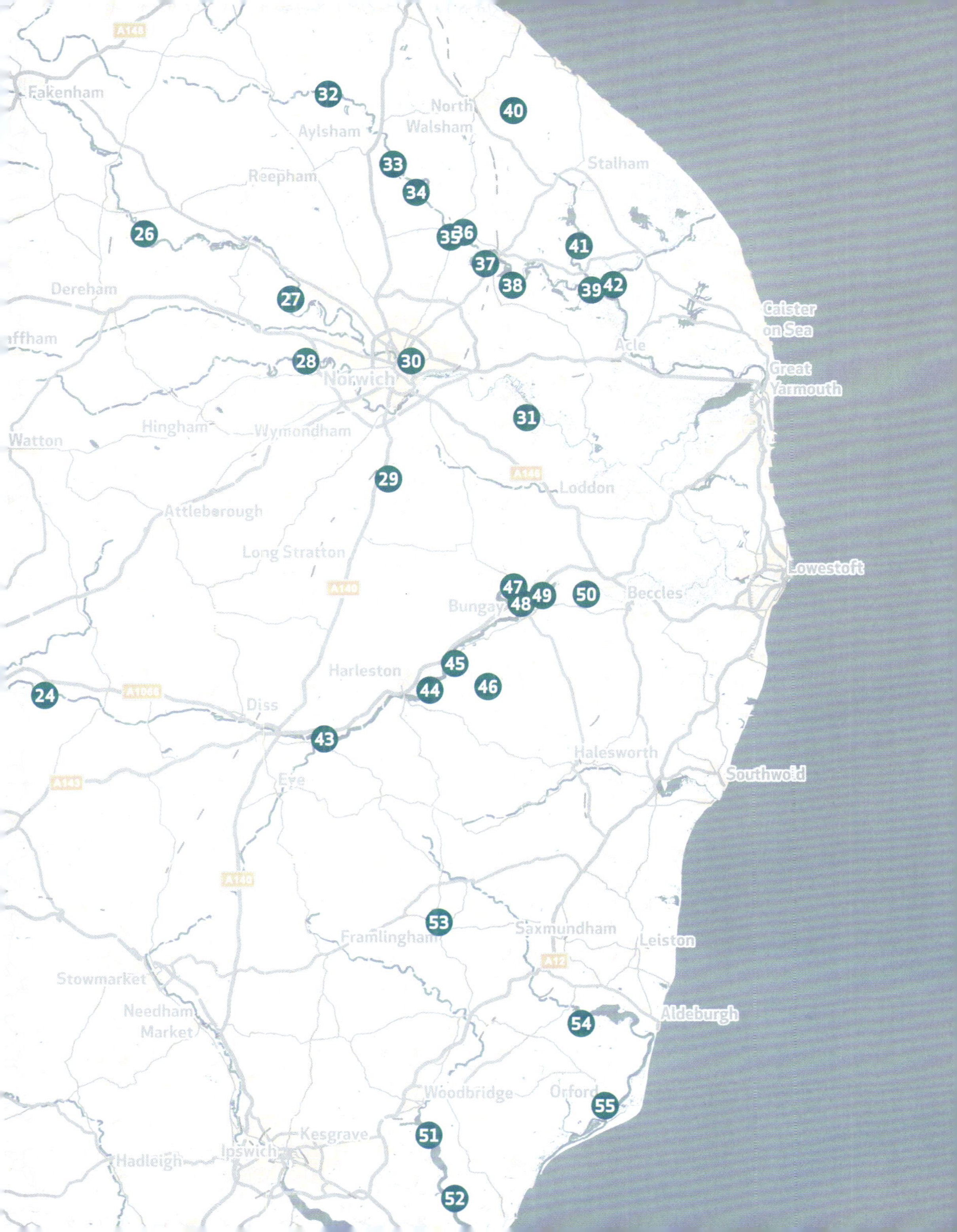
A148
Fakenham
32
North
Walsham
40
Aylsham
Stalham
33
Reepham
34
26
35
36
41
37
38
39
42
Dereham
27
Caister
on Sea
affham
Acle
28
30
Great
Yarmouth
Norwich
31
Hingham
Wymondham
Watton
A146
Loddon
29
Attleborough
Long Stratton
Lowestoft
A140
47
48
49
50
Beccles
Bungay
45
Harleston
44
46
24
A1066
Diss
43
Halesworth
Southwold
A143
Eye
A140
53
Saxmundham
Framlingham
Leiston
A12
Stowmarket
Needham
Market
54
Aldeburgh
Woodbridge
Orford
55
Kesgrave
51
Ipswich
Hadleigh
52

'In Grantchester their skins are white; They bathe by day, they bathe by night'

From 'The Old Vicarage, Grantchester,' Rupert Brooke, 1912

Grantchester village is a good place to end your explorations. The Orchard Tea Garden has served tea from its meandering gardens for well over a hundred years. A great sweep of meadow reaches down to the water's edge, and the deckchairs and low wicker tables are a wonderful place to refuel after a long punt or swim.

It was here that Brooke and the young Bloomsbury Group spent long summers camping and river bathing. Virginia Woolf, who once went naked night-swimming with Brooke near here, christened her Grantchester friends the 'Neo-Pagans'. Their vision was of a simpler, gentler lifestyle, closer to nature, with strong values of reciprocity and friendship.

These idyllic times in Cambridge were short-lived. Rupert Brooke died tragically just a few years later in the First World War, aged 28. He was widely recognised posthumously for his poetry, including 'The Soldier', and became a symbol of the innocence of youth and the appreciation of simple pleasures and pastimes. When his contemporary Bertrand Russell returned to Grantchester after the war, he said of Brooke's death: 'I am feeling the weight of the war much more since I came back here…with all the usual Grantchester life stopped. There will be other generations – yet I keep fearing that something of civilisation will be lost for good…'

So visit Grantchester, punt, and swim, and ensure Brooke's legacy lives on. Brooke would certainly be pleased to know that in 2024, Sheep's Green on the Cam was designated as a bathing water site, one of the first river sites in the UK, marking the culmination of a multi-year campaign led by the Cam Valley Forum, a local environmental group. The initiative began in 2020, inspired by the successful designation of the River Wharfe at Ilkley. It engaged over 500 residents, with 93% in favour of the designation, and recorded bathing rates of up to 478 bathers in a single day, all of which provided the necessary evidence. This serves as a case study for other groups, as the designation mandates regular water quality monitoring and compels water companies to address pollution issues. Anglian Water has since committed to investing £5 million to upgrade the Haslingfield sewage works. It's one of the key ways to drive improvement in our local rivers.

To the east of the region if Suffolk. As the Stour forms Suffolk's border with Essex, so the Waveney forms its border with Norfolk. The villages in the flat area between the rivers Blyth and Waveney, known as 'The Saints', boast no fewer than eleven medieval churches and provide the water for the famous local brewery of St Peter's (44-45). The Waveney was also the local river of Roger Deakin, the modern father of wild swimming, whose beautiful and seminal book, *Waterlog*, detailed his journey swimming through Britain by river, lake, and sea. Outney Common is one of the best places to swim, with excellent riverside access for more than a mile (47). Deakin paddled his canoe, 'Cigarette', along here as part of a Radio 4 documentary exploring the natural history of the river.

To the north the nearby landscape of the Norfolk Broads National Park is a unique low-lying patchwork of interlocking rivers and lakes. It was originally believed to have been formed as the result of natural processes. It was not until the 1950s that Joyce Lambert proved otherwise. She showed that the sides of the deep lakes should be gently sloping if naturally formed, but instead they were steep. She also analysed the high demand for peat as fuel in the Middle Ages, suggesting the lakes were, in fact, flooded peat quarries abandoned in the fourteenth century as sea levels began to rise and inundate them.

Once perfectly clean and clear, the Broads have suffered poor water quality due to agricultural runoff from intensive farming and sewage outflows during heavy rain, leading to severe eutrophication and ecological decline. The upstream reaches remain mostly clean, and the Bure, north of Buxton and Lamas, offers one of the prettiest river swimming stretches. Downstream, several projects are working to remove nutrients using reed bales. Significant restoration efforts are underway, particularly at sites like Barton and Hickling Broads, where clearer waters indicate recovery. Local campaigns, such as clean-up events led by Angling Direct and ongoing advocacy by the Broads Society, have played a vital role in lobbying water companies and farmers, tackling litter, and raising awareness. Projects like Hoveton Great Broad's ecological restoration offer hope, although more needs to be done over the coming years.

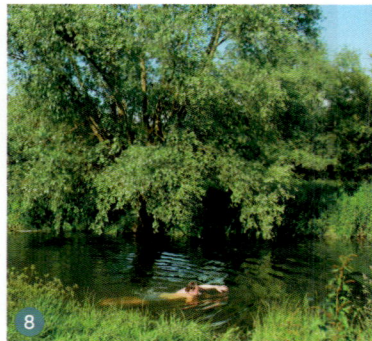

GREAT OUSE

1 GRAFHAM WATER 🅴
Secluded, sunny pebble beaches and lakeshore walking area. From Grafham village follow Church Hill to lane-end parking or follow footpath from behind church. No Swimming signs, so better to pay for an OWS session from main Grafham Water Visitor Centre 1km outside village (PE28 0BH, £7 on NOWCA app). Bike hire and refreshments available here too.
5 mins, 52.3033, -0.3028 ❓

2 SOUTHLAKE WATERPARK 🅴
Swim in sheltered freshwater lakes in the Cambridgeshire countryside. Lifeguarded OWS and other water sports with a café and hot showers. Turn off the A1 into Little Paxton, taking a sharp L off the High Street after the village. Follow the road taking a R then following the road L (Great N Rd, Little Paxton, PE19, 5YF 07377 949952, southlakewaterpark.co.uk).
5 mins, 52.2567, -0.2594

3 OFFORD CLUNY, R GREAT OUSE
A lovely downstream stretch of the river with many weir pools. Or head upstream to bathe opposite St Peter's Church. Find path between Buckden Marina (PE19 5QS) and the narrow bridge (Station Lane). Pass weir pool on L (swim if no fishermen) or continue, cross footbridge, and head upstream to opposite church (PE19 5RH), 800m.
10 mins, 52.2874, -0.2213

4 BRAMPTON, R GREAT OUSE
The river is wide and secluded with some beaches and diving spots. Approaching Brampton from S on B1514, turn R down River Lane by Notcutts Garden Centre (PE28 4NF). At bottom walk R upstream along riverbank.
2 mins, 52.3142, -0.2116

5 HOUGHTON MILL, R GREAT OUSE
Wide meadows and calm, deep water make this a brilliant summer location. There are fun millstreams for paddling and a NT mill and café too, plus you can hire rowing boats. The Mill is well signed from Houghton, on A1123 between Huntingdon and St Ives. Park at the Mill (PE28 2AZ, 01480 301494) and swim from here, or walk W down the path, beyond the caravan site, bearing R across the wooded mill streams to reach open riverbank. Or cross at the lock and explore the opposite bank (Hemingford Meadows), also accessible from Hemingford Abbots (PE28 9AR).
10 mins, 52.3282, -0.1171

6 LAKE ASHMORE, HEMINGFORD 🅴
Lifeguarded OWS in a grassy, tree lined gravel lake. NOWCA. Gore Tree Rd, PE28 9BP, 07894460784, lakeashmore.co.uk
2 mins, 52.3107, -0.1038

7 NEEDINGWORTH/OVER, R GREAT OUSE
The river flows through the empty meadow and lake landscape of Ouse Fen. From Needingworth follow signs to The Pike & Eel (Overcote Lane, PE27 4TW, 01480 463336) then follow the path N (downstream) to find a place to dip. Or access from Over on opposite bank. Rope swing upstream.
20 mins, 52.3314, 0.0055

8 UPPER CUTS, SETCHEL FEN
In remote open countryside, the Great Ouse has shrunk as it meanders through bucolic countryside. 4km N of Cottenham (B1049) park on track R, just before bridge and bend, and take river footpath upstream to L for up to 5km.
10 mins, 52.3215, 0.1631

9 LITTLE THETFORD, OUSE VALLEY WAY
Beautiful and wild, with 'Ship of the Fens' cathedral views to Ely. Little Thetford is just S of Ely off A10. Head to level crossing, cross over and bear R down track, then follow river.

10 mins, 52.3570, 0.2537

RIVER CAM

10 GREAT SHELFORD, R CAM
Clear river pool in the young Cam, with water lilies. Shelford Delicatessen on the High Street for afterwards. At far end of recreation ground. Entrance is almost opposite the deli (8a Woollards Lane, CB22 5LZ, 01223 846129).

5 mins, 52.1429, 0.135

11 GRANTCHESTER MEADOWS, R CAM
Over two miles of meadows and swimming from Sheep's Green (now with Designated Bathing Water Status) past Hodson's Folly, then through Grantchester Meadows, to The Orchard Tea Garden. Deep banks make this good for diving, but it can be muddy! Some weeds but clean. Continue walk to Grantchester to find popular swimming hole next to the Orchard Tea Gardens. From A603/Barton Rd take Grantchester St by lights and find footpath at bottom, L, heading to river and fallen tree 200m (Paradise Pool). Or continue and park in the car park at bottom of Grantchester Meadows. There's a good pool within 150m on a bend, or explore riverbank 30 mins to Grantchester tea rooms (CB3 9ND). For a longer riverside walk, set out from the The Mill (CB2 1RX) at Sheep's Green.

5 mins, 52.1907, 0.1046

12 MILTON COUNTRY PARK
Seasonal supervised OWS and full moon swimming in gravel lakes in the park (No Swimming other times). NOWCA booking app. Cambridge Road, Milton, CB24 6AZ, 01223 420060, miltoncountrypark.org

2 mins, 52.2371, 0.1619

13 WICKEN FEN, UPWARE
Filtered and purified by the reed beds of the famous nature reserve, Wicken Lode is clear, clean and beautiful. Be silent. Head for the Five Miles Inn in Upware near Wicken A1123 (CB7 5ZR, 01353 721654) with pleasant gardens along the River Cam (lots of river to explore along here). Turn R. After 200m take the footpath L by sluice/bridge leading to footbridge after 300m.

15 mins, 52.3033, 0.2613

FENS AND NENE

14 BLOCK FEN, MEPAL
Very remote, abandoned former sand and gravel pits and lakes used for angling, swimming and occasional jet-skiing. From Mepal take the A142 W, pass the outdoor centre (CB6 2AZ) on L and at roundabout take road signed Block Fen, which turns L to become a dirt road with lake to R and many more beyond. Nearby the New Bedford River at Sutton Gault (Gault Bridge, 52.3962, 0.0979) is desolate, long and straight.

2 mins, 52.4349, 0.1034

(PE11 3NG) on the A151 take Slipe Drove turn just S of river, follow approx 1.3km and park L next to the lone small barn. Cross ditch opposite barn and small, wooden bridge across the marsh at telegraph pole. Crest the levee to reach the river. Or walk along footpath from West Pinchbeck.

2 mins, 52.7962, -0.2370

RIVER LARK

18 JUDE'S FERRY, R LARK

Riverside pub and limit of the navigable section with excellent footpath access. Downstream is deeper but with boats. Isleham was a popular site for traditional 'total immersion' baptisms mentioned by Roger Deakin. Upstream was navigable until the 1920s all the way to Bury, so there are historic navigation rights and a system of 'staunch' locks (the first after 1km at King's Staunch, 52.3412, 0.4807, arrives opp bank to Worlington). Jude's Ferry pub for afterwards (IP28 8PT, 01638 712277).

5 mins, 52.3455, 0.4610

19 WORLINGTON, R LARK

Pretty riverside picnic area on this lovely chalk stream. Park respectfully on narrow lane by church (IP28 8SG) then follow footpath N for 400m.

5 mins, 52.3455, 0.4610

20 MILDENHALL, R LARK

Wooded river pools on riverside walk. Park on Old Mill Lane (52.3356, 0.5316), turn by Bull Inn (IP28 6AA, 01638 711001). Follow river path downstream 500m. Continue 1km to town river meadows. Across metal footbridge, then 300m, there are popular pools below sluices (or from King Street / Jubilee Fields car parks, IP28 7HG).

10 mins, 52.3372, 0.5262

21 ICKLINGHAM & CAVENHAM HEATH

Fun deepish pool under the bridge on t.ny lane, just E of the village off A1101 (signed 6'6"). Or more remote, follow West St from village (by old schoolhouse) and continue to Temple Bridge. Downstream are concrete weir pools. Or follow the river down through the open access land of Cavenham Heath (52.3264, 0.5784).

10 mins, 52.3227, 0.6005

LITTLE OUSE & WISS

22 LAKENHEATH FEN, R LITTLE OUSE

Remote and wild river swimming in the Little Ouse among lakes and a vast RSPB nature reserve, restoring a traditional fenland habitat. Take either

15 TEN MILE BANK, DOWNHAM MARKET

A quiet, broad stretch of the Great Ouse with pontoons and grassy banks N to Denver Sluice and S to Brandon Creek. A little lane, perfect for cycling, follows on one side and the Fen River Way footpath on the other. Remote, beautiful fenland. From the bridge at Ten Mile Bank (PE38 0HB, off A10 5km S of Downham Market roundabout) explore along the riverbank lane 5km N or S. Train at Downham Market and Littleport.

2 mins, 52.5525, 0.3586

16 BAWSEY COUNTRY PARK, KING'S LYNN ⓘ

Beautiful blue lake with sand beaches, birch-covered hill and heathland. Brickyard Lake is very popular for swimming but No Swimming and home to a monthly swim trespass, but you can enjoy the beach instead. N on A149 King's Lynn bypass. At hopsital take B1145 signed Gayton to find rough entrance on R after 3km.

5 mins, 52.7469, 0.4838 ⓘ

17 PINCHBECK SLIPE, R GLEN

Arrow-straight, slow-moving river in nature reserve of flood-meadows. Easy access to spot nesting birds and for a relaxing, secluded swim. From West Pinchbeck

of the downstream embankments, from Lakenheath Station. If you take the N bank you can continue as far as Shippea Hill Station to return by train (via Redmere Drove track 52.4581, 0.4189, about 9km). Or there's bumpy off road byway access 4km to Botany Bay 52.4479, 0.4674.
5 mins, 52.4454, 0.4674

23 SANTON DOWNHAM & BRANDON LOCK
Pretty chalk stream by bridge at St Helen's picnic spot (IP27 0TT) in Thetford Forest. Chalky riverbed, beach up to 1m deep and rope swing. There's a very cute single nave church here too. It's a 4km riverside walk from Brandon Station. Or swim downstream of Brandon below the weir/lock where it's much deeper and better for a long swim. Walk down on riverside path from Ram Inn on High Street (IP27 0AX) or park at leisure centre and take track (Church Rd, IP27 0JB).
2 mins, 52.4530, 0.6863

24 KNETTISHALL HEATH, R LITTLE OUSE
Sandy beach and pretty, shallow weir pool, next to car park and fields. Perfect for picnics and little ones. From A1066, 2 miles W of Garboldisham, take road S signed Gasthorpe. R at crossroads after a mile signed 'Country Park' to find

parking and river on R after a mile.
2 mins, 52.3899, 0.8725

25 LYNFORD WATER, ICKBURGH WISSEY
Wonderful series of sandy bays and lakes among trees. Lynford Arboretum opposite. N of Mundford (A1065) turn R down Lynford Road a mile, past Lynford Hall Hotel, to find Lynford Water car park on L, then 200m N. Supervised OWS through peakopenwatersports.com You can also try the fun plunge pool below the weir 1km upstream on the R Wissey (52.5224, 0.6972, also driveable at lane end, through Ickburgh village).
2 mins, 52.5194, 0.6821

WENSUM & YARE

26 SWANTON MORLEY, R WENSUM
Family friendly river beach and paddling, weir and rope swing. Head N out of Swanton Morley, past church, until road swings round to R after ¾ mile to find bridge and gate on L. Further weir 300m upstream.
5 mins, 52.7268, 0.9909

27 RINGLAND RIVER GREEN, R WENSUM
A small pretty village green area by the river with paddling and rope swings, by little road

143

32 BLICKLING MILL, R BURE

Lovely clear pool below mill with paddling and a deeper section where water rushes out from under the arches. Interesting pyramid mausoleum in nearby Blickling Estate Woods. On tiny lanes (NR11 6PX) between Itteringham and Ingworth, ½ mile N of NT car park on the NW of the Blickling Estate, from which you can also follow woodland walk E to the mausoleum 52.8193, 1.2135. 20 mins, 52.8279, 1.2099

33 BURGH NEXT AYLSHAM & OXNEAD

Gorgeous, easy church-side swim downstream of wooden footbridge. Park on lane by church (NR11 6TR) and follow track adjacent. 1km downstream is more beautiful, easy riverside with very few boats. Park at Oxnead Bridge and swim down to the mill (52.7681, 1.2980). 2 mins, 52.7770, 1.2869

34 BUXTON MILL POOL, R BURE

A huge mill pool with a strong race, right by the road. More secluded upstream. Look for a large white mill building (NR10 5JE) just outside Buxton on the road to Lamas. Upstream footpath is on the river's R bank, accessed via front of mill. Also on the Bure Valley Railway from Wroxham. 5 mins, 52.7566, 1.3144

35 HORSTEAD, R BURE

Popular swim spot with big bubbly pools below the bridge/sluices at Horstead Mill (park on Mill Rd, NR12 7AU). Or upstream of the village find hidden wooden platform behind the Tithe Barn, keep church on L (Rectory Rd, NR12 7EP, 52.7303, 1.3508). It can be weedy in summer but this 2km stretch of river up to Mayton Bridge at Little Hautbois (NR12 7JR, with small car park) is idyllic and perfect for canoes. The riverside path runs along the N bank. 3 mins, 52.7242, 1.3551

36 COLTISHALL RISING SUN, R BURE

Swim upstream towards Horstead or downstream towards Belaugh from the grassy banks near this village pub. The Rising Sun (NR12 7EA, 01603 737440) is on Wroxham Road coming E out of Coltishall. Enter the river via the ladder on the green to the L of the pub as you face the river, near a wooden footbridge. 4 mins, 52.7277, 1.3710

37 CAEN MEADOW, R BURE

Gradual sloping entry on a sandy beach into the clear water of the River Bure, at the

in summer. From Newton Flotman take the A140 N and then take the second R onto Mill Lane. There is space for a few cars to park just before the ford. The road through the ford is now closed to traffic, but you can cycle or walk across the footbridge. The roads to the E are perfect for cycling. Entry into the shallows near the road. Near the bridge, you can swim against the current in deeper water. 1 mins, 52.5471, 1.2815

30 COW TOWER, R WENSUM

Swim under an artillery tower built in the 12th century to defend Norwich from France, and from English rebels entering the city by the river. Park at St Helen's Wharf or free parking nearby on a Sunday. Keeping the river on your L, follow Riverside Walk until you see the tower, where entry to the river is to the R along the bank. Swim upstream to the L. 5 mins, 52.6339, 1.3084

31 ROCKLAND BROAD, R YARE

Broad river swims on the less touristy R Yare river. Watch out for boats. From the Rockland Staithe car park (NR14 7HP), walk on footpath NE to the Broads. 10 mins, 52.5920, 1.4460

bridge. Parking adjacent (NR8 6HX). 1 mins, 52.6792, 1.1651

28 BAWBURGH MILL, R YARE

Popular with families, dip in a millpond then picnic along the river. Harts Lane runs through Bawburgh. Park next to the green near the King's Head. Cross the grass and enter the water via the sloped bank. 2 mins, 52.6338, 1.1833

29 SHOTESHAM FORD, R TAS

A refreshing ford surrounded by trees off quiet country lanes. Popular with local swimmers all year round, and with families

bottom of a picturesque meadow, perfect for a long midsummer picnic. Coming into Wroxham from the S, turn L off Norwich Road after the petrol station onto Castle Street then turn R onto Church Lane. There is space to park, respecting residents' parking. Go through the wooden gate at the entrance to the meadow. After a short path, you will see the meadow and river.
4 mins, 52.7049, 1.3969

38 SALHOUSE BROAD, WOODBASTWICK
One of the few Broads lakes you can easily swim in, with beachy area and canoe hire. Car park on N side of road ½ mile W of the Fur and Feathers (NR13 6HQ, 01603 720003) in Woodbastwick. Pretty walk from car park and WC. Lakeside refreshments at The Hungry Otter.
15 mins, 52.6893, 1.4288 🏊🛶🖼️

39 ST BENET'S ABBEY, R BURE
Riverside Anglo-Saxon monastery, abandoned in the 1530s. Ruined windmill inside. Busy, open Broads stretch, so watch for boats. It's a high bank but there's a small beach 200m downstream towards cross. Car park at end of several unsigned lanes S of Ludham (52.6884, 1.5222).
5 mins, 52.6858, 1.5231

RIVERS ANT & THURNE

40 EBRIDGE MILL
A large millpond in the North Walsham & Dilham Canal, popular with local swimmers. Take Happisburgh Road SE out of N Walsham for 2 miles until you reach the free car park on R. Cross the small wooden bridge over the lock to find the metal steps into the pond. The Canal Trust allows swimmers and sometimes you'll share the space with model boat enthusiasts.
2 mins, 52.8160, 1.4300

41 HOW HILL, RIVER ANT
Classic Broads river with three windmills, How Hill Trust (free Secret Gardens) and Toad Hall Cottage museum. How Hill car park (52.7162, 1.5108) and then follow footpath down to museum. Turn R and head upstream 200m where the busy broad widens a little and is less busy. Tricky entry through reeds/steep banks.
5 mins, 52.7178, 1.5083 🏊🖼️🍴

42 WEAVER'S WAY, R THURNE
Swim from the reeds with windmills on the skyline at this wide, wild and iconic stretch of the Broads. Thurne is signed off the B1152 about halfway between Acle and

Martham/Potter Heigham. Head for The Staithe (NR29 3BU) opposite the Lion Inn (NR29 3AP, 01692 670796). Walk down to the main river then head upstream/N for 10 mins and enter the river through the reeds (watch for boats). Camping at Clippesby Hall (NR29 3BL, 01493 367800) and Bureside Holiday Park (NR29 3BW, 01493 369233).
10 mins, 52.6897, 1.5488 🏊🛶🖼️ℹ️⛺

RIVER WAVENEY

43 HOXNE, R WAVENEY
Long stretch of river, with multiple rope swings and a ladder for access. Hoxne

is a charming, mid-Suffolk village with interesting history. Head to The Swan Inn afterwards. Park in the village, then walk N, uphill, towards Green St, then turn R to Water Mill Lane and after 100m bear L, down Fisher's Lane. Follow riverside path 500m, cross bridge and turn L.

15 mins, 52.3579, 1.2053

44 MENDHAM, R WAVENEY

A wild, wonderful, meandering stretch of the mid-Waveney – warm and not too deep. Otters, kingfishers, and overhanging willows. From Mendham Road Bridge (IP20 0NH) walk downstream on left bank (fishing path) for 200m to pool. Or upstream through meadows to wild, hidden reedy pools (bear L on footpath from church in Mendham and ½ mile to reach the river).

10 mins, 52.3934, 1.3307

45 HOMERSFIELD, R WAVENEY

Secluded river dip with swing. Then visit nearby St. Peter's brewery for local ales (NR35 1NQ, 01986 782322). 2 miles N of Mendham (IP20 0NH) on a tiny lane (Regional Cycle Route 40) find footpath on L after IP20 0NS, just before Valley Farm on R at fork.

2 mins, 52.4129, 1.3605

46 SOUTH LAKE, SOUTH ELMHAM

Secluded one-acre lake set in a wildflower meadow, IP20 0PS. No lifeguards, basic changing facilities. Summer only. wildswimsouthelmham.co.uk 07879697427

5 mins, 52.3961, 1.3998

47 OUTNEY COMMON, R WAVENEY

Ancient common land, popular for canoeing and swimming. Turn off A143 onto B1332 at the roundabout signed Ditchingham and find footpath/track immediately on L (parking at Smokey Joes, NR35 2JL, 01986 894776). Follow path through woods, then bear L over bridge. Bear R along river bank to large pool with willows and sandy bottom, plus rope swing (500m). Or keep exploring upstream. Canoe hire from Outney Meadow Caravan Park (NR35 1HG, 01986 892338)

10 mins, 52.466, 1.4325

48 FALCON MEADOW BUNGAY, R WAVENEY

Lovely riverside meadows in backwaters of this small free-spirited town with many independent cafés and shops. Park along Ditchingham Dam (NR35 2JG).

5 mins, 52.4572, 1.4413

49 WAINFORD WEIR, R WAVENEY

A long swim through the Broads along the River Waveney to Ellingham, then enjoy a secluded sauna. From Mettingham head W on the B1062 and turn R onto Wainford Road, going over two bridges. Park in the layby on R then return over one bridge and turn R through a gate. Access to the river is on a shallow channel to the left of the weir via a platform. The nearby Secret Sauna can be hired by groups (secretsauna.com). Great coffee spot in The Silo for afterwards (NR35 2RU).

2 mins, 52.4582, 1.4575

50 GELDESTON LOCKS, R WAVENEY

Descend a ladder into the tidal River Waveney behind The Locks Inn. Swim upstream then enjoy a pint in this community owned pub (NR34 0HS, 01508 830033, thelocksinn.com). Leaving Gillingham to the W, continue 2km into Geldeston then turn L onto Station Road, and L again onto Lock's Lane. Behind the beer garden you will find the boating ladder. You can also access the river on the other side of the footbridge (52.4631, 1.5157) although this can be muddy and difficult to exit at low tide.

5 mins, 52.4633, 1.5169

SOUTHERN SUFFOLK

51 WALDRINGFIELD, R DEBDEN

A pretty village on SW shore of the R Deben with easy access to wide stretch of river. It's best to swim at high tide due to muddy bank and currents. Watch out for boats from the sailing club. Big car park behind the Maybush Inn (IP12 4QL).

2 mins, 52.0690, 1.3301

52 RAMSHOLT & METHERSGATE QUAY

A small shoreside hamlet with pub on the NE bank. Wide, atmospheric stretch of river and interesting birdlife. High tide due to muddy bank. Watch out for boats and strong currents. Park by Ramsholt Arms (IP12 3AB, 01394 411209). For something much more remote, there's a quay with ladder and beach 3km upstream at Methersgate. Footpath from All Saints Church Sutton (IP12 3DU) via Methergate Hall to 52.0690, 1.3298 (or canoe up with the flow).

2 mins, 52.0228, 1.3613

53 FRAMLINGHAM MERE AND RUINS

Beautiful lake below the ruins of Framlingham Castle. Take New Rd N from the mini-roundabout in Well Close Square (IP13 9DS) then find footpath on R after 300m. Lots of local cafés and gastro food at The Crown Hotel (IP13 9AP, 01728 723521).

3 mins, 52.2252, 1.3416

54 IKEN CLIFF, SNAPE

Old-world tidal backwater with lagoon, beach and riverside church. High-tide swimming in water warmed over mud flats. Canoe hire (Apr–Oct, 07979517186, Ikencanoe.co.uk). Turn off B1069 just S of Snape Maltings, signed Orford. Then L after a mile (Iken), then first L to picnic parking (IP12 2EN).

2 mins, 52.1511, 1.511

55 ORFORD QUAY & BUTLEY JETTY

Pretty Orford has a popular quay. The River Alde is tidal and can have strong currents. Multiple points of access around the quay. But from main car park bear L for a sheltered section between the quay and Orford Sailing Club. Watch out for boats. A circular walk could take you downstream and back up Butley Creek a remote tidal creek with rowboat ferry jetty to jump from, at high tide only (52.0804, 1.4905).

2 mins, 52.0909, 1.5395

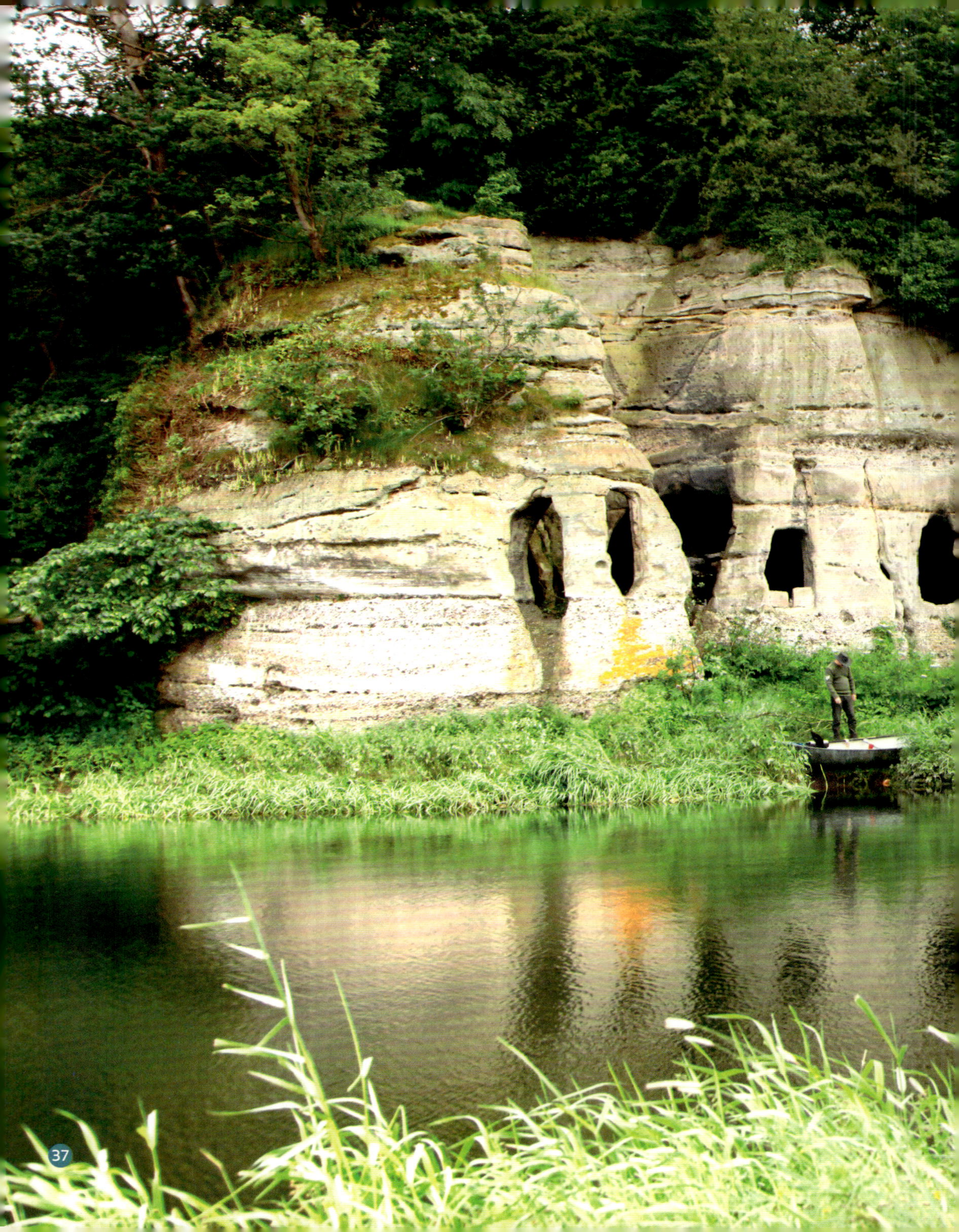

SOUTHERN MIDLANDS

The great River Trent, artery of the vast coalfields and industrial heartlands of the East Midlands, collects rivers from far and wide, including major rivers like the Derwent, Dove, and Tame. Just shy of the Thames in total length, it passes through some beautiful swimming scenery. Essex Bridge (22), the longest packhorse bridge in the UK, with 14 of its original 40 arches remaining, was built in 1550 for Queen Elizabeth I. Above it lies the forested Cannock Chase, which features a series of lakes and pools on Stony Brook (25).

Downstream, near Derby, seek out the extraordinary caves of 'Anchor Church,' carved out by the river and inhabited by hermits and saints since the sixth century (37). In earlier history, the river was a major transport route for the coalfields, but since their decline, the National Forest project has begun regenerating former colliery pits and slag heaps. One of the prettiest sites is at Oakthorpe, a perfect vision of regeneration (35). This once-bustling colliery is now meadow and woodland, and where the land subsided from a subterranean mine collapse, a wild lake has formed, waiting for you to take a dip.

To the east, Rutland may be the smallest county in England, but not in vision. When Rutland Water opened in the 1970s, it marked a bold shift in how reservoirs were conceived—not just as utilitarian infrastructure, but as places for people. Built by Anglian Water with recreation at its heart, it was one of the first reservoirs in Britain to feature a public beach, complete with imported sand and designated swimming zones (53). This progressive attitude stood in contrast to the more restrictive policies seen elsewhere, where reservoirs were often fenced off and guarded against human contact. At Rutland, however, visitors were invited in: to swim, to sail, to picnic on the shores and explore nature reserves teeming with birdlife. It embodied the spirit of the 1973 Water Act, which encouraged water authorities

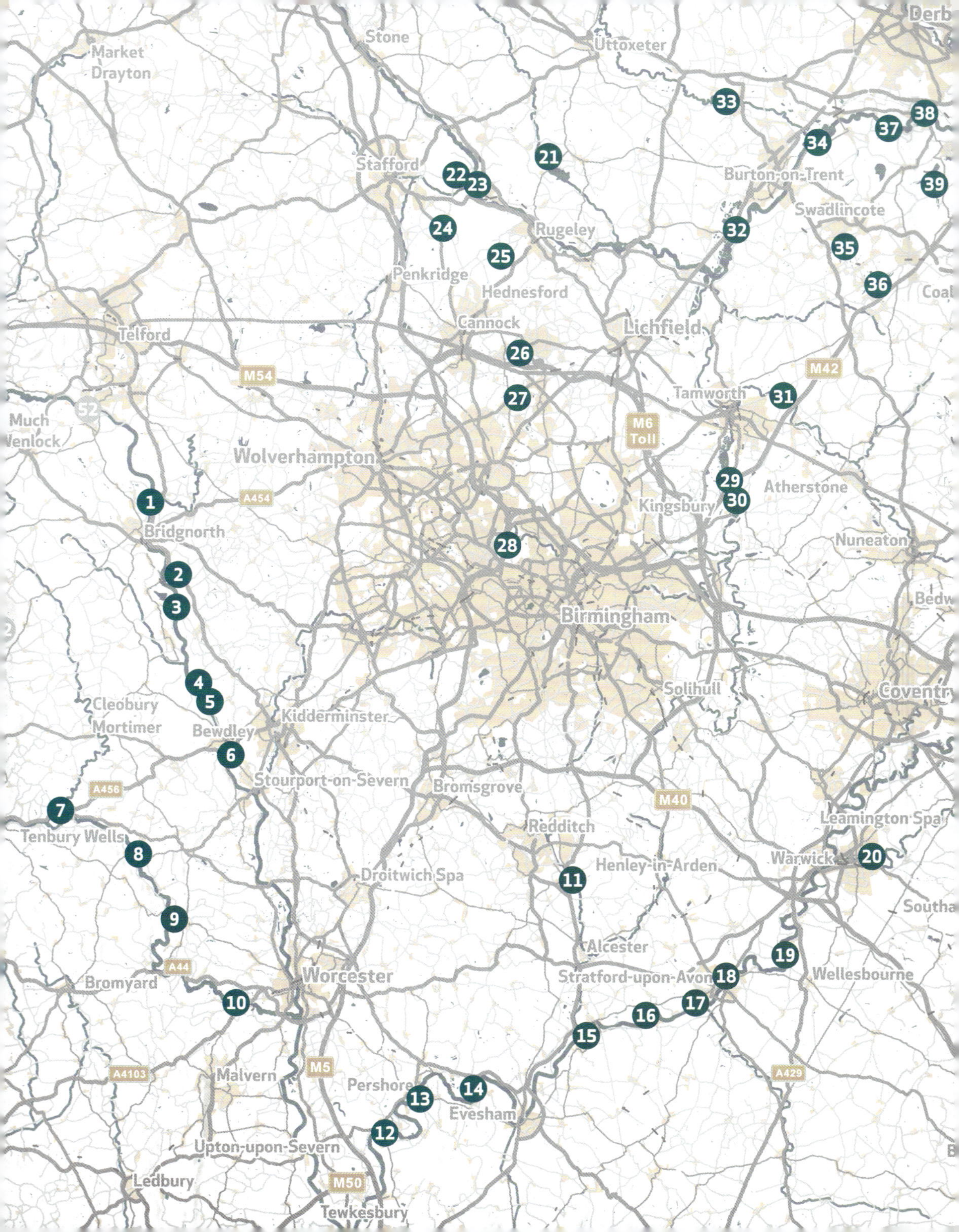

Stone
Uttoxeter
Derb
Market Drayton
33
38
37
34
21
Stafford
22
23
Burton-on-Trent
39
Swadlincote
24
32
Rugeley
35
25
Penkridge
36
Hednesford
Coal
Cannock
Lichfield
Telford
26
M54
M42
Tamworth
31
27
Much Wenlock
M6 Toll
Wolverhampton
29
Atherstone
1
A454
30
Kingsbury
Bridgnorth
28
Nuneaton
2
3
Birmingham
Bedw
4
5
Solihull
Coventr
Cleobury Mortimer
Kidderminster
Bewdley
6
Stourport-on-Severn
Bromsgrove
A456
M40
7
Leamington Spa
Tenbury Wells
Redditch
8
Henley-in-Arden
Warwick
20
11
Droitwich Spa
Southa
9
Alcester
19
Stratford-upon-Avon
18
Wellesbourne
Bromyard
A44
Worcester
10
17
16
15
A4103
M5
Malvern
A429
Pershore
14
13
Evesham
12
Upton-upon-Severn
Ledbury
M50
Tewkesbury

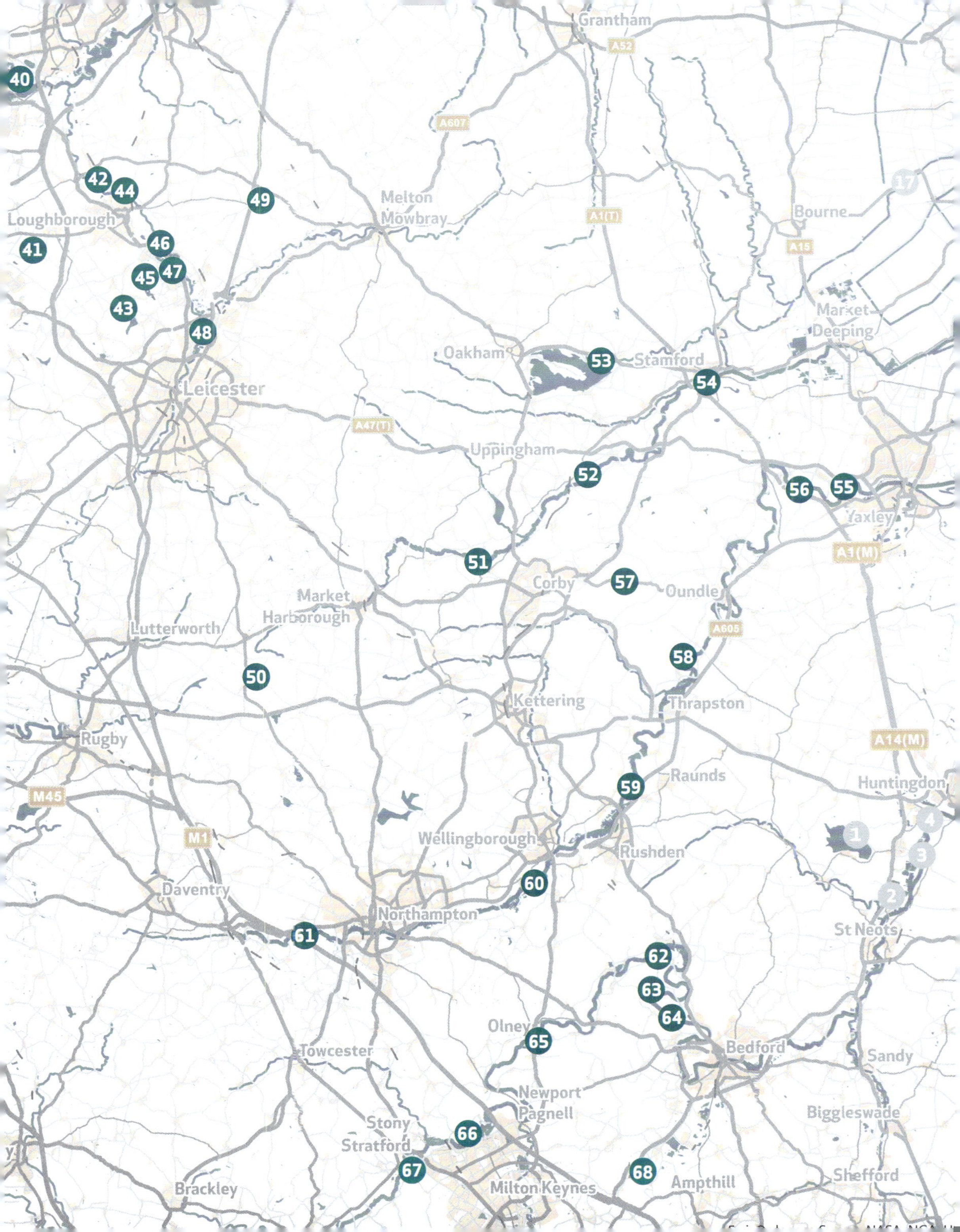
Grantham
A52
40
A607
42
44
49
Melton Mowbray
A1(T)
17
Bourne
Loughborough
46
41
A15
45
47
43
Market Deeping
48
Oakham
53
Stamford
54
Leicester
A47(T)
Uppingham
52
56
55
Yaxley
51
A1(M)
Corby
57
Oundle
Market Harborough
Lutterworth
A605
58
50
Kettering
Thrapston
Rugby
A14(M)
59
Raunds
Huntingdon
M45
4
1
M1
Wellingborough
Rushden
3
60
Daventry
2
Northampton
61
St Neots
62
63
64
Olney
65
Bedford
Sandy
Towcester
Newport Pagnell
Biggleswade
Stony Stratford
66
67
68
Ampthill
Shefford
Brackley
Milton Keynes

to actively facilitate public enjoyment, including swimming, the most accessible water sport of all. Decades later, Rutland Water remains a model for how access, conservation and utility can coexist—an early and enduring example of water managed for both people and purpose. In a similarly hopeful initiative, Severn Trent Water's £78 million Green Recovery Bathing Rivers programme, seeks to upgrade over 49 km of river, primarily the River Leam upstream of Leamington Spa (20), by reducing sewage spills through storage capacity and surface water seperation.

Olney is to the south, a charming market town on a beautiful stretch of the River Great Ouse that has long held a tradition of river bathing (64). Just downstream from the stone bridge at the town's north end is a historic bathing place—once popular with Victorian and Edwardian swimmers. The river here is wide and gently shelving, and the meadows on both banks offer grassy access and space to spread a towel or picnic blanket. You'll find remnants of steps or stonework where locals used to wade in, and in summer, children still paddle while families picnic under weeping willows. Upstream and downstream of Olney, you'll find long, meandering sections through pasture and wooded banks, with deeper pools, slower bends, and fewer people. These spots are less formal, but often more magical—perfect for a quiet dip, a heron's call echoing in the still air.

In the south-west of the region, the Malvern Hills in western Gloucestershire rise suddenly and steeply, affording views out of proportion to their modest height. From here, you can see across the plains of the Severn, towards Shakespeare's Avon and the Midlands. The rocks of the Malverns are hard and resilient, and some of the most ancient on the planet, formed more than 600 million years ago. The curative powers of the spring waters that well up beneath them are among the best known in the world: Tennyson came here after a nervous breakdown, Florence Nightingale stayed in 1897, and Charles Darwin visited three times.

The waters were first bottled over 150 years ago and have been consumed by the royal family for more than a century. If you want to drink the water, there are over 70 drinking fountains dotted across the hills, but if you want to swim in it, there is only Gullet Quarry. This old stone quarry opened in 1818 as a source of stone for Malvern town. The cliffs and crevices that surround it have quickly returned to nature in the thirty years since it closed, and the famous spring waters have filled it, creating an aquamarine amphitheatre over 100 metres wide. It's a deep and wild place, like journeying to the centre of the earth. As I swam under the tectonic folds and curling faults laid down during the earth's early formation, buzzards circled high above, alighting on the cliff-top trees. I pondered the aeons of time and great subterranean forces condensed in the tiny crucible around me and I felt rather small and insignificant. (Sadly, due to a number of tragic drowings of young lads, swimming is now prohibited and the site is heavily fenced. It is no longer included in the listings).

The Vale of Gloucester stretches beneath and carries the wide meanders of the River Severn in its final stages before reaching the estuary. The Severn is the longest river in the UK, and I was keen to try swimming in it. There are a number of pleasant spots, such as Trimpley, Arley and the Old Foot Ferry (3-5). Near Worcester the Teme joins and upstream Bransford Bridge is a superb deep gladed meader with jumps (10).

I was also keen to explore Shakespeare's countryside from the winding perspective of the Warwickshire Avon. Much of the river is navigable, which means the water is always deep and there are no problems with access, but large boats cannot pass beyond Stratford. Up to Warwick, the river is wild and even more beautiful beautiful, such as Alveston and Hamton Lacey (19).

I set off late in the day from Charlecote Mill, one of only a small handful of surviving commercial working watermills in the UK. Most of the processes are as they would have been over 200 years ago, and wherever possible, grain is still sourced from local farms. I dawdled downstream long into the warm evening before stopping for the night among tall grasses on a remote section of bank.

That summer night, as darkness fell, I strung up the hammock and watched a full moon rise across the meadows. Then, at around eleven o'clock, when the moon was bright, I slipped into the water. The river was silent, and the swans were sleeping in the reeds. There was just the soft sound of the water trickling as I broke the pool of silver light. Unzipping my tent early the next morning, the sweet fresh river beckoned for another swim. Dew had covered everything but was burning off quickly as I struck camp, and I covered several pre-breakfast miles before arriving at Stratford-upon-Avon for a superb riverside brunch (18).

SEVERN & TEME

1 ASTLEY ABBOTTS, RIVER SEVERN
A delightful dip in the Severn from a secluded section of riverbank. From B4373 N out of Bridgnorth turn R onto Stanley Lane. Follow 2km, past golf club, to WV16 4SR and here turn R house to park on L before gated road. Path to river is at corner of road to R.
5 mins, 52.5562, -2.4072

2 COMER WOODS, DUDMASTON
A lovely woodland walk and cycle route past the secluded Brim Pool. A great picnic spot on the grassy banks. Head S on A442 from Bridgnorth. Just after Quatford (WV15 6QL) NT Comer Woods pay car park signed L for easy cycle access to extensive paths. Or 2.4km after Quatford, opp entrance to Dudmaston Estate (NT), turn L signed Claverley and park in Old Sawmill car park R after 600m. Walk back to signed footpath opp just before farm building. Follow path to woods and turn L. Brim Pool is furthest.
15 mins, 52.5012, -2.3725

3 THE OLD FOOT FERRY, RIVER SEVERN
A delightful swim in the River Severn where the old chain ferry used to cross. A great place to launch a kayak to Upper Arley. From E of the River Severn, head S from Bridgnorth on A422. After 7.2km, turn R at signs for Hampton Loade and parking for River Severn. Car park at end of road, next to river. NT pay car park.
1 mins, 52.4764, -2.3745

4 UPPER ARLEY, RIVER SEVERN
A wide and tranquil section of the Severn, perfect for a swim or launching a kayak or paddleboard. The Riverside Tearoom serves delicious, home-made refreshments and lunches. This is also a stop on the Severn Valley Railway with walks along the Severn Way. From E of the River Severn, head onto Arley Lane from A442 N of Kidderminster. Park in riverside pay car park. From W head to Arley car park (DY12 3NF) from B4194 N of Bewdley. Footbridge across river. A good exit point for a longer kayak down from The Old Foot Ferry (see listing).
2 mins, 52.4191, -2.3467

5 TRIMPLEY, RIVER SEVERN
A tranquil walk through dappled sunlit woods down to the reservoir and river. Various entry points to the river and an island to swim to and explore. No Swimming policy on the deep, man-made reservoir, which has a pumped-in supply. Head in N out of Trimpley, turn L signed Trimpley Reservoir, dir DY12 1PH. Reservoir car park L after 2km. Walk down through woods to river. Turn L and find river entry point just outside reservoir border.
5 mins, 52.4047, -2.3325

6 DEVIL'S SPITTLEFUL, RIVER SEVERN
One of the largest heathland habitats in the county, dominated by bell heather and at its best in late summer. A chance for a swim or kayak launch, and an impressive rock outcrop (the spade- or spittleful) and cave give panoramic views. Heading S from Bewdley on B4194, dir DY12 2TQ, pass under A456 bridge and after 100m turn L into Blackstone Riverside car park. Easy entry point for swim or kayak on bend of river.
10 mins, 52.3643, -2.3063

7 NEW BRIDGE, R RAWTHEY
Paddling and shallow rapids below bridge. For a deeper pool, follow the riverside footpath on L bank 800m downstream to just above the weir. Heading E out of Sedbergh on the A684, there is easy parking in a lay-by by the sports field. Then follow path down to river. Further S find shallow swim and jump at Millthrop Bridge (54.3170, -2.5223). Also check out Birks Pool, once the

Sedbergh School pool, 1.5km downstream (parking by footbridge 54.3158, -2.5382 then cross bridge to rectangular pool upstream. Walk further up river to more pools (no access from Birks village).

2 mins, 52.3222, -2.5164

8 STANFORD BRIDGE, RIVER TEME

Gentle section of the Teme with beaches and deeper pools on the bend downstream. A great secluded stretch on which to spend a lazy afternoon. In Stanford on B4203 park at The Den Cafe Bar at Mill Farm (WR6 6SP) opp footbridge. Walk over bridge and follow footpath back around the river to the L under the trees.

5 mins, 52.2896, -2.4199 🏊🚶⛺🛶🏖

9 KINGSWOOD COMMON, RIVER TEME

A secret stretch of riverside with old stone weir, beach and pools. Ideal for a paddle or swim upstream. On the B4204, steep hill from Martley down to Ham Bridge (WR6 6QT) park halfway down hill in lay-by on R (52.2419, -2.3696) and follow signed footpath from other side of road to river.

15 mins, 52.2405, -2.3752 🏊🚶🏖

10 BRANSFORD, RIVER TEME

A deep meander with tree swings and jumps from high earth embankments. Perfect for a picnic with the kids. Park at The Fold Cafe (WR6 5JB), follow nature trail out the back and L path to river.

10 mins, 52.1772, -2.2984 🏊🚶🍴⛺🏖🏃

STRATFORD AVON & LEAM

11 STUDLEY, RIVER ARROW

Great place to swim in a deep bowl at a bend in the river, overlooked by Studley Parish Church, and not far from the grand Gothic Revival castle (now a hotel). Head E out of Studley on Church Rd to B80 7AB. Park L by the church or around bend by cemetery walk on or back to kissing gate and follow footpath to river. Road becomes footpath beyond bend for a view of the castle.

5 mins, 52.2713, -1.8835 🏊🏖🛶

12 ECKINGTON BRIDGE, RIVER AVON

Roadside picnic area by medieval bridge and easy access to a lovely river swim. Signed off A4104 just before bridge 800m N of Eckington, WR10 3DD. For more secluded swim walk over bridge and head R, across field to Swan's Neck (52.0794, -2.1028)

1 mins, 52.0786, -2.1144 🏊🚶🍴⛺🏖

13 PERSHORE OLD BRIDGE, RIVER AVON

Now closed to vehicles, this bridge was built about 1413 by monks, supposedly after the abbot drowned when he fell from the stepping stones. A delightfully tranquil stretch of river for a swim. Head S out of Pershore on B4084 past WR10 1AX over river and park in Bridges Car Park L. Head through gate to R and follow river upstream for 100m.

10 mins, 52.1044, -2.0708 🏊🚶🏖

14 CROPTHORNE MILL

One of Roger Deakin's favourite places, featured in 'Waterlog', with a variety of spots to get in above and below the weir. Follow Mill Bank S out of Fladbury for 800m, over Jubilee Bridge and park in picnic area to L just after bridge. Follow footpaths back across meadow to various swim spots.

5 mins, 52.1122, -2.0051 🏊🏖

15 MARLCLIFF, BIDFORD-ON-AVON

Swim and jump into the deep water below the wooded slopes on this wide, slow-moving bend of the Avon. Signed Marlcliff off B4085, turning L down track where The Bank bends R to B50 4NT and parking by waterside. Alternative swim at Bidford Bridge, 1.5km upstream at: 52.1635, -1.8566.

1 mins, 52.1531, -1.8657 🏊🚶🏖⭐

16 WELFORD-ON-AVON

Enjoy the walk down past quintessentially English thatched cottages to a lovely wide, tranquil section of the Avon, with a millpond and weir. Take your pick of places to swim. Retreat to the marvellous Bell Inn for a cosy pint to follow your dip. Signed from B439 4 miles W of Stratford. From Bell Inn (CV37 8EB) head past church to bottom of Boat Lane. Follow permissive path to R.

10 mins, 52.1688, -1.7922 🏊🚶🏖🍺

17 DOGLEG, RIVER AVON

A tranquil bend of the Avon, perfect for a relaxing swim. Park at Greenway car park (CV37 9AL) S of Stratford on A4390. Head S on cycleway to Stannells Bridge over the Avon. Enter water here or take footpath to R before bridge, along river to bend. Be mindful of private gardens further along.

15 mins, 52.1784, -1.7311 🏊🚶

18 STRATFORD & ALVESTON

'The Old Bathing Place' in Stratford is a large lawn for sunbathing and picnicking, and a gentle curve in the River Avon for swimming, where previous generations learnt. Watch out for boats: it can get very busy with rowers, tourist cruisers, and hired motor boats. Head NE out of Stratford-upon-Avon on A439 past CV37

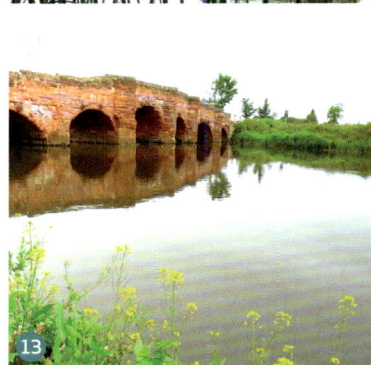

Gardens in town, upstream of the weir (52.2887, -1.5281). 7km NE of town is lovely Avon Wild Camping on the riverside with paddling and some deep bits (52.3484, -1.4966, CV8 3DR).

10 mins, 52.2831, -1.5001 ◭

CANNOCK CHASE

21 BLITHFIELD RESERVOIR PENINSULA
A quiet, secluded beach can be found on the tip of the peninsula, a pleasant place to relax and watch the varied birdlife, including goosander and wigeon. Check for blue-green algae blooms if you paddle. On B5013 N out of Abbots Bromley, take L at fork just after WS15 3EJ, on Newton Hurst Lane. Blithfield Walks signed L after 1.5km. Take signed footpath from car park through woods or walk on road to end of peninsula.

25 mins, 52.8195, -1.9175 🚶▶

22 THE BROAD WATER, TIXALL
When asked if the canal could cross his land, Lord Clifford agreed only if it could be made to look like a lake in front of his house, to match his Capability Brown grounds. The result, also known as Tixall Wide, makes an unusual swim. Head E out of Tixall dir ST18 0XN, park in lay-by L by railings and trees after 800m. Cross road and walk on to take bridleway R by octagonal house down to canal, cross and turn R onto towpath. Variable water quality.

15 mins, 52.8019, -2.0250 🚣🅿🚶⛵

23 ESSEX BRIDGE, RIVER TRENT
A beautiful location below a substantial 16th-century packhorse bridge on the edge of Shugborough Estate. Park in Great Haywood and walk down Trent Lane (ST18 0ST) 150m, under railway and over first bridge. Can get busy on hot days, follow footpath downstream for more secluded swims.

3 mins, 52.8007, -2.0085 🚶⛵🍴🏕

24 BROCTON QUARRY POOLS
Wild, serene and secluded lake in a former gravel pit, with trees sweeping down to the water and an island. There is a bird hide at the north-west corner. Head N from Cannock on A34, turn R before Brocton, signed Pye Green. After 800m (past ST17 0SS), just after Cannock Chase markers, park in lay-by L and take footpath back through woods, descending on far side.

10 mins, 52.7654, -2.0473 🚶❓⛵🍴🚂🚾

25 STONYBROOK POOL, CANNOCK CHASE
Sandy lakes in open heath and woodland of Cannock Chase. Upper (Fairbook) pools very

6YP. Dedicated car park R after 800m with path down to river. Or 3km upstream, the community owned riverbank and garden in Alveston. From the Ferry Inn (CV37 7QX, 01789 269883) take Ferry Ln and continue along footpath or descend by old ferry steps (Swiffen Bank, 52.2049, -1.6525)

1 mins, 52.1989, -1.6936 🚶🚣🏕🍴🚾

19 HAMPTON LUCY, RIVER AVON
Swim tucked away on a gentle stretch of the Avon just above the mill and weir, or swim down from Wasperton. Turn R off A429 S of Warwick signed NT Charlecote Park. Then R to park in Hampton Lucy. Walk back over both bridges and take bridleway on L, just after Charlecote Mill. Halfway through second field, cross stream on L and head to river. Wasperton river path for fishermen from pull-in at 52.2295, -1.6079.

10 mins, 52.2151, -1.6205 🚶❓🏕◭

20 LEAM VALLEY NATURE RESERVE
Thanks to a new clean-up initiative, the Leam, a tributary of the Avon, is much more appealing for swimming. From Radford Rd Car Park, CV31 1LQ, on E edge of Leamington Spa, cross footbridge and head upstream for up to 1km and swim anywhere. People also swim from Jephson

popular with anglers, but lower Stonybrook pool much more secluded. Take Penkridge Bank Rd W out of Rugeley 600m, forest is signed L on Birches Valley (dir WS15 2UQ), car park 130m on L. Walk or cycle on new path behind car park up valley to find two lakes, followed by two more 800m further up.

15 mins, 52.7446, -1.9759 ▣❓⌂

BIRMINGHAM AREA

26 CHASEWATER
Gravel-based, clear lake ideal for a secluded evening picnic. Great place to watch birds or enjoy a cycle, too. No Swimming signs, but there is NOWCA-organised swimming from the Watersports Centre (52.6630, -1.9520) twice a week in summer. Use discretion. Take no through road Church St from roundabout at Uxbridge Arms in Chasetown (WS7 3QL). Park at the end of the road. Take footbridge over A1495, follow path down to lake, and walk along the bank to find a quiet spot.

15 mins, 52.6712, -1.9518 ▣⌘⌂❓

27 RYDERS HAYES MERE
A lovely, wild spot, idyllic for a paddle with the wildlife: it is very deep and cold further out, so stay in the shallow ends well inshore of the islands. In NE end of Pelsall travel N to end of St Johns Road (WS3 4EZ) where it turns to become Fairburn Crescent and park by sign for cycle path. Follow path to R, through gate and horse field, over stile and down to lake. Footpath from Ryders Hayes Lane (WS3 4EQ) leads to other end.

15 mins, 52.6371, -1.9547 ▣▽⌂⌣⌘🍴⌗

28 SWAN POOL, SANDWELL VALLEY
A surprisingly welcoming place for a cooling swim in clear water. Signs encourage swimmers to assess their own risk rather than prohibiting them. Be mindful of anglers. Mountain bike trails in the woods. Signed from A41/Holyhead road up Park Lane (B21 8LE). Follow 2.4km N, past cemetery, to car park L after pedestrian crossing, with path down to lake.

4 mins, 52.5247, -1.9661 ▣⌂👥⌣⌘⌣

29 MIDLAND OPEN WATER, TAMWORTH ▣
Award winning open swimming lake, privately owned and very well looked after. Open Mar to Oct. Signed off A51 6.5km S of Tamworth, 1.5km N of Kingsbury. Tamworth Rd, Tamworth, B78 2HZ.

1 mins, 52.5747, -1.6923 ▣⛱

30 KINGSBURY, RIVER TAME
A gentle section of the Tame ideal for a

paddle or swim. Crystal-clear lake adjacent used by jet bikes. From A5 at S end of Kingsbury on A51, just N of roundabout with A4097 turn into dead end stub of Kingsbury Rd (B78 2DG) and park R before footbridge. Path to river on R. Lake over footbridge.

4 mins, 52.5592, -1.6833 ▣⌂⌘

31 ALVECOTE POOLS
The River Anker pools alongside sweeping meadows and grazing cattle. Perfect for a quick dip or punt around in a kayak. Nearby, Pooley Country Park offers visitors another lake, beautiful, wooded walks and wetlands, and the remains of Alvecote Priory nestled under the chestnut trees alongside the canal. Just NE of Tamworth follow Shuttington Rd NE from The Pretty Pigs pub, (B79 0ED, 01827 63129) for 1.5km as it becomes Polesworth Rd and bends right. 800m after bend pull off by gate R (room for 1 car) and walk through to river, or park by bridleway at bend and walk.

2 mins, 52.6395, -1.6266 ▣⌘⌣

R TRENT & R DOVE

32 TUTBURY CASTLE, RIVER DOVE
A deep, rural stretch of the Dove above a

weir, with a view back to Tutbury Castle ruins on the bluff. Tutbury Mill picnic area is signed on A511 roundabout at N of Tutbury (N of DE13 9LZ). Park and follow path over meadows, along millstream to weir, 1.2km.

15 mins, 52.8613, -1.6986 ▣⛱⌂

33 WALTON-ON-TRENT
Rare serene section of the Trent offering seclusion and a rope swing, next to one of the country's newest nature reserves, a wetland in an old quarry where you may yet hear a bittern boom. From crossroads in the centre of Walton-on-Trent head W on

Station Lane (dir DE13 8EN), cross river and continue 800m to park in Tucklesholme Nature Reserve on R. Follow path around wetland to gate on R near elbow in the river.

15 mins, 52.7651, -1.6851 🚶🚳🛶🅿🏕🧍🚶

34 NEWTON SOLNEY, RIVER TRENT

Several easy entry points from grassy banks along the river for a day adventuring, exploring and kayaking. In Newton Solney, Trent Lane becomes a path to river near DE15 0SE. River is wide and can be fast flowing, strong swimmers only.

3 mins, 52.8308, -1.5851 🚶🛶🏊

35 ALBERT VILLAGE LAKE

Large expanse of open water in a flooded pit, perfect for a paddle or dip next to a pretty, young woodland. Take a stroll or cycle and spot a menagerie of birdlife. No-swimming rules here, except when supervised sessions are running. Car park SW end of Occupation Rd, on the edge of Albert Village (DE11 8HD) and follow path to lake.

10 mins, 52.7526, -1.5510 🅿❓🏕🚲🧍🚻

36 THORTIT LAKE, OAKTHORPE

A remnant from the mining era, this pond in Willesley Woods is bordered with wild meadow and lend itself to a short dip or picnic, depending on signage. Take Ashby Rd E out of Donisthorpe, Oakthorpe Picnic Site signed 800m on R. Follow footpath into grass clearing, take R fork down to little cove. Also named Saltersford Brook.

10 mins, 52.7239, -1.5099 🅿❓🏕🧍🚶

37 ANCHOR CHURCH, RIVER TRENT

Exceptional grotto cave thought to have been the home of St Hardulph, a 6th-century anchorite. Safe swimming in this gentle offshoot of the Trent. Head N from Ticknall on Ingleby Lane for 3.2km dir DE73 7HW. Park on R in lay-by just before bend in Ingleby. Follow footpath through gate

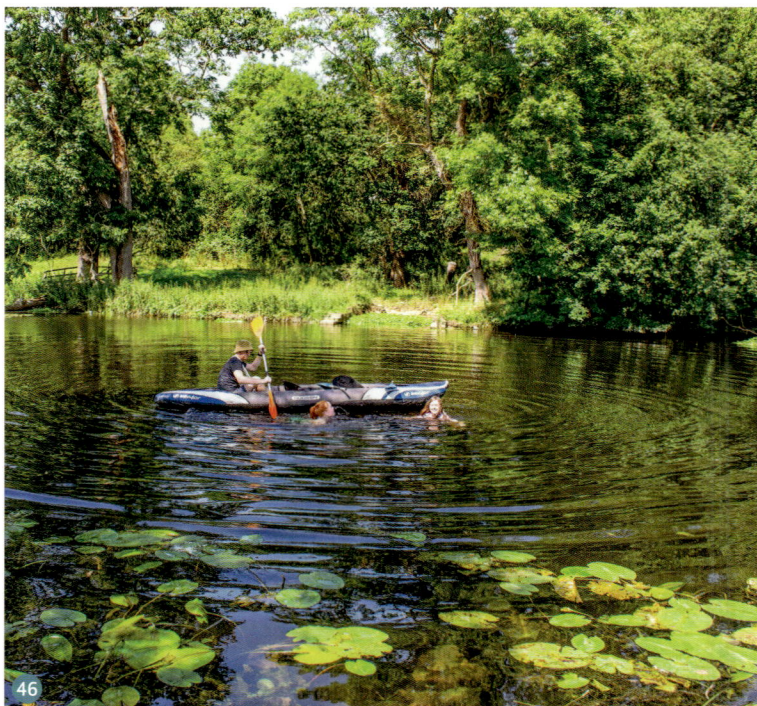

opp 1.5km down to and along river to crag. In high water you may need to follow path above crag and drop down.

25 mins, 52.8415, -1.4975 🚶🧍🛶🏕🚲🦮

38 SWARKESTONE BRIDGE, DERBY

Britain's longest stone bridge, at nearly a mile including the causeway section, is where Bonnie Prince Charlie turned back his Jacobite rebels and ended his advance on London. Some fancy they can still hear approaching hoofbeats on quiet nights. On A514 heading N through Swarkestone, car park of Crewe & Harpur pub is on L (DE73 7JA). Walk down to bridge. Path L down to entry point, or cross bridge, turn R signed Ingleby and find path down to river R after 50m. River is wide and can be fast flowing, strong swimmers only.

1 mins, 52.8529, -1.4534 🚶🛶🏊

39 STAUNTON HAROLD & SPRING WOOD

Staunton Harold Reservoir near NT Calke Abbey is a popular place for a lakeside walk or cycle with wildflower meadows, bird hides and a children's playground. But head to aptly named Spring Wood Nature Reserve and you will be rewarded with quiet woodland that is carpeted with bluebells in late spring. Take B587 S of Melbourne past

DE73 8BJ, turn R signed Calke after 3.2km. Park at Calke Car Park overflow L after 800m. Gate into wood opp and 20m to R of car park entrance. Follow path through reserve over wooden walkway and 200m after end of walkway take L spur to the bird hide. Discretion and evening access advised.

10 mins, 52.7995, -1.4409 🛶🧍🏕🚶

40 DRAYCOTT BEACH, RIVER DERWENT

A tranquil meander on the River Derwent with a gently sloping beach. Lovely little picnic spot. From A6005 in Draycott turn S on Market Street and follow 2.4km, past St Chad's Church (DE72 3QH), to park in lay-by R where road comes alongside river. Head over bridge and downstream to beach.

4 mins, 52.8777, -1.3300 🚶🛶🏕🏊🦮

RIVER SOAR

41 BLACKBROOK RESERVOIR

Constructed in 1796 to feed the Charnwood Forest Canal, which has long since vanished. A bridleway leads up to an old viaduct bridge, from which it is possible to explore the deeply wooded shores. The old quarry before the bridge is sometimes used by climbers, though the land above is private. On A512 at crossroads SW of

Shepshed, turn onto Charley Rd signed Oaks in Charnwood. Follow 1.2km (past LE12 9EW) and park in lay-by L across from gravel track (One Barrow Lane). Cross rd and follow track 500m to bridge, quarry to R.

5 mins, 52.7488, -1.3149

42 NORMANTON ON SOAR

Easy swims up- and downstream, or take advantage of the old chain ferry for access to walks along the riverbank. Park on the main street in village (LE12 5HB). Slipway is down Soar Lane, beside pub (easy kayak launch here). For chain ferry (operates May to September) head S, signed through gate R 130m beyond the church. Lovely, gentle stretch of the Soar also at Zouch, 1.5km away: 52.8068, -1.2471.

1 mins, 52.8019, -1.2339

43 SWITHLAND WOOD QUARRY

The most flora-rich woodland in Leicestershire spreads a sumptuous carpet of bluebells each spring. 300-year-old trees provide habitats for varied wildlife, whilst volcanic outcrops lure young limbs to clamber. The jewel, though, is the old slate quarry with beautifully clear water and prominent jumping locations for the

brave. Swimming permission is granted by request, though the locals simply wait until after 6pm. From Cropston, head N on Reservoir Rd, which becomes Roecliffe Rd. Swithland Wood South Car Park 1km on R. Follow R fork path, quarry fence 500m on L.

10 mins, 52.7046, -1.2033

44 STANFORD, RIVER SOAR

A quiet stretch of river with many access points, including a metal footbridge that takes you across to a secret island where you can wild camp and paddle the loop or swim when the water is high. Take Meadow Lane N out of Loughborough, dir LE12 5PY. Just after crossing the river, park L under railway bridge and follow track along river. For island, continue to bend, turn R and park in small lay-by L after 180m by footpath sign. Path through gate opp to river: 52.7892, -1.1951.

5 mins, 52.7934, -1.2011

45 SWITHLAND RESERVOIR

Remote, mirror-like reservoir in the SSSI wooded valley of Charnwood. A quiet, narrow lane runs alongside, leading to the waterworks, with the shore fenced. Some Deep Water and No Swimming signs, but secluded. At S end of Woodhouse take

School Lane fork at church (LE12 8UZ), follow for 1.2km (becomes Brand Lane at national speed limit signs) and turn L on Rushey Lane signed unsuitable for motors. Follow 1.5km to park R at sharp L bend. Waterworks beyond.

8 mins, 52.7283, -1.1767

46 BARROW UPON SOAR

A lovely swim or kayak on a gentle meander of the grand River Soar. Follow it with great food at The Moorings pub, where you can also launch your kayak. In Barrow-upon-Soar park at The Moorings pub (LE12 8PN), cross bridge and turn R along towpath 600m. Grassy banks and some beach areas for entry.

5 mins, 52.7534, -1.1574

47 1860 BRIDGE, MOUNTSORREL

A beautiful, arched, red-brick bridge, formerly used to carry slate from the local quarry, provides a stunning backdrop for a cooling evening swim. Park at The Waterside Inn (LE12 7BB), cross road and follow footpath along river to bridge.

5 mins, 52.7330, -1.1428

48 KING LEAR LAKE, WATERMEAD PARK

Former gravel pit used by the local triathlon

to paddle and swim. Hambleton Peninsula is also lovely to explore, with views to the submerged church. Rutland Water Sykes Lane Car Park (LE15 8PX). Signed off A606, E of Oakham. Parking is charged on entry per car. Kid's aqua park nearby.

2 mins, 52.6629, -0.6149

RIVER NENE

54 STAMFORD, RIVER WELLAND

A lovely section of river with numerous beaches and deeper sections upstream. If you get a chance, grab a pint and pizza at the Tobie Norris after (see listing). Park at the Cattlemarket car park in Stamford (PE9 2WB). Walk N over the footbridge and turn L onto Meadows footpath. Walk 500m along river to small beach on bend.

10 mins, 52.6461, -0.4843

55 FERRY MEADOWS COUNTRY PARK

Nene Outdoors operates a 400m OWS loop from Gunwade Lake. There are several other lakes in the park, with easy paths and shoreside picnic tables to enjoy, all fed by freshwater from the River Nene which runs alongside. 2 miles from the A1 and centre of Peterborough, nenepark.org.uk

2 mins, 52.5661, -0.3156

56 WATER NEWTON, R NENE

Pretty circular river walk with weir and swimming, near station and Peterborough. From Water Newton off A1 W of Peterborough, cross at the mill lock (PE8 6LY), walk upstream to the weir and then return via the lower river section and footbridge. Also reached from Castor across the railway line, or via Ferry Meadows cycle route. Or walk 1½ miles down Nene Way from Wansford station.

15 mins, 52.5640, -0.3706

57 YOKE HILL LEISURE

Lifeguarded wild swimming and paddleboarding lake on the outskirts of Corby. 07308 378734

2 mins, 52.4949, -0.5874

58 WADENHOE, R NENE

A lovely riverside footpath, and pretty church, make this a wonderful place for messing about in the water. The riverside pub may reopen in due course. Park in Wadenhoe village PE8 5ST and follow the river path towards the church to choose your spot along the meadow below.

3 mins, 52.4383, -0.5155

59 STANWICK LAKES, R NENE

Another network of lake gravel pits (dug

---

club, with a namesake statue by the western bank. Beautiful, clear water but check for blue-green algae and anglers. From Syston follow Wanlip Rd and just after roundabout and the Hope & Anchor (LE7 1PD) turn L into pay car park before road joins A46.

5 mins, 52.6868, -1.1059

49 SWIM SIX HILLS, MELTON MOWBRAY

A new addition to the OWS family. Very inclusive, friendly and supportive of all abilities. Children welcome. Cafe on site. Take A6006 W out of Melton Mowbray. After 17km turn L onto Six Hills Lane. Signed off rd 1km on R. Six Hills Lane, Melton Mowbray, LE14 3PR.

1 mins, 52.7854, -1.0334

RUTLAND & R WELLAND

50 WELFORD & SULBY RESERVOIR

Built to feed the canal, with open, grassy shores, locals often swim or kayak here in the summer. Enjoy a tranquil walk across the causeway to find the earthworks of lost Old Sulby village, lying either side of the path, perfect for a picnic. Entering Welford from the N on A5199 after passing The Wharf Inn (NN6 6JQ, 01858 575075) take L at the bend, cross over the bridge, to car park L

---

after 300m. Old Sulby 52.4278, -1.0383.

4 mins, 52.4247, -1.0424

51 COTTINGHAM, RIVER WELLAND

Tranquil section of the Welland near old windpump. Pebble beach perfect for kids, leading into a gloriously deep pool near the bridge. Take Ashby Road N from Middleton dir Ashley (past LE16 8YJ) 600m to bend L. Park carefully if barrier on track straight on is locked, and walk on along bumpy track to the bridge, 400m.

5 mins, 52.5103, -0.7678

52 TURTLE BRIDGE, RIVER WELLAND

This quiet stretch of the Welland shelves gently down to deeper pools with a rope swing upstream. Perfect for a family picnic. From A47 just S of Morcott, take B672 at LE15 9EB, signed Caldecott. Drive 1.2km, to bend R, turn L and park immediately in end of bridleway. Walk 800m down bridleway to river.

10 mins, 52.5763, -0.6320

53 RUTLAND WATER BEACH

Seasonal, supervised lake beach - the first inland bathing location in England to have a Seaside Award. Long sandy shoreline and a 2,800 square metre area in which

---

to build Wellingborough) with a cycle trail along old railway. Some used for fishing so continue on to the R Nene and footbridge. Well-signed car park and visitor centre (NN9 6GY) off A45 Stanwick roundabout 10 miles E of Wellingborough. Bear N through lake to find white footbridge over river. Nearby Stanwick Lakes Nature Reserve has activities for kids and organised OWS sessions (NN9 6GY, stanwicklakes.org.uk)

20 mins, 52.3406, -0.5812 ❓

60 SUMMER LEYS, WELLINGBOROUGH

Explore this network of wild gravel lakes along the R Nene, or take a dip in the river. Find dead-end road a mile W of Wollaston off the Hardwater Rd. There are wild lakes on R of the road or continue up to Nene river bridge ½ mile. Walk L 200m to Summer Leys lake shore and river banks. Or explore R to a smaller lake and another larger lake beyond (under pylons).

5 mins, 52.2677, -0.7007 ❓

61 KISLINGBURY MILL POOL, RIVER NENE

Charming, disused village mill pond, perfect for a splash around with the family, with deeper pools by the footbridge. Kislingbury is signed from A4500 roundabout just W of Northampton. Follow road 1.2km, turn R on Mill Lane, past NN7 4BD to bend L at end and park on road. River across road, footbridge L.

2 mins, 52.2288, -0.9845

RIVER OUSE

62 FELMERSHAM, GREAT OUSE

Easy family beach by bridge or numerous swim spots downstream for a longer swim. Very easy access for canoes. Access from benches and bridge in village (Hunts Lane, MK43 7JP), or follow bridleway 300m downstream on opposite bank.

1 mins, 52.2123, -0.5485

63 PAVENHAM, GREAT OUSE

A wonderfully bucolic loop of the Great Ouse with willows, a deep swim and rope swings. Pass The Cock pub (MK43 7NJ, thecockatpavenham.co.uk), then L down Mill Lane and follow the footpath down to the river. You can continue downstream all the way to Park End Church.

10 mins, 52.1868, -0.5570

64 OAKLEY, GREAT OUSE

A wide, peaceful stretch of the river, deep above the weir. South of Oakley (MK43 7RU) 200m, past Saint Mary's Oakley (Church Lane) to find path on R after bridge.

5 mins, 52.1654, -0.5316

65 OLNEY, GREAT OUSE

Shingle beach and beautiful views back to Olney Church. Follow the footpath behind St. Peter and St. Paul Church (MK46 4AD, Church St) and continue 200m to large beach. Continue on footpath along the river all the way to Clifton Reynes. Or park at Olney Football Club (MK46 4DW) on East Street - beach at end of playing fields.

5 mins, 52.1483, -0.6965

66 HAVESHAM RUIN, GREAT OUSE

A ruined riverside church in a quiet area

of lakes on the N edge of Milton Keynes. Turn L off Wolverton Rd at the canal bridge/Black Horse Inn (MK14 5AJ, theblackhorsegreatlinford.co uk), a mile E of Wolverton Station (or walk/cycle from the station, 2 miles). Follow track along canal, then into open fields, to find ruin of St Peter's Church after ½ mile on L and river behind. Other lakes to L.

15 mins, 52.0776, -0.7331

67 PASSENHAM, GREAT OUSE

Pretty riverside picnic area with slipway to clean waters on the upstream NW edge of Milton Keynes. Between Claverton and Stony Stratford off A5 (MK19 6EW). Or from A422, go through Passenham village and turn L at Calverton Road Car Park on R.

1 mins, 52.0497, -0.8527

68 LIDLINGTON LAKE

Huge, exposed, easy-access lake, surrounded by open fields. Some sailing. On lanes 1 mile NW of Lidlington village and station.

2 mins, 52.0484, -0.5677

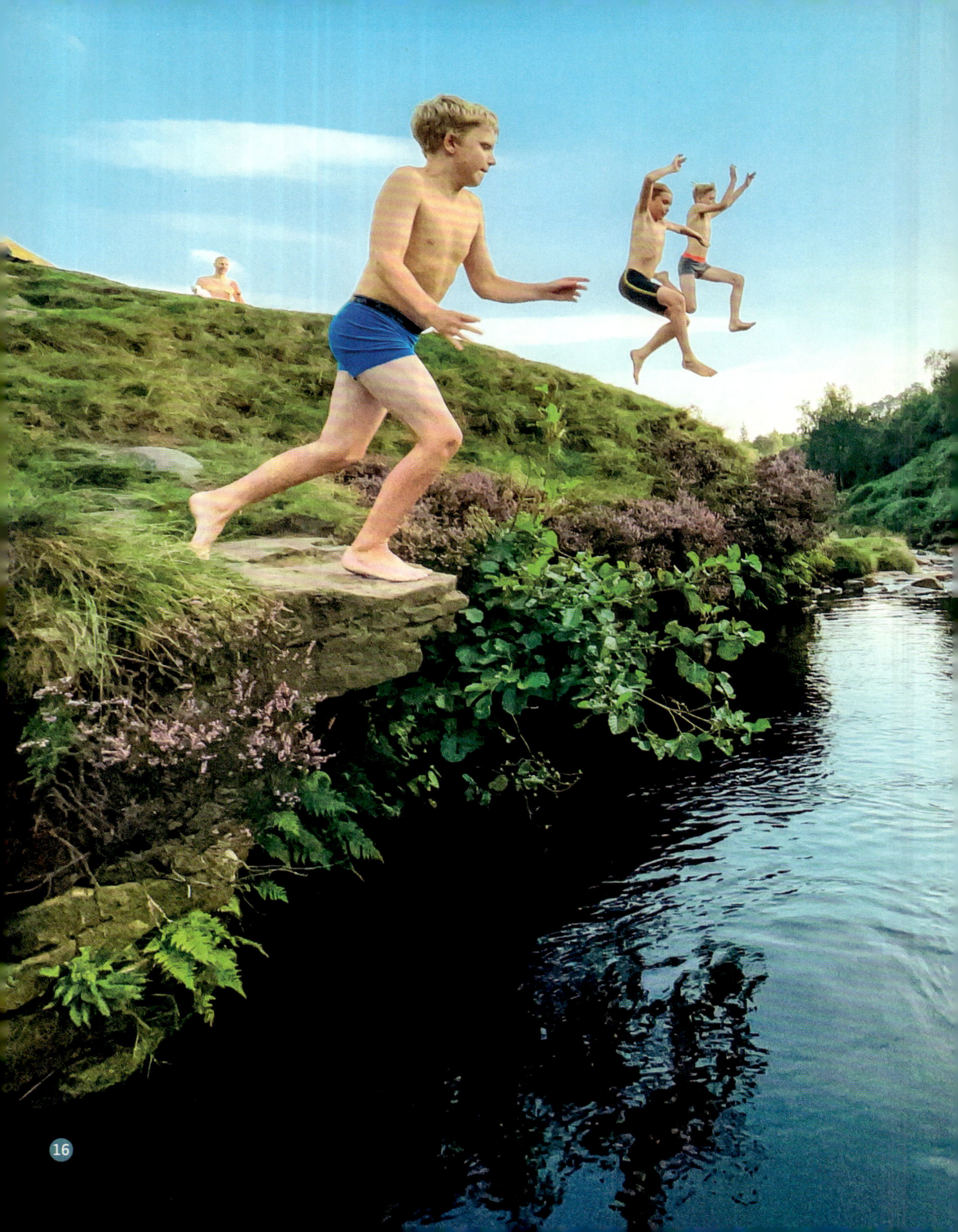

PEAK DISTRICT &
EAST MIDLANDS

On 24 April 1932, over 600 walkers from nearby cities ventured onto the moors, which were then reserved solely for grouse shooting, during the Kinder Scout Marches mass trespass. Six participants were arrested, but their efforts ultimately led to the establishment of Britain's first national park, the Peak District, in 1951. Today, this historic protest has inspired hundreds of swimming groups across Britain to swim 'trespass' in reservoirs on the same date each year, including those in the High Peak, to establish a right to swim in these beautiful lakes.

The Derwent Valley features the three reservoirs of Howden, Upper Derwent, and Ladybower. The young Derwent River that feeds these reservoirs is a playful, bubbling brook at Slippery Stones (16), which was once a treacherous packhorse crossing. It now provides hours of enjoyment as a great spot to leap into one of the many deep, peaty pools.

As I set off downstream in search of more delights along the Derwent, rain clouds rolled in from the west. Few screen moments are as iconic as when Colin Firth, playing Mr Darcy in the BBC's Pride and Prejudice, swims in the lake at Pemberley, emerging dripping from the water, his shirt unbuttoned and clinging to his chest, his breeches sodden, and his dark hair a tangled mess. This scene helped establish Firth as a romantic icon. Both Lyme Hall and Chatsworth House have portrayed Pemberley, but Chatsworth's River Derwent is the more popular location for a summer swim (29). Landscaped by Capability Brown, the mountain river was deepened and straightened between two weirs. Soft red sands line the banks, and with the light low, once the coach crowds have departed, the still waters invite a long and most aristocratic swim.

To the south-west, on Axe Edge Moor, at the headwaters of the River Dane, there's an altogether more riotous little creek that

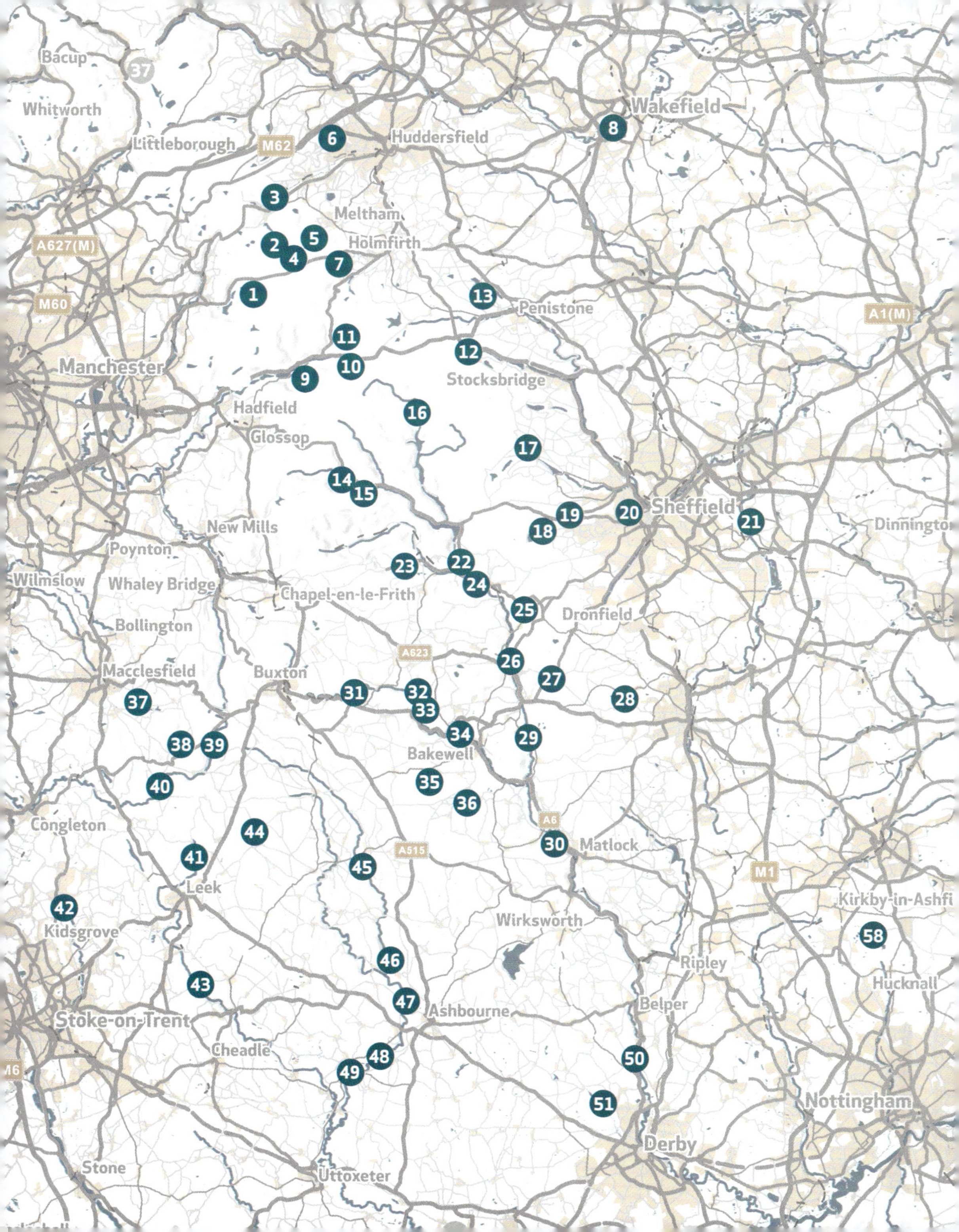
Bacup
37
Whitworth
Littleborough
M62
6
Huddersfield
Wakefield
8
3
Meltham
A627(M)
2
5
Holmfirth
4
7
M60
1
13
Penistone
A1(M)
11
12
Manchester
10
9
Stocksbridge
Hadfield
16
Glossop
17
14
15
20
Sheffield
19
21
18
Dinnington
New Mills
Poynton
23
22
Wilmslow
Whaley Bridge
24
Chapel-en-le-Frith
25
Dronfield
Bollington
A623
26
Macclesfield
Buxton
27
31
32
28
37
33
34
38
39
29
Bakewell
40
35
36
A6
Congleton
44
30
Matlock
41
A515
45
M1
Leek
42
Kirkby-in-Ashfi
Wirksworth
Kidsgrove
58
46
Ripley
43
Hucknall
47
Belper
Stoke-on-Trent
Ashbourne
Cheadle
48
50
M6
49
51
Nottingham
Derby
Stone
Uttoxeter

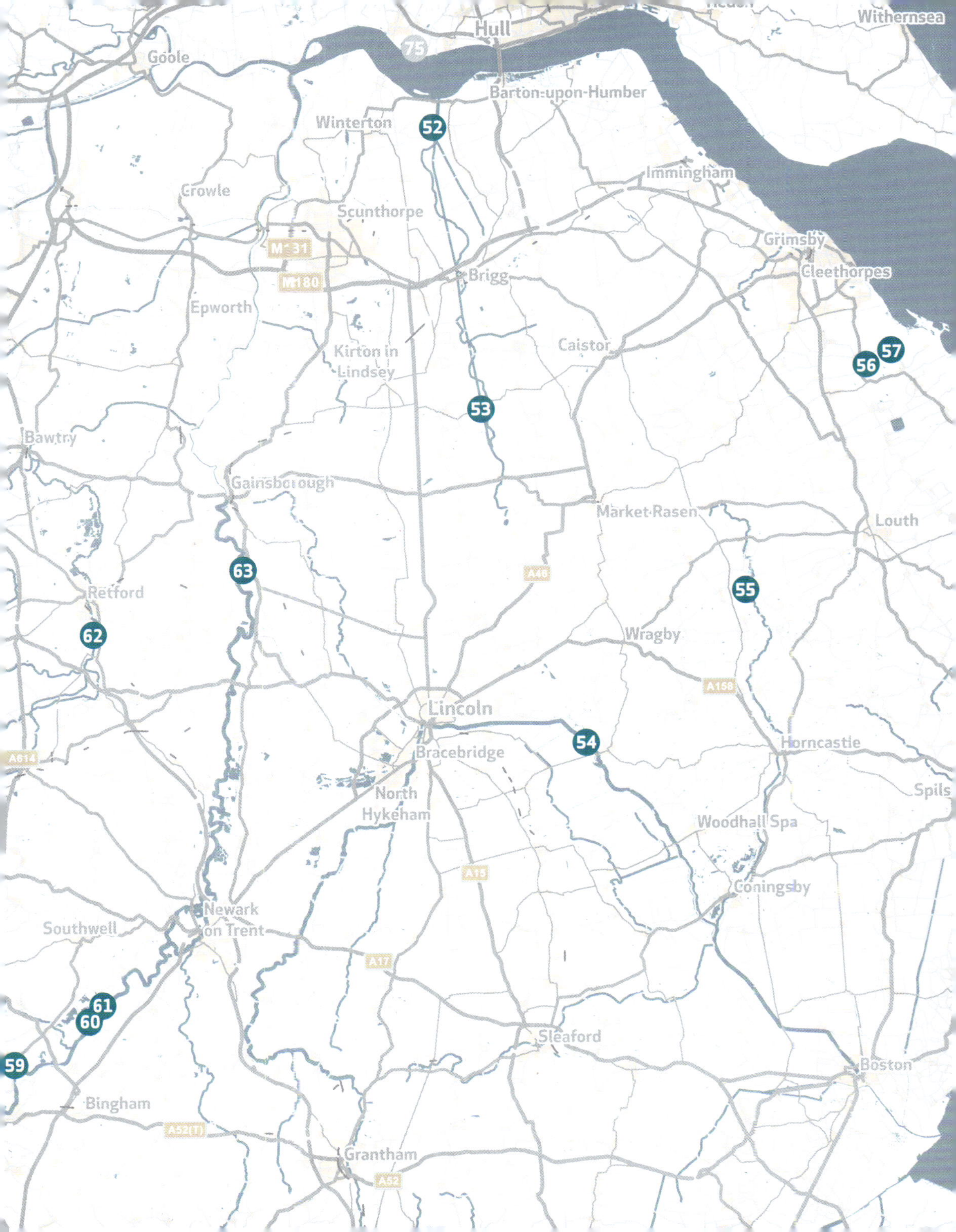

Hull
Withernsea
75
Goole
Barton-upon-Humber
Winterton
52
Immingham
Crowle
Scunthorpe
Grimsby
M180
Brigg
Cleethorpes
Epworth
Caistor
Kirton in Lindsey
57
56
53
Bawtry
Gainsborough
Market Rasen
Louth
A46
63
55
Retford
62
Wragby
A158
Lincoln
54
A614
Bracebridge
Horncastle
Spils
North Hykeham
Woodhall Spa
A15
Coningsby
Newark on Trent
Southwell
A17
61
60
Sleaford
59
Boston
Bingham
A52(T)
Grantham
A52

29

29

44

gushes down the hillside along narrow grassy banks before dropping into a pool beneath two medieval bridges. This is Three Shires Head, named for the convergence of the three counties of Derbyshire, Staffordshire, and Cheshire at the old packhorse bridge (39).

Residents of nearby Flash, the highest village in the country, once used this giddy political geography to their advantage, holding illegal boxing matches on the no-man's land of the bridge, where no county sheriff could arrest them. Renowned for counterfeiting 'Flash' money, they would come to Three Shires Head to exchange it for goods.

The moor was deserted as I approached across the hillside, squelching through the remnants of a week of summer rains. Dark clouds had obscured the sun again, and a warm westerly wind whipped at my coat. The storms of the previous days had transformed the mountain tub into a raging, frothy cauldron. Giant ferns billowed about like bendy palms in a tropical typhoon, and enormous bubbles the size of footballs spiralled around the pool. Overheated and sweaty from my walk, I stripped and plunged in, buffeted by the currents of the wild jacuzzi. A cluster of bubbles took off in a gust and floated down the valley before becoming caught on the gorse.

That night, at the remote Mermaid's Inn, which overlooks The Roaches from several miles away, I heard the legend of a local beauty accused of witchcraft by a spurned admirer and drowned in a nearby tarn known as the Mermaid's Pool, also marked on maps as Blake Mere (44). Three days later, the man was found dead in the pool, his face torn by talons. Now, no animal or human dares to approach it. In Celtic times, small pools and standing waters were viewed as doorways between the terrestrial and spirit worlds. Generally, these pools were seen as bringers of life and fertility, but the spirits could be unpredictable. The next morning, the pool made a chilly wake-up call, but I emerged unharmed, even invigorated. Its bottom is solid and the view superb, but the water is very dark and there are No Swimming signs. You'll need to decide yourself if this rite of passage is worth it.

The White Peak forms the headwaters of the Dove, one of the most beautiful rivers in the Midlands, beginning at Dovedale, a truly spectacular limestone gorge (46,47). Here, the river is mainly shallow, but there are deeper sections beneath the ancient rock caves and limestone cliffs of Dove Holes and Raven's Tor. At Lover's Leap, a young woman, having heard that her fiancé was killed in the Napoleonic Wars, threw herself from the cliff but was saved when her billowing dress caught in the trees. The entire White Peak area consists of old coral that once lay at the bottom of a 350-million-year-old tropical sea. You can still find fossils of ancient crinoids, or 'sea lilies', by the stepping-stones at the south end of the dale, and Thorpe Cloud Hill is actually the remains of an old tropical atoll on the seabed.

Rivers such as the Lathkill were harnessed to power mills by the Romans, with galena serving as the local currency. Take a walk through the verdant Lathkill Dale to discover hidden remnants of this era scattered along the riverbanks. Bateman's House was built over a mine shaft, still accessible today via a ladder to see the water pump. Further along is the old packhorse bridge and the engine house of Mandale Mine. Another remnant of industry, the Monsal Trail is a disused railway route that links swimming spots and nature reserves (33).

To the east of the Peak District, in Nottinghamshire, the River Trent meanders slowly through the countryside, providing perfect spots like Burton Joyce for a leisurely swim or kayak (59).

Lincolnshire, with its flat fenlands, vast expanses of unspoilt coastline, and rolling wolds, also attracted the Romans, who developed an infrastructure of forts, three great roads, dykes, inland ports, and straightened rivers. These waterways, once thriving and busy as they connected the bustling trades of the area with Europe, now offer plenty of serene opportunities for those wishing to swim, kayak, or simply splash about. Brandy Wharf and the Louth Navigation Canal are lovely for swimming (53, 57), or you can join the locals who leap off the listed suspension bridge at Horkstow (52). The Branston Island Loop is ideal for a longer swim (54), while Low Pond Lake offers seclusion amid nature (55).

NORTHERN MOORS

1 GREENFIELD WATERFALL
Delightful cascades and natural infinity pools make this an unforgettable walk. Plenty of secluded spots for the adventurous - you can continue up for the most limber to climb the Trinnacle rock (see entry). Take A635 E out of Greenfield 2km to Binn Green RSPB car park at OL3 7NN. Follow track down to dam and turn L onto main footpath. Walk for 2km past 2 reservoirs and turn R up Greenfield Brook gorge at weir. Continue up and cross river for Trinnacle.
45 mins, 53.5394, -1.9431 🅿🚻🚻🚻

2 WESSENDEN FALLS
Truly magical, secret waterfall hidden behind a sea of rhododendrons. Picnic, then skinny-dip in the plunge pool. Blake Clough waterfall nearby is also worth a look. Head S out of Marsden along Binn Rd just past HD7 6HQ and park in lay-by R at head of track to reservoirs. Walk down track 2.5km to lay-by on R opposite farmhouse (53.5758, -1.9176). Head down hill from lay-by to R, across stream, under the rhododendrons to pool. Blake Clough waterfall at 53.5728, -1.9252.

45 mins, 53.5751, -1.9181 🅿🚻🚻🚻🚻

3 SPARTH RESERVOIR, MARSDEN
Small reservoir at the northern end of the Peak District where thanks to a local campaign, you are allowed to swim. Borders the Huddersfield Narrow Canal. Best visited early morning or evening as this is a popular spot. Park at either Marsden or Slaithwaite and walk along the canal towpath.
20 mins, 53.6091, -1.9179

4 WESSENDEN HEAD RESERVOIR, MELTHAM
The highest of a string of stunning reservoirs situated in the Wessenden Valley on Marsden Moor with spectacular moorland views. Wild and remote. No Swimming signs, although people do, so make your own choice. Park at Wessenden Head car park on Wessenden Head Rd (HD9 4EU). From the car park, cross the road and follow the Pennine Way track. Look for a steep track L down to the water's edge and a beach with several entry points. Water levels can vary and it shallows out in parts.
20 mins, 53.5652, -1.8952 ❓

5 FAIR NOOK SPRING
A sliver of aquamarine, crystal-clear, spring-fed water awaits visitors to this

quarry. Much used by youngsters over the generations, some parts can be fenced, but the site is in open access land. Leave it tidier than you find it. Take Wessenden Head Rd SW out of Meltham for 2.5km, past HD9 4HW. Pull off near gate of old quarry road at 53.5795, -1.8747. Follow road for 300m to disused building and turn L onto track before it. Follow 400m looking out for a trail on L through bushes down to water.

20 mins, 53.5800, -1.8706

6 LONGWOOD COMPENSATION RESERVOIR

A picturesque reservoir tucked away on the edge of Longwood with a long history of swimming, especially in school holidays. No Swimming signs. Park on Holmefield Rd (53.6496, -1.8485) then walk 100m up the track to the reservoir. Access is by climbing over the dam wall to a gently sloping beach. Entry is on the L of the dam. Watch out for broken glass. Avoid the R side where there is an outlet and trees.

10 mins, 53.6513, -1.8495

7 DIGLEY RESERVOIR, HOLMFIRTH

A beautiful tree-fringed Pennine reservoir, situated just within the Peak District National Park. No Swimming signs but popular with local swim groups with trees to hang your clothes on while you swim! Gets deep quickly and some roots to navigate. From Holmfirth, head W along Greenfield Rd, then turn L at the Ford Inn. After several sharp bends, the car park is in a disused quarry just before you reach the reservoir. From the car park, turn R onto a track, going up and down a slope. Keep L where the path splits, and continue towards the trees. There is also lovely 500m walk upstream along Marsden Clough which takes you to Blackpool Bridge (53.5593, -1.8681), a beauty spot where people used to swim in the black pools beneath the bridge, suitable for a paddle and a dip.

15 mins, 53.5616, -1.8408

8 'BOB' LAKE, PUGNEY'S COUNTRY PARK

One of a chain of lakes in the vicinity of Pugney's Country Park. Bob is a man made lake, part of the flood plain for the R Calder. Popular with local swim groups. From the M1 take J39 towards Wakefield. Take the 2nd exit at the 1st roundabout then continue towards Wakefield then take a L turn at the next roundabout (at the Swan and Cygnet pub). Head towards the pub car park to 3 lay-bys before the pub. The lake is beyond the grassy mound and the easiest spot to enter the water.

5 mins, 53.6595, -1.5138

LONGDENDALE

9 THE CRUX, WILDBOAR CLOUGH

Take the meandering path through twisted trees and then scramble up to the seclusion of this waterfall and plunge pool. Take Woodhead Rd/B6105 N out of Glossop about 5km, to park after SK13 1JF at Torside pay car park by reservoir. Walk up to cycle path and follow L 300m, then take signed path for Wildboar Clough R. Follow footpath about 1.5km through woods and up rocky gorge to waterfall.

60 mins, 53.4785, -1.8809

10 MIDDLE BLACK CLOUGH

A beautiful scramble up the side of a waterfall suitable for all the family, with dipping pools and paddling all the way up. Take a picnic and make a day of it. On A628 NE of Glossop, 3.2km E of junction with A6024, turn down slip road opp lay-by to car park for Three Black Cloughs (SK13 1JE). Follow path 600m with Etherow River on your L. Just after steep path to R, and small clearing in trees, the path crosses the river. Keep following with river now to R as you head uphill to falls.

60 mins, 53.4876, -1.8263

Royal Oak pub (SK13 8QY) and park in large lay-by R (53.4022, -1.8050). Take signed path S 500m, over river to wall corner. Follow wall for 800m until it ends, then take path W down to brook, and 200m S to find larger falls.

30 mins, 53.3958, -1.8103 🏊🚶

16 SLIPPERY STONES

A pretty stretch of the young Derwent River with grassy banks and a deep pool, perfect for jumps, leaps and somersaults. Water crystal clear, but tinted brown from the peat, and some claim it's fizzy like cola. From A57 13km W of Sheffield take road signed Derwent Valley Dams. If possible, follow 12km to head of Howden Reservoir (past S33 0BB) and park at end. Walk about 1.5km upstream to pool 300m above footbridge. At weekends, car access restricted to Fairholmes car park after 4km - bring a bike for the rest! A further 3km upstream is a delightful swim 100m upstream from the foot of Lower Small Clough (53.4670, -1.7713).

25 mins, 53.4546, -1.7470 🏊🍴🚶🏞🚻

17 AGDEN RESERVOIR ❓

A beautiful, tree-lined reservoir with crystal-clear water and various walks around it. No Swimming signs. Head W out of Low Bradfield (S6 6LB) from cricket club and take first R signed Strines. Follow 800m to park on R in lay-by after bend. Path around water just over wall.

5 mins, 53.4297, -1.6144 🏊❓🚶

SHEFFIELD

18 WYMING BROOK NATURE RESERVE

A superb gorge lined by majestic pine trees, mossy crags and endless waterfalls. Perfect for a river walk or a paddle in the pool at the bottom. From Redmires follow Redmires Rd 2km W from edge of village, past S10 4LJ. Entrance with car park on R.

---

11 WITHENS BROOK

A pretty waterfall with plunge pool. River walk downstream to more pools. Park in small lay-by at end of farm track on A6024 at Heyden Bridge, without blocking gate (53.5044, -1.8520). Cross stile next to metal gate, follow track alongside stone wall. Path steepens, keep R at fork, bear L along low rocky ridge, keeping Withers Brook to R. 700m beyond sheepfold is first swim.

45 mins, 53.5089, -1.8317 🏊 🚶 🏞 🏊

12 LANGSETT RESERVOIR, BARNSLEY

A scenic reservoir surrounded by ancient woodland at the NE edge of the Peak District National Park. Popular with local swimming groups, although there are No Swimming signs. Park at Langsett Barn Car Park, off the A616, 5.5km W of Stocksbridge. Entry on N side of reservoir is where the stone wall ends and wooden fence starts, sunnier and deeper. For the S side, more beachy and discreet, entry is at 53.4926, -1.6863 or 53.4940, -1.6845.

5 mins, 53.4986, -1.6859 ❓

13 ROYD MOOR RESERVOIR, PENISTONE

A scenic reservoir NW of Penistone, abundant in birdlife and fringed with oak

---

woodland. Popular with local swim groups. No Swimming signs. Parking on Royd Moor Rd at 53.5335, -1.6632. Follow track to reservoir and keep L on footpath through woods to S of reservoir to an area with beachy, sloped access to the water.

10 mins, 53.5390, -1.6689 ❓

HIGH PEAK & HOWDEN

14 FAIRBROOK WATERFALLS

Small meadows, purple heather, shady trees, and cascading small waterfalls on a remote but easy walk, ideal for families, with some of the pools deep enough for jumps. Pass Royal Oak pub (SK13 8QY) and park in lay-by (53.4098, -1.8295). Follow road on S 400m taking path R down and over stream via stepping stones. Continue W for 500m to falls.

20 mins, 53.4058, -1.8366 🏊🚶

15 BLACKDEN BROOK WATERFALL

Walk beside, or if you are more adventurous scramble up, a series of small waterfalls that make up the infinitely pretty Blackden Brook. Shallows for paddling and deep pools for plunging provide something for everyone in this tranquil location. Take A57 E out of Glossop for 11.5km after passing

Follow footpath R dir Rivelin Dams.
15 mins, 53.3693, -1.5963 🏊🧗🚶🪑🔁

19 RIVELIN VALLEY TRAIL
A popular plunge pool on the outskirts of Sheffield. Extended river walks with various paddles downstream. Head W out of Sheffield on A57 and park in Rivelin Valley Conservation parking lot (S6 6GF). Cross road and follow path downstream, keeping river to your R. Plunge pool 300m.
10 mins, 53.3811, -1.5642 🏊 🔁

20 CROOKES VALLEY PARK, SHEFFIELD
Spring-fed former boating lake and reservoir (the Old Great Dam), situated at the heart of public parkland in the Crookesmoor area of Sheffield, 2km from the city centre. No Swimming signs but local swim groups do. Very popular with families so can be busy. Park in Crookes Valley Rd (free parking in bus lane outside peak times), Mushroom Lane or Oxford St. Entry to the water is at Dam House Jetty with several other access points around the lake.
10 mins, 53.3831, -1.4932 ❓

21 TREETON DYKE
There are a number of good access points at this delightful lake frequented by anglers, swans and mallards. Also used by powered vehicles, and has 'no swimming' signs, so exercise judgement. From Sheffield Rd/B6200 turn into Falconer Lane (S13 9ZL) and find parking (limited). Follow path through gate at end of lane to lake.
15 mins, 53.3767, -1.3477 🏊❓

RIVER DERWENT

22 BAMFORD MILL
Pretty bridge and stepping stones across the Derwent lead to a secluded and peaceful swim with rope swing. Park in Bamford; some space to pull off along The Hollow (S33 0DU). Follow The Hollow down

to mill, then footpath to river and across stones, turn R to rope swing.
10 mins, 53.3466, -1.6939 🏊🍴🚶🪑

23 PEAKSHOLE, HOPE VALLEY
A gem of a swimming spot: languid waist-deep water in a secluded S bend. Park in Castleton car park and head E on A6187. After 600m follow footpath to R. Just after wooded area, river bends to L. Swim spot is on S bend after 100m.
20 mins, 53.3434, -1.76114 🏊

24 HATHERSAGE STEPPING STONES
A delightful couple of swim spots around the Hathersage Stepping Stones. The water can be fairly deep and fast flowing in places. Take A6187 W out of Hathersage. Park carefully on R under railway bridge after 2km. Cross road and follow footpath to river and Stepping Stones. Various entry points up and downstream. Derwent Valley Way on other side of river offers circular walks.
15 mins, 53.3305, -1.6756 🏊

25 PADLEY GORGE
Mossy, twisted oaks and the bubbling Burbage Brook make this beautiful woodland gorge a popular spot for local photographers. There are some bracing

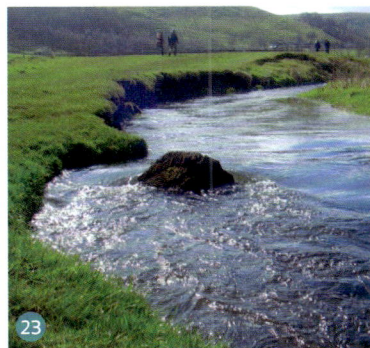

plunge pools for the brave. Busy in summer. In Upper Padley (S32 2JA) park by Grindleford Station Cafe, cross railway and follow Padley Gorge Trail footpath on R. Waterfalls near wooden bridge after 500m, pool a further 500m.
20 mins, 53.3122, -1.6181 🏊🧗🚶🪑🔁🐕♿

26 CALVER BRIDGE, RIVER DERWENT
Probably the best place in the Peaks for a long, secluded river swim. Beautifully bracing water and jumps from bridge. Simply delightful. From Froggatt take A625 dir Calver (S32 3WY) and park in

There is also a long stretch of sheltered, secluded river upstream of house and bridge before cricket ground.
10 mins, 53.2199, -1.6125

30 MATLOCK SWOOSH
A gentle 1km float/swim down the river through very pretty countryside. Head W on Derwent Valley Way from where it crosses the A6 in Matlock. After 15mins/2km footpath meets a bend in the river. This is the entry point. Exit on the L (N) shore. Scramble up the steep, rocky bank under the bridge to the footpath by the railway line. Check exit point before you start.
15 mins, 53.1441, -1.5805

lay-by L just before bridge. Follow footpath downriver or walk 750m up to Froggatt Bridge for a leisurely swim back.
2 mins, 53.2748, -1.6342

27 WHITE EDGE POOL
A delightfully secret little roadside pool, hidden by a bridge. Head NE out of Baslow on A621. After 5km park at intersection with Clodhall Ln. Pool beneath bridge to SW of the crossroads.
5 mins, 53.2622, -1.5850

28 LOWER LINACRE RESERVOIR
Crystal-clear but cold waters are surrounded by attractive woodland trails. There are bluebells in spring and a good spot for a picnic. From Overgreen, head E on B6050 (dir S42 7AX), reservoirs signed R after 750m. Car park after 500m and path to water.
10 mins, 53.2480, -1.4976

29 CHATSWORTH, RIVER DERWENT
Perfect place for a day out with family in a stunning landscaped parkland. Calm, deep river pools above downstream weir, shallows to paddle in below. Use discretion. Park at Calton Lees pay car park off B6102 N of Beeley (DE4 2NX). Follow paths down to river in park and walk upstream for weir.

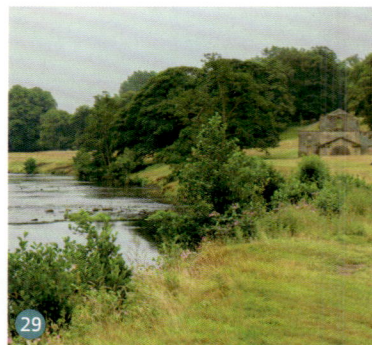

RIVER WYE

31 CHEE DALE
This is one of the finest dales in this area, abundant with wild flora and limestone crags and worth exploring. Follow the footpaths below the cliffs along the River Wye to the stepping stones. Park at Topley Head lay-by, 5.6km E of Buxton (500m NW of turning to SK17 9TG). Follow footpath from E end down, across the Monsal Trail, and head through Blackwell Mill Cycles. Cross bridge and follow footpath to R along river for 20 mins. Path can be muddy and floods after heavy rain.
30 mins, 53.2516, -1.8208

32 WATER-CUM-JOLLY DALE
Wonderfully named dale with a wide expanse of river making beautiful reflections of cliffs above an old mill weir. Head upstream for clear water and a deeper swim. From Monsal Head (DE45 1NL), head NE signed Cressbrook between hotel and car park. Follow 1.5km and park R by road near Cressbrook Mill. Follow signed concessionary footpath through holiday rentals to river.
10 mins, 53.2524, -1.7446

33 MONSAL DALE, RIVER WYE
Well-loved verdant valley overlooked by the iconic Headstone Viaduct, with many swimming opportunities along the River Wye at the end of the Monsal Trail Tunnels. In Monsal Head (DE45 1NL) drop down from bridge viewpoint by woodland path and head 750m L on bank to swimming above or below weir. Cross on footbridge to return by a circular loop.

15 mins, 53.2395, -1.7353 🚉🍴🚶🏊

34 ASHFORD-IN-THE-WATER, RIVER WYE
Delightful riverside pools above a weir, with deep, clear sections and some shaded areas. Heading E on A6, 230m after A6020 signed Ashton-in-the-Water, take L down short dead end over old bridge (opp turn to DE45 1PY) and park. Follow footpath downstream 750m.

15 mins, 53.2223, -1.6939 🚉❓🍴🚶

35 LATHKILL DALE, MONYASH
River emerges from a cave into limestone valley. Shallow weirs and pretty waterfall. Descend on path, by toilets on B5055, 1km E of Monyash. Paddling only.

15 mins, 53.188, -1.7303 💬

36 YOULGREAVE, RIVER BRADFORD
Short but perfectly formed river known for the clarity of its water. Stroll along and take a dip in the shallow 'swimming pool' above the little weir. Follow Bradford Rd S from Youlgreave Church (DE45 1WL), keeping L at fork, park near footbridge and walk 200m upstream. For a longer walk, take Alport Lane from church dir Alport (DE45 1LG) 750m, park in lay-by L, walk over river and take footpath R.

10 mins, 53.1732, -1.6854 🚉🍴🚶

SOUTH WEST

37 TEGG'S NOSE COUNTRY PARK
Stunning parkland featuring beautiful green rolling hills on one side and a view across the Cheshire Plain with Jodrell Bank radio telescope on the other. There are four reservoirs to explore in this area. No Swimming signs, and anglers. From A537 E out of Macclesfield turn R after 3.2km signed Tegg's Nose (dir SK11 0AP). Pay car park L after 800m. Follow the Saddler's Way down to reservoirs. Alternatively avoid hills by starting at the Leather's Smithy pub (SK11 0NE).

30 mins, 53.2442, -2.0791 🍴🚶

38 WILDBOARCLOUGH, CLOUGH BROOK
Picnic, plunge and paddle amongst the flat rocks in this delightful stretch of

the dappled Clough Brook. Head N into Wildboarclough on Nabbs Rd, SK11 0BD, past the Crag Inn and park 150m further up in lay-by on L opposite bridge. Walk back down to the little wooden bridge on L just before the pub.
1 mins, 53.2141, -2.0276 🏊🏞🚶🍴

39 PANNIERS POOL, THREE SHIRE HEADS
Situated at the point on Axe Edge Moor where the counties of Cheshire, Derbyshire and Staffordshire meet, a picture-perfect pair of packhorse bridges are the backdrop for a series of delightful pools and waterfalls. Ideal for a cooling dip after a warming walk. Head NE on A54 from Allgreave (SK11 0BJ) for 4km and park in lay-by L. Walk on 200m to signed footpath over stile R and follow path SE to water and then downstream to bridges. 1.2km in all.
30 mins, 53.2137, -1.9874 🏊🍴🚶👨👣⛰🅿

40 WINCLE, RIVER DANE
Enjoy a swim against the current in one of the deeper pools at the bend of this picturesque section of the River Dane. After your dip reward yourself with a visit to the nearby Wincle Brewery. In Wincle village (SK11 0QE) follow road E and park on L just before bridge. Walk over bridge

and follow footpath to L. Path down to river after 200m.
5 mins, 53.1841, -2.0525 🏊🏞😊

41 TITTESWORTH RESERVOIR
A popular place for walkers, cyclists and birdwatchers. Numerous beach-like areas ideal for a paddle, but No Swimming signs. Exercise discretion. Head E from The Lazy Trout in Meerbrook (ST13 8SN) and turn R into entrance just after dam to pay car park. Follow footpath around woodland area and past the second inlet to quieter areas.
15 mins, 53.1333, -2.0108 🏊🚶🏞🅿🚶

42 KNYPERSLEY SERPENTINE POOL
Country Park with 114 acres of old estate woodland, waterfalls, grottoes, follies and lakes. The lower reservoir is used by anglers, but shoreside paths lead on up to the more secluded upper lake and pool. Greenway Bank Country Park signed from A527 S of Biddulph, 2km to entrance with car park L, before ST8 7QX.
15 mins, 53.0966, -2.1662 ⛰🅿

43 CONSALL FORGE, RIVER CHURNET
Once home to a thriving lime furnace, the area now offers a peaceful and tranquil swim in the river - with the sighting of a

steam train on some days! From Consall (ST9 0AE) follow signs for Consall Forge no through road 2.8km then L at fork for Black Lion pub. Park in car park at end. Follow river on for 200m.
5 mins, 53.0416, -2.0028 🏊🚶🅿🚊

44 MERMAID'S POOL / BLAKE MERE
Tiny moor-top pool by roadside. Dark and foreboding, but deep with solid bottom and no 'submerged metal' like the scare-monger No Swimming signs say. Steeped in legend with views of The Roaches. 1km N of Mermaid Inn (ST13 8UN, 01538 300253).
2 mins, 53.1486, -1.9413 📷

DOVEDALE

45 PIKE POOL
One of the most famous locations in the canonical 'Compleat Angler', with a dramatic shaft of limestone overlooking a deep, luxurious swim. Nearby is the curiously named Frank i' th' Rocks cave. Head S out of Hulme End, take first L after campsite, signed Beresford Dale. Park carefully on R at end, beyond SK17 0HQ. Walk on to river, turn L before ford and follow footpath to pool before wooden bridge.
15 mins, 53.1271, -1.8096 🏊🚶🚉😊⛰

175

51 CUTLER'S BROOK
A secluded pool below a weir, dappled in sunlight, at the edge of the Kedleston Estate. Plunge, paddle and picnic. Park near Kedleston Country Hotel (DE22 5JD, some pulling off R shortly up Inn Lane). Head back down road to footpath sign R (52.9595, -1.5139). Follow path to and over brook, follow brook to R to pool.
25 mins, 52.9568, -1.5212 🏊🚶🏕

LINCOLNSHIRE

52 HORKSTOW BRIDGE
The beautiful Grade II listed suspension bridge is a fantastic place to leap into the Ancholme. Popular with locals on a hot day. From South Ferriby take High St/B1204 S 1.5km, turn R onto Bridge Lane by DN18 6BE, drive to limited parking at end. Follow footpath down to river near bridge.
2 mins, 53.6583, -0.5282 🏊🛶🍴

53 BRANDY WHARF, RIVER ANCHOLME
An interesting swim or kayak in the narrow, diverted section of an old river that is now as straight as a Roman road! Take Waddingham Rd/B1205 from South Kelsey 3.2km to Brandy Wharf. At second bend after bridge, turn L down track to river. Swim or kayak down to bridge.
2 mins, 53.4556, -0.4717 🏊🛶⛺

54 BRANSTON ISLAND LOOP
Swim the loop past Mrs Wright's former lock house at Bardney, around the lush, green fields of Branston Island, where the River Witham and Old River Witham join. There may be fishing: use discretion. Park in Bardney by Heritage Centre LN3 5UF. Cross road and follow Water Rail Way up to Bardney Lock. Use metal steps down into water on RH side to swim anticlockwise. Be aware that you need to exit on L side after the fishing site to navigate the weir before re-entering the water to finish the swim.
20 mins, 53.2157, -0.3477 🏊🛶🏊🚶🏕

55 LOW POND, DONINGTON ON BAIN
A secluded lake, dappled by shade, offering the perfect spot for skinny-dipping on a hot summer's evening. Follow B1225 south of Ludford 7.2km, past LN8 6JT, turn L signed Donington on Bain. Follow 750m and park on verge R as road bends L: 53.3268, -0.1664. Follow footpath over stile and R at field end, past first lake.
20 mins, 53.3247, -0.1557 🏊🚶⛺🏕

56 TETNEY BLOW WELLS
Artesian springs once used for a watercress farm and to provide the locals with water.

46 STEPPING STONES, DOVEDALE
The perfect family day out: stunning scenery and refreshing paddles and dips in the River Dove. Walk on to Reynard's Arch and cave. Signed off A515 just N of DE6 1NH, 3.2km N of Ashbourne. Deeper pools beneath Dove Holes upstream (53.0795, -1.7883) nearer Milldale.
10 mins, 53.0597, -1.7760 🏊🏕⛵🚶🏠💧

47 OKEOVER BRIDGE, RIVER DOVE
The small but beautifully formed River Dove winds its way through this lowland area. Here, a stony beach leads to a deep section for swimming by the bridge, where there is a traditional New Year's Day jump. Follow Mapleton Rd from Ashbourne to park at Okeover Arms, Mapleton (DE6 2AB). Walk on to next L to bridge.
2 mins, 53.0302, -1.7570 🏊🏕🍴

48 TOAD HOLE FOOTBRIDGE, SNELSTON
Simple, white-painted bridge over the River Dove. Swim, picnic, relax. On B5033 S out of Ellastone, take L onto Sides Lane signed Snelston at Norbury (DE6 2EQ). After 2.4km, pull off L at footpath opp turning R. Follow footpath to river.
3 mins, 52.9905, -1.7877 🏊🏕

49 ELLASTONE, RIVER DOVE
The idyllic, meandering River Dove pools near the bridge, offering the perfect spot for a refreshing dip. Head upstream near weir and downstream of bridge for other swim options. Head SE of Ellastone on B5033 past DE6 2GY, park in lay-by R just before bridge and follow path R from kissing gate to river. Cross bridge to explore upstream footpath on L.
5 mins, 52.9787, -1.8231 🚶🏕

SOUTH DERBYSHIRE

50 DUFFIELD, RIVER DERWENT
Immerse yourself in the cooling waters of the River Derwent and idle in the gentle current under the dappled shade against the quintessentially English backdrop of the village cricket team playing nearby. In Duffield follow Makeney Rd (DE56 4BD) E over bridge and turn R on Church Dr. Follow 800m beside railway to car park L by cricket club and cross cricket pitch to bend in river to NW. Various jetties and gaps in vegetation. If busy, park in Duffield and follow path past medical centre (DE56 4GG), under bridge to cricket pitch.
5 mins, 52.9893, -1.4832 🏊⛵🚶🏕🚗

Crystal-clear waters, but be wary of very cold temperatures and signs saying no swimming. Pipistrelle bats haunt the trees at dusk. Park in Tetney close to footpath from Church Lane, opposite Primrose Lane (DN36 5PJ). Follow path through field to first blow well in front of you to L of field

15 mins, 53.4872, -0.0103 🏊❓🅿️♿

57 LOUTH NAVIGATION CANAL

Despite its less than appealing name, this river is no longer used for navigation and is ideal for a long swim down through leafy green pastures. From A1031 in Tetney, take Tetney Lock Rd E 3.2km and over bridge to park near DN36 5UW. Walk back over bridge to take path L. Enter river after 100m on bend. Exit at sluice 400m down, or continue on for a longer swim.

5 mins, 53.4976, 0.0196 🏊🏊

NOTTINGHAMSHIRE

58 NEWSTEAD ABBEY, RAVENSHEAD

Just beyond the quirky cannon fort is a great spot for a discreet swim, with the abbey ruins and Byron's home across the water. Walking in the park is free. In Newstead follow Tilford Rd over railway (past NG15 0BT), turn R down Station Ave and follow to end. Park at barrier, continue walking and turn L at lake. Swim spot just past fort. To visit the ruins, house and gardens, too (£), use main gate on A60 in Ravenshead.

10 mins, 53.0792, -1.1992 🏊❓🍴🏊🚶🏔️

59 BURTON JOYCE, RIVER TRENT

Wide 750m swim or kayak with the flow along the River Trent. Some fast currents so competent swimmers only, and be careful of rocks on exit. Park near to The Nelson pub. Take path from car park over railway lines and grass to riverside path and turn R. Walk 1.5km to The Ferry Boat Inn (NG14 5HX) for easy access, and swim back to The Nelson.

25 mins, 52.9854, -1.0338 🏊🔽🏊

60 HOVERINGHAM LAKES SAILING CLUB 🅿️

Supervised swimming sessions 2-3 times a week, all year round at S end of lakes. Super water clarity. Notts County Sailing Club, Hoveringham Lane, Nottingham, NG14 7JX. loveopenwater.co.uk/nottingham-open-water-swimming

1 mins, 53.0166, -0.9444 🏊🅿️

61 HOVERINGHAM LAKES & TRENT

A pretty riverside walk along the Trent to the secluded N end of tranquil, spring-fed gravel pits. Great picnic spot. Or swim along

the river. E out of Bleasby, over crossroads onto Boat Lane past NG14 7FT, and car park at end (53.0325, -0.9185). Follow footpath R upstream for 500m. River swim at 53.0300, -0.9220.

15 mins, 53.0232, -0.9300 🏊🚶🍴

62 EATON BRIDGE, RIVER IDLE

A great spot for cooling off in the river on a hot summer's day. On A638 just S of Retford, turn off to Eaton (DN22 0PR). Park just after bridge by footpath sign on R. Walk back over bridge and enter river by bench on R. Further entry points along bank for 100m where bank shelves to beach.

4 mins, 53.2943, -0.9371 🏊🍴

63 SEGELOCUM, RIVER TRENT

A serene section of the River Trent, just walk upstream and then swim with the flow. The tiny Norman church of St Nicholas is worth a visit. Park at St Nicholas Church in Littleborough (DN22 0HD, E of Sturton le Steeple) and walk down to river. Footpath to L offers grassy bank for easy access. Walk 750m, keeping an eye out for the beautiful Chateau between the trees on opposite bank.

5 mins, 53.3399, -0.7573 🏊⛰️🍴

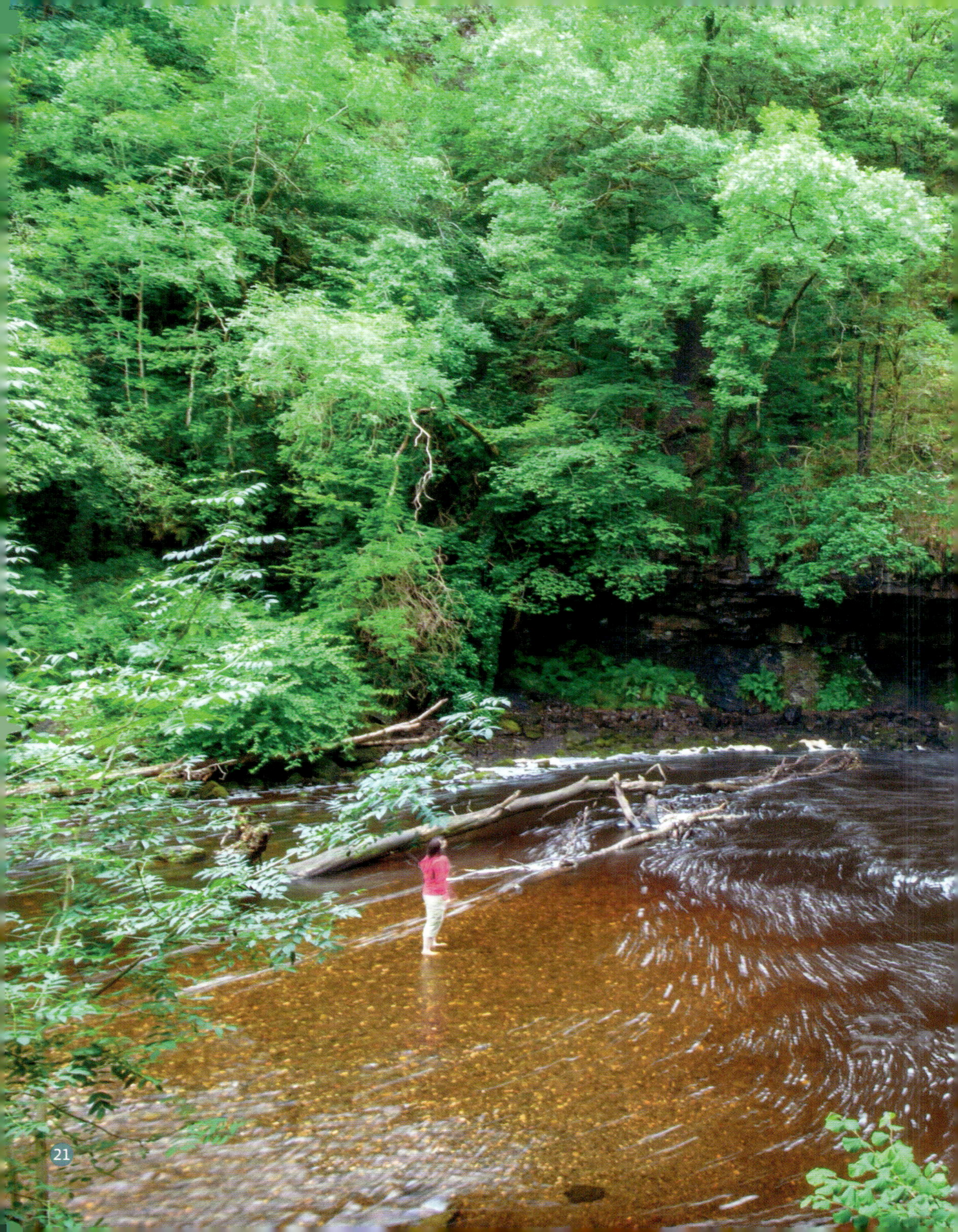

WEST WALES TO BRECON BEACONS

The great rivers of West Wales, the Teifi, Cleddau, and Tywi, provide a wealth of swimming opportunities, but the real drama begins in the western uplands of Bannau Brycheiniog (Brecon Beacons). Coed-y-Rhaiadr means 'waterfall woods', and you won't find a more impressive network of forest lidos and cascading water anywhere in Wales. The route to the waterfalls near Pontneddfechan ('bridge of the small Neath') is found through an old gate inscribed simply 'Waterfalls' in wrought iron. Soon, the sound of rushing water fills the woods. If you follow the trail for twenty minutes or so, you'll come to a large rocky outcrop on the right, above a mini canyon through which you can snorkel, enjoying clear views of the underwater rock formations in the abyss below. Further on, there's a large junction pool beneath a footbridge where families swim and older children jump (21).

The next waterfall along, Sgwd Gwladys, or Lady Falls, is named after the daughter of King Brychan, who ruled here in the tenth century (21). The falls occupy a giant amphitheatre rimmed with a lip of dark black gritstone. The great bowl holds a wide pool of gentle water and a shingle beach. Moss and fern grow in profusion in this misty microclimate, and many say this is the most beautiful waterfall in Wales. I arrived at midday, and the sun was high enough to light up the sunken woodbine and ragwort-draped glade. A slender chute of water cascaded from a high ledge beneath slopes of oak and beech. Tiptoeing into the pebble shallows, I dived into the deeper parts of the plunge pool and swam underwater in the peaty darkness, hearing the drone of the water hum between my ears and feeling the movement of the falls vibrate across my skin. Breaking the surface close to the far wall, I clambered out onto a ledge of wet rock that leads around behind the falls.

If you're well equipped and have time, you may be able to bushwhack your way up a further kilometre through the forest above Lady Falls to find the falls of Einion Gam, named after

Lampeter
Aberteifi
/ Cardigan
Newcastle
Emlyn
5
7
8
9
10
Newport
A487(T)
4
6
Fishguard
11
2
1
13
A40(T)
12
Carmarthen
3
St. Clears
Whitland
Haverfordwest
A40(T)
Narberth
Laugharne
Pembroke
Tenby
Llanelli
Loughor

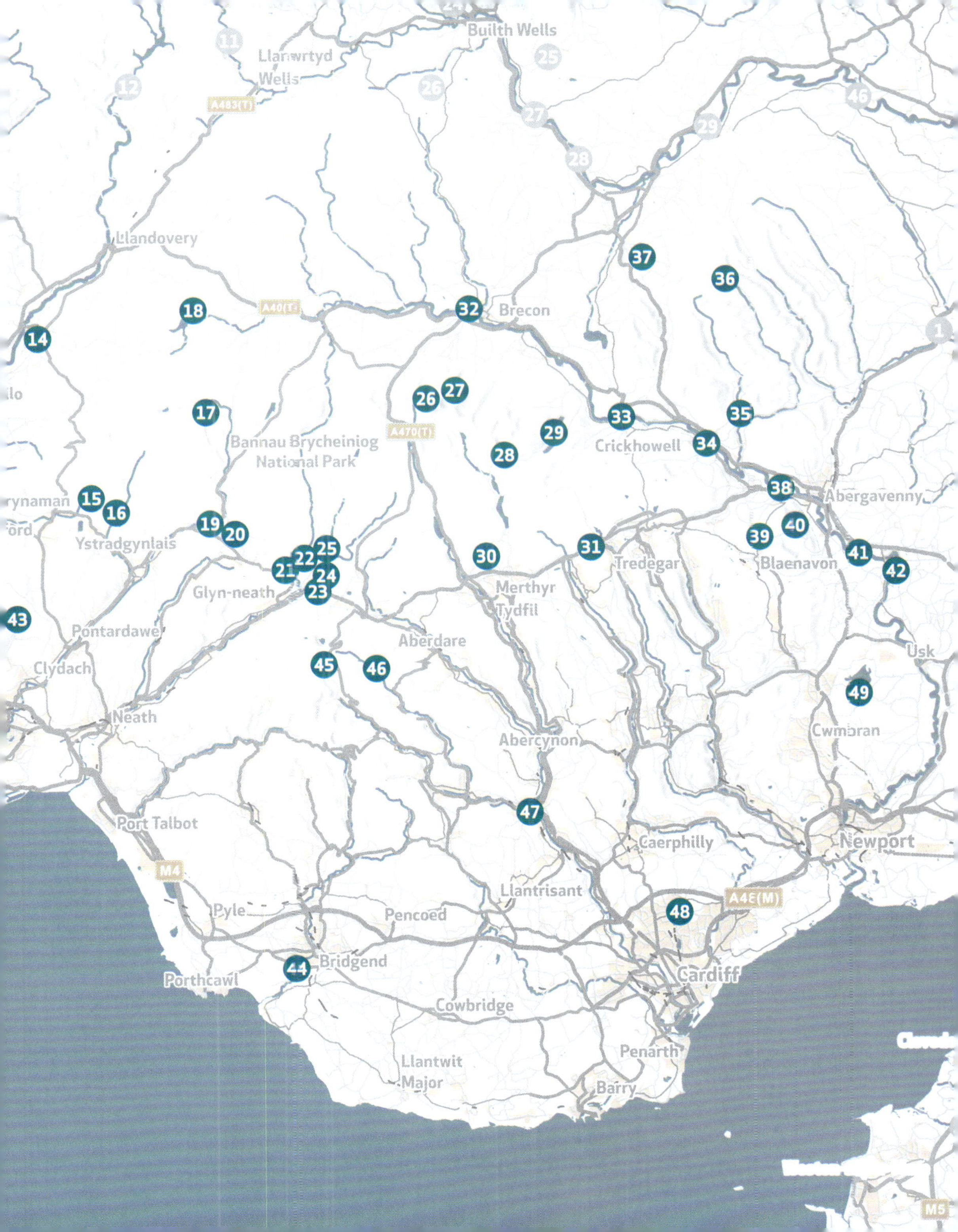

Builth Wells
Llanwrtyd Wells
A483(T)
Llandovery
A40(T)
Brecon
A470(T)
Bannau Brycheiniog National Park
Crickhowell
Abergavenny
Ystradgynlais
Glyn-neath
Merthyr Tydfil
Tredegar
Blaenavon
Pontardawe
Clydach
Aberdare
Usk
Neath
Abercynon
Cwmbran
Port Talbot
Caerphilly
Newport
M4
Llantrisant
A48(M)
Pyle
Pencoed
Bridgend
Porthcawl
Cardiff
Cowbridge
Penarth
Llantwit Major
Barry
M5
11
12
25
26
27
28
29
46
37
36
18
32
14
26
27
33
35
17
29
34
28
38
15
16
19
20
40
39
25
22
21
24
31
30
41
42
23
43
45
46
49
47
48
44

25

17

17

Gwladys' lover. This waterfall is twice as tall, and its pool is cut into a sheer-sided ravine. Back at the footbridge and junction pool, a rather precipitous path leads on to the Horseshoe Falls and two perfectly elliptical pools, like emerald lidos, lying deep in the forest (21).

In the parallel valley of the Melte, leading up to Ystradfellte, there are yet more waterfalls. At one of the most famous, Scwd yr Eira, an ancient drovers' road passes behind the flow (25). In another, the entire river disappears into the caverns of Porth yr Ogof, one of the largest cave systems in Europe. This extraordinary landscape was laid down in layers of time. The oldest limestone was formed from the shells of sea creatures that inhabited the early tropical seas, and these soft layers have been eroded into plunge pools. The harder red sandstones and gritstones above were compressed from the desert sands that covered the earth just before the dinosaurs, and these form the hard lip at the top of the falls. Finally, there are the carboniferous, or coal-bearing, seams, the remains of the first forests that colonised the earth once the seas and deserts receded. Warped, compressed, and contorted, all these aeons of time are visible in the waterfalls.

To the west is the Black Mountain, an area of sinkholes and limestone karst. Llyn y Fan Fach is one of two high tarns that sit beneath the peak (17). For many centuries, legend has told of a 'Lady of the Lake' who will rise shimmering on the first Sunday of August at two o'clock in the afternoon. I camped up here with a friend one midsummer. A wall of bare scree rises on the south side of the lake, and many miles of central Wales' most remote interior drop away in undulating vistas to the north. We ventured into the grey, glassy waters at the end of the day, just as the sun was becoming pink in the sky. Having reached the middle, we watched in amazement as great sheets of summer mist began to roll in and surround us on the water. Our distant tents disappeared beneath the shrouded veil, and great wisps of ghostly vapour rose slowly up the mountain wall. We made for the shore, feeling the lake might suddenly erupt in some supernatural horror, and stood there shivering and waiting, peering out for our camp. Then, just as quickly as the mist had come, it was gone, and the burning evening glow dried us as the sun sank like a fireball in the sky.

To the east the Bannau Brycheiniog form the centrepieces of the National Park. The ridge path along Pen-y-Fan and Cribyn is popular on a summer day, but few know about the waterfall that cascades down into the Usk, set into the side of the steep mountain and invisible from above. The valley of Nant Sere is the most remote: a series of moss-covered waterfalls in a deep, sheltered vale filled with patches of ancient oak woodland and shallow pools amid mountain bracken (27). At least five falls drop down this mountainside, and after a hard walk up to the summits, there's nothing more idyllic than to descend and dip in each one.

The Usk Valley collects the sparkly waters from these peaks and channels them through beautiful pools in the valley below. Carving through soft pink sandstone, it is a shallow river for much of its length but occasionally opens out into beautiful hidden swimming holes, perfect to while away a weekend of wildlife spotting and swimming. Bats may be seen in the early evening swooping over the river; purple- and green-winged orchids can be found, and in the spring, there are crab apple, wild cherry, and plum blossoms.

One such area is around the little village of Crickhowell, halfway between Brecon and Abergavenny. It's a medieval town beneath Table Mountain – Crug Hywel – from which it takes its name. There is good paddling and plunging in the pool beneath the bridge and a small weir by some stone steps (34). An old right of way stretches across the river, and if you swim across, you'll notice that the bridge appears to have seventeen arches from one side but only sixteen from the other.

Some miles upstream, you'll find Llangynidr. From the narrow medieval bridge, the river runs rocky and shallow below, forming small rivulets between island clumps of butterwort and shingle. The bedrock is as gentle to the touch as soapstone but struck through with cream and red quartz bands. Upstream rounded eddy holes hold little piles of pebbles, and pillars of rock stand like miniature wind-carved tors, etched by the current and flow (33).

Picking my way down the rough bankside path from the bridge, I was searching for a particularly idyllic swimming pool discovered by a friend. Just as I was about to give up and return to the bridge, the alto tinkling of the shallow water began to lower into the baritone of a deeper pool. A few minutes ahead, the river poured over a low ledge into an area of still water extending from bank to bank, with flat sunny picnic ledges and sculpted stones on which countless local families must have hung their clothes (33).

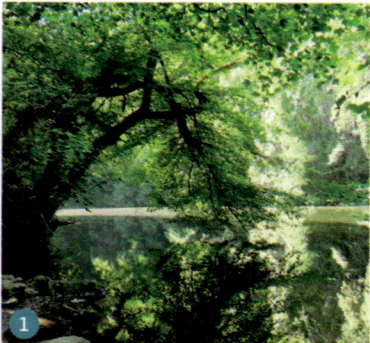

3 CLEDDAU DDU, LLAWHADEN

After visiting the superb castle, desend to the stone bridge for a swim (SA67 8DJ). Explore further for pools and little beaches upstream. Parking/ path at 51.8215 -4.7942 to find corner pool after 1.5km.

2 mins, 51.8316, -4.7885

4 NEVERN, R NEYFER

Perfect corner pool with small waterfall before a woodland gorge walk into the Nevern gorge. Park near Trewern Arms (SA42 0NB, 01239 820395) and take downstream footpath before bridge, 400m. There's also a very nice pool on the upstream section (52.0211, -4.7894) for those walking to Felindre Farchog.

5 mins, 52.0243, -4.8002

TEIFI VALLEY

5 TEIFI GORGE, CILGERRAN

The Teifi gorge is a steep, forested section of the lower reaches of the river. Ferns and creepers hang from the cliffs over the dark, deep waters, home to otters and rich in birdlife. Dip under the shadow of Cilgerran Castle, or make a committing swim journey all the way down to the Teifi Marshes. Also good for canoeing and paddleboarding. A footpath runs along the river from the Welsh Cilgerran is signed off the A478 S of Cardigan. The riverside car park is down dead end, signed from the village shop, past SA43 2SS. Downstream are steps. Walk back towards shop for Pumporth Road to the castle.

2 mins, 52.0558, -4.6310

6 FFYNONE WOOD WATERFALLS

A surprisingly large waterfall for a tiny stream, flowing into a deep pool. There are rope swings galore, dens and tree climbing. Turn S off B4332 just E of Newchapel, signed Cwm-ffynnone. After 1¼ miles find a large car park on R past SA37 0HQ. Follow track 800m up past lake and through woods.

15 mins, 52.0136, -4.5698

7 CENARTH, RIVER TEIFI

Cenarth is a tourist honeypot, famous for its coracles and the picturesque falls where salmon leap in autumn. There are waterfalls above the ancient bridge and a huge pool beneath. The Coracle Centre (entry fee) tells the story of the Teifi fishermen and their coracles – once common across Wales. W of Newcastle Emlyn on A484 (near SA38 9JL), with a large cash-only car park by bridge. A boardwalk leads upstream and it's a good

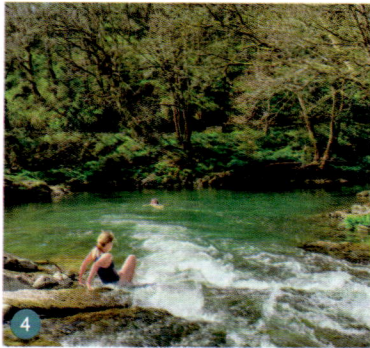

NORTH PEMBROKESHIRE

1 SEALYHAM WOODS, LAKE & RAVINE

Enter this enchanting ancient beech wood to find a mossy gorge, waterfalls and an old stone bridge over the Anghof river. There is a vast lake, from the slate-quarrying era, connecting to a fascinating man-made stream ravine (fun on an inner tube).N from Haverfordwest on A40, just N of Wolf's Castle, turn R into cul-de-sac Quarry Lane (SA62 5ND, park here or layby off A40 just beyond). Follow footpath at end and bear R at junction down towards stream. 300m upstream, beyond activity camp, is the lake.

10 mins, 51.908, -4.9675

2 ROSEBUSH QUARRY, MYNYDD PRESELI

A deep blue lagoonand some fine ruins are the lasting relics of these 19th-century slate quarries. The lagoon was originally dug as a pit, allowed to flood and then used as a reservoir to drive the dressing shed's turbine. Good bilberry foraging. Between Fishguard and Narbeth on B4313 turn into Rosebush village. Park and walk up the dead-end lane, beyond the cottages SA66 7QX, to find the dressing shed ruins L after 500m and path up to lake R.

10 mins, 51.9359, -4.7959

place to launch a canoe. There's also access to riverside footpath and space to pull off a mile downstream on A484 from 52.0528, -4.5417. Museum open Easter–September not Saturdays. (01239 710980).
2 mins, 52.0455, -4.5252

8 NEWCASTLE EMLYN, RIVER TEIFI
A loop of the river near the town centre is overlooked by an easily accessed ruin on a steep mound. There's loads of riverbank here, from which to swim or boat, and a weir too. Or just have fun rolling down the slopes. Well-signed from the main high street (A475), past SA38 9AF.
2 mins, 52.0391, -4.4631

9 HENLLAN BRIDGE & WATERFALL, TEIFI
An exciting section of easily accessible gorge, deep pools and woodland upstream of the attractive arched stone bridge. Take A484 E of Newcastle Emlyn, turn L over bridge for B4334/Henllan (signed Teifi railway, dir SA44 5TE). A footpath on R after bridge leads upstream to pools after 50m. Or explore downstream to Pwll Glas, a big river bend and beach with trickier access (continue on road 100m to find path on L via church).
2 mins, 52.0347, -4.3978

10 MAESYCRUGIAU, RIVER TEIFI
In the quiet upper reaches of the Teifi, this little river walk leads to a deep pool near an old church and ruin. Below the bridge are luscious pools and lawns; they are private, but you could swim down past them. Signed Maesycrugiau from A485 in Llanllwni. Continue 1¾ miles park L and walk on 150m to find path on R before the Pont Llwni stone bridge, SA39 9LT. Follow the river footpath up from the bridge through woods. There are rapids and pools before arriving at a ruin and a large, deep pool.
5 mins, 52.0496, -4.2257

TYWI/TOWY VALLEY

11 ABERGORLECH & TALLEY ABBEY
The footpath opposite the forest car park leads upstream into an adventurous wooded gorge on the Cothi, a beautiful undeveloped tributary of the Tywi (B4310, at SA32 7SJ, 12km N of Llandeilo). There's also a river pool opp the ancient Black Lion (SA32 7SN, 01558 685271). Talley Abbey Lakes is 4km to the E, with majestic ruins by a double lake nature reserve. Follow the W shore to explore (51.9774, -3.9907). To explore downstream, try the laneside footbridge at 51.9356, -4.1298,

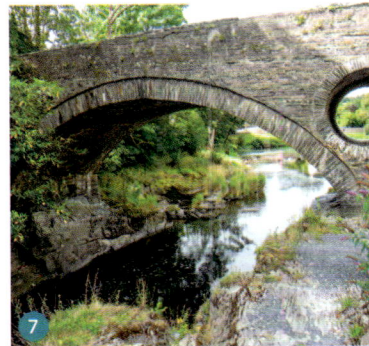

14 AFON SAWDDE

Easy spot for a picnic, paddle and plunge, in meadows with a small weir by the road. Just S of Llangadog on A4069, turn R (dir Bethlehem, SA19 9BU) to parking before bridge. Better weir to the L 180m. Near sewage works so avoid after heavy rain.

3 mins, 51.931, -3.8826 🏊🌊

BLACK MOUNTAIN

15 PWLLYMERCHED, RIVER AMMAN

A traditional swimming hole in a high mountain stream. It's small, but remote and wild, so you will probably have it all to yourself. Turn off A4068 E of Rhosaman, dir SA9 2WN, and park at the cattle grid after 250m. Bear L onto dirt track 500m NW across the moor for the stone sheepfolds, then on again to where the river bends.

15 mins, 51.8197, -3.8237 🏊⛰

16 AFON TWRCH

On a section of river that feels wilder than its post-industrial location would suggest, a pretty cascade empties into a deep pool next to an enormous ruined kiln. Downstream, a small weir creates a deep pool beneath fun for a quick dip. From Ystradowen village car park (SA9 2YP) continue on road down to stone bridge, cross and take footpath L 400m to weir pool (51.8017, -3.8028). Continue 1km, crossing the river on footbridge, then take path R past kiln and down to river bend.

30 mins, 51.8096, -3.7959 🏊🚶🏚

17 LLYN Y FAN FAWR & STREAM

Legend-rich, wild lakes under the shadow of the Black Mountain's steep escarpments. NB Llyn y Fan Fach has No Swimming signs due to drinking water supply. Park on lane at 51.8696, -3.66727. Ascend via the Nant y Llyn with waterfalls along the way.

30 mins, 51.8791, -3.6961 🏊📷🚶

18 USK RESERVOIR

Set in forested mountain scenery, and mostly encircled by a track and lane. The north road has south west-facing beaches, great for picnicking and paddling but sadly No Swimming signs, so it's your choice. On A40 Trecastle turn by antiques shops and follow 4 miles to pull off L, beyond LD3 8YF.

2 mins, 51.9502, -3.7097 🌊🏊❓

19 TAWE AT ABERCRAF

Popular with local families in summer, the Tawe has pools of various depths underneath the footbridge, or you could explore further downstream nearer to the road bridge to find a larger, deeper pool.

then upstream footpath to find beach opp, 1.5km. Or the iron footbridge at 51.8863, -4.1494 with wooded shores.

1 mins, 51.9818, -4.0568 🏊🚶⛰🌊🏃

12 CASTELL DRYSLWYN

Captured by Edward I in 1287, a dramatic ruin stands on an isolated knoll on the banks of the Towy valley above the road. There is good river swimming from the far bottom end of the car park, although current can be strong. Push through the balsam, following the fishing path. Or head downstream a little through the fields for more bank. Eventually you come to a huge gravelly meander with beaches and deep pools (no official right of way, so be discreet). 11km W of Llandeilo take B4297.

10 mins, 51.8624, -4.1013 🏛❓

13 LLANDEILO

Convenient spot next to swinging bridge in fields close to the town. Well used by local swimmers. Park in station car park (or arrive by train) and cross tracks with care using designated crossing spot. Turn L and follow path to swinging bridge, cross over to find beaches below.

5 mins, 51.8846, -3.9859

Space for 2-3 cars in layby opp St David's Church (SA9 1TJ). Follow footpath R from layby past house and field to find footbridge after 300m. For downstream spot, turn off A4067 onto Heol Tawe then L onto Station Road. Follow footpath past stables and under bridge to river.

5 mins, 51.8015, -3.6919

20 HENRHYD FALLS

The tallest waterfall in southern Wales, with a drop of 27m and a small plunge pool below – you can also walk behind. Sessile oaks cling to the cliff walls. Follow the footpath downstream along the Nant Llech another 1.6km for a smaller waterfall with a larger pool, and the ruins of Melin Llech mill by a footbridge. Signed from the A4221 via Coelbren. Continue through the village beyond SA10 9PG then turn L to NT car park. Walk through gate, steeply downhill to river, cross the bridge and turn L upstream

15 mins, 51.7942, -3.6641

WATERFALL WOODS

21 SGWD GWLADUS & EINION GAM

A graceful column of water in a wooded amphitheatre falls 10m into the large, deep plunge pool of 'Lady Falls'; you can

climb behind and dive back in. Entering Pontneddfechan from B4242, find woodland 'waterfall woods' through metal gate behind Angel Inn L (SA11 5NR, 01639 722013, parking opp). About halfway is a little canyon stretch for jumping and swimming (51.7639, -3.5978). Eventually arrive at a large junction/confluence pool below footbridges, another lovely swim spot. Cross first bridge and bear L up the Afon Pyrddin 400m for the main falls. (Bear R to continue on the main Nedd to Horseshoe and then Ddwli falls, see next listing). Upstream further is the imposing Einion Gam, 21m high and rarely visited. It requires some criss-crossing of the stream, but you are rewarded with a huge plunge pool, best in the morning sun. Bear up R above falls, then 1km (51.7718, -3.6088).

30 mins, 51.7714, -3.6011

22 NEDD FECHAN WATERFALLS

The graceful arc and large pool of Ddwli on the Nedd Fechan is one of the quieter waterfalls in the area, you'll often be only in the company of dippers and wagtails. As for Sgwd Gwladus but at confluence bear R over bridge. You'll pass Sgwd y Bedol (Horseshoe Falls) after 700m, also great fun with a big, deep jump and a further 400m to Sgwd Dwli. The Pont Melin car

park at the N end is only open off season.

5 mins, 51.7771, -3.5876

23 DDINAS SILICA MINE & SYCHRYD FALLS

Once the most important silica mine in the world. One path leads into the lower Sychryd gorge falls, under the great folds of Bwa Maen. Confident scramblers could climb this following the route of the old tramway, along a precipitous track along the canyon wall, with remains of rusting old mine trucks in the river below. If this wet short-cut doesn't appeal, a climb up and over the sheer Craig y Ddinas (a hill fort said to be inhabited by fairies), leads to the upper gorge. The Sychryd waterfall and large plunge pool thunder below a bridge which leads to the long silica mine tunnel. Popular for gorge scrambling. Parking as for Gunpowder Works (see entry). Follow accesible path around back of rocks to lower gorge. Or bear L on a steep path up and over Craig y Ddinas, turning right on a narrow downhill path for the upper gorge and bridge (51.7598, -3.5711).

20 mins, 51.7577, -3.5689

24 GUNPOWDER WORKS, AFON MELLTE

A large, deep pool beneath a ruined weir, good for jumps and next to the old gunpowder works. Explore upstream through sylvan glens to find the upper weir and pools, then discover the upper waterfall with deep canyon pools. Entering Pontneddfechan from B4242, bear R past the Dinas Inn and turn right at village hall (SA11 5NU) over bridge to car park on left. Return over river on foot, turn R past hall and walk on track upstream. This is private land until barrier but walkers usually tolerated. Continue 1km to footbridge with weir, pools and ruins. Alternatively take path from car park uphill with river on L, and turn L after 800m to descend to footbridge. Lower river path non existent following landslip. Continue another 500m for the upper weir, and 500m again for the waterfall, keeping to river R (near side).

15 mins, 51.7639, -3.5671

25 YSTRADFELLTE FALLS, AFON MELLTE

A dramatic and very popular gorge with many waterfalls, best in hot weather! Go early morning or evening to beat the crowds. Often more dramatic than the others listed, but with smaller pools. The upper Clun Gwyn is best accessed from the west of the river, before crossing to lower Clun Gwyn, a tiered waterfall, and our favourite: y Pannwr, with large pool at the base. Then on to yr Eira (on the Hepste) – a big pool, and you can walk behind the falls. The Mellte can become treacherous after heavy rain. Entering Pontneddfechan from B4242, follow road up L at the Dinas Inn. After 2½ miles, before SA11 5US, find car park R by cattle grid. Follow footpath down 500m, past Clyngwyn bunkhouse to footbridge. Cross and follow waymarked paths on river L. Y Pannwr is at 51.7813, -3.5631, on the lower green path. Yr Eira is another 500m on from here.

20 mins, 51.7838, -3.5625

BANNAU BRYCHEINIOG

26 LLYN CWM LLWCH & CORN DU

High in the beautiful Cwm Llwch valley, a remote tarn with a gently shelving shore and superb view. A good approach to the summit ridge of Corn Du and Pen y Fan. From B4601 W approach into Brecon from A40, turn first R into Ffrwdgrech Rd and follow straight for about 3 miles, past LD3 8LD, to road-end Nant Cwm Llwch car park beyond gate. Continue 3.2km up the valley to the lake.

30 mins, 51.8878, -3.4516

27 NANT SERE WATERFALLS & WOODS
A string of enchanting, moss-covered shallow waterfalls in magical woodland, under a heather-covered hillside in a secret valley. Amazing mossy hummocks can be found in the woods below. Spectacular approach by bushwhacking down from Cribyn or Pen y Fan ridge to S as part of a loop. Or from B4601 W approach into Brecon from A40 turn by church dir LD3 8LL to end of road (Cwmcynwyn Farm pay parking L), continue on bridleway 300m then follow wall all the way along to stream 800m (small waterfall) and continue up another 800m. Probably nicest walk is from Cwm Gwdi car park at 51.9127, -3.4203 (over cattle grid ½ mile E of LD3 8LE, National Trust pay & display), then around bottom of Allt Ddu, 3.2km.
35 mins, 51.8936, -3.4195 ⊞

28 BLAEN-Y-GLYN FALLS, CAERFANELL
Find your perfect pool on this popular mountain stream. The deepest are downstream of the footbridge, some with grassy banks. Above the bridge there are rock slides and paddling leading up to the tallest falls. Beyond and above is a quieter stretch with orchid meadows, shallow pools and ancient oaks, continuing for half a mile. From Pontsticill follow the reservoir road, signed Talybont-on-Usk. About 1¼ miles after CF48 2UT top car park is off L, but it's easier to continue down to bottom parking area, another ¾ mile, just before bridge. Follow the river path up from the bridge (far side) and, as you go, then choose your pool to swim in on the way back.
20 mins, 51.8485, -3.365 ⚠ ⊞

29 TALYBONT RESERVOIR ❷
Sheltered by trees and with grassy banks this gently shelving reservoir warms up nicely in summer. There's bird hide from which to spot pochard, tufted duck, mallard and teal. As for Blaen y Glyn falls

(see listing), but continue NE 3 miles from the bridge. Find a gate in fence R, and bird hide (just under a mile SW from the dam wall). This is a Welsh Water reservoir so swimming is not allowed, with signs advising this here. If you dip, take all precautions and be discreet. Bigger parking and picnic area mile on.
2 mins, 51.8641, -3.3097 🅿❓❷ ⊞

30 PONT-SARN BLUE POOL
The Taf Fechan churns through a narrow, deep chasm under the old bridge to reach what's known locally as the Blue Pool – more black than blue. You can find further pools downstream in ancient woodland, or upstream under the viaduct. Further north are the lost remains of Vaynor Church. Take A470 N from Merthyr Tydfil, turn R onto A4054 then L through Trefechan. Space for a few cars on roadside next to Aberglais Inn or for one car down nearer bridge on L (turn R before pub). On W of stone bridge take path R following river downstream to find waterfall pool and separate pool above.
3 mins, 51.778, -3.3854 ⚠ ⊞

31 PARC BRYN BACH LAKE, TREDEGAR ❸
Supervised OWS courses in 36 acre lake in Tredegar. NP22 3AY. Tel: 01495 369687.

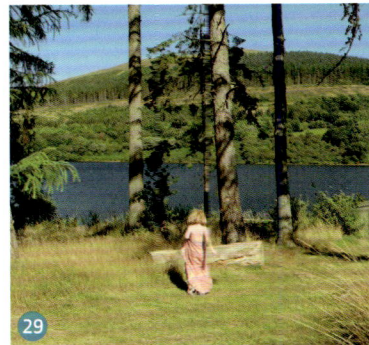

May - Oct. 1 or 1.5 hour sessions £7.50. Min age 11. parcbrynbach.co.uk.
2 mins, 51.7841, -3.2692

USK & BLACK MOUNTAINS

32 USK PROMENADE, BRECON

Pleasant stretch of deep water above the weir. Pedalos to rent, easy swimming and grass banks for picnics. Cradoc Rd towards cemetery and bear L signed for promenade, past LD3 9LL to large car park on L.
2 mins, 51.9505, -3.4034

33 LLANGYNIDR, RIVER USK

Just upstream of the old bridge are deeper pools, shallower rapid sections and plenty of flat rocks for picnics. Downstream by a wooded crag is a large pool below a waterfall good for a jump, but this can be shady in the afternoon. More excellent and secluded pools downstream 400m. The whole of the Usk has private fishing rights, so do not swim if fishermen present. Signed off A40 11km SE of Brecon. Cross the bridge, turn R and park by post office café/shop. A path behind leads down to riverbanks. Downstream of bridge on same bank a path leads to the waterfall 800m (51.875, -3.2230). 1.6km further downstream is Dyfnant riverbank

(51.8707, -3.2038), but also popular with fishermen. Just E of NP8 1PX cross the roadside canal bridge (good point for canal canoe access too) then turn L.
5 mins, 51.8749, -3.2349

34 CRICKHOWELL, RIVER USK

A large, deep pool beneath the arched stone bridge. Paddling, picnics and shallow pools upstream along riverside path. Access from steps below green, opp Bridge End Inn (NP8 1AR, 01873 810338, parking by old chapel). Avoid if fishermen are present.
2 mins, 51.8561, -3.1405

35 UPPER CWM BRIDGE, LLANBEDR

Old stone packhorse bridge over the bracing Grwyne Fechan stream. Pool below, and beach with small waterfall pools just upstream. In Llanbedr (NP8 1SR) follow the dead-end lane past church, becoming a footpath down to the river.
5 mins, 51.8767, -3.1028

36 GRWYNE FAWR RESERVOIR

It's a long walk up into the upper reaches of this remote valley, but efforts are rewarded with a fine Victorian dam and lake, and a bothy. The water is deep and cold, in high water the far end has ledges popular for

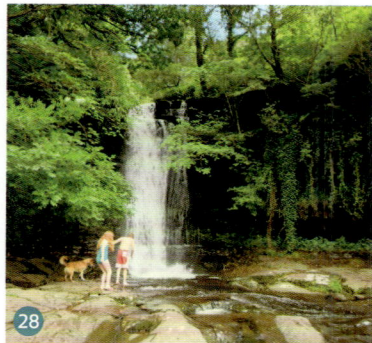

jumping. The reservoir is Welsh Water managed and swimming is discouraged. From A465 Llanvihangel Crucorney (signed Llanthony), turn L after 1¼ mile signed Partrishow/Forest Coal Pit. Continue straight for 7½ miles (1¾ miles N of/past NP7 7LY) to Myndd Du forestry car park near road end. Walk on to gate and bear R up trackway, arriving at top of dam.
45 mins, 51.9709, -3.1189

37 PWLL-Y-WRACH WATERFALL

By name and local legend this was the 'witches pool', where suspected witches were tried by immersion. Today it is a peaceful, wooded glen, vibrant with woodland flowers in springtime. In Talgarth turn up Bell St by the Bridge End Inn. Continue ¾ mile (past turning to LD3 0DU) to reserve signboard and some parking R.
15 mins, 51.9862, -3.2109

38 LLANWENARTH, RIVER USK

Walk across the field from the church to this long pebble beach with an island to explore and deeper spots downstream. Heading W out of Abergavenny bear first L after hospital past NP7 7EL. Continue to church ¾ mile to find parking R, footpath on L.
5 mins, 51.8248, -3.0581

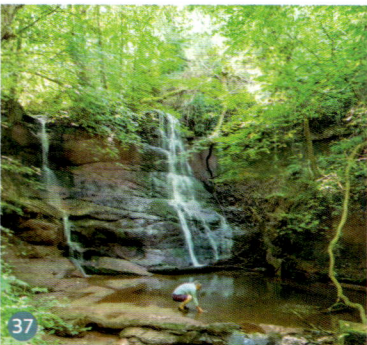

39 KEEPER'S POND & PUNCHBOWL

There are superb views from this high-level 'pond' (Pen-ffordd-goch), and it's popular with swimmers all year round, with a mobile visiting sauna (sawna.co.uk). Built in 1817, the water once supplied the Garn Ddyrys iron forge below, and you can still see the remains of old furnaces and huge, weirdly shaped slag. Hill's Tramroad passes below which linked the ironworks at Blaenavon via the Pwll Du limestone quarry, a place of rock walls and wilderness, to the canal at Llanfoist below the Blorenge. It included the longest horse-drawn tramway tunnel in Britain and the route is now known as the Iron Mountain Trail. On B4246 a mile N from Blaenavon, find pond and car park opp turn off for NP4 9SS. Also explore the old coal and ironworks lake at 51.7961, -3.1120 on the hillsides to the west.

2 mins, 51.791, -3.0817

40 PUNCHBOWL LAKE, BLORENGE

This forested cwm was carved by glaciers and now shelters an islanded lake. There are big views and a large tree to climb by the embankment. The walk down is via an old trackway lined with twisty veteran beeches. On hill to transmitter, find a bridleway by stone wall and cattle grid (51.7949, -3.0476

parking for one car, more parking back up the hill in layby). On the old Iron Mountain tramway path, linking to Keeper's Pond.

10 mins, 51.7988, -3.0424

41 ST CADOC'S AT THE BRYN, RIVER USK

A path leads down to the river near the church (look out for the ancient yew growing in the graveyard wall). There are beaches and a pool downstream. Upstream, beyond the railway bridge, are more pools and an island. B4598 at Penpergwm SE of Abergavenny, signed The Bryn (dead end) over A40. Follow round to village end and St Cadoc's past NP7 9AP and park on junction grass verge. A footpath leads down lane L through the gate into field and down to river.

5 mins, 51.7794, -2.9718

42 CLYTHA, RIVER USK

Beautiful riverside at Clytha. The NT Clytha car park at 51.7719, -2.9273 gives access downstream. Also explore 800m upstream of bridge via path (same bank) for secret, very secluded beaches at 51.7755, -2.9563, good for bivvying.

20 mins, 51.7669, -2.9306

GLAMORGAN & VALLEYS

43 CWM CLYDACH, LOWER CLYDACH

Paddle below the ancient stone packhorse bridge in this secret wooded valley. Create a loop via Carn Llechart stones, part of the Cwm Clydach Walk. From B4603 in Clydach head NW through Craig-cefn-parc and then turn R to Pont Llechart/SA6 5TL; 300m beyond postcode, find footpath on L signed Mynydd Carnllechart (park R by bridge just beyond – nice little pool below). Continue 1.6km N. Main pools 500m upstream of stone bridge at 51.7401, -3.9097.

20 mins, 51.7361, -3.9062

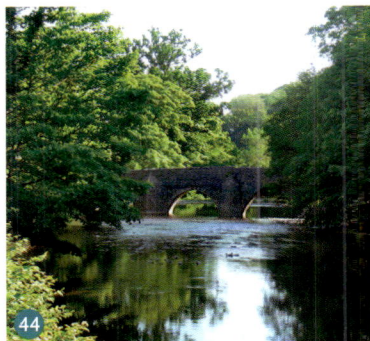

44 DIPPING BRIDGE, MERTHYR MAWR
Deep pool below ancient stone arched bridge, look for the holes where farmers used to push sheep into the water to wash them. Prone to flooding after a high tide, popular with local children in summer. Leaving Bridgend W on A48, turn onto New Inn Road, for postcode CF32 0LR. Parking next to bridge for 2-3 cars.
0 mins, 51.4935, -3.5988

45 RHONDDA FAWR WATERFALLS
Two high waterfalls plunge and tumble over verdant cliffs to collect in this large dammed pool; other smaller falls are found nearby. N from Treherbert on A4061, 2½ miles beyond turn to CF42 5PH, Hendre'r Mynydd car park is on R. Cross road and down the slope SW.
5 mins, 51.7034, -3.5663

46 RHONDDA FACH WATERFALL
On splendid open moorland, a cycle route and track follows the mountain stream to a waterfall plunge pool. This links up with Castell Nos reservoir, set under a medieval motte. A 1¼ mile N of Maerdy/CF43 4BE on A4233, find car park on L. Follow the cycle route SW then NW for 2.8km, perhaps

returning S 800m to Castell Nos if you fancy a second dip.
40 mins, 51.7006, -3.5081

47 LIDO PONTY, PONTYPRIDD £
Grade II listed lido with 3 pools heated to 28 degrees. CF37 4PE. Tel: 0300 004 0000 Open Apr - Sep £3.50. Online bookings only lidoponty.co.uk
2 mins, 51.6017, -3.3388

48 LLANISHEN & LISVANE RESERVOIR £
Lifeguard supervised reservoir swimming in Cardiff. 90 minute sessions £10. CF14 0BB. Tel: 02920 740454. Reduced number of sessions in Autumn / Winter. Min age 12 years. book: lisvane-llanishen.com
2 mins, 51.5321, -3.1731

49 LLANDEGFEDD LAKE, PONTYPOOL £
Lifeguard supervised reservoir swimming. 2 hour sessions £10. NP4 0SY. Tel: 0330 0413 381. Min age 12 years. Book ahead online: llandegfedd.co.uk
2 mins, 51.6829, -2.9723

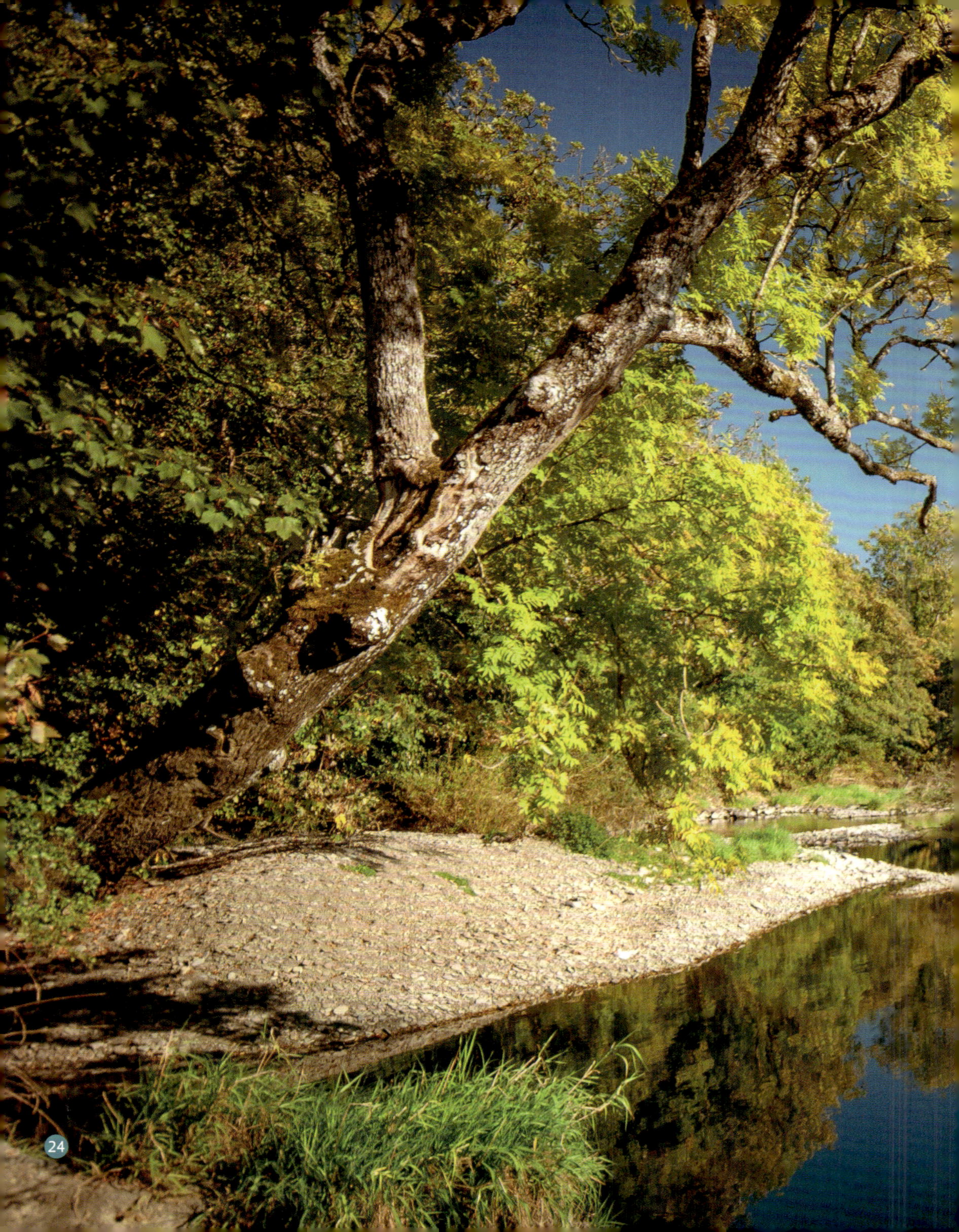

CAMBRIANS TO THE MARCHES

Wolf's Leap is a tight rocky canyon on the River Irfon, set above a series of deep river pools (10). Rugged and beautiful, the valley winds its way down from the rooftop wilds of central Wales and serves as a sanctuary for the once-rare red kite.

The canyon takes its name from the last wolf in Wales, allegedly seen jumping to freedom here in the sixteenth century. Wolves were perceived as vermin and hunted to extinction. The same fate almost befell the red kite, which was reduced to just a handful of breeding pairs by the end of the nineteenth century. These mountains were their lonely refuge, but a huge conservation effort has led to their recovery across the UK.

The journey to these hills can feel rather epic. I made it in a conked-out 1979 campervan, driving in from Tregaron in the west, up and over twenty miles of narrow mountain lanes. My van overheated and was saved by a call to the AA from the lonely telephone box at the junction of two mountain roads high on the moors of rhos pastures, a wetland mosaic of heather, grass, and bog.

The River Irfon appears as you descend down the Devil's Staircase, with the landscape opening up into a wide crag-edged valley. The pools themselves are at the outflow of a small slot canyon, which forms the metre-wide Wolf's Leap. This narrow crack of churning water has cut deep into the rock and eroded potholes and chambers. The pool is small but deep, featuring great sloping slabs of Cambrian rock, some of the oldest in the world.

Well known as a swimming river, the Irfon was once used by local churches as a place for baptisms. Downstream from the Leap is the wash pool (11), also used by drovers, for whom the river marked the beginning of a cattle-herding route to East Anglia. As many as one thousand animals at a time would be brought by this pool, sometimes under the guidance of just one man and his dogs.

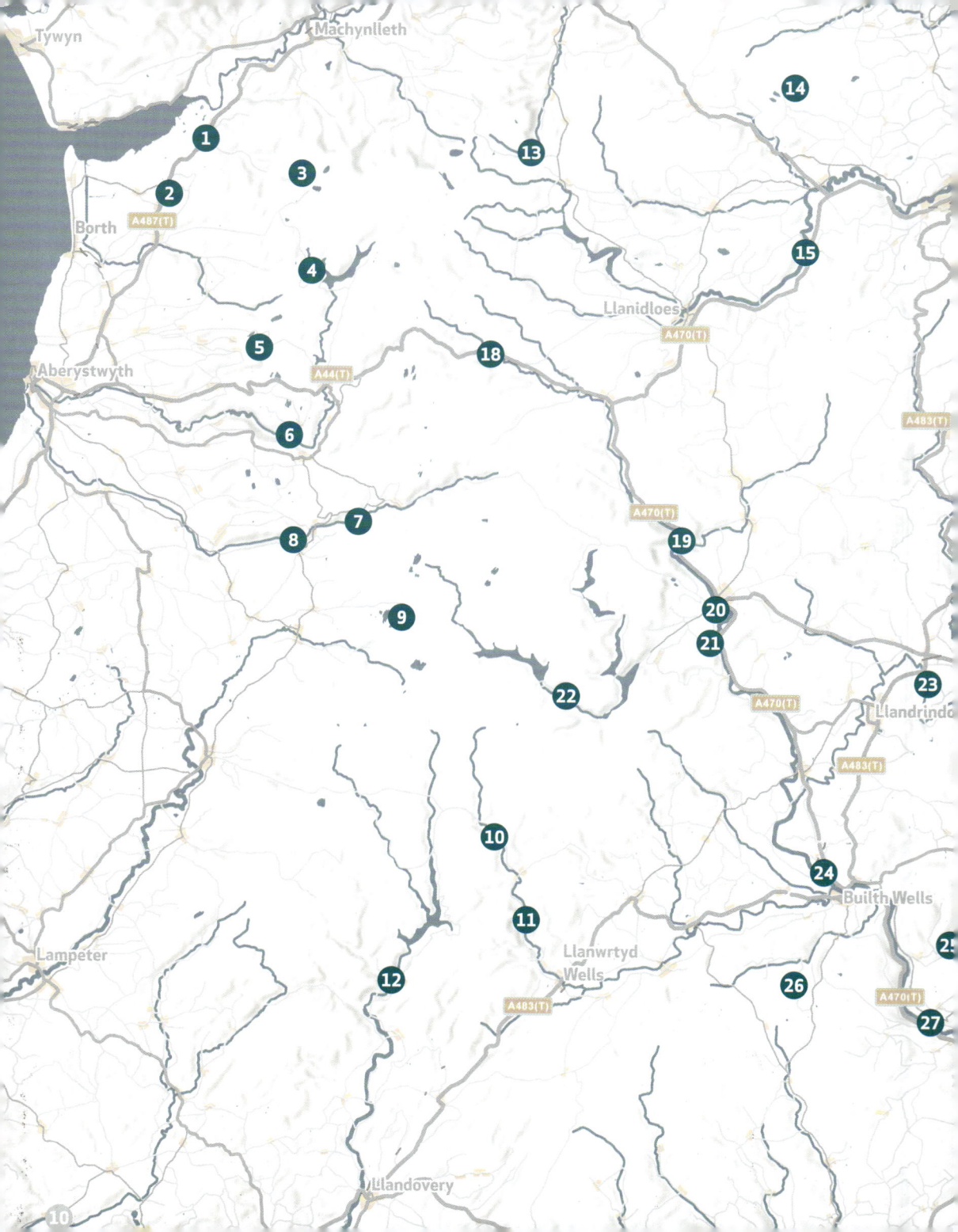

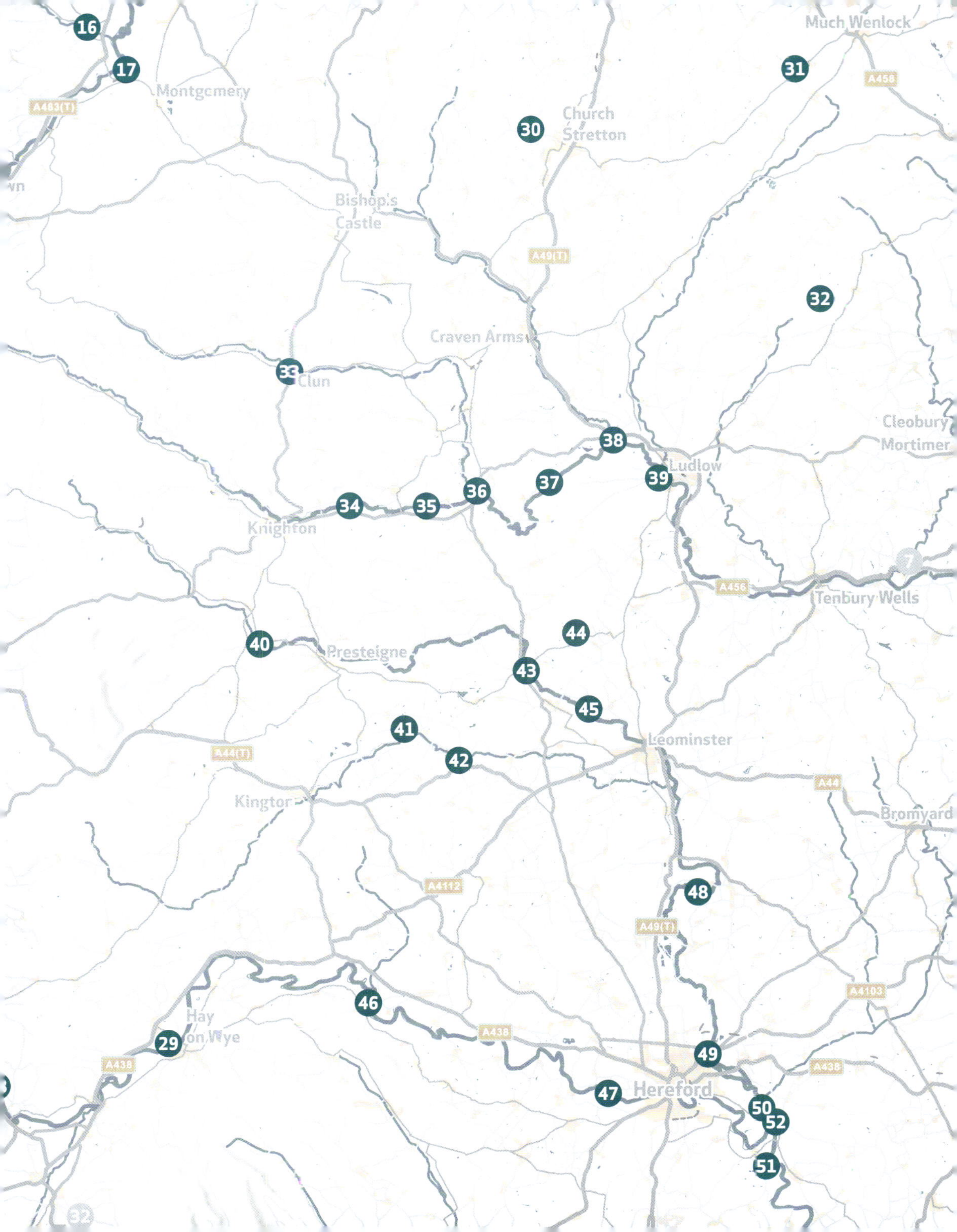
16
17
Montgomery
A483(T)
Much Wenlock
31
A458
30
Church Stretton
Bishop's Castle
A49(T)
32
Craven Arms
33
Clun
Cleobury Mortimer
38
Ludlow
37
39
36
34
35
Knighton
7
A456
Tenbury Wells
44
40
Presteigne
43
45
Leominster
41
42
A44(T)
A44
Kington
Bromyard
A4112
48
A49(T)
A4103
46
Hay on Wye
29
A438
A438
49
A438
47
Hereford
50
52
51
32

Downstream, the tiny town of Llanwrtyd Wells was once famous for its natural springs. These days, they have fallen into decline, but in an effort to diversify and attract tourists, the town...has introduced the world championship for 'bog snorkelling'. Competitors must complete two lengths of a 60-metre trench cut through the peat bogs of Waen Rhydd in the quickest possible time, wearing snorkels and flippers, but without using any conventional swimming strokes. A triathlon has also been introduced, as well as mountain-bike bog snorkelling, which involves cycling underwater through the trench. With over a hundred participants each year, entries have included snorkellers from Russia, Australia, New Zealand, and Ireland.

Far to the east, the Teme – part Welsh, part English – means 'the dark one' in ancient Celtic and is one of several rivers that drain the Welsh Marches. It is wild and beautiful and is locally known for its annual coracle regatta at Leintwardine (36). Coracles are one of the oldest boat designs in Britain and were used by Bronze Age Britons and invading Romans alike. They are oval in shape, rather like half a walnut shell, and are traditionally made from interwoven willow rods tied with willow bark, covered in horse or bullock hide, and sealed with a thin layer of tar. Designed for use in swiftly flowing shallow streams, such as those on the Welsh border rivers, they don't have a keel and only need a few inches to float. This makes them very light – perfect if you're a poacher and need to flee – and highly manoeuvrable.

It's just as well that the Teme at Leintwardine is an excellent swimming river because the coracle's manoeuvrability makes it inherently unstable – spinning round on the spot and all too easily tipping you in. If you haven't yet honed the necessary skills, the Leintwardine coracle regatta is the perfect place to combine some training with plenty of opportunities for an involuntary river dip. The village's main swimming stretch runs from the road bridge upriver past the rope swing to a sizeable pool where the River Clun joins the Teme. With gardens running right down to the river, these banks have a rather civilised and homely feel. A little further on, the meadow opens out, and the river runs fast over wide pebble rills with some deeper holes and lively currents.

The Teme, which eventually joins the Severn, is just one of the many rivers that drain from the Radnorshire hills and form this historic stretch of the Welsh Marches, a borderland of battlegrounds and fiefdoms that the Normans attempted to control from 1066 onwards. The River Lugg runs parallel a few miles to the south and eventually joins the Wye. At the head of its valley stands the church of Pilleth, meaning 'the pool on the hill'. In 1402, it was the site of one of the bloodiest and most important battles in a thousand years of Welsh wars of independence. Despite the great massacre that occurred here and the burning of the church, its holy well is still revered for its healing powers. Tadpoles and great crested newts also seem to thrive in its shallow waters and there are more pools nearby at Discoed (**40**).

It was not until we had travelled another twelve miles downstream from Pilleth, well past Presteigne, that a friend and I actually found somewhere for a proper swim in the Lugg. Just outside Leominster, near the village of Eyton, in a perfect rural landscape, you will find several weirs and river pools (**45**). The Arrow runs close by, and we began searching for a shallow ford that was the location of an idyllic toddlers' picnic party he had attended thirty years before and wanted to relocate. We found the site, homing in using a photo as a guide, and a mile upstream discovered a long weir pool that provided a deeper swim in dark, peaty water through a tree-lined avenue of emerald alders.

The Arrow eventually joins the Lugg downstream of Leominster, and we stopped for an afternoon dip at Bodenham (**48**) before continuing on for some miles to Lugg Meadows near Hereford. These are the largest known modern examples of 'Lammas' meadows in Britain, with ownership divided into strips marked by dole stones. The meadows are still managed in accordance with this medieval system, and an active commoners' association controls the grazing rights. With its intermittent gravel beaches and deeper pools, we partly swam and partly waded the length of the Lugg that evening, floating in the low light past banks awash with cow parsley and meadow shank (**49**).

The Elan Valley is sometimes known as the Welsh Lake District and was the romantic inspiration for Shelley's early years. It is also the Welsh Wye's first major stop on its journey from its source in the Cambrian Mountains towards the literary haven of Hay-on-Wye. Shelley – the idealist, revolutionary, and great romantic poet – first visited his uncle's estate in the Elan when he was 18, walking there from Sussex over the course of a week. Already having a reputation as a strange but fun-filled young man, he used to bathe in the mountain streams and sail toy boats down the currents, sometimes with a cat on board. He fell in love in the valley and tried to make a life there with his first wife, but when they failed to acquire a house, the marriage collapsed. She drowned herself in the Serpentine in London two years later. He lost his life at sea in Italy at the age of 29. The Elan stream in which Shelley used to bathe, and both the valley homes he loved so much – Cwm Elan and the manor house Nangwyllt – were also drowned by a series of Victorian reservoirs in the late nineteenth century. These impressive dams and vast lakes were created to supply water to Birmingham at the height of its population growth. While swimming is not officially allowed in the reservoirs (but fine in the Claerwen and Rhiwnant waterfalls, 22) it is still possible to swim in the Elan at the pool where it meets the Wye a few miles downstream. In the spring, the water flows in from the top layers of the reservoir and is not too icy. In summer, the authorities begin to release water from the bottom sluices, causing the temperature to drop dramatically (21).

The Wye continues south from the Elan junction, often shallow but sometimes pooling where it meets rocky seams. Pen-doll Rocks at Builth Wells is a particularly impressive series of pools and rapids. Wildlife along this stretch includes ravens, red kites, buzzards, herons, kingfishers, peregrines, and otters (24). As it reaches the north escarpment of the Brecon Beacons, the Wye is forced to turn abruptly north-east and arrives in the charming, bookshop-filled town of Hay-on-Wye—a place that loves to swim. The Warren, a twenty-minute walk upstream from the town centre, is the ideal spot to paddle, skim stones, or watch hapless canoeists negotiate the rapids from the long pebble beach (29). Further upstream, the river is deeper, allowing for a longer swim. During the Hay Festival, you'll find it packed with people from all over the world, propped up on one elbow, reading with their picnics and Pimms.

These grassy banks have been used to catch rabbits since medieval times, but in the 1970s, a scheme was proposed to convert the Warren into a caravan park. Local businesses and residents were so horrified that they decided to club together to purchase the field.

A '20 Club', set up to find twenty supporters, quickly mushroomed into the '300 Club', which continues to run to this day. The outpouring of community spirit catalysed by this swimming hole led to other community initiatives and restoration projects. Anyone can join the Warren Club, and membership is still £13, as it has been since 1973, though non-members are free to use the area.

ABER & THE YSTWYTH

1 FURNACE WATERFALL, CWM EINION

Don't let the busy roadside location put you off, this is a wonderful waterfall with deep pool to swim in, with a verdant canopy surrounding it. Cwm Einion is known as the Artists Valley and is associated with the story of Saint Einion and local legends of spirits and faeries. Good car park just across road (SY20 8PQ) and buses stop here too. On A487 between Aberystwyth and Machynlleth, in the village of Furnace, find waterfall next to old waterwheel.

2 mins, 52.5383, -3.9400

2 CWM CLETWR, TRE'R-DDÔL

Follow the good path up behind the village (by converted church) into a wooded valley and nature reserve. There a small waterfall with a deep plunge pool (SY20 8PP).

10 mins, 52.5100, -3.9704

3 LLYN CONACH & BEYOND

This is perhaps as remote as you can get by road in Wales. The forestry tracks head higher and higher, passing endless wild swimming lakes and wild camping spots. Turn off A487 Tal-y-bont by the White Lion and Black Lion, and follow signs for Nantymoch, past turning to SY24 5HL. At top, about 5 miles from pub, turn L onto wide forest gravel track (R is to Nant-y-Moch, see listing), then L after ¾ mile at crossroads and continue 1¼ miles, past lovely little (unnamed) tarn below R (52.5068, -3.8642), to find L turn to Llyn Conach. Back to main track continue E past New Pool lake and the historic Anglers Retreat cabin (R) on the way to Llyn Penrhaeadr (52.5228, -3.8408). These are all used as fishing lakes, so give the usual courtesies.

5 mins, 52.5207, -3.8594

4 NANT-Y-MOCH & PLYNLIMON

High in the barren uplands of the Cambrians lies this twisting reservoir with long shale edges, many inlets and an empty road hugging its southern shores. Rising above is the hulk of Plynlimon, the highest point in the Cambrians (752m) and source of both the Severn and the Wye. The road here feels like an epic journey in itself, even in a car, and passes several ruined mines and smaller lakes. As for Llyn Conach (see listing), but continue on tarmac road R (SE) at the 5 miles junction. Pass lovely Llyn Nantycagl on L after ½ mile, to reservoir after 2 miles (there are quirky fireplaces in the woods, just off the road at 52.4780, -3.8606). The main beach shore is after another 2 miles; continue up to 3 miles beyond this, turning L after the dam, to explore the little island/peninsula (52.4777, -3.8120) and the flanks of Plynlimon. At the road end (gates at Maesnant), take the R track (public byway) another mile up to the Afon Hengwm. Also reached following lane N from Ponterwyd (SY23 3JX).

5 mins, 52.4706, -3.8508

5 LLYN RHOSGOCH & MYNYDD MARCH

A trio of pretty tarns adorn the ancient roadway that traverses Mynydd March. Although fishing lakes, they are popular for swimming. Further along are the easily accessible Buwch a'r Lo (cow and calf) standing stones, just a few of the many Bronze Age remnants that pepper the area. From centre of Penrhyn-coch, E of Aberystwyth, follow Pendam Mountain Road E about 5 miles, past SY23 3EX, to reach Llyn Pendam. Turn R opp car park signed Ponterwyd for easy Llyn Blaenmelindwr. From here a footpath on R heads down to Rhosgoch, secluded and wilder. Standing stones ½ mile further E on lane (52.4332, -3.8799).

5 mins, 52.4308, -3.8942

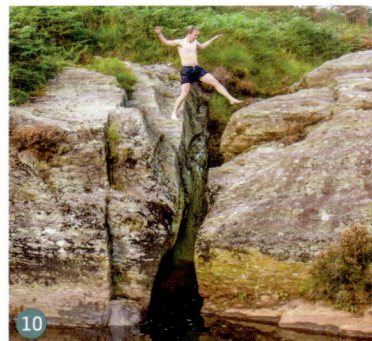

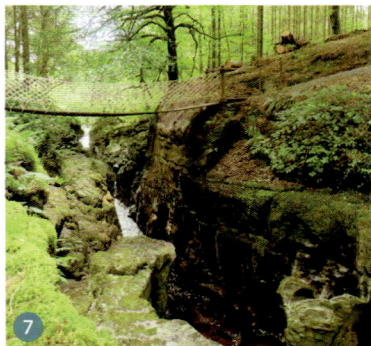

6 CWM RHEIDOL WATERFALLS

A tiny lane winds its way up this gentle rocky valley, passing a butterfly centre, ancient woods and many lovely pools and falls. It eventually reaches a super waterfall pool with beach at road end. More adventures on foot beyond. Turn off A44 at Capel Bangor 3 miles E from Aberystwyth, signed Cwmrheidol. After 1¼ miles at a R bend, with a small dirt layby to R, steps lead down to a deep river pool with big gravel banks (52.3915, -3.9600). Continue another 4½ miles, past the Butterfly House, Rheidol Power Station, Rheidol

Falls bridge, and SY23 3NB, to layby and gate on R signed Statkraft. There is a deep wooded gorge with good jumps (52.3866, -3.8710) just downstream above bridge, alas with 'keep out' signs. Finally, 180m on, at 'end of route' sign, find parking for 3 cars L, signboards and a gate on R down to the main beach and falls. The adventurous can follow the road to the remote waterfall and epic pools of Gyfarllwyd at 52.3817, -3.8492 (steep bushwhack and river scramble required).

2 mins, 52.3858, -3.8686 ▣▮▯▦▨❀

7 CWM YSTWYTH, HAFOD ESTATE

A fine house was built here in the late 18th century, complete with a network of picturesque paths and bridges that showed off the many waterfalls and wooded ravines. The house is now a pile of rubble, but the walks are being restored, and include a range of canyons and gentle river pools. From the bridge at Pont-rhyd-y-groes (N of SY25 6DN) follow B4343 just over ½ mile to the accessible entrance. Bear R on B4574, signed Hafod, for another 1 mile to main car park at church on R. Head down by Mrs Johnes Flower Garden on the main estate road. Downstream 200m on the bend are picnic tables and a deep river

pool on the Afon Ystwyth. Upstream ½ mile is Pont Dologau (52.3445, -3.8054), where you can scramble into the Ystwyth gorge. There are also lovely pools beneath the wobbly chain bridge another ½ mile upstream (52.3465, -3.7997). The Gentleman's Walk leads to Melyn waterfall (52.3424, -3.8015) and the Cavern Cascade (52.3389, -3.7998) on the Nant Gau but the latter is closed off at time of writing.

20 mins, 52.341, -3.8105 ▣▮▰▨▦❉▨▨

8 YSTWYTH LOWER GORGE

A sculpted slot canyon widens into a wooded gorge with a waterfall and deep pools. It's a tricky scramble down, but explore up the canyon for a real adventure. From Pont-rhyd-y-groes, take fork SY25 6DQ by bus stop, signed B4340. Follow ½ mile, past café and waterwheel, to bend to find route down into woods on R and some room to park (52.3303 -3.8669). Follow woodland down to a steep rock scramble down to the river bed, then scramble upstream 50 m to the waterfall and canyon.

5 mins, 52.3312, -3.8647 ▣▮▯▦▨

9 LLYN EGNANT, TEIFI POOLS

With easy access and stunning southerly views, this remote family of high lakes makes for a sublime adventure on a sunny day. Together they form the headwaters of the River Teifi at the start of its journey to Cardigan Bay. Tracks lead off to most of the lakes, and if nobody is fishing, a swim and wild camp shouldn't be an issue, though some of the lakes do now have No Swimming signs. Egnant is the last lake and has a track right along its shore. Llyn Bach is hidden beyond, only a little way on foot. Leave B4343 about 7 miles N of Tregaron at Ffair-Rhos, turning by Teifi Inn for SY25 6BW. Continue 3¾ miles, passing R turns for Llyn Teifi and Llyn Hir. Where road turns to track ('unfit for motor vehicles' sign in Welsh) turn R for Egnant. Llyn Bach is at end of lake, about 200m to R on foot (52.2861, -3.7770). Follow the stream W of Claerddu bothy (down a small track N of Llyn Hir) for a small waterfall pool (52.3056, -3.7735), or walk the Cambrian Way 2km N to remote and wild Llynnau Fyrddon twin lakes (52.3206, -3.7610).

2 mins, 52.2912, -3.7738 🏊🏔️⛺❓

IFON & TYWI

10 WOLF'S LEAP, RIVER IRFON
A valley of wild beauty, open and sunny with flat rocks. Above the small deep pool is a narrow, sculpted slot gorge. You can also explore the upper parts of the gorge and climb down inside. From Washpool (see listing) continue on to Abergwesyn and turn L signed Llyn Brianne/Tregaron at postbox. Continue 1¾ miles to uneven road sign and find pool below L, ½ mile before LD5 4TF. Also approach from Fannog, Llyn Brianne (see listing) in the other direction.

5 mins, 52.1788, -3.6949 🏊

11 WASHPOOL/PWLL BO, RIVER IRFON
Large roadside pool overhung with gnarled oaks, traditionally used for washing horses. Swim up into the deep gorge section with its scenic crag and waterfalls. From Llanwrtyd Wells take Abergwesyn/Coed Trallwm road. Continue 3 miles to find forestry sign and parking on R and obvious pool, 300m before LD5 4TN.

2 mins, 52.1362, -3.6678 🏊🏔️🍂

12 TOWY WATERFALLS
Follow the Towy river up into the foothills of the Cambrians to find a double waterfall at the confluence with the Doethie near Twm Sion Cati's cave and RSPB Nature Reserve. Beware high water levels and cold water released from reservoir. Descend from Llyn Brianne or take Cilycwm Rd from Llandovery and continue about 9 miles

dir Rhandirmwyn. Turn R at Towy Bridge Inn, crossing iron bridge. Continue 1 mile then park in layby on left just past turning for bridge signed Troedyrhiw. Cross the bridge and walk R on lane for 1.2km to a small outcrop of rock on R and narrow path through trees down to river junction. NB If coming from Llandovery there is also a good gorge swim right by the tiny lane to SA20 0UH, near Cilycwm (-3.8016, -3.8016). Although Llyn Brianne has a bylaw against recreational water use, many do swim and camp at Fannog (52.1482, -3.7416).

5 mins, 52.105, -3.7802 🏊🏕️🔄🔄

UPPER SEVERN

13 DYLIFE POOL & FFRWD FAWR
You can view the spectacular Ffrwd Fawr falls from the road as they crash over 35m down the cliffside. But only locals know about a different, hidden waterfall pool, concealed in a deep cleft upstream. From Llyn Llanidloes continue on B4518 N and turn dir SY19 7BP and Dylife. Large layby and signboard on R with dramatic views of waterfall and Twymyn valley after ½ mile. Continue to 175m past cattle grid for small pull-off on R, with plateau below and tricky scramble down to the hidden waterfall.

Nearby Llyn Clywedog reservoir (52.4864, -3.6342) is very deep and has shingle beaches at the northern end. Technically no swimming allowed and there are signs to that effect, but people do.

5 mins, 52.532, -3.6682 🏊🏔️🔄🔄❓🏔️

14 LLYN Y TARW, MYNYDD CLOGAU
A trio of wild lakes hiding in the high, rolling emptiness of Mynydd Clogau (420m). Llyn Mawr is a nature reserve, Llyn Du is for fishing, while Llyn y Tarw is the quietest of the three, best for a swim or wild camp. From A470 1.5km SE of Clatter, turn

(signed Bwlchygarreg) and follow the lane. After 3.2km, 200m after turn to SY17 5NE, find bridle path on R and some parking. Walk 1.2km NE, or take bridle path L for Llyn Mawr.

15 mins, 52.5657, -3.4481

15 LLANDINAM GRAVELS, RIVER SEVERN

The meanders of the young Severn are blessed with shingle beaches and deep pools. Tread lightly, as this is a nature reserve with many insects, wading birds and even otters living and breeding in it. In summer the bordering water meadows are decorated with wildflowers. Signed Broneirion/Nature Reserve from A470 just N of Llandinam. Cross the river on narrow bridge, then turn L along a disused railway track dir SY17 5AU. About 1.5km down find reserve parking L.

10 mins, 52.4814, -3.4387

16 BERRIEW, RIVER RHIW

A pretty village stream that feeds the Severn. You'll find grassy banks and small waterfalls and pools above the stone bridge. Park in Berriew and walk upstream beyond bridge dir SY21 8PJ. Pools at 50m, but fence ends after 100m.

1 mins, 52.5992, -3.2028

17 RHYDWHYMAN, CAERHOWEL

The ancient Roman road crossed the River Severn here, defended by Forden Gaer fort, just 500m to the N. A perfect place for an easy dip on B4385. Opp the turn to SY15 6HD, find a wooded area by the river.

1 mins, 52.5775, -3.1700

UPPER WYE & ELAN

18 PONT RHYDGALED, RIVER WYE

The meeting point of the young Wye and Tarrenig, with a pool and beach below the forestry track bridge and several waterfalls downstream.7 miles W of Llangurig A44, 270m W of SY18 6SY, find Tarrenig forestry car park. Follow track from car park to bridge pool, or continue S and turn L down track for waterfalls, about 200m.

5 mins, 52.428, -3.7011

19 PONT MARTEG, RIVER WYE

Mossy, ancient woods cloak this hidden gorge, with a footbridge and small pools for paddling. On A470 3 miles N of Rhayader, park in layby opp turn to St Harmon. Go through gate and across bridge. Or follow narrow lanes (cycle route 8) to find a secret spot a mile downstream under old railway with a white beach, deeper pools and rope

swing (52.3237, -3.5454).Park in gravel layby (52.3141, -3.5309) and NW along disused rail line.

5 mins, 52.332, -3.5403

20 RHAYADER BEACH & FALLS

Swim in the waterfall that gives the town its name. There's also a pretty gravel beach, south facing and secluded, at the bottom of the rugby club. A path leads to the river from behind the Triangle Inn LD6 5AR. Or head down Water Lane past LD6 5AN to rugby club car park. Follow path at R of car park entrance along the river to very end of playing fields.

5 mins, 52.2962, -3.5116

21 ELAN JUNCTION POOL, RIVER WYE

A wide junction pool and footbridge on footpath and open access land. Deepish section to jump into from the bank. But may be No Swimming due to fishing. Limited park at bend/track beyond LD1 6NP.

2 mins, 52.2788, -3.516

22 CLAERWEN & RHINWNANT VALLEYS

Up the Elan valley from Rhayader is a mini-gorge and plunge pools by the road, and a secret mountain-valley walk with pools all along its happy way. 2 miles SW of Elan

village turn L over bridge signed Claerwen Dam. Continue 3½ miles, past Rhiwnant turn off on L (by telephone box and parking) to 300m before LD6 5HF. A rocky section of the river comes close to the road on L with deep pools and waterfall; park by salt bin. Also explore the Rhiwnant Valley for a waterfall and lovely confluence pool at 52.2314, -3.6453 with mine ruins above and more falls. Although technically not allowed, people also swim at Penygarreg (52.302, -3.619), with a secluded picnic area, beaches and an island. Above it, Craig Goch enjoys open access all along its northwestern shore below Pont ar Elan.

2 mins, 52.2514, -3.6359

MID WYE TO HAY

23 ALPINE BRIDGE, RIVER ITHON

Beauty spot popular with the Victorians, little visited now. Sunken gorge in the river with deep pools below a bridge. Take A483 N from Llandrindod Wells for 2 miles. Just before LD1 5ST and church, after bridge, take unsigned road R. Continue 1½ mile beyond to pull off on R after bungalow. Take path SW through old stile gate across field to river bridge. Shaky bridge is also pretty, with shallow paddling and a church hidden in

a meadow (52.2419, -3.3418).

5 mins, 52.2585, -3.3338

24 PEN-DDÔL ROCKS, RIVER WYE

An exciting stretch of the Wye, narrowing through rocky cliffs near Builth Wells. Upstream the water is deeper, passing through a small gorge with rock formations. Downstream find safe, white-sand bays. A mile N of Builth Wells on A470 find small layby on L directly opp entrance to Penmaenau Caravan Park, just before LD2 3RD. Stile in fence in layby leads down steep bank to rapids.

2 mins, 52.1613, -3.4195

25 RIVER EDW WEIR

The Edw stream transforms into deep water at the weir, with a rope swing and pool. The valley is quiet and open, with picnic tables by the water and old quarries over the lane. Perfect for family picnics. Leave Aberedw E past pub then find small weir and picnic spot after 1½ miles, ½ mile beyond LD2 3UR.

1 mins, 52.1244, -3.3138

26 FARMERS' WELSH LAVENDER, BUILTH

Swimming pond and sauna on lavender farm with exceptional views of surrounding countryside. Gift shop and cafe. LD2 3HU, 01982 552 467. Jun - Aug £5. Book ahead for sauna. welshlavender.com

2 mins, 52.1035, -3.4436

27 ERWOOD BRIDGE SLIPWAY, RIVER WYE

The slipway track below the road bridge makes this an easy spot to access the grassy shore and beach, where you can play in the rapids and rocky pools so typical of this section of the Wye. You can launch a canoe here and paddle downstream to Glasbury or Boughrood . Local company 'Want to canoe?' can arrange hire with drop-offs and pick-ups. Turn off A470 S of Builth Wells signed Aberedw to find new path on far side of bridge. Parking near craft centre (LD2 3SJ)

2 mins, 52.0848, -3.3293

28 BOUGHROOD, RIVER WYE

A large, very secluded pool lies in a kink of the Wye above the rapids. Pull off A470 by suspension bridge 350m N of turning to LD2 3TQ (park on grass). Walk S on verge over bridge to find footpath L just after, and follow S for a mile. Do not swim if people are fishing.

3 mins, 52.0541, -3.2803

29 THE WARREN, HAY-ON-WYE

A deservedly popular stretch of meadow owned by the community. There's a long, white shingle beach, shaded by trees, a pool and shallows below the rapids and deeper section above. A beautiful setting. In Hay turn opp the Swan Hotel (HR3 5DQ), past St Mary's Church. After 500m, drive/walk down bumpy track R to car park at bottom. Or walk upstream from Hay 10 mins; footpath at end of Wyeford Rd (HR3 5BJ). Canoe hire available from our friends 'Want to Canoe?' just outside Hay at Racquety Farm (01497 820604)

3 mins, 52.0761, -3.1369

NORTH SHROPSHIRE

30 CARDING MILL & LIGHTSPOUT FALLS

Sitting in a sheltered glen at the top of New Pool Hollow, this disused reservoir was built in 1902 to power the textile mill in the valley below. Owned by the NT, swimming is permitted. Continue up north west to Lightspout Hollow to find a remote waterfall – no pool but fun for a soaking. Signed Carding Mill Valley from B5477/ High Street in Church Stretton. Continue about a mile, beyond SY6 6JG, to road end parking (NT). Cross stream on first

fcotbridge and climb SE for Hope Pool Hollow. For waterfall, continue up valley on second footbridge, then bear L up next side valley W to 52.5504, -2.8405.

15 mins, 52.5464, -2.8321 ⚓🚶

31 LEA QUARRY, WENLOCK EDGE

Enjoy spectacular views from the Wenlock Edge ridge. Below are the dramatic turquoise waters of Lea Quarry - the blue colour is from dissolved limestone. Sometimes the way down to the lake is open and people swim. Wenlock Edge Car, TF13 6DQ then footpath up NE to above quarry. Interesting kilns at 52.5751, -2.6126. May be No Swimming, so seek permission and observe signs.

15 mins, 52.5770, -2.6109 ⚓❓🚶🅿

32 BOYNE WATER, BURWARTON

Beautiful, peaty, warm water in a very secluded, tranquil location in the Clee Hills. Set in open-access land. Said to hold parts of aircraft that foundered on Brown Clee Hill. Park in Burwarton and head out of village di-Cleedownton to pick up footpath to R after 5 mins (52.4593, -2.5660). Follow footpath across fields and around N side of Lyster Dingle, turning L to water. Can be muddy.

40 mins, 52.4587, -2.5904 ⚓🦮🚶♿🅿🚻

SOUTH SHROPSHIRE TEME

33 CLUN CASTLE

Swim at a bend of the River Clun below a wonderful ruined Norman castle. Lots to explore. In Clun head W on High St/B4368 (SY7 8JB), and follow signs for castle L onto Bridge St, over river, then immediately R to car park on R. Follow signs from car park. Free entry to the castle.

5 mins, 52.4218, -3.0342 ⊞⚓🦮🏕

34 WESTON, RIVER TEME

This secret swimming spot, best reached by bike, is surprisingly deep and enjoys a large shingle beach. There's a bridge for Pooh Sticks and an overgrown castle motte on the south bank to discover too. 3.2km E of Knighton on A4113, turn L signed Stowe, then after crossing river R dir Buckton/Weston. After 2.4km, at SY7 0BB, find postbox, stile and gate. Very limited parking by house. Follow path down to railway cottage, cross lines and continue S 100m to the footbridge. Deep pool and beach below.

5 mins, 52.352, -2.9841 ⚓🦮🚲

35 PARSON'S POLE BRIDGE, RIVER TEME

There is some paddling just upstream of this pretty single-track bridge, but the

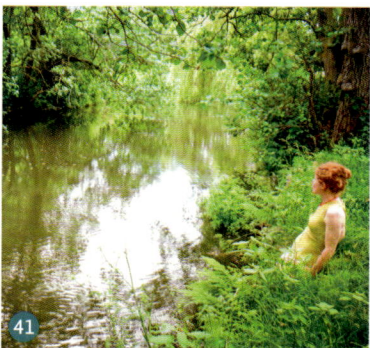

easy access near the bridge: ideal for an afternoon in the sunshine. Follow the River Teme upstream for secluded, deep pools and beaches for paddling. Park on Rosemary Lane, opp Lion Hotel (SY7 0JZ). Walk upstream from bridge to rope swing and beach. Also, follow Herefordshire Trail SW of Leintwardine for 3.5km to secret weir and pool further upstream at 52.3523, -2.9190.

8 mins, 52.3595, -2.8777

37 DOWNTON GORGE, RIVER TEME
Dramatic swim in a deep gorge hidden among trees. Remnants of old mill, weir and caves to explore. Deep pools in beautiful surroundings. Downton signed from A4113 W of Ludlow, near SY8 2LB. Park in layby to L just after crossroads and Downton sign. Carry on downhill and take footpath to L across field to weir, bridge and river. Take footpath R along river 2km, below castle to Castle Bridge. Explore gorge upstream of here. Various swims along route.

30 mins, 52.3639, -2.8170

38 BROMFIELD CHURCH, RIVER TEME
A super church with ceiling murals. Beyond is a bridge and weir, with riverside path and deep swimming upstream. Or continue into Ludlow to swim below the castle, or onto Ashford Carbonell beach. Turn off A49 for A4113 Knighton, then immediately L dir SY8 2JP, to find church and parking L. Bridge is 200m further. Ludlow Teme is at SY8 1EG by the Green Café.

5 mins, 52.3858, -2.7638

39 LUDLOW & ASHFORD CARBONELL
The imposing castle ruins provide a historic backdrop to a gentle swim in the river meanders below, away from the tourists in the town. Pay car park for Linney Riverside Park near SY8 1EG. Various entry points along bank. Downstream 3km is Ashford Carbonell village, with a large pebble beach and wonderful deep pool. Down bridleway opp Church Ln, SY8 4BY (52.3329, -2.7022).

2 mins, 52.3660, -2.7257

ARROW & LUGG

40 DOLLEY OLD BRIDGE, RIVER LUGG
Offa's Dyke crosses the River Lugg here, with a coppice grove, gravel beaches with paddling and some deep pools for a dip. Great fun for kids. W of Presteigne on B4356 take turn on bend 350m W of LD8 2NQ, signed Cascob. After a mile, by postbox and barn, park opp by gate. Take footpath by gate, continue 350m

across 2 fields to river bridge. Pools are downstream.

10 mins, 52.2811, -3.0597

41 STAUNTON ON ARROW, RIVER ARROW
Grassy riverside and lovely deep water upstream of the weir, good for jumping and diving. Staunton on Arrow is signed from B4355, 3 miles N of Kington. After 1½ miles find gate and footpath on R with space for one car, HR6 9HS. Follow hedge down to river. There is also a footbridge and sunny riverbank path just downstream of the village at Gig Bridge (52.2331, -2.9240); it's deep here too, above the weir at Court of Noke manor.

2 mins, 52.2373, -2.9392

42 PEMBRIDGE, RIVER ARROW
Stone bridge with a pebble beach perfect for paddling. Downstream is all open access meadow land with tight meanders and deeper swims spots. Shop and tearoom in village. On A44 through Pembridge, turn R by New Inn (HR6 9DZ). Follow 400m to parking L just over river.

2 mins, 52.2212, -2.8935

43 MORTIMER'S CROSS, RIVER LUGG
River meanders, shingle pools and beaches are set within a water-meadow nature reserve and guarded by many ancient, hollow willows. Public footpath but may be No Swimming due to anti-social behaviour. Park on R near bridge at HR6 9PE, and find footpath downstream. Cross two fields for the meanders by the water meadows.

10 mins, 52.2671, -2.8370

44 FISHPOOL VALLEY, CROFT CASTLE
Bottom of five spring-fed estate lakes on NT land. Also on a public footpath from 52.2879, -2.7956. May be No Swimming.

15 mins, 52.2863, -2.7953

45 EYTON, RIVER LUGG
Discover over a mile of secluded deep pools and beaches, weirs and footbridges, with shallows meandering through open pasture and little wooded glades. Very pretty and rarely visited. B4361 N from Leominster, turn L signed Eyton/Lucton after a mile. Then L dir HR6 0AQ, signed Aston/Lucton, after another mile (park on verge here). Find third set of double steel gates on L after a mile, before first house and follow track 400m, bearing R at end, towards to river, bridge and weir 400m. Cross bridge and head downstream for deeper sections and second weir.

15 mins, 52.2474, -2.7849

best spot is at the weir downstream, with a rope swing and long deep stretch above, and little shingle beaches and pools below. Private but well used – be respectful. At Brampton Bryan (SY7 0DH), 4.8km W of Leintwardine on A4113, turn N signed Buckton. The bridge is 800m on; no parking. Stile on L after bridge for paddling below, but for weir take rough path before bridge on R before, along field edge 600m.

10 mins, 52.3518, -2.92

36 LEINTWARDINE, RIVER TEME
Rope swing, beaches and a weir all with

46 BREDWARDINE BRIDGE, RIVER WYE

A pebble beach alongside the elegant bridge when flows are low provides a beautiful setting for a swim or jumps from the base of the bridge. From Bredwardine turn R opposite Red Lion (HR3 6BU) signed Hereford and follow 800m, over river to lay-by L 100m up hill beyond. Walk back down over river, turn L over stile onto footpath to shingle beach.

5 mins, 52.0967, -2.9697

47 BREINTON SPRING, RIVER WYE

A delightful spot on the River Wye for a picnic and a swim. See also the fresh water spring and the pretty St Michael's Church Park in car park in Lower Breinton, HR4 7PG. Head down sloping path to riverside walk, and spring. Church in orchard to L. Earthworks to R are remains of Breinton Camp, an old moated house.

5 mins, 52.0498, -2.7691

48 RIVER LUGG & BODENHAM LAKE

Take a dip in the deep pools of the meandering River Lugg with a long, sandy stretch of beach at this point. The river here borders Bodenham Lake Nature Reserve with beautiful gravel lake, meadow and orchards to explore. Signs say No Swimming so look out for otters instead. In Bodenham park at Church Walk, HR1 3JU. Follow path through church over footbridge and follow footpath W along the river. Best access to Bodenham Lakes is from the Reserve entrance and car park 52.1547, -2.6959, signed from the village.

15 mins, 52.1533, -2.6939

49 LUGG MEADOWS, HEREFORD

Secluded beach at the point where two tributaries of the River Lugg meet on meadows near the outskirts of Hereford. Tall banks and trees make this the perfect spot for paddling, a picnic or even a skinny-dip in the deeper pools either side of the beach. Follow A465 N out of Hereford dir Worcester, to Aylestone Park car park L (HR1 1JJ). Cross road, walk back to gated track and follow path 500m straight over meadows to river.

10 mins, 52.0701, -2.6858

50 HAMPTON BISHOP, RIVER LUGG

An ideal spot for a skinny-dip in a secluded stretch of the gentle River Lugg. At this point a deep, wide pool graduates down from pebble beach. In Hampton Bishop (HR1 4JY) take unsigned Church Lane N

from bend in Rectory Rd 150m and park at end. Follow track R for 200m.

3 mins, 52.0423, -2.6406

51 HOLME LACY, RIVER WYE

Remote pastoral plain giving easy access to the river and a beach. St Cuthbert's church stands alone by the river to the south in a bucolic graveyard. Downstream, access the river from the old railway bridge at Ballingham. Entering Holme Lacy from Hereford bear R (signed Holme Lacy House). After ½ mile turn L signed Church Rd. After ½ mile kissing gate on L by bend (parking for one) before church at HR2 6LX. Or pass Church Rd and continue another 1½ miles for the bridge and track on L to river (51.9925, -2.6347).

2 mins, 52.0121, -2.6367

52 MORDIFORD BRIDGE, RIVER LUGG

A relaxing swim under the old bridge towards some gentle rapids. Explore upriver following the Wye Valley Way or down river to join the confluence with the Wye. From Mordiford (HR1 4LN) follow Wallflower Row/B4224 W just over bridge and park in lay-by L beyond parapets. Cross road and follow path N down to pebble beach.

2 mins, 52.0349, -2.6288

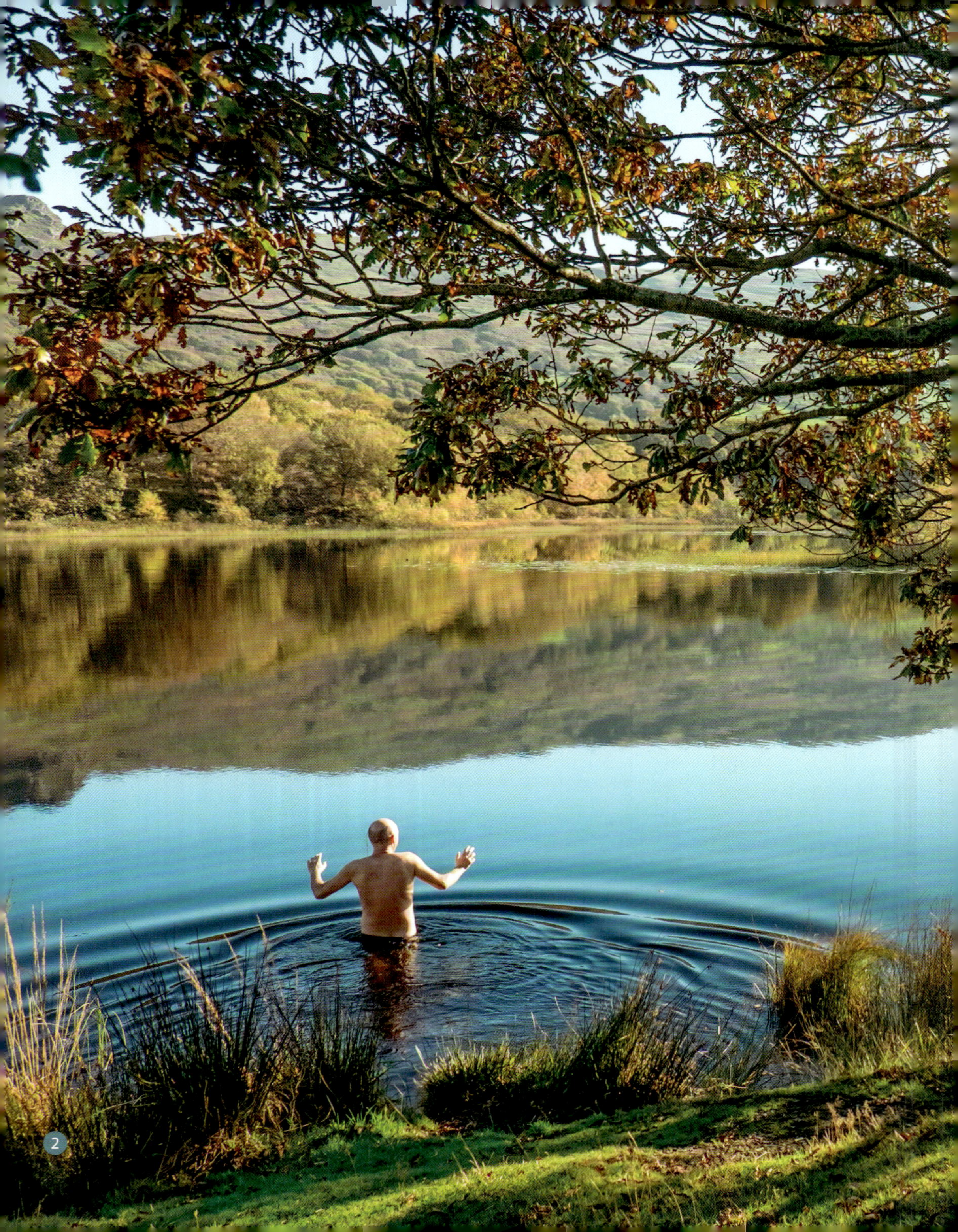

NORTH WALES & CHESHIRE

During the eighteenth century, the northernmost part of Wales was still one of the wildest and least charted regions of Europe. Yet it was increasingly renowned for its beautiful waterfalls and became fashionable among adventurous artists of the aesthetic movement searching for the ultimate 'picturesque' scene.

One intrepid travel writer keen to capitalise on this trend was the eccentric Reverend William Bingley, a peripatetic pastor and naturalist from Suffolk who had taken it upon himself to bring tales of the wild waterfalls of Wales to London. North Wales, delineated from two excursions through all the interesting parts of that highly beautiful and romantic country, was intended as a guide for future tourists. It was published in London in 1804 and sold over 300 copies.

One of his most memorable descriptions is of Rhaeadr Du – the Black Cataract – a 'deep and horrid chasm' in a little-visited woodland near Maentwrog in the northern Rhinog Mountains (2). The best time to go is in early September when the water has been warmed, the oak leaves are still green, and blankets of moss cover the forest floor. Sheer, steep, rocky cliffs soar upwards, trees grow out sideways, and buzzards circle above. Huge tangles of fallen trunks litter the riverbed, but a string of quiet pools lie between, as calm as glass

The canyon is much more peaceful than when the vicar visited it 200 years ago. Upstream, the gorge was dammed and the waters diverted in 1925, leaving the river almost empty. The result is an eerie calm, but it offers wonderful swimming and sunbathing on the large dried-up bedrocks.

Follow the old coach road from sublime Llandecwyn lake (2) or from the hydrostation the path stretches up the hillside past a slender medieval bridge overgrown with ivy. After a sweaty ten-minute climb, with the ravine on your left, you'll hear the gentle

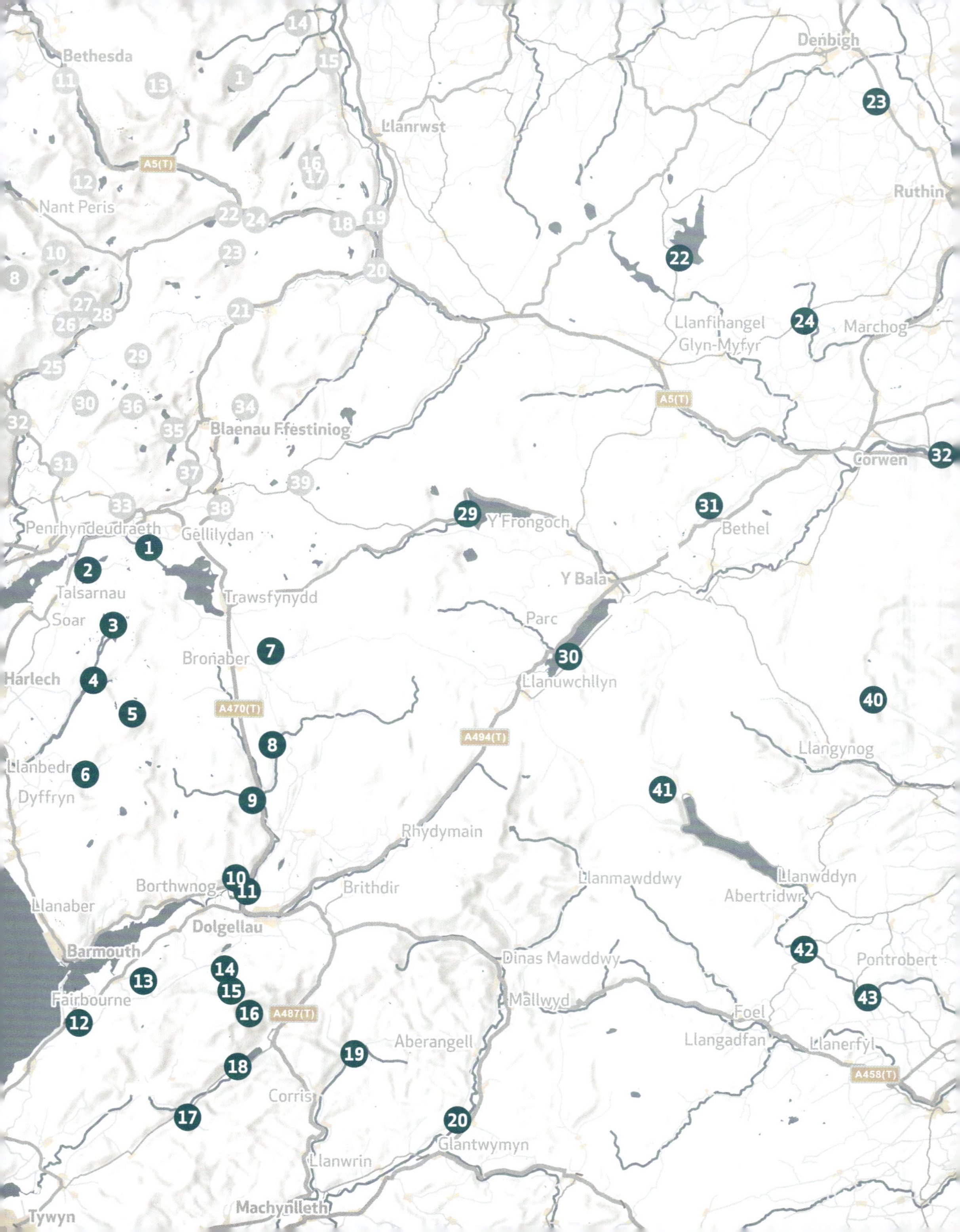
Bethesda
Llanrwst
Denbigh
A5(T)
Nant Peris
Ruthin
Llanfihangel
Glyn-Myfyr
Marchog
A5(T)
Blaenau Ffestiniog
Corwen
Penrhyndeudraeth
Gellilydan
Y Frongoch
Bethel
Talsarnau
Trawsfynydd
Y Bala
Soar
Parc
Bronaber
Harlech
Llanuwchllyn
A470(T)
A494(T)
Llangynog
Llanbedr
Dyffryn
Rhydymain
Llanmawddwy
Llanwddyn
Abertridwr
Borthwnog
Brithdir
Llanaber
Dolgellau
Barmouth
Dinas Mawddwy
Pontrobert
Fairbourne
Mallwyd
A487(T)
Foel
Aberangell
Llangadfan
Llanerfyl
A458(T)
Corris
Glantwymyn
Llanwrin
Machynlleth
Tywyn

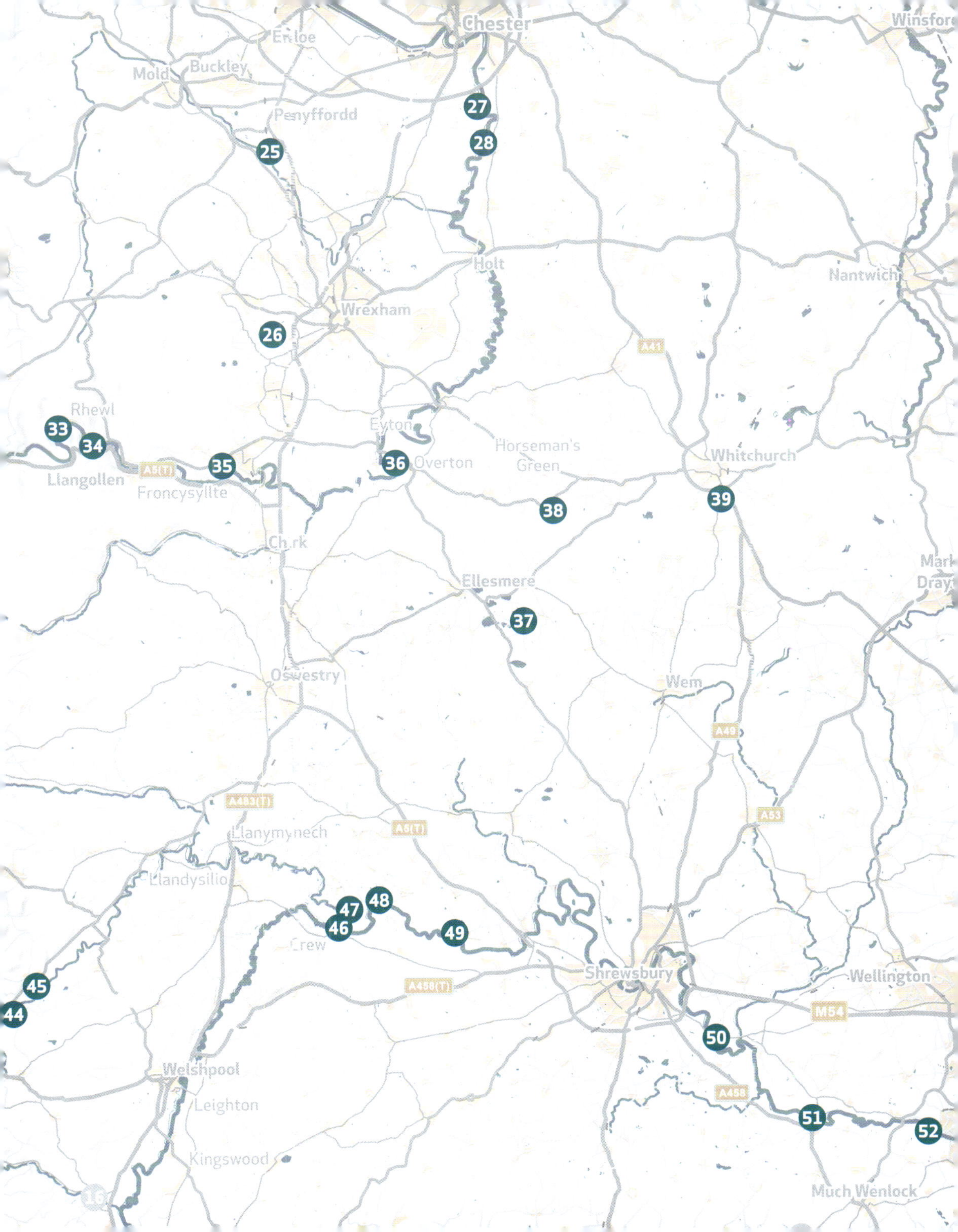

Chester
Winsford
Ewloe
Mold
Buckley
Penyffordd
27
28
25
Holt
Nantwich
Wrexham
26
A41
Rhewl
33
34
Eyton
Llangollen
A5(T)
35
36
Overton
Horseman's Green
Whitchurch
Froncysyllte
38
39
Chirk
Ellesmere
37
Oswestry
Wem
A49
A483(T)
A5(T)
A53
Llanymynech
Llandysilio
47
48
46
49
Shrewsbury
Wellington
A458(T)
45
44
M54
50
Welshpool
Leighton
A458
51
52
Kingswood
Much Wenlock

'In this cataract, which is surrounded by dark and impending scenery, the water is thrown with vast impetuosity… The banks closed in above my head, leaving but a narrow chasm, from which the light was excluded by the dark foliage on each side… I found myself entering, to appearances, into the mouth of a deep and horrid cavern…'
From Bingley's North Wales, 1804.

sound of falling water. Down through the trees, a bobsleigh run of rapids tips a slender column of water over the chute of Rhaeadr Du and into a perfect plunge pool below. At midday, the sun is high enough to light up the glade, but the cold may be intense – you'll be lucky to do more than rocket around the pool a few times, squeal, and scrabble out. With the surface of your skin dilating and blood rushing to the extremities of your body, this is cold dipping at its most therapeutic. Drying off in the tingling warmth, your skin stinging, the world seems sharp and clear, with the muggy layers purged.

There are many other beautiful gorges and waterfalls in southern Eryri. Deep in Coed-y-Brenin forest, accessible via the extensive network of mountain bike trails, two waterfalls lie at the one-time heart of Welsh gold production (7). The gold from this valley near Dolgellau made Princess Diana's wedding ring and has been the royal choice since Roman times. The last commercial operation closed down in 1998, but there are still many old workings along the gorge. The most prominent are by the plunge pools of Rhaeadr Mawddach. The building here generated power for the mines, and they say the old tailings still contain traces of gold. Why not try panning for some of your very own royal Welsh gold?

Southern Eryri is a glaciated landscape and contains many true 'cwm' lakes (known as 'corries' in Scotland). They have been scooped out of mountain walls by 10,000-year-old glaciers and usually formed in a northern or easterly direction, in the shadow of the ancient afternoon sun. One of the most famous and dramatic is Llyn Cau in the deep cliff-faced cwm of the beautiful Cadair Idris near Dolgellau (16), but my favourite is Llyn Eiddew Bach (3), part of a series of wild mountain lakes that is very dear to me. It's in the heart of the northern Rhinogs, Snowdonia's least-visited region, close to a 3,000-year-old roadway that once linked Ireland with Stonehenge. I spent some time living on the farm close by and would always leave a bottle of bubbly stashed and chilling on the lake bottom, tied to a secret piece of string, in preparation for weekend picnics. On the shallow side of the tarn are grassy, sheep-mown banks perfect for playing frisbee and paddling in the water. On the deep side are cliff ledges for sun lounging and for those who like to jump. A backdrop of bronzed September bracken, bony stone peaks, and glimpses of the Irish Sea completes the sense of awe and beauty.

The highlands of north Wales provide the waters for the Dee, Vrynwy, and Severn, which flow towards Cheshire and Shropshire, 50 miles to the east. The meres and mosses here are some of the last remaining fragments of ancient peat bogs in the country. They form one of our most important habitats in Britain, with new species still being discovered.

The meres are particularly well known for dragonflies – including the White-faced Darter and the Southern Hawker – and swimming in the lake is a fantastic way to get up close without disturbing them. As you glide through the water, your nose peeping above the surface, you are just another part of the lake's ecosystem.

There are important mere at Colemere and Hanmere (37, 38) where swimming is not encouraged, but a dip should be OK if discreet. Delamere – the forest of the meres – is Cheshire's most important area of wetland, to the north. The lakes were laid down 10,000 years ago at the end of the last ice age. It was the same glaciers that scoured out the cwms and tarns of the mountains. As the melt took hold, huge iceberg-sized chunks fell away from the undersides of the glaciers and became trapped in pockets of earth and mud on the newly revealed ground. When they finally melted and collapsed, they left large depressions – kettle holes – that evolved into freshwater lakes. Some were then colonised by sphagnum moss, which would entirely fill the shallows, soaking up rainwater and swelling like a sponge to many times its original size to form higher wetland areas called 'mosses'. These endangered lowland bogs have unique flora and fauna and have been drained, farmed, or destroyed in many other parts of the country.

Hatchmere, nestling in the corner of Delamere, is a serene, reed-banked lagoon that has been popular with wild swimmers for generations. A small bay leads to sandy shallows that can reach 24 degrees Celsius at the height of summer. Late afternoon sun filters through the forest canopy. Dark, dappled green waters stretch out ahead, and jewel-blue dragonflies whirr low over the water. Sadly, today, although a small part of Hatchmere had been a popular bathing place for decades, there is no longer access following a major struggle between local residents, a private fishing club, and the wildlife trust. One of the key issues was the disturbance of silt and trapped nutrients caused by people walking on the lake bottom. This case raises interesting questions about how nature conservation and swimming can best coexist.

several manganese mines to Llyn Du (not the one on Rhinog Fawr). Nearby is beautiful Llyn Caerwych with sea views. Head N from Harlech on B4573, turn R after 3 miles for Eisingrug (unsigned), after 1 mile take narrow dead-end mountain road R 150m after pond. Follow past turning to LL47 6YB, find parking ½ mile later at road end. Bear R (initially S) to climb track 2.5km to lake, bearing R after 1.2km. Llyn Caerwych is NW at 52.8958, -4.0227 (15 mins). Llyn Du is E at 52.8867, -3.9974 (30 mins).

30 mins, 52.8905, -4.0141 🏔️⛰️🎏📷❄️

4 NANT STEICYN POOLS, CWM BYCHAN

Sparkling clear mountain stream with many enticing plunge pools. The most obvious is on L of the lane on the way up to Llyn Cwm Bychan. Follow it upstream to discover a second set, running in a little gorge above tiny off-grid cottage.

15 mins, 52.8625, -4.0305 🏊⛰️🏔️🐟

5 LLYN DU, RHINOG FAWR

At the top of the Roman Steps below Rhinog Fawr, with infinity pool views over Mynydd Bach and the sea, this is a perfect high-level spot to swim and wild camp on the roof of the world. Follow road past LL45 2PH and Nant Steicyn pools (see listing) to the end at Cwm Bychan Farm (paid parking and camping). Follow the Roman Steps (actually a medieval packhorse path) up as if for Rhinog Fawr, well signed.

90 mins, 52.8457, -3.9978 🏊🏕️📷

6 AFON CWMNANTCOL POOLS

The waterfall at the Nantcol campsite is huge (pictured, day pass available, LL45 2PL). But the secret pools are secluded and delicious. Pass the campsite, then 3km further laong lane. Parking difficult - don't block gates or tracks - and follow footpath to the stream, then upstream 200m.

5 mins, 52.8151, -4.0367 🏔️⛰️📷

---

park in layby on A496 just N of the Magnox hydro station and bridge (LL41 4HY). A footpath follows the L bank of stream up to the falls, 1.5km. From here, a bushwhack/scramble up around the falls 300m arrives at the ruined bridge (52.9286, -3.9843) and another 400m to the slide pool (52.9270, -3.9817) below the main gorges. The R bank approach descends on a public footpath from a lane (the one by the parking) at 52.9270, -3.9817 and provides access down into the gorge, but there is no parking on the lane. Canyoning companies run gorge adventures here e.g. Snowdonia Adventure Activities (01341 241511).

20 mins, 52.9305, -3.9847 🏔️⛰️👨🎏❄️📷🚗🐟

2 LLYN TECHWYN ISAF, LLANDECWYN

Just below the superbly-sited hilltop chapel is this idyllic roadside lake. Or beyond the chapel, on the old coaching road, is bigger Llyn Techwyn Uchaf. Head for LL47 6YR., take fork bearing up L.

2 mins, 52.9188, -4.0357

3 LLYN EIDDEW-BACH & TARNS

This perfect tarn in the remote northern Rhinogs has cliffs for jumping and fabulous views. From here an impressive old mining track heads up Moel Ysgyfarnogod past

RHINOG MOUNTAINS

1 RHAEADR DU, LLENNYRCH

Set in a remote and magical gorge, this 'black waterfall' cascades into a large plunge pool. It was much admired by Victorian travellers, but is now little visited. Head upstream, beyond a ruined bridge, the remains of the old Harlech road, for another waterfall with rock slab slide into a large pool. More pools continue above in a zigzag gorge, eventually reaching the base of the dam. There's access from either side, which could make a loop. The simplest is to

COED Y BRNEIN

7 LLYN GELLI-GAIN, TRAWSFYNYDD

A perfect wild-camping tarn with an island in rugged territory. If the walk in puts you off, there is also a sweet little river pool off the quiet lane nearby. From A470 in Bronaber turn E dir LL41 4UY and follow 1 mile to park at 52.8690, -3.8937 (by cattle grid and 'bus shelter'). Take hillside track from gate SE then NE around peak. River pool is at Pont Dôl-y-mynach, 1.6km S at 52.8629, -3.8826.

30 mins, 52.8777, -3.8825 🏊🏕️🚗💧🏃

8 PISTYLL CAIN & GOLD MINE

Impressive waterfalls with pool at the bottom and nearby gold mine ruins. According to local legend a cave near the waterfall is haunted by a tortured man! If this doesn't put you off, it is a lovely area for a walk and swim. Climb above the Mawddach falls to reach the recently derelict ruins of Gwynfynydd goldmine. There's a further shallow swim in a pool underneath the stone bridge above Rhaeadr Mawddach. 6 miles N of Dolgellau on A470 turn R for LL40 2HS at end of Ganllwyd (where speed limit ends), cross bridge and continue 1¼ miles to Tyddyn Gwladys car park at road end. Walk 1.6km on track upstream, admiring the river pools, to find Pistyll Cain joining from the L. A rocky scramble leads to the base of the falls. There are warning signs so take all usual precautions. Cross footbridge to larger Rhaeadr Mawddach (no swimming). Climb up above waterfall and continue along river on track to find stone bridge with pool and ruins at 52.8351, -3.8761. The main Gwynfynydd mine workings are up incline into forest above L. Also accessible from the Coed-y-Brenin mountain biking trails (LL40 2HZ, 01341 440728).

20 mins, 52.8304, -3.8806 🏊🚶🅿️📷🚴💧

9 CWM CAMLAN FALLS

Follow the Gamlan river as it tumbles through woodland and up onto open hillside, with jewel-in-the-crown waterfall Rhaeadr Du (not to be confused with waterfall of same name at Llennyrch). There are several pools for dipping; if the water isn't thundering down, scramble down carefully to a large pool below the waterfall for a wonderful swim. This is a Special Area of Conservation, don't damage the vegetation. On A470 at Ganllwyd, park in National Trust car park on roadside, cross road and find path next to village hall. Follow path

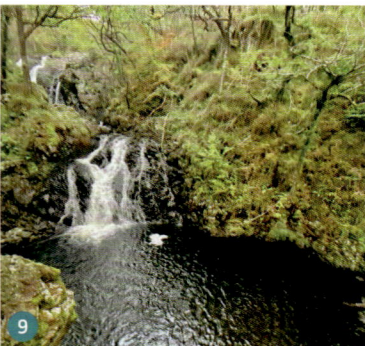

upstream, branching left as track climbs to find footbridge and waterfall. Return to track to explore upstream.

20 mins, 52.8023, -3.8970 🏊⚷▼🧗🏊

10 LLYN TAN-Y-GRAIG

Follow the New Precipice Walk along an old mountain tramway, and enjoy stunning views down the Mawddach. The first part is flat and wheelchair friendly. It then descends to the super clear Llyn Tan-y-graig, a glassy lake, backed by forest and with views out over Cader Idris. Turn off the A496 into Taicynhaeaf (opp Penmaenpool wooden toll bridge). Continue for 2 miles, bearing R at the chapel (before LL40 2TU), up through several gates, to reach the parking area.

20 mins, 52.7628, -3.9105 🏊🏞️🚶

11 PONT LLANELLTYD, RIVER MAWDDACH

A late-18th-century stone bridge watches over a huge shingle pool and beach edged with grassy banks. Cymer Abbey ruins are also nearby, adjacent to a caravan park. Signed Cymer Abbey from A470 just S of Llanelltyd (NW of Dolgellau). Abbey at LL40 2HE, but turn L to find parking by river /old bridge first.

1 mins, 52.7561, -3.9011 🏊🐟

NORTH CADER IDRIS

12 BLUE LAKE, GOLWERN QUARRY

Legendary 'Blue Lake' in an amphitheatre of cliffs, once accessible, but tunnel now blocked by landowner due to exessive littering and social media. You are still free to explore, with its sea views and mine remains. Discreet anchor bolts have been for abseiling access. Others have reported a dangerous scramble down on the SE face. Not advised. Included here in the hope it might one day open again. Park/path starts 52.6919, -4.0405.

20 mins, 52.6890, -4.0411 ▼❓

13 LLYNNAU CREGENNEN & ARTHOG FALLS

Set in a secret valley below Cader Idris, these NT-managed lakes are sublime, with a boathouse, stunning sea views and mystical peaks rising around. The sunsets from here are worth the climb. Swimming is contentious here, especially in the first lake which is popular for fishing, and there are signs to that effect, discretion advised. Combine this perhaps with a visit to nearby Arthog Waterfalls. Enjoy a steep walk up the picturesque, waterfall-filled wooded gorge with some little plunge pools to reach a pool under a clapper bridge. On A493 ½ mile E of

Arthog, turn signed Cregennen Lakes just N of LL39 1YT. Continue up the lane 1½ miles to find first lake L and car park on R. For waterfalls, you may find space for 1 car ¼ mile after turning off A493 at the entrance for Pant Phylip (LL39 1LQ). Don't block gate or turning. Continue 200m through gate for the stream bridge (permissive path). The waterfall path heads steeply up about 880m. Otherwise from A493 take footpath opp St Catherine's Church.

2 mins, 52.7103, -3.9875 🏔️📷

14 PENRHYN-GWYN WATERFALLS

Beyond the usual attractions of an old slate quarry – a ruined mill and waterwheel, old inclines, a vast overgrown quarry pit and amazing views – follow the secret track and you'll enter a steep sylvan glen boasting two beautiful waterfalls and plunge pools, and a dark, mysterious tunnel. From the Ty Nant car park take Pony Path path (52.7187, -3.9297). After the farm follow L branch of stream through a copse 200m, then L through gate, soon leading to the mill ruins (waterwheel pit) on open access land. Climb incline to second main level for the track (52.7161, -3.9220) and contour around 100m NE to stream. Take care.

20 mins, 52.7165, -3.9195 🧗🪨

15 LLYN GAFR & LLYN Y GADAIR

Two lovely tarns – Gafr at 410m and Y Gadair at 560m – below the great mountain wall of Cader Idris, with expansive views and few visitors. Good for wild camping. The main path ascends from Gwernan lake LL40 1TL, or make your own way across country from the Penrhyn-gwyn. Park at Ty Nant car park. Pony Path path starts 200m W, over bridge and past possible further field parking. Follow to just after the farm (was a hostel) then follow L branch of stream through a copse 200m, then L through gate, soon leading to the mill ruins, waterwheel pit below. Climb incline to second main level (52.7161, -3.9220) and contour around 100m NE to stream (52.7165, -3.9195). Take care. Continue to follow stream up to path, then S to lake.

60 mins, 52.7055, -3.9139 🏕️🏔️⛰️

16 LLYN CAU, CADER IDRIS

A huge, dramatic glacial cwm in the crater of Cadair Idris set beneath 400m-high mountain walls. It's a 350m ascent up from the car park, past numerous falls and pools, so even if the lake is cold you'll be warm when you arrive. Shady by afternoon. 6 miles S of Dolgellau on A487, turn R after the Minfford Hotel (LL36 9AJ) to find main

car park on B4405. Cross bridge through woods and follow stream up hillside via Dol Idris path to arrive at lake after 3.2km. You are about halfway up Cadair Idris if you want to continue!

60 mins, 52.6941, -3.8987

SOUTH CADER IDRIS

17 NANT GWERNOL & BRYN-EGLWYS

Sparkly little woodland waterfall pool, perfect for nymphs. A Cascade Trail (marked yellow) leads up the wooded valley from the station and reaches the small pool almost immediately. Follow the Quarryman's Trail (marked blue) through the reforested remains of the once-busy Bryn-Eglwys slate quarry: an incline, winding-house and some vast, tree-filled pits, one of which has a waterfall cascading into it. In Abergynolwyn (LL36 9YA) walk up from behind the community centre to Nant Gwernol station (or take the train from Tywyn). There are also the busy Dolgoch Falls in the next valley SW, LL36 9UW, with a viewing platform, 52.6191, -3.9884.

10 mins, 52.6413, -3.9501

18 TAL-Y-LLYN & LLYN MWYNGIL

Stretching out along the lush valley floor under the southern flanks of Cader Idris, this is a tempting lake on a summer day, and not too cold either. Stop at the no-frills Pen-y-Bont Inn for a post-swim pint. Take the B4405 dir Tywyn from the A487, follow towards LL36 9AQ, and reach the lake after 1 miles; limited parking in a couple of laybys. The Pen-y-Bont (01654 782285) is on the R at the far W end of the lake, after the Ty'n-y-cornel Hotel, and you could follow the lane from here along the N shore of the lake, beyond the Old Rectory – it's a public byway.

1 mins, 52.6673, -3.9082

19 AFON DULAS POOLS

Oak-wooded stream gorge just by the road, leading to a little waterfall and pool with rope swing. On A4870 at Corris, take R for Aberllefenni, towards SY20 9RX. After 2 miles turn R, continue ½ mile to a large layby on R on bend. Descend, open access.

2 mins, 52.67403, -3.8108

20 PONT RHYDYGWIAL, RIVER DOVEY

Good riverside banks for paddling, picnic and a dip, if nobody is fishing. At Cemmaes, 8 miles E of Machynlleth on A470, turn into Maes-y-Llan, past SY20 9PS, and continue to river bridge.

2 mins, 52.6405, -3.7243

DENBIGHSHIRE

21 TWT HILL & CLWYD, RHUDDLAN CASTLE

There are fine views of 13th-century Rhuddlan Castle from Twt Hill motte, the upstream site of the original castle, built in 1087. Below is the river Clywd – ships once sailed all the way here to supply the castle from the sea. From Rhuddlan Castle car park (opp LL18 5AD) follow Hylas Lane and take footpath forking R at bend, which leads towards the river bank and up to Twt Hill.

5 mins, 53.2869, -3.4618

22 LLYN BRENIG ⬛

Supervised OWS sessions. Lifeguarded reservoir swimming. Sun & Fri mornings, seasonal. 2 hour session, £7.50. Min age 12. llynbrenig.com. Other shores of the lake are exposed, or mainly for bird watching or fishing.

2 mins, 53.0798, -3.5420

23 ST DYFNOG'S WELL

Steps lead down into this sacred pool, a short woodland walk behind the church. Opp the King's Head, Llanrhaeadr, LL16 4NL. From back L of the churchyard a path leads up the stream 300m.

5 mins, 53.1592, -3.3778 🏊

24 BOD PETRYAL POOL

Large woodland lake with trails, perfect for a dip and very easy to get to. Follow B5105 from Clawdd-newydd W. After 3 miles take L signed Melin-y-wig before LL21 9PR. Forestry car park is on R.

3 mins, 53.0477, -3.4373 🏊🏞️♿

FLINTSHIRE

25 STRYT-ISAF LAKE, WREXHAM ⬛

This old sand-and-gravel lake was always nice for a discreet dip on a hot day, accessed from the public footpath at N end, across railway. Now it has been bought by a community project (parkinthepast.org.uk) you'll need to use your judgement. The S end has OWS sessions and tent saunas (saunacwtch.co.uk)

5 mins, 53.1311, -3.0498 🏊❓

26 PLAS POWER FALLS, CLYWEDOG

The weirs along the Clywedog supplied power for the many important surrounding ironworks and corn mills. The sylvan valley trail through damp woods is a botanists' dream, and you'll also find one of the best-preserved sections of Offa's Dyke. From Bersham old ironworks, LL14 4LL,

head W 250m past St Mary's church to find horseshoe weir on R (53.0371, -3.0393). Park here. Take a dip and follow river upstream on far bank to the more impressive waterfall weir, 800m further along the Clywedog Trail. Offa's Dyke crosses river here. Another mile upstream leads to Nant Mill country park and visitor centre (53.0434, -3.0620). Further upstream are the Minera Lead Mines and country park. Downstream you can explore more of the Clywedog at the Erddig country park, S of Wrexham.

10 mins, 53.0381, -3.0487 🏊🏞️♿

27 RIVER DEE, ECCLESTONE

Convenient riverside car park, from which to reach the water for swimming or canoeing. Fills up early in summer. Footpath heads both up and downstream, but upstream leads to the beautiful Crook of Dee meander. From Ecclestone take Paddock Rd dir CH4 9JE, following L past gates to ferry parking at end of road.

10 mins, 53.1534, -2.876 🏊🚶

28 IRON BRIDGE, RIVER DEE

This is undoubtedly one of the finest remaining examples of a Thomas Telford cast-iron bridge. Spanning a wide, bucolic stretch of the river Dee, with footpaths up and downstream. Make yourself visible with swim hat / tow float as motorised boats do use this stretch. In Aldford (CH3 6HX), park at church side entrance and take footpath through white gates and across fields down to woods and river bridge, 800m.

10 mins, 53.1349, -2.8711 🏊

BALA & RIVER DEE

29 LLYN CELYN

Llyn Celyn occupies an important place in Welsh history, it having been created by the controversial flooding of the community of Capel Celyn in the 1960s. It is a peaceful, quiet spot now and the best swim would be had from the picnic spot at its W end, although as a Welsh Water reservoir, swimming isn't permitted, take all usual precautions. On A4212 a mile SW of LL23 7NY.

2 mins, 52.9487, -3.7183 🏊🚶

30 LLYN TEGID/BALA, LLANGOWER

The largest natural lake in Wales, also called Bala Lake, with gravel shores and swimming freely allowed, though it suffers from blue-green algae in the summer so be cautious. There's a very easy cove by Llangower

No parking but you may be able to fit one car near entrance to Caerau Gardens. Walk another 800m on track and L down across open access land to SE shore.

15 mins, 52.9534, -3.5163

32 CARROG BRIDGE, RIVER DEE

River meadows, beach and pools by an old stone bridge, perfect for an easy swim and picnic. Then enjoy lovely river views and real ale on the terrace of the friendly Grouse Inn. Turn off A5 at Llydiart y Parc, dir LL21 9BD signed Carrog, and after ½ mile park R before river bridge. Cross to kissing gate at bridge and follow riverside footpath upstream for 800m. Grouse Inn is over bridge (LL21 9AT, 01490 430272).

2 mins, 52.9799, -3.3218

33 RHEWL, RIVER DEE

Easy roadside paddle and swim spot, surrounded by trees and countryside. If you are travelling on the Llangollen steam railway you can also find your own private spot near Deeside Halt. Start as for Horseshoe Falls (see listing) but continue past car park to Rhewl. There take L for LL20 7YT and follow L past the Sun Inn to find pulling off space mile further along, where road runs along river. Leave

enough space for a passing place. Deeside Halt pools are above the little weir 300m downstream of the halt, at 52.9736, -3.2276. Can also be accessed from A5, find parking area just E of Tollgate Cafe cross road, take footpath, crossing rail line to river.

1 mins, 52.9905, -3.2285

34 HORSESHOE FALLS, RIVER DEE

Set in parkland in a beautiful valley, the graceful curve of this weir may be beautiful but it creates dangerous currents – never swim below the weir and avoid when current running strong. The pool above is deep and can be calm, easily accessed from the footpath. Built by Thomas Telford in 1804–06, to supply the Llangollen canal. A5 heading W from Llangollen, take R signed Ruthin over river by the train station in Berwyn. Turn L at end, uphill to the pay car park on L, ½ mile before LL20 8BT. Follow riverside path to falls.

5 mins, 52.9816, -3.1996

35 CYSYLLTAU BRIDGE, RIVER DEE

Follow the wooded footpath along the river, enjoy fine views of Pont-Cysyllte Aqueduct, and discover plenty of places to stop for a paddle or bathe. From Froncysyllte A5

station car park, and more shore to explore, lined with ancient oaks, leading on to campsite at Pant Yr Onnen. Take B4403 just S of Bala, follow 2½ miles along lake Bala, ½ mile before (E of) LL23 7DA. Cross tracks to shore.

2 mins, 52.8757, -3.6331

31 LLYN CAER EUNI

A secluded and sheltered lake hidden in rolling moorland, perfect for a summer picnic and swim. On the A494 3½ miles NE of Bala, turn into Sarnau (LL23 7LG) and continue 1 mile to gate at road end.

take B5434 1 mile, dir LL20 7YS, and park before bridge on R. Cross bridge and find riverside path down on R.

3 mins, 52.9707, -3.0913 🏊❓

36 OVERTON, RIVER DEE
Remote meander of the Dee in open fields with a sunny shingle beach. Explore the riverbank both ways on the Wat's Dyke Way. On A528 (A539) mile NW through Overton, look out for two ornate wooden gates into woods, just before LL13 0HF. Parking for one here. Descend on footpath through woods, bear R on reaching the open fields downstream to the river 200m.

10 mins, 52.9715, -2.9464 🏊❓

SHROPSHIRE MERES

37 COLEMERE COUNTRY PARK
In an area of glacial lakes, Cole Mere is one of the more easily accessible, with a quiet shore path on open access land where a dip might go unnoticed, but be discreet. Blue-green algae possible. Orchids decorate the hay meadows in spring. Signed from the A528, 2 miles S of Ellesmere. Follow road taking L fork after crossroads, past turning for SY12 0QL, then L at T-junction to lakeside car park. Follow path around to wooded N shore for quieter spots. Some also swim from NW shore of Ellesmere (52.9122, -2.8815).

5 mins, 52.891, -2.8402 🏊❓🐦✤

38 HANMER MERE
Wander through the woods past carpets of bluebells until you reach an open meadow and small, secluded, sandy beach, perfect for a swim. Hanmer is signed 9.5km W of Whitchurch on A539. Park at Glendower Place (SY13 3DF) and follow footpath through gate on corner 500m L through woods, keeping the mere on your R.

10 mins, 52.9469, -2.8147 🏊🚶✤

39 ALDERFORD LAKE 🅿
This pretty lake, with good water quality, is a spot popular with wild swimmers and triathletes. It is also a peaceful place for a walk or bring your own kayak or paddleboard. Fees apply. Cafe on site. From roundabout on A41 just south of Whitchurch (SY13 3JQ) take B5476 signed Wem. Entrance L after 500m.

4 mins, 52.9522, -2.6742 🏊🧒🐕🏕

BERWYNS & R VYRNWY

40 PISTYLL RHAEADR & LLYN LLUNCAWS
One of the highest waterfalls in Wales thunders down a vertical cliff and then escapes through a circular hole. Small pools for plunging are below the footbridge. Adjacent are tea rooms, loos and campsite, so it can get quite busy. Take the path to the top for far reaching views, or walk high up into the hills through the stunning Nant y Llyn valley to Llyn Lluncaws, a pretty glacial tarn tucked below the cliffs of Moel Sych. Signed Pistyll off the B4580 in Llamrhaeadr-ym Mochnant. Follow single-track road 4 miles to end, past SY10 0BZ. Parking £5. You can also park 800m before, and walk in on footpath (52.8513, -3.3677). For Llyn Lluncaws (52.8741, -3.3797),

follow the path or E of falls, cross the Nant y Llyn river and continue N following it upstream for 2.6km.

5 mins, 52.8546, -3.378 🔺📷

41 RHIWARGOR FALLS
Also named Pistyll Rhyd-y-meinciau, a multi-tier set of falls on the Afon Eiddew, cascading steeply down with several small pools, including a super infinity pool. Scramble up the different levels on a rough path alongside. Additional pools above the waterfall. A 1.6km walk W of the picnic site at NW end of the lake.

2 mins, 52.8087, -3.5538 🥾🧒🏊🐕📷

42 PONT LLOGEL, RIVER VYRNWY
An old stone bridge and wooded gorge with an easy-access riverbank walk for over 3 miles along Ann Griffiths Walk (and Glyndwr's Way). Deep enough for a swim under the bridge. E4395 over river a mile N of SY21 0QD. Forestry car park at N side of bridge.

1 mins, 52.7277, -3.4348 🏊🔺🚶

43 DOLANOG FALLS, RIVER VYRNWY
Very impressive wooded waterfalls and weir below white cliffs. Enjoy a deep section above the rope swings and all the way up

so best on bikes, but this is a well-known swimming spot. On A495, 2 miles S of Meifod, turn at traffic lights, to and past SY22 6HR and over New Bridge across Banwy. Just after, find stile on L down to river beach, be aware that this is not an official right of way. Beach and pool upstream (turn R up lane after bridge and drop down, or go over gate before bridge), but possibly private. From Meifod side of traffic lights, a footpath leads 800m upstream to a weir. Or swim all the way down to Meifod (see listing).

3 mins, 52.6928, -3.2692 🏊❓

45 BRONIARTH BRIDGE, MEIFOD
Open, sunny and deep with fine views, this is perhaps the easiest place to swim on the beautiful Vyrnwy. Turn off A495 in Meifod, dir Recreation Facilities and SY22 6DA past rugby club/tennis courts to find Broniarth Bridge and limited verge space on far side. Riverside footpaths head downstream for a 1.6km (L bank to a beach).

2 mins, 52.7073, -3.2499 🏊🚶

UPPER SEVERN

46 SEVERN/VYRNWY, CREWGREEN
A glorious stretch of deep, tranquil water

where the Severn and Vyrnwy meet. Perfect for jumps, dives and swimming. At E end of Crewgreen (SY5 9AT) take lane N signed Melverley (National Cycle Route 81) for 500m. Park R just before bridge and follow footpath R down, then L under bridge.

5 mins, 52.7359, -2.9966 🏊🍴⛺🏕

47 MELVERLEY, RIVER VYRNWY
Upstream of Melverley the footpath follows the meandering river Vyrnwy through empty lowland pasture for over four miles with a couple of good access points for a dip or long linear swim. St Peter's black-and-white church on the bank is one of the oldest of its kind, rebuilt in the 15th century after Owain Glyndŵr burnt it to the ground. There is a Jacobean pulpit and a chained Bible. Leave B4393 at Crewgreen, opp SY5 9BS, for Melverley. After 1 mile the church is signed L (SY10 8PJ, dead end). Follow footpath N past caravan park to explore the river meanders. Upstream there is vehicular byway access to a remote section of the river from SY10 8PQ (about ½ mile on a dirt track), and the road meets the river again ½ mile SE of SY10 8QJ.

2 mins, 52.7425, -2.9903 🏊⚓✝

to the old road bridge. Some deep pools downstream too. Explore more river pools downstream along Glyndŵr's Way. Below B4382, ¼ mile E of Dolanog (beyond SY21 0LQ). Some parking on L adjacent to river or car park at postcode.

1 mins, 52.7036, -3.3812 🚶🧗

44 NEWBRIDGE, RIVER BANWY
On the Banwy where it meets the Vyrnwy, you'll find a glorious section of deep river pools either side of the New Bridge, studded with beaches and ancient trees. Uncertain access, and no parking space

48 ROYAL HILL, RIVER SEVERN

Grassy banks, shingle beaches and a pub on one of the few access points to the Severn on this stretch. Swim upstream or down, but be aware that there is no road or footpath access along the river banks. This does make it a haven of wildlife and tranquility. As for Melverley (see listing) but continue past church turning to take next R to SY10 8ES. Large layby with footpath down to river opp the Royal Hill Inn and campsite (01743 741242).

2 mins, 52.7498, -2.9627

49 SHRAWARDINE, RIVER SEVERN

A lovely, grassy-banked section of the young River Severn with an easy entry point next to the ruined railway bridge. A good take-out point if kayaking from Royal Hill (see listing). In Shrawardine take lane NW dir SY4 1AJ (National Cycle Route 81). Park by last houses, follow footpath sign to L to river.

15 mins, 52.7330, -2.8996

50 ATCHAM, RIVER SEVERN

Dip your toes at this calm, shallow bend in the River Severn or walk upstream and swim down through the languid, deeper waters. Park at Atcham, 2.4km from Shrewsbury ring road on B4380. Long lay-bys on road W of and opp Mytton and Mermaid Hotel (SY5 6QG). Footpath at E end of old bridge down to a shallow sandy beach.

5 mins, 52.6790, -2.6812

51 CRESSAGE, RIVER SEVERN

Access points on both sides of the river, offering a great opportunity to wallow in the water under Cressage Bridge. Watch out for nettles! From Cressage (SY5 6DE) take the B4380 N. After 600m, take footpath on L just before bridge and follow down to the riverside. Walk or cycle from village.

7 mins, 52.6378, -2.6010

52 IRONBRIDGE, RIVER SEVERN

A glorious gorge swim under the iconic Ironbridge. Enter the water under the cooling towers at Dale End car park and swim down under the bridge to easy exit point at Severnside. Head NW out of Ironbridge along river on Wharfage to Dale End car park on L (TF8 7NJ). Short walk to river. Exit at Severn Side path to L: 52.6270, -2.4825.

3 mins, 52.6272, -2.4853

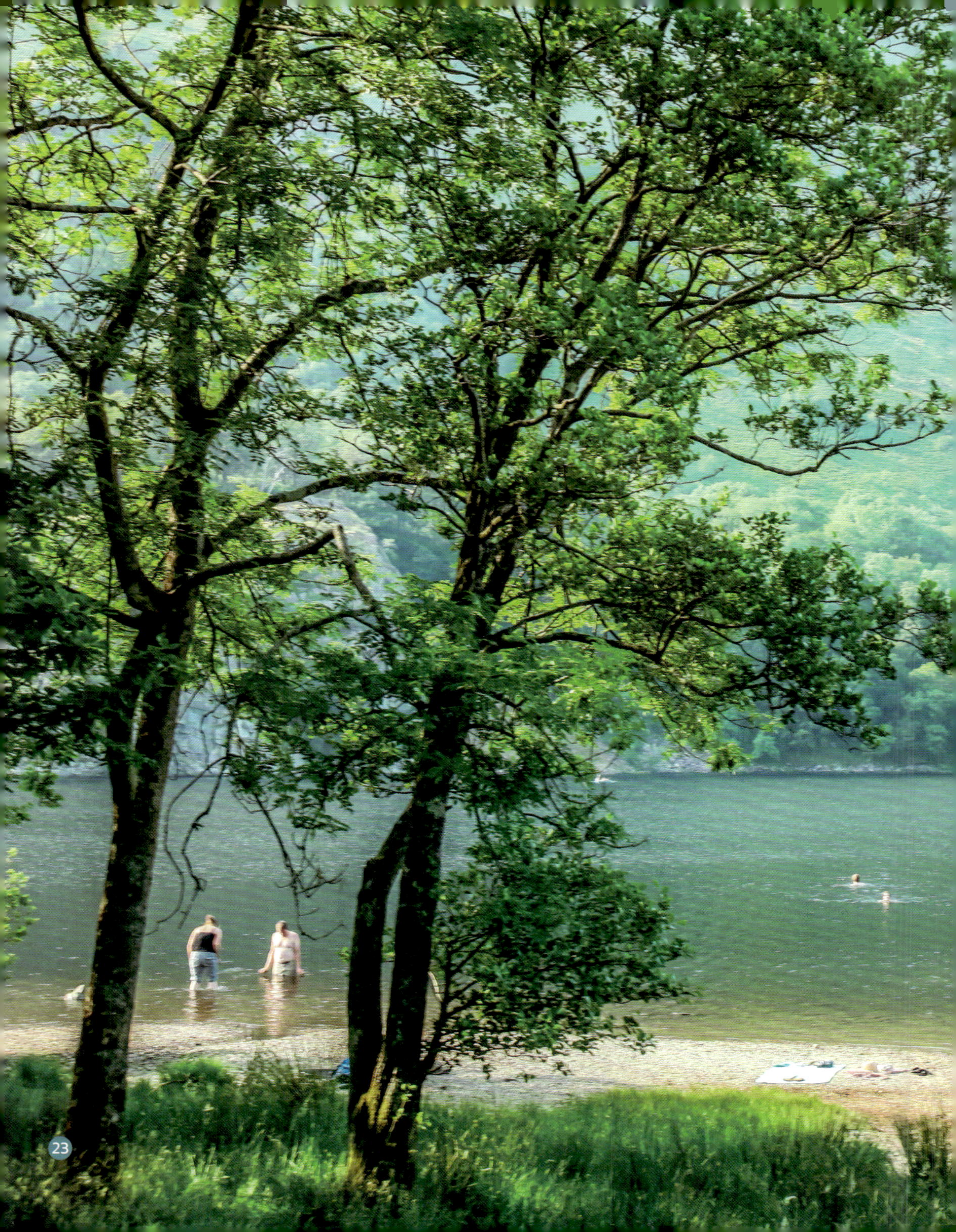
23

NORTH ERYRI SNOWDONIA

Llyns are those magical lakes that appear as you're sweating your way to the top of the mountain. Swimming in them provides total immersion in the landscape and the ultimate sense of the wild.

Getting in, and out, of a tarn is as much a part of the ritual as the swim itself. For me, it has to be a dive. First, I peer down to check for sea monsters among the rocky shapes of the dark bottom. Then, with a lurch of adrenaline, I leap in and am under the water, scrabbling up through a riot of rising bubbles towards the surface before breaststroking to the side, gulping little sips of the sweet spring water as I go. As I reach the shallows and wade out of the primordial depths, my skin is already tingling. I may have only managed 50 yards, but there's an unnatural sense of elation and achievement – my head is in focus, the world is in perspective again, and all my grogginess has been washed away. No sooner am I dry than I turn to dive in again.

Swimming over the iconic massif of Yr Wyddfa/Snowdon, the highest peak in England and Wales, with its pyramid pinnacle and sea views, provides the ultimate llyn safari. The mountain has long been a place for wild bathing as well as mountaineering excellence. George Mallory, the ill-fated Everest explorer, was also a fanatical lake swimmer who used the mountain to train for the first British ascent. Accompanied by some of the finest thinkers of his time – E. M. Forster, John Maynard Keynes, the Huxley brothers, and other members of the Cambridge Apostles – an opportunity to bathe always rounded off a mountain day and complemented the new socialist ideology, which embraced a closer connection with the 'great outdoors'.

My route is six miles from south to north, returning by bus and staying the night at the eccentric old mountain hotel of Pen-y-Gwryd. The route begins at Llyn Dinas (25), beneath the precipitous rocky knoll of Dinas Emrys, a fifth-century castle

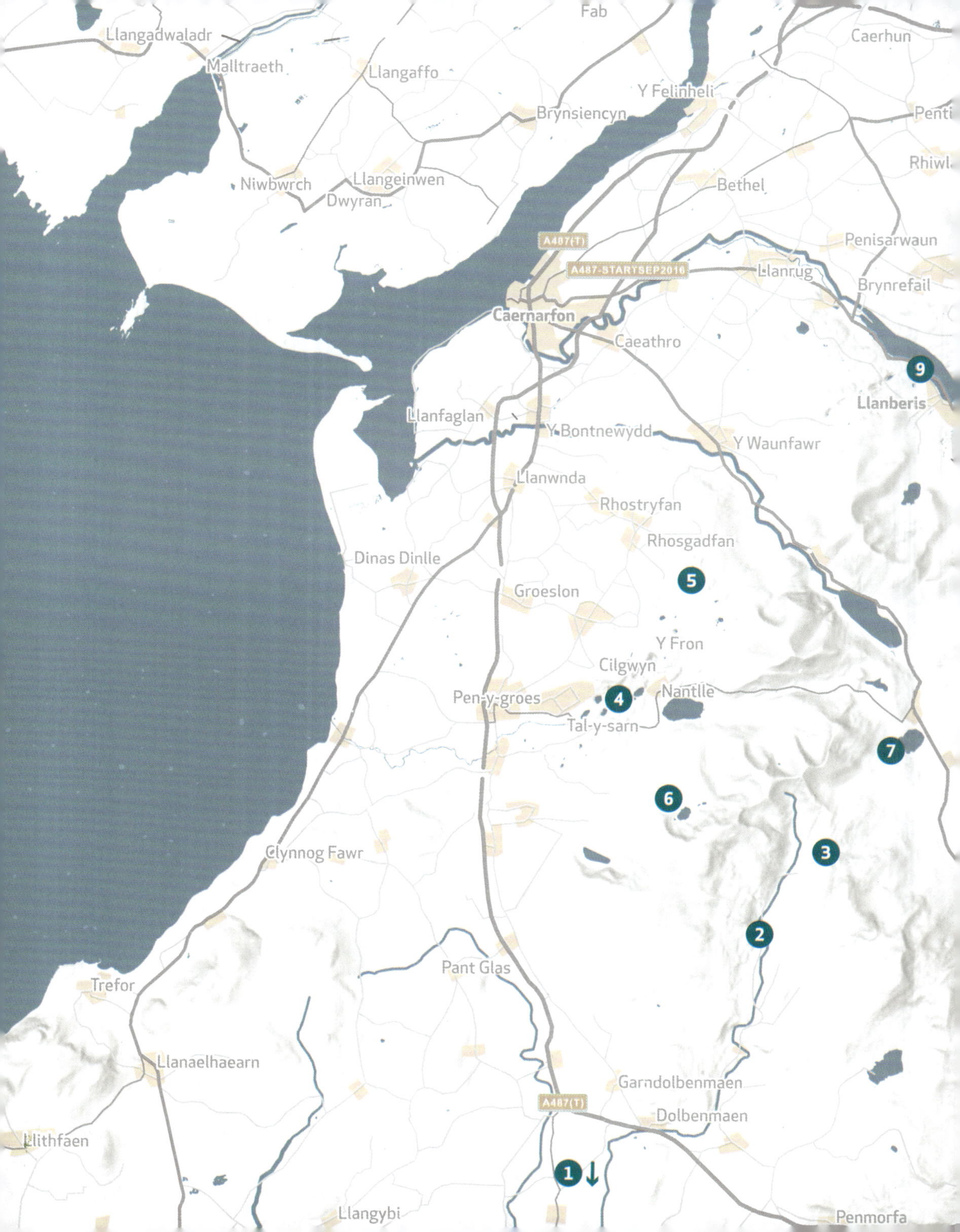
Fab
Llangadwaladr
Malltraeth
Llangaffo
Caerhun
Y Felinheli
Brynsiencyn
Penti
Rhiwl
Niwbwrch
Llangeinwen
Dwyran
Bethel
A487(T)
Penisarwaun
A487-STARTSEP2016
Llanrug
Brynrefail
Caernarfon
Caeathro
9
Llanberis
Llanfaglan
Y Bontnewydd
Y Waunfawr
Llanwnda
Rhostryfan
Rhosgadfan
Dinas Dinlle
5
Groeslon
Y Fron
Cilgwyn
Pen-y-groes
4
Nantlle
Tal-y-sarn
7
6
3
Clynnog Fawr
2
Pant Glas
Trefor
Llanaelhaearn
Garndolbenmaen
A487(T)
Dolbenmaen
Llithfaen
1
Llangybi
Penmorfa

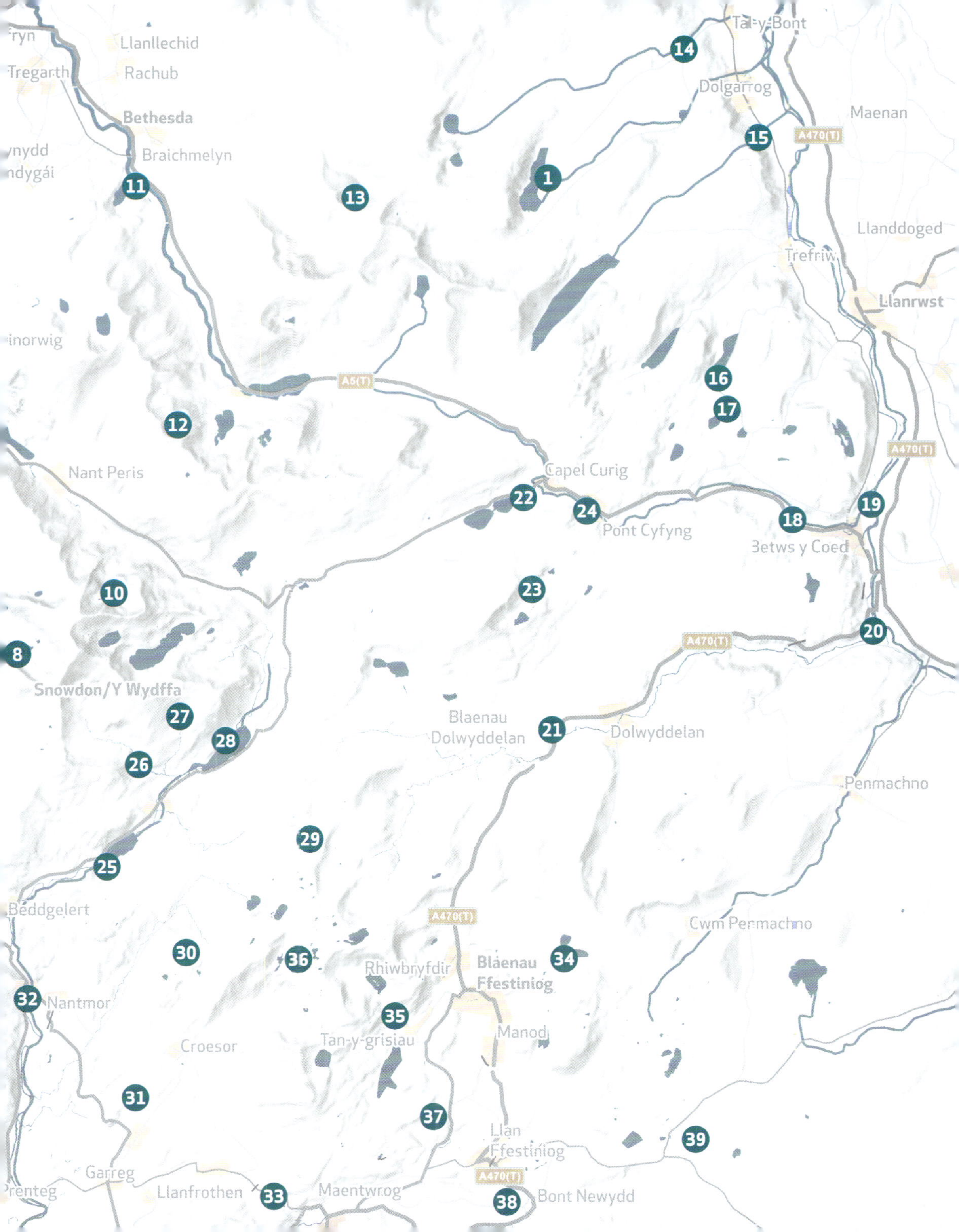

Ta-y-Bont

14

Dolgarrog

Maenan

Bethesda

15

A470(T)

Braichmelyn

Llanllechid

Rachub

Tregarth

ryn

ynydd
ndygái

11

13

1

Trefriw

Llanddoged

Llanrwst

inorwig

12

A5(T)

16

17

Nant Peris

Capel Curig

22

24

Pont Cyfyng

18

19

A470(T)

Betws y Coed

10

23

20

8

A470(T)

Snowdon/Y Wydffa

27

28

Blaenau
Dolwyddelan

21

Dolwyddelan

Penmachno

26

25

29

Cwm Permachno

Beddgelert

30

36

Rhiwbryfdir

34

Blaenau
Ffestiniog

32

Nantmor

35

Tan-y-grisiau

Manod

Croesor

31

37

Llan
Ffestiniog

39

Garreg

A470(T)

renteg

Llanfrothen

33

Maentwrog

38

Bont Newydd

stronghold where the original red dragon of Wales emerged from a pool and defeated the white dragon of the Britons. This crag-bounded lake makes an impressive and historic starting point, lined with gnarled oaks, craggy outcrops, and parched gorse.

Two miles up the road, at Nantgwynant, the Watkins Path begins. Within half an hour, a series of large plunge pools and waterfalls appears on the right. Cascading down the mountain, deep blue and decked with rowan, this sunny, south-facing stream is popular with Snowdon walkers (26).

As you continue, you'll pass more pools and the Gladstone Memorial, where in 1892 the elder statesman, after being prime minister four times, made a plea for justice for Ireland and Wales. The path turns and rises steeply up to the southern ridge of Snowdon and then on to the summit before heading over onto the Llanberis path that follows the course of the railway.

Perfect weather. Explored Craig-yr-Ysfa, three new climbs, bathing each time on the way back.

Mallory's letters, 1907. (He and his climbing partners took to bathing with obsessive zeal and wondered if life would ever be so good again.)

From a mile below the summit, you can drop down to the right, to the tiny tarn of Llyn Glas, with its magical little wooded island (10). The tarn overlooks the Llanberis Pass and the sea, but it's a very rough, steep scramble (and a 300-metre descent) to the plateau on which it's perched. Alternatively, turn off left instead, to Llyn Du'r Arddu, a deep blue lake, stained by copper and set under the craggy cliffs of 'Cloggie' (Clogwyn du'r Arddu). This 100-metre sheer rock wall is legendary among climbers and rescue helicopter pilots. So fearsome is the location that legend says birds will not fly over the lake.

From here, the River Arddu drains the heather moors for three miles, and the path continues, tracking the railway, past Hebron mountain railway station. The road heads to the tree line, where you'll find another series of amazing plunge pools cascading into Llanberis and Llyn Padam (9). Or a westerly descent could take you to Llyn Nadroedd, and then down to the extraordinary blue crater of Glanrafon quarry (8)

You're almost home, and after such an expedition, you deserve a night at the classic mountain hotel of Pen-y-Gwryd, high on Pen-y-Pass. When Mallory and Irvine failed to return from Everest in 1923, it was 30 years before Hillary led the first ascent. Pen-y-Gwryd was where his team trained and is filled with climbing antiquity. After a long day on the mountains, enjoy the great Victorian bathtubs, the outdoor sauna and swimming lake, and a hearty five-course meal that appears on the dot at seven o'clock, announced by a gong.

To the east of Snowdon, on the great massif of the Moelwyns and Cnicht, between Blaenau Ffestiniog and Snowdon, is another network of mountain-top lakes. Llynnau Diffwys are a pair that are rather shallow, though this does mean they warm up quickly (36).

These lakes stand at the head of Croesor's U-shaped valley, with views down the mountains, across the sandy flats of Traeth Mawr, and out to sea. You will also find nearby the crumbling remains of the mining town of Rhosydd, one of the largest, highest slate mines in North Wales. There are over twenty tarns up here, all within a couple of miles of each other, and you can make a fantastic ten-mile mountain walk from the sea at Portmeirion or Penrhyndeudraeth through Croesor (via its small but perfect waterfalls and infinity pools, 31) to Blaenau Ffestiniog, taking the mountain railway back to your starting point.

The slate mines above Croesor were just one of many that have left blue lagoons, filling with clear, blue water – like cobalt jewels on the mountainside. The rich mineral seams of North Wales made many investors rich, but just as many poor.

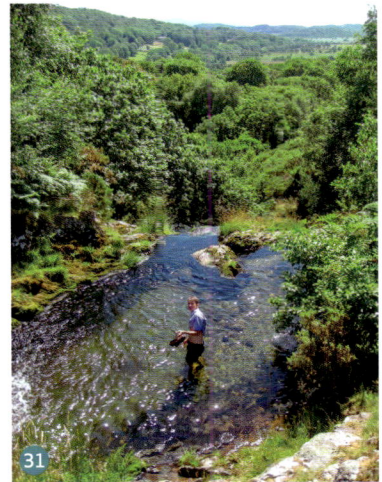

The Prince of Wales quarry at the head of the remote and beautiful Cwm Pennant valley was a wildly optimistic undertaking. An entire village was built to house 200 workers, a tramway was routed for many miles up the mountain, and a reservoir was constructed to provide the constant water supply essential for running the machinery of a mine. You can still see the dam, a double-skinned dry stone wall that would have been filled with clay (3).

The remains of an old waterwheel are some way below, next to the ruined dressing sheds. Here, the water-powered machines would have helped split and grade the slate before it was loaded onto the mountain railway. Although 200 years have passed since the reservoir was built, it still remains, its pool of unused water perfectly clear blue. Sheltered in its little valley, it is serene and romantic, surrounded by the fading ruins of a long-gone industrial age, with steep banks of heather growing along its edge.

PENNANT VALLEY

1 AFON DWYFOR, LLANYSTUMDWY

A bend in the river with a pretty pool popular with families, just along the riverside path from David Lloyd George's birthplace and final resting place. Park sensitively in the village - best spot 130m E of the museum (LL52 0SH). Follow signs from bridge to Lloyd George's grave ('bedd') 120m E of LL52 0SW, then continue on the riverside path for 1.2km.

15 mins, 52.9317, -4.2636 🚶🍴👶🏳️

2 CWM PENNANT POOL

It's not deep but this is the most easily accessible pool on the Dwyfor river, just below a road bridge and popular with families, who picnic on the grassy banks enjoying the beautiful secret valley setting. From Llanfihangel-Y-Pennant, ¾ mile beyond LL51 9AX. Space to pull off by the bridge.

1 mins, 53.006, -4.189 🚶🏊

3 PRINCE OF WALES QUARRY

A clear blue lagoon in a hidden cleft, at the head of one of the most remote and beautiful valleys in Snowdonia. The water once fed the Prince of Wales quarry which only operated for 13 years. Quarry ruins to explore and a carpet of bluebells in late spring. From Penmorfa (A487 W of Porthmadog) follow the signs to Cwm Pennant via Woollen Mill, and continue 4 miles, through several gates, to road end and car park. Follow path 300m up to ruined mine manager's house above on R, then continue up, bearing R up old railway, to reach ruined watermill and factory 200m. Follow stream valley to find old reservoir 200m above. Bring a map!

20 mins, 53.0236, -4.1657

NANTLLE & RHYD-DDU

4 DOROTHEA QUARRY LAKE & RUINS

A vast, wild site with many fascinating overgrown ruins, like a Welsh Angkor Wat. Circumnavigate the lake to discover old railways and a beam pump house. Over 100m deep in places, the lake is the culmination of many flooded quarry pits. Swimmers are welcome at the diving pontoon, at the end of a rough vehicle track. Currently open to the public, but development plans afoot. Park near the roundabout at the far E end of Talysarn (LL54 6AF). Follow access track E: after 70m a stile R leads to a swimming lagoon in fields, 100m on is a new security gate. Continue on main track 700m to reach the parking for the main dive/swim location (open to vehicles) at listed lat long. But bear L on footpath for ruined Talysarn Hall and barracks on R at 53.0559, -4.2439. Beyond the lake dive site, detour off E along the deep tramway cuttings, and find many more ruins to the N and E. Circumnavigate lake to find to find the magnificent Cornish beam pumping engine at 53.0542, -4.2435, with a second lake to the SW with tall island.

15 mins, 53.0561, -4.2393 🚶🚗🔽

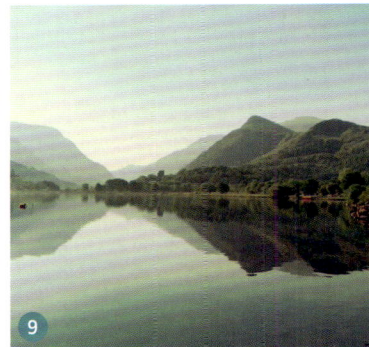

5 MOEL TRYFAN BLUE LAGOON

Set under Dolomite-like pinnacles in a lunar landscape of slate ruins (you may still see the odd quarry truck here), find four iridescent blue open-access lakes and the mini peak of Moel Tryfan with sunset views out over the Llŷn. Entering Y Fron from W on A487, turn L at telephone box (dir LL54 7BT) and park immediately on R, by track. Follow track 400m up NE to reach first crater lake (53.0740, -4.2245, skirt round on its L to find way down). Continue on NE on quarry tracks another 800m to reach the main trio of lakes.

20 mins, 53.0816, -4.2138 🏊🚩📷

6 LYNNAU CWM SILYN

Two super-clear, blue tarns, looking out to sea. Perfect for catching a midsummer sunset swim. Space for 2-3 cars through gate at the very end of the mountain lane beyond LL54 6RT. Follow track E for 1.6km. Upper lake is deeper. Nearby Llyn Cwm Dulyn has a similar aspect, but is lower and closer to road, at 53.0238, -4.2531, via LL54 6EA.

20 mins, 53.035, -4.2214 🏊📷

7 LLYN-Y-GADER QUARRY & CYCLE

The old quarry tramway, now the Lôn Gwyrfai cycle path, runs along the shores of Llyn-y-Gader to quarry ruins with a blue lake crater, and continues all the way to Beddgelert. Park as for Llyn Nadroedd (see entry), but take path on opp side of road. Follow 800m around lake; when path turn E, the quarry is 100m above to W.

20 mins, 53.0453, -4.1429 🚴🏊

8 LLYN NADROEDD & GLANRAFON QUARRY

One of a trio of beautiful tarns in west-facing Cwm Clogwyn. Superbly clear and super cold! Take footpath from main car park just S of Rhyd-Ddu A4085 (LL54 6TN). Take Rhyd-Ddu path for Yr Wyddfa / Snowdon but veer L around Llechog ridge; in total some 4km of walking and 300m of climbing. Descend via Glanrafon, a huge azure quarry crater, Access to water is via a tricky scramble scree on NW edge, only for adventurous, but interesting ruined barracks, waterwheels and a mill, all from 1875 (53.0655, -4.1188).

90 mins, 53.0677, -4.098 🏊⛰📷

LLANBERIS

9 LLYN PADARN SHORE

A large, glacial lake, perfect for a quick canoe or swim among wooded islands, coves and peninsulas – all created by slate waste. From A4086 at the far N end of Llanberis, almost opposite turn into town (dir LL55 4PX), turn towards lake to find several different separate parking/drive-on beach areas among the trees and a sauna (saunawales.co.uk). Good spot for an easy overnight.

2 mins, 53.1273, -4.1332

10 LLYN GLAS & CWM GLAS

This enchanting wild tarn has an island, on which grow two picturesque Scots pines. It sits in the secret Cwm Glas, one of the least trodden areas of Yr Wyddfa -Snowdon, with an infinity-pool view to the pinnacles of Crib Goch rising up before you. From here you can ascend to Llyn Bach and on up the scrambling ridge of Gyrn Lâs/Crib y Ddysgl (the Cwm Glas horseshoe).1½ mile NW of Pen-y-Pass on the A4086 (LL55 4NY) there is layby parking, by the Cromlech boulders, and a few more spaces ¼ mile further. Often full by early morning. Walk 400m past these to second bridge and follow Cwm Glas Mawr up, then head L to tarn. A map is needed, as there are few paths.

80 mins, 53.0807, -4.0638

11 OGWEN BANK, BETHESDA

If you ignore the mobile homes, this is as beautiful as any river scene, with a view up the Ffrancon valley, a stone bridge, ancient oaks, waterfalls and a huge pool for swimming, and popular with locals in the summer. Scramble up slate on the other side of the bridge to peer down into the flooded part of Penrhyn quarry, once the biggest slate production site in the world. Easy parking in layby off A5 by entrance of the caravan park (LL57 3LQ). Walk down entrance way to bridge.

2 mins, 53.1681, -4.0561

12 CWM CLYD LAKE

This little glacial lake has a peninsula, towering mountains and epic Ffrancon valley views. At 600m it's an imposing place to swim. From the NT Ogwen Cottage visitor centre, parking and kiosk (off the A5 at LL57 3LZ), climb up to Llyn Idwal. Bear R at the lake, then climb up to the W between Pinnacle Crag and Castell y Geifr.

60 mins, 53.1168, -4.0412

13 CWM CASEG & LAKE, CARNEDDAU
Swim surrounded by towering cliffs at Llyn Caseg, set in a remote glacial valley in the magnificent Carneddau range. From Bethesda drive beyond LL57 3UD to park at road end at pump station. Follow path E upriver 5km to lake. After 1.6km find tunnel which leads to a quarry chamber (53.1805, -4.0185).

90 mins, 53.1656, -3.9785 🏊🧭🏕🏔

VALE OF CONWY

14 AFON DULYN WATERFALL
Excellent waterfall with a big pool, just off the lane, in ancient woods. In Tal-y-bont, turn as for Llyn Eigiau (see listing), and continue ½ mile to double hairpin bend and grit bin R just beyond (no parking), where path descends to stream. Ford and continue upstream. Not an official right of way but path regularly used.

5 mins, 53.1975, -3.8622 ✴🧭❓

15 AFON DDU GORGE
Gorge scramble popular with activity groups, with smallish pools and falls. Passes through an SSSI for plant life so don't clamber on the vegetation. Approaching Dolgarrog from S on B5106, find car park

R after narrow bridge and LL32 8JG. Cross road and climb tarmac road, taking footpath on L to stream (see noticeboard and map of scramble). Exit above main waterfall to L, and return down on tarmac road.

5 mins, 53.1785, -3.8359 🏊🧭▼

16 LLYN GEIRIONYDD & KLONDYKE
A particularly accessible and popular swimming lake, with car park and little lane along its entire length, but in beautiful scenery. There's a slipway for canoes and dinghies, a meadow for picnics at S end and. A gorge scramble with tunnel leads down to the fascinating Klondyke mine ruins from the N end (53.1421, -3.8475). Lakeside car park well signed just beyond LL27 0YX.

2 mins, 53.1268, -3.8501 🏊🧭🏕🐟🦮

17 CORS BODGYNYDD
Two beautiful lakes backed by mountains sit in a strange land of hummocked hillocks and wetland bog – ancient spoil heaps from zinc mining 400 years ago, now re-wilded. The first lake, just a moment from the road, has an old dam wall with deep water for a swim. Gates to the reserve on the R, just beyond turn off L for LL27 0YZ and limited parking. Walk in 150m, bearing off R to the dam wall.

5 mins, 53.1201, -3.847

18 MINER'S BRIDGE, RIVER LLUGWY
Fun gorge with steeply sloping bridge and pools. The best pool and waterfall is 100m upstream with some good jumps; some easy riverside scrambling required. Heading W out of Betws on A5, take L to park in Rhes Dolydd street (LL24 0BU). Cross A5 and continue W 40m to find stone stile and steps down to river. After 100m reach Miner's Bridge stairs. Head upstream. Or walk from Betws bridge on the far river path (L bank), 1.6km.

10 mins, 53.0962, -3.8238 🧗🛶

19 CONWY & LLUGWY CONFLUENCE
Bring a picnic and enjoy an afternoon playing on the gravel beaches at the confluence of the rivers Conwy and Llugwy. With an inner tube you can ride the gentle rapids. Follow path from end of Station Rd car park in Betws-y-Coed (LL24 0AG) to river, under railway and downstream 400m to confluence. Footpath continues around the golf course and back to start by crossing the lines again via the station bridge.

10 mins, 53.0995, -3.796 🛶🏊🏕🚶

235

20 FAIRY GLEN, RIVER CONWY

A picturesque gorge with access for £1 per person plus £2 for parking. Bring cash. The big grassy junction pool is good for a longer, sunnier swim and family picnic. Upstream the gorge has some large rocks to sit on and a deep section down the middle to swim through (if not in spate). The path down can be tricky when wet. Also find Llyn yr Afanc, a huge, easy-access river pool named after a mischievous, mythical beaver of local legend, beneath the A470 bridge. S of Betws-y-Coed take A470 (dir Blaenau Ffestiniog). Signed on L just before bridge (dir LL24 0SL). For Llyn yr Afanc, turn R after bridge.

15 mins, 53.0725, -3.7953 🏊🚶👪⛱

21 DOLWYDDELAN CASTLE QUARRY

This brooding 13th-century castle tower stood sentinel over the Lledr valley. There's a free carpark for it on A470 and a deep quarry pool hidden 100m to the W of it.

2 mins, 53.0515, -3.9089

CAPEL CURIG

22 LLYNNAU MYMBYR, CAPEL CURIG

Twin lakes at the foot of Moel Siabod, where thick pine forest meets the water's edge at the valley floor, and a postcard view of the peaks of Yr Wyddfa, Y Lliwedd and Crib Goch is laid out ahead. Can be windy On the A4086 W of Capel Curig, pass Plas y Brenin outdoor centre (pyb.co.uk for courses & accommodation) and find pull-in on L at LL24 0ET. Walk back towards centre and take gate on R down steps to lake. Cross bridge and turn R, to find various paths leading to lake shore. For second lake, drive 600m further W and find large layby near boulders and path down to lake.

5 mins, 53.1010, -3.9190 🏊🚶⛱

23 FOEL QUARRY & LLYN Y FOEL

Tucked below the crags of Moel Siabod, this old flooded slate quarry pool with waterfall cascading into the far end is a sheltered, sunny spot to swim. Nearby is natural lake Llyn y Foel, wonderfully situated below the Ddaer Du ridge. Park as for Cyfyng Falls (see listing), cross bridge and take second footpath on R. Climb 1km on lane which becomes track, go through gate and continue 1.5km, past reservoir to quarry pool. Llyn y Foel is a further 800m SW.

40 mins, 53.0814, -3.9160 🏊⛲🚶⛰🔻

24 CYFYNG FALLS, RIVER LLUGWY

The falls themselves are notoriously

dangerous, with a turbulent pool beneath a towering waterfall and steep rock walls. The site is well used by local lads in summer, but because several deaths have occurred, it has been fenced off with 'private' and 'no swimming' signs. Upstream are easier pools, one a large deep pool with rope swing in a pretty meadow. 50m W of Bryn Glo on A5 (LL24 0DT), find a small layby on L, often full from early morning, pay car park at Bryn Glo. Cross bridge, turn R to follow river upstream. Large river pool in meadow at 53.0981, -3.8966 and further pools near Cobden hotel at 53.1004, -3.8967.

15 mins, 53.0981, -3.8966 🚶🚗🏊👪❓🅿🌳

NANT GWYNANT

25 LLYN DINAS, BEDDGELERT

A mile-long valley lake at the foot of Snowdon with stunning craggy backdrop. Accessible directly from the main road. Has become popular with paddle boarders, and for picnics. 2 miles NE of Beddgelert on A498. ½ mile after Sygun Copper Mine find parking on L. Cross road for footpath over footbridge to far shore.

5 mins, 53.0224, -4.0664 🚶🅱🏊🌊

26 CWM LLAN FALLS, WATKIN PATH

Cascading down the mountain, deep blue and decked with rowan, these sunny, south-facing pools are incredibly popular with both walkers returning from Yr Wyddfa and in their own right. Footpaths lead on up to Cwm Llan ruins or Merch falls (see listing). Park at Pont Bethania pay car park off A498 N of Beddgelert, opp LL55 4NQ turning, and follow Watkin Path signs. There is a deep pool for a dip right next to the bridge at Pont Bethania too.

30 mins, 53.0441, -4.0551 🚶🅱

27 MERCH FALLS & LLIWEDD MINE

Situated on remote mountainside beneath the Y Lliwedd ridge, this copper mine has huge chambers and many old artefacts. It sits at the head of the Merch river stream with many remote waterfalls, slides and pools to discover. Ascend from Hafod-y-Llan NT farm and campsite (LL55 4NQ).

90 mins, 53.0544, -4.0406 🚶🅱🌳

28 LLYN GWYNANT & ELEPHANT ROCK

Stunning lake surrounded by mountains with beaches and easy access along much of the eastern side. Make your way round to Elephant Rock (Penmaen-brith) cliff for epic jumps from all heights. Nantgwynant

campsite on the lakeside, makes for a perfect base. The cliffs are obvious on the far NW shore of the lake. There's some limited space on the roadside at 53.0475, -4.0174, 50m NE from entrance to YHA Bryn Gwynant (LL55 4NP) where the shoreside footpath and beaches begin, and you can swim from here. To get to the Elephant Rock, follow the footpath through the campsite to the footbridge upstream, then double back towards the rocks, 1.2km, keeping below the mountain wall. Scramble down to shore at end. Or reach by boat from the road.

10 mins, 53.0492, -4.0244 🚶🏊🌊

29 LLYN EDNO & PLUNGE POOLS

Reached from the tiny lanes above Nant Gwynant, this is a wild and remote lake with large rock slabs on its E side for diving in. The route up traces the tiny Afon Llynedno with some magical hidden plunge pools, one at the bottom of a gorge cleft (53.0293, -4.0149). The whole stream is worth exploring in full. Parking is tricky, so arrive early in season (53.0249, -4.0338).

45 mins, 53.0282, -3.9946 🚶🅱

GLASLYN & CROESOR

30 LLYNNAU CERRIG-Y-MYLLT

The ridge of Cnicht conceals a land of wild enchanting lakes. This pair, at 410m, are completely hidden by crags and perfect for a summer wild swim and camp after an ascent of Cnicht. Park just N of the Nantmor Mountain Centre (Gelli lago), a mile S of LL55 4NL, and head up past the hostel on the footpath, bearing up to the R along a wall after 1.2km. After about 450m, over another wall, find first lake.

50 mins, 53.0042, -4.0384 🚶🏕️🏞️🖼️

31 AFON CROESOR WATERFALLS

Follow the tiny stream up a secret valley below Croesor, amongst rowan and ancient trees, to find a series of magical deep pools and waterfalls. Many are big enough to jump and swim in. On A4085 ½ mile NW of LL48 6SG (beyond Croesor turning) the road crosses a bridge and turns hard L. Park on L (limited space) and take the track on R. After Gelli, the final house, keep to the stream. The first pools are very deep and shady – good for jumps – but the stream soon opens out after 200m.

15 mins, 52.973, -4.0562 🚶🖼️

32 PONT ABERGLASLYN, NANTMOR

A secret swim in a wooded gorge with pebble beach and deep river pools. In summer the water can reach 22°C, warmed by its route through Gwynant. Swim up and under the bridge or down into the junction pool. Park at the Aberglaslyn car park on A4085, between the bridge and the turning into Nantmor dir LL55 4YG. Take path through woods to L of toilets to reach bridge. Hop over wall opp kissing gate, down to beach. Not an official public right of way so be respectful if asked to move on. Also explore the riverbank path upstream from the bridge for many smaller pool and waterfalls.

5 mins, 52.9943, -4.0945 🚶❓🖼️

33 LLYN MAIR, TAN-Y-BWLCH

With a backdrop of wooded hills, this clear lake decorated with lily pads is easily accessible from the small picnic area by road. You could even arrive at Tan-y-Bwlch Station on a Ffestiniog Mountain Railway steam train. On A487 E of Porthmadog, turn L at Oakley Arms (01766 590277) dir LL41 3AQ, and continue ¾ mile to car park on R, picnic area opp. The adventurous could also climb up to Llyn y Garnedd reservoir 1.2km to the NE (52.9584, -4.0010).

2 mins, 52.9519, -4.0072 🚶🖼️♿

BLAENAU & FFESTINIOG

34 LLYN BOWYDD, BLAENAU FFESTINIOG
For slate mine history lovers, old reservoir on the mountain tramway that linked to amazing Cwt-y-Bugail mine ruins, (53.0043, -3.8886). Walk up through and above Maenofferen quarries. Footpath from end of Walter Terrace, LL41 3BE.
60 mins, 53.0028, -3.9047 ▲

35 CWMORTHIN WATERFALL & LAKE
A deep pool below a rock cleft in a series of cascades. Adjacent are the remains of the old wheelpit and other mine workings. Very easily accessed below the parking area. A great excuse to explore the ruins of this fascinating valley further. Continue on for Llyn Cwmorthin and ruins and the walk up to Rhosydd quarry (see next).
2 mins, 52.9905, -3.9645 🚶🏊

36 LLYNNAU DIFFWYS & CLOGWYN-BRÎTH
There are many beautiful high lakes amid the Moelwynion peaks. Llynnau Diffwys are a favourite pair and the northerly tarn has an island in the centre and views out to the sea. Perfectly located after a descent from Cnicht. Llyn Clogwyn-brîth, nearer the Rhosydd quarry ruins, is an old quarry reservoir and offers good swimming surrounded by sheltering cliffs. Park in the Cwmorthin car park above Tanygrisiau (52.9890, -3.9623) and follow the Snowdonia Slate Trail to the tips, then a further 1km NW of the ruined buildings. From the ruins continue 500m N to find Llyn Clogwyn Brith at 53.0007, -3.9909.
80 mins, 53.0027, -3.9987 🏊⛰🏞🚶🏊

37 AFON GOEDOL WATERFALLS
The Goedol flows from Tanygrisiau Reservoir, through plantation woodland and Celtic Rainforest, some of which is a National Nature Reserve, with several deep sections of gorge and falls. On A496 S of Tanygrisiau, park in layby on R at LL41 4BN. Follow footpath next to gate, turning R when path splits, to reach bridge with pool underneath. Cross bridge R to find waterfall upstream.
10 mins, 52.9689, -3.9508 🏊 🏊🏊 🚻

38 CEUNANT CYNFAL
Magical, remote gorge with huge waterfalls and exciting swimming and scrambling. A mile south-east of Llan Ffestiniog at Bont Newydd take lane opp LL41 4PY then turn right to find footpath on right into woods after 70m (52.9494, -3.9181).

39 AFON GAM WATERFALL & BLUE POOL
Deep in the wild lands of the Migneint moors, a short walk leads to an impressive waterfall and on up to a dramatic blue pool in the old quarry. From B4391 E of Llan Ffestiniog, take B4407. Park after mile at Llyn Dubach (52.9638, -3.8686). Cross road, walk back 75m and follow vehicle track. Waterfalls are below R after 200m. Continue, bearing L to reach flooded quarry pit. Another good waterfall further up the road at 52.9696, -3.8617, no parking.
15 mins, 52.9641, -3.858 🚶🏊

239

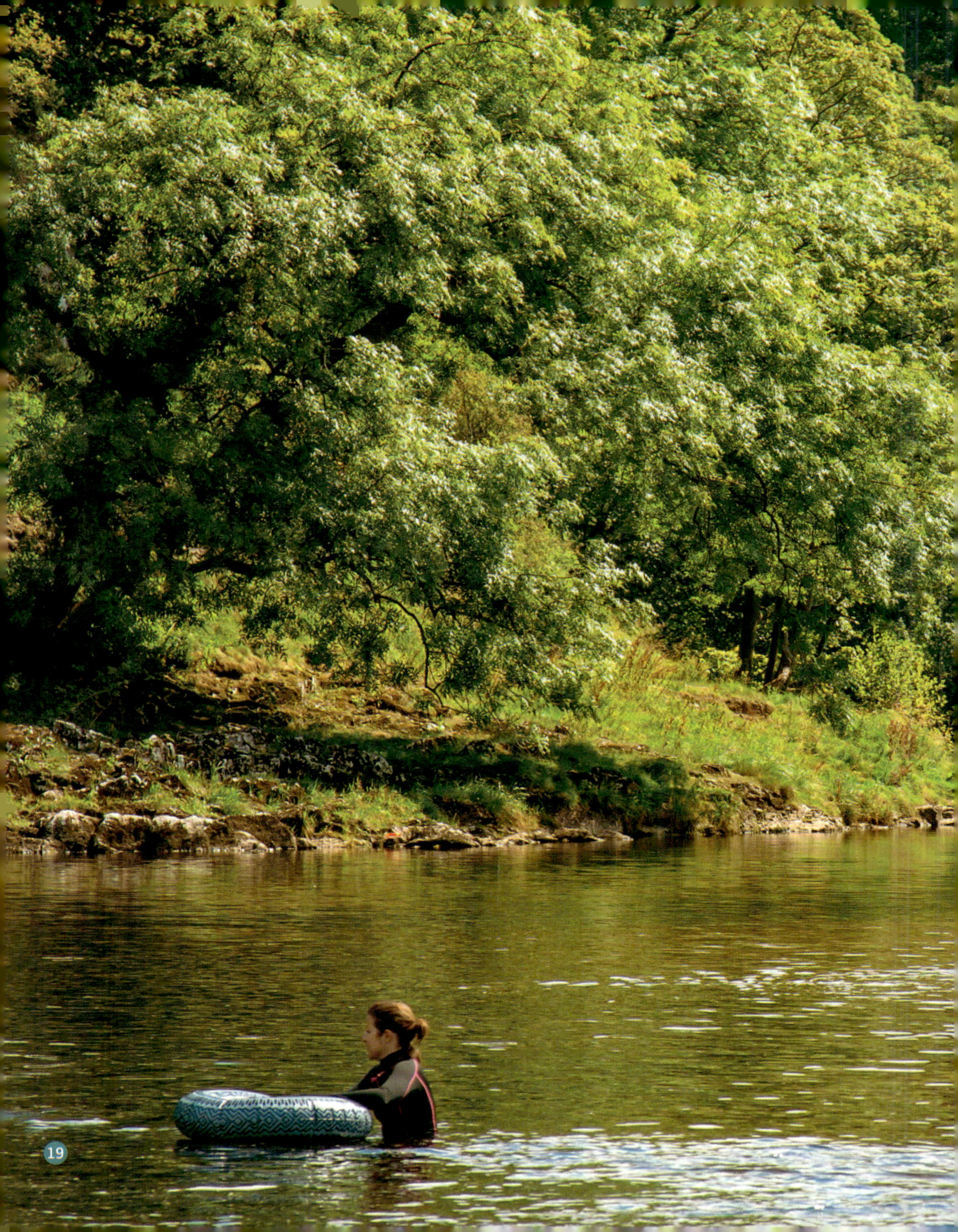

WHARFEDALE & BOWLAND

At Stainforth on the River Ribble, just a few miles north of Settle, a caravan park has grown up around one of the river's most popular swimming holes (13). It's always busy through the summer and deservedly so. There is a series of shallow rapids by an old packhorse bridge where children fish and paddle.

The water then tumbles down a waterfall into a deep, black, smooth-sided plunge pot with an old iron ladder. On any day in summer you can sit and watch the antics of children and parents alike testing their nerve by jumping into the cauldron from higher and higher vantage points. Downriver, fields open out in a wash of peace and buttercups, and further large pools provide a place for longer swims.

Catrigg Force is just a mile's walk from Stainforth but much more secret (14). Water squeezes down through a slot in the tall rock structure via an upper pool, into which you can climb, and down into the lower pool. It's only large enough for a quick plunge but the cathedral-like setting deep in this wooded glade more than makes up for that in awe and wonder.

The reason for all these waterfalls is the limestone geology and the legacy of glaciation. At Gordale Scar, ten miles away, a 400-foot-deep ravine is all that remains of a great underground river cave the size of the Channel Tunnel, while nearby at Malham Cove a waterfall with the power of Niagara once flowed over a vast inland cliff. This cliff can still be seen, stained grey and overgrown with ferns and shrubs. Several miles upstream, Malham Tarn, a mile-wide lake, is all that remains of the great river that once fed it, now home to curlews, mallards and greater crested grebe. It's a wildlife reserve and rather exposed so best to have a dip at Janet's Foss instead (15).

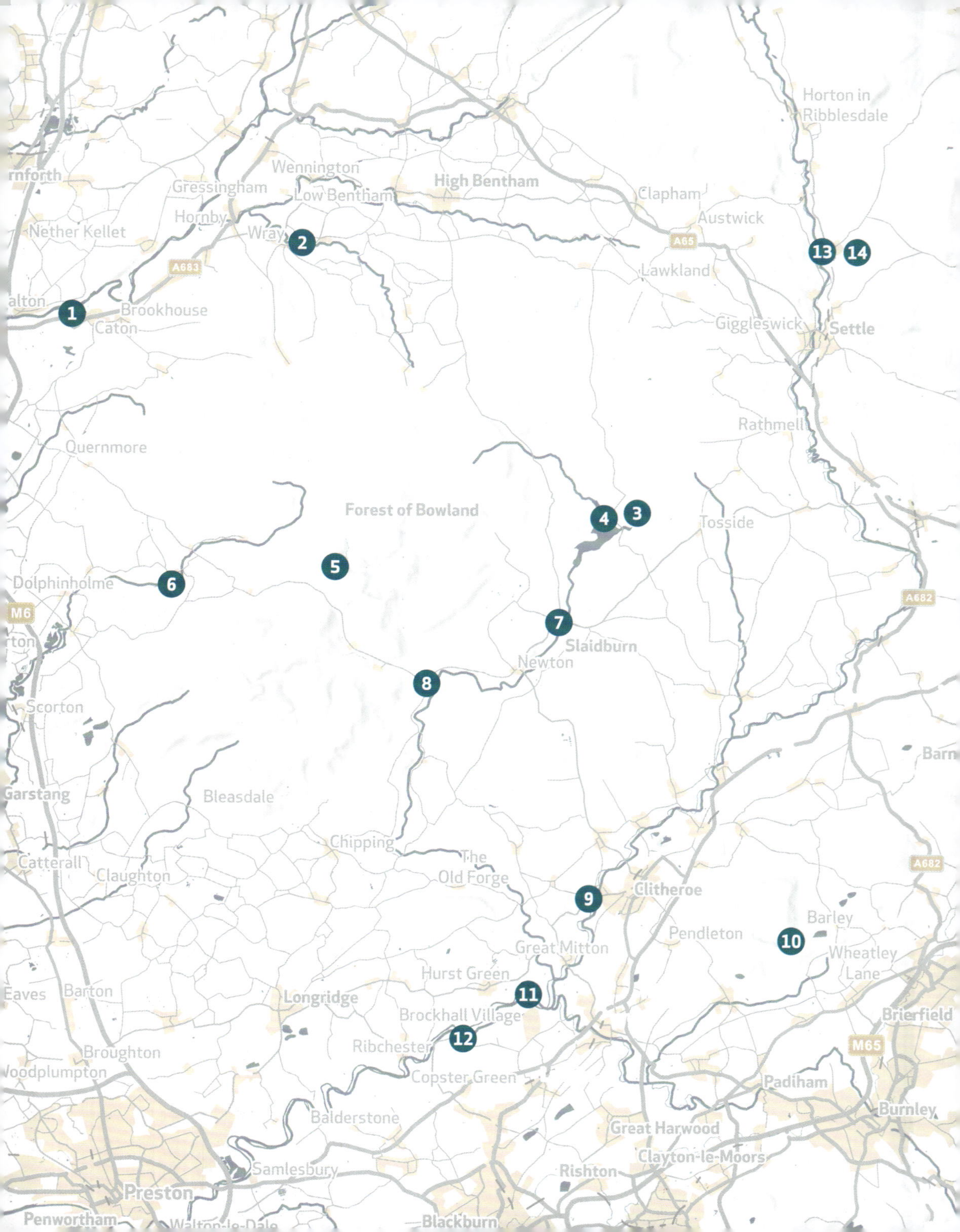
Horton in Ribblesdale
rnforth
Wennington
Gressingham
High Bentham
Low Bentham
Clapham
Hornby
Austwick
Nether Kellet
Wray
2
A65
13
14
A683
Lawkland
alton
1
Brookhouse
Caton
Giggleswick
Settle
Rathmell
Quernmore
Forest of Bowland
4
3
Tosside
5
Dolphinholme
6
M6
A682
7
rton
Slaidburn
Newton
8
Scorton
Barn
Garstang
Bleasdale
Chipping
The Old Forge
A682
Catterall
Claughton
9
Clitheroe
Barley
Pendleton
10
Great Mitton
Wheatley Lane
Hurst Green
Eaves
Barton
11
Longridge
Brierfield
Brockhall Village
12
Ribchester
M65
Broughton
Woodplumpton
Copster Green
Padiham
Burnley
Balderstone
Great Harwood
Clayton-le-Moors
Samlesbury
Rishton
Preston
Penwortham
Walton-le-Dale
Blackburn

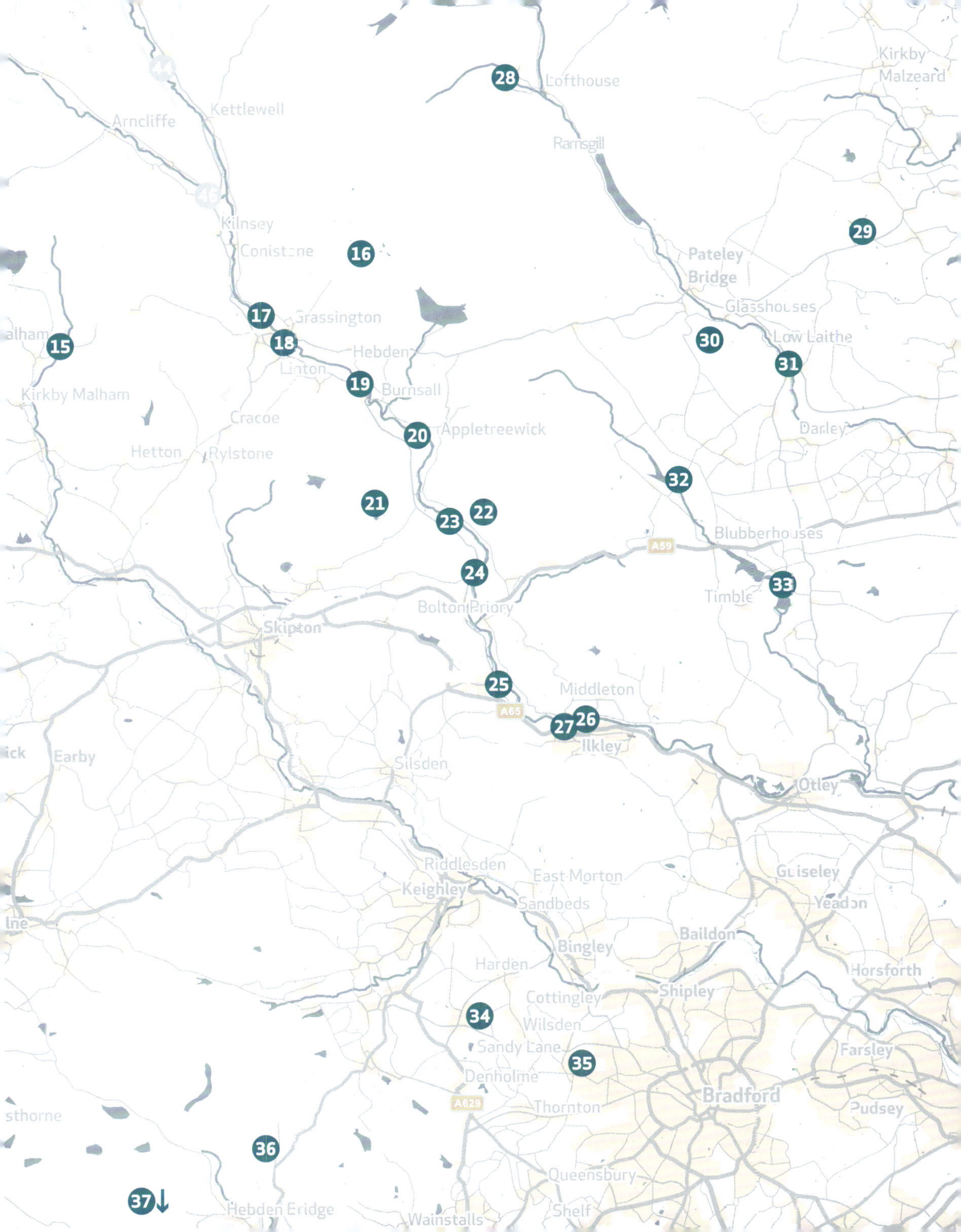

Kirkby
Malzeard
28
Lofthouse
Kettlewell
Arncliffe
Ramsgill
Kilnsey
Conistone
16
29
Pateley
Bridge
Glasshouses
17
Grassington
15
alham
18
Hebden
30
Low Laithe
31
Linton
19
Burnsall
Kirkby Malham
Cracoe
20
Appletreewick
Darley
Hetton
Rylstone
32
21
22
23
Blubberhouses
A59
24
33
Timble
Bolton Priory
Skipton
25
Middleton
A65
27
26
Ilkley
ick
Earby
Silsden
Otley
Riddlesden
East Morton
Guiseley
Keighley
Sandbeds
Yeadon
lne
Baildon
Bingley
Harden
Horsforth
Shipley
Cottingley
34
Wilsden
Sandy Lane
35
Farsley
Denholme
Bradford
A629
Thornton
Pudsey
sthorne
36
Queensbury
37
Hebden Bridge
Shelf
Wainstalls

18

18

19

To the east, Upper Wharfedale is the classic Yorkshire Dale: rectangular hay barns in every field, green meadows filled with wild flowers and beautiful rivers dotted with pools and falls.

High up on the fells of Moss Top and Chapel Moor the headwaters of the Wharfe begin to collect, filtering down through sinkholes, trickling through cracked limestone fissures before reappearing in tiny tributaries and streams. The Wharfe gathers pace through Langstrothdale, is fed by Littondale (see Yorkshire Dales chapter, **43-46**) then flows through the pools of Amerdale Dub and Ghaistrill's Strid (**17**) before arriving at Grassington, one of Yorkshire's most picturesque swimming villages (**18**).

Most people gather on the river meadows to the south of the village. Here you'll find families in rubber dinghies and children wielding fishing nets. At the weir people slide down the smooth chute or swim in the larger clear pool above. Further down there is a waterfall by a footbridge and stepping stones to a riverbank church. The connoisseurs, however, head upstream of Grassington to Ghaistrill's Strid, a series of cascades and rapids: the perfect place to while away the day swimming in rocky pools, chasing minnows and 'tubing' the rapids. Above the falls, and alongside an idyllic grassy knoll, the river is forced down a 100-metre bobsleigh run. Only a modicum of skill is needed to navigate the chute – the current takes care of the rest. The best method is to lie down head first on the ring so you can steer yourself with your arms – if you sit on the ring you tend to spin round and round. Our group was soon running time trials for sets of three descents, including the run back up the hill. If you're very daring, and the river is low, it's possible to surf the white water without a ring at all, though you may end up bruising a knee or an elbow. Keep your head down, eyes up and arms in front. Stay streamlined but flexible and let the current curl you around the corners and guide you around any obstacles. The trick is to move with the flow like an eel and make only small body adjustments.

The walk from Grassington downstream follows an avenue of sycamores and oaks, passing the pretty falls and stepping stones at Linton (**18**) before arriving in the outskirts of Burnsall at Loup Scar, a faintly Jurassic-like limestone scar (**19**). You might well be disturbed by the spectacle of young men throwing themselves off the cliffs of the scar into the plunge pool below as part of a well-known local rite of passage. The small pool is certainly deep enough for those who wish to test their mettle, but the full jump requires a degree of judgement as an overhanging cliff must be cleared. There have no doubt been serious accidents here. If there are no jumpers the pool is also excellent for a gentle swim and you can sit with your legs dangling in the water over its perfect edge almost as if you are at a properly excavated swimming pool.

Just below the rapids there is a larger river pool before passing behind the old Anglo-Saxon church of St. Wilfred's and heading on to the village bridge. On hot days the village green in Burnsall heaves with families. The field next door is turned into a large car park and the river is choked with a flotilla of the kiddy dinghies sold from the village shop and various makeshift stalls. The shallows below the bridge are popular with children, while upstream, alongside the pub, you can even find grown men drifting around in toy boats while ordering drinks from the bar (19).

From here it's only a mile or two down the rapids to Appletreewick, a delightful stretch of Wharfedale with a riverside campsite (Masons), two pubs, one with a traditional cruck barn (Craven Arms), some houses and a pleasant set of meadows with river pools and even an island (20).

Bathing morning and dusk in this peaceful place became the routine of our days. I had arranged to explore the area and test out the local swimming holes with a group of friends. Emerging from our tents we would slowly gather at breakfast time beneath the old hazel, dive into the cool peaty waters and swim several lengths of the long pool. Then we would loll about on the short grass and dry in the morning sun, sipping tea and reading papers, sometimes putting up a hammock between the trees if we felt energetic. Soon we were planning the day's excursion but by dusk we would re-congregate, sometimes lighting up the island with candle lanterns and swimming silently in the inky waters beneath the rising stars.

Downstream of our happy home at Appletreewick is the Bolton Abbey estate and we made several expeditions to test the waters and teashops there. The great ruins of this major monastic enclave sit on a bend of the river above a stretch of pebbly beaches. During the hottest days it becomes a Yorkshire Costa del Sol: a mass of swimmers and sunbathers mixed with suntan lotion and sloppy ice cream. Upstream the river is deep enough for swimming, downstream it is shallow enough for paddling and stone skimming (24). Taking the water, ruins and landscape together it's not surprising it attracts so many people, literally thousands.

Some miles upstream the 'Strid' section of river is less crowded. The river here runs through a notorious cataract with fantastical curving rock shapes. The water is so deep that it is almost motionless on the surface. When in flood the level rises quickly creating treacherous under-surface eddies. Although the Strid is very narrow it is 20 feet deep in places and its profile is hourglass shaped. Underwater there are many hidden caves and pockets in which you would not want to get trapped.

A 'strid' in old provincial English literally means 'a narrow passage between precipitous rocks or banks, which looks as if it might be crossed at a stride'. A number of people have died trying to jump the gap, or venturing too close to the edge, and the dangers are particularly acute during heavy rains.

We peered into the Strid respectfully and decided to swim several hundred yards below it instead, where the river has returned to its normal width (23). The bluebell-rich beech and oak woods have been opened up by a series of tracks and are a Site of Special Scientific Interest, renowned for summer migrants from Africa including the wood warbler, redstart and pied flycatcher. Arriving by the middle of May they find the insect-rich vegetation and mild valley climate irresistible. The yellow and white wood warbler nests at ground level and can be hard to spot, though its call of a whistle followed by a harsh trill is difficult to miss. The pied flycatcher is scarce, though nesting boxes have been placed around the woods.

We swam breaststroke under the lush beech trees while a warbler whistled sweetly from the bank. Some of us swam up close to the Strid and peered in from the safety of our downstream position. The curving rocks rose up above us and we thought soberly of the water's potential power and fury.

FOREST OF BOWLAND

1 CROOK O'LUNE, CATON

Just off the motorway at Lancaster, this is a wide stretch of mature river with beaches and long swims. Easy access. From M6 / J34 take A683 towards Caton and turn L after around 3km, signed 'Crook O' Lune Picnic Site'. Beaches below bridge or river walks up and down stream.

5 mins, 54.0763, -2.7312 🏖🚗🌀

2 HINDBURN BRIDGE, R HINDBURN

Pretty cascades and shallow pools just upstream of the old stone bridge. 1.2km E of Wray via Main St (signed Higher Tatham Fells), at turn for LA2 8ND. There's a footpath upstream on near side of the bridge. No parking here.

2 mins, 54.102, -2.5926 🌀

3 BOTTOMS BECK WATERFALLS

Several dark pools cascade down through the forest, reached on a forest cycle trail. From School Lane car park, follow the lakeshore road 400m then the forest track on L (with barrier, signed red and blue trail) and continue for 1.5km.

25 mins, 54.0056, -2.3898 🏖🚶🌀🚴

4 STOCKS RESERVOIR

This vast, shallow reservoir is surrounded by woodland and low hills. It warms up nicely in the summer and you might be tempted to take a discreet dip, though respect fishermen and birdwatchers. There are paths around the whole perimeter, and a disused railway on the NW shore. 5km from Slaidburn on the Tosside road, turn L at the crossroads signed Clapham and Gisburn Forest (a little before BD23 4SY). 300m after the church there's a track on the L with a good orchid meadow in summer – the R track leads to water's edge – or continue on and over the causeway to School Lane car park (around 3km total) and follow paths up to the N arm of the reservoir. At low water levels a large beach appears all around the reservoir, making it much easier to explore.

10 mins, 54.0036, -2.4099 🏖🚗🌀

5 BRENNAND TARN, TROUGH OF BOWLAND

Just off the famous Trough of Bowland road, but well hidden, is one of the few natural tarns in Bowland. Legend has it that the gold plate from Whalley Abbey was hidden at the bottom of the tarn during the dissolution of the monasteries. A prehistoric axe was found near here. From the cattle grid at the very highest point of

the Trough road (small parking area) head N across the moor for 1km (bring a map or GPS). 3km up (NW) from BB7 3BJ, and just under 5.5km from Dunsop Bridge as the crow flies.

25 mins, 53.9858, -2.5718 🏖🌀🚶

6 ABBEYSTEAD LAKE, RIVER WYRE

A pretty lake with a woodside path leading downstream to a striking curved weir, the ruins of Catshaw cotton mill, which burned down in 1848, and a stone waymarker on the Wyre Way carved with a leaping salmon (look out for the stepped salmon ladder at the weir). From the school in Abbeystead (LA2 9BQ) head E 400m and turn R after the bridge. After another 400m take footpath R, joining the river and leading down to the old weir after 1.2km. Continue on to the footbridge below the weir; for the cotton mill detour L up Cam Brook into Catshaw woods here. Over the bridge, head L 800m for the salmon marker, R to return to the village via the lake shore and Far House Barn.

20 mins, 53.9792 -2.6705 🏖🚶🌀🚗

7 SLAIDBURN, RIVER HODDER

Popular paddling and swimming spot, both up and downstream of the bridge (try the deeper junction pool just upstream). Riverbank Tearooms, loos and two car parks. Slaidburn on B6478, BB7 3ES

1 mins, 53.9665, -2.4363

8 DUNSOP BR & WHITEWELL, R HODDER

The Dunsop stream babbles down to meet the Hodder at a large junction pool, downstream of a footbridge with gravel banks and some beachy bits. You can also continue 1.2km downstream along the riverbank footpath to stepping stones at Langden Brook junction pool. Also good paddling from the stepping stones at the excellent riverside Inn at Whitewell downstream (BB7 3AT, 01200 448222). From the village car park in Dunsop Bridge, turn L along road then first R down driveway to BB7 3BB, alongside stream. Cross the bridge and turn R onto footpath with riverbank on the R.

5 mins, 53.9443, -2.5163

RIBBLE VALLEY

9 EDISFORD BRIDGE, R RIBBLE

A popular and easily accessible picnic, parking and paddling spot downstream of the old bridge. 1.5km W of town on B6243, just beyond BB7 3LA turn L (signed

camping). At the campsite turn R to find the riverside car park.

1 mins, 53.8679, -2.418

10 UPPER OGDEN RESERVOIR, PENDLE HILL

A little lake that could make a nice cooling dip on the route up to the top of famous Pendle Hill. There's parking at the signed picnic site in Barley. Cross the main N/S road to take the track/road by the village hall (Barley Green, BB12 9JU). Follow the easy reservoir road up to the second lake, 2km.

25 mins, 53.8532, -2.2958

11 JUMBLES ROCKS, R RIBBLE

The Ribble flows wide and graceful through meadows, and passes rapids and a beach at the confluence with the Calder. An old ruined bridge is just upstream next to Lower Hodder Bridge; now named Old Hodde, Brandywine or Cromwell's Bridge. This is where Oliver Cromwell and 8,000 troops crossed en route to the Battle of Preston in 1648. There are shallow rapids and a pebble beach next to it. 2.5km E of Hurst Green on B6243, find a place to park and then turn R onto footpath to Winckley Hall (private road). Bear R and pass BB7 9PN and then Fox Fields down to river (1.2km from road). Continue 1.2km

upstream for large beach at confluence. Continue on up the B6243 for Cromwell's Bridge and more riverside footpaths.

20 mins, 53.834, -2.4541

12 MARLES WOOD, R RIBBLE

Superb rapids and pools, with a large river pool downstream. 1.2km W of Dinckley, just before PR3 3XR, find car park on R and descend through woods down to the river, bearing R along bank.

5 mins, 53.8182, -2.4934

STAINFORTH & RIBBLE

13 STAINFORTH FORCE, R RIBBLE

A series of river pools and falls beneath an old packhorse bridge. Grassy banks, paddling and a deep cauldron into which the brave jump. Set below a caravan park, but peaceful stretches in the field downstream. Peaty water. Stainforth is 5km N of Settle (B6479). Park in village and carry on up main road 200m on foot. Turn L down Dog Hill Brow dir BD24 0DP, and descend 400m to bridge (where there's some limited parking in the off season). Main fall is 200m downstream. Continue to the Eel Pool, a long, deep basin where the water slows to pass through a gorge (54.0988, -2.2798).

10 mins, 54.0997, -2.2791

14 CATRIGG FORCE

One of the most beautiful waterfalls in the Dales. Set in a wooded chasm on the moor edge, with a small pool and double fall beneath towering rocks. From the green in Stainforth (facing BD24 9PF) walk R (E) up the lane, becoming a track up hillside. After 800m take the path down to the woods and falls below L.

20 mins, 54.0994, -2.2580

15 JANET'S FOSS

Small but beautiful clear plunge pool and waterfall, perfect for families and set in a wooded glen just off the lane near Gordale Scar. Cave up to the R, allegedly home of Jennet, a fairy queen. Sadly it's a bit busy, so expect spectators if you swim. From Malham village, head E towards Gordale Scar. Take the path on the R about 300m before the campsite (BD23 4DL); parking tricky, there's a layby between the path and the campsite, or it's less than 1.5km from Malham.

2 mins, 54.0657, -2.1365

UPPER WHARFEDALE

16 BLEA BECK DAMS & MINE RUINS

Three remote wild-lake reservoirs – they actually warm up well under the summer

17

17

19

19

sun – plus the bleak ruins of long-gone lead and baryte mines, flue tunnels and a great chimney standing in the moor. Follow the track E another 1.2km for two further lakes. It's exposed up here, so choose a calm day to visit. From Grassington take the dead-end lane to Yarnbury (BD23 5EQ) where there's a signboard about the Grassington lead mines. Turn R across the cattle grid up and into the ruined mine area.
20 mins, 54.0985, -1.9551 🚶🏔⚠️❓ⓘ

17 GHAISTRILL'S STRID, GRASSINGTON
Exciting rocky pools with chute. Upstream

rapids have a narrow-gorge cataract, which is fun on inflatable rings but dangerous in flood/high water conditions – be careful. Lower pools have interesting snorkelling and a larger area for a longer swim, but watch out for submerged rocks. By the main road bridge in Grassington (BD23 5NH) follow the main river path upstream for 800m to the flat rocky ledges and pools beneath rapids. The upper section above the falls is accessed by the riverside footpath behind hedges, 200m, and makes a good picnic spot. Continue another 300m into Lower Grass Wood for secluded river pools.
20 mins, 54.0766, -2.0153 🚶🏊🚷🧍

18 GRASSINGTON WEIR & LINTON FALLS
A large, grassy area of riverside common with two weirs, a water slide, a waterfall, an ancient church and stepping stones. Very popular and good fun. Park in Linton at the car park (opp turning to BD23 6BQ). Cross the river at Linton Falls on the footbridge. Best swimming is above the upper weir. There's a smooth stone slide on far side by the ruined millhouse – fun with inflatables – or head downstream 200m for beaches, the stepping stones and the 12th-century riverside church of St Michael's. Look out

for the tall erratic boulder in a field next to the church, with deep scar marks where it was dragged along by the glaciers.
5 mins, 54.0668, -2.0016 🚗🚶🏛🚶‍♂️ⓘ

19 LOUP SCAR, R WHARFE, BURNSALL
A fantastic stretch of grassy riverside incorporating river, meadow and beaches, with the limestone cliffs and the gorges of Loup Scar. There's a terrifying jump here from the path on river R, into a small very deep plunge pool. In summer there will probably be a bunch of lads attempting it. The village itself, below the bridge, is very busy, sometimes with hundreds of swimmers and families. Follow the riverside path upstream from village bridge/Red Lion (BD23 6BU, 01756 720204), about 800m past the church, to Loup Scar gorge, with a very deep rectangular plunge pool beneath cliff.
15 mins, 54.0517, -1.9558 🧍🚷🚶‍♂️ⓘ

20 APPLETREEWICK, R WHARFE
Idyllic rocky pool in the river with a small island and bay, rapids upstream and a large shingle beach on far bank downstream. There's a good rope swing on far side, with grassy banks and a field for picnics. The water has many submerged underwater

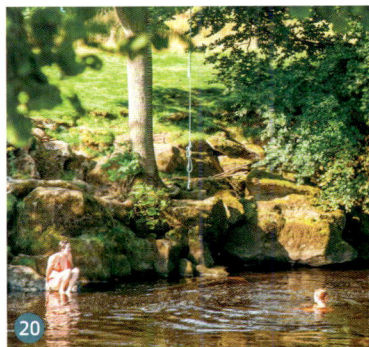

rocks, which makes diving dangerous. Just over 3km off the B6160 between Grassington and Bolton Abbey. Opposite the New Inn (BD23 6DA, 01756 720252), find gate and follow the farm track down the field to the river. The pool is 200m downstream; Mason's riverside camping is just upstream.

5 mins, 54.0332, -1.9213

21 LOWER BARDEN RESERVOIR
Under wide skies, on lonely moors, this is the place for those longing for a large expanse of water. N bank is best, but be discreet if you dip. 5km S of Burnsall on B6160, turn R signed Eastby/Embsay. After 2km there's a cattle grid and parking (BD23 6AR). Walk down the track to the reservoir, 800m.

20 mins, 54.0089, -1.947

22 VALLEY OF DESOLATION & WATERFALL
Evocatively named after a storm that devastated the area in 1826, the valley has a pretty waterfall (Posforth Gill) with a small pool and a stream leading into a little glen. No dogs allowed on the estate paths. Signed Storiths off the A59, 1.5km E of Bolton Abbey roundabout. Continue around 3km to BD23 6AW, to find a small

parking area on R, and by a 12% gradient sign, a gateway into parkland on R. Follow the permissive path around the hillside, keeping to the L, to reach the footbridge after 800m with the waterfall below, and the valley beyond.

20 mins, 54.0057, -1.8816

23 BELOW THE STRID, R WHARFE
A deep, shady stretch of river runs through this nature reserve and woodland. Above is the Strid gorge (do not try to swim in the cataract itself – people have died here), but below, the river is wide and deep with a pleasant stony bottom. Dappled and glorious on a sunny day. A long swim is possible up to the end of the Strid, and downstream until the river shallows out. At weekends the path alongside the river can be busy. Around 3km N beyond Bolton Abbey on B6160, 1km beyond BD23 6AN, find The Strid car park and visitor area (and caravan park) on R. Pay for parking and walk down through woods to admire the cataract. Follow path downstream 300m beneath end of the cataract and drop down to rocky riverside.

10 mins, 54.0024, -1.9019

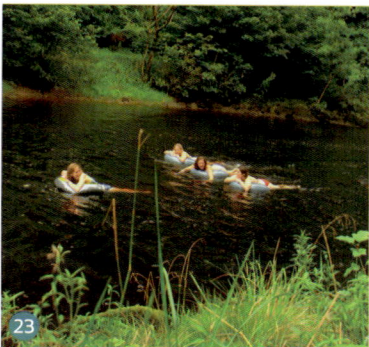

24 BOLTON ABBEY, R WHARFE
Enjoy the riverside ruins, and throngs of paddlers and swimmers, at Costa del Bolton. There are stepping stones and a deeper pool just downstream. Popular, but fun. Park in the large village car park or continue up the valley for the riverside Sand Holme car park on R (400m past BD23 6AL); go R (downstream) where the driveway splits and park where you wish along 1.2km of river, then walk downstream to the ruins.

10 mins, 53.9841, -1.887

LOWER WHARFEDALE

25 ADDINGHAM, R WHARFE
Popular village paddling and swimming spot from the far side of the suspension bridge. Mostly shallow but the water is deeper and faster opposite. Good for picnics. Explore upstream and downstream for more pools. 9.5km E of Skipton (LS29 0QX, park in Bark Ln by bend and follow footpath down to river.

5 mins, 53.9443, -1.8727

26 ILKLEY LIDO
Large, lagoon-shaped 1930s, unheated lido, bounded by an immense grassy sunbathing area on the north side of the River Wharfe in the spa town of Ilkley. Onsite cafe serving snacks and ice cream. Also has a heated indoor pool. www.bradford.gov.uk/lido 01943 600453

2 mins, 53.9319, -1.8202

27 OLD BRIDGE, ILKLEY
At a bend in the river, the water slows to form a wide pool for a tranquil swim. From the A65 W of town, find limited parking in Stockeld Way (LS29 9HQ) then cross ancient bridge and walk 200m upstream to bend. Families might want to head for the wide, shingle beach near the suspension bridge on Denton Rd at 53.9316, -1.8163 with shallow entry and deeper water in the main river, perfect for summertime picnics.

10 mins, 53.9292, -1.8333

NIDDERDALE

28 POOLS ABOVE HOW STEAN GORGE
A pretty walk leads down over the gorge and upstream through meadow to a glade and a plunge pool under a rocky undercut. From Lofthouse follow the signs to How Stean Gorge walk/café (800m), but continue past to park at the farm hamlet of Stean 800m further on (HG3 5SY). Walk

back out a liitle way and take footpath or
down to and across the gorge. Bear L into
fields and continue upstream 500m until
the path follows the streamside with pools
and flat (slippery!) rocks.

10 mins, 54.1612, -1.8681

29 EAVESTONE LAKE
A wooded footpath hugs the north
shoreline of this neglected ornamental lake
which occupies a deep, rockbound valley.
Purple rhododendrons and tree branches
overhang, luring you in for a discreet dip.
The south shore is owned by Yurtshire, a
luxury glamping and wellness spa. Between
Ripon and Pately Bridge on the B6265
turn for Eavestone (dead end) 2.5km W
of Risplith. About 800m before HG4 3HD
a footpath leads into the woods, R. The
keen might also like to visit Lumley Moor
Reservoir, with good access all around the
lake (54.1318, -1.6580, HG4 3PN).

5 mins, 54.1062, -1.6529

30 GUISECLIFF TARN
A secluded little wooded tarn, nestled in
the hillside, sheltered by Guisecliff Woods,
bounded by rocks and visible from Guise
Cliff above. From Yorke's Folly towers
continue E and drop down into the woods
L after 300m to find a track, then continue
E 800m.

20 mins, 54.0675, -1.7452

31 SUMMERBRIDGE, R NIDD
Secluded stretch of the River Nidd with
a beautiful wide pool above the weir,
bordered by trees and offering easy entry
into the water. Look out for kingfishers. Just
off the B6165 between Ripley and Pateley
Bridge, find roadside parking in village then
follow the footpath behind the school down
to the river and continue upstream to weir
and pool.

5 mins, 54.0588, -1.6976

32 THRUSCROSS RESERVOIR
The highest and youngest of the Washburn
reservoirs. Thruscross Reservoir was
completed in 1966, drowning part of the
village of West End which emerges during a
drought. There's a path all the way around.
It's No Swimming but locals do, discreetly.
Make your own decision. Park beyond dam
(54.01728, -1.7639) and walk along N
shore.

15 mins, 54.0172, -1.7639

33 SWINSTY RESERVOIR
A large reservoir lake with a south-west
facing beach by the wooded picnic and
parking area. From Fewston village and
church (HG3 1SU) head S to find the parking
area on the R after 800m. Please be
discreet if dipping and head along the path
away from the road.

5 mins, 53.9797, -1.7014

HEBDEN & BRADFORD

34 GOIT STOCK FALLS, HARDEN BECK
A mighty waterfall and a good pool along
this woodland walk near Bingley. Take
footpath 1.5km upstream from bridge in
Harden (B6429 to Cullingworth).

20 mins, 53.8263, -1.8844

35 CHELLOW DEAN RESERVOIR, BRADFORD
One of two picturesque Victorian
reservoirs, bordered by oak, beech and
ash woodland and particularly attractive
in autumn. Popular with local swim groups
and swimming seems to be tolerated.
There is a level path all round with several
spots to enter the water. Abundant with
birdlife, including buzzard and osprey. Small
car park just off Haworth Rd (53.8139,
-1.8315).

10 mins, 53.8094, -1.8228

36 LUMB HOLE, CRIMSWORTH DEAN BECK
Picturesque waterfall and plunge pool
surrounded by ferny cliffs. On Crimsworth
Dean Beck near Stone Booth Farm, N
of Pecket Well. Or walk / cycle up from
Hardcastle Crags car park (bottom of
Midgehole Rd N of Hebden Bridge).
Occasional access issues.

40 mins, 53.7790, -2.0132

37 GADDINGS DAM
High and wild, often dubbed England's
highest beach. This old reservoir is a
well-known local swim with a pub at the
bottom to reward your efforts. Climb
track by Shepherd's Rest Inn (OL14 6JJ,
01706 813437), just W of Lumbutts, S
of Todmorden. Parking is an issue here so
if possible, use public transport to reach
the dam. There is an hourly bus the T6 or
T8 from Todmorden to the start of the
footpaths up to the dam.

30 mins, 53.6992, -2.0793

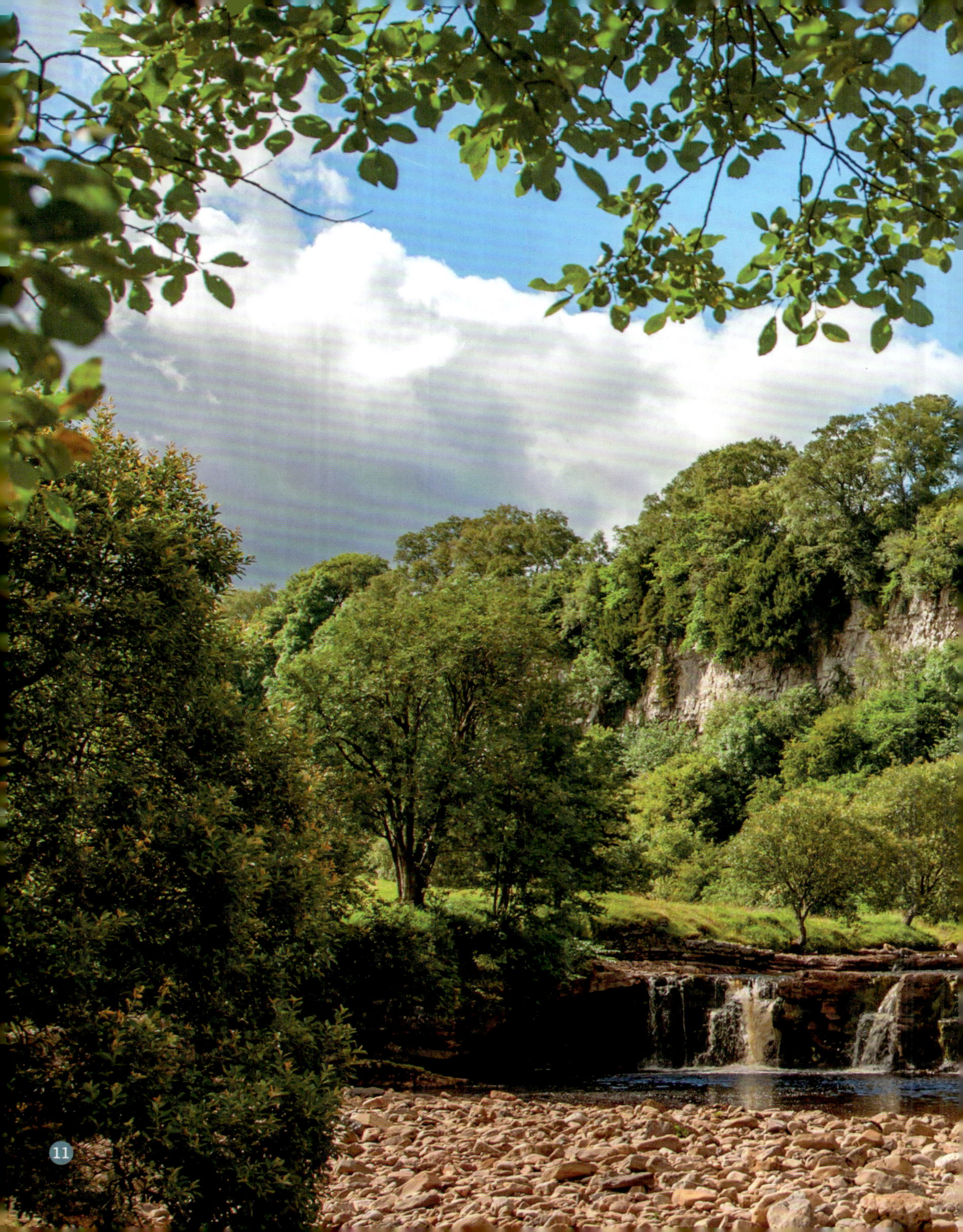

YORKSHIRE DALES

I stepped onto a remote and windy station halt as the train pulled away with a judder, creaking higher on the 'long drag' over the Settle-Carlisle moors. From here, I would attempt to descend through the watery bowels of Hell Gill (9).

Hell Gill is a collapsed limestone cave system, now a deep slot canyon and geological curiosity. It offers the opportunity to plunge and paddle down an ancient underground river system, approximately 500 metres in length, without the need for specialist knowledge.

My local guide was Rob, an outdoor instructor. Together, we climbed up Lunds Fell, past Hell Gill waterfall and Hell Gill farm, to a small medieval bridge spanning a deep fissure. This bridge has long marked the county border between Yorkshire and Cumbria: Dick Turpin leaped to freedom across it on Black Bess, and Mary, Queen of Scots, was escorted this way to her imprisonment at Bolton Castle. Legend has it that Satan himself created this gash, which, though only a few yards wide, resembles a fault line opened by an earthquake. Ash trees overshadow crumbling sandstone cliffs that almost touch in places, while the water gushing through narrow chasms and pools below is heard rather than seen.

We entered further upstream, where the stream tumbles down into the gorge via stepped pools. The sky was overcast, but no rain was forecast, and the entire stream catchment was within view—an important consideration when entering a slot canyon. The brown limestone karst walls were curvaceous and plump, undulating like an ileum, pitted with dimples that made the water echo and our voices boom, as if we were inside Jonah's gut.

As we descended, the canyon walls rose higher, the light dimming, yet the sky and trees remained reassuringly visible above.

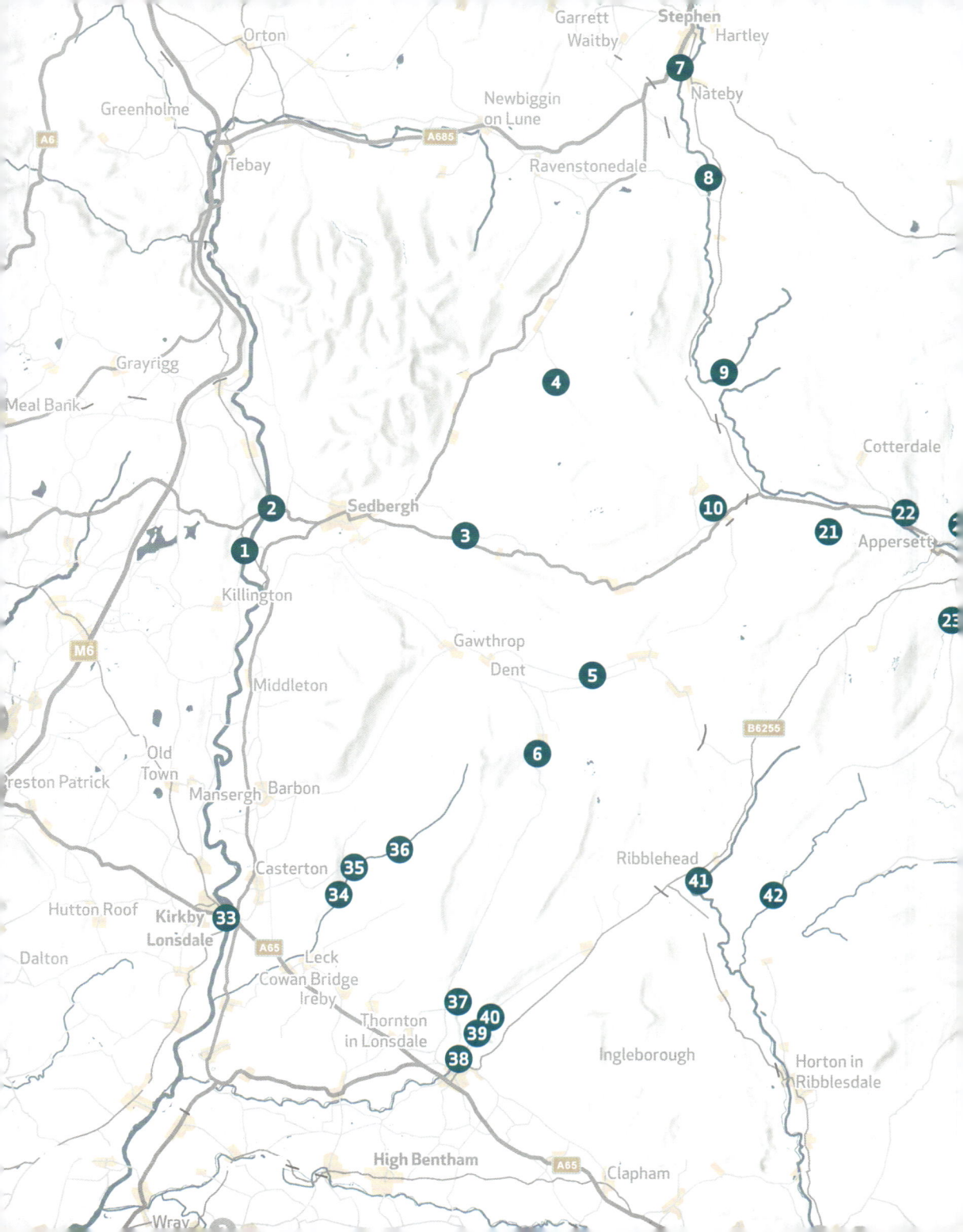

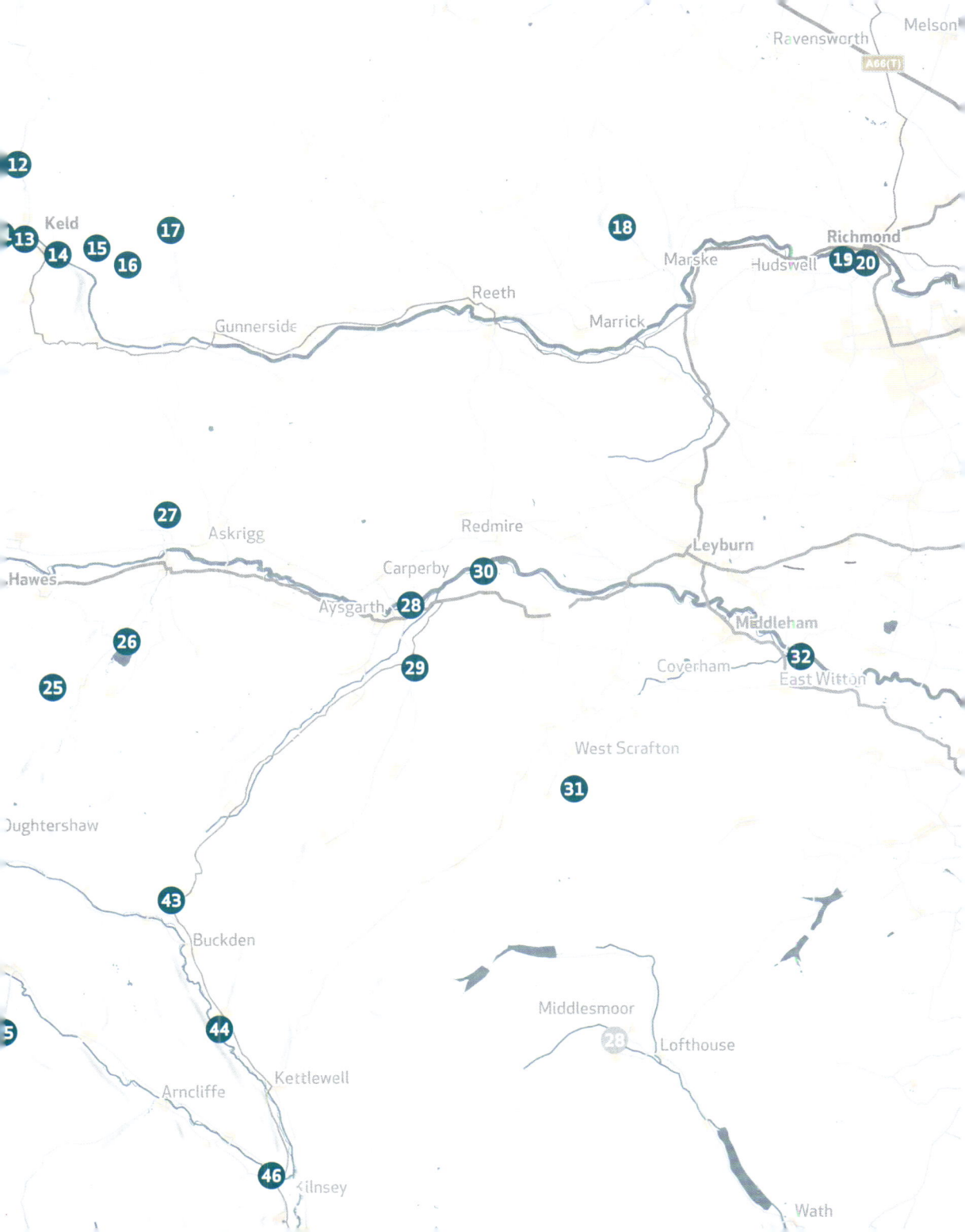

I was only out of my depth at one point, in a deep plunge pool where you must swim after sliding down a boulder beside a waterfall. There is usually a rope tied to help you back up if you wish to retreat, but if it isn't there, you should return and enter from the bottom of the gorge instead. There are also some accessible upper ledges to escape to in case of unexpected rain.

This brown limestone karst is also found across the moors in Upper Swaledale. The village of Keld boasts five excellent waterfalls with plunge pools. This region is so remote that in the seventeenth century, the nearest consecrated land was over three days away. After following the river below, you can walk the 'Corpse Road' back over the high limestone plateau.

Kisdon Force is the most spectacular set of falls, featuring two huge pools beneath great basalt-like pillars, thundering deep in the woods (14). The high pool is the larger, at least 100 metres across, with ledges around its edge, while the lower pool is deeper: dark and foreboding, with steep walls.

At Park Lodge campsite in Keld, behind the café and down a track to a river, you will find several shallow falls flowing across hot, flat rocks with shallow pools that warm up nicely during the day. At night, the campsite's riverside fires send reflections shimmering across the river pools, and in the morning, you can swim in your own private plunge bath (14).

Finally, Wain Wath Falls, located a mile beyond Keld, is the most popular and accessible of the Keld swims. Prettily situated under limestone cliffs, there's even a garden, a little gate, and a bench on which to hang your towel (11).

Slot canyons with long catchments are particularly dangerous, as unseen localized rainfall upstream can create flash floods. Kolob in Zion Park, USA, gained international notoriety in 1993 when a group of scouts lowered themselves into a flooding canyon with no means of retreat.

The south-west corner of the Dales, around Settle and Ribblesdale, is one of the best-known areas for waterfalls. For more waterfalls than you can possibly swim in a day, you should try the Ingleton Waterfall Walk, which features a truly superb series of falls and plunge pools (37-40). Established

in 1885, the walk attracted thousands of visitors who traveled by the new railway from Manchester and Bradford to see its geological wonders. By 1888, it was drawing over 3,000 visitors a day, even with an entrance fee of 2d.

On the western side, Pecca Falls and Thornton Force (37) are now on open-access land, though no one will thank you for attempting to park in these narrow lanes. Thornton Force is the more popular, a classic strata waterfall with an upper layer of 330-million-year-old Carboniferous Great Scar limestone and lower layers of 500-million-year-old Ordovician sandstone. The pool is open, south-facing, and on a hot day, you will find many people wading, swimming, and clambering on the rocks. Below, Pecca Falls flows through a wooded glen, and its many plunge pools are perfect for those who enjoy scrabbling on the rocks and diving into dark pools. For the full Gollum experience, however, seek out Yordas Cavern, just up the lane.

GARSDALE & DENTDALE

1 BEEHIVE DUB, R LUNE
Pools with rocks to sunbathe on and jump off upstream of Killington New Bridge. Further upstream is the chain of dubs. It is best to swim across to opposite bank at Beehive and walk upstream to assess these deep pools before attempting to swim back downstream. Take care and keep an eye on water levels and flow, particularly in the narrow channels. 5km SW of Sedbergh with limited parking in small lay-by by Killington New Bridge then follow footpath upstream to first set of pools and rocks at the Dub.
2 mins, 54.3114, -2.5815

2 LINCOLN'S BRIDGE, R LUNE
Tree-fringed, deep, meadowside pool. Heading W out of Sedbergh on the A684 for around 3km to limited parking in small lay-by just before Lincoln's Bridge on L. Then look for footpath sign (Luneside Farm) just before stone bridge and follow path downstream to pool.
5 mins, 54.3246, -2.5675

3 GARSDALE, R CLOUGH
Series of pools in a wooded limestone gorge beneath a pretty packhorse bridge in the shadow of the Howgills. Deeper pools are upstream of bridge. Interesting geological rock features including Tom Croft Cave with two entrances either side of a dividing rock pillar 200m upstream. Travelling E on A684 from Sedbergh, find parking bay on L (54.3156, -2.4716) and follow signpost (Sedgwick Trail) 300m towards bridge and pools in ravine.
5 mins, 54.3162, -2.4656

4 ULDALE FALL, R RAWTHEY
A series of beautiful waterfalls and pools of ever-increasing height, each with a good plunge pool, culminating at the impressive falls of Uldale Fall. Park at Rawthey Bridge (A683 8km NE of Sedbergh) and follow the river upstream 2.5km. Or follow the lane by the bridge past CA17 4LN, then first R, park where the road forks after 1.5km, and walk 800m on L fork to end. Bear R and take footpath on L down to the river to explore.
10 mins, 54.3638, -2.4182 🚶🏞️🏕️🏊

5 IBBETH PERIL & HELL'S CAULDRON
The Ibbeth Peril is a large plunge pool in the often-dry bed of the River Dee, where local witch Ibby is supposed to have drowned unlucky drunks. To the L of the waterfall there's a cave, leading to a long passageway

and large cavern. Enter only in sustained dry weather: the Peril pool can rise fast and the caves can flood. 800m scramble downstream is Hell's Cauldron, with a waterfall and a deep pool in a narrow slot canyon. The whole gorge can be explored but does require scrambling. Between Dent and Cowgill (leave Dent signed Hawes/Ingleton via Newby Head). 800m W of LA10 5TQ, find a small turn into a car park area on R with path and footbridge leading off 100m W along the road you can scramble down below the waterfall pool.

5 mins, 54.2729, -2.3988 🟥🏊🚶🚲

6 GASTACK BECK WATERFALL

An impressive little waterfall with a deep plunge pool and undercut cave, situated right by the lane. Explore further pools downstream from the bridge. High on the Ingleton–Dent road. From Dent, turn opposite Sedgwick memorial fountain with Dent Brewery on your L and after ¾ mile turn R signed Igleton/Clapham. The falls are just over a km on R (about 1.5km past Butterpots, LA10 5QY).

1 mins, 54.2489, -2.4275 🏊🚶🚲

EDEN DALE

7 STENKRITH BRIDGE, R EDEN

The river has sculpted pools and eddy holes in the limestone bedrock, with a small, deep canyon and waterfalls. Leaving Kirkby Stephen on the B6259 to Nateby, find a path into Stenkrith Park on L, just before the road bridge over the river (opp CA17 4SZ – car park just over the bridge on R). Follow the river upstream 200m to find the small canyon and deeper sections.

5 mins, 54.4608, -2.3535 🏊🚶

8 CATAGILL SCAR, R EDEN

A secret pool and beach as the river bends R out of a wooded ravine downstream from Pendragon Castle ruins. 4.5km S of Nateby on B6259 turn R at Pendragon Castle (red squirrels sign, shortly S of CA17 4JT). After 500m a byway crosses at a cattle grid. Turn R (you are allowed to drive down here if you want) and continue 800m then descend steep slope to a big river pool. Continue another 300m for more plunge pools and pretty little waterfalls. Idyllic.

15 mins, 54.4271, -2.3384 🏊🅿🚶🏃♿

9 HELL GILL, GARSDALE HEAD

A very deep and narrow canyon, almost enclosed, with a stream and impressive rock formations. t descends in easy steps, coming to a 1m-waterfall and deep plunge pool (sometimes a rope is here – but you shouldn't rely on the depth of the pool for jumping without checking first from below) before emerging to daylight. Good scrambling skills are useful: never climb down what you cannot get back up. From Garsdale Head (Moorcock Inn, LA10 5PU, 01969 667488) follow B6259 N dir Kirkby Stephen (or 13.5km S from Kirkby Stephen). After 4km, at Cumbria border sign, turn R onto track. There's parking for one car

river and rock shapes downstream and good paddling. Head NW 800m from Keld (dir Kirkby Stephen) on B6270 to find falls on R, 200m after the turning to W Stonesdale (DL11 6DZ). Limited parking.

1 mins, 54.4095, -2.1803 ⬛🔲🔲

12 STONESDALE BECK & GILLS

Pretty pools and falls with easy access just off this mountain pass. There are also ruins of an engine house and old lead mine that worked the same seam as the Gunnerside mines but deeper (not safe to enter). From B6270 800m NW of Keld, turn for W Stonesdale at DL11 6DZ and after 3km reach the tiny bridge over the Stonesdale Beck (1.5km after the turning for DL11 6EB). There's a large green container and a ruin here. The first waterfall is just below the bridge downstream, the second another 150m downstream.

3 mins, 54.4319, -2.1786 ⬛🔲🔲

13 CURRACK FORCE, STONESDALE BECK

This connoisseur's waterfall is well hidden and shaded among trees where the water tumbles over the rock face, scouring out a deep plunge pool. From B6270 800m NW of Keld, turn for W Stonesdale at DL11 6DZ and park on the roadside L. Walk up the hill and on the second bend a track leads to the R and crosses the beck. The waterfall is below. You can potentially follow the beck down 100m to the where it joins the Swale and Rainby waterfalls.

10 mins, 54.4094, -2.1759 ⬛🔲🔲

14 KISDON FORCE & PARK LODGE

Spectacular double waterfalls in a wooded gorge. The top one is 5m high with an 80m-wide plunge pool – open and awe-inspiring for a big swim. The bottom one is 12m high with a deep canyon plunge pool – dark and scary but good for brave jumpers! Also take a look at the pretty waterfall and small pool on East Gill just upstream – a better option for kids and picnics. From Keld (DL11 6LJ) take the bridleway opp Rukin's/Park Lodge and car park entrance (signed Swale Trail/ Coast to Coast). After 250m the L path drops down to the footbridge then up past East Gill waterfall. However, stay on the upper R path for another 250m, and take the L turn along a rocky path down. Those staying at Park Lodge riverside campsite can explore the impressive waterfalls upstream of the campsite, below Swaledale Yurts (54.4088, -2.1753).

15 mins, 54.4040, -2.1578 ⬛🔲🔲🔲

by railway. Cross railway and follow track. Where it splits, impressive Hell Gill Force with pool is 100m on, below track on L, but follow R up track 600m to farm, then 300m to stone bridge (NE). 100m downstream is the exit of Hell Gill canyon, and this is the safest way to explore; you may not be able to ascend to the top. Or follow wood boundary 250m up hillside to see the stream disappearing into the canyon entrance.

20 mins, 54.3669, -2.33 🔲🔲🔲

10 CLOUGH FORCE, R GRISEDALE

Deep waterfall pool on a little-visited stream near Garsdale Head station. From the station (LA10 5PP, with overflow car park SE of tracks) go down to the main road (A684), turn L then first R fork for Grisedale and find field gate on R after 200m. Climb into open access land then continue 500m, bearing down into the valley.

10 mins, 54.3249, -2.3356 🔲🔲🔲

KELD & SWALEDALE

11 WAIN WATH FORCE, KELD

Wide and graceful roadside waterfall with a very pleasant plunge pool, limestone cliffs and grassy banks for picnics. Interesting

15 SWINNER GILL CANYON & POOLS

A deep canyon with waterfall pools, cascades and mining ruins upstream from Crackpot Hall. Try to find the surprise tunnel at the very far end of the upper gill – part natural, part excavated. From Muker village car park (DL11 6QG) cross bridge to village store. Follow lane to R of store towards hay meadows. Follow flagged path to end of the meadows. Turn R, crossing a bridge over the R Swale. Then bear L onto a bridleway. Continue for 1.5km then just before the mouth of Swinner Gill on R, follow a steep unmarked footpath up the grass slope, with a fence and plantation on the right, to join a more obvious path. Cross the beck and follow the path on the other side of the gorge. Look R for a series of falls and plunge pools below. Back on the main path, continue over a craggy section to the head of the gill, and a larger waterfall, pools and mine workings. You can scramble down to the plunge pool.

30 mins, 54.4060, -2.1373 🏞️🚶🐟⛰️🏊🗿

16 MOSS DAM

Wild and high on bleak Ivelet Moor, this is one of the largest and least-known set of lakes in the Dales. They were built around 1842 to supply water to a hydraulic engine

in the Gunnerside mining area below. The three adjacent, broadly rectangular ponds are defined by 3m-high flat-topped earthen banks with gently sloping drystone internal faces. Set on the N side of Black Hill, best explored from the top of Swinner Gill (1.5km) or Gunnerside Gill (2.5km), or on a walk between them.

45 mins, 54.4008, -2.1211 🚶🏕️⛰️

17 GUNNERSIDE GILL

A fascinating gill, rich in lead-mining ruins, such as the Blakethwaite smelt mill and hillside flues, leats, old dams and limekilns and several waterfalls including this one beneath the footbridge with a decent plunge pool. The path starts along the stream from the bridge in Gunnerside – parking off the road by DL11 6LA. About 4-5km up to the main ruins and waterfall beneath Gunnerside Moor.

60 mins, 54.4114, -2.0986 🏞️🚶🏊

RICHMOND & SWALEDALE

18 ORGATE FORCE, MARSKE BECK

A little-visited waterfall, with a plunge pool on the river's R bank. Take dead-end lane, 150m S of bridge in Marske 1.5km to end (towards DL11 7LZ, tricky parking),

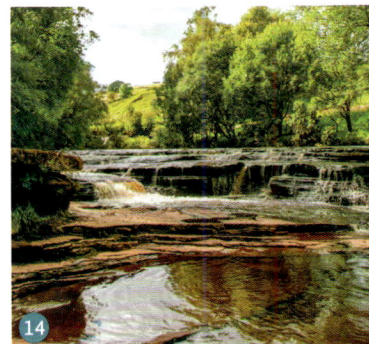

about 600m. Ash Force is at 54.3564, -2.2615.

10 mins, 54.3235, -2.2346 ⬛⬛⬛

23 AYSGILL FORCE, GAYLE
Lesser-known but impressive 10m-waterfall over dramatic dark rock in a shady, secret setting. Deep plunge pool. From the bridge in Gayle follow the Kettlewell road S just under 1.5km – best on foot or by bike, as no parking space. 200m before DL8 3SF see ladder stile and follow footpath down to river, then downstream 200m.

5 mins, 54.2901, -2.2101 ⬛⬛⬛

24 HARDRAW FORCE
At 30m, this dramatic column of water is claimed to be England's highest single-drop waterfall in the open air. It's also where Kevin Costner famously exposed his tan lines in Robin Hood: Prince of Thieves. Access (paid, with heritage centre, 01969 667572) is behind the 13th century Green Dragon Inn, Hardraw (DL8 3LZ). Signed No Swimming but many do.

5 mins, 54.3198, -2.2021 ⬛⬛⬛⬛⬛

25 BARDALE BECK, MARSETT
This secluded and remote beck meanders down through open moorland until it meets the Hawes limestone. Here it descends through several waterfalls and plunge pools into an interesting ravine with carved rocks and deep water at Wipera Side Cave. From Countersett continue on to Marsett (DL8 3DG) and follow the footpath upstream along the river for 1.5km. Follow beck downstream to explore falls and cascades.

20 mins, 54.2703, -2.1615 ⬛⬛⬛⬛⬛

26 SEMER WATER
Legend has it there's a city beneath the water, drowned by a wandering hermit angered at being treated meanly. There's a wide, rocky beach and easy access to the

---

then walk R on the bridleway track to the beck, and follow upstream 200m. Or walk upstream on the bridleway along the other side of the river in Marske (past DL11 7LU, 2.5km)

5 mins, 54.4117, -1.8618 ⬛⬛

19 RICHMOND FOSS, R SWALE
Pretty, town-centre waterfall swimming hole with many pools to play in, and beachy and wooded shallow shores upstream with the ruined castle perched above. Popular but easy access near the town centre. Follow Riverside Rd downstream from the old bridge past the castle to the waterfalls car park (just before DL10 4JR).

2 mins, 54.4005, -1.7434 ⬛⬛⬛⬛

20 ROUND HOWE, R SWALE
Just upstream of Richmond, a meadow riverside walk with a long beach and deep pools. Excellent for families or a long swim. Park in the Round Howe car park, also signed Richmond Caravan Park (DL10 4TJ) off A6108 1.5km W of Richmond. Cross footbridge and walk downstream 800m to large meadow area.

10 mins, 54.4005, -1.7341 ⬛⬛

WENSLEYDALE

21 MOSSDALE GILL
Impressive gill and little-known 10m-waterfall above the abandoned Wensleydale railway line viaduct. Tricky access – you need to make your own route for this adventure. On A684, 2.5km W of Cotter Force (see above), park in layby opp turning to at DL8 3LS. Take footpath opposite Thwaite Bridge 400m to a large waterfall under the old railway viaduct. The main waterfalls are 800m further upstream. If you don't fancy gill scrambling, the best route is to take the track which bears R up and over the old railway line to the W, then onto the open access land and down again. Bring a map!

20 mins, 54.3176, -2.2749 ⬛⬛⬛

22 COTTER FORCE
Expansive flows over fabulous, crisply multi-tiered rock slabs hung with ferns and moss down to a deep, wide plunge pool. Explorers could venture up Cotterdale to the waterfalls of East Gill too (Ash Force). 6.5km E of Garsdale Head, or 1.5km W of Appersett, on A684, 200m E of turning for DL8 3LP, find stone river bridge with parking on R. Tarmac path up river to falls,

water. You will need to wade out to find some depth. It was sketched and painted (though titled Simmer Lake) by Turner. Signed Countersett/Semer Water from the centre of Bainbridge. Head for DL8 3DD, then take next left after and park just over bridge by the shore (modest charge, payable at Low Blean Farm).

1 mins, 54.2843, -2.1224 🚗🚶🐟

27 LOWER WHITFIELD GILL FALLS, ASKRIGG

The best of a series of lesser-known pools and waterfalls in a beautiful wooded ravine. Mill Gill is tall and impressive, but Lower Whitfield is the best one for a dip. Park in Askrigg (car park at DL8 3HJ) and head for DL8 3HN (signed dead end). This becomes Mill Lane. Take the footpath around the mill to R, then cross onto the beck's R (S) bank via the footbridge. Stay on this bank all the way up the beck. 800m brings you to Mill Gill double falls (no pool), another 800m to the lower Whitfield Gill falls (large pool, below a footbridge) and just under another 800m to final waterfall (Whitfield Gill, much higher with small pool). You can also drive almost up to the topmost fall: leave Askrigg on Moor Road, turn L onto Low Straights Lane for DL8 3JF, but continue past it on the byway to the end.

30 mins, 54.3232, -2.1009 🚶🚗🏊🐟

28 LOWER AYSGARTH, R URE

Follow the woodland path down past the middle falls to the quieter lower falls with countless pools along the way. The water drops in perfect, tiered cascades, creating some enticing oblong plunge pools. From the far end (Lower Falls) you could explore along the river rocks further downstream for even more pools and rapids. There's a big car park just under the bridge S of DL8 3TH, or on the opposite bank at DL8 3SR. Follow river's L bank downstream 800m.

10 mins, 54.2951, -1.9736 🚗🏊🐟🚶

29 CAULDRON FALLS, WEST BURTON

Two beautiful waterfalls with good pools in a village – the lower falls, beneath the bridge, are deeper. This is a very pretty village. Signed, SE of Aysgarth off the A684. Park in village, towards DL8 4LA; there's a one-way system. Near DL8 4JP a narrow lane leads down to the river and bridge. The falls are upstream.

2 mins, 54.2758, -1.9716 🚗🐟🐾

30 REDMIRE FALLS, R URE

For real peace, well away from the summer crowds, head for Redmire Force. There are acres of grassy pasture, ancient oaks, limestone cliffs and deep pools including a huge deep-water area below the lower falls. Above the waterfalls the river is also deep and the shore is wooded with sandy bays. Park in Redmire village and follow the dead-end lane down to Mill Farm (DL8 4HB). There is a footpath signed Redmire Force upstream through fields.

15 mins, 54.3054, -1.9353 🚗🐾🏊🐟

31 GREAT FORCE, SCRAFTON MOOR

A ferny, tree-fringed secret ravine with cascades and a small pool. From West Scrafton take bridleway past houses opp and across the bridge from Methodist

chapel DL8 4RT. Bear R on footpath where it splits off towards Lead Up Gill and after about 800m drop down to find the falls.

30 mins, 54.2385, -1.8884

32 COVER BRIDGE, R URE

Some deeper pools on the River Ure downstream of the Cover Bridge Inn with riverside garden. From the Cover Bridge Inn (DL8 4SQ, 01969 623250) cross the bridge S and take the riverside footpath on the L. After 800m there's a deeper section where the Ure joins, above the old weir opposite the mill. Or explore further downstream.

10 mins, 54.2789, -1.7692

LECK BECK & LUNE

33 DEVIL'S BRIDGE, KIRKBY LONSDALE

Swim beneath one of the finest medieval bridges in the country, dating from 1370. There are rapids and a very deep channel beneath the bridge (popular with scuba divers) and a sandy beach upstream. Heading E, turn L off the A65 just after LA6 2DE and park on L. Follow to bridge at end; path up the river's R bank leads to the beach. Paths downstream too.

1 mins, 54.1984, -2.5908

34 LOWER LECK BECK/EASE GILL

A series of wonderfully secluded pools and ancient oak-wooded gorges with two good waterfalls, almost as good as those on the official Ingleton Waterfall Trail – just without anybody there. Skinny dip away… As for Whittle Hole, but continue another 1.5km downstream. Or, more directly, follow the footpath sign down the lane 1.5km before LA6 2JP, then bushwhack down passing to the R of the island of conifer woods, and drop down SE about 1.2km to the valley bottom to explore. The falls are above and below the tight bends.

20 mins, 54.2056, -2.5317

35 WHITTLE HOLE & LECK BECK

About 2.5km downstream of Cow Dub, and 800m down from Ease Gill Kirk, the water reappears into a pretty pool and falls with a rocky overhang. On a limestone shelf just below the waterfall is the attractive cave entrance to Whittle Hole. As for Cow Dub, but go directly to Ease Gill Kirk, then downstream 800m.

30 mins, 54.214, -2.5236

36 COW DUB WATERFALL, EASE GILL

A deep, shady waterfall pool in the upper reaches of Ease Gill/Leck Beck. When flowing, the water swirls and then sinks in the bottom of the pool to enter nearby

County Pot. From S of Casterton A683, near golf club, follow the High Casterton/Bullpot road past LA6 2JP, to road end and Bullpot Farm (8km total). Follow the track opposite the farmhouse E, then bearing SE across Casterton Fell and finally following S along field wall to gill (2.5km). Or follow footpath past farm S 1km along the wall to Ease Gill Kirk, then follow the ravine 1.5km upstream.

30 mins, 54.2195, -2.4998

INGLETON WATERFALLS

37 THORNTON FORCE, R TWISS

This impressive waterfall has a huge lip of gritstone and a large pool. It's popular with bathers and is on the official marked Ingleton Waterfall Trail (fee charged) but there's also a little-known public right of way should you prefer, which extends down past several more falls to Pecca Falls. The Waterfall Trail begins in Ingleton and is very well signed (just NE of LA6 3ET, £11/£5.50 child) and this waterfall is at the far N end, just over 3km. It can be accessed more quickly over open-access land/public footpaths, from lanes N of Ingleton. Leave Thornton in Lonsdale dir Dent. About 1.5km beyond LA6 3PJ find a double-walled track on the R and some parking. Follow the track on R down to the stream, then follow the R bank downstream about 800m, past the footbridge. Or continue downstream another 800m on open access land as far as Pecca Falls – deep pools and a steep gorge.

15 mins, 54.1727, -2.469

38 INGLETON SWIMMING POOL £

A 1930s heated 20m pool gloriously situated in a riverside glade. Small shop. Sammy Lane, LA6 3EG, 01524 241147

2 mins, 54.1552, -2.4686

39 CHEMIST'S HOLE, R DOE

Secluded, deep pool in an idyllic setting at the end of the Ingleton Waterfall Trail, formed in part of an old limestone quarry fringed with woodland and enclosed by a steep rock face. Keep an eye on water levels as it is unsafe to swim here when the river is in full spate. From Main St in Ingleton village, keep L of the Village Kitchen Café, continue onto Thacking Lane to metal gate at the end. Go through gate and continue to lower path. Then follow rough paths over a small hill to a small wooden bridge over a stream with waterfalls and a metal entry gate (Ignore signs saying you cannot go further as this is open access land). From this gate follow the decent path until you drop down almost to the riverside and

Chemist's Hole. Look for some flat rocks where the river emerges from a small gorge.

20 mins, 54.1630, -2.4589

40 BEEZLEY FALLS, INGLETON

This pretty canyon pool is also on the Ingleton Waterfall Trail, but at the N end of on the return loop, on the River Doe. Head for Ingleton to complete the official walk (near LA6 3ET, £11/£5.50 child). To access this fall via the footpath instead, head out of Ingleton towards LA6 3JQ via the Chapel le Dale top lane. About 1.5km before this postcode, a footpath crosses the road and there is very limited parking on verge L about 300m on. Follow the footpath track down to the river. There's no access to falls below this point.

5 mins, 54.1674, -2.4528 🖼

RIBBLEHEAD

41 THORNS GILL BRIDGE, GAYLE BECK

Gayle Beck is actually the River Ribble in its infant state. Below Gearstone Lodge is a little-known gorge with pools to explore and clamber through and a beautiful packhorse bridge. Combine with Katnot Cave, just upstream. From the Ribblehead viaduct head up Blea Moor Rd (B6255) and park in layby R just before Gearstone Lodge (LA6 3AS). Turn back downhill and after 400m take the footpath on L by the barns down to Gayle Beck to find the bridge and gorge. There's a bridleway before this (at the end of the parking) that leads you down to Katnot Cave.

10 mins, 54.2101, -2.3426 🖼✝🏊

42 LING GILL BRIDGE

A series of small weirs create some pretty, small paddling pools on this remote beck From Horton in Ribblesdale head to High Birkwith Farm (BD24 0JQ) and park just beyond. Follow the bridleway, turning L after 500m to join the Pennine Way. Continue another 1.5km.

30 mins, 54.2056, -2.3034 🖼🚶🏊

LITTONDALE

43 CRAY GILL AND CROOK GILL FALLS

Secret waterfall pools along Cray Gill and Crook Gill. From the pub (closed) in Cray, walk on the footpath past Mount Pleasant farm BD23 5JB down the Cray Gill about 800m. Go through a gate marked with a NT sign into the woodland and continue. To access Cray Gill waterfall look for a track on the L that doubles back to the falls. For Crook Gill Falls (54.2050, -2.1010), return to the main footpath and just before a

stone packhorse bridge, turn R for 50m to a 6m-high waterfall that cascades down a limestone cleft into an oval plunge pool.

5 mins, 54.2047, -2.0997 🖼🚶

44 STARBOTTON, R WHARFE

This is an idyllic stretch of the young River Wharfe with a footbridge and meadows. Deep enough for swimming downstream. Entering the village from the S on the B6160, park on the L by the double-walled track to bridge, before BD23 5HZ. Take the track down the river 300m. The Fox and Hounds in the village is a good pub with inglenook, real ales and food (01756 760269).

5 mins, 54.1649, -2.0746 🖼🚶

45 HESLEDEN BECK WATERFALLS

Secluded set of pools and falls at the bottom of a magical, remote valley under Pen-y-Ghent. 800m W of BD23 5QL in Litton, dir Nether Heselden, turn L down the dead-end byway track. Park over river and walk upstream on the water-meadow track towards Hesleden Beck. It's just under 3km to the first small pools, and there's a bigger pool above the stream junction under 'snorkel cave'. Or drop down via the footpath near the cattle grid, 1.5km E of BD23 5QR.

15 mins, 54.1642, -2.1905 🚶🖼✝🏊

46 SKIRFARE BRIDGE, R SKIRFARE

Delightful pool in a twist of the river. This is a wonderfully remote spot yet very accessible as it is so close to a minor road. Just off the B6160 between Kettlewell and Kilnsey. Immediately after crossing the stone bridge over the R Skirfare, turn L over cattlegrid onto Armistead Barns and large grassy car parking area overlooking the river.

2 mins, 54.1194, -2.0473

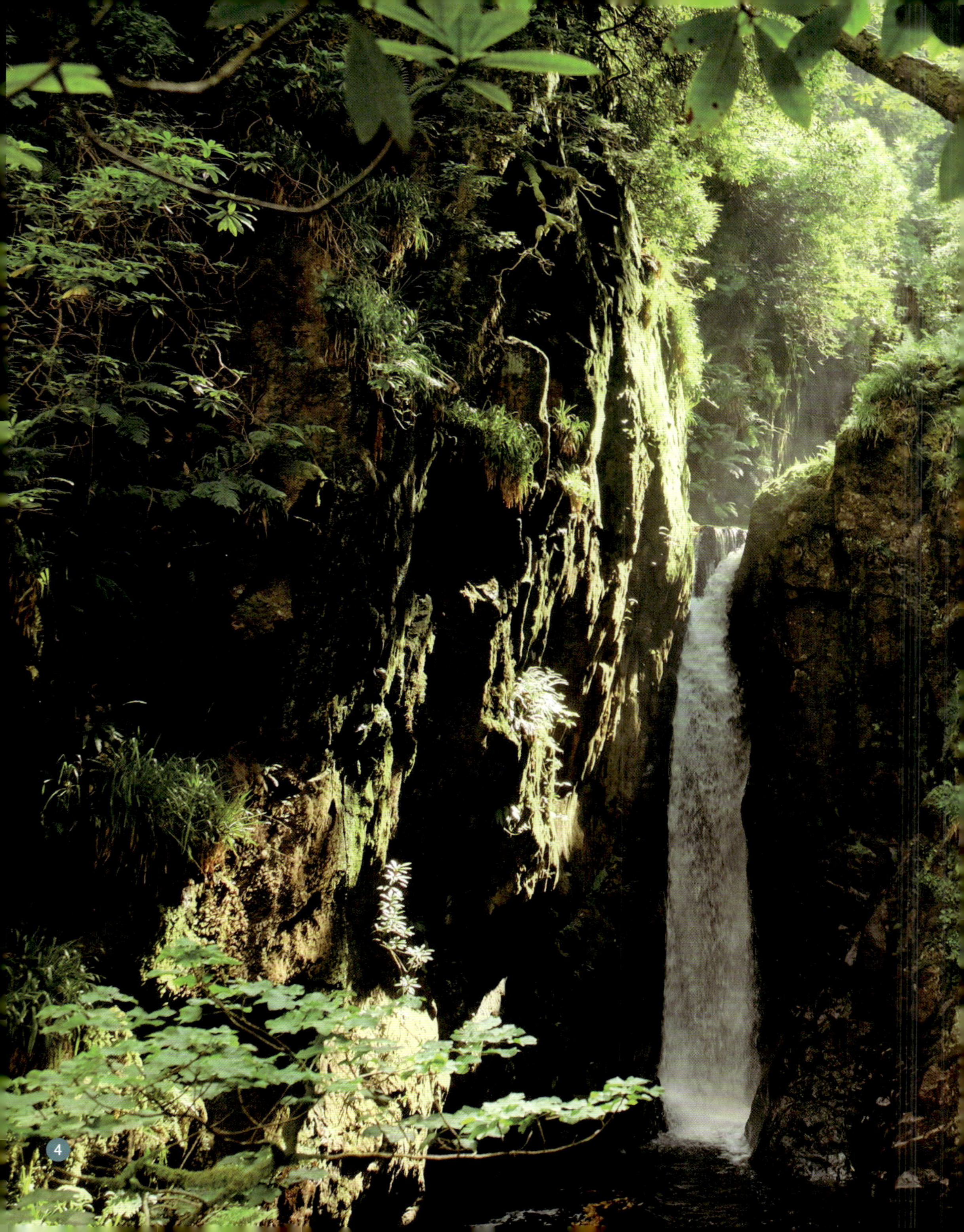

SOUTH LAKE DISTRICT

The beautiful Esk is renowned for its magical pools and waterfalls, sharing the same bright white geology and crystal waters as Wasdale. Arriving in Boot, a short walk from the pub, you'll find a lovely wooded pool called Gill Force, just upstream from a riverside church (3). Along its 15-mile length, there are many more pools, and even the tributaries are impressive, such as Stanely Ghyll, a high shoot which pitches into a deep jungle pool (4). The next day, I took a day trip high into the mountains to the legendary 'Tongue Pot' and Esk Falls, sampling many of the dips along the way (1). Tongue Pot is located just beneath the packhorse bridge at the head of the dale, about an hour's walk from the road. Here, in a cleft of the mountain burn, a long emerald pool has formed beneath a waterfall at the confluence of two rivers. A pebble beach shelves down on one side, and an oak tree overhangs the water. Sheer rock walls rise up on each side, making this place famous for jumps. The oak's knotty roots create excellent handholds for scrambling out of the water before diving back in.

Climbing higher through Esk Falls, a series of perfect plunge pools extends right up to the Great Moss mountain plateau, above which the shimmering Scafell Pike looms. Further smaller pots link back down again via Lingcove Beck, with rocks that are grey and sinuous, streaked with white quartz (1). Each forms a perfect place to lie in the sun as the waters roar by. When the sun is shining, there is no better place on earth to be.

Parallel to Eskdale to the east is another valley rich with childhood memories. Ulpha Bridge on the River Duddon has been a favourite spot for family swimming for generations (9). The grassy banks and cherry trees provide a choice of shallows or deeper pools. The little post office sells sandwiches, coffee, newspapers, ice creams, and fishing nets. Many families while away entire days here, and the bridge jumping—from a respectable fifteen feet— provides ongoing entertainment throughout the afternoons.

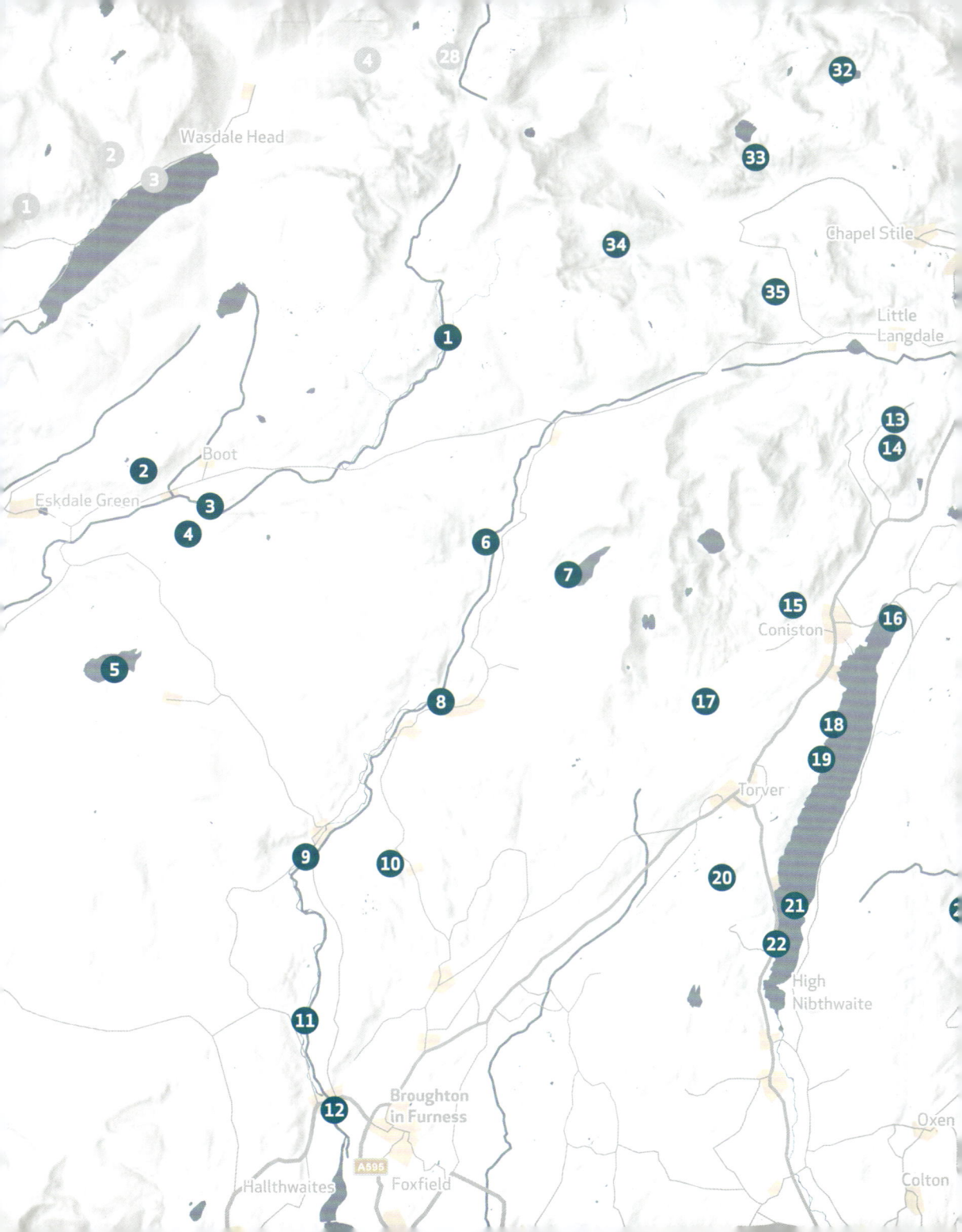

Wasdale Head

Chapel Stile

Little Langdale

Boot

Eskdale Green

Coniston

Torver

High Nibthwaite

Broughton in Furness

Hallthwaites

Foxfield

Oxen

Colton

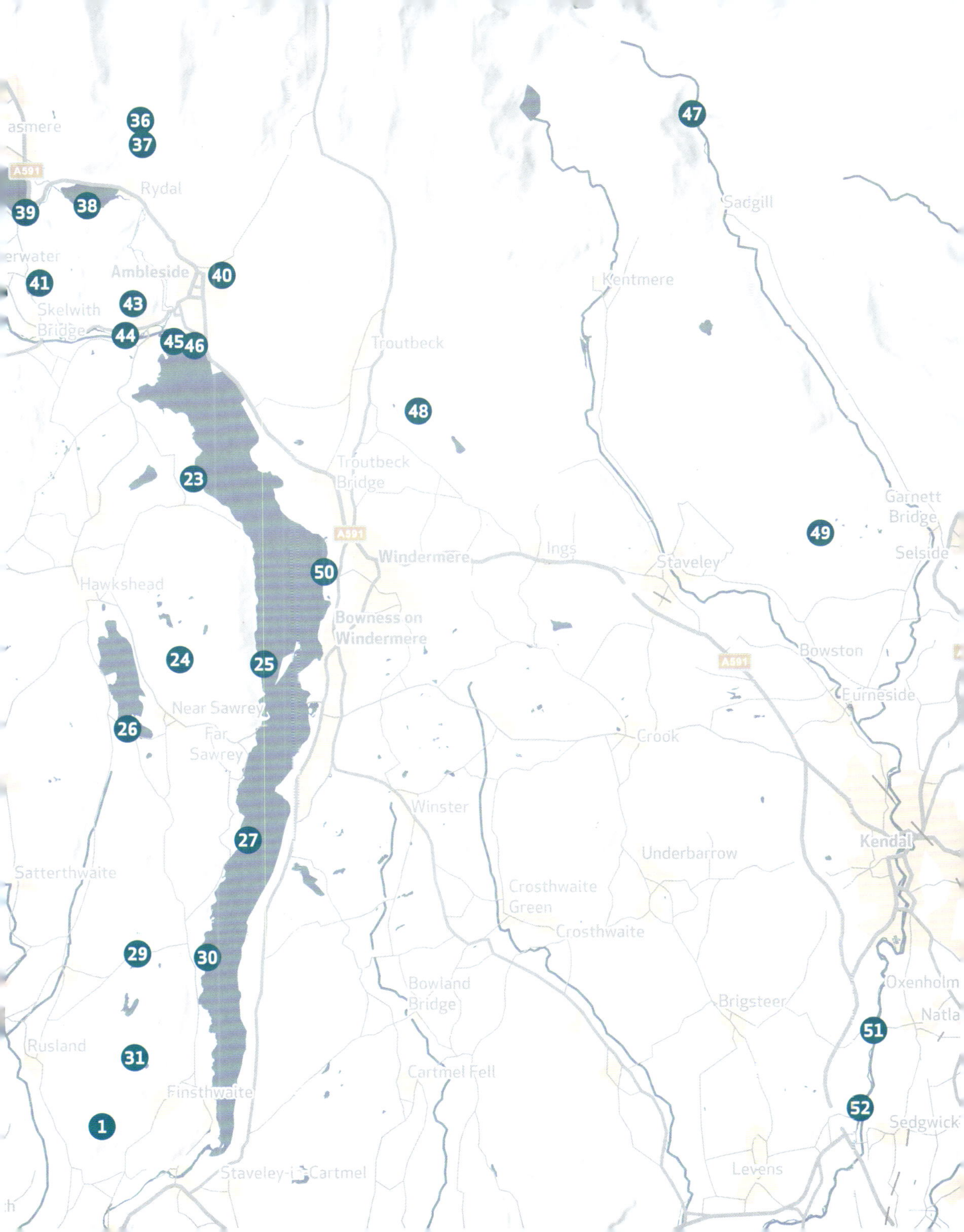
asmere
36
37
A591
Rydal
38
39
erwater
Ambleside
40
41
43
Skelwith Bridge
44
45
46
47
Sadgill
Kentmere
Troutbeck
48
23
Troutbeck Bridge
Garnett Bridge
49
Selside
A591
Windermere
Ings
Staveley
50
Hawkshead
Bowness on Windermere
24
25
A591
Bowston
Burneside
Near Sawrey
26
Far Sawrey
Crook
Winster
27
Kendal
Underbarrow
Satterthwaite
Crosthwaite Green
Crosthwaite
29
30
Bowland Bridge
Oxenholme
Brigsteer
Natla
51
Rusland
31
Cartmel Fell
Finsthwaite
52
Sedgwick
1
Staveley-in-Cartmel
Levens

'There are no natives on the island now,' said Roger. 'They may have been killed and eaten by other natives,' said Titty. 'Anyhow, this is the best place for a camp,' said John. 'Let's put the tents up at once.'
Arthur Ransome, Swallows and Amazons

Further up the Duddon valley, craggy hills create a rugged backdrop as the road twists and turns, meeting the river here and there. Beyond the hamlet of Seathwaite are the rocky pools of Birk's Bridge (6) on the edge of Dunnerdale Forest. Set in a canyon overshadowed by dappled sunlight and beneath an old packhorse bridge, the water is still, deep, and clear. It's possible to swim right up and under the bridge into a small gorge beneath a waterfall. The road continues up to Hardknott Pass and the old Roman Fort, eventually connecting with Eskdale and its string of swims, creating a perfect wild swimming driving tour.

To the east lies Coniston. Peel Island—Wildcat Island in Swallows and Amazons—can be found off the south-east shore of Lake Coniston (21). Old woodland, gravel beaches, and rocky promontories provide superb swimming, walking, and canoeing.

Swallows and Amazons by Arthur Ransome tells the stories of the Altounyan family, who visited the Lakes over several summers during the 1920s. The adventures of Titty, Roger, Susan, and John have captured the imagination of children and teenagers for generations. Their adventures begin when they spot the distant Wildcat Island and mount an expedition to reach it. After learning to sail their clinker dinghy, Swallow, they eventually reach the island and camp there, settling into a routine of watching for enemies, making campfires, and fetching milk and eggs from the shore. Eventually, they meet another group of children on the island who have a boat called Amazon, and they get up to various mischiefs together, drinking ginger beer, swimming, and bothering Captain Flint on his houseboat.

Peel Island is now owned by the National Trust, and camping and fires are no longer allowed, though you will see many people sailing and canoeing there in summer. It is no more than 100 metres long and has steep rocky sides, but in the south-west corner, you'll find both the 'Secret Harbour' and the beach described in the books. Anyone who has taken a boat in here, manoeuvred around the submerged rocks, splashed ashore, and scrambled over the rocks needs little convincing that they are on Ransome's island. It's from the beautiful rocky headlands in the woods at Low Peel Near that you can swim to the island, a crossing of some 100 metres (21).

There are several other swimmable bays up the east coast, but the most popular beach is on the western side along the grassy banks of Brown Howe, close to where the Amazon Family had their home (22). Arthur Ransome was inspired by his own childhood holidays spent in the Lake District. Each summer, as he and his siblings arrived, they would rush down to the lake, dip their hands in the water, and make a wish. When they left, they were 'half drowned in tears'. Nibthwaite, the tiny village where they stayed, is at the south end of Lake Coniston and still retains an air of simple, carefree summers.

The mountains, rivers, and waterfalls of the Lake District were also the literary inspiration for William Wordsworth, of course, and many of his influential circle. The area around Rydal Beck was the setting for many of his walks, swims, and musings. Rydal Mount was Wordsworth's base for eight years, his most beloved home, and the place from which he courted his future wife, Mary Hutchinson. There are many pools in the parkland and fells above Rydal, but one was so special to him that he named it after Mary and dreamed of building a cottage there.

We may never know the pool's true identity, but he described it as 'far among the ancient trees', and I have wondered whether Rhydal Bower could be it, enclosed by ancient oak and rowan trees (37) or Buckstones Jum, set in open fells on the edge of the wooded estate. It's a perfect triangular pool with a shingle beach in a bay between two flat slabs of granite, the water pouring in over the rock lip and scouring out a deep pool, perfect for swimming (36). From up here, a wide lakeland vista opens up, stone walls criss-crossing down the valley, and Rydal Water glinting below.

Wordsworth believed that nature was the crucible through which we must pass before our spirit can be independent. Many people who travelled to visit him in his remote home were touched by a sense of liberation and joy as they immersed themselves in the landscape. 'I have satisfied myself that there is such a thing as that which tourists call romantic... It was a day that will stand out like a mountain, I am sure, in my life,' wrote Charles Lamb after spending a day wading up waterfalls and streams. But returning to London, he soon spiralled into depression. 'You cannot conceive the degradation I felt… from being accustomed to wander free as air… and bathe in rivers without being controlled by anyone… I had been dreaming I was a very great man.'

ESKDALE

1 TONGUE POT & ESK FALLS

There's a series of lovely pools along the higher reaches of the River Esk. The legendary Tongue Pot is the best, set beneath an ancient packhorse bridge with high jumps possible into deep water. There are many more pools as you explore upstream on the Esk and Lingcove Beck; Esk Falls has the biggest pool. Follow road E from Boot past Woolpack Inn (CA19 1TH) to park by the telephone at the bottom of Hardknott Pass ('road unsuitable' signs) and follow riverside path up through Brotherilkeld Farm for 3.2km to confluence and bridge. Kail Pot is a sunny, shallow pool on the way up to Tongue Pot (54.4106, -3.2073).

40 mins, 54.4212, -3.1926 ♨☷🚻🚶

2 BLEA TARN, ESKDALE

A steep walk up but wonderful sunsets. A beachy area on S side. The water is peaty and a little brown – even though 'blea' means blue, which is why there is more than one Blea Tarn or Blea Water in the Lakes. Follow the path up from behind the track at Beckfoot Station, Eskdale (CA19 1TG).

40 mins, 54.3967, -3.287 ♨☷🚶🏕🌳

3 GILL FORCE, RIVER ESK

A small rocky gorge with pool in the Esk, just downstream of Boot. Shady and secluded. At Boot turning, 200m S of Boot Inn (CA19 1TG, 0194 67 23711) take opposite lane leading to St Catherine's Church by the river (700m, bear right through farm where route splits). Turn L, following river upstream for 250m to find narrow gorge and footbridge with pools below. Alternatively, walk down the river (on N bank) about a mile from Doctor Bridge, down dead-end turning just before the Woolpack Inn (CA19 1TH, 0194 67 23230) or up from Dalegarth Bridge or Stanley Force.

20 mins, 54.3902, -3.2663 ♨☷🚶🚻

4 STANLEY FORCE & DALEGARTH BRIDGE

One of Lakeland's most graceful falls, with a shimmering chute falling 20m into a deep plunge pool. It's hidden in a mossy and verdant, tropical-looking ravine reached by crossing several bridges and scrambling along a slightly tricky path. You can also swim in the deep pools beneath Dalegarth Bridge – some jump from the bridge, and there are rope swings. Turn R off the road from Eskdale to Dalegarth, after Beckfoot station (CA19 1TF) opp old schoolhouse with two solid porches. Cross Dalegarth

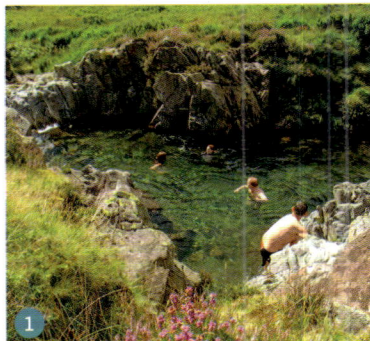

Bridge and find the car park on the L after 200m. Carry on by foot up the road, bearing L. After 300m you'll see a gate into the woods on the L. Follow the track upstream for 800m.

20 mins, 54.3851, -3.2732 🏞🚶🛶

5 DEVOKE WATER
Said to be the largest tarn in the Lakes. High on Birker Fell, with a great expanse of mountain all around and a tiny islet called Watness Coy. The old ruins of the fishing house stand lonely on the shore of the windswept waters. A great place for a big swim. The dramatic mountain road links Ulpha (LA20 6DT) and Eskdale Green (CA19 1TS). The bridleway is marked by a black and white signpost halfway between them, pointing to Stanley Force in one direction. Devoke is 1.2km up the opposite track. Holehouse Tarn is another hour beyond, an ultra-remote tarn with far-reaching sea views (54.3344, -3.3018)

15 mins, 54.3602, -3.296 🏞🏔🧺🚻

RIVER DUDDON

6 BIRKS BRIDGE, DUDDON
A deep stone gorge with ledges, platforms and crystal-clear water under an old packhorse bridge. Swim upstream from the rocks to the waterfall. Shady but great for jumps and diving. From Ulpha Bridge (see entry) continue N on lane, through Seathwaite and 3.5km beyond to reach Forestry Commission Birks Bridge car park on L (beyond LA20 6EF). The little stone bridge is 200m before.

5 mins, 54.3837, -3.1808 🏞🚶🏊🍴

7 TARN BECK & SEATHWAITE
These waterfalls plunge down through craggy outcrops and provide a remote dip on the way up to Seathwaite Tarn reservoir, one of the wilder lakes in the area. Tarn Beck makes a fun gill scramble with narrow gorges – follow it all the way from the road. 1.2km N of the Newfield Inn (LA20 6ED), turn R signed 'Coniston unfit for cars'. After 200m turn L and follow the public road up towards Tongue House and then follow the stream up into the fell. Bring a map.

30 mins, 54.3777, -3.1552 🏞🚶🏔

8 TARN BECK & WALLOWBARROW
The confluence of Tarn Beck and the Duddon forms a large pool. Continue upstream to the footbridge and into the Wallowbarrow gorge, where there are more deep and beautiful pools. The crag above is well known for climbing. You'll find a gate into the woods opp School House, shortly W of Newfield Inn (LA20 6ED). Very limited parking. Cross the bridge and head downstream to the confluence (150m) then upstream into the gorge and to the next footbridge/stepping stones. Cross and keep exploring upstream if you wish (300m).

10 mins, 54.3544, -3.1947 🏞🛈

9 ULPHA BRIDGE, DUDDON
A popular, picnic-friendly area of grassy riverside with a long deep section under the bridge, good for jumps. Shallows downstream. Easy parking. Village post office and shop nearby. Lovely. Turn off the A595 for Ulpha and continue 6km to near LA20 6DT. Why not walk upstream a km (river's L bank) and find the huge stepping stones at Crosby Bridge (54.3322, -3.2300), and another km for more stepping stones and a deep pool and rapids at Jill's Folly (54.3373, -3.2177).

2 mins, 54.3263, -3.2366 🏞🚶🍴

10 STICKLE TARN
A remote and dramatically sited tarn above Dunnerdale, W of Seathwaite. Shallow, but this at least means it warms up. 4km from the Newfield Inn, Seathwaite (LA20 6ED)

towards Broughton Mills, the lane reaches the summit pass where there is layby parking (before LA20 6BA). Follow the path W 400m up to Stickle Tarn.

10 mins, 54.3251, -3.2104 🚶🚵ℹ️🚩

11 RAWFOLD BRIDGE, DUDDON

A deep pool with slabs and ledges for jumping beneath an old stone-arched footbridge. Few people visit here. Turn off the A595 for Ulpha and after a km or so you will find the footpath sign on the L (LA20 6DR) down across the fields. No parking – perhaps easier from the opposite bank via Beckfoot.

15 mins, 54.2965, -3.2369 🚶🚵ℹ️

12 DUDDON BRIDGE

Shortly downstream of the road bridge the river opens up and becomes deep and wide, just before it turns tidal. There's a large pool above a pinch point. If you explore downstream a mile you'll come to sand flats. Opposite the junction of the A595 and the Ulpha road (direction LA20 6DR, limited parking on R), by bridge traffic lights, there's a footpath into the woods. Follow this 400m to the riverbank.

10 mins, 54.2803, -3.2278 🚶🚵

CONISTON & AREA

13 HODGE CLOSE QUARRY

An exciting flooded quarry in a deep, seemingly inaccessible amphitheatre, reached by an extraordinary descent into a jungle quarry. It's popular with divers, and you can get near the water's edge where you see the caves and railway track. Only for the very adventurous - check you can get out of water before you get in. 3½ miles S of Skelwith Bridge on A593 turn R signed 'Hodge Close only'. Follow to parking about 300m before LA21 8DJ. Walk past Hodge Close cottages (200m) to find public path on the R. After 50m descend into overgrown Parrock Quarry on R (54.4076, -3.0517) and after 100m climb through cavern which links through to the water's edge below.

15 mins, 54.4062, -3.0538 🚩🚶🚵

14 HOLME FELL LAKE

This is one of our favourite little lakes, and a great escape on a sunny day. It's an old reservoir on the route up Holme Fell, used for the mines below. It's deep enough to dive in from the old dam wall, and small enough that it warms up nicely in the sunshine. From the SE corner of Hodge Close quarry, a path leads up through woods, past old mine ruins 300m. Keep climbing on the upward path (don't bear R along the wall path) and you reach the lake after 300m more.

15 mins, 54.401, -3.0547 🚶🚵ℹ️🚶🏃

15 CHURCH BECK GILL

This is a well-known gill scramble. There are some deep pools and two waterfalls, on which this is the easiest to access. Follow the path up towards Coniston fell from behind The Sun (LA21 8HQ, 0153 94 41248). The beck is down on your R all the way. There's a gravel path to it after 300m at 54.3719, -3.0856 and the waterfall is upstream. Or join cragsadventures.com (0153 95 96317).

20 mins, 54.3721, -3.0855 ⛰️🚶🅿️📹

16 MONK CONISTON

Very accessible SW-facing tree-lined beach with a good jetty pontoon if you like jumping! Can be a bit windy. E of Coniston on the B5285, turn at the top of the lake, signed E of Lakes/Brantwood (towards LA21 8AA). Park at Monk Coniston car park after 150m on the R. There is a beach right here or follow the path S down the shore 200m for the jetty.

3 mins, 54.3697, -3.0545 🚵🚶🅿️⛵ℹ️🚩

17 TRANEARTH/BANISHEAD QUARRY

This remarkable flooded quarry has a grand waterfall pouring into it where the adjacent stream has breached the leat banks. It's a slightly tricky descent, but once down you can swim straight out into the very deep water. Look out for the adit tunnel, which reappears out of the quarry via a stream gorge. Park at the junction 200m N of the Church House Inn on A593, for Crook Barn Stables (LA21 8BP). Head up the lane, past Scarr Head bungalow and up the track for 1.5km

30 mins, 54.3545, -3.1126 ⬛🅅🐕⬛⬛

18 HOATHWAITE TO CONISTON HALL

Backed by meadows and ancient parkland, with silver beaches, this is a popular stretch and is situated between the two campsites of the same name. Ideally you would enjoy this stretch while camping here (Hoathwaite is much more peaceful but Coniston Hall is closer to the shore). Alternatively you can sometimes park at busy Coniston Hall (lakeside after LA21 8AS) or Hoathwaite campsite and walk down on the footpath (turn off the A593 800m N of Torver, as if for LA21 8AX, then immediately L again).

20 mins, 54.3503, -3.0729 ⬛⬛⬛⬛⬛

19 TORVER COMMON, CONISTON

This is one of our favourite spots. Very quiet and backed by ancient woodland, with a good jetty to jump from. Best in the morning, as it loses the sun in the afternoon. Arrive by ferry, or take the beautiful walk through Torver woods, about 1.5km. Continue past the Hoathwaite campsite turning, past Brackenbarrow Farm (LA21 8AX), to find the next farm track on L with footpath (tricky parking). Walk along the track round to the back of the farm (200m), and then take the R fork towards and through the woods and down to the lakeshore.

25 mins, 54.344, -3.0766 ⬛ℹ⬛⬛⬛

20 TORVER TARN

A lovely little swimming lake in a relatively unvisited place, also known as Thrang or Throng Moss Tarn. This is a natural feature, but its height was raised many years ago by this small dam in order to increase the water supply for a former wood mill below at Sunny Bank, which manufactured bobbins, axe handles and pill boxes. Take the unsigned lane, nearly opposite Brown Howe car park on A5084. Head to Stable Harvey Farm at LA21 8BN. 60m before the farm gate and wall, take grassy bridleway

track on L (not footpath along wall) and follow it down and along the contour about 1.2km, due N. There's also a (harder) route up from Torver Beck/Torver Common gate, further N on A5084 at Sunny Bank.

20 mins, 54.3226, -3.1075 ⬛⬛ℹ⬛⬛

21 PEEL ISLAND, CONISTON

An inspiration for Wild Cat Island in Swallows and Amazons. Swim out the 100m to it and explore the woods and find the 'secret harbour' – two rocky spurs that shelter a tiny bay where Titty landed her boat. There are also some pretty beaches on the mainland shore, but parking is tricky. No wild camping! Turn off the B5285 E of Coniston (signed Brantwood/E of Lake) to follow the E shore. Continue 6.5km to Rigg Wood parking then another 800m along the road to the beach and Peel Woods.

5 mins, 54.3175, -3.0849 ⬛⬛⬛⬛

22 BROWN HOWE, CONISTON

A car park, woods, slipway, toilets, grassy banks and a long stretch of beach make this a deservedly popular beach for families and those with small boats. On A5084, a mile S of Sunny Bank, just before LA12 8DW. Toilets.

2 mins, 54.3105, -3.0906 ⬛⬛⬛⬛⬛

WEST OF WINDERMERE

23 HIGH WRAY BAY/WRAY CASTLE

The quintessential Windermere lakeshore. A sheltered, shelving, grassy bay backed by ancient oaks, with two old stone boathouses. Signed Wray/Wray Castle off the B5285 2.4km S of Clappersgate. After 1km find the bridleway on the L, by the gatehouse for Wray Castle. Or if you're a NT member park in Wray Castle for free and walk along the shore. The castle has loads of kids' activities so is a great rainy-day option too.

10 mins, 54.3954, -2.9626 🏊🚲🚶♿

24 MOSS ECCLES TARN

Beatrix Potter bought this tarn in 1926 and planted the water llies here. She enjoyed spending sunny evenings on the grassy banks of the tarn, and its believed to have been the inspiration for The Tales of Mr Jeremy Fisher, one of her most beloved children's stories. From the NT car park in Near Sawrey (LA22 0LF), cross road and follow Stones Lane. Continue along track up to the tarn for 1.2km

20 mins, 54.3625, -2.9670 🏊🚶

25 LILIES OF THE VALLEY ARCHIPELAGO

In the 18th century tourists rowed out to pick the wild lilies that once grew here. You're free to land here, though the lilies are rare and must not be picked. You can explore the larger Thompson Holme beyond. Belle Isle is private. From the ferry on the W shore (B5285) follow the road 'Lake Shore/Harrowslack' to parking near LA22 0LR. It's less than 100m to the nearest island.

5 mins, 54.3616, -2.9409 🚣🏊🚲♿🌿

26 ESTHWAITE WATER

Lying between Coniston and Windermere, Esthwaite Water is often overlooked and is much smaller and more peaceful. There's easy access from the laneside car park. 3km S of Hawkshead dir Grizedale/Newby Bridge past LA22 0QF. Café gallery shop (now closed) and then long-stay car park on L.

1 mins, 54.35, -2.9833 🏊

27 RAWLINSON NAB, WINDERMERE

A remote, wooded peninsula on the lake shore, with a little S-facing beach. A good place to find peace on the otherwise busy shore. Follow the shore road N from Lakeside. After 4km turn R signed Cunsey/ferry, opposite the second gatehouse for Graythwaite Estate. Head for LA22 0LU (Cunsey Farm) and 500m before on R

there's a cottage with jetty (Hammerhole), then a farmhouse and barn and a footpath to the lakeshore. Park here by the barn and follow the path for 500m N up the shore. You can make a loop by continuing up the shore and returning on the lane (5km).

5 mins, 54.3297, -2.946 🏊🚶🛶

28 HOB GILL TARN & SCULPTURES

A shallow, hidden, un-named tarn in Grizedale Forest. Probably built to help power the old iron works at Force Mills in the valley below. The Lady of Water sculpture is on the beck which drains the tarn below to SE. Small parking area on R

Oaks Wood, reaching the shore after 400m. Follow the shore N for another 800m.

20 mins, 54.3085, -2.9587

31 HIGH DAM & BOBBIN MILL

Two idyllic lakes, hidden in Scots pine and larch woodland in low foothills, with plenty of places to swim and paddle from rocky headlands. Possibly our favourite mid-level tarn. It was formed in 1835 when the original Finsthwaite Tarn was enlarged to provide power for a waterwheel at Stott Park Bobbin Mill (now intriguingly restored – in its day it provided literally millions of wooden bobbins to the Lancashire weaving and spinning industry). Finsthwaite, with its whitewashed stone cottages, has a fascinating church, St Peters, with an unusual squat steeple and a timber framed porch. From Newby Bridge (A590) head to and through Lakeside and follow signs for Stott Park Bobbin Mill (800m, LA12 8AX, paid tours on certain days. Book in advance.) bearing L at fork on bend. Turn R up into woods after 300m and park. Walk uphill for about 15 mins, past the first, smaller lake, and you'll arrive at a larger lake. Turn Rover the wooden bridge and there are numerous entry points.

15 mins, 54.2903, -2.9813

LANGDALE PIKES

32 EASEDALE TARN AND SOUR MILK GHYLL

The cascades were once known as Churn Milk Force, and Dorothy Wordsworth likened them to a 'broad stream of snow'. A fun wet scramble up to Easedale Tarn – a vast hollow, gouged out by glacial action. Shortly past LA22 9QJ follow the no through road straight on where the road bends: this becomes the path up to the tarn. NB there is another Sour Milk Ghyll at Seathwaite, Borrowdale.

45 mins, 54.47, -3.0702

33 STICKLE GHYLL

A well-known gorge walk, with some chutes and deep pools. It's quite wide, so you can walk around most of the waterfalls. Continue all the way up to the tarn for a final swim, or explore Dungeon Ghyll too (more of a dry scramble). The walk begins behind Lanty Slee's distillery and tavern (LA22 9JU). It's about 1.5km up to Stickle Tarn (good for a dip), and the best waterfalls are halfway up. Join a half day course with cragsadventures.com (0153 95 96317).

45 mins, 54.4541, -3.0971

under trees at corner of wood, 300m S of LA12 8LN in Satterthwaite. Follow track along wood edge, turning L into woods after 150m. Sculpture at 54.3139, -3.0263

15 mins, 54.3167, -3.0327

29 GREEN HOWS TARN

A very quiet, little-visited yet very easily accessible tarn. As for Rawlinson Nab (see entry), but turn L by the first Graythwaite Estate gatehouse, signed Rusland. Continue on 800m, past LA12 8BQ, and just beyond the cottage there is a gate and track on the L, with the lake, just as the road bends R. Green Hows Upper Tarn can be reached via a vehicle track off the road, but is less pretty.

2 mins, 54.3092, -2.9804

30 SILVER HOLME, WINDERMERE

A perfect, tiny island, an easy 20m swim just offshore, with a grassy top and flat rocks for jumping. Long Tongue is a diminutive peninsula just to the S. 3km N of Lakeside on the shore road, pass two YMCA entrances on the R (LA12 8BD). 20m further along on the R is a footpath sign and wooden fence. (There's room for one car to park, just, or you might be able to park at the YMCA.) The path leads into Great

34 WHORNEYSIDE FORCE, OXENDALE BECK
Small plunge pool below high waterfall, a good place to refresh after Crinkle Crags. Best in morning sun. Park at Old Dungeon Ghyll (if eating there, LA22 9JY) and follow byway up valley 2.6km, crossing at second footbridge.
45 mins, 54.4383, -3.1404 🚶🏊‍♀️⛰️♿️🚻👥🅿️

35 BLEA TARN, LANGDALES
A famously picturesque little tarn, but popular too. The Langdale Pikes rise above on the skyline, and the shore is backed by trees and beaches, with a small rock outcrop. The sediment in the bed of Blea Tarn has not been disturbed since the last ice age. Follow B5343 up to the end of Great Langdale, past Lanty Slee's distillery and tavern. Just after Old Dungeon Ghyll Hotel, the road turns sharp left and eventually reaches the tarn and car park, 300m after LA22 9PG.
5 mins, 54.4296, -3.0909 🅿️🚶🏊‍♀️🌲🐾

AMBLESIDE & RYDAL

36 BUCKSTONES JUM, RYDAL BECK
High on the edge of the fells, and visible from all around, the stream turns a corner and plunges into a deep triangular pool with huge, smooth rock slabs. There's a large pebble beach with views down to Rydal Water. Beautiful. Is it Jum or Jump – no one can agree! 2.4km NW of Ambleside on A591, turn R at the Rydal Lodge Hotel (LA22 9LR) signed Rydal Hall and Rydal Mount. Park on the roadside by St Mary's church (or car park near LA22 9LW, across the bridge to SE, signed Under Loughrigg) and continue up the lane, becoming a good track, for 2.5km. Keep to the R and along the wall at the edge of the woods – don't take the footpath L at Hart Head Farm. As you reach the fell and the track flattens, you'll see the triangular pool on R.
30 mins, 54.4611, -2.9788 🅿️🚶🏊‍♀️

37 RYDAL BOWER, RYDAL, AMBLESIDE
Hidden deep in the woods below Buckstones Jum, this deep pool lies in a narrow, dark cleft between rock walls and a waterfall, crowned with rowan. Very deep and cold with a cliff to jump from. A magical secret place. From Buckstones Jum (see entry) continue downstream 400m through various waterfalls to come to a large rocky outcrop, through which the stream flows. There's a small grassy entrance below and a tree to hang your clothes on. Alternatively, we first found this place by exploring

33

281

20 mins, 54.4443, -3.0145

40 STOCKGHYLL FORCE, AMBLESIDE

Victorian posters used to advertise 'bathing under the fall – towels provided'. This is a tall falls in oak woodland with a small plunge pool below. Take the little lane from the Salutation Hotel (LA22 9BX) next to the Market Hall. Follow the signs. Look out for the 'penny tree' stump.

10 mins, 54.4327, -2.9536

41 LOUGHRIGG TARN

With the Langdale Pikes rising up behind and gently shelving shores, this is a perfect little lowland tarn without too many people. It's fun to stay at the little campsite adjacent, but there's a good footpath around the whole lake to take a dip anywhere. Some of the lanes are no entry, so take the High Close turning L off the A593 (LA22 9HE), 800m E of Skelwith Bridge Hotel. After 1.6km pass LA22 9HF and then the tarn, to find a footpath R which takes you down to the shore.

5 mins, 54.4314, -3.0102

42 ELTERWATER, RIVER BRATHAY

An easily accessible and perfectly picturesque lake shore and river bank, backed by ancient woodland and the Langdale Pikes skyline. Very popular, but find a quiet spot on the lake beach or try swimming down from the lake along the river (get out before the falls!). There's a big pay car park on the B5343 about 500m up from Skelwith Bridge Hotel (LA22 9NJ) dir Elterwater. Follow the path to the river. Downstream passes lots of deep river pools and heads to Skelwith Force (with a pool beneath); upstream leads to the lake shore with beach.

20 mins, 54.4295, -3.0244

43 LILY TARN

A small, shallow tarn, almost a pond, with a tiny island and wonderful views. It's rather shallow and silty for a proper swim but it does warm up quickly! Park as for Brathay Bridge (see entry), walk back to the junction of B5286 and A593 and take path opposite by phone box.

20 mins, 54.4276, -2.9812

44 BRATHAY BRIDGE, CLAPPERSGATE

Not particularly wild, but there's a lovely roadside pool just above the bridge. If there's enough water in the river, it's fun to paddleboard or float from Skelwith

upstream on the waymarked waterfall path behind Rydal Hall and then crossing the wall onto the open access land (you can park there if using the Old School Room Tea Shop LA22 9LX, 0153 94 32050).

35 mins, 54.4567, -2.9782

38 RYDAL WATER

This is a very popular lake, but it's relatively warm with good beaches on the S side. Plus you can swim out to the Little Isle. Parking on main road between Rydal and Grasmere at White Moss parking (LA22 9SE). Cross the road and follow the river to the footbridge. Cross, head into the woods away from the river and pick up the path R along the bottom of the fell to the lake shore (1.2km). Alternatively, park in the main Rydal car park (near LA22 9LW, across the bridge to SE, signed Under Loughrigg) and follow the road to the lake shore.

15 mins, 54.4455, -2.9954

39 GRASMERE BEACH & ISLAND

A good albeit popular shale beach by the weir. The small, wooded island in the middle was a favourite of Wordsworth, who would row out here for fishing and picnics with his sister. Parking on main road between Rydal and Grasmere at White Moss parking (W of

all the way down to this point, passing through several deep, large river pools. This section has few footpaths so is otherwise inaccessible. However, respect fishermen and give them a wide berth. There's layby parking on B5286 opposite the Brathay Trust Training Centre entrance, LA22 0HP, by the junction signed Skelwith Fold (NB also nice spot by the bridge and church). To float down to this point, start at Skelwith Bridge A593 (parking by the bridge, near LA22 9NW).

2 mins, 54.4218, -2.9836

45 ROMAN FORT, BRATHAY PARK

This is a tranquil spot where the Brathay River enters Windermere and you can swim hidden by the reeds. You can also explore the extensive foundation remains of the Roman fort of Galava, once connected to the port of Ravenglass via the road that runs over the Hardknott Pass. Park near the Wateredge Inn/Waterhead Car Park (LA22 0EP), bear L and wander through Borrans Park to the far end and into the field (200m) to the fenced fort area and reedy neck of the Brathay.

15 mins, 54.4207, -2.9686

46 WATERHEAD ROW BOATS & JETTIES

Right by the road, but fun if you're in Ambleside with time to kill. Hire a row boat from the pier or swim/jump from the one of the jetties if there are no boats. Traditional wooden row boats from £26/hr. Opposite the Waterhead pay car park (LA22 0EP), or park at the pier itself if hiring (LA22 0EY). windermere-lakecruises.co.uk

2 mins, 54.4199, -2.9622

EAST OF WINDEMERE

47 CLEFT GHYLL, SADGILL

A series of cascades and pools on the R Sprint leads into a narrowing gorge with a deep pool above the beautiful and remote Longsleddale. Continue on for Wrengill Quarry above, with a waterfall over a vast cavern, cave system and ruins. Park at Sadgil by bridge and walk up the rough byway 1.8km to the start of the access land. A gate leads down to the stream on L at 54.4594, -2.8049 but continue up another 300m to the start of the mini gorge and be prepared to rock hop up through the pools to the final waterfall. The mine ruins are another 1km upstream at 54.4698, -2.8106.

40 mins, 54.4620, -2.8076

48 DUBBS RESERVOIR & WATERFALLS

A small, remote reservoir and stocked trout lake. Little-visited, with waterfalls on the fell above. Travelling W on A591 from Kendal, turn R just after Ings (LA8 9QQ), signed High Borrans. After 3km turn R up on the gravel track (no through road sign) and you come to the reservoir after 800m. If you're feeling energetic you can bushwhack up to the Sour Howes cascades (small plunge pools) 800m above on the R, on the 320m contour at 54.410, -2.8807.

2 mins, 54.4077, -2.8928

49 GURNAL DUBS

Delightful out-of-the-way tarn with a small slate-built boathouse at the western end. From Hundhowe Farm, Staveley (LA8 9AB) follow the bridleway up via Ghyll Pond and Potter Tarn. Or, with less climbing but slightly longer, from Birk Field (LA8 9QU) via Potter Tarn too.

40 mins, 54.3851, -2.7681

50 MILLERGROUND JETTY,

Pretty wooded lakeside common land with several beaches, boathouses and a good jetty for jumps, if no ferries. East parking at Rayrigg on A592 (LA23 1BP)

2 mins, 54.3782, -2.9221

RIVER KENT

51 HAWES BRIDGE, PRIZET, RIVER KENT

After a leisurely stretch through Kendal, the River Kent picks up speed as it drops into several miles of gorges and small waterfalls. Under this old bridge the river funnels down a chute into a series of deep pools. Look out for the minor road signed Prizet/Natland off A591 just S of Kendal. Continue to the old stone road bridge (before LA9 7QG). There's a footpath downstream on far bank (also footpaths upstream on both banks) and this leads on down to the old mill rapids where gunpowder was made (800m – take care as there are bits of metal) eventually arriving at Wilson Place suspension bridge (LA8 0JZ). Limited parking.

2 mins, 54.295, -2.7521

52 WILSON PLACE, RIVER KENT

A charming little suspension footbridge, wooded shores, open meadows and some pleasant river beaches. Come off the A591 S of Kendal at the A590 junction, but take the Hincaster exit at the roundabout. Turn L after 400m signed to the tea room and caravan site. On the opposite bank of the river from LA8 0JZ.

5 mins, 54.2809, -2.7563

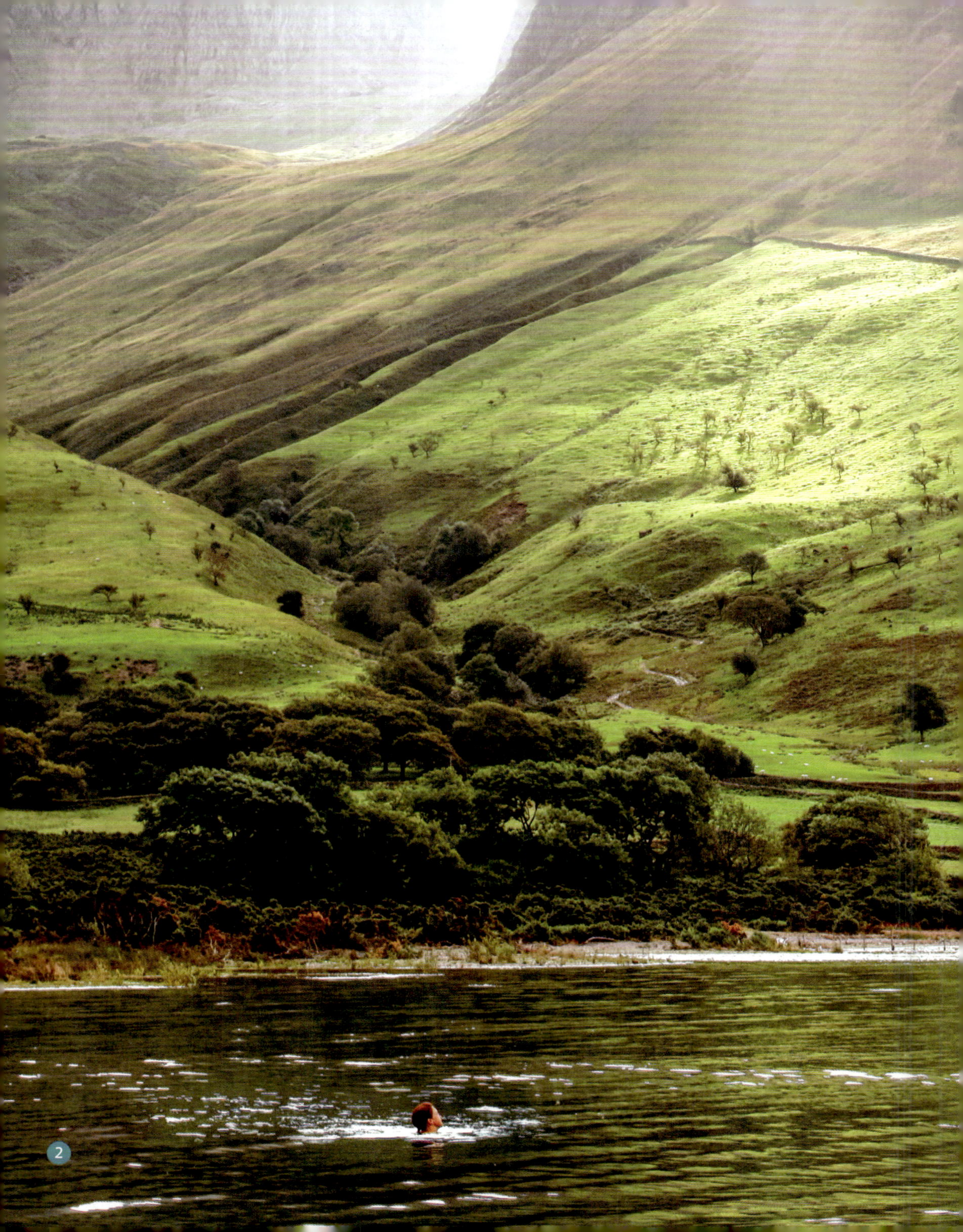
2

NORTH
LAKE DISTRICT

The sun was falling in golden pools in a small bay where a group of walkers and swimmers had congregated to catch the last rays of the day. Steep white scree slopes plunged 500 metres into the lake on the opposite shore.

Scrambling down to the shoreline, grimy from a day of driving, the cool water instantly quenched my skin. Striking out over the white quartz lake bed, the water was as clear as the Mediterranean. Small clumps of freshwater grass soon waved beneath me, and the mountains of Whin Rigg and Illgill Head rippled in broken reflections around me (3).

There are many little white bays along the three-mile length of Wastwater, several fringed with great boughs of Scots pine. The whole area is tinged with the pinks and blues of the white volcanic granite that underlies the region, a material so pure and hard that it creates virtually no sediment or nutrients, keeping the lake free of algae and making it the clearest in the Lake District.

This valley of Wasdale is certainly a place of extremes: Wastwater, England's deepest lake, is overlooked by Scafell Pike, its highest mountain. It even contains the country's smallest church, so perhaps it's not surprising that it's also home to some of its tallest tales. The World's Biggest Liar competition was first won by Will Ritson, landlord of the Wasdale Head, in 1872. The competition was resurrected by Copeland Borough Council in 1974 and has attracted competitors from Australia and Canada, featuring classics such as the foxhound that could fly because its mother mated with a golden eagle (1989 winner) and turnips so huge that the Lakes folk could quarry sheep pens from them (1992).

You'll understand, then, why I didn't believe a story about a garden of gnomes that lives 50 metres down at the bottom of the lake, guarded by a picket fence. As it turns out, the story is true. The lake is popular with divers because it's so clear and deep. However,

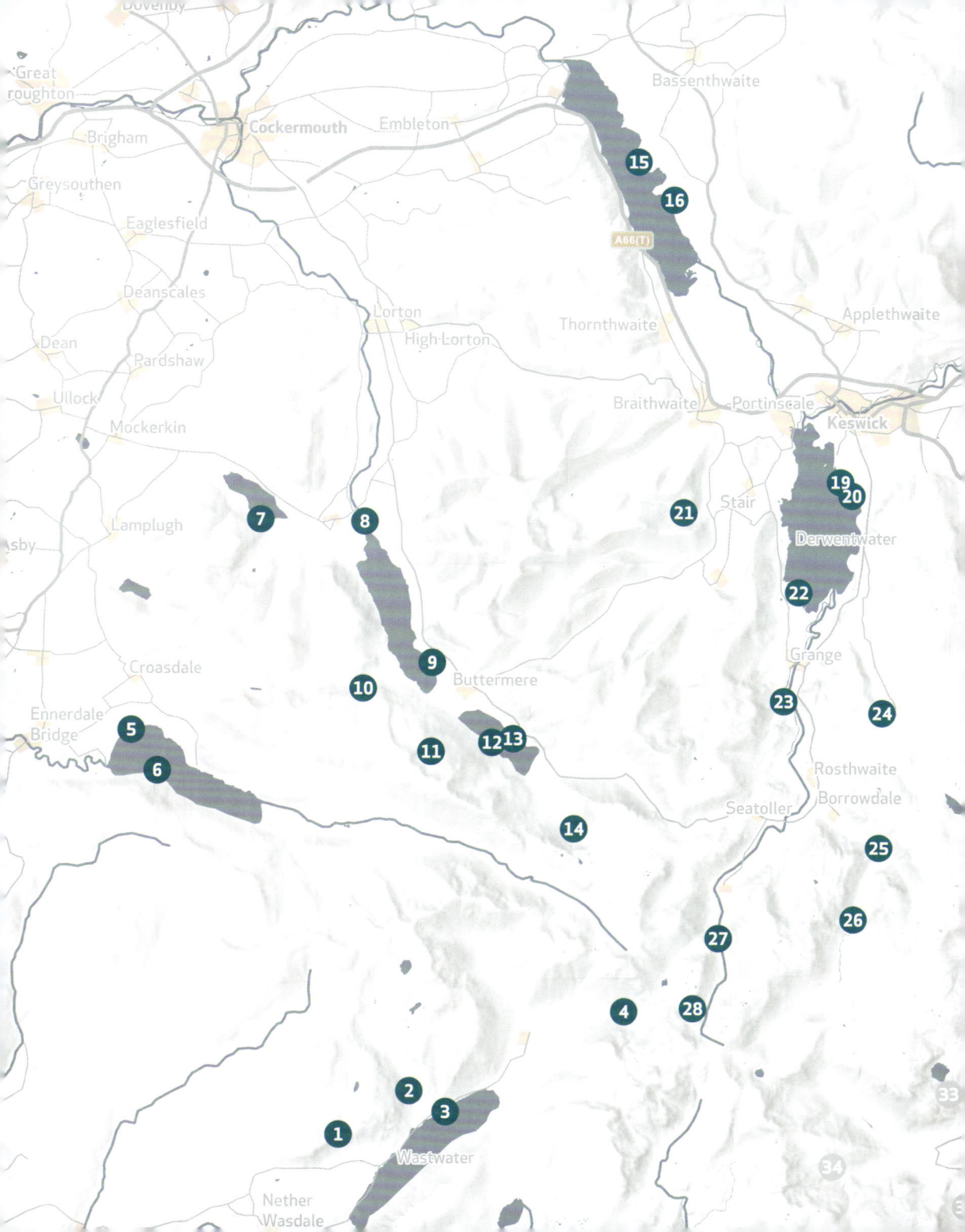

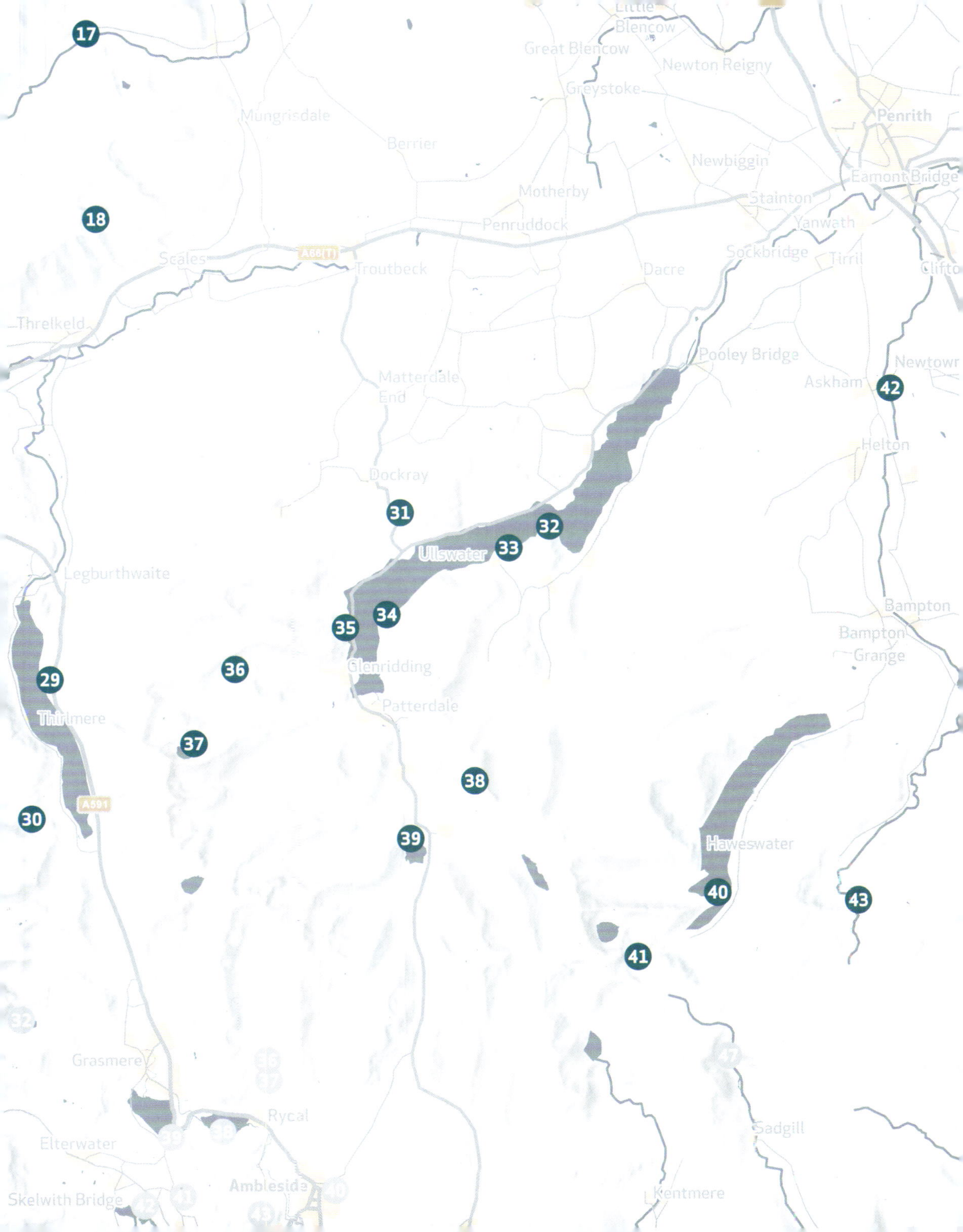
Little
Blencow
Great Blencow
Newton Reigny
Greystoke
Penrith
Mungrisdale
Berrier
Newbiggin
Motherby
Eamont Bridge
Stainton
Penruddock
Yanwath
Scales
A66(T)
Troutbeck
Sockbridge
Tirril
Dacre
Threlkeld
Pooley Bridge
Matterdale
End
Askham
Helton
Dockray
Ullswater
Legburthwaite
Bampton
Bampton
Grange
Glenridding
Thirlmere
Patterdale
A591
Haweswater
Grasmere
Rycal
Sadgill
Elterwater
Ambleside
Skelwith Bridge
Kentmere
17
18
29
30
31
32
33
34
35
36
37
38
39
40
41
42
43

because there isn't much for divers to do or see on the way down, a series of extraordinary artificial 'sites' have been built up to keep them amused. Apparently, the underwater gnome garden is growing.

Across the heights of Scafell to the north-east, Borrowdale is considered by some to be the most beautiful valley in the Lakes. A steep-sided vale, running ten miles from its sources beneath Scafell down to the shores of Derwent Water, it is spectacular and remote, with waterfalls, deep pots, and high tarns.

An old lady who lived on St Herbert Island in Derwent Water once told Beatrix Potter the story of a squirrel that swam out from the mainland to collect nuts each summer. The lake is scattered with wooded isles, and the story and location became the inspiration for The Tale of Squirrel Nutkin, in which the squirrel and his friends built a raft of twigs and used their tails as sails to reach the island. Now the lake is a little too busy with ferries for my liking, though there are still plenty of places to bathe along the shore, and squirrels do still swim here.

My favourite swim is further upstream, near Seathwaite. From this tiny village, centred around the very civilised Langstrath Country Inn, a steep track leads to camping fields along the banks of Langstrath Beck. Just 15 minutes further upstream is Galleny Force (25), a series of river pools sparkling as they overflow, overshadowed by twisted and teal-green mountain oaks. They are not deep, no more than three feet in places, but make a great place to snorkel with their hypnotic array of underwater light and shade. Galactic bubbles stream over the waterfall, and sunbeams laser across the sandy river floors. I spent much of my first afternoon in Borrowdale floating about in these crystal-clear pools, burning my back in the sun as I chased minnows and gazed down at the great wobbling underworld.

Beyond Galleny, the valley walls steepen, peregrine falcons soar above the fell, and the map marks the remote bluffs of Eagle Crag, Heron Crag, Bleak How, and Great Hollow. Climbers report several caves in this vicinity, and a couple of miles ahead, under the mountain eye of Scafell Pike, lies Blackmoss Pot, a cliff face above a wide cavity in the rock and a deep, clear cauldron of water (26). There are many more pools upstream too.

The best way into Blackmoss is to swim upstream. The pot walls gain in height gradually, so you have time to admire the curves and gain your bearings. This pot has long been a place of initiation, legend, and superstition. In recent years, teenagers have gathered here from Whitehaven and Cockermouth most weekends to swim in circles in the pool and dare their friends above to jump. It's not particularly high or dangerous – about fifteen feet – but many stand for hours trying to summon up the courage in vain. As any old hand will explain, you should make your decision to jump during a thorough reconnaissance beforehand. Then, as you approach for the real thing, you can clear your mind and step out, relaxed in the knowledge that there is nothing left to consider. If you dither at the edge, looking down and filling your head with dizzy vertigo, hours can pass in torture.

Beyond Blackmoss, you can follow the river for several more miles as it becomes wilder and higher, with more 'pots' and pools to find. If you follow it to its source, you can swim in Styhead Tarn and Sprinkling Tarn, both large and just as spectacular (27). The temperatures can be chilly but no worse than a mountain stream, and the water tends to heat up throughout the day. Sprinkling Tarn has a small swimming island near the edge, linked to land by a causeway of stepping stones. From up here, the views down Borrowdale to Derwent Water are sublime.

To the north-east, Ullswater offers some of the most diverse wild swimming in the Lake District. Although popular, the lake is long and narrow, bordered by steep fells and quiet bays that feel far removed from the busy tourist spots. Early morning is ideal, when the water is still and the light soft across the valley. Popular spots include Kailpot Crag (32), with deep clear water perfect for jumps or a longer swim, and Sandwick Bay, which offers a gentle, pebbled entry point (33). Aira Force is on the north shire, with many gladed pools below (31) and Side Farm provides a perfect campsite with west-facing sunsets (34).

From here Helvellyn rises, offering some fine pools and ghyll scrambling along Glenridding Beck (36), up to the Red Tarn (37). But for real remoteness, head to secret waterfall of Swindale (43), or Small Water above Haweswater (43)..

WASTWATER & WASDALE

1 GREENDALE FALLS & TARN

Greendale is a south-facing gill with some good deep plunge pools among a quick succession of waterfalls. Continue up to the source tarn for a bigger swim. Turn for Gosforth off the Wast lakeshore road, towards CA20 1AU. 800m brings you to the hamlet of Greendale. The clear path up the fell is immediately on the R where you can also park. The waterfall is 1.2km and the tarn another 1.6km

20 mins, 54.4452, -3.3235 🏊🚻🚶🏕️🅿️

2 NETHER BECK POOLS

Nether Beck is a bubbly little stream that plunges down the mountain with views back to Wastwater. There are many small waterfalls on the way. It's quiet up here and you can explore all the way to the ravine, which is a fun place for scrambling. There's also a grove of ancient yew trees on the mountainside above the path to the L. 1.2km before Overbeck Bridge (see entry) park by cattle grid and little bridge over Nether Beck. Follow the rough path along the river's W bank. The first pools are after 800m, and if you look up to Iron Crag on the L you'll also see the yew grove. Another 1.5km leads to the ravine.

20 mins, 54.4546, -3.2973 🚶🏊🅿️🌳🅿️

3 OVERBECK BRIDGE, WASTWATER *

England's deepest lake, with white quartz beaches and clear water. There's road access all along the shore and a dramatic mountain backdrop. Good pub and NT campsite. One of the most remote of the large lakes and well worth the effort of exploring. Signed Santon Bridge/Wasdale from the A595 W coast road between Ravenglass and Whitehaven. Or from Ambleside via the dramatic Hardknott Pass (challenging – and not advised in winter)

and Eskdale. From Nether Wasdale pass the youth hostel, and after a 1.6km there are some good beaches by the T-junction to Gosforth. Turn R and continue another 2.4km (Wasdale Head) and there's a better beach at Overbeck Bridge, with car park on L by stream. Continue to end of lake for Wasdale Head Inn and camping (CA20 1EX, 01946 726 229).

2 mins, 54.4501, -3.2838 🏊🅿️🌳🅿️

4 LINGMELL BECK & DUBS, SCAFELL PIKE

The turquoise hue of the pools along the Scafell ascent are famous, and this is the best, at the confluence of Piers and Spouthead Gills, just big enough for one. From Wasdale Head (CA20 1EX) follow the main path but keep to the lower stream path, about 2.6km. For those continuing up Scafell, seek out tiny, shallow Lambfoot Dub as well, above the Corridor Route (54.4653, -3.2037).

90 mins, 54.4718, -3.2177 🏊🅿️🌲🅿️

ENNERDALE

5 ANGLERS' HOTEL, ENNERDALE WATER

There used to be a wonderful lakeside hotel and little jetty at this site, but in 1960 it was demolished to make way for raising

the water level. The scheme was never completed. The shore shelves gradually, so it's good for kids and paddling, especially with water shoes. Easy access, but less known. On the lane between Ennerdale Bridge and Croasdale, a lane is signed 'Ennerdale Water ½' and takes you down past How Hall Farm, to the shore and some parking on the L.

20 mins, 54.5323, -3.4007 🅿🏊🚻🚗

6 ROBIN HOOD'S CHAIR, ENNERDALE

Explore under Angler's Crag for the deepest and clearest water. You can swim anywhere from the shore path, but it's worth heading for the little grass-topped rocky headland called Robin Hood's Chair. The lake is signed from Ennerdale Bridge. Pass CA23 3AS and find the car park at the lane end. Take the lane to towards the shore, but bear off R along the S shore, W, for 1.2km (Bear L for the Anglers' Hotel site.)

15 mins, 54.5236, -3.391 🅿🚶

CRUMMOCK & BUTTERMERE

7 LOWESWATER BOAT & SQUIRRELS

A bridle path follows the wooded far shore of this outlying lake. Secluded, except for the occasional fisherman and plenty of red squirrels. Nearby Holme Wood bothy is great for a rustic lakeside stay. 800m W of Loweswater, dir Mockerkin, turn L down unmarked lane, before the lake. Park at Maggie's Bridge and continue on to Watergate Farm, then on through the woods.

20 mins, 54.5782, -3.353 🅿🏕🚻🚗🏊🚣

8 RIVER COCKER, CRUMMOCK HEAD

Shortly after the River Cocker leaves Crummock Water it twists and turns through a woody dell, creating a lovely deep swimming hole. You can also explore the upper shore and swim from the boathouse beach. Easiest access is along the forest track from Scalehill Bridge. Park at National Trust Lanthwaite car park, 150m SW from Scale Hill Hotel (CA13 9UX). Continue along the track (SE) and you'll see the bend in the river after 800m on your L. Continue another 1.2km to reach the lake and boathouse beach (54.5758, -3.3137) or to the rocky, secluded beach at (54.5664, -3.2994).

15 mins, 54.5778, -3.3144 🅿🚗

9 WOODHOUSE BEACH, CRUMMOCK

Beautiful silver gravel beaches lining SE shore of Crummock Water. Woodhouse

perimeter, no motorised craft allowed, and beautiful sunsets at mid-summer. On the NE shore is a long strand of silver beach with an intriguing tunnel cut through the rocks and wonderful views. Boats can be hired at Gatesgarth Farm. There is no parking on the B5289, so the best option is to park at the E end of lake at bottom of pass, at Gatesgarth Farm car park (54.5237, -3.2457, £4 pay display), then walk 800m to join lake path, then another 800m along shore. From W end, Buttermere village, park beyond Buttermere Court Hotel (01768 770253, CA13 9XA) and follow footpath through Wilkinsyke Farm.

25 mins, 54.5306, -3.2592 🚶🏊⛰️♿

14 WARNSCALE BECK INIFINITY POOL

Views to Butternere and Haystacks make these little infinity plunge pools deservedly popular (see cover image of this book). Park at Gatesgarth Farm pay car park on Honister Pass road (54.5237, -3.2457). Take main footpath (signed Honister Hause) and after 1.2km bear off R to cross footbridge over beck. Then 100m up. Afterwards continue up to the tiny hidden bothy Dubs Hut and quarry ruins (54.5035, -3.2298). Fans of infinity pools should also seek out Comb Beck on S flank of Buttermere, shallower but much less known (54.5245, -3.2650), from the same parking, but head W around lake, taking the upper path via crags (25 mins).

30 mins, 54.5113, -3.2365 🏊🚶⛰️🐕♿

BASSENTHWAITE LAKE

15 SCARNESS, BASSENTHWAITE LAKE

Pebble beach and fun jetty, next to the lodge park. Great for sunsets and views of Lakeland's NW fells, although the A66 can be noisy. Park at end of lane (CA12 4QZ, 54.6635, -3.2105) and follow the signed footpath L. For something more remote we love the idyllic lakeside chapel of St Bega, said to have inspired the opening of Tennyson's Morte d'Arthur (54.6479 -3.2001).

5 mins, 54.6561, -3.2134 🚶🌲♿

16 ST BEGA'S CHURCH, MIREHOUSE

Idyllic lakeside church, said to have inspired the opening of Tennyson's Morte d'Arthur. Layby parking on lane, and signed track (54.6530, -3.1943). Or there's a lovely, longer walk in through Mirehouse estate and gardens on the public footpath (Dood Wood car park, A591, 54.6426, -3.1870).

15 mins, 54.6479, -3.2001 🚶❓

---

beach is near the road, just below some conifers, with islands offshore, or Nether How beach is accessible from the village. From National Trust Buttermere car park, 500m NW of Buttermere village centre (CA13 9UZ), path leads down through woods to both beach areas. Or, if you're early and in a rush, keep going 800m and a gate in the wall on the L leads down from the road (limited roadside parking).

10 mins, 54.547, -3.2892 🚶🏊🐕♿

10 SCALE FORCE, CRUMMOCK

Scale Force is Lakeland's highest waterfall, and tumbles down the northern flank of Red Pike above Crummock Water. It's hidden in a verdant, narrow ravine and provides a very exhilarating plunge in its small pool. The walk there from Buttermere passes along the beautiful beach shore at Nether How. Follow the lane to the L of the Buttermere Court Hotel (0176 87 70253, near CA13 9XA), turn L at the bottom of the car park then as the lane bears R, take the bridleway on R, across the valley bottom water meadows and across the stream footbridge. After 1.6km following the shore path, bear L up Scale Beck to the falls, the path deteriorates rapidly. From the lower falls you'll need to scramble up a slippery

slab of rock on the L to get to the base of the main chute with pool.

30 mins, 54.5414, -3.3148 🚶📷📖

11 BLEABERRY TARN, BUTTERMERE

Wild feeling tarn with craggy peaks of Red Pike and High Stile looming above. The water appears dark but is crystal clear. Water shoes recommended! Parking at Buttermere car park, next to Buttermere Court Hotel (CA13 9XA). Follow path to N tip of lake and over footbridge. Climb through woods, then follow path W towards Sourmilk Gill before reaching tarn.

30 mins, 54.5278, -3.2895 🚶📖

12 BURTNESS WOOD, BUTTERMERE

More remote and secret SW shore is good for morning sun. Backed by a woodland of mainly native trees and larch, carpeted with soft green mosses, including some rare species. Park at Gatesgarth Farm car park (54.5237, -3.2457) and follow the bridleway to Peggy's Bridge and along the SW side of the lake.

25 mins, 54.5298, -3.267 🚶🐕♿

13 HASSNESS TUNNEL, BUTTERMERE

The perfect swimmer's lake, Buttermere has an excellent path around its entire

NORTH FELLS

17 RIVER CALDEW/BOWSCALE TARN

Big, brandy-brown river pool beneath waterfall rapids, in remote valley with juniper bushes, reached on a narrow track. The energetic can scale the fell to swim in Bowscale Tarn. Heading N on the lane from Mungrisdale, turn L at the Mosedale Meeting House (near CA11 0XQ, signed Swineside, at telephone box). After 1.6km Roundhouse old farm complex on L marks path up to Bowscale tarn. Continue another 1.5km to car parking area on L. Pool is immediately below. Carrock tungsten mires are also worth a visit, 800m above the river pool on the gated track.

1 mins, 54.6839, -3.045

18 SCALES TARN & SOUTHER FELL

Follow the beautiful Glendermackin mountain stream, with secret waterfall, to the perfectly round mountain corrie of Scales Tarn at its source. Return via the mysteriously haunted Souther Fell, famed for apparitions on Midsummer Eve! Park by telephone box in Mungrisdale (just N of Mill Inn CA11 0XR, 01768 779632). Head up track past Bannerdale View cottage and follow river path, with Souther Fell up on

your L. After 3.2km there is a little waterfall in a steep gorge (tricky descent, 54.6433, -3.0147). 500m later cross footbridge for ascent to the tarn.

100 mins, 54.6436, -3.0416

DERWENT WATER

19 LORD'S ISLAND, DERWENT

Once the home of the Earl of Derwentwater and his great house (you can still make out the foundations). It's now an enjoyable 100m swim to the island for those that fancy attempting it. As for Calfclose Bay (see entry), then walk N along shore for 300m.

5 mins, 54.5866, -3.1382

20 CALFCLOSE BAY, DERWENT WATER

Beautiful beach with an unusual split boulder sculpture marking 100 years of the National Trust. Depending on the season it may be semi- or fully submerged. Park at Great Wood car park (off B5289 about 2km S of Keswick). Cross the road and head through the woods for the nearest shore (about 200m; the second cove has the sculpture). Canoes and rowing boats can be hired from nearby Friar's Crag CA12 5DJ

5 mins, 54.5836, -3.1339

21 STONEYCROFT GHYLL SCRAMBLE

Adventurous little gill with small slides and deep pools. Descend to the stream at the road bridge and paddle/wade up through the slot canyon until the waterfall, or join an organised group. More pools/caves to explore in the higher reaches too. Follow Regional Rte 71 from Braithwaite towards Little Town for 2km. 300m after turning to Uzzicar Farm, find parking on L. Follow the miners' track opposite parking area up the valley to reach the stream higher up, or walk down the road for 500m to bridge and head up the stream from there. Join a led expedition at cragsadventures.com (0153 95 96317).

15 mins, 54.5799, -3.1962

22 MYRTLE BAY, DERWENT WATER

This stretch of secluded wooded bays and coves is perhaps the best of its kind in the Lakes. Explore Myrtle Bay, Abbot's Bay, Otter Island and Brandelhow boathouses. Join the wide gravel track (Cumbria Way) on the Grange to Newlands road (54.5542, -3.1595, about 100m S of Manesty holiday cottages CA12 5UG – park on the road). Bear L where it joins the lake shore at Great Bay after about 1.2km. Alternatively continue N another mile on the lane

293

towards Newlands, past Manesty caravan park, and drop down on the path L to the landing stage from 54.5634, -3.1631. Paddleboards for hire from nearby Lodore Landings (CA12 5UX).

20 mins, 54.5625, -3.1535

23 GOWDER DUB, RIVER DERWENT

Popular stretch of river for swimming, thanks mainly to its location below Hollows campsite. Lovely big beach with shallows and deeper stretch for a longer swim downstream. Park at the Bowderstone car park (about 600m S of turning for Grange on B5289), cross the road and follow the river path upstream 300m to reach the bend. Or via the campsite (CA12 5UQ, 0176 87 77298) from the opposite shore. Explore further 'dubs' and pools upstream following the Cumbria Way. One of the better stretches is Stang Dub (54.5284, -3.1557) where the Stonethwaite Beck joins (also accessible from Rosthwaite on the footpath past the Flock-in cafe, towards the river footbridge, direction Rigghead quarries).

5 mins, 54.5388, -3.1589

24 WATENDLATH TARN

Pretty and easily accessible tarn by a farm with a tearoom and good beachy areas.

Brownish water and a sharp drop-off into deeper water. Signed Ashness Br/ Watendlath from the B5289 towards Grange from Keswick. Cream teas and parking at the Caffle House tearoom (CA12 5UW). Bear round to the R of the lake on the footpath to swim. There's fishing here too, so don't disturb their sport.

5 mins, 54.5363, -3.1224

BORROWDALE FELLS

25 GALLENY FORCE, STONETHWAITE

Two sets of sparkling pools and cascades (the lower ones often missed), with grassy knolls and ancient rowan trees. Not deep, but fun for plunging, snorkelling and picnics. 10km S of Keswick (B5289), after Rosthwaite, turn L at crossroads with post box in wall signed Langstrath Country Inn (carry on along lane beyond CA12 5XG) and follow lane to Stonethwaite. If camping, continue on rough track for further 600m to park at Stonethwaite riverside campsite (0176 87 77234). The path above the campsite leads through the woods 800m to find first set of pools, below on L, followed by the main pool after another 200m.

15 mins, 54.5073, -3.1234

26 BLACKMOSS POT, LANGSTRATH

Iconic deep pot/mini-gorge with 15-foot cliff for jumping (actually quite tame). Popular with teenagers at weekends. Fun to swim upstream into the gorge and pot. From Galleny, continue along the river path a further 2.4km. It's about 200m after Blea Rock, the house-sized boulder on far L, 100m off the path. More pools further upstream (Swan Dub, Tray Dub).

30 mins, 54.4918, -3.1328

27 STOCKLEY BRIDGE, GRAINS GILL

An ancient stone packhorse bridge with a lovely pool just below it. Take the main track up through Seathwaite Farm (CA12 5XJ, car park adjacent) for 1.6km to the bridge. The track crosses here and continues on up to either Sprinkling Tarn or Styhead Tarn.

20 mins, 54.4877, -3.1828

28 SPRINKLING TARN, ROSTHWAITE

A high tarn (600m) in the shadow of Scafell Pike, with island for jumps and dives and excellent swimming. Good for wild camping. Styhead Tarn is also close, and Lambfoot Dub (see entry). From Wasdale Head (CA20 1EX, car park) via Moses Trod path to Styhead and on SW. Also feasible from Seathwaite to the N (signed from CA12 5XH) and Great Langdale to the SE (LA22 9JY car park at Old Dungeon Ghyll Hotel dip in Angle Tarn on the way).

20 mins, 54.4725, -3.1922

THIRLMERE

29 THIRLMERE & INFINITY POOL

Lake beach and infamous infinity pools above. The reservoir was created by the construction of a dam in 1894 to provide water for Manchester. Technically No Swimming but it's popular for paddling on the beaches below Station Coppice layby pay car park (A591). The series of waterfalls are high on Fisherplace Gill above, best accessed on the bridleway behind the King's Head Inn and camping, 700m N along the main road (CA12 4TN) From there it's about 1km and 150m ascent. At the falls, take care as a slip could be fatal and in high flow you could be swept over the lip.

20 mins, 54.5435, -3.0592

30 HARROP TARN

The waters of Harrop Tarn have a unique golden shimmer and you can swim amongst beautiful yellow waterlilies. Signed Armboth off A591 at S end of lake (CA12 4TP). Continue 1.7km to Dob Gill Car Park (CA12 4TP). Take the footpath heading SW up to forested fell, following Dob Gill. After 700m, continue right around tarn to N shore to small gravel spit.

10 mins, 54.5134, -3.0661

ULLSWATER

31 AIRA BECK WATERFALLS

Beautiful series of waterfalls above Aira Force. First are some enchanting small falls and plunge pools in the trees. Continue downstream to a wooden bridge, High Force, with ledges great for jumping. Continue further downstream and finally you come to a stone bridge at Aira Force itself. The best approach is actually from above. Take the Dockray (CA11 0JY) road off the A592 along Ullswater. After 1.5km, and beyond the NT Aira Force car park R, find large double layby (54.5815, -2.9344). Park and walk down across the meadow to find the first pools.

30 mins, 54.5793, -2.9289

32 KAILPOT CRAG, HOWTOWN

This high, craggy cliff beneath Hallin Fell plummets into deep water. Great for jumps and snorkelling. Wood behind, beach alongside; it's a great spot. Take the ferry to

Howtown and follow the shore path 1.6km SW. Or take Howtown road from Pooley Bridge at N end of Ullswater; you will pass several beaches en route and Park Foot camping (CA10 2NA, 0176 84 86309) has lakeshore pitches. Follow 6.4km to Howtown pier (tricky parking) or approach from Sandwick Bay (see entry)

20 mins, 54.5763, -2.8734

33 SANDWICK BAY, ULLSWATER

Beautiful, tree-backed bay on the edge of Hallinhag Wood, hidden away on the remoter S shores of Ullswater. There's some parking at Sandwick (turning 2.4km SW of Howtown, before CA10 2NF). Follow the footpath through the far right gate, over the stream, and continue to the shore.

10 mins, 54.5716, -2.8886

34 SILVER BAY & LINGY HOLM ISLAND

Juniper and heather hug the crags and a little path leads down through the bracken to this secluded silver shingle beach If approaching from Side Farm/Patterdale you'll pass offshore islets and rocky outcrops, and you might like to swim out to Lingy Holm islets, about 50m from the shore. There's oak woodland here and Silver Crag (271m) makes a great mini climb,

returning on the upper path. If you plan to enjoy the refreshment at the Side Farm tea shop (CA11 0NL, 0176 84 82337) you can park here (signed on R coming down into Patterdale, before the church). The path goes along the back of the campsite and continues for 2km. Look out for the path to Silver Bay after you've rounded Silver Point on the R.

40 mins, 54.5573, -2.934

35 MOSSDALE BAY & NORFOLK ISLAND

This is a fun and very easily accessible stretch of shore, right by the road with a mossy knoll. If you have a canoe, you can paddle out to Norfolk Island – it's very small but has some fun boulders to jump from (take care). Park at one of the layby parking areas at 54.5526, -2.9489 (CA11 0NQ).

2 mins, 54.5545, -2.9493

HELVELLYN AREA

36 GLENRIDDING BECK DUB

Lovely little waterfall and deep pool hidden in a wooded fold of the beck, on the main path to Helvellyn, 600m W of the YHA. The whole beck is superb for ghyll scrambling and gorge walking.

20 mins, 54.5456, -2.9904

37 RED TARN, HELVELLYN

718 metres above sea level and nestled beneath the shadow of Helvellyn's craggy peak, this is one of the finest swimming spots in the Lake District. From Glenridding car park (CA11 0PA), follow road to YHA Helvellyn (CA11 0QR) and, after 300m, cross footbridge and veer R to follow Glenridding Beck (see entry). After 2nd footbridge, follow path SW along Red Tarn Beck all the way up to Red Tarn. Or arrive in style via the superb Striding Edge ridge scramble.

80 mins, 54.5296, -3.0058

38 ANGLE TARN, BANNERDALE

One of the most enticing spots in the Lake District, with three rocky islands, ledges and places to dive. Fabulous views. Few visitors. A fun gill scramble up Angletarn Beck from Hartsop (CA11 0NY) near Patterdale.

90 mins, 54.5214, -2.9015

39 BROTHERS WATER, HARTSOP

Just 500m wide in every direction, this is one of the smallest lakes in the Lake District, but is surprisingly cool and refreshing for a swim. Easy access. 3.2km S of Patterdale on the A592, park at Cow

Bridge (CA11 0NZ). Follow the riverside path S, upstream towards lake. After 400m, take path down to shore.

5 mins, 54.5089, -2.9254 🏊🚶

HAWESWATER & SWINDALE

40 THE RIGG & CORPSE ROAD

This distinctive wooded peninsula drops steeply into Haweswater – in dry weather and at low water large beaches appear. From here you can swim out to Wood Howe islet over the flooded village of Mardale (occasionally exposed at very low water). On the opposite shore the Old Corpse Road rises, on its way to Shap Abbey. From Bampton follow the Haweswater road (via CA10 2RP turn) to Mardale Head parking (often overspills up road) at 54.4891, -2.8218. Take the main path, heading for the mountain, but turn R immediately, along the wall, round to the wooded Rigg and its steep shore. Easier, you can stop at one of the wider stretches near gates and drop down to the shore.

20 mins, 54.4973, -2.8114 🏊🔵✝️

41 SMALL WATER & ROCK SHELTERS

It's a good hike up to Small Water but it makes a beautiful swim in crystal waters.

There are numerous strange rock shelters on the far bank in case you decide to camp. From here you can climb up to High Street plateau. As for the Rigg peninsula (see entry), but take the main track up the mountain, keeping R.

60 mins, 54.4835, -2.8411 🏊🔵🔵🏔️

42 RIVER LOWTHER, ASKHAM

A scramble down to a wooded, rocky gorge with deep pools. A little shady but good fun. This is a pretty village with two pubs, two community-run heated outdoor swimming pools and Askham Hall with its fabulous kitchen-garden restaurant. Park near the bridge and follow the path upstream 150m, on the opposite bank to the church. The swimming pool is next door to the Queen's Head Pub and shares facilities with Askham Village Hall (CA10 2PN, 01931 712999). It's also fun to cycle/walk through the Lowther parkland along the footpath to Low Gardens Bridge (two bridges in fact, 54.6181, -2.7431).

5 mins, 54.6064, -2.7467 🏊🔵🔵🏠🔵🔵

43 SWINDALE BECK WATERFALLS

Brilliant series of high falls and deep pools in this remote and less-visited valley. Perfect for secluded swimming, but quite a

walk in. From M6 at J39 head to Shap, then L following signs for Rosgill. 500m after Rosgill and crossing the river, take hairpin L signed Swindale. Park at road end CA10 2QT, walk up to farmhouse (or someone can do a drop-off there – but no parking), then follow beck up for 1.6km. The main waterfall pools are on the L but there are many good deep slab pools higher too.

40 mins, 54.4956, -2.7591 🚶🔵

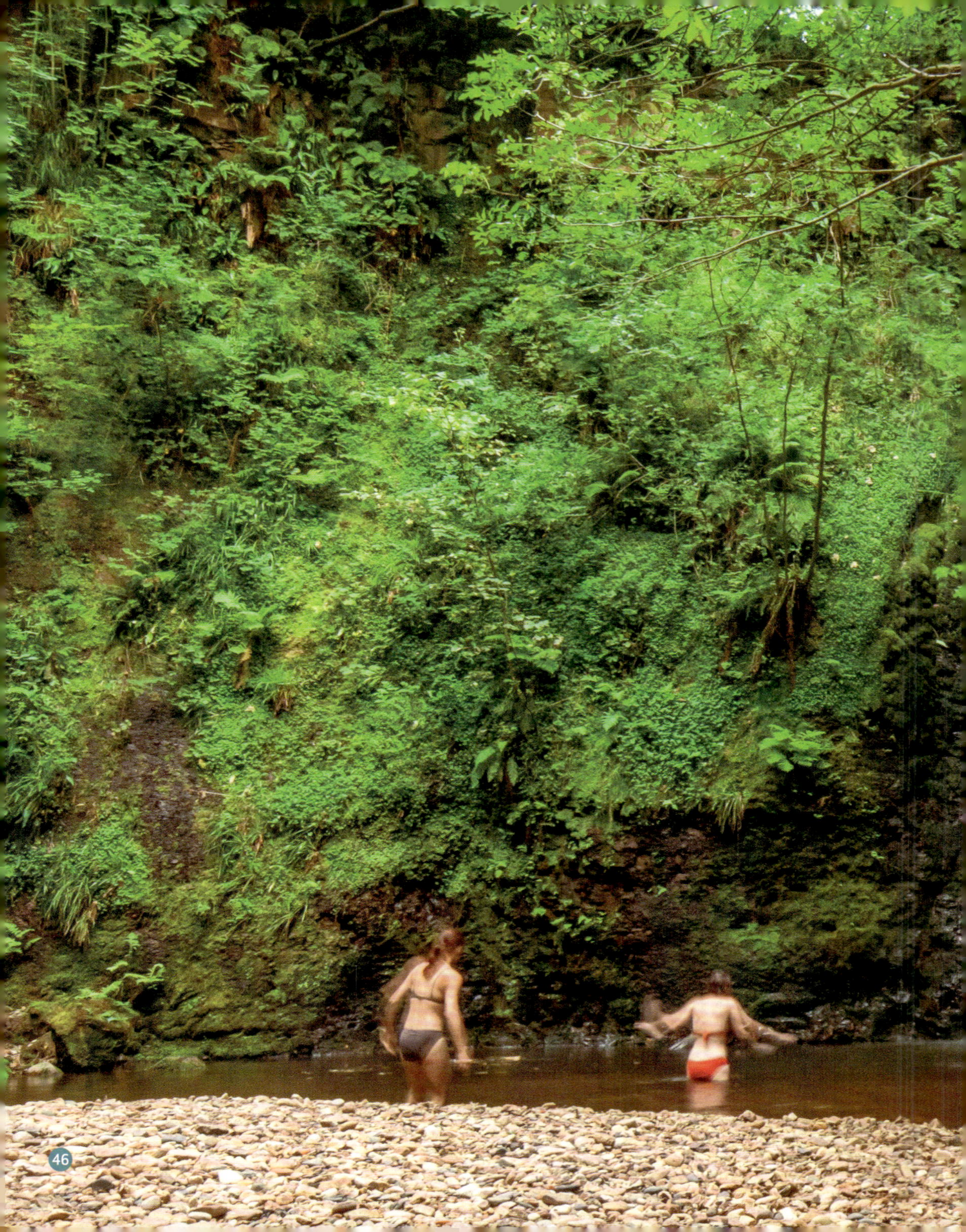

PENNINES &
YORK MOORS

Heading along the spine of Lune Moor, great long trails of pink cloud reached into the sky. I camped by moonlight in a large meadow on the banks of the River Tees, close to Low Force (22), before continuing on to Hadrian's Wall. The plan was to find the shrine of the water goddess Coventina and swim in the same spots as the Romans at Chesters Fort and Broomlee (6,8).

The North Pennines traditionally marked the last frontiers of Roman Britain; a great march of barren hills and plunging dales that grew more desolate as they reached the border with the Picts. For the southern Mediterranean Roman soldiers stationed here in the second and third centuries AD, the wet climate must have been very different from their dry and dusty homeland. They brought with them an adoration for springs, running water and river gods, all of which were to be found aplenty in ancient Britain. At Brocolita Fort on Hadrian's Wall, they built one of the best-preserved 'nymphaeum' shrines in the country. The water temple consisted of three altars to the part-Celtic, part-Roman water goddess Coventina. The inscriptions show her reclining with flagons and palms, protecting the three springs with her nymph assistants.

The great wall was begun in AD 122 and acted as a working defence for over two hundred years. Its remains run intermittently across the countryside; in some places, a ragged ruin – much was taken to build the roads of Newcastle in the eighteenth century – but in more remote parts, there are miles of surviving fortifications with milecastles and forts still standing among crags and tarns. In this central Pennine section, the wall hugs a long dolerite escarpment, a natural defence, with lakes forming in the depressions below.

The Romans were very keen bathers, and though there was a bathhouse at Brocolita, it couldn't compare to that at Chesters Fort, three milecastles down the River Tyne at Chollerford. With

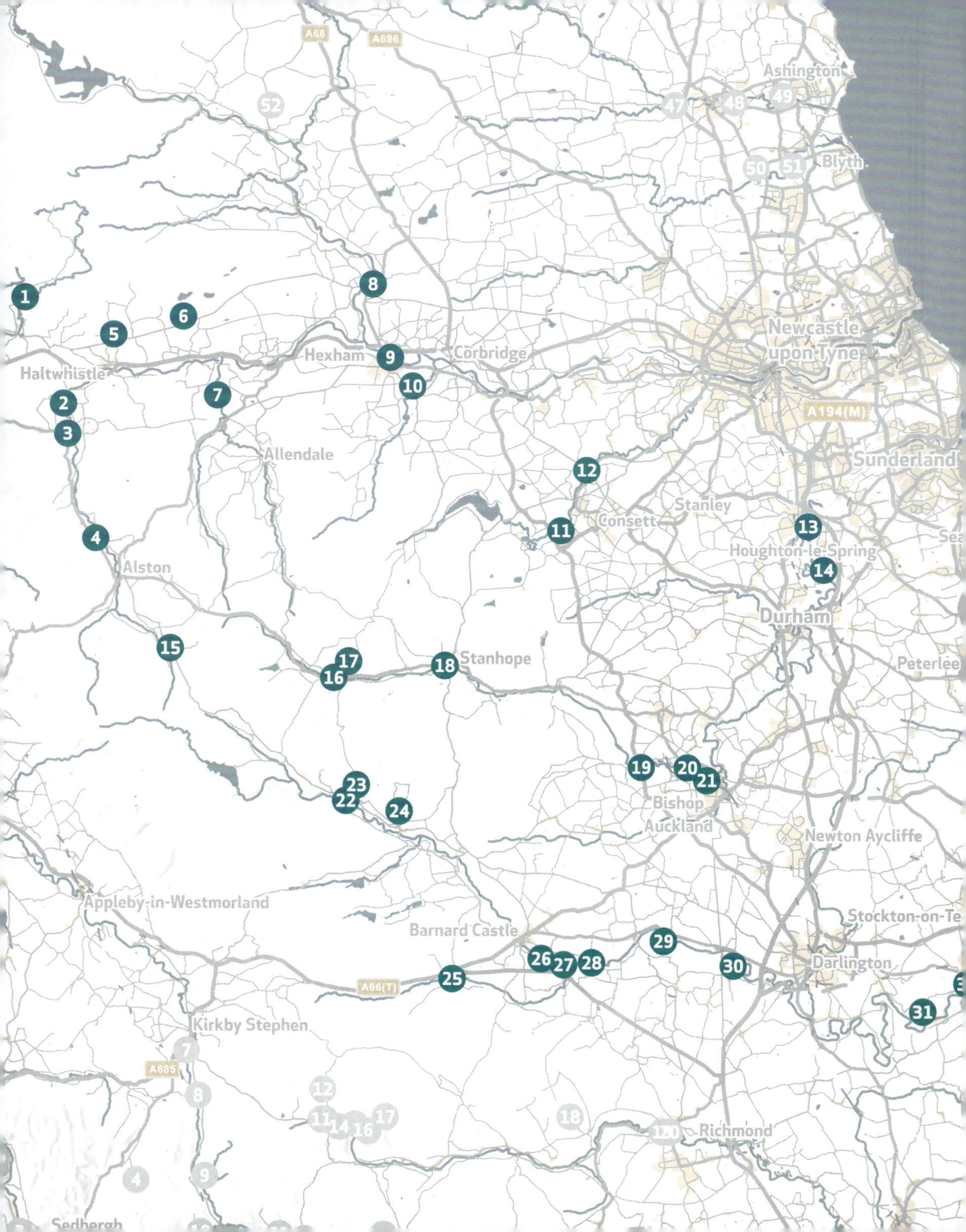
A68
A696
Ashington
Blyth
Haltwhistle
Hexham
Corbridge
Newcastle upon Tyne
A194(M)
Sunderland
Allendale
Stanley
Consett
Houghton-le-Spring
Durham
Alston
Stanhope
Peterlee
Bishop Auckland
Newton Aycliffe
Appleby-in-Westmorland
Barnard Castle
Stockton-on-Te
Darlington
A66(T)
Kirkby Stephen
A685
Richmond
Sedbergh

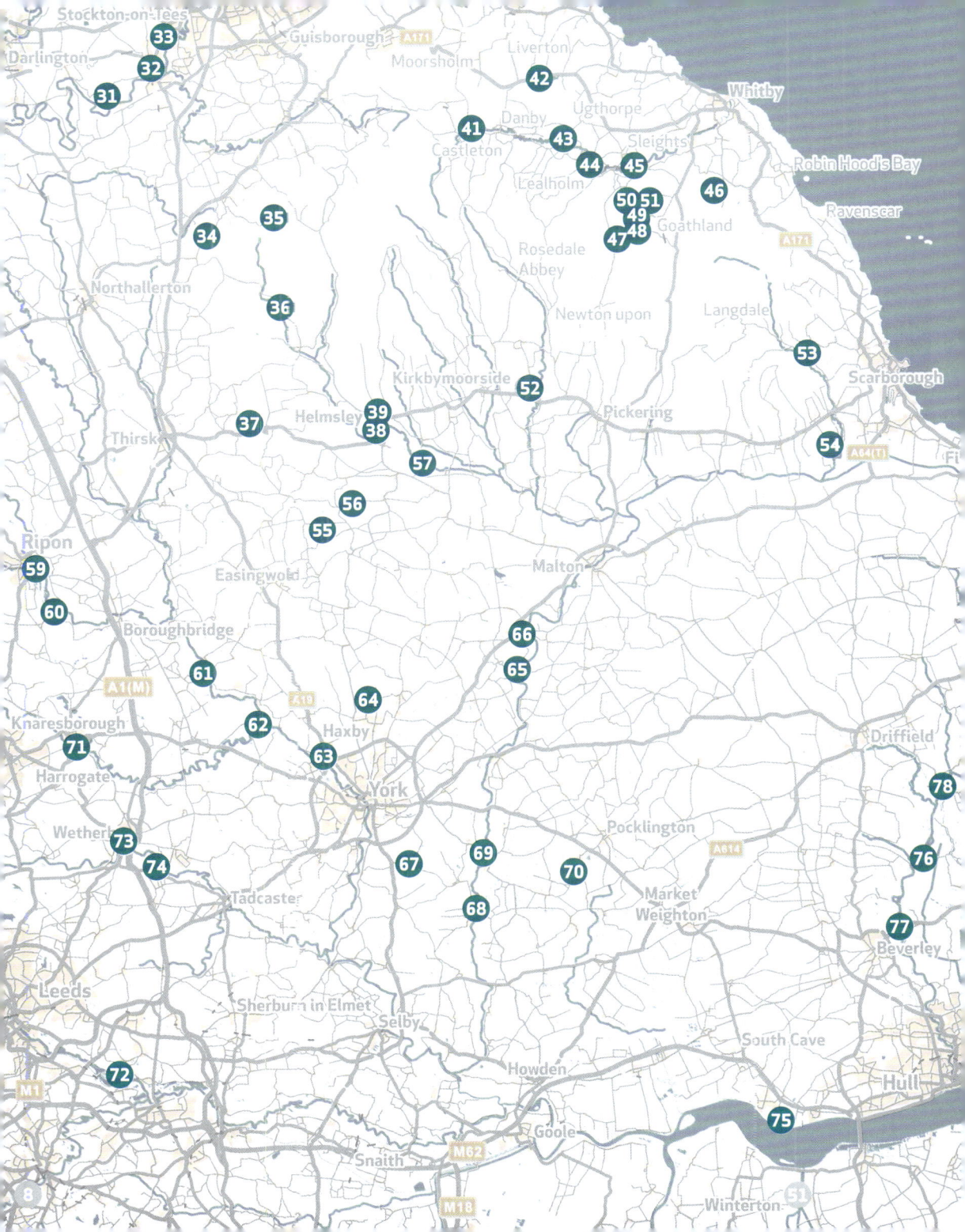

its endless supply of river water, they were able to build a large bathing house complex. Its sixteen interconnecting chambers contained warm, hot, and steam rooms, and, of course, the cold plunge pools that are so central to Roman hydrotherapies. There was once a great Roman bridge here, and you can now paddle in the stream among the original bridge stones, scattered around like blocks from the Colosseum, or swim downstream at Chollerford. Some years ago, old Roman coins were found among the rocks, and there are doubtless other treasures lurking in the riverbed.. The Romans were also excellent swimmers – it was a requirement for a Roman soldier to be able to swim across a river in spate with full battle kit – but they would have had little challenge here. The river is mainly shallow in the vicinity of the ruined bridge, but there are deeper holes if you explore a little way downstream on the far bank (8).

The main Roman swimming was at Housesteads Fort, the most extensive and best-preserved of Roman wall fortifications, and three milecastles to the west of Brocolita. Broomlee Lough is just 500 yards down from the fort, across the moor into no-man's land. Today, the local farming families still gather here once a year for their summer swimming party in the overhanging eaves of Dove Crag. The tarn is large, mainly shallow, and surprisingly tepid, but at this crag end, the water is deeper, and the cliffs provide enough shelter from the wind for the mallard, tufted duck, goldeneye and coots that make forays out from the reeds to paddle under the great Northumberland sky. The National Trust owners are not so keen, however, so try Crag Lough instead (6).

While the Pennines are primarily made of limestone and gritstone, the North York Moors to the south-east are predominantly sandstone and shale, forming large areas of heather moorland. Sutton Bank offers the finest view in England, according to the real James Herriot. From here, you can see for miles across the Vale of York to the Dales. Halfway down the escarpment, romantically nestled in the woods, is the emerald oval of Gormire Lake (37). The water of Gormire Lake is quite warm, and you'll most likely be the only person swimming there when you go. This is a quiet and secluded place to visit among broad-leaved woodlands: a breeding place for coot, great crested grebe, and mallard, sheltered by higher ground. A steep path leads down from Sutton Bank, the top of the escarpment. Alf Wight, better known by his fictional name James Herriot, had his veterinary practice in Thirsk (Darrowby in the books) about five miles away. He often visited Gormire Lake.

The tarn was formed 20,000 years ago by glacial erosion, and folk tales and legends of Gormire abound, many involving horses. One tells of a local knight who tricked the Abbot of Rievaulx into lending him his white mare. The mare would not respond to his commands, jumped off Sutton Bank, and plunged him into the lake, with the Abbot behind transformed into the devil. Ambitious schoolmaster John Hodgson was so inspired by this tale and a recent trip to the white horses of Wiltshire that in 1857, he and 31 volunteers decided to carve out their own horse from the escarpment. It was badly damaged by a hailstorm in 1896 and fell into disrepair after the First World War, but was renewed in 1925, and today it is the most northerly white horse in England.

The steep, twisting road that leads up to Sutton Bank threatens horrible things to caravans as it rises onto the Yorkshire Moors proper. From here, 40 miles of heather and gorse flow in undulating ridges to the sea. There are few large rivers, but several smaller becks and woodland waterfalls near the coast at Whitby. One of the best falls is just below the famous village of Goathland, through which the North Yorkshire Moors Railway steams. Goathland is the setting for TV's Heartbeat, and the station was also used for Hogsmeade Station in the Harry Potter films – the shop on the platform was transformed into the Prefects' Room, and the ladies' toilets became the Wizards' Room. The Thomason Foss waterfall is approached from the picturesque Becks Hole pub and bridge a mile down the road. It's a short walk up through woods to a west-facing rocky pool in a sunlit glade, where families often come to play in rubber dinghies and swim under the falls (50).

Even closer to Whitby, on the other side of the A169, is Falling Foss, romantically set in deep woods by the fairy-tale cottage of Midge Hall (46). Set over a deep black chasm into which a small stream flows, smoke was billowing from the chimney, and in the evening light it was a scene reminiscent of Hansel and Gretel. It's a fair trek to reach the bottom of the falls, backtracking and then picking a way along the overgrown stream bed. Standing on the shingle beach looking up, the waterfall flows down the jet-black cliff like a white veil, breaking into hundreds of competing rivulets.

We dived in and swam over to sit on the ledges beneath the water. In the cooling evening air, this was certainly a cold dip, but the dark green mosses and jungle-like setting made this place feel strangely exciting: like finding a secret passageway to a lost world.

TYNE & HADRIAN'S WALL

1 CRAMMEL LINN, R IRTHING
Spectacular 7.5m-waterfall, Northumberland's biggest. Vast pool on wild moor strewn with derelict military tanks, as adjacent to military training area. Check red flags. Popular spot on a hot day. Head 1.5km W of Gilsland, over bridge and uphill past Gilsland Spa. Continue for another 2.5km and take 'no through road' R turn over cattle grid. Find parking by signed footpath on R after 1.5km, on far edge of forest.

10 mins, 55.0202, -2.5637

2 FEATHERSTONE CASTLE, R SOUTH TYNE
A superb, accessible swim spot near Featherstone Castle. Suntrap sandy beach on hot days. Deeper water towards the centre of the river, shallows for paddling and flat rocks on the opposite bank for jumping. Beautiful situation. River can be flashy here. On the A69 heading towards Carlisle, 1 mile beyond the Haltwhistle turn-off, turn L on to Bellister Bank and continue for 1.5km, then take a slight R turn and continue for a further 1.5km, passing Haltwhistle Campsite, to parking on R before footbridge over river. Follow footpath on L of riverbank to beaches. Also check out Featherstone Bridge, a km downstream with beach, deep pools and flat, rocky slabs (54.9504, -2.5077).

5 mins, 54.9415, -2.5141

3 LAMBLEY VIADUCT, R SOUTH TYNE
Pebble beach and pools beneath the impressive Lambley Viaduct with its elegant stone arches. The 260m-long structure once carried trains from Alston to Haltwhistle, transporting coal and lead from the surrounding mines. Follow the A689 N to Lambley. After Lambley village take R turn and follow road for 2km to Lambley Viaduct South Tyne Trail car park on L at 54.9298, -2.5015. Follow way-marked South Tyne Trail, then cross viaduct then footpath to R to footbridge to pebble beach on other side.

20 mins, 54.9191, -2.5085

4 KIRKHAUGH, R SOUTH TYNE
Peaceful swim spot by new footbridge over the River South Tyne. Mostly paddling with some deeper pools and large pebble beach. Near Kirkhaugh station on Alston narrow-gauge railway. Perfect picnic spot. From Alston follow the A689 N for around 3km towards Slaggyford. After Nook Farm Shop, find lay-by parking on L at 54.8352, -2.4752. Cross road to follow Pennine Way towards Dyke House, then continue over railway bridge at Kirkhaugh station. Cross field to footbridge over river.

20 mins, 54.8407, -2.4721

5 CAWFIELD QUARRY, HADRIAN'S WALL
Picturesque lake with cliffs in a former quarry. Above is one of the most scenic stretches of Hadrian's Wall along the sheer crags of Whin Sill. 'No Swimming' signs, although it's popular with swimmers, so make your own choice. Cawfield is clearly signposted from the Military Road. Park in Cawfield's car park by the lake.

1 mins, 54.993, -2.4499

6 CRAG LOUGH
The most magical of the four lakes along the wall, Crag Lough sits directly below the sheer Whin Sill crags. It is a natural eutrophic lake, so be mindful of blue-green algae. From Steel Rigg car park, continue E along the wall for 2km, past the dip of Sycamore Gap, to woodland on L. Just before gate a small path leads down to shore. Alternatively, pass through gate to open meadow and shoreline.

20 mins, 55.0065, -2.3610

7 PLANKEY MILL, R ALLEN

Beautiful wooded riverside walks through NT Allen Banks and Staward Gorge. Beach with rocky slabs and deep pools around 1km downstream of Plankey Mill (54.9449, -2.3152). Continue downstream for more beaches and pools. 3 miles SW of Haydon Bridge on the A686. Parking Allen Banks NT pay and display car park (NE47 7BP).

50 mins, 54.9482, -2.3166 🚶🏊🅿️⚠️🏕️

8 CHOLLERFORD, R NORTH TYNE

Deep, calm stretch of the Tyne upstream of Chollerford bridge and weir, with several entry points along the riverside path. Chollerford is 5km N of Hexham. Parking at Chesters Roman Fort (closes 5.30pm). Walk along road to roundabout, cross bridge and follow riverside path upstream.

20 mins, 55.031, -2.1184 🏊🚶

9 TYNE GREEN, R TYNE

Good access to the Tyne from steps and jetty by the 18th-century bridge with beautiful parkland and mature trees. From Hexham follow Haugh Lane straight across roundabout on to the A6079, then turn L on to Tyne Green Road and signs to country park (NE46 3HR) and parking.

2 mins, 54.9767, -2.0960 🏊🚶🏊🚻

10 SWALLOWSHIP POOL, DEVIL'S WATER

The steep, sandstone walls of a secluded gorge shimmer in the calm waters of this deep, clear pool on the evocatively named Devil's Water. This is a delightful location reached by a pretty woodland trail. Lay-by parking by Kingswood Education and Outdoor Centre (NE46 1TP), N of Linnels Bridge on the B6306. Take footpath into woods, past Duke's House to fork in path near ruins of Five Gates House. Turn R along path through Scots Pines. Turn R when path ends and follow path above Devil's Water to steep, uneven path to burn and pool.

30 mins, 54.9555, -2.0672 🏊🚶🏃‍♂️🅿️⚠️🏕️

DERWENT & LOWER WEAR

11 ALLENSFORD PARK, R DERWENT

An accessible and shaded stretch of the Wear with deep pools for swimming, beaches and paddling. Café at campsite in park. Heading N from Castleside on the A68, take R at Allensford Park to car park and river. To visit nearby Wharnley Burn Falls, a pretty hidden waterfall in a tranquil wooded ravine, cross road to footpath to L of bridge. Follow path upstream to waterfall (54.8446, -1.8849).

2 mins, 54.8476, -1.8765 🏖️🏊🚶

12 EBCHESTER BOATHOUSE, R DERWENT

The boathouse stands next to a weir, forming a large, wide, calm pool on the River Derwent, giving easy access to the water from a small jetty. Popular with rowers, kayakers and swimmers. Driving W through Ebchester on the A694, turn R on to the B6309, Chare Bank, and the boathouse is on the L at the bottom of the hill. Limited parking on a lay-by by the boathouse.

2 mins, 54.8932, -1.8438 🏊🛶

13 LUMLEY BRIDGE, R WEAR

Leisurely stretch of river in the shadow of Durham's cricket ground. Popular with paddleboarders and the rowing club. Easy access from a jetty at the Riverside Sports Complex by Lumley Bridge. From Chester-le-Street follow the B6313 to Park Road N/A167, then turn L at roundabout on to Ropery Lane and Riverside car park.

2 mins, 54.8514, -1.5601 🏊

14 FINCHALE PRIORY, R WEAR

Paddling and pools at a meander of the River Wear as it flows past the expansive ruins of 12th century Finchale Priory. From High Carr Rd in Durham, at roundabout take 3rd exit on to Finchale Rd. Continue on to Old Pit Ln, then at roundabout take 2nd exit to stay on Old Pit Ln. At next roundabout take 3rd exit on to Finchale Rd/Ave, then L turn at prison. Road swings to R. Continue to parking at bottom of hill by priory (site closes at 5pm). More secluded spots with deeper pools, beaches and a rope swing on the opposite bank reached by crossing the footbridge and following the riverside paths upstream through Cocken Wood (54.8178, -1.5383) or parking at Cocken Road car park (lay-by) at 54.8196, -1.5388 and following path or steps down to river.

5 mins, 54.8187, -1.5403 🚶

UPPER WEAR

15 ASHGILL FORCE

Spectacular 16m-curtain waterfall that you can walk behind, by way of a rocky shelf, when not in flood. Situated in a beautiful deep gorge with pools for paddling and dipping in. Many smaller waterfalls further downstream with deeper pools. Park in Garrigill (lay-by parking S of village at 54.7649, -2.3955). After a few hundred metres, follow footpath sign on L, then cross Windshaw Bridge to South Tyne Trail. Follow river upstream for 1.5km, passing small waterfalls and plunge pools.

35 mins, 54.7588, -2.3762 ⚠️🧗

16 ST JOHN'S CHAPEL, R WEAR

Gorgeous natural swimming pool with falls just off the Weardale Way. Grassy bank for picnics and a wide beach. Park in St John's Chapel (on the A689). Then walk to river and follow the Weardale Way riverside path downstream for 800m to pool. Further upstream, find shallows and more pools near old stone bridge at Ireshopeburn (54.7420, -2.1936).

15 mins, 54.7374, -2.1665 🏊🚶🌊

17 SLITT WOOD WATERFALLS & TARN

A picturesque trail through ash and wych elm woodland beside a series of waterfalls, pools ending in a small lake. The step-like rocks are due to repeated layers of limestone, sandstone and shale wearing away at different rates. At the end of the trail are the remains of Slitt and Middlehope Mines, with pools and a tunnel you can swim through. Travelling W along the A689 in Westgate (Front Street) look for lay-by on R to park (54.7372, -2.1479). Walk W along Front St, turning R just before the Primitive Methodist Chapel (one of the best preserved of its kind in the north). Follow footpath, keeping R at the houses with the burn on the R. Cross footbridge, pass High Mill and go through a kissing gate into the woods, following burn on L. After 1km climb up W to find the circular mineworks reservoir/lake hidden behind embankment with spectacular sunset views (you can also drive up and park here on the lane, to start the walk higher up, 54.7462, -2.1539). Or bear up E to the old ironstone quarry at West Rigg Opencut.

5 mins, 54.747, -2.1475 🚶🧗

18 STANHOPE OLD BRIDGE, R WEAR

Deep pools with slabs and ledges beneath an attractive old stone bridge. Stepping stones further downstream towards village. From Stanhope head W on the A689, then take L on to the B6278 to parking in lay-by on L just before bridge. Cross bridge to river access on opp bank. Stepping stones at 54.7473, -2.0156.

2 mins, 54.7466, -2.0244 🏊🚶🧗

19 WITTON-LE-WEAR, R WEAR

A pleasant stretch of the Wear with a beach area, paddling and a pool deep enough for a swim up to 70m. From Witton-le-Wear follow road, Clemmy Bank, S to Witton Bridge. Park on L just before bridge and follow riverside path downstream to swim spot.

5 mins, 54.6717, -1.7722 🏊🚶🏊

20 ESCOMB VILLAGE, R WEAR
Wide beach and river pools deep enough for swimming near Escomb lake. Park in Escomb village by church (DL14 7SY). Follow Dunelm Chare and footpath behind church to river. Historic St John's Church is the most complete Saxon church in England with the earliest surviving example of a sundial in its original setting.
5 mins, 54.6665, -1.7021

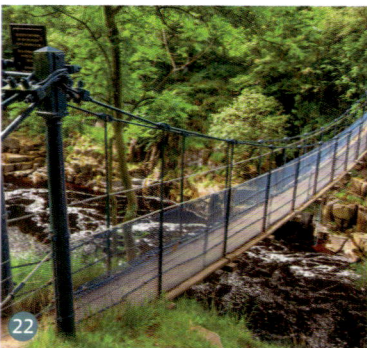

21 BISHOP AUCKLAND, R WEAR
Popular with families and teenagers, this lovely stretch of the Wear has several beaches and is deep enough for a decent swim. Never feels overcrowded as there is plenty of room for everyone. Parking at rugby club layby (54.6638, -1.6874).
5 mins, 54.6647, -1.6906

UPPER TEES

22 LOW FORCE, R TEES
Lesser-known sister of High Force, about 2.5km downstream with a deep pool on a side channel by a wooded island reached across dry rocks (54.6495, -2.1654) and a long gorge beneath the Wynch Bridge. Located 6.5km NW of Middleton-in-Teesdale on the B6277. Park at lay-by by junction, 200m after Bowlees Visitor Centre sign. Follow path down to bridge and falls (300m). Afterwards continue along the Pennine Way to admire thundering High Force and 700m beyond is Bleabeck Force, a delightful waterfall on a tributary of the Tees, small pools and paddling. Basic riverside camping 2.5km downstream of Low Force on opp bank at Low Way Farm, Holwick (DL12 0NJ, 01833 640506).
5 mins, 54.6464, -2.1505

23 SUMMERHILL FORCE & GIBSON'S CAVE
Several pretty woodland plunge pools with paddling, leading to a waterfall and large cave overhang with plunge pool. Easy access for paddling/swim halfway between the falls and the cave at 54.6525, -2.1439. The cave is named after William Gibson, a lovable 16th-century rogue who hid here while on the run. From Bowlees Visitor Centre car park (DL12 0XF), keep R to follow riverside path upstream to Summerhill Force then beyond for cave.
10 mins, 54.6528, -2.1414

24 HUDESHOPE BECK WATERFALL
Hudeshope Beck cuts a deep gorge, forming a pool and scouring caves into its banks. The pool makes a great swim spot and those daring enough might jump from the waterfall with care. Perfect secluded picnic spot with a bit of adventure. Around 1km downstream another low waterfall forms a wide pool, creating a shaded swim spot in a river gorge. From the B6277 through Middleton-in-Teesdale, turn R on to Town Head to King's Walk on the L. Parking after 1/3 mile in lay-by on L. Follow King's Walk to a section of steel barriers on the L to find the waterfall. Scramble down from either side of the bank and walk up gorge to pool.
15 mins, 54.6387, -2.0822

25 MILL FORCE

A bend in the River Greta, close to the town of Bowes, forms a wide pool and waterfall, perfect for swimming. From Bowes take the road S to Gilmonby. At the bridge over the river there is a small lay-by on R before bridge, where you will also find the footpath to the falls.

5 mins, 54.5145, -2.0134

26 EGGLESTONE ABBEY BRIDGE, R TEES

Beneath the high arch of Egglestone Abbey Bridge, the River Tees cuts through, forming a deep gorge with rocks and pools ideal for swimming. Daring young locals climb the rocks to plunge into the river below. Approx 2.5km E of Barnard Castle. Take Newgate out of Barnard Castle, then turn R on to the road signposted for the A66. Follow this over Egglestone Abbey Bridge and turn R at the lights, where there is a lay-by on the R. Return to the bridge to find the Teesdale Way on the E side of the bridge. Descend to the bridge and pools.

5 mins, 54.5296, -1.8993

27 THE MEETING OF THE WATERS

The tumble of huge rocks where the Rivers Greta and River Tees meet makes for a dramatic scene that inspired artist J.M.W Turner. It also forms deep pools, perfect for a cooling swim. Approx 5km E of Barnard Castle. Take Newgate out of Barnard Castle, then turn R on to the road signposted for the A66. Follow this over Egglestone Abbey Bridge, turning L. Follow road to parking at various lay-bys at Manyfold Beck (W of Rokeby Hall). Follow Teesdale Way footpath, which skirts a field next to the river, through woods to Mortham Lane and the pools.

15 mins, 54.5251, -1.8707

28 WHORLTON, R TEES

Beautiful stretch of the Tees that was once a public lido. Cascades tumble over stone slabs into various deeper swimming pools. There are several access points with a shallow entry point at 54.5257, -1.8316. Whorlton is 6.5km E of Barnard Castle. Park in Whorlton village and follow footpath in front of church over the wall and through graveyard. Follow steps on L down to river, then cross stepping stones to riverside path.

5 mins, 54.5266, -1.8349

29 GAINFORD, R TEES

Idyllic swim spot on a bend in the River Tees with a wide pebble beach in one of England's prettiest villages (Stan Laurel, of Laurel and Hardy fame, went to school here). Paddling and deep pools for swimming. Head W from High Coniscliffe on the A67 for 5.5km. At Gainford, turn L on to High Green then continue to village green for parking near St Mary's church (54.5461, -1.7382). Follow riverside footpath through woodland behind church for 400m to beach. Gainford Spa is one km upstream (54.5500, -1.7495), offering a deeper, longer swim. Here the mineral spring flows from an artesian well, discovered in an attempt to drill for coal in the 19th century. The hope was that Gainford would become a spa resort but this never happened. Steep entry to water.

10 mins, 54.5427, -1.7428

30 HIGH CONISCLIFFE, R TEES

Deep pools, shallow rapids and a large pebble and sand beach on a secluded stretch of the R Tees between High Coniscliffe and Merrybent. Further beaches downstream. From Merrybent, head NW on the A67 for 3km in direction of Barnard Castle. At High Coniscliffe, pass St Edwin's Church on L and take R to street parking in West Close, Ulnaby Lane (54.5339, -1.6551), just before school. Cross road and follow footpath to L of turreted wall to riverside path. Avoid anglers by continuing downstream. Follow grass path to beach. Continue downstream for other spots at 54.5243, -1.6512 and 54.5260, -1.6373.

10 mins, 54.5246, -1.6535

LOWER TEES

31 NEWSHAM HALL, R TEES

Here the River Tees winds through scenic countryside, with an entry into the water from the grass bank which can be overgrown in summer. Take the Aislaby road from Egglescliffe (S of Stockton-on-Tees)

and bear L (straight on) for Newsham Hall. Continue to parking bay on L after 1.5km. Follow Teesdale Way sign diagonally across field to river.

5 mins, 54.4909, -1.4102

32 YARM, R TEES

A tranquil stretch of river accessed via a small wooden platform, just behind the Blue Bell pub. From Yarm head towards Egglescliffe, crossing the historic bridge. Parking is tricky so turn L on Aislaby Road to park on verge by school playing fields (54.5125, -1.3624) and walk back along the Teesdale Way, which comes out opp pub. Take footpath at side of pub on to riverside path to jetty.

10 mins, 54.5117, -1.354

33 PRESTON PARK, R TEES

Accessible swim spot from the floating pontoon in Preston Park, with the possibility of an upstream swim to Yarm bridge. Café onsite. Situated 4km N of Yarm on the A135. Well signed. Free parking at Butterfly World, TS18 3RH. Head towards play area and river to find pontoon.

5 mins, 54.5355, -1.3375

HAMBLETON HILLS

34 COD BECK, OSMOTHERLEY

Surrounded by a coniferous woodland beneath remote moorland, this picturesque lake has a shoreside footpath and sheltered beaches. Leave the A19, taking the A684 Northallerton, and follow signs to Osmotherley. Turn L in village and continue 2.5km to 2 car parks. 'No Swim' signs but many do. Use your own judgement. Upstream is the Sheepwash, offering mostly paddling and an idyllic picnic spot (54.3882, -1.0665).

2 mins, 54.3854, -1.2829

35 BRIAN'S POND, SCUGDALE

Climb on to the moor at the end of this beautiful, remote valley to find a shimmering moorland tarn and crags for scrambling. From Swainby, off the A172, follow the high street and take a L fork on to Scugdale Road. Follow this road to the very end, to a lay-by before a group of houses. A bridleway to the L of the houses leads up through Barker's Crag and on to the moor. Keep to the bridleway as it runs directly to the pond.

30 mins, 54.399, -1.1972

36 BLOW GILL, HAWNBY

Mini waterfalls and cascades leap over rocks as water pours down Hawnby Moor into small pools at this delightful roadside stream. Great for paddling and picnics but it is a steep clamber down to the beck so take care. 2 miles NW of Hawnby on the road to Osmotherley. Park at the spacious Hazel Head Car Park and walk 300m to bridge over the gill.

5 mins, 54.3312, -1.1889 🏊🅿️

37 GORMIRE LAKE

Sheltered by ancient Garbutt Wood and brimming with birdlife, this enchanting tarn, fed by an underground spring, was formed by glacial erosion more than 20 000 years ago. According to local legend it is bottomless, a portal to hell, used by the devil himself, and the water crawls with leeches (there is some truth to this). Some issues with swimming here so be discreet if you dip. Park at Sutton Bank Visitor Centre. Follow footpath signs for Cleveland Way. Continue for 500m. Take L and descend into Garbutt Wood to lakeshore. Path is steep and can be boggy when wet.

30 mins, 54.2427, -1.2283 🏊🅿️🚶

38 CASCADES, R RYE, DUNCOMBE PARK

Gnarled ash trees line the banks along this lovely section of the River Rye in Duncombe Park. The Cascades are popular with local kids, who come here to cool off in summer. Deeper bathing pools up and downstream. This was the former medieval deer park for Helmsley Castle, and many of the ancient trees date back to this time, including ancient pollarded oaks, ash, lime and beech. Heading into Helmsley on the A170 from Thirsk, turn L on to Buckingham Square, then L again through gates to Duncombe Park parking (YO62 5EB). Follow footpath through woods.

30 mins, 54.2373, -1.0665 🏊🅿️🐾

39 HELMSLEY OPEN AIR POOL £

A 25-metre, heated outdoor pool, flanked by a wide grassy seating area, and situated in a picturesque location on the fringes of the pretty market town of Helmsley. Unheated in autumn. Baxton's Sprunt, Helmsley, YO62 5HT, 01439 408010

2 mins, 54.2511, -1.0640 £

40 HOB HOLE

Local beauty spot next to Baysdale Beck in a steep bracken-carpeted valley. Some pools for dipping in between shallows that tumble over the rocks and stones. Idyllic picnic spot for families. From Young Ralph Cross, take L signposted 'Westerdale'. Follow road for 4km to village, then continue on Upper Esk Road for 1.5km. Parking after ford on L.

2 mins, 54.4575, -0.9963 🏊🅿️⛺🐾

41 CASTLETON, R ESK

A steep grassy bank descends to a pleasant stretch of river with deeper pools upstream of the stone bridge. The Esk picks up pace here so be mindful of river levels and flow. S of Castleton, park on grassy verge (New Rd) at the junction of New Rd and Station Rd just after the stone bridge. Then follow river upstream to pools.

2 mins, 54.4660, -0.9433 🐾

42 SCALING DAM RESERVOIR £

Large freshwater lake, surrounded by heather moorland, offering organised open-water swimming sessions, once a week. Scaling Dam Sailing Club, https://members.

plunge pool beneath the main falls. The approach is uneven and wet, so good footwear is essential. Follow the B1416 S from Whitby and turn R after 5km, signed 'Newton House/Falling Foss'. Follow Foss Ln for 1.5km to car park. Take footpath into the woods, signposted 'Hermitage', keeping R. Just before the Hermitage, take the L path down the slope along stone trods. Cross the first footbridge, then follow riverbed upstream to bottom of waterfall.
30 mins, 54.419, -0.6327 🚶🧗

GOATLAND WATERFALLS

47 NELLY AYRE FOSS

A secluded waterfall hidden in a copse of trees with a plunge pool and rocky ledges for drying off on afterwards. More plunge pools downstream. Head SW out of Goathland with Mallyan Spout Hotel on R and go across roundabout. Continue for just over a km to parking on R before cattle grid. Find footpath on L, signposted 'Nelly Ayre Foss', alongside New Wath House. Continue to end of wall and start of perimeter fence. Follow fence round and find narrow path down to falls. Scramble down last bit.
20 mins, 54.3858, -0.749 🚶🧗

48 THE TARN, GOATHLAND

Nestled in a bowl of upland hills and circled by swallows and skylarks, this peaty moorland tarn has a tussocky shore with small slope for entry on S side of tarn. From Goathland, pass the Mallyan Spout Hotel on R and go straight ahead at roundabout to parking on grass verge on R (54.3944 -0.7318). Follow footpath sign on to moor for 800m.
15 mins, 54.3900, -0.7345 🚶🧗🏕🚶🏕

49 MALLYAN SPOUT

This picturesque waterfall, the highest in the North York Moors, has charmed visitors since Victorian times. Water tumbles over

scalingdam.org, 01287 643026.
3 mins, 54.5035, -0.8561 🚶🏊

43 LEALHOLM, R ESK

There are three crossings of the Esk at Lealholm, the bridge, a ford and this set of stepping stones by the village green, which are definitely a favourite with younger visitors. Deeper pool upstream of the Board Inn and more options downstream along riverside footpath. Park in car park at Lealholm.
2 mins, 54.4583, -0.8257 🚶🏊🏕

44 BEGGAR'S BRIDGE, R ESK

Beautiful stretch of the River Esk with deep pools beneath the medieval Beggar's Bridge with a beach a few metres downstream. Follow the footpath into East Arncliffe Woods to find a deep pool upstream of the weir. From Glaisdale, follow road towards Egton Bridge. Beggar's Bridge is about 800m along on R, just under railway bridge. In East Arncliffe Woods, entry point is at 54.4367, -0.7922.
2 mins, 54.4387, -0.7921 🚶🏊🏕🚶

45 GROSMONT, R ESK

A deep pool and rapids on a meander of the River Esk near Grosmont with further pools upstream. Although not deep, the rapids can be fast flowing so take care. Just off the old toll road between Egton Bridge and Grosmont. From Grosmont, follow road towards Egton, passing footbridge on L, to parking at end of toll road. Follow track to path to river on L.
5 mins, 54.4379, -0.735 🚶🚶🏊

46 FALLING FOSS

A dramatic waterfall that drops 10m into a wide pool. Pass smaller pools along May Beck as you wander through the ancient woodland, before reaching the deeper

a steep-sided 20m drop. Spectacular after rain but take care as rocks can be slippery. Plunge pool and more pools and swing upstream. Heading N on the A169, take L turn at signpost for Goathland, passing Goathland Viewpoint car park on L. Continue to Goathland village and take L at roundabout to park on verge. Walk back towards Mallyan Spout Hotel and follow signpost 'Footpath Mallyan Spout' and descend into woods. At junction at bottom, path to L leads upstream to Mallyan Spout.

20 mins, 54.3978, -0.7321 🏞️

50 THOMASON FOSS

A very pretty waterfall that leaps over rocky ledges of the Eller Beck into a deep plunge pool. It is tucked away in a wooded dell and is reached by a narrow path and a final rocky scramble. Afterwards, pop into pocket-sized Birch Hall Inn at Beck Hole with its traditional sweet shop. Heading N on the A169, take L at signpost for Beck Hole. Continue to roadside parking on hill before you descend into Beck Hole. Walk into village (800m). Follow signposted footpath by bridge in centre of village to falls.

25 mins, 54.4079, -0.7284 🚶🏞️

51 WATER ARC FOSS

Spectacular, little-known waterfall with plunge pool upstream of Thomason Foss. Further plunge pools and large flat rocks to L and R of footbridge. Tricky, precipitous descent so take care. From Goathland follow signs for Beck Hole and park at top of this road. Find footpath opp, through a snicket, and head into a field towards railway bridge (look out for steam trains) and steep steps down to riverside. Cross footbridge and turn L along footpath to end, then take steep path on L down to falls.

15 mins, 54.4079, -0.7243 🚶🏞️🐟🏞️🌿❀

NORTH RIDINGS

52 SINNINGTON, R SEVEN

A pebble beach at a sharp bend in the river, shaded by a canopy of trees with some dappled light. Rope swing and fallen tree trunk to scramble across. From Pickering, follow the A170 for 6.5km then turn R to Sinnington. Continue on Main Street to parking at village hall (donation). Follow road to L of village hall, with river on L, to woodland footpath. Continue along riverside path, round a sharp L-hand bend in river, to a shallow ford used by horse riders. Beach is to L. Also paddle spot at 54.2669, -0.8596 with small beach and pool.

20 mins, 54.2691, -0.8691 🏞️🐟🍴

53 HACKNESS, R DERWENT

A tranquil stretch of the Derwent flowing through beautiful Hackness, with a riverside footpath and narrow paths down to the river. Look out for kingfishers which nest here. From Hackness, head S on Storr Ln, then turn L on to Mowthorp Rd for 800m. Before Everley, take R turn, crossing bridge to parking on L at Wrench Green. Cross road to follow riverside footpath.

2 mins, 54.2957, -0.5137 🏊🚶🏕️♿

54 NORTH YORKSHIRE WATER PARK ⭐

The largest natural water sports lake in North Yorkshire, with weekly open-water swimming sessions. Café and gravel and grass camping pitches, plus inflatables. Long Causeway Rd, Wykeham, Lakes YO13 9QU, 01723865052.

1 mins, 54.2258, -0.4851 🏊🚣🛶🏕️🏠🍴£

HOWARDIAN HILLS

55 OULSTON RESERVOIR

A secluded fresh water lake, this is the source of the River Foss which rises in nearby Foss Crooks Woods. From Yearsley village, take North Moor Ln, then turn L, signposted 'Oulston', for 1.5km. Park in lay-by on L at 54.1663, -1.1307. Walk up road

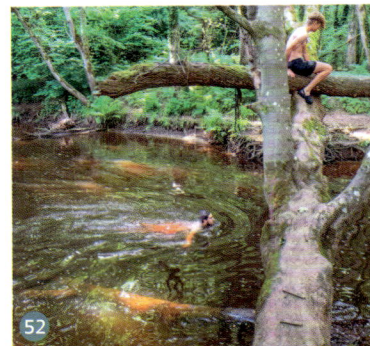

exit points before entering the water. Follow Low St Agnesgate at back of cathedral then L down Low Mill Rd and cross footbridge by ford. Follow river down Fisher Green for 800m to confluence. 20 mins

5 mins, 54.1329, -1.5027 🏊

60 NEWBY HALL, R URE
Wide expanse of river swimming opposite the stately home. 1.5km E of Bishop Monkton, past HG3 3RQ, find footpath on L, leading to river. Stock up between them at Lister's Farm Shop for Newby Hall.

5 mins, 54.1004, -1.4792 🅿

61 ALDWARK TOLL BRIDGE, R URE
Popular local swim spot beneath the old toll bridge on a tranquil stretch of the River Ure before it feeds into the Ouse further downstream. Jetty is to L of bridge. A toll keeper still collects a small fee for crossing the bridge. Follow the road S out of Aldwark for 800m, then turn R at T-junction to cross bridge. Toll at end (coins). Turn immediately R after bridge to car park by river. Upstream 5km, a short walk from Myton-on-Swale, over the grand iron bridge, is another good pool at 54.0892, -1.3447 where the Ure and Swale meet (YO61 2QY).

1 mins, 54.0534, -1.2887 🅿👫🛶🚶

62 BENINGBROUGH, R OUSE
A river beach at the confluence of the rivers Nidd and Ouse, popular with families in the summer. Deep enough for swimming with a tree swing for jumping into the water. Avoid swimming too close to the riversmeet as there are sometimes strong currents and turbulent eddies. From Beningbrough, head N for 800m, then turn L at T-junction to parking in small parking area (54.0207, -1.2012). Follow riverside footpath through woods to river.

10 mins, 54.0149, -1.2182 🅿👫🍴🛶🚶

63 NETHER POPPLETON, R OUSE
Easy sloped access to the Ouse from a sandy beach reached via a stroll past a 16th-century tythe barn and through a moated field. Follow the York ring road (A1237) anti-clockwise and take the R turn for Nether Poppleton on to Millfield Ln, then R turn on to Church Ln (2km) to parking at end by tythe barn. Follow footpath through moated field under Skelton Bridge then along riverbank to beach.

20 mins, 53.9908, -1.1347 🅿🚶

64 CHALONER POND, HAXBY, YORK 🏊
Tranquil wild swimming pond set on a working family farm. Occasional saunas,

to footpath sign on L. Follow track towards Pond Head Farm and turn R through kissing gate. Follow footpath beside the field then into woods. Reservoir is just off path on L. Technically no swimming but locals do.

20 mins, 54.1616, -1.1354 🅿

56 GILLING LAKES
The largest of three lakes, 'lower fish pond' has several wooden jetties stretching out into the water around the perimeter of the lake. Can be affected by blue green algae. From Gilling East, follow the road (Pottergate) past the Fairfax Arms as it becomes a narrower lane. Continue to the end for limited parking or park in the car park on the L by the cottages and walk to reach the footpath. Follow the footpath into the woods to the lake just ahead. For the other two lakes, follow the lakeside footpath on the L.

5 mins, 54.1816, -1.0969 🅿🚶

57 NUNNINGTON, R RYE
As the Rye snakes through Nunnington, it creates a plethora of small pools and beaches with a deep pool by the old railway bridge (54.2123, -1.0069). From Helmsley, follow the A170 towards Thirsk for 800m, then turn L on to the B1257 for 6.5km.

Turn L after Birch Farm on to Lack Ln for 800m. Verge/roadside parking with care. Walk past East Newton Hall to riverside footpath. Either cross ford or turn L to footbridge to cross over, then double back downstream to swim spots.

20 mins, 54.2123, -1.0069 🅿🏊🚶

RIVERS URE & OUSE

58 WEST TANFIELD, R URE
A wide expanse of river above a weir and next to the village meadows. You will need to wade upstream for deeper water. Cross the bridge S out of the village (HG4 5JQ) and take the footpath on L downstream 800m to the weir. Also accessible directly from the lane opposite, which leads to Thornborough henge. Deeper pools can be found beneath the bridge in front of the Bull Inn (54.2032, -1.5876).

10 mins, 54.2038, -1.5789 🚶🏠

59 RIPON, R URE
The scenic River Skell descends for 20km through the wild, remote moorland of Dallowgill Moor intersecting the National Trust's Fountains Abbey and Studley Royal to its confluence with the River Ure here. It is a fast flowing stretch of river so check your

yoga and pilates sessions. chalonerpond.
co.uk, 07773 771373.

2 mins, 54.0331, -1.0773 💷

RIVER DERWENT

65 HOWSHAM MILL, R DERWENT

Tiny island housing a Georgian Gothic
watermill with a deep stretch of river above
the weir. More suitable for experienced
swimmers as entry from the river bank
is steep. The island is occasionally closed
for educational events so check Howsham
Mill website. Follow the A64 E from York
for 14km. Take R turn just before petrol
station, signposted 'Harton' Follow road for
1.5km, then turn R out of village. Continue
straight for 1.5km. Parking on R just over
bridge. Walk under bridge with river on L
Cross footbridge to island. Continue past
the mill and weir to a tree and rope swing
and metal ladder to access the water (may
be submerged if water level is high).

10 mins, 54.0558, -0.8865 🚗🅿️🅰️

66 KIRKHAM ABBEY, R DERWENT

A languid stretch of the river as it meanders
through the Derwent Valley past the
romantic ruins of Kirkham Priory. Grassy
banks with a steep entry to the water, using
gnarled tree roots as handles and footholds.
Travelling E from York on the A64, after
the R turn for Barton, continue uphill and
filter R, signposted 'Kirkham', on to Onhams
Ln. Cross railway crossing to parking over
bridge by abbey (YO60 7JS) Return over
bridge to gate on L to access riverbank.

5 mins, 54.0827, -0.8801 🚗🅿️🅰️🏰

RIVER WHARFE & SOUTH

67 POOL BRIDGE FARM, YORK 💷

Family-run wild swimming venue with
four unique lakes set in an idyllic location
brimming with wildlife. Wood-clad lakeside
saunas and campsite. Whelcrake Ln, YO19
4SQ, 07928 359 420, poolbridge.co.uk

2 mins, 53.9097, -1.0254 🚗🅿️🏕️💷

68 WHELDRAKE, R DERWENT

The river weaves through the seasonally
flooded hay meadows of the wildlife-rich
Lower Derwent Valley here and this tiny
beach offers easy access into the water.
From Wheldrake, head E on Main St, then
continue on to Church Ln for just over 3km
to a L turn on to Ferry Ln and parking at end.
Follow footpath beside river to small beach.

5 mins, 53.8758, -0.9396 🚗🅰️

69 SUTTON BRIDGE, R DERWENT

Just below the weir and lock, this grass-
fringed stretch of the Derwent offers
an easy entry point and a secluded basin
for swimming. From Elvington, follow the
B1228 for 300m to parking in Riverside
Gardens on L. Cross road and follow
footpath through snicket to churchyard.
Then find metal gate on L to riverside path
and river.

5 mins, 53.9179, -0.9303 🚗🅿️🅰️

70 ALLERTHORPE LAKELAND PARK 💷

Shallow man-made lake which warms up
quickly in summer. On-site café, camping,
inflatables and swimming sessions.
Melbourne Road, Pocklington, YO42 4RL,
01759 301 444.

1 min, 53.9037, -0.8145 🚗🅿️🅰️🚶🏞️

LEEDS AREA

71 KNARESBOROUGH LIDO, R NIDD

A wide, shallow basin, tucked between two
weirs, flanked on one side by a small gorge
and a caravan park on the other. This is a
popular spot with local swim groups. Toilets
and refreshments from the Watermill
Cafe. Limited parking in Wetherby Rd (HG5
8LL) then walk through the caravan site or
access the riverside from Wetherby Rd at
the Watermill Cafe sign. Alternatively, park
in Conyngham Hall car park for easy parking
and access to the river at the far end of the
car park (HG5 9AY).

5 mins, 53.9983, -1.4512 🍴

72 CAROLINE'S AT ST AIDAN'S, LEEDS 💷

Once an open cast coal mine, this popular
wild swimming lake is now managed by the
RSPB. With good parking and relatively
easy entry into the water from a grassy
shoreline, this is a much-loved swim spot
that teems with birdlife. Stick to the
designated entry point to avoid disturbing
wildlife and eroding the banks. 14.5km
SE of Leeds. Park in RSPB reserve (LS26
8AL) during opening hours (fee, free to
members). Alternatively, there is a lay-by
near the start of Wood Ln (53.7579,
-1.3918). 5 mins

2 mins, 53.7501, -1.3956 💷

73 WETHERBY, R WHARFE

Small pebbly beach offering entry into
the water for an upstream swim at a
meander of the river. Park in Wetherby
Leisure Centre car park, Lodge Lane (LS22
5FN) then follow the riverside path 500m
upstream, passing sports fields on the L.

Look out for a bench where you will find a
small, pebbly beach to access the river.

10 mins, 53.9276, -1.3905 🚤

74 BOSTON SPA, R WHARFE

Beautiful, wide tree-fringed section of
the River Wharfe as it winds through the
former 18th century spa town. Park in the
car park next to the church (LS23 6DR).
Head to the bottom of the car park, cross
the field and go through a gap in the hedge
then turn R onto path. Turn L to the river and
walk upstream past the weir. Access by the
metal railings or continue to Jackdaw Crag,
a limestone outcrop hanging above the
river (53.9125, -1.3577). Be aware that the
riverbed shelves quickly and deeply here.

5 mins, 53.908_, -1.3487

HULL TO HUMBER

75 WELTON WATERS ADVENTURE CENTRE £

Water adventure centre situated next to
a peaceful stretch of the River Humber,
offering open-water swimming in the
sheltered lagoons. Onsite café. https://
www.wwac.org.uk, 01482 668277.

2 mins, 53.7149, -0.5489 🅿️🚤🚤

76 BASWICK LANDING, RIVER HULL

Peaceful stretch of the chalk-fed River
Hull with a river beach for a wild swim just
upstream of the nature reserve at Tophill
Low. Can be weedy in high summer. From
Brandesburton, follow Mill Ln for 5km,
crossing bridge at Burshill to car park with
honesty box.

2 mins, 53.913_, -0.3665 🚗🅿️🅰️🚤

77 TICKTON, R HULL

Small beach on a tranquil stretch of the
River Hull just downstream of Pulfin Bog
Nature Reserve. From Beverley, follow
the A1035 for 2km. After crossing the
road bridge over the River Hull, take R for
Tickton, then immediately R again on to
Weel Rd and verge parking.

5 mins, 53.8615, -0.397 🚗🅿️🅰️🚶🚣🅰️

78 FRODINGHAM LANDING

Branch of the scenic Driffield Navigation
with easy access into the water. Can be reedy
in summer. A tow float is advisable to ensure
you are visible to paddleboarders, kayakers
and canoeists who all launch here. The wharf
is off the B1249 on L, just over one km W
of North Frodingham. Honesty box with
suggested donation of £5 for parking to help
towards upkeep of the canal. 🚗🅿️🅰️🚤

2 mins, 53.9674, -0.3418 🚗🅿️🚣

BORDERS &
NORTHUMBRIA

Despite taking in the country's most densely populated cities, the central belt also plays host to beautiful countryside and a surprising array of waterbodies, including many fine disused Victorian reservoirs. To the south Dumfries and Galloway remains a best kept secret that repays its visitors in charm without the crowds. Formed officially in 1975 by merging the various historic counties lying in the south east of the country, the region stretches from the Irish Sea in the east to The Borders in the west, with the north of England to the south. Bisected by several south-flowing rivers with evocative names - Cree, Kith, Annan and Ken - Dumfries and Galloway epitomises the variety of landscapes Scotland offers, from intricate and windswept coastlines to lush forests and lonely hills.

Galloway Forest Park remains the big draw, with what some claim to be the largest forest in the UK and some spectacular 'highland' scenery, including glens, lochs and river pools, such as the pretty Otter Pools (18) as well as impressive waterfalls: note the Gray Mares Tail (16) is not the Grey Mares Tail (23) the other side of Moffat, 50 miles away to the north-east.

Arran lies offshore to the west, at the extreme western end of the Highland Boundary Fault, which runs across Scotland to Stonehaven and marks the geographical dividing line between Highlands and Lowlands. Its position and history make these complex rock formations of interest to hill walkers, rock climbers and the amateur geologist. The dividing line of the Fault shaped Scotland not only geologically, but socially and culturally as well, and Arran packs a punch in terms of variety. There are few places in the country with such diversity of flora, fauna and landscape on show in such a small area. Straight off the ferry there are sights to behold, with Goatfell rising in the distance with beautiful Blue Pools of Glen Rosa (2) mere minutes away offering dreamy waterfall dips – don't miss out on a walk, swim and camp in this wonderful glen.

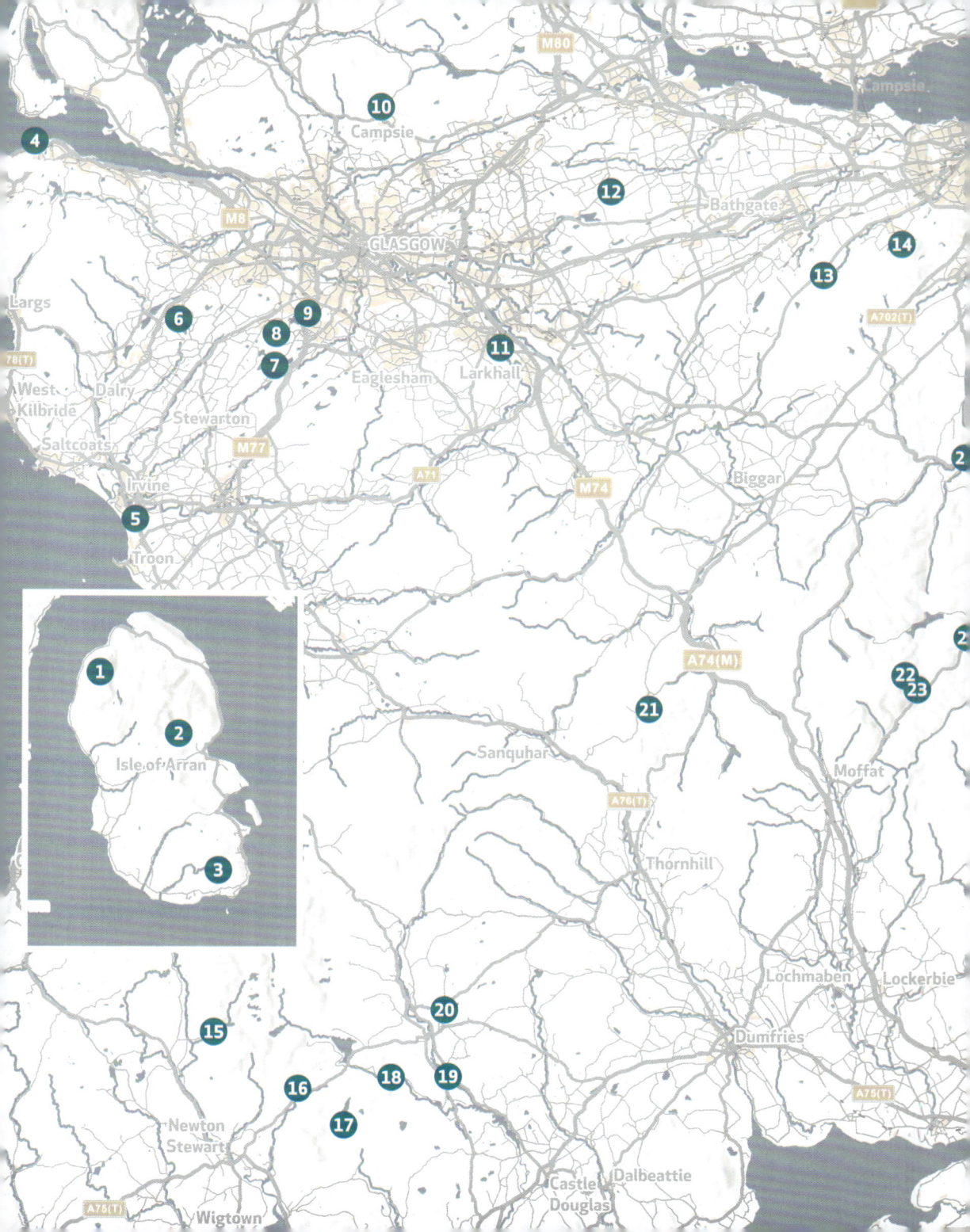

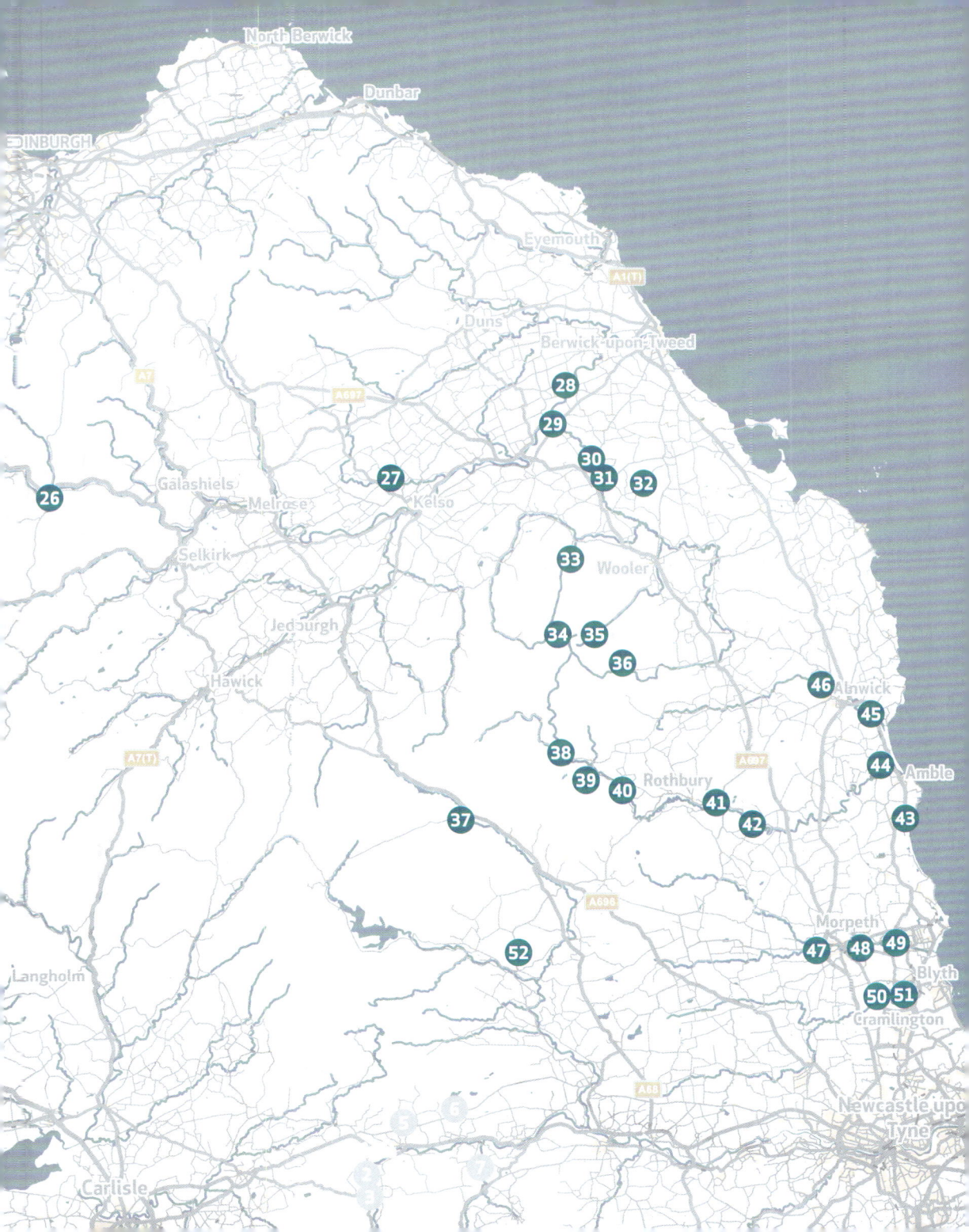

North Berwick

Dunbar

EDINBURGH

Eyemouth

A1(T)

Duns

Berwick-upon-Tweed

A697

28

29

30
31   32

Galashiels

Melrose

Kelso

A7

26

27

33   Wooler

Selkirk

34   35

36

Jedburgh

Hawick

46 Alnwick

45

A7(T)

38

39   40   Rothbury

41   44 Amble

42   43

37

A697

A696

Morpeth

47   48   49

Langholm

52   Blyth

50   51

Cramlington

A69

Newcastle upon Tyne

Carlisle

'Says Tweed to Till Whit gars ye rin sae still? Says Till to Tweed Though ye may rin wi' speed And I rin sla For aye one ye droon I droon twa!'
Traditional poem

The Borders feature the whole plethora of Scottish staples - winding rivers, ancient forests, historic villages and bothies located deep in remote and secluded hills. With the Tweed and the Teviot bisecting the territory on their meandering journey to the sea. Many of the attractions lie along the River Tweed, one of the grandest salmon rivers in Scotland and surely a contender for the most beautiful. Flowing east from the Lowther Hills down to the North Sea at Berwick-Upon-Tweed in England, it is the source of many adventures, passing by the great riverside castle at Peebles (25), and on thourgh Innerleithen, Melrose, Kelso and Coldstream, all of which are well worth a visit (26-29). The River Teviot also approaches the sea heading east from the south, and along which sits the town of Hawick.

To the south-east, across the border, lie the Cheviot Hills and a Northumberland borderland contested for centuries by chieftains and smugglers. Deep remote valleys are rich in river pools and on the northern edge you can swim to Scotland across the River Tweed.

All is peaceful in the county now and much is protected in the fabulous and remote Northumberland National Park with Kielder Forest and the Cheviot hill range. Three river dales drain the Cheviots: the Harthope, the Breamish and the Coquet. The best-known pool on all of these is Linhope Spout on the Breamish, renowned for its unfathomable depth (36).

It's a long walk to the Spout but the high plume is worth it. It tips down a straight chute into an almost perfect cylindrical plunge pool on the edge of a wooded Breamish dale. Popular with walkers and families cooling off in the summer, there is a fun six-foot ledge from which you can jump. For the wildlife enthusiast, Linhope Burn attracts breeding birds like the dipper and grey wagtail – always on the move in their search for caddis-fly and other aquatic invertebrates. You may well also see an oystercatcher scurrying along the river bank.

The River Coquet is easier to reach, but feels just as remote (38-42). A winding mountain lane runs for many miles to the head of the dale. Here it meets the Scottish border and the remains of Chew Green Roman Fort, an old staging post on the road from York to Scotland.

I followed the road to Linbriggs and Shillmoor and a stretch of perfect river pools bounded by grassy moor (38). The current was just strong enough to pick me up and propel me down the chute of the mini-waterfall. Although the river is generally shallow, it's possible to swim down for at least half a mile, mainly carried by the flow, with a few strokes here and there to keep up the momentum.

The valley to the north of the Linhope and the Breamish is Harthope, one of the emptiest of the Cheviot valleys with a long approach walk. The plunge pool is magical, deep and cave-like with mosses climbing up the steep black grotto walls (35). Finding Harthope Spout, hidden in the crevice of a wooded hollow, is quite an achievement and it makes a wonderful place to skinny-dip.

The Harthope and Breamish rivers both join the Till, which flows north into the Tweed. This, in turn, forms the border with Scotland in its final 20 miles. The Union Bridge was the longest suspension bridge in the world when it opened in 1820 and finally linked the east coasts of England and Scotland. Oddly the Scottish end is actually south of the English side! It has long been famous for eloping couples keen to wed under more liberal Scottish law: marriage on the Scottish side is legal even without the 'reading of the banns' for three Sundays prior to the ceremony. A better place to swim in upstream at Norham (28).

Given all this border history it seemed a good place to attempt to swim across the frontier. A friend and I arrived late one August afternoon for the challenge, the meadow beneath the bridge awash in head-high crimson balsam. Parting the flowers to find the riverbank we stepped down into the pebbly river shore and began to walk out into the alarmingly brisk current. The wide stream proved shallow enough to wade but after a little orientation – swimming breaststroke against the flow and practising landing ourselves on the bank – we began our migration attempt, striking out at an upstream angle to try to hit the opposite side square on, and checking from time to time that we could still feel the riverbed with our feet. The passage was remarkably easy and the feeling of running the stream invigorating – so much so that we swam between the two countries several times before finding somewhere to get a cup of tea.

ISLE OF ARRAN

1 COIRE FHIONN LOCHAN

Secluded and serene mountain loch with two white beaches at either end. A refreshing place for swimming, in every sense. Limited lay-by parking in the tiny village of Thundergay (about 2.5km N of KA27 8GD). Head E on a signposted and well-constructed path opp parking that winds through the houses and hills for about 2.5km to the lochan.

45 mins, 55.6619, -5.3405 ⛰️📶👣

2 BLUE POOLS, GLEN ROSA

Gorgeous clear pools on beautiful Glen Rosa glen, leading up to Goatfell. There's a circular walk from behind the Arran Brewery, with car park opposite. Follow the path along the edge of the forest, onto moorland and the pools are just above the footbridge, 3km

45 mins, 55.6019, -5.2043 👣🏊

3 LOCH GARBAD

Placid loch favoured by fisherman seeking solitude (and trout). It can be combined with a visit to Eas Mòr waterfall and fascinating woodland library for a varied excursion. Park in the car park off the A841, opposite the Kildonan turning (dir KA27 8RR) in the S of the island. Follow the good path N. Where the path forks beyond the waterfall viewpoint, take the fork signposted 'Loch Garbad 1 mile'. Follow the path to the loch, returning the same way. To visit the library, turn R at the fork.

35 mins, 55.4676, -5.1346 🪧🏊

CENTRAL BELT

4 GOUROCK OUTDOOR POOL £

Scotland's only heated outdoor saltwater pool, with spectacular views of the Clyde estuary. Seasonal Opening, part of Inverclyde Leisure. Parking right outside on Kempock St (PA19 1NA)

5 mins, 55.9611, -4.8225

5 SHEWALTON WATER

These former sand and gravel pits are commonly known as Booker's Pond as parking is at the nearby Cash N Carry. Easily accessible just off the A78 on the outskirts of Irvine, park at Bookers and then follow a well-trodden path N.

5 mins, 55.5886, -4.6462

6 BARCRAIGS RESERVOIR

Easy access from B776 S from Howwood, take first right after Bowfield Hotel (PA9 1DZ) onto Glenhead Road. Follow road along reservoir. Parking very limited in small layby and on verge, access over wall or via gate further along.

5 mins, 55.7867, -4.5726

7 WHITE LOCH

Located just off the B769 between Newton Mearns and Stewarton this popular loch is an accessible and safe place to swim. Limited parking in small car park (G77 6QB)

5 mins, 55.7412, -4.4060

8 GLANDERSTON DAM

Shimmering below Duncarnock hillfort, a very scenic spot and generally very quiet Water around the shore is quite weedy but this clears up about 50m from the shore. Park in area by the field gate (55.7754, -4.3963) and cross the pasture 500m. There's also Walton Dam, right on the lane.

10 mins, 55.7727, -4.4033

9 WAULKMIL GLEN RESERVOIR

Handy city lake swim. Car park at 55.7975, -4.3548 at end of Coarelet lane. Walk up to waterworks and bear L around to E shore for best acces

15 mins, 55.7926, -4.3491

10 CAMPSIE GLEN WATERFALLS

Pools along the Campsie Glen with two points of access. For a longer walk, start at Clachan of Campsie car park just off the A891 in Lennoxtown, walk N upstream as signed. Alternatively the Crow Road car park off the B822 NW of Lennoxtown, access to Glen down a steep path, continue N upstream

20 mins, 55.9952, -4.2231

11 CHATELHERAULT COUNTRY PARK

W facing beach under crags. Swim against the curremt. Free parking at visitor centre then woodland walk down.

10 mins, 55.7592, -4.0156

12 BLACK LOCH

Tranquil spot between Airdrie and Falkirk. Park off B829 in small car park signed for Black Loch. Follow wide, surfaced path along the bank of the Black Loch on the S side of Limerigg Wood for easy access.

5 mins, 55.91284, -3.8245

13 HARPERRIG RESERVOIR

Beautiful moorland lake popular with swimmers and paddle boarders. Easy car park right by the shore, just off A70.

2 mins, 55.8309, -3.4556

14 HARLAW & THREIPMUIR RESERVOIRS

Interlinked reservoirs at the foot of the Pentlands. Popular with paddle boarders and swimmers but also fishermen, Harlaw is backed by lovely pinewoods. Threipmuir is more open with stony beaches. Recommended parking is at the large Threipmuir Car Park (EH14 7JS). Follow signs to Threipmuir and Harlaw beyond.

10 mins, 55.8616, -3.3199

DUMFRIES & GALLOWAY

15 LOCH TROOL

Narrow, freshwater loch surrounded by dense woodland and rushing waterfalls with good paths around its shores. On the northern side of the loch is Bruce's Stone, a large boulder erected to commemorate the Battle of Trool in 1307. Park at the Loch Trool Trail car park (DG8 6SS) and follow the green waymarked path. Cross the bridge over the Water of Trool and take a L at each of the two junctions. Cross a second bridge, entering a campsite and take another L at the fork. Follow the signs for the Southern Upland Way which soon leads L over a tiny bridge. Then take a R onto a footpath that leads up through the trees where the loch will soon come into view.

Continue on good paths around its shores.

180 mins, 55.0817, -4.5074

16 GRAY MARES TAIL & PALNURE BURN

A high chute and very deep plunge pool. Crazies leap from the top into it. Reached along a pretty streamside path with more falls and pools along the way (Buck Loup, Foot Loup). Look out for the 5 carved stone faces too in an abandoned sheepfold (55.0237, -4.3606). From roadside 'Queens Way' forestry car park on A712 (55.0198, -4.3621), cross bridge and then 1km upstream (signed path, circular forest walk). Downstream on the Palnure Burn is another set of pools, beneath tumbling waterfalls. S on A712 for 600m and take forestry track on L with parking at bridge. The pools and Clugie Linn are just below ((55.0116, -4.3694).

15 mins, 55.0253, -4.3621

17 LOCH GRANNOCH

Wild and remote loch with golden sandy beach in the heart of Galloway Forest. Ruined boathouse and derelict hunting lodge add a spooky feel. Great for wild camping. Follow 3796 NW from Gatehouse of Fleet for 10km. Turn R at junction signed Cairnsmore of Fleet NR. Pass the visitor

centre and drive under viaduct to park in one of the lay-bys. Continue along the track with viaduct behind you, turning R at first fork, following National Cycle Route 7. Continue downhill and L on forest track by cottage. Follow track round to L and, after 2.3km, turn L at fork, leaving the cycle route. After 1.6km follow track to R, past forestry gate and up steep hill, leading on to loch.

90 mins, 54.9889, -4.2827

18 OTTER POOLS

Popular spot on the River Dee, where the river widens into an attractive series of shallow pools in the heart of the Galloway Forest Park. Ideal spot for a picnic with benches, toilets and a car park. Follow the A712 NE from Newton Stewart for 17km to find Raiders Road on R. This is a forest drive open to vehicles from April - October. There's a £3 fee to use the road. Park at the Otter Pool car park (DG7 3SB).

1 mins, 55.0366, -4.2007

19 LOCH KEN

14km freshwater loch located in picturesque Glenkens, the wildest and largest glen in Galloway. A popular destination for water sports, served by the Galloway Activity Centre. Kenmure Castle sits at the northern shore of the loch. There are several car parks placed around the shores of the loch that offer pleasant views and easy access to the water (DG7 3NQ).

2 mins, 55.0375, -4.1018

20 HOLY LINN, DALRY

Waterfall with large, deepish pool on the Garple Burn was used as a place of worship by the Covenanters. Park on A702 near field gate (55.1081, -4.1132) and follow field track.

10 mins, 55.1039, -4.1084

LANARKSHIRE

21 GLEN FRANKA

Lovely deep, clear former reservoir, near highest village in Scotland. At end of 1.3km track. Park at 55.4102, -3.7621

30 mins, 55.4013, -3.7558

22 LOCH SKEEN

Sublime Uplands loch backed by the White Coomb - the highest of the Moffat Hills. Feeds the high Grey Mare's Tail waterfall (see x). A bracing yet rewarding wild swim. Park at the Grey Mare's car park (DG10 9LH) and continue as for Grey Mare's Tail

(see entry). Continue shortly on to Loch Skeen.

60 mins, 55.4319, -3.3084

23 GREY MARE'S TAIL

One of Scotland's most spectacular waterfalls, it takes a dramatic 60m plunge through a deep scar in the Moffat Hills that starts at Loch Skeen (see entry) and ends on the floor of the glen in Moffat Dale. A steep walk heads up alongside the waterfall and continues to the loch. Park at the Grey Mares car park (DG10 9LH) and follow the path that leads W of the burn until a fork is reached. Keep R and cross a footbridge to follow the steeply climbing path until the crest of the waterfall is reached. Continue on to Loch Skeen if desired.

50 mins, 55.4222, -3.2932

24 ST MARY'S LOCH & LOCH OF THE LOWES

Large and impressive interlinked lochs, two of the finest in the Scottish Borders. A brilliant spot for a wide range of water-based activities - canoeing, swimming, paddleboarding and sailing. A 15km path loops the entire St Mary's Loch. A very popular spot and one to be mindful of your impact on others. Park at the James Hogg memorial car park at TD7 5LH. Various

options exist, with good swimming and canoeing spots right in front of the car park.
5 mins, 55.4722, -3.2054 [icons]

RIVER TWEED & BORDERS

25 THE DOOKITS, PEEBLES

Popular spot with a rope swing, large boulders, easy access and beautiful setting just below Neidpath Castle. From the large free Neidpath Road Car Park, opposite Hay Lodge Park W of Peebles A72 (EH45 8NX), enter the park, down to the Tweed and upstream.
10 mins, 55.6515, -3.2098 [icons]

26 TOLL WOOD, INNERLEITHEN

Beautiful and easily accessible section of the River Tweed. Great for paddling and picnicking. Park at the Toll Wood car park signed of Traquair Road on the N bank of the Tweed, just before the bridge heading out of Innerleithen towards Traquair. River banks in either direction offer spots to dip and sit. Accessible also via walk from Traquair House.
5 mins, 55.6126, -3.0601 [icons]

27 STICHILL WATERFALL

Hidden waterfall set in a wooded glade.

It seems improbable that the peaceful Eden Water could result in such a beautiful waterfall. A secluded spot for a dip. Not the easiest to access and various options available. Park at the car park in Stichill village (TD5 7TA) and follow the B6364 1km S until 200m past the start of the trees, where there is a gap in the wall on the R. Go straight ahead to a bridge, then turn R and follow the path upstream alongside the river 1km. Please be considerate of locals and do not disturb what is a very tranquil spot.
35 mins, 55.6307, -2.4682 [icons]

28 NORHAM, R TWEED

A peaceful and accessible stretch of the River Tweed. Upstream is Norham Bridge and Canny Island, offering the chance to swim the short distance from England to Scotland. Scenic riverside walks with further picnic and paddling spots both upstream and downstream at Horncliffe. From Norham village centre, follow road N down to river for 400m to parking area. Follow path L to beach and swim spot. Canny Island is 800m upstream at 55.7166, -2.1736.
1 mins, 55.7222, -2.1647 [icons]

RIVER TILL

29 TWIZEL BRIDGE, R TILL

Situated in a picturesque gorge beneath a lovely Tudor arch bridge, this section of the Till has some deep pools near the bridge and a beach by the broken weir with pools and shallower rapids. Located just of the A698. Park on L just after Twizel Bridge at 55.6826, -2.1838. Follow footpath signed 'Twizel Castle' by parking area, then drop down to riverbank and follow path around to weir for beach and swim spot at 55.6836, -2.1866.
5 mins, 55.6837, -2.1867 [icons]

30 ETAL WEIR, R TILL

Fun swim spot at the end of pretty Etal village. Some rapids to play in and deeper pools for swimming, with paddling by the small weir. Grassy bank and picnic tables. Heading N on B6354 in Etal village, turn L and continue past castle on L to a small parking area by river.
2 mins, 55.6491, -2.1201 [icons]

31 FORD BRIDGE, R TILL

An accessible deep pool with a rope swing on a meander of the river by the stone bridge, with shallow entry from a

small beach. Near Ford Bridge Campsite. Head W out of Ford, crossing B3654 and stone bridge to large parking area almost immediately on L behind trees.

2 mins, 55.6303, -2.0982

32 ROUTIN LYNN WATERFALL

On a path leading up to Goatscrag Hill, find this pretty, secluded waterfall in a hidden ravine, falling about 6m into a sun-dappled pool of the Broomridgedean Burn. Combine with a visit to the largest carved outcrop of rock art in Northern England nearby (55.6240, -2.0270). From Ford, follow the B6353 towards Heatherslaw, then turn L at end of village towards Kimmerston. After 2.5km, turn L at T-junction and continue for 2.8km to parking on R by roadside on no through road (55.6231, -2.0276). Follow footpath opposite (worn signpost for Routin Lynn Farm) for 100m, listening for rushing water to L. Scramble down path through woods down to falls.

10 mins, 55.6247, -2.0300

CHEVIOT HILLS

33 HETHPOOL LINN, COLLEGE BURN

Screened by trees beside a footpath, a channel of deep pools has formed between the cleft of the rock walls of the College Burn, leading from the waterfall. A magical place for a summer's evening dip. Head N from Wooler on the A697 and after 4km keep L on to the B6351. Continue for 6.5km through Kirknewton and take L for Hethpool. Continue past Hethpool House to car park on L. Walk back along road to gate on R and footpath signposted 'St Cuthbert's Way'. At second field cross stile on L, pass through field then a second field and cross footbridge to reach paths down to burn on R.

20 mins, 55.5500, -2.1569

34 THE HEN HOLE AND THREE SISTERS

This dramatic gorge cuts an enormous slice out of the steep, west-facing slopes of the mighty Cheviot, creating a channel for the Three Sisters Waterfall, which pours into the Hen Hole. End your journey here or scramble on to the summit of the Cheviot, the county's highest hill. Limited number of parking passes issued each day for car park at Mounthooly Bunkhouse, obtained from College Valley website (£). From parking at Mounthooly Bunkhouse (NE71 6TU), follow footpath behind bunkhouse, passing woodland on R and continuing through valley before turning a corner to Hen Hole and waterfall. Alternatively, park

at free Hethpool car park and follow burn to Mounthooly as above (extra 8km).

60 mins, 55.4760, -2.1794 🧍🏕️🚶🛶📖⭐❄️

35 HARTHOPE LINN, HARTHOPE BURN

Magical, hidden waterfall and plunge pool in a tiny, wooded gorge at the foot of the Cheviot and Hedgehope Hill. Further fun upstream above the falls, where a cataract has created a natural water slide. Signed 'Harthope Valley' from the Anchor Inn in Wooler. Park at road end at Langleeford (55.4939, -2.0790) and walk 3.5km up Harthope Burn. Pass through gate on L to find falls.

60 mins, 55.4759, -2.1159 🧍🏕️🚶🛶📖🍴

36 LINHOPE SPOUT, LINHOPE BURN

Spectacular 18m-chute of water falling into a deep plunge pool where daring souls leap off ledges into the clear, cool waters of the Linhope Burn. Situated in a pretty glade beneath the Cheviot Hills and prehistoric hill forts. Travelling N on the A697, pass through Powburn then take L turn signposted 'Breamish Valley' and keep on through village, past haugh land and pretty paddling and picnic spots, to end of public road. Continue 2.5km on foot

through hamlet and on to open moor. Signed to spout below on R.

45 mins, 55.4474, -2.0678 🧍🏕️🚶🛶📖🍴

RIVER COQUET

37 HINDHOPE LINN, KIELDER

Spectacular waterfall with a refreshing plunge pool in an enchanting dell of old Scot's Pine and larch, reminders of the ancient forests here. Park at Blakehopeburnhaugh car park at the N end of Kielder Forest Drive, off the A68. Pass through gate over River Rede on to gravel track and after a few metres take R turn on to woodland path to falls.

20 mins, 55.2936, -2.3489 🚌🚴🛶🏊🅿️🛶🍴

38 IRVING POOL, R COQUET

Idyllic swim spot surrounded by open meadows and moorland. Plunge pool, some rapids and a small waterfall. Buckham's Bridge, once the haunt of whisky smugglers, is 2.5km further on with shallow rapids and paddling spots (55.3681, -2.2064). Follow the River Coquet from Rothbury and B6341 to Alwinton. Cross River Coquet at Linbriggs farm and continue for 1.2km to park by river.

2 mins, 55.3593, -2.1748 🛶🏕️🛶🚶

39 HARBOTTLE LAKE, HARBOTTLE

Secluded moorland tarn just over the brow from the mythical Drake Stone, perfect for a wild swim after a hike up the Harbottle Hills. Shallow entry at NE corner. From Rothbury follow B6341 for 6.5 miles, then turn R onto Greenside Bank for 7km to car park on R at end of Harbottle village. Cross road and head R to footpath sign on L after a few metres. Cross field to gate and follow forest perimeter N through another gate and onto narrow track up to the Drake Stone, then descend hills to lake. Note MCD signs.

5 mins, 55.3333, -2.1316 🧍🏕️🚶🔻🛶🛶

40 HOLYSTONE, R COQUET
Delightful meadow-side riverbank next to footbridge with some tree shade. Paddling and deeper pools. Head S out of Harbottle, then just before Sharperton (before the river bridge) turn R and continue for around 80m to parking on L and footpath across field to bridge and riverbank.

2 mins, 55.3222, -2.0687

41 ROTHBURY STEPPING STONES
Stepping stones over shallow rapids with deeper pool to the right. In Rothbury, head towards Cragside on the B6344. Turn R opp

almshouses for parking and river. Follow footpath downstream for further river access points. Alternatively, for meadow-side paddling and pools head 2km upstream beyond Beggars Rigg car park to kissing gate on L then follow path into field to a meander of the river and beaches (55.3042, -1.9296).

1 mins, 55.3098, -1.9061

42 PAUPERHAUGH BRIDGE, R COQUET
A tranquil stretch of the River Coquet beneath the attractive stone five-arch Pauperhaugh bridge with a slope by the weir. From Rothbury, follow B6344 for 5km to Pauperhaugh and parking in pull-in over bridge.

2 mins, 55.2887, -1.8435

ALN & COAST

43 LADYBURN LAKE, DRURIDGE BAY
A freshwater lake with a stone jetty, surrounded by woods and meadow. Stepping stones halfway around the lake which kids love hopping across. Picnic tables. Open daylight hours. From Amble follow the A1068 S for 4.5km, then take L turn signed 'Druridge Bay Country Park'. Parking is first L up the rise, in the water

sports car park. One-hour free parking at machine.

1 mins, 55.2938, -1.5780

44 WARKWORTH HERMITAGE, R COQUET
Swim across the pretty River Coquet to the fascinating Medieval hermitage carved out of the rock face, once a private chapel. Look out for the unusual multi-trunk yew. From behind Warkworth Castle follow the path upstream along the river for 300m to where the little ferry boat usually waits to cross. Beaches upstream.

10 mins, 55.3462, -1.6206

45 LESBURY WEIR, R ALN
A pretty weir pool near Alnmouth, sheltered by trees. Just N of Alnmouth roundabout (A1068) at Hipsburn find footpath/gate on L, 100m before new river bridge at Lesbury. Roadside parking in either Hipsburn or Lesbury.

10 mins, 55.3966, -1.6371

46 HULNE PARK, R ALN, ALNWICK
Just upstream of Monk's Bridge in Hulne Park. Sandy beach with paddling and deep enough for a longer swim. Perfect picnic spot. Ruins and follies to explore in the park. In Alnwick, park in Ratten Row at

entrance to Hulne Park (55.4167, -1.7166).
Follow Red route, passing Duchess Bridge.
Just after Monk's Bridge, find beach a
few metres upstream. (Park opens 11am
- 4pm. Park may close on certain days.
Check website or call Estate Office 01665
510777).
40 mins, 55.4255, -1.7235 🏊🏕🐟🚶🛈

R WANSBECK & BLYTH

47 MITFORD CASTLE, R WANSBECK

Deep section of river, with a small beach
downstream of the stone bridge, as it
loops away from the romantic ruins of
11th-century Mitford Castle. The castle,
which sits on an adjacent hillock, became
the HQ of notorious kidnapper Sir Gilbert
Middleton in the 14th century and was used
to hold prisoners. From Morpeth follow the
B6343 for 3.5km through Mitford, then
take a L turn to cross bridge to parking on L.
Follow footpath down from bridge on R
2 mins, 55.1638, -1.7328 🏊🏕🖼

48 LADY CHAPEL WOODS, R WANSBECK

A delightful woodland trail passes the site
of a ruined chapel to a secret, dappled
swim spot at a bend in the river with deep
pools, little rapids and stone ledges. There
are a couple of picnic benches in a clearing
of the trees nearby. From Morpeth follow
the A192 then the A196 towards Bothal
After 5.5km cross river bridge, then take
immediate L to car park (55.1698, -1.6232).
Follow footpath through woods, passing an
intriguing coat of arms carved in the rock
face, the Jubilee Well (dated 1887) on the
R and picnic benches on the L, then follow
path down to beach at river bend. Other
swim spots en route, including a deep pool
at 55.1671, -1.6554. Also check out shallow
paddling and deeper pool at Bothal Castle
stepping stones in Bothal village (55.1718,
-1.6238).
25 mins, 55.1661, -1.6566 🏊🏕🖼🚶

49 WANSBECK RIVERSIDE PARK

A calm, smooth stretch of the River
Wansbeck for an upstream or downstream
swim with plenty of riverside parking.
Children's playground and caravan site
nearby so not particularly wild. Head E of
Morpeth on the A197 for 8km, then turn R
on to Sheepwash Road (A1068) and L on to
Wellhead Dean Road, keeping L for parking
at Riverside Park.
1 mins, 55.1711, -1.5945 🏊🏊

50 PLESSEY WOODS, R BLYTH

Woodland paths wind down to the riverside
for paddling and swimming at the wooden
jetty or find the small beach and deep pool
at the bottom of the steep steps to the
river (55.1115, -1.6289). Take care as the
riverbed has sharp rocks. Cafe at the visitor
centre. From the junction of the A1 and A19
at Seaton Burn, head N on the A1068 for
7km. Country park is signed on L. Walk past
visitor centre, through woods and head L to
follow route down to riverside.
20 mins, 55.1178, -1.6281 🏊🏕

51 HUMFORD MILL, R BLYTH

Stepping stones over the river leading to a
pretty riverside walk through Humford
Woods. Shallow paddling here with
deeper pools upstream by the weir.
From Bedlington follow the A193 from
roundabout towards Blyth, turning R then R
again, following track to parking at Humford
Mill car park (NE22 5RT).
2 mins, 55.1194, -1.5809 🏊🐟🚶

52 HARESHAW LINN, BELLINGHAM

Cross six charming bridges through ancient
woodland to a dramatic 9m-waterfall. There

are several smaller falls on the way up; the
secluded second fall has an enticing plunge
pool (55.1574, -2.2514). This beautiful,
wooded valley was a favourite with the
Victorians, who came here for recitals and
performances. Bellingham is 17 miles N of
Hexham on the B6320. Take the Otterburn/
Redesmouth road from the main street and
turn L immediately after crossing stream to
car park (NE48 2BZ or 55.1453, -2.2520).
Well-signposted circular walk of 5km.
60 mins, 55.1627, -2.2499 🛈

HIGHLANDS & PERTHSHIRE

Glen Coe is famous for its wild and dramatic scenery, but it is a lesser known valley running to the south that holds its most spectacular swimming pools and gorges. A haven for climbers and wild campers, Glen Etive is a place you could spend many days exploring (16).

Picking up a friend in Glasgow on her first visit to Scotland we drove north past Loch Lomond in the evening light before climbing up through the craggy lakes of Rannoch Moor as dusk fell. Arriving at King's House Inn at Glen Coe we pitched our tents in the darkness with the black outline of Aonach Eagach towering over us against the indigo sky. Apart from catching the occasional glint of foam flashing in our headlights, we could only hear the nearby river and hope we hadn't camped too close to its edge.

The whole valley was still in shadow when we awoke the next morning but the sun had caught the top of the mountain and was playing with wisps of cloud. Here, under the dark guardian of Buchaille Etive Mor – The Great Shepherd of Etive – we found ourselves by the most fantastic series of river pools you can imagine. A few yards away our grassy bank dropped into a gentle river lido in a wide meander with a shingle beach and a hundred yards downstream it tumbled into a long gorge with deep lagoons and purple-streaked cliffs.

It was to this beautiful glen that Deirdre, foremost heroine in Irish mythology, came to escape Conor Mac Nessa and his warriors. Her twisted yellow tresses and grey-green eyes were said to lure the gods and mesmerise the mortals. That morning, as the shadow line edged down the mountain wall and the sun broke the high peaks with blinding rays, there was something of her colours in the dawn sky. The tiny road follows the river for over eight miles down to the remote and enchanted sea loch of Etive. The gorge by which we camped remains my favourite place but there are many other swimming holes as well. A mile upstream there

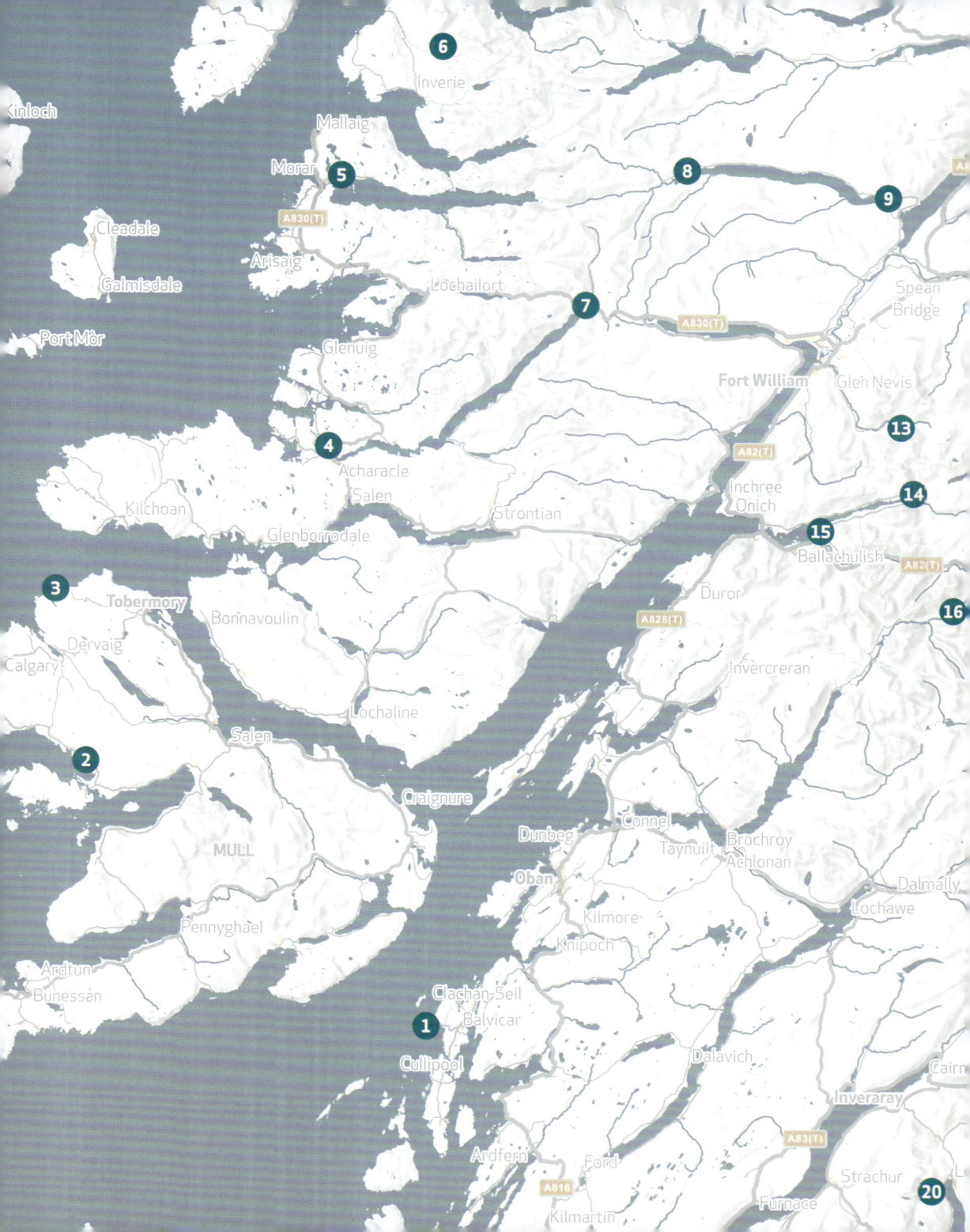

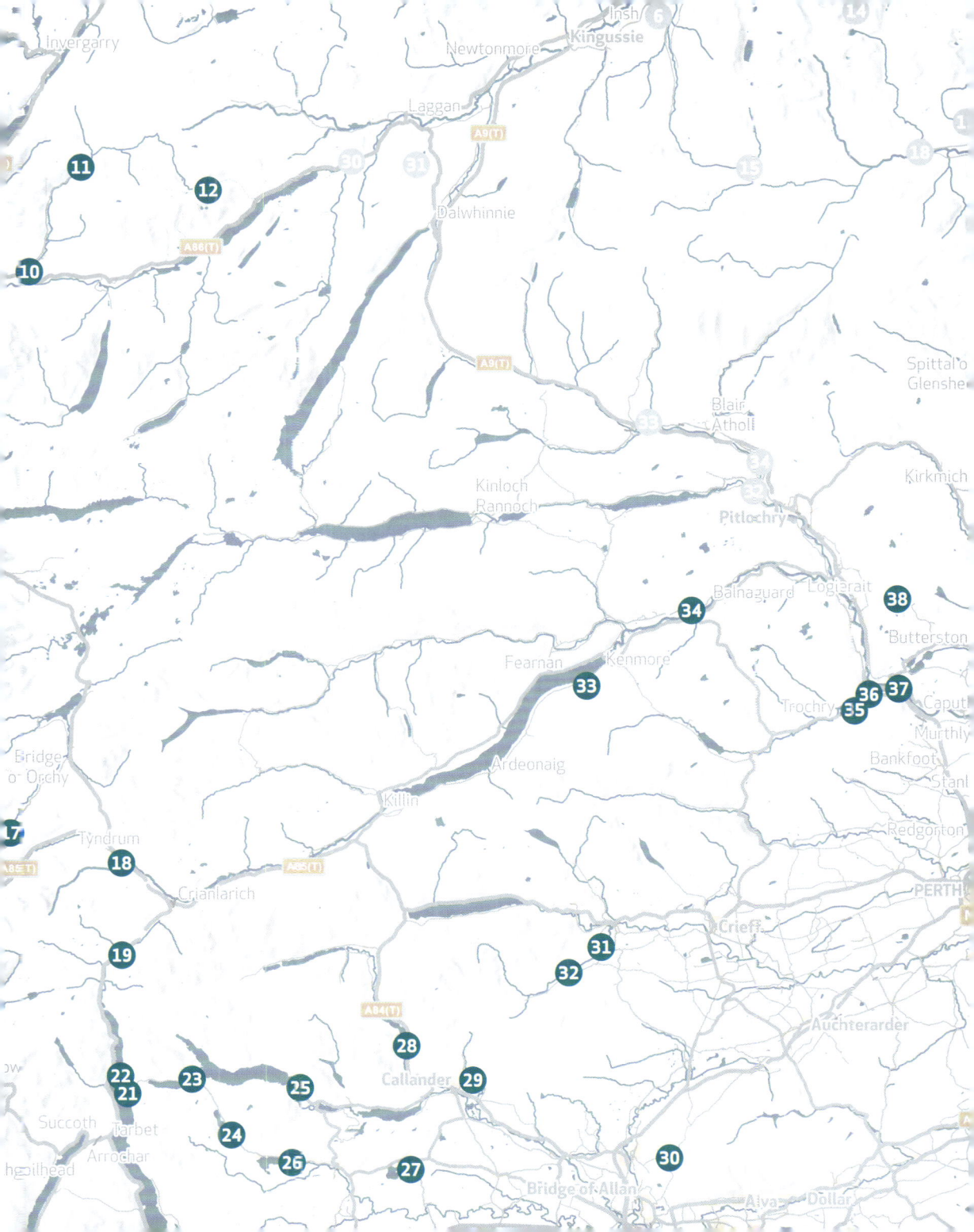

Invergarry

Kingussie
Insh 6
Newtonmore

14

Laggan

11
12
A9(T)
Dalwhinnie
A86(T)

30
31

15

18

10

A9(T)

Spittal o'
Glenshe

Blair
Atholl

33
Pitlochry

Kirkmich

Kinloch
Rannoch

Balnaguard
Logierait
38

34
Butterston

Fearnan
Kenmore

33
36 37
Trochry 35
Caput

Ardeonaig
Murthly

Killin
Bankfoot
Stanl

Bridge
o' Orchy
Redgorton

7
PERTH

Tyndrum
18

Crianlarich
A85(T)

Crieff

19

31
Auchterarder
32

A84(T)

28

22
23
25
Callander
29

21
Succoth
Tarbet

24

Arrochar
26
27
30

goilhead
Bridge of Allan
Alva Dollar

are good shallows for children with a small island and further on the river plunges through a waterfall to open onto a long pool. Two miles before the road head of Glen Coe are deep plunge bowls scooped out of the blue stone, each a bathing place to while away a whole day.

Thirty miles to the north of Glen Coe, on the other side of Fort William, you'll find the Dark Mile, a long line of beech trees and a stone bridge across the Caig Burn. To the right the Eas Chia- aig Falls tumble into a deep, dark pool known as the Witch's Cauldron (9). An old woman was accused of casting her evil eye over Lochiel's cattle, causing them to fall ill and die. When she fell into the pool and drowned the cattle miraculously began to recover from their illness. There are three tiered pools and, while the lower is the largest, the upper two have wildly contorted rock striations that are particularly noteworthy. There may have been some witch-like trickery going on the day we were there. Having dipped in the Witch's Cauldron we headed further up the remote lane to find somewhere to swim in Loch Arkaig (8). We quickly passed an unusually early crop of red and white toadstools on the roadside, the magic mushroom Fly Agaric. Suddenly a stone on the road cut open not one but two of the tyres on the car. We had no phone reception and were stranded by the loch overnight. This gave us plenty of time to explore the white shingle beaches and swim but we couldn't help but feel we had been tricked by the Witch's Cauldron and her toadstools.

To the south the national park of Loch Lomond and the Trossachs is home to several lochs and waterfalls imbued with Sir Walter Scott's legends and heroism, from Rob Roy's bathtub (19) on the Falloch to the Lady of the Lake's island on Loch Katrine (25). The Lady of the Lake has many incarnations in British folklore, but Scott's epic poem of 1810 is perhaps the best known. Set on Loch Katrine it features several young chief sons fighting for Ellen's love during the Jacobite uprisings a hundred years before. It's from Ellen's Isle (Eilean Molach) on Katrine that Malcolm Graeme, Ellen's true love, swims to shore in a fit of rage after his fight with Douglas. There are several other islets nearby and it is quite possible, with boat support or in a group, to swim between them still. Access to these islands, and the entire loch, is only open to cyclists and walkers on a private, ten-mile road. The cycleway does make a beautiful way to explore this remote and dramatic woodland with its countless places to swim and camp undisturbed.

Loch Lomond, to the west, was heavily associated with another of Scott's poems: 'Rob Roy'. Based on the real Rob Roy MacGregor, the poem, published on Hogmanay 1817, became so popular that a ship needed to be commissioned to take copies of the book from Leith to London, making Scott a rich man.

Rob Roy was painted as a colourful Scottish Robin Hood by Scott, though his adventures were heavily romanticised. He fought the upper classes, plundered cattle and joined the Jacobean rebellions with a dangerous band of 500 men. Many of Rob Roy's adventures were set on Loch Lomond, also made famous through Robert Burn's love ballad 'Auld Lang Syne'. This is the largest freshwater lake in Britain, set beneath the high peaks of Ben Lomond, and is dotted with islands to the south.

From Loch Katrine and the Trossachs a ten-mile, single-track road through unspoilt country brings you to Inversnaid, the location of Rob Roy's lochside hideaway. This cave can be found among great fallen rocks, its entrance quite obscured, only feet above the waterline. You can step out of the cave almost into the loch to swim (22). A few miles north, at the head of the loch on the river Falloch is Rob Roy's 'bathtub'. This is a stunning setting for swimming and picnics with a great shiny black rock vat set beneath the Falls of Falloch. Almost 100 feet across, with steep sides, it is one of the largest plunge pools in Britain and certainly makes an impressive place to take a bath (19).

In 1715 Rob Roy became heavily involved in the first Jacobean uprising. His men seized every boat on the Loch and assembled them at Inversnaid. He then set off to fight at the great battle of Sheriffmuir near Dunblane, 30 miles away, where the Earl of Mar was attempting to take Stirling. The battle was fought across the Wharry Burn, now a more peaceful series of small falls known as the Paradise Pools by the families who visit them from nearby Stirling (30).

The shingle beach, plunge pools, rock slides and open meadows are set only a few miles from the motorway, making this an easy day out from Glasgow or Edinburgh. The famous Sheriffmuir Inn sits on the moor above and marks the site of the brutal and inconclusive battle. It was also once home to a famous wrestling bear. It now makes a pleasant après-swim location for a warming hot toddy.

'Then plunged he in the flashing tide. Bold o'er the flood his head he bore, And stoutly steered him from the shore… Fast as the cormorant could skim. The swimmer plied each active limb; Then landing in the moonlight dell, Loud shouted of his weal to tell.'

Malcolm Graeme swimming from Ellen's Isle, in Lady of the Lake by

MULL & OBAN

1 EASDALE ISLAND, SEIL, OBAN

Many old steep-sided slate quarries now filled with Mediterranean-blue water, right next to the sea. Off A816 S of Oban, follow signs to Seil (B844) and Easdale. From Ellenabeich, cross to island by ferry and walk NW to quarries, 400m. The L-shaped one is the usual swimming one.

15 mins, 56.2927, -5.6615

2 EAS FORS, BALLYGOWN, MULL

Cliff-top plunge pools overlooking sea. 16km S of Calgary on B8073, 3.2km N of Oskamull. Pools above and below road leading down to main fall into sea.

5 mins, 56.5031, -6.1541

3 DÙN ARA BATHING POOL

A hidden bathing pool revealed at low tide, constructed to provide shelter from the waves. Good place for spotting seals and sea otters. From Glengorm Castle coffee shop car park (PA75 6QE, but take R fork inside castle gate) cross bridge and follow the track through a gate and out onto grassy land to N of castle. Continue through a 2nd gate before swinging R on a fainter grassy path downhill, which soon reaches a T-junction. Turn R heading towards gate before crossing a stile and heading NW down the field, crossing a 2nd stile. Path goes through 3 more gates then curves L beside a crag where the ruin of Dùn Ara stands. The bathing pool (signposted) is further along path by the sea.

45 mins, 56.6405, -6.1989

MOIDART TO KNOYDART

4 SHIEL OLD BRIDGE

Deep large river pool beneath old stone bridge. Follow Dorlin Rd towards castle, layby for parking on L after bridge. By roadside on L, on lane to the castle.

2 mins, 56.7562, -5.8065

5 LOCH MORAR

Wildly beautiful 12-mile long loch surrounded by woodland and open hillside. The deepest loch in the British Isles. Turn L off the B8008 from Mòrar and park in one of the lay-bys between on the N Shore and Bracara (PH40 4PE).

10 mins, 56.9718, -5.79

6 EAS O CHAORAINN, KNOYDART

Waterfalls and deep pools in the heart of Knoydart. Perhaps the remotest waterfall swim in Britain? Great tavern when you return. Good campsite. Take the ferry from Mallaig to reach Inverie. From the Old Forge Inn (PH41 4PL, 01687 462 358) turn R and find forest track on R after 30m. Follow for 3km, bearing R at junction, another 3km down to the Guiserein river. Long Beach Campsite is 15 min walk from pub (PH41 4PL, 01687 347422).

90 mins, 57.0738, -5.6449 🅿🏕⛺🏔

SPEAN BRIDGE

7 LOCH SHIEL

Wonderful loch surrounded by spectacular Highland scenery close to famous Glenfinnan viaduct. At the head of the loch stands the Glenfinnan monument to the Jacobite rising that started here. Park at the pay & display NTS car park, just off A830 opp turning to PH37 4LT, and cross the road towards the loch. If busy, quieter access from the pier and slipway on NW edge of loch (56.8682, -5.4449).

10 mins, 56.8692, -5.437 🏔⛺🚃🚻

8 LOCH ARKAIG

Swim wild from the enchanting and remote white pebble beaches of Loch Arkaig. Perfect wild camping. Continue 11km on from the Witch's Cauldron.

5 mins, 56.976, -5.2917 ⛺🏔🖼

9 THE WITCH'S CAULDRON, CLUNES

Eas Chia-aig. A series of three falls and pools set in quick succession by roadside. Interesting rock formations. Follow the Lochy river N of Fort William (B8004 / B8005) for 19km, bearing L at Gairlochy. 1.6km beyond Clunes forest, find the bridge and picnic spot. The first pool by the bridge is deep and large. Above are more pools accessed via footpath.

5 mins, 56.9548, -5.0012 🚻🚷⚡🔽

10 ACHADERRY LOCHAN, ROYBRIDGE

Peaceful lochan with a picnic table by the water's edge. Leave the car in the centre of Roybridge, next to the shop (PH31 4AE) head E over the river and follow signs for Bohenie, then take a R into Achaderry estate and finally Lochan Walk. Additional swim spot at 'the meetings' just south of Roybridge. Wide, deep pool at the confluence of the rivers Roy and Spean. Swimming contests were once held here (56.8848,-4.8383).

30 mins, 56.8946, -4.8251 🔽🚷⚡🍴

11 RIVER ROY

Multiple plunge pools and deep bowls along the length of this wide stretch of

river. Easily accessible from road. From RoyBridge, follow Braeroy Road, passing the memorial hall, for 13km. There are numerous spots along the river, particularly by the bridge near the end of the public road, where there is space to pull off.

5 mins, 56.9776, -4.7511 🚷⚡🖼

12 COIRE ARDAIR & CREAG MEAGAIDH

Remote lochan under towering cliffs of Creag Meagaidh. Beautiful and wild. Good for camping. From the car park at Creag Meagaidh reserve at Aberarder on the A86, follow the tarmacked path to the north of the car park, past a whitewashed farmhouse with picnic tables. At fork, follow signs for Coire Ardair. A good path hugs the N side of the glen, with ever-increasing views of the cliffs ahead.

120 mins, 56.9593, -4.5677 🔽🚷🚷⚡🔄

GLENCOE & GLEN EITIVE

13 WATER OF NEVIS & STEALL GORGE

Beautiful river in steep-sided gorge, with Ben Nevis behind. Just beyond the Glen Nevis Rope Bridge, the river widens and deepens enough to swim. Wild camping in the adjoining meadows. Cross the rope bridge for one of the most picturesque and

16

16

spectacular waterfalls in Scotland, Steall Waterfall. The 120m cascade is the perfect backdrop to an already stunning glen (no pool). From Fort William take the road that winds up the glen (PH33 6SY) to the Upper Falls car park at the road end. Follow the rocky but obvious path up into the higher reaches of Glen Nevis, following the river.
20 mins, 56.7723, -4.9814 ▥▽▣▦▩▦▨▧

14 GREY MARE'S TAIL
Impressive waterfall, with water cascading for 50m in a single leap. For adventure lovers, Vertical Descents run canyoning sessions down the falls (01397 747111). From the car park next to the church in Kinlochleven (PH50 4QT), follow signed Grey Mare's Waterfall path out of the park. Take a L at a T-junction and follow this to the falls.
30 mins, 56.7190, -4.9632 ▣▣

15 GLEN COE LOCHAN
Sequoia and Douglas fir grow in abundance around this tranquil little lochan with easy access for swimming. Leave A82 at Glencoe village (PH49 4HX) and take L signed for Lochan immediately after crossing river. From car park at end, follow well-signed Lochan Trail. Wheelchair friendly.
30 mins, 56.689, -5.0968 ▣▣▣▣▣▣

16 GLEN ETIVE
Dramatic glen with many wonderful pink rock river pools, waterfalls and canyons, easily accessible from the little road. Great wild camping. This first set of pools is one of the best. Heading NW on A82 (Glen Coe) turn L 1.1km after the Kings House Hotel (PH49 4HY, 01855 851259). After 3.2km, the first main waterfall with plunge pools is visible on L near road. Continue further downstream to Eas An Fhir Mhoir, a much higher falls with large tub above (56.6184,-4.9239). A further 2km past the Alltchaorunn farm bridge on L, find large river pool in road bend and, just downstream, a 150m long deep rocky canyon (56.616,-4.9682). More waterfalls at (56.6161,-4.9809). For a real campsite try Red Squirrel 11km further along the A82, Glen Coe (PH49 4HX, 07538 763695).
3 mins, 56.6252, -4.9052 ▣▣▣▽

WEST LOCH LOMOND

17 EAS URCHAIDH FALLS
Beautiful ravine with interesting rock formations set amongst ancient pinewoods. Not recommended if river in spate. Glen Orchy Car Park on B8074 (PA33 1BD). Best

swimming is downstream of the bridge.
1 mins, 56.4477, -4.853 ⬛⬛⬛⬛

18 RIVER FILLAN PLUNGE POOLS

Secluded and little-known plunge pools hidden just off the West Highland Way. Turn off the A82 for Dalrigh (FK20 8RX) and follow the road swinging L to car park. Head R out of car park and take L past several houses. Take a further L following track down to a small beach by the River Fillan. Pools lie a short distance upstream on the main river.
10 mins, 56.4236, -4.6934 ⬛⬛

19 FALLS OF FALLOCH, CRIANLARICH

Huge plunge pot under a great waterfall known as Rob Roy's Bathtub. Spectacular great lido provides a large area in which to swim and dive. From Crianlarich A82 head S, car park signposted. Follow the wood and walk downstream for further pools. Historic Drover's Inn at Inverarnan (G83 7DX, 01301 263 108).
3 mins, 56.3502, -4.6928 ⬛⬛⬛

20 LETTERMAY BURN, LOCHGOILHEAD

Waterfall pools and rock slides, plus jumps when the water levels are high. From Lettermay, follow the gravel track SW past Lettermay House (PA24 8AE) – part of Cowal Way. After 100m the track splits, go R another 100m and down track through gate to river. Walk up river 800m for three waterfalls. Path on S side is tricky; cross for an easier path.
20 mins, 56.1612, -4.9317 ⬛⬛⬛

TROSSACHS & CALLANDER

21 INVERSNAID, LOCH LOMOND

These small, sandy beaches not far from the Inversnaid Hotel (FK8 3TU) are a great place from which to swim in Loch Lomond and easily reached on the West Highland Way path, which runs all the way up the east side of Loch Lomond. Park at Inversnaid Hotel (FK8 3TU, 01877 386223). Follow the West Highland Way path S down the loch for various little beaches and coves.
15 mins, 56.2391, -4.6844 ⬛⬛

22 ROB ROY'S CAVE, LOCH LOMOND

Remote stretch of northern Loch Lomond on West Highland Way. Swim from Rob Roy's Cave. From Inversnaid Hotel (FK8 3TU, 01877 386223) follow Highland Way 1.2km N along loch to find cave signposted and marked with white letters on rock. Inversnaid can be reached from Aberfoyle or by ferry/Waterbus from Inveruglas or Tarbet A82.
15 mins, 56.2534, -4.6947 ⬛⬛⬛⬛⬛

23 LOCH ARKLET

Viewpoint and camping spot with an excellent panorama over to the Arrochar Alps. Black grouse gather in a 'lek' on the foreshore, so come in the evening in early summer to watch the males strutting their stuff. Great place for a picnic. Take B829 road leading W from Aberfoyle to Inversnaid, passing Lochs Ard and Chon. Arklet is reached shortly after. There is space to pull a car off the road beside a gate (56.2508, -4.5878). Take path down to loch
5 mins, 56.2507, -4.592 ⬛⬛⬛

24 LOCH CHON

Amazing wild swimming spots with several leafy islands. Beautiful woodlands throng the crinkled shores. Loch Chon lies on the W side of B829, along the winding road W out of Aberfoyle. As you head N there are two car parks 600m apart on the E side of the loch. Access is better from the first; the second is for the campsite.
2 mins, 56.2056, -4.5347 ⬛⬛⬛⬛

past FK8 3RA and the car park for the Inchmahome ferry. After 500m park in Lake of Menteith Car Park and cross road to small beach.
2 mins, 56.1776, -4.2771 ⬅🛶🎣♨🚗🛟🚻🏊

28 LOCH LUBNAIG
Sparkling loch nestled in the shadow of Ben Ledi. There are several good entry spots to the pebble shore from two car parks off the A84, 4km N of Kilmahog/FK17 8HD. The beach in front of the café car park is a safe and comfortable entry spot. Road side parking available if car parks closed.
2 mins, 56.2774, -4.2834 ⬅🚗🏕🍴🏔🛟

29 BRACKLINN FALLS, CALLANDER
Popular waterfall in Callander on the Keltie Water, with further pools upstream. Car park signed off A84 in Callander. Follow signed path for pools. Continue on to Scout Pool (56.2631, -4.1973) via new bridge and woodland walk (2km) or take road from car park. Further pools 1km along the road at Braeleny farm.
15 mins, 56.2497, -4.188 ⬅

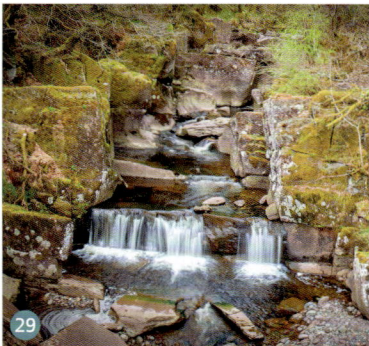

25 ELLEN'S ISLE, LOCH KATRINE
Swim to the famous islet in this beautiful loch setting. Follow signs for Trossachs Pier (A821 N of Aberfoyle). From car park bear R and continue 2.5km by foot or cycle along loch shore.
30 mins, 56.2437, -4.4365 🚴🛟

26 LOCH ARD
A brilliant swimming spot in the Trossachs, also very popular for canoeing and kayaking. Easily accessed from the B829 roadside with lay-by parking, or through forest walks on the S side of the loch. Loch Ard Forest is signed from the B829 W of Aberfoyle. For walks, start at Loch Ard Forest Car Park (FK8 3TG) signed in Milton.
5 mins, 56.1832, -4.448 🛶🚗🏔🛟

27 LAKE OF MENTEITH
Tranquil loch that is the only natural 'lake' in Scotland – a couple of others so named are man-made. Its islands are home to Inchmahome Priory, a beautiful ruined monastery, and Talla Castle, seemingly built of stone taken from the priory. There is an attractive beach just off the road. Popular with local fishermen. Priory/ Lake of Mentieth Fisheries is signed down the B8034 off the A81 E of Aberfoyle. Go

DUNBLANE & COMRIE

30 SHERIFF MUIR PARADISE POOLS
Plunge pool with a fun rock slide into the Wharry Burn. Take Glen Road E out of Dunblane, turn L at Kippenross Home Farm, then R at final T junction, follow Sherrifmuir Road S towards Cauldhame (FK15 0LN) for 1.5km crossing a weak bridge. Climb gate R down through open field into wooded gorge below pylons.
5 mins, 56.1872, -3.9046 🚶⬅

31 THE LINN A' CHULLAICH, COMRIE
Comrie's very own pool is a lovely hidden place for a dip on the Waters of Ruchill. It has a small stony beach where you might find locals warming up with lunch by a campfire. Head W from Comrie and cross

humpback bridge off A85 signposted for Ross. After 1km at warehouses take L fork and after 1.5km, park on L by the river.
2 mins, 56.3561, -4.0036

32 SPUT A'CHLEIBH, WATERS OF RUCHILL
Secluded and exciting little canyon below falls with rope swings. Great for jumps. Signed Cultybraggan Camp from B827 Comrie, park by the little stone bothy (56.3339, -4.0470) and bushwhack down.
10 mins, 56.3357, -4.0501

UPPER TAY

33 FALLS OF ACHARN & KENMORE
Wonderful wooded gorge with tumbling waterfalls and a small man-made cavern and balcony, known as Hermit's Cave, built in the 18th century to provide picturesque views of the falls. Great place to spot red squirrels. Park in Acharn Village (PH15 2HT) on S of Loch Tay. Follow path signed for walk as it ascends into the woods and to the cave before continuing to upper falls. Afterwards enjoy a longer swim from popular Kenmore beach (56.5836, -3.9965), perhaps out to the Ilse of Spa.
30 mins, 56.5639, -4.0241

34 ABERFELDY, R TAY
The River Tay is its most perfect here, with fine pebble beaches, deep pools and plenty of access. Park at the golf club car park, just N of town bridge. Take riverside trail downstream to beach after 200m. Or there's a little bay with big stones just 200m W out of town, path down through trees (56.6179, -3.8769).
5 mins, 56.6234, -3.8729

35 RUMBLING BRIDGE, R BRAAN
Dramatic falls with many pools and ledges up and downstream. Walk 1.5km up from the Hermitage or park at Rumbling Bridge car park, signed on R off the A822, 3km S of Dunkeld.
10 mins, 56.5517, -3.6338

36 THE HERMITAGE, DUNKELD
Beautiful woodland trail and pools along the Braan leading to Ossian's Hall overlooking Black Linn waterfall. Well-signed National Trust for Scotland site, off A9, W of Dunkeld. Best pools are upstream of bridge and waterfall.
15 mins, 56.5557, -3.6179

37 BIRNAM, R TAY
A hidden sandy beach on the Tay in the shadow of the mighty Birnam Oak tree. Access from Oak Road off Perth Road (PH8 0BJ). On-street parking on Perth Road or outside Birnam Arts (PH8 0DS). Extend walk upriver for further swimming at confluence with River Braan (56.5631, -3.5908)
10 mins, 56.5614, -3.5750

38 LOCH ORDIE
A secluded hill loch reached by a long (8km) scenic walk through the Atholl woods and heather moorlands north of Dunkeld. A very peaceful and refreshing spot for a swim. Park at Cally car park just N of Dunkeld (PH8 0EP). From here follow signed Atholl Woods path past The Glack, Mill Dam, Rotmell and Dowally Lochs. At Raor Lodge turn R past the house. For return walk, turn R through rhododendrons and before the house, turn R uphill and go through gate in deer fence. Follow rough track along side of hill to Mill Dam and pick up the track you took on outward route back to the car park.
150 mins, 56.6322, -3.5767

CAIRNGORMS & RIVER DEE

High above Loch Ness, in the Monadhliath Mountains, the enchanted River Findhorn gathers its waters, preparing to carve out a string of gorges and river pools inhabited by gods and satyrs.

As one of the longest rivers in Scotland, the Findhorn is famous for its mystical qualities and rich legends. It has associations with Macbeth at nearby Cawdor Castle, where King Duncan is said to have been murdered, and more recently with the spiritual eco-village of Findhorn, where residents believe the river is sacred and marks a border between the earth and spirit worlds.

At Randolph's Leap, a narrowing gorge overlooked by shelves of yew and Scots pine woodland, the black, peaty waters of the Findhorn twirl and swirl through fissures (3). The river passes over large stones carved and curved by flood eddies, opening onto a wide, calm pool dotted with islands and bays. On the sunny afternoon I visited, it indeed seemed like the perfect place to meet Pan and his nymphs, to frolic and gambol with the satyrs. As you wander through these woods, look out for the two flood stones, protected in iron cages, resembling gravestones. They mark the upper reaches of the great Muckle Spate of 1829, likely the greatest flood in British history.

After a sultry week in August, a thunderstorm erupted over the Monadhliath Mountains. It rained for three days and three nights, washing away all the bridges except for nearby Dulsie (2). The position of the stones shows how high the waters rose, climbing over 10 metres and consuming vast tracts of land on both sides of the valley. The bridge at Dulsie survived only because the gorge it spans is so high; the spate came within a foot of its central keystone. This is a well-known beauty spot, with a path above the bridge leading down to rocky shallows. Below the bridge lies a large area of calm, deep water where a waterfall joins from the right bank beside a small sandy bay. Silver and downy birch shade

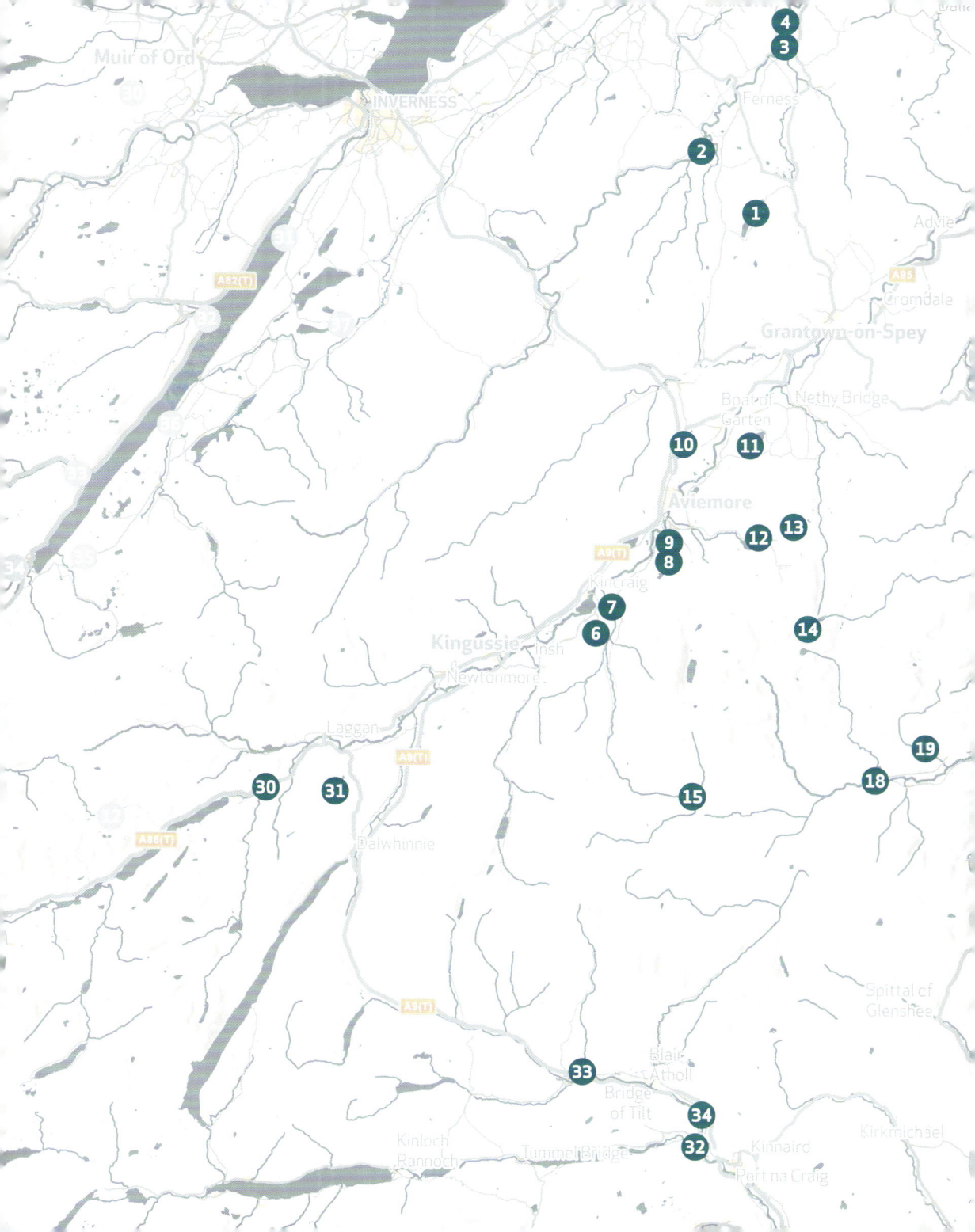

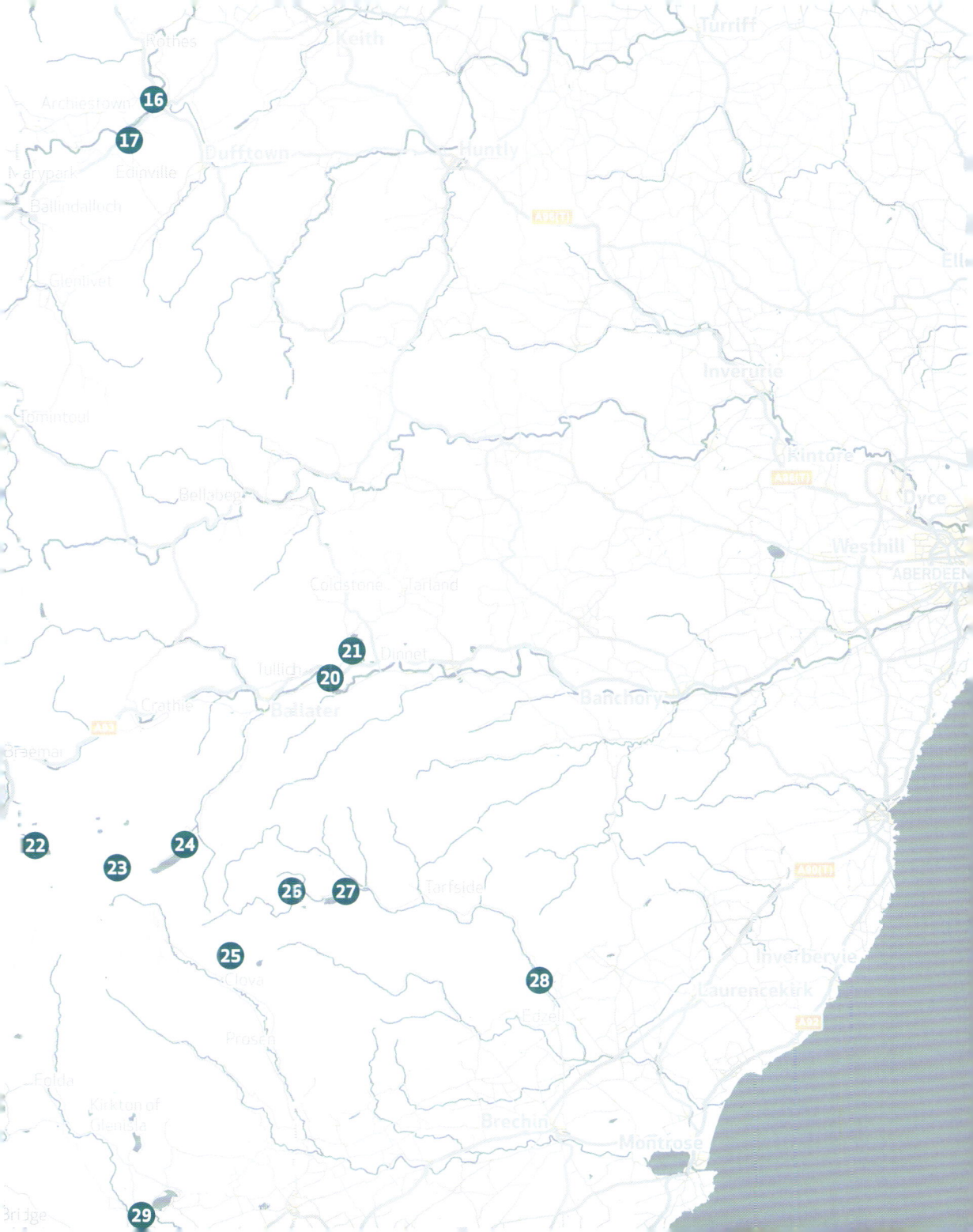

the riverbanks, accompanied by rowan, willow, and bird cherry, alongside great stands of aspen, now rare in Scotland. Dippers and ospreys are occasionally seen, and if you look carefully, you might spot a rock remarkably similar to a rhinoceros bathing in the pool below.

To the south, the Cairngorms National Park is the wildest landscape in Britain. Home to four of Scotland's five highest mountains, the range is a rocky massif, encrusted with snow and ice for most of the year. As one of the coldest plateaus in Britain, it harbours wildlife typically found in the Arctic.

At lower, warmer levels, this granite geology has produced beautiful rivers and lakes. At Feshiebridge, the river flows through smoothed strata of deep grey, layered with vanilla quartz and blueberry granite (7). There are narrow pools and rapids upstream, and on a hot day, the rocks act as solar heaters, absorbing the sun's rays and transmitting heat to the water. Under the bridge, the water tumbles in a helter-skelter, cutting deep circular eddies and creating a moonscape of fantastic shapes. The pool beneath the bridge is large, clear, and still. On the left bank stands a solitary Caledonian Scots pine, at least two hundred years old, its trunk furrowed and its long, lichen-clad branches arching down to sip from the river. Its old roots provide perfect nooks and crannies to curl up and sleep among the soft litter of pine needles. Opposite lies a sandbank of pure white rounded pebbles, an inviting spot to swim to. As you dive into the water, you are struck by its clarity. Unlike other Highland streams, the Feshie is not peaty; instead, the water casts a golden yellow glow onto the riverbed, allowing you to snorkel between the rock shapes, gazing at millions of years of geological history. For a big trek explore the pools of its upper reaches in Glen Feshie and the Eidart Falls (15)

On the edge of the Rothiemurchus estate next door, the tree-lined Loch an Eilein sits at the foot of the mountains, with an island at its centre featuring a ruined, ivy-clad castle (8). Shrouded in early morning mist, it presents a quintessential Scottish image. Estimated to be at least 600 years old, the castle fell into disuse several hundred years ago, but its stones have been protected by its island location ever since, allowing a small forest to grow within. While the estate probably does not encourage swimming across to the island, the experience is serene nonetheless. The loch waters lie still beneath the gently shelving banks, and although the castle is only a hundred yards from the shore, the backdrop of the Cairngorms rises thousands of feet high. Where the castle wall meets the water, there's a small doorway through which you can clamber. Inside, the old hall features a tumbledown fireplace and trees growing through the roof. Wildflowers have sprouted in the kitchen range, and a family of crossbills has nested under an old stone seat in the small garden.

A further twenty miles south-west up the whisky-famous valley of the Spey, the Pattack tributary offers more pools and opportunities for swimming (30). Strathmashie community forest is justifiably popular with wild campers who prefer not to stray too far from their cars. Within a few metres of the car park, you arrive at a large amphitheatre-like bathing pool, idyllically situated among cliffs and waterfalls, with ample space to swim and even a small beach.

In Scotland, it is legal to wild camp an appropriate distance from buildings, but this means that the most accessible beauty spots are often littered with fire pits and toilet paper. Although the Cairngorms may be the wild home to endangered species such as twinflower, capercaillie, dotterel, and mountain hare, it seemed unlikely that I would find them at Strathmashie.

While the Spey flows to the northeast, the Royal Dee runs to the southeast. There's a wealth of royal history here. You'll find Queen Victoria's bridge over the Linn of Dee (18), the stately Balmoral Castle, and extraordinary ice-age geology. This area has traditionally been a summer holiday destination for the royal family since Queen Victoria and Prince Albert purchased the estate and built their Gothic castle in 1852.

There are some beautiful swimming spots along the Dee. Downstream from Balmoral is Cambus o' May – literally, the 'bend in the valley' – featuring a quaint white suspension bridge donated by a gentleman from Kent in 1905. This area has a deep section, and the sandy banks and flat rocks are popular in summer for picnics and swimming. The Deeside railway line used to run this way, and Cambus o' May station was regarded as one of the most picturesque in Scotland, so much so that the directors of the Great North of Scotland Company had a special meeting wagon shunted out to it for their board meetings.

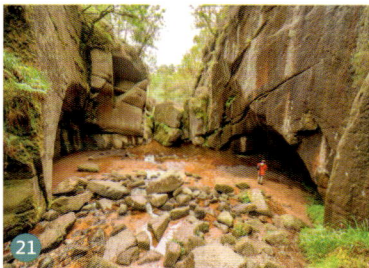

Just a mile up the valley is the Burn o' Vat. You're standing in the riverbed of a once massive whirlpool. The glacial meltwaters that carved out this great cave-ravine 10,000 years ago were ferocious; the rounded sides and arched roof indicate where boulders would have churned and scoured in the force. Stumbling upon this curiosity when the woods are empty is an eerie experience. You can swim across the road, in Loch Kinord (21)

Upstream of Balmoral and six miles west of Braemar – the home of the Royal Highland Games – you will find Victoria Bridge over the Linn of Dee, opened by Her Majesty in 1857. Here, the river passes through a furious and deep rocky gorge before slowing into sunny, shelving pools. From here, you can also continue to the Linn of Quoich, a series of smaller waterfalls and rapids popular with families. This is a fun but steep stretch of river with some plunge pools to dip into if you are cautious. If you look carefully at the river rocks, you'll see the Earl of Mar's Punchbowl, a natural pothole about a metre across, from which the Earl of Mar is reputed to have served hot whisky and honey punch to his Jacobite hunting colleagues in 1715. Three hundred years later, however, the bottom of the pothole has worn right through.

"We came to the Pass of Killiecrankie, which is quite magnificent; the road winds along it, and you look down a great height, all wooded on both sides, the Garry rolling below. I cannot describe how beautiful it is. Albert was in perfect ecstasies." — Queen Victoria's journal, 1844

Referring to it as "my paradise in the Highlands," Queen Victoria retreated to Deeside after being widowed. She suffered greatly after Albert's death and took refuge in her memories of their times together, with their visit to the Pass of Killiecrankie, 25 miles to the southwest, being one of her favourites. This was one of Prince Albert's favourite places, featuring many accessible waterfalls. Here, the third major Cairngorm river system, the Garry, flows south before joining the Tummel at Pitlochry, and in turn the Tay towards Dundee. In a magnificent wooded gorge, a key battle of the Jacobite uprising was fought. The Soldier's Leap is the narrowest part of the gorge (34), across which some soldiers are thought to have leaped while trying to flee in 1689. Further below, hidden from the visitor centre and car park, lies the river pools that Queen Victoria and Prince Albert excitedly looked out over in 1844.

On a midsummer day, with a warm breeze rustling the leaves, I swam out into the blue of a wide pool, reaching the white shingle bank on the far side. There I lay, eyes closed, feeling my skin tingle and dry in the morning sun. Otters, pine martens, red squirrels, and flycatchers inhabit this gorge, but all I spied that day were flecks of white cloud floating on a jet stream high above.

FINDHORN VALLEY

1 LOCHINDORB CASTLE, GRANTOWN

A ruined castle set on an island on a quiet and little-known loch. Signed L off A939, 7 miles N of Grantown-on-Spey.

5 mins, 57.4057, -3.708 🏔🏔🏖

2 DULSIE BRIDGE, R FINDHORN

Ancient bridge and gorge with rapids above and deep pools, waterfall and sandy cove below. Quiet. Dulsie is signed off B9007 (via A939, S of Nairn). Park in signed layby by bridge and follow upstream path for view of gorge and paddling. Climb downstream from bridge on river's L bank to access deep river pools opposite waterfall. Submerged rocks downstream so take care. Just upstream of bridge (go under it) there is a very small sandy cove. Route here via Cawdor Castle (8km from Nairn) to visit inspiration for Macbeth (IV12 5RD, 01667 404401).

5 mins, 57.4507, -3.7814 🏊🏖🏔

3 RANDOLPH'S LEAP, R FINDHORN

Stunning wooded gorge on River Findhorn leading down to rocky headland with access to river beaches and very large river pool and islets. Some shallows for paddling. Follow A940 S of Forres and bear L on B9007 following signs to Logie Steading. 800m beyond Logie find parking and gate down into Randolph's Leap woods. Bear down to L to see the Leap, shallows and head of gorge. Bear down to R to find headland and large river junction pool with islands. Look out for the flood marker stone. Warm up with tea afterwards at Logie Steading (café and craft centre, 01309 611378, IV36 2QN).

10 mins, 57.5272, -3.6708 🏖🍴

4 LOWER FINDHORN GORGE

Great cliff jumping spot. Very steep access from remote forestry track. Bring map or contact Ace Adventures in Relugas for guidance (IV36 2QL, 01309 611769, river bugging, canyoning etc).

20 mins, 57.5453, -3.6699 🍴🏖

5 RIVER DEVERON

Wide, beautiful river with some deep pools. Great place to spot kingfishers and other birdlife. Starting from Duff House (AB45 3SX), head SW for 800m to the river. Follow it upstream for a further 4km to reach Bridge of Alvah. Nearby swim at the popular Inverboyndie beach (57.6714, -2.5551)

15 mins, 57.6527, -2.5308 🚶🏖➕

AVIEMORE AREA

6 UATH LOCHANS

Four small, sparkling lochans amid magical wild woodland scenery. Follow the easy boardwalk path around the water or climb upwards to Farleitter Crag for fantastic views down over the lochans. Take the Glenfeshie turning from the B970 (dir PH21 1NX) 11km S of Inverdruie. After 1.6km take R to park at Uath Lochans car park after 400m. Follow the boardwalk path to lochan or red marker posts up to Farleitter Crag.

90 mins, 57.096 -3.9194 🏖🚶🏕➕

347

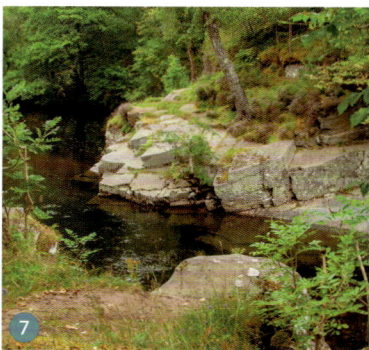

7 FESHIEBRIDGE, KINCRAIG

Fabulous clear water flows down rapids into huge river pool with white shingle beach opposite. Interesting rock shapes and patterns. Rest under the large Scots pine on the bank. A great fun location and one of the few with clear, non-peaty water. As for Loch an Eilein but continue on B970 to Feshiebridge. 5km beyond Eilein turn off. Park close to bridge to find pool downstream.

2 mins, 57.1156, -3.8982 🔽

8 LOCH AN EILEIN, ROTHIEMURCHUS

Another tiny ruined castle on an enchanting lochan island. A busier place, but great fun to swim out to and explore. Or just paddle at the loch edge. Signed Rothiemurchus / B970 from the roundabout at S end of Aviemore. After 1km, turn R (Inshriach / B970), then L again after 1.7km (Loch an Eilein). Bear R 700m along loch edge to reach castle island.

10 mins, 57.149, -3.822 🔽🖼️🏞️

9 LOCH MOR (LILY LOCH)

Small quiet loch with lilies. Sometimes weedy. Take path on L by Milton Cottage 800m before reaching Loch an Eilein.

15 mins, 57.1634, -3.8216 🔼

10 LOCH VAA

A hidden gem just off the A95 NE of Aviemore towards Boat of Garten. Park in the small car park by the cemetery or the larger one just S of the railway bridge. Access can be steep. From cemetery car park climb up bank into the trees, then down the other side. Go left and down towards the shore.

10 mins, 57.2361, -3.8031 🏧

11 LOCH MALLACHIE

Beautiful forest loch surrounded by Scots pine. Part of an RSPB reserve, together with nearby Loch Garten, which is a brilliant place to spot ospreys in the spring and early summer. To walk through forest to loch, park in Garten Woods car park opp Boat of Garten turning from the B970, 800m S of PH24 3BY. Follow Red Trail through trees to Loch. For ospreys and Loch Garten, take Loch Garten turning from B970 at PH24 3BY and follow 2.4km for RSPB Osprey Centre (PH25 3HA).

60 mins, 57.2351, -3.7139 ♿🚶🏕️✿

12 LOCH MORLICH

Rightly one of the most popular swimming spots in the Cairngorms with its large sandy beach, easy access and views of some of Scotland's highest mountains. Take the B970 E of Aviemore towards Glenmore. Park in one of the car parks just before The Pine Marten Bar/Glenmore Lodge (PH22 1QU). Gets very busy in good weather.

5 mins, 57.16716, -3.7019 🏔️

13 LOCHAN UAINE

Tranquil lochan ringed with sandy beaches, set amid ancient Scots pine forest. The clear turquoise waters are attributed to fairies washing their clothes, giving it its other name, The Fairy Loch. Easily accessible but there can be leeches here. Ryvoan bothy lies beyond. Starting from Glenmore Forest visitor centre (PH22 1CY) follow the path that runs E to Glenmore Lodge. Continue past a sign for Nethy Bridge, and follow the good path as it winds through forests and over several small bridges to Lochan Uaine.

60 mins, 57.1751, -3.6549 🚶🏔️❓✿

14 LOCH AVON

Secluded, deep mountain loch with crystal clear waters. Nan Shepherd, iconic local writer, poet and academic wrote of the loch (also known as Loch A'an), 'gazing into its depths, one loses all sense of time'. From the car park at the Cairngorm ski centre (PH22 1RB), head up the path to the W side of Coire Cas to the Fiacaill a' Choire Chais ridge. Descend straight ahead into Coire Raibert and Loch Avon should be visible far below. Follow the steep, rocky path on the E bank of the stream to reach the water. Return by the same route. Serious undertaking in bad weather.

180 mins, 57.0997, -3.6352 🔻🍴❓🏊🏖️🏔️

15 EIDART FALLS, GLEN FESHIE

Deep large pools and waterfalls with clear

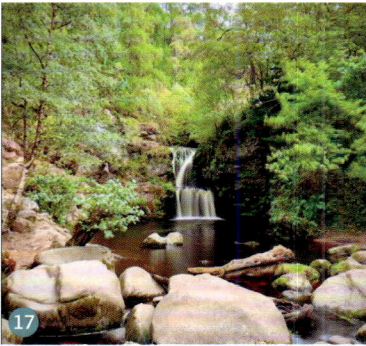

water in this truly wild river valley. Take the Aclean / Glen Feshie Hostel road, just before Feshiebridge, all the way to the road end. Then it's a beautiful 16km riverside trek on a good path to these impressive series of falls and pools. Look out for Allt na Leuma waterfall on creek to L too (56.9814, -3.8334).

240 mins, 56.9763, -3.7886 ▣▲

SPEYSIDE

16 OLD CRAIGELLACHIE BRIDGE

Classic Speyside beach, pools and rapids under the old turreted iron Telford bridge. Good access up and downstream on the Speyside Way and easy parking.

2 mins, 57.4911, -3.1936 🏃

17 LINN FALLS, ABERLOUR

Big deep pool under double waterfall, popular with swimmers. An easy walk or well maintained path from main road A95. Park outside Charlestown of Aberlour cemetery and the path is opposite.

15 mins, 57.4613, -3.2262 ▣▣▣

RIVER DEE

18 LINN OF DEE, BRAEMAR

A dramatic slot canyon cutting under an elegant Victorian bridge leads to deep pool and river beach. From Braemar, follow Linn of Dee Road (signed Inverey) for 8km to reach bridge and Linn of Dee parking. Walk downstream 100m for beach pool.

2 mins, 56.9884, -3.5435 ▣

19 LINN OF QUOICH, R DEE

Plunge pools set in woods and the Earl of Mar's Punchbowl - a round hole carved by the river from the rock. Continue along the road a further 5.5km from Linn of Dee (past Mar Lodge) to road end in open meadow. Head upstream 300m to footbridge and pools (Punchbowl is above bridge) but for

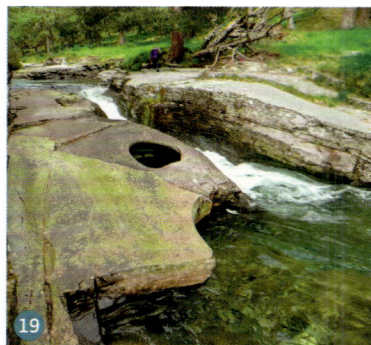

best pools continue another 800m to the upper falls.

15 mins, 57.0123, -3.4765 ▲▼

20 CAMBUS O' MAY BRIDGE, DEE

Pretty gently shelving river beach above elegant white Victorian suspension footbridge. Deep sections and large flat rocks on the nearside. Heading E on A93 from Ballater, pass Cambus o' May Hotel (6.5km, AB35 5SE, 01339 755428) and find turn off opposite, signed. Follow old railway line footpath back up river 200m to bridge . Beach is on far side.

5 mins, 57.0659, -2.9568 ▾⚓⚑

21 LOCH KINORD & BURN O' VAT

On one side of road is a path to lovely Loch Kinord with standing stone, perfect for a proper swim. On other side is a woodland stream leading into to a deep ravine with caves, Burn O' Vat, a fascinating relic from the ice age. Continue 500m beyond Cambus o' May, turn L (B9119) and find Vat visitor centre car park after a mile with path up into woods L or loch on R.

10 mins, 57.0857, -2.9273 ▾⚓⚑

SOUTH EAST CAIRNGORMS

22 LOCH CALLATER

Easily reached but with a wild feel; hemmed in by mountains making for an atmospheric swim. It has a comfortable bothy at its head and forms part of the ancient Jock's Road, a drovers' route across the mountains to Glen Clova. This track is an easy cycle. Park at the large car park off the A93 opp Auchallater Farm (AB35 5XS). From the car park follow the obvious track through the hills to the head of Loch Callater, ignoring any turns and forks along the way. It is possible – and recommended – to walk around the loch, although the inflow river at the far end of the loch may have to be waded.

50 mins, 56.9431, -3.3535 ▾⚓⚑▲B⚑

23 DUBH LOCH

Set below Creag an Dubh Loch, one of the UK's largest and finest mountain cliffs, this is the epitome of wild Scotland -lonely and unspoiled for a wild swim. Leave the B976 S of Ballater on minor road by bridge, signed Glen Muick. Park at the large Spittal of Glen Muick car park at the road end, past AB35 5SU. Walk down the W shore and take a R fork after Glas-allt-Shiel Bothy. Follow this path up and over to Dubh Loch.

150 mins, 56.9266, -3.2432 ▾?▾⚓⚑

24 LOCH MUICK

Grand, 2-mile loch within the boundary of the Balmoral estate and enclosed by steep mountains, including the famous and atmospheric Lochnagar. On the north shore sits Glas-allt-Shiel, once Queen Victoria's summerhouse, now a bothy with sloping lawn down to sandy beach. Park as for Dubh Loch (see entry). Muick is a short distance beyond. A good path rings the entire body of water. 2–4 hours circuit

10 mins, 56.9437, -3.1526 ⚑⛺⚓▮B

25 LOCH BRANDY

Remote loch, high above Glen Clova, hemmed in on three sides by precipitous cliffs. A circuit above the loch gives amazing views both over Angus and across to Deeside and Lochnagar. From car park by Glen Clova hotel (DD8 4RA), a good path passes the bunkhouses at top of car park and continues onto the open hill, passing through gate. Stay on path to loch. To make a complete circuit, walk clockwise, L up and around rim of the corrie.

60 mins, 56.8621, -3.0909 ⚓⚑▾

26 FALLS OF UNICH

Beautiful, hidden falls; brilliant for swimming and wild camping. From Loch Lee (see entry) continue along track on N side of loch past the turn to Inchgrundle House and a boarded-up cottage in a small plantation. Continue up the glen until the falls can be spotted on your L side. Cross a small bridge L and follow the path to the falls.

120 mins, 56.9093, -3.0088 ▾⚓▮▾

27 LOCH LEE

Attractive loch set in a rolling glen with small hydro scheme on one of the burns flowing into it. The walk in passes ruins

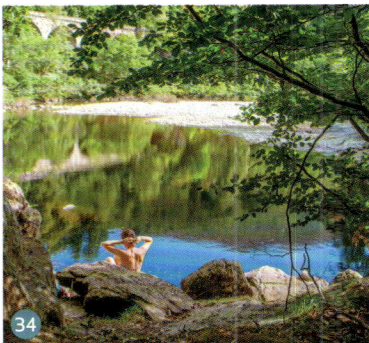

of sandstone Invermark Castle and an attractive church, while track beside the loch leads to the Falls of Unich (see entry). From the B966 at Edzell take minor road for Invermark up Glen Esk to its end at DD9 7YZ. Signed car park R before the end. Walk on along the road to loch, passing castle with the Water of Lee on your L and church at water's edge.

20 mins, 56.909, -2.9359 🏊🐾🏕🚶🚗

28 ROCKS OF SOLITUDE

Pass through mystical 'blue door' into enchanting woodland. Swim in the deep pool at Burn Beach or through the narrows upstream to another pool. Admire the Rocks of Solitude, a granite ravine where salmon can often be seen leaping. In Edzell, there is signed access to the river down a track beside the garage (just S of DD9 7TA). Take a L when you reach river and follow good path on L bank. At Gannochy Bridge, cross the road and bridge, then L through an obvious blue door to continue the walk on the opposite side of river. Burn Beach is 30 mins from the door.

60 mins, 56.8437, -2.6756 🚶🏰🏕🚶🚗🐕

29 REEKIE LINN FALLS

A pair of falls named for the mist that rises as the water cascades through a narrow gorge. Deep plunge pool at the base of the lower falls. Look out for the cave next to the pool and a stone hut perched on the cliff edge above. Park at the Bridge of Craigisla (S of PH11 8QG), a few miles N of Alyth on the B954. Reaching the plunge pool requires a scramble. From car park, cross bridge and follow the B954 for 5mins to find gate in wall. Follow lane into woodland and towards the base of the fall. This was once a well-trodden path but can now be overgrown so bushwacking may be required.

20 mins, 56.669, -3.2103 🅿🚶🏕🏰

30 PATTACK FALLS, STRATHMASHIE

A large calm pool with beach beneath a waterfall on River Pattack in Strathmashie community forest. Right by road and popular with wild campers, so the site can be messy. 7km W of Laggan on A86, look out for car park on L, then 50m. Further narrow pools immediately above. Or continue a mile upstream for more falls and the remains of Druim an Aird village.

2 mins, 56.9816, -4.3609 🅿🏕🏔

31 LOCH CAOLDAIR, LAGGAN

A beautiful hidden loch, surrounded by birch woods and interesting crags. Sandy beach at E end. Wild. 5.5km S of Laggan (A889, Dalwhinnie direction) and 50m before the white cottage (Halfway House bothie), find bridge, parking space and footpath to R, leading 2.5km up to loch.

30 mins, 56.9791, -4.2677 🏔🚶

32 LINN OF TUMMEL

Impressive pools by these roadside falls where river Garry and Tummel meet. The road continues along the wild shores of Tummel and Rannoch lochs. Signed Clunie/Foss off A9 between Pitlochry and Killiecrankie. Follow road 3km to car park (PH16 5NP). You can also take a longer woodland walk to the other bank from Soldier's Leap visitor centre (PH16 5LQ).

3 mins, 56.7185, -3.7327 🅿🚶🏰🐕🚶

33 LOWER FALLS OF BRUAR

Scenic and popular woodland gorge with waterfalls, stone bridges, a natural arch and caves to explore. Signed Bruar/B8079 off A9 N of Pitlochry. Park at House of Bruar (PH18 5TW) and follow signed footpath up through woods to the first bridge and falls. Scramble down to the pool.

15 mins, 56.7739, -3.9341 🅿🏰🐕🚶

34 SOLDIER'S LEAP, KILLIECRANKIE

A beautiful gorge opening out to a large, hidden river pool. Access is a scramble but peaceful and private once there. Railway line passes above L. White pebble beach on far side. Find Soldier's Leap visitor centre (National Trust for Scotland), well signed on old B8079 N of Pitlochry. Follow paths down to the Soldier's Leap, a narrow chasm, but bear down to the L, via an informal path through steep woodland, to reach flat rocks by large river pool, about 100m downstream of the Leap itself.

5 mins, 56.742, -3.774 🚶🏰🐕🚶

NORTH WEST HIGHLANDS

The Faerie Pools on the Isle of Skye are so clear that you have to stare to see if they even contain water. They lie serenely in a sheltered glade of lilac rocks and rowan trees, while the misty towers of the Black Cuillin mountains rise menacingly above.

Skye attracts visitors from all over the world for its breathtaking scenery and some of the most inaccessible wilderness left in Britain today. Rising like great Gaudí spires above giant basalt cliffs, the Black Cuillin Mountains are the remnants of massive volcanoes composed of gabbro, an intensely hard, ancient green igneous rock usually found beneath the ocean. Riddled with deep scars and ridges from millions of years of relentless rain and extraordinary geology, they feature some of the clearest and most colourful waterfalls in the UK, plunging down the mountains to the ocean. High in the hills are several 'Faerie Pools,' renowned in local folklore for their association with enchanted beings.

The best known are on Allt Coir a Mhadaidh in Glen Brittle (5). I arrived in the evening just as the peaks above had cleared for the first time in days. A crimson light glowed on An Dia laid peak, and the water pipe gully that runs from top to bottom gaped open like a liverish wound. A mile up from the road, the first sunken glade appeared like a safe haven within the mountain. The waterfall, pool, and stream were all banked with berries and ferns, sheltered from the wind.

The pools, tinged with pinks and greens, are lined with smooth rock, resembling the inside of a woodturner's bowl. Two are linked by an underwater arch, and with goggles on, I swam back and forth, examining the faerie underworld. The rock face was encrusted with pieces of quartz, emitting an almost phosphorescent emerald glow. Deep down on the pool floor, ingots of rock shimmered on the sandy bed. I stayed in the water, mesmerised, for almost twenty minutes before realising how chilled I had become and quickly made my way home as dusk fell.

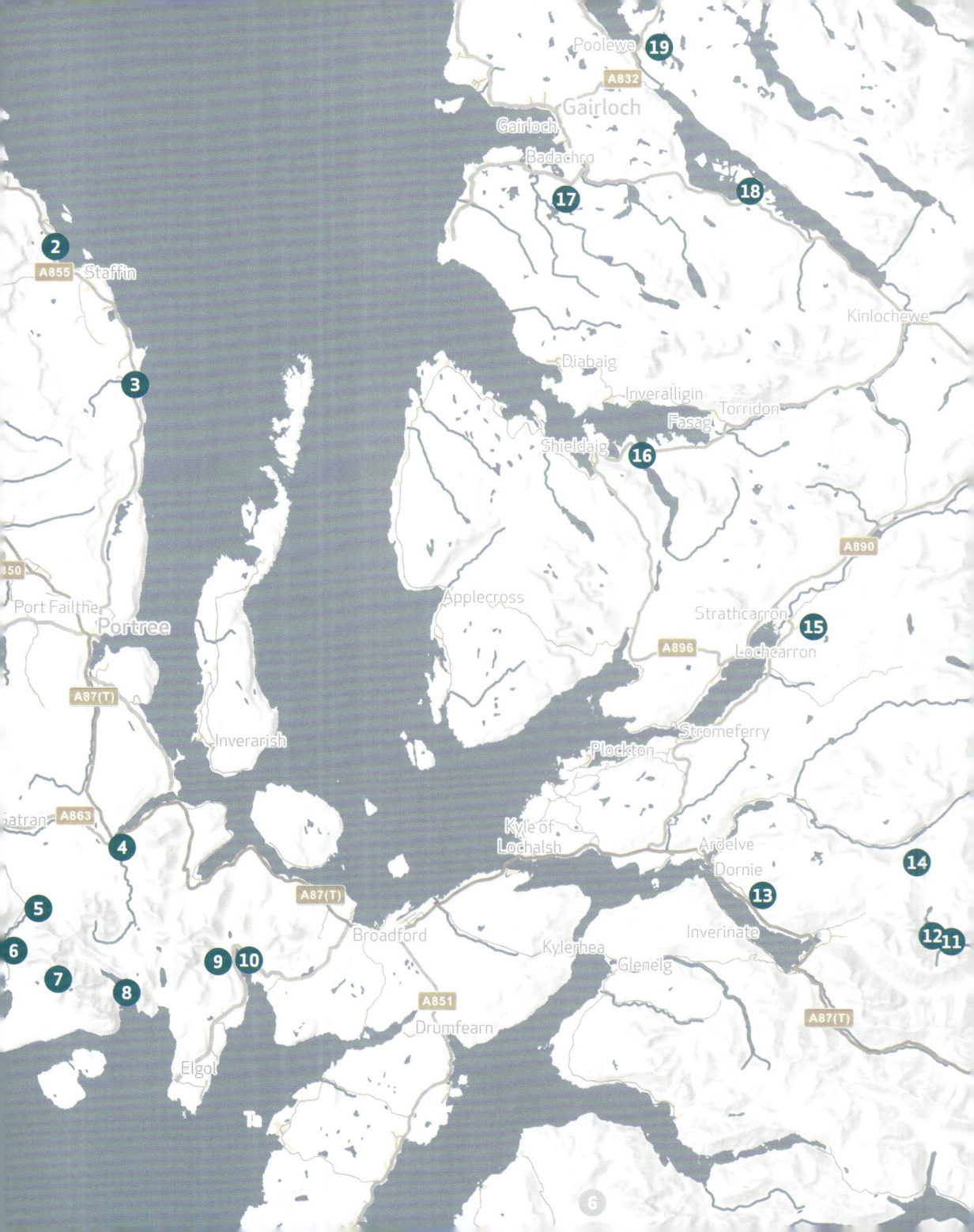

Poolewe

19

A832

Gairloch

Gairloch

Badachro

17

18

2

A855

Staffin

Kinlochewe

3

Diabaig

Inveralligin

Torridon

Fasag

Shieldaig

16

A890

Applecross

Strathcarron

A50

15

Port Failthe

A896

Lochcarron

Portree

Stromeferry

Plockton

A87(T)

Inverarish

Kyle of
Lochalsh

Ardelve

14

Dornie

13

Satran

A863

Inverinate

4

A87(T)

5

Broadford

12 11

6

Kylerhea

Glenelg

7

9 10

8

A851

Drumfearn

A87(T)

Elgol

6

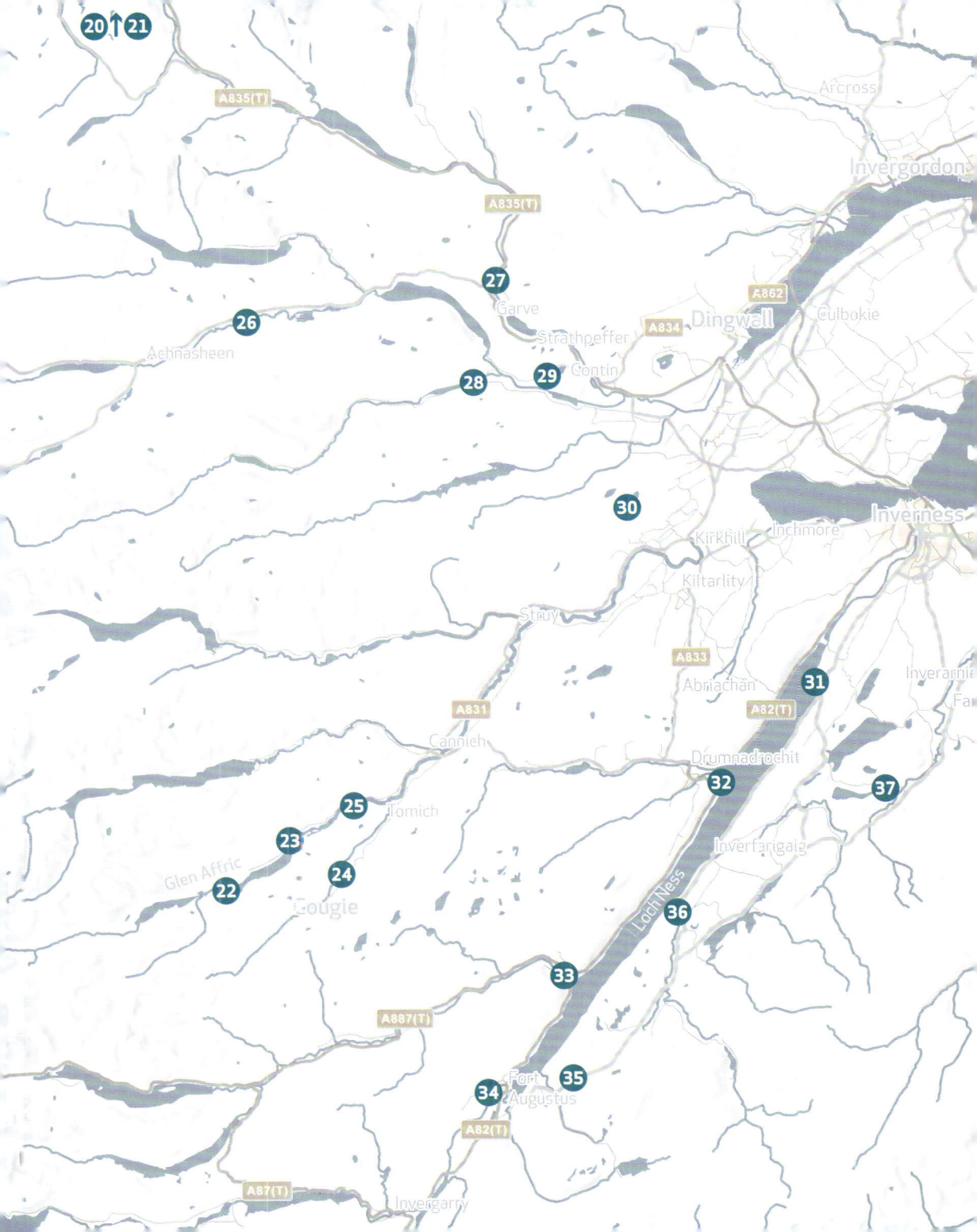

You'll find more faerie pools off the Glen Brittle road and additional ones in the burns draining the Red Cuillins on the Torrin side (6,7). Skye faerie legend tells of the local chief MacLeod, who fell in love with a Faerie princess. The King of the Faeries, Oberon, agreed to the marriage but only on the condition that after a year and a day, the princess must return to her own people. The marriage took place, and a son was born, but the princess had to return to the Land of Faeries. She abandoned her child at Faerie Bridge near Dunvegan. At Uig, just north of Dunvegan Castle, you can find Rha Falls, a large plunge pot, and a mile further into the hills, the famous Faerie Glen, a glacial curiosity dotted with many small, conical-shaped hillocks overgrown with thick, green turf rising several metres in height (1). The landscape is scattered with bleating sheep and occasional strange yellow mushrooms of unknown power or use. I found a tiny loch there with a small brook running through it and a circle of stones shaped like a spiral. According to legend, girls who dance naked on the spiral will have their dearest wishes fulfilled, but that day the circle lay bare.

For more Scottish supernatural, it would be churlish to miss the chance for a swim with the Loch Ness monster. The ruins of Urquhart Castle seemed the most impressive place to dip, but determined to avoid the crowds and coaches, we walked up the road a bit and dropped down through a steep field of yellow mullein and butterflies to reach a more peaceful section of the shoreline (32). More than once during its troubled 700-year history, Urquhart was able to hold out because it could be resupplied by ship. As I swam a little way out into the castle's hidden bay, I had a fish-eye view up to the battlements and could see first-hand the great rocky bluff on which it was built. If you really want to swim with Nessie, though, she'll undoubtedly prefer the many more peaceful bays on the south side of the Loch, so do explore those (31,35,36).

From Drumnadrochit the road winds up into Glen Affric, refuge for one of Scotland's largest remaining stands of rare, ancient Caledonian pine. You'll also find Scotland's second highest waterfall here and a loch with an archipelago of forest-clad islands. Scots or Caledonian pine once comprised the great ancient forests of Scotland. This magnificent tree is entirely different from the regimented rows of conifers seen in forestry plantations. Baobab-like in its grace and statesmanlike in its size, its boughs make graceful open arcs, and its bark is gnarled and red. No two are ever the same. The Affric woods begin as you approach Dog Falls, where several old pines stand cantankerously by the riverside (25). Ten minutes downstream, you'll come to plunge pools ideal for bathing, with hot rocky shelves to lay out a towel and dip a toe. Further below are the main falls, a narrow plummeting chute into a gorge. A footbridge crosses some way down, and from here, it is possible to swim in the deeper water and explore the cliffs on either side.

As the lane winds further up into the glen, views of Loch Beinn a Mheadhoin appear, with its scattering of closely interconnected forest islands (23). There is something about an island—a place of adventure yet retreat—that is irresistible and island-hopping even more so. Examining the map, we located a point on the shore where the straits narrowed to only a hundred yards. From there, we circumnavigated the nearest island in an afternoon—part swimming, walking, and canoeing—before striking out for the second.

The road actually ends as Loch Affric begins (22). From here, truly wild territory unfolds, reaching into the heart of the Highlands, where the forest has stood for over 8,000 years, since after the last ice age. Bonnie Prince Charlie hid here after the Battle of Culloden, and many of the trees are over 500 years old. Roe, sika, and red deer are all present; watch for them at dawn or dusk on the open hills above the tree line. Pine martens have increased in number over the past ten years, although their nocturnal habits make sightings unlikely. Red squirrels, otters, and brown and blue hares may also be found. Keep an eye out for buzzards, golden eagles, or dippers by the water's edge. You may even encounter a wildcat or an adder.

On our return, we camped in deep forest near Plodda Falls (24) in the parallel valley of Abhainn Deabhag. Here lies one of the most spectacular falls in Scotland, yet we were alone as we descended through the Douglas fir forest the next morning. From the old Victorian viewing platform, perched on the edge of a 150-metre-high precipice, miles of woodland opened out across a great tropical gorge. A treetop dawn chorus was in full swing, and down below, we could see a giant pool. The path to the bottom of the falls was slippery and difficult, but the pool was still and calm, with wood sorrel on the banks and only a small stream flowing into it from way up high. Once upon a time, many people must have visited this place—an old wrought-iron walkway is still visible around the edge—but we swam in the great gorge as if no one had been here for years, with just a circling buzzard above and the birdsong filtering through the trees.

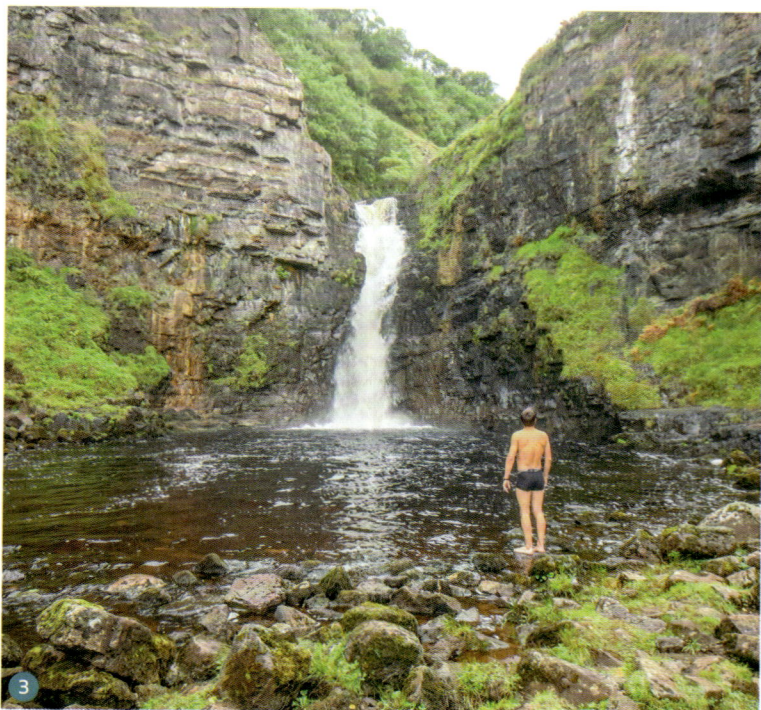

1 RHA BURN & FAERIE GLEN, UIG

Magnificent double waterfall with large plunge pool, just out of town. As you enter Uig from S, bear R on A855 Staffin road, then find footpath and steps up on R, just before bridge. Many more waterfalls up the valley. Also visit the enchanting Faerie Glen with fairy mounds, basalt columns and a little roadside pond. Back S from Uig on A87, turn L after a mile, signed Shaeder (57.5837, -6.3266).

5 mins, 57.5935, -6.3602 🌀

2 LOCH SHIANTA

A pretty walk downhill through woodland leads to a vibrant emerald green lochan with incredibly clear and cold spring water. There's also a hidden holy well. Small car park area off A855 (57.6467, -6.2430)

10 mins, 57.6473, -6.2395 🧍

3 LOWER LEALT FALLS

Big plunge pool at base of tall, dramatic coastal waterfall. There are ruins of a diatomite factory (fossilised silica) on the way down and on the beach. A large layby parking area is just above on A855.

10 mins, 57.5649, -6.1512 🧍🏊

4 ALLT DARAICH BURN, SLIGACHAN

Pretty pool and waterfall at base of interesting slot canyon with more pools above for those who like scrambling. Cross old bridge and main river from Sligachan Hotel (IV47 8SW, 01478 650204) and bear R up stream 600m.

15 mins, 57.2863, -6.1636 🧍🏊

5 FAERIE POOLS, GLEN BRITTLE

Famous 'Allt Coir a Mhadaidh' pools and waterfalls, tinged with pink and blue hues, set under the mystical peaks of the Black Cuillins. Crystal clear water and underwater arch to swim between pools. From Sligachan Hotel (A87) follow A863 / B8009 and turn L (signed Glen Brittle) just before Carbost (Talisker Distillery - yum). After 6km find 'Fairy Pool' car park on L. Cross road and follow clear path down and then up valley, keeping to L of stream for 1.2km to find several pools. Good jump into the underwater arch pool.

20 mins, 57.2497, -6.2554 🌀🏊

6 ALLT A' CHOIRE GHREADAIDH

Also in Glen Brittle, parallel but further S, this is a less visited set of mountainside pools. Further S along the road to youth hostel and Loch Brittle. Also try Coire na Banachdich waterfall and pools (57.2113, -6.2763) and Brittle river itself, in pools alongside road. Great seashore campsite and hostel (IV47 8TA, 01478 640404).

20 mins, 57.2243, -6.2823 🏕🏊🏖

7 COIRE LAGAN

This tiny turquoise lochan is surrounded by the spectacular jagged peaks of the Cuillin range. A spectacular, yet icy cold swim. From the car park for the Fairy Pools (see entry) follow road S to park at end by Loch Brittle, after IV47 8TA. Take path leading E uphill, ignoring path heading S along loch. When path splits, take L fork and continue climbing. After passing shore of Loch an Fhir-bhallaich, keep straight, ignoring path veering off to R, taking the steeper, rockier climb to the l p of the coire. Some mild scrambling required near top. Return same way.

180 mins, 57.2073, -6.2335 🚶♿🚗⛴

8 LOCH CORRUISK, ELGOL

The wildest loch in Britain? Surrounded by the high mountain walls of the Cuillins. From Elgol (IV49 9BJ) follow the coastal path 8km NW or take a half day or full day boat trip on the Bella Jane (0800 7313089) or Misty Isle (01471 866288).

200 mins, 57.1993, -6.1579 🏔⛴🚶🏞

9 FAERIE POOLS, BLA BHEINN

Dramatic waterfall gorge and pools on route up to Bla Bheinn, East Cuillins. From Broadford (A87) follow B8083 (Elgol). 3km beyond Torrin find bridge and follow path up R of stream to find main waterfall (Allt na Dunaiche) after 1.2km. If ascending search out Loch Fionna Coire on the edge of the world (57.2145, -6.0795)

20 mins, 57.2181, -6.0574 🏔🏞

10 TORRIN POOLS

A small but deep marble pool at the bottom of a cleft gorge, in the shadow of Blaven on Loch Slapin. You can scramble up the waterfalls for more pools. Just 20m off the coast road, 200m N of Torrin.

2 mins, 57.2190, -6.0234 🚗🏞

CENTRAL HIGHLANDS

11 ALLT GLEANN GHNÌOMAIDH

Fantastic, remote plunge pool with crystal clear water. Start at the NTS car park in Morvich (IV40 8HQ). Follow signs for Glen Affric via Gleann Licht, taking the wide track along the River Croe, passing a red roofed mountaineering hut. Ignore path off R and cross 2 footbridges. Follow path over Alt Grannda gorge, past the waterfall and down the other side of the pass to Camban Bothy. Follow the path to a confluence of rivers (57.2285, -5.1940). Cross the first footbridge, and follow the path L into Gleann Ghnìomaidh. The plunge pool is roughly halfway up Gleann Ghnìomaidh and marked by a free-standing fin of detached rock. 2½ hrs from Camban Bothy.

150 mins, 57.2312, -5.2507 🚶🏊🚶

12 LOCH A' BHEALAICH

Large and tranquil loch in a remote setting of grand mountain scenery. A great spot for secluded wild swimming. Follow directions for Allt Gleann plunge pool (see entry). The

loch is further up Gleann Ghnìomaidh. 3–4 hours from Camban Bothy.

210 mins, 57.2347, -5.2716 🚶🏊🚶

13 COIRE DHUINNID, LOCH DUICH

Dramatic SW facing valley and switchback waterfalls above famous loch-side Castle Eilean Donan. Pass Eilean Donan (A87) heading SE. After 6.5km, at Inverinate, turn L (signed Carr Brae viewpoint). Cross bridge (800m) and after another 300m find cottage and track on R. Follow track up valley for 1km. Also loch side by castle.

20 mins, 57.2588, -5.4586 🏞🏔

14 FALLS OF GLOMACH

Magnificent and remote 113m waterfall; one of Britain's highest and often called Scotland's best. It is well worth the walk in, with pools both up and downstream of the falls. Start at the NTS car park at Morvich (IV40 8HQ). Follow the road upriver, ignoring two L branches to cross the bridge at Innichro/Innis a' Chròtha and follow signs from here. Keep L then R at two forks as the path passes through forestry. After crossing a bridge and leaving forestry the path follows a well-worn stalkers' route up to the falls.

180 mins, 57.2786, -5.289 🚶🏞🚶

15 STRATHCARRON GORGE & COULAGS

Wooded gorge with pools. The best is hidden at the head, by two waterfalls, at the confluence of two streams. From Strathcarron level crossing and station (A890) follow river bank upstream for 2.5km, above gorge, to eventually drop down to confluence (also path via Achintee). Or simply explore gorge at river level until you can go no further. Also pools at nearby Coulags (57.4576, -5.4118).

30 mins, 57.4197, -5.4041 🏞

WESTER ROSS & NORTH

16 BALGY FALLS, LOCH TORRIDON

Falls on path to Loch Damph secret beach. Take path through small gate, 50m E of Balgy Bridge (A986 E of Shieldaig) and continue 800m to falls. Another 1.2km (cross river) leads to jetty and beach.

10 mins, 57.523, -5.5932 🏕🏞

17 FAIRY LOCHS, BADACHRO

Series of peaceful lochans in the hills, more properly called Lochan Sgeireach. Remains of USAAF Liberator that crashed here in 1945 can still be seen. 150m SE of the Shieldaig Hotel (IV21 2AW), take the public signed path. The route is marked by cairns; turn L at the first cairn sign, and again at the next. Path is boggy in places. Stay on the track following the cairns, it reaches a high point with good views before descending to the Fairy Lochs.

30 mins, 57.6765, -5.6777 🐦✝🏞

18 LOCH MAREE ISLANDS, GAIRLOCH

Another Scots pine forested archipelago with superb swimming and wild camping. Plenty of places to explore and swim but this is our favourite. Bushwhack N to shore off A832 about a 1.5km E of Loch Maree Hotel (IV22 2HL). Also beach and picnic benches nearby (57.6894, -5.5439)

60 mins, 57.6815, -5.4753 🏔🏊🏞🏕🏞

19 LOCH KERNSARY

Wild loch with great views over to Fisherfield and the Torridon hills. Walk N from the centre of Poolewe (IV22 2JX). At the end of the speed restriction, after a long white house there is a footpath signed for Loch Kernsary. This passes through the Cnoc na Lise woodland to reach the shores of the loch. It is possible to make a complete circuit of the loch, but only on much rougher paths.

30 mins, 57.7673, -5.5759 🏞🏊🏵

20 FALLS OF KIRKAIG

The Falls of Kirkaig, impressive even at just 20m. The plunge pool beneath the fall is accessible via a rope but check exit before swimming. Multiple river pools on the walk to the falls if preferable. Along the river From Lochinver, take the minor road S to Inverkirkaig (IV27 4LR). Follow along the shore, then inland to car park on R at sharp R bend and bridge. Walk E, taking the R lower path that leads towards the forest, signed Inverkirkaig Falls,

90 mins, 58.1092, -5.2061 🏞📖

21 WAILING WIDOW / ALLT CHRANAIDH
A short 250m scramble along the rocky river gorge leads to a giant waterfall and a deep pool in a classic Assynt mountain landscape. There's a rough layby on A894 (NC500) where it crosses the river. You can also swim in Loch na Gainmhich above which feeds it, where there's a large parking area, good for overnights.
120 mins, 58.2178, -4.9933 🏞🚶🏔❄

GLEN AFRRIC

22 RIVER AFFRIC
A short walking loop that follows the River Affric on a small promontory between two lochs. From Cannich, turn left onto the minor road signposted for Glen Affric. The car park is about 16 km along this road. Follow the blue waymarkers downhill to the river.
30 mins, 57.2629, -4.9858 🏕🚶🏞🏊🚵♿

23 LOCH BEINN A MHEADHOIN
Glorious islanded lake, rich in original Caledonian pine. Many places to swim from shore and potential to swim out to islands if you are in a group. Continue past Dog Falls car park for a further 5km up Glen Affric and look out for car park/picnic spot and a

100m channel swim to one of the islands. 1.6km further along road, find large layby above sandy beach linked to island. Great for wild camping (57.2831, -4.9279)
5 mins, 57.2926, -4.9159 🏞🏊🏖

24 PLODDA FALLS, GLEN AFFRIC
Deep, large, black plunge pool (30m) at base of Scotland's second highest waterfall. Remains of Victorian viewing gangways around pool. Tricky scramble down into this forested canyon. Tomich is signed L at the power station off the Glen Affric road from Cannich (A831). Continue 5km beyond Tomich hotel, eventually on forestry track, to Plodda Falls forest parking. Drop down through woods, to view-bridge to admire panorama and the pool below, then down via steep, slippery path for a plunge.
15 mins, 57.2723, -4.8593 🏞🏊

25 DOG FALLS, GLEN AFFRIC
Beautiful stretch of river among woods of Scots pine in this famous glen. Good plunge pool in stretch above falls or deep canyon below falls. From Cannich (A831) follow the Glen Affric road for 8km to find the Dog Falls forest car park on L. Admire the Scots pines by the river and follow path downstream 250m to find rapids and fun

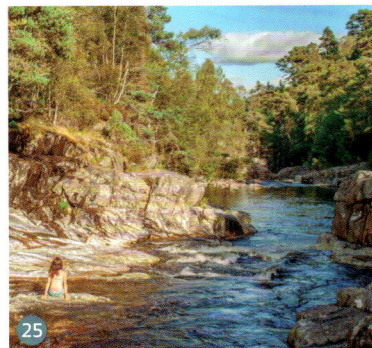

plenty of parking in the forestry car park.
2 mins, 57.5698, -4.6313 ▼

30 LOCH NAM BONNACH
Remote and peaceful loch, great for a swim in a wilder setting. Start from the end of the public road (no parking here, limited space to pu 57.56604, -4.71200 ll the car off the road beforehand) at Drumindorsair (N from IV4 7AQ) and take the track through the gate on the L, which then turns R. Head uphill to a gate, pass through. Stay on the main track, ignoring turn offs.
45 mins, 57.4905, -4.5445 ▼🏊🏞️⛺

LOCH NESS

31 DORES BEACH, LOCH NESS
Pebble beach on the shores of Loch Ness for a swim away from the crowds. Can be included in a circular walk through Aldourie woods, with further secluded bays and an old pier where Nessie was once sighted. From the Dores Inn car park (IV2 6TR), take path behind Nessie spotter's caravan down to beach. For woods, take the path behind beach, through a gate and follow the E side of the loch heading N.
5 mins, 57.3858, -4.3396 🚶♿🚻

32 URQUHART CASTLE, LOCH NESS
Trek down through these fields to find this secluded place to access the shoreline and swim out to Urquhart Castle, far away from all the crowds. Park at the huge Urquhart visitor centre just S of Drumnadrochit. Continue up main road 300m on foot (NE, towards Drumnadrochit). As road bends to L find gate into field on R and walk down to shore, bearing R down to wooded shoreline.
15 mins, 57.3264, -4.4431 🏞️📷

33 INVERMORISTON, LOCH NESS
Waterfalls and two old highland bridges. From main car park by Millennium Hall, head S back to bridge and take path on L

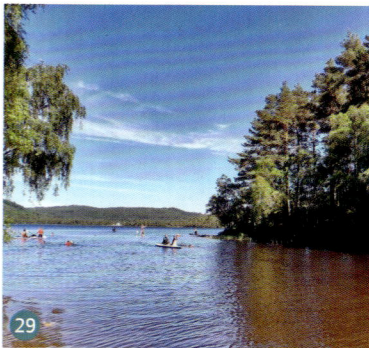

plunge pool, and then another 200m to footbridge and deep canyon below main falls (access further down, swim back up). Continue over footbridge along Coire Loch waymarked trail to reach secluded lochan with water lilies and rare dragonflies (57.3126, -4.8344)
5 mins, 57.3133, -4.8456 ▼

STRATHBRAN & CONON

26 RIVER BRAN & LOCH A'CHUILINN
Old box girder bridge and with pebble beaches in the open, empty Bran valley,

perfect for wild camping. 3km E along A832 the road skirts the loch with easy access for a long swim (57.6112, -4.8542).
2 mins, 57.6029, -4.9602

27 LITTLE GARVE & ROGIE FALLS
Huge pool below the historic bridge on Black Water. Many more pools up and downstream. Easy forest parking and well signed off A835. Rogie Falls is better known 4km downstream on A835, with a calmish section under the fun suspension bridge (57.5889, -4.6031) but be wary of currents. It's also busier and closer to the main road.
2 mins, 57.6272, -4.6871 ▼🚶

28 RIVER MEIG NATURAL ARCH
An old fish trap weir which creates a large pool. Below adventurers can scramble downstream through the gorge for pools and a small natural arch after 350m. Trail head 57.5665, -4.7115 on little lane then descend 100m. On follow lane and swim in loch above the dam.
5 mins, 57.56604, -4.71200

29 LOCH ACHILTY
Beautiful little loch that warms up easily. Beach and picnic tables in the trees and

and down to the river to find rocky pools, grassy banks and the pretty hexagonal summerhouse above. Glenmoriston Arms Hotel in the village is a good traditional hotel and tavern (IV63 7YA, 01320 351206) and there's also St Columba's Holy well.

5 mins, 57.2114, -4.616

34 RIVER OICH
Serene river set amongst Scots pine. Good chance to see red squirrels. From Fort Augustus take minor road signed Auchteraw to the Forestry Commission car park (just past PH32 4BW). Follow the yellow River Oich trail, well waymarked from car park.

60 mins, 57.1413, -4.6992

35 LOCH TARFF, LOCH NESS
Serene and beautiful little roadside loch. Warmer and quieter than Loch Ness. Beach and offshore islets. From Fort Augustus follow B862 (off General Wade's military road) NE to loch for 8km. Continue on to explore less visited SE shore of Loch Ness (B852) or Loch Mhor (B862). Good wild camping.

2 mins, 57.15, -4.6062

36 FALLS OF FOYERS & LOCH NESS
A short walk leads to a view of one of the best waterfalls in Scotland; this crashing mass of water has inspired much poetry and writing. The vast plunge pool can be viewed from above, but a spectacular 1km walk skirts the top of the canyon down to the river (the adventurous could try some scrambling back up the gorge to access plunge pools) and across the bridge and campsite to the placid shores of Loch Ness, where the swimming is easy. From the centre of Foyers (450m S of IV2 6XU), cross the road in front of the shop and café and follow good path down to the falls viewpoint, passing several information boards. Cameron's Tea Room is recommended, further along the road.

5 mins, 57.2489, -4.4913

37 LOCH RUTHVEN
RSPB reserve at broad, tranquil loch that is home to half the UK's population of Slavonian grebe. The loch lies on the S side of Loch Ness, just under 1.6km off the B851 (dir IV2 6UA). From the reserve entrance follow a short path up the S side of the loch to a bird hide.

10 mins, 57.3226, -4.263

Wild Swimming Britain

1000 hidden dips in the rivers, lakes and waterfalls of Britain

Photos:
Daniel Start
Sarah Banks
Nikki Squires
Matt Heason
Joe Bird (cover)
& and those credited

Words:
Daniel Start
Sarah Banks
Nikki Squires
Georgina Duckworth
Nia Lloyd Knott
John Weller
Danya Harris
Kimberley Grant

Editing:
Patrick Naylor
Philip Nice
Ann Landman
Lisa Drewe

Distribution:
Central Books Ltd
50, Freshwater Road
Dagenham, RM8 1RX
020 8525 8800
orders@centralbooks.com

Published by:
Wild Things Publishing Ltd.
Freshford, Bath, BA2 7WG

We love feedback!
Please send updates to:

WILD THINGS PUBLISHING

hello@wildthingspublishing.com

Acknowledgements Acknowledgements To the forebearers of wild swimming: Roger Deakin, Kate Rew and Rob Fryer. With heartfelt thanks to the friends and colleagues who helped find and test all these swimming holes, come rain or shine, and who supported us on the journey, particularly to: Petra Kjell, Ciaran Mundy, Eve Stebbing, Owen Davis, Tom, Katie, Amelia and Rueben Alcott, Emily Walmsley, Julian Hodgson, Olivia Donnally, Annie Vanbeck, Fiona Smith, Anna Pemberton, Nick Hemley, Belinda Kirk, Biddy Hodson, Carl Reynolds, Tamara Giltsoff, atherine Howarth, Roma Backhouse, Lucy Odling-Smee, Chloe Kinsman, Oliver Bullough, Nick Cobbing, Sam Coughlan, Joanna Johnston; Rosie Jones, Naomi and Suna Nightingale; Lucy Tisserand; Roderick, Tiggy and Wilbur Wiles; Douglas King-Smith; Luke and Amanda Hudson; Natalie Start; Caroline Wilson; Maria Glauser; Jack Thurston; Tom Currie; Tor Udall.

Discover the local Wild Swimming Walks series

Regional Wild Guides with land and water adventures

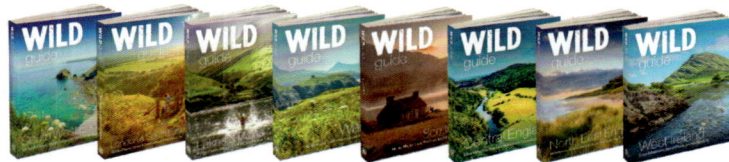

Plus other Wild Swimming adventure guides